Exponential Inequalities

Foreword

David B. Oppenheimer

When the Covid-19 pandemic began, one frequently heard the phrase, 'we're all in this together'. We weren't. The rich got richer and the poor got poorer (and sicker). Outside of medicine, the professional classes quickly adjusted to working from home (or a second home in the country), remaining relatively comfortable in a suddenly very unsafe world. But for the working class and the poor, and especially for working class and poor women and disadvantaged minority group members, at the intersection of low income/wealth and disadvantaged status the pandemic was and remains brutal.

Professors Shreya Atrey and Sandra Fredman of Oxford, two of the leading theorists in the field of equality law (closely associated, respectively, with intersectionality and substantive equality), are to be commended for bringing us this diverse and discerning collection of authors, a mix of leading scholars and new voices from six continents. The essays in this excellent collection document how the pandemic exacerbated inequality exponentially around the globe, and how those who were already worse off to begin with sunk ever deeper into poverty and danger. For this alone the book is worth reading. But this is only the beginning.

The authors each take up the question of how equality law addresses the inequalities created and/or accelerated by the pandemic. For all the differences in the substance, procedure, remedies, and theories of equality law across six continents, the answers merge; equality law had almost no application to the inequalities caused by the pandemic. It was rarely invoked. It was sometimes worse than useless, as it created the false impression that there were legal solutions extant when there were not. For this alone the book is worth reading. But this is still only the beginning.

The authors then ask in two dozen voices, as if a chorus, why equality law has failed us in these crises of inequality. Their answers overlap like harmonizing chords. Equality law looks backward, not forward. It focuses on individual harm and individual rights limited by national borders. It privileges formal equality over substantive equality or equity. It ignores obligations of international law. It rarely keeps up with social change, leaving it reliant on categories that are incomplete. Thus, it generally fails to recognize poverty or migration status or geographical isolation as protected categories. It relies on litigation. It relies on judicial orders that are frequently disregarded. It relies on lawyers. It relies on bureaucrats. It relies on state funding. It relies on cases instead of policy. It relies on democratic participation. It expects those who are rendered voiceless to speak out. The standard of proof is too high. The remedies available are inadequate. It generally rejects the reality of intersectionality (except when White men complain of 'reverse' discrimination). For this alone the book is worth reading. But there's more.

It is said that a crisis is a terrible thing to waste. In crises we look for new ideas, new solutions. We test the tools designed to address the crises, and prepare to fix them if required. We become more creative. We do our best work.

Read this book not just for the data documenting the pandemic's inequalities, though that would be enough. Read this book not just for the description of how equality law has failed, though that would be enough. Read this book not just for the critique of equality law, though that would be enough. Read it for the authors' proposals for reform. Read it for the compelling arguments to protect socio-economic rights, to rethink discrimination law procedures and remedies, to recognize theories of substantive equality and equity, to apply feminist economics, to embrace intersectionality, to take seriously policies of redistribution, to re-examine the meaning of 'disadvantage', to explore alternatives to the litigation model of dispute resolution, to demand oversight and accountability, to redefine proportionality, and to adopt positive duties. And then do something.

David B. Oppenheimer
Berkeley
August 2022

Acknowledgements

The contributors of this book and our research assistants—Chelsea Wallis and Mihika Poddar—have been an excellent team to work with. It is their intellectual energy and commitment to equality law that has sustained this project during an otherwise difficult time with the pandemic.

The research for this book has been made possible by the British Academy/Leverhulme Small Research Grant and the Society of Legal Scholars Annual Seminar Fund. The Department for Continuing Education at Oxford has supported this research, not least by supporting the team led by Christy Callaway-Gale at the Oxford Human Rights Hub in producing the *Exponential Inequalities* podcast series, which serves as an excellent companion to this book. Our editors at the Oxford University Press—Alex Flach and Paulina dos Santos Major—have provided input at crucial junctures.

Our sincere thanks to all.

SA & SF
Oxford, June 2022

Contents

List of Contributors	xi
List of Abbreviations	xix

1. Introduction: Exponential Inequalities: What Can Equality Law Do? — 1
   Shreya Atrey and Sandra Fredman

PART I UNDERSTANDING EXPONENTIAL INEQUALITIES

2. Protecting Workers' Equal Rights during Crisis and Recovery: Constitutional Approaches in 193 Countries — 19
   Aleta Sprague, Amy Raub, and Jody Heymann

3. Addressing Intersecting Inequalities through Alternative Economic Strategies — 43
   Diane Elson and Marion Sharples

4. Social Security, Exponential Inequalities, and Covid-19: How Welfare Reform in the UK Left Larger Families Exposed to the Scarring Effects of the Pandemic — 61
   Aaron Reeves, Kate Andersen, Mary Reader, and Rosalie Warnock

5. The Proportionality of an Economic Crisis — 79
   Meghan Campbell

6. Intersecting Crises and Exponential Inequalities: The View from Hong Kong — 97
   Kelley Loper

PART II ADDRESSING EXPONENTIAL INEQUALITIES

SECTION A: COMPARATIVE AND INTERNATIONAL LAW

7. New Directions Needed: Exponential Inequalities and the Limits of Equality Law — 123
   Colm O'Cinneide

8. More than an Afterthought? Equality Law in Ireland during the Pandemic — 145
   Mark Bell

9. A Public Policy Approach to Inequality 161
   Jessica Clarke

10. Responding to Exponential Inequalities in Australia: Beyond the Limits of Equality and Discrimination Law 183
    Beth Gaze

11. The Interaction of Laws Enabling Gender Equality with Other Legal Regimes: Limiting Progress in Times of Crisis 200
    Helena Alviar García

12. Equal Access to Vaccines: Exposing the Limits of International Human Rights Law? 213
    Catherine O'Regan

SECTION B: VULNERABLE GROUPS

13. A Life Course Approach to Addressing Exponential Inequalities: Age, Gender, and Covid-19 233
    Alysia Blackham

14. Disability in Times of Emergency: Exponential Inequality and the Role of Reasonable Accommodation Duties 255
    Anna Lawson and Lisa Waddington

15. Remote Working, Working from Home, and EU Sex Discrimination Law 276
    Jule Mulder

16. Covid-19 and Exponential Reproductive Rights-related Inequalities in Brazil 295
    Marta Machado and Taís Penteado

17. A Life of Contradictions: Group Inequality and Socio-economic Rights in the Indian Constitution 311
    Aparna Chandra

18. An Equality-sensitive Approach to Delivering Socio-economic Rights during Crises: A Focus on Kenya 335
    Victoria Miyandazi

19. The Role of Equality Law in Expanding Access to Social Goods and Services in South Africa: Lessons after the Pandemic 353
    Catherine Albertyn

Index 373

List of Contributors

Catherine Albertyn is the National Research Foundation (NRF) South African Research Chair in Equality, Law, and Social Justice and a professor of law at the School of Law University of the Witwatersrand, Johannesburg, South Africa. Her research focuses on the meaning and interpretation of equality in the South African Constitution, law, and jurisprudence, as well as the role of the law, rights, and courts in enabling, advancing, or preventing the achievement of substantive equality in South Africa. Catherine is an attorney of the High Court of South Africa, a member of the Academy of Science of South Africa (ASSaf), and an editor of the *South African Journal on Human Rights* and the *Oxford Human Rights Hub Law Journal*. She has previously served as a Commissioner of the Commission for Gender Equality and the South African Law Reform Commission.

Kate Andersen is Research Associate at the University of York. Her research explores the intended and unintended consequences of new social security policies. Kate is especially interested in investigating how government justifications for welfare reforms compare with the everyday lives of people in receipt of social security benefits. Her research also particularly focuses on how welfare reforms impact women. She has published an article titled 'Universal Credit, Gender and Unpaid Childcare: Mothers' Accounts of the New Welfare Conditionality Regime' in *Critical Social Policy* (2020).

Shreya Atrey is an Associate Professor in International Human Rights Law at the Faculty of Law, University of Oxford, and is based at the Bonavero Institute of Human Rights. Her research is on discrimination law, feminist theory, poverty, and disability law. Her monograph, *Intersectional Discrimination* (OUP 2019), which won the runners-up Peter Birks Book Prize in 2020, presents an account of intersectionality theory in comparative discrimination law. Shreya is the Editor of the *Human Rights Law Review*. She is an associate member of the Oxford Human Rights Hub and an Official Fellow of Kellogg College.

Mark Bell is Regius Professor of Laws and a Fellow of Trinity College Dublin, the University of Dublin. He was Head of the School of Law (2018–2021). Prior to his appointment at Trinity, he was a professor at the School of Law, University of Leicester, where he was also Head of the School of Law (2011–2014). Mark has published regularly on Anti-discrimination Law and Employment Law, particularly in relation to EU law. He is co-editor of *International and European Labour Law: A Commentary* (Nomos 2018). Mark is co-Director of the Disability Rights Working Group of the Berkeley Center on Comparative Equality and Anti-Discrimination Law. He is a member of the Board of Directors of the Irish Centre for European Law and the Editorial Board of the *International Journal of Discrimination and the Law*. He has conducted research for the European Commission and the International Labour Organization, as well as non-governmental organizations.

Alysia Blackham is an Associate Professor at Melbourne Law School, the University of Melbourne. Her research focuses on the intersection of employment law, equality law, and public law, using empirical evidence to cast new light on legal problems. Funded by the Australian Research Council as part of the Discovery Early Career Researcher scheme, in 2017 Alysia commenced the project DE170100228 'Addressing Age Discrimination in Employment'. The project explored the ways in which age discrimination law is enforced in Australia and the UK, and the barriers to effectively addressing age discrimination at work. A monograph based on that research, *Reforming Age Discrimination Law: Beyond Individual Enforcement* was published by OUP in 2022. Alysia has published extensively across leading journals and in legal and interdisciplinary forums. Her first monograph, *Extending Working Life for Older Workers: Age Discrimination Law, Policy and Practice* (Hart Publishing 2016), won second prize in the UK Society of Legal Scholars' Peter Birks Prizes for Outstanding Legal Scholarship in 2017. Alysia has worked as an academic in Australia, Sweden, and the UK, including as the Turpin-Lipstein Fellow and College Lecturer in Law and Director of Studies at Clare College, Cambridge and an Affiliated Lecturer at the Faculty of Law at the University of Cambridge.

Meghan Campbell is a Reader in International Human Rights Law at the University of Birmingham and Deputy-Director of the Oxford Human Rights Hub. Her scholarship centres on the right to equality and has examined equality in relation to intersectionality, the Sustainable Development Goals, socio-economic rights, climate change, poverty, and the limitation of rights. Her monograph *Women, Poverty, Equality: The Role of CEDAW* (Hart Publishing 2018) offers an interpretation of equality and non-discrimination in UN Convention on the Elimination of All Forms of Discrimination against Women to ameliorate women's poverty. She is the co-editor of *Human Rights and Equality in Education* (Policy 2018) and *Feminist Frontiers: Climate Justice and Gender Equality* (Edward Elgar Publishing 2023). In her role as the Deputy Director of the Oxford Human Rights Hub, she has worked in collaboration with the World Health Organization and the UN Office of the High Commissioner of Human Rights to produce the documentary *A Right to a Better World*, exploring how the Sustainable Development Goals and human rights can be harnessed to achieve sexual and reproductive health. She is the co-founder of the *University of Oxford Human Rights Hub Journal*, which has been cited by numerous apex courts.

Aparna Chandra is an Associate Professor of Law at the National Law School of India University, Bengaluru. She teaches and researches on constitutional law, human rights, gender and the law, and judicial process reform. She has previously worked at the National Judicial Academy, Bhopal, National Law University, Delhi, and as a Tutor at the Yale Law School, USA.

Jessica Clarke is a Professor of Law at Vanderbilt Law School. She writes on anti-discrimination law, with a focus on sex, gender, and sexuality. Her work has appeared in law journals including the *Columbia Law Review*, *Harvard Law Review*, *NYU Law Review* and *Yale Law Journal*, as well as other outlets including the *New England Journal of Medicine*, *Los Angeles Times*, and *Harvard Business Review*. She has twice received the Dukeminier Award for the best legal scholarship on sexual orientation and gender identity.

Professor Clarke graduated from Yale Law School and clerked for Shira Scheindlin of the US District Court for the Southern District of New York and Rosemary Pooler of the US Court of Appeals for the Second Circuit. Before entering the academy, she was a litigation associate at Covington & Burling in New York. From 2011 to 2018, she taught at the University of Minnesota Law School, where she received the Stanley V. Kinyon award for teacher of the year. In the fall of 2016, she was the Walter V. Schaefer Visiting Professor at the University of Chicago Law School and, in the fall of 2022, she was a visiting professor at Harvard Law School.

Diane Elson is Emeritus Professor of Sociology at the University of Essex, UK and a former Chair of the UK Women's Budget Group (2010–2016). She chaired the Commission on a Gender Equal Economy set up by the Women's Budget Group (2019–2020). She has been a member of the UN Committee for Development Policy (2013–2021), adviser to UN Women and Vice President of the International Association for Feminist Economics (2004–2006). She was awarded the 2016 Leontief Prize for Advancing the Frontiers of Economic Thought by the Global Development and Environment Institute at Tufts University. She has published widely on gender equality, human rights, and economic justice. Her recent publications include: (with R Balakrishnan and J Heintz) *Rethinking Economics for Social Justice: The Radical Potential of Human Rights* (Routledge 2016); 'Financing for Gender Equality: How to Budget in Compliance with Human Rights Standards' in N Burn and Z Kahn (eds), *Financing for Gender Equality: Realizing Women's Rights through Gender Responsive Budgeting* (Palgrave Macmillan 2017); 'Securing the Social and Economic Rights of Women in Economic Policy Making' in N Reilly (ed), *Human Rights of Women* (Springer 2018).

Sandra Fredman is Professor of the Laws of the British Commonwealth and the USA at the University of Oxford, and a professorial fellow at Pembroke College. She was elected a Fellow of the British Academy in 2005 and became a QC (honoris causa) in 2012. She has written and published widely on anti-discrimination law, human rights law, and labour law, including numerous peer-reviewed articles. She has authored four monographs: *Comparative Human Rights* (OUP 2018); *Human Rights Transformed* (OUP 2008); *Discrimination Law* (3rd edn, OUP 2022); and *Women and the Law* (OUP 1997), as well as two co-authored books: *The State as Employer* (Mansell 1988) with Gillian Morris, and *Labour Law and Industrial Relations in Great Britain* (2nd edn, Kluwer 1992) with Bob Hepple. She has also edited several books: *Human Rights and Equality in Education* (Policy Press 2018) with Meghan Campbell and Helen Taylor; *Discrimination and Human Rights: The Case of Racism* (OUP 2001); and *Age as an Equality Issue* (Hart Publishing 2003) with Sarah Spencer. She was awarded a three-year Leverhulme Major Research Fellowship in 2004 to further her research into socio-economic rights and substantive equality. She is South African and holds degrees from the University of Witwatersrand and the University of Oxford. She has acted as an expert adviser on equality law and labour legislation in the EU, Northern Ireland, the UK, India, South Africa, Canada, Malaysia, and the UN. She is also a barrister practising at Old Square Chambers. She founded the Oxford Human Rights Hub in 2012, of which she is the Director.

Helena Alviar García holds an SJD from Harvard Law School, an LLM from the same institution, and is a lawyer from Universidad de Los Andes in Bogotá, Colombia. She is a professor at Sciences Po Law School. She served as Dean of Los Andes Law School and held tenure as full professor (*profesora titular*). An expert in law and development, property, feminist approaches to law, and transitional justice, she has been invited to participate in global networks regarding these issues. She is the author of books, book chapters, academic papers, and essays, including *Legal Experiments for Development in Latin America* (Routledge 2021); 'La Lucha por el Género en la Transición' in Isabel Cristina Jaramillo (ed), *Género en Transción* (Springer 2020); and 'Neoliberalism as a Form of Authoritarian Constitutionalism' in (co-edited with Günter Frankenberg) *Authoritarian Constitutionalism: Comparative Analysis and Critique* (Edward Elgar Publishing 2019).

Beth Gaze is a Professor at the Melbourne Law School in the University of Melbourne, Australia. She has taught and researched in anti-discrimination law for many years, and is co-author with Associate Professor Belinda Smith of *Equality and Discrimination Law in Australia: An Introduction* (Cambridge University Press 2017). Beth has been a member of several state and federal tribunals, and has been a consultant to both state and federal governments. She has conducted empirical research funded by the Australian Research Council into subjects including enforcement in anti-discrimination law, the experience of participants in social security appeals tribunals, and adverse action claims under the Australian Fair Work Act. She is currently conducting research into the implementation of Victoria's Gender Equality Act 2020, causation in discrimination law, and enforcement and compliance in discrimination law.

Jody Heymann is Founding Director of the WORLD Policy Analysis Center and Distinguished Professor at the UCLA Luskin School of Public Affairs, Fielding School of Public Health, and Geffen School of Medicine. Heymann has authored and edited over 500 publications analysing laws, public policies, and constitutional rights worldwide, including *Advancing Equality* and eighteen other books. Among these are *Making Equal Rights Real* (Cambridge University Press 2012), *Children's Chances* (Harvard University Press 2013), *Raising the Global Floor* (Stanford University Press 2009), *Disability and Equity at Work* (Oxford University Press 2014), *Profit at the Bottom of the Ladder* (Harvard Business Press 2010), and *Forgotten Families* (Oxford University Press 2006). Heymann has worked with leaders in North American, European, African, and Latin American governments, as well as a wide range of intergovernmental organizations including the World Health Organization, the International Labour Organization, the World Economic Forum, UNICEF, and UNESCO. She has received numerous honours, including election to the National Institute of Medicine in 2013 and the Canadian Academy of Health Sciences in 2012. Heymann's research findings have been featured in thousands of articles in the national and international media.

Anna Lawson is a Professor of Law and Joint Director of the Centre for Disability Studies at the University of Leeds. She is a Fellow of the Academy of Social Science and an honorary Master of the Bench at the Middle Temple Inns of Court. Her research focuses on disability equality and human rights, with a focus on issues of discrimination, accessibility, access to justice and public space.

Kelley Loper is an Associate Professor and Director of the Master of Laws in Human Rights Programme in the Faculty of Law at the University of Hong Kong. She is also Co-Editor-in-Chief of the *Asia-Pacific Journal on Human Rights in the Law* and sits on the advisory board of the Berkeley Center on Comparative Equality and Anti-discrimination Law. Her work focuses on the implementation of international human rights law in domestic contexts, especially Hong Kong. She has researched and published on several related topics, including human rights treaties and refugee protection; the rights to education and legal capacity in the Convention on the Rights of Persons with Disabilities; sexual orientation and gender identity discrimination; dignity as a constitutional value; and gender constitutionalism. She teaches international human rights law and equality and non-discrimination. In addition to her academic work, she serves on the board of the Hong Kong Dignity Institute and is past Chairperson of the Hong Kong Refugee Advice Centre. She has advised numerous other local and international organisations on a range of human rights issues.

Marta Machado has been a full-time professor at FGV São Paulo Law School since 2007 and Director of the Centre for Racial Justice and Law, Associate Dean of the Academic Master's and PhD Programmes since 2019. She gained her Master's (2004) and PhD (2007) in Philosophy and Theory of Law from the University of Sao Paulo. She is currently a senior researcher at the Brazilian Centre of Analysis and Planning (CEBRAP); Global Fellow at the Centre on Law & Social Transformation (University of Bergen); Fellow at the International Reproductive and Sexual Health Law Programme, University of Toronto School; Associate Researcher at the Oxford Human Rights Hub; and one of the main investigators at Maria Sibylla Merian Centre Conviviality-Inequality in Latin America (MECILA).

Victoria Miyandazi is a Lecturer in Law at the University of Embu, an Associate Advocate at Okubasu, Munene & Kazungu Advocates LLP, and a former Researcher at the Oxford Human Rights Hub. She holds a doctorate from the University of Oxford, where she was a Rhodes Scholar. Dr Miyandazi researches, teaches, and writes on Equality Law, Human Rights, Constitutional Law, Administrative Law, Property Law, and Comparative Law. She has published widely in these areas and continues to contribute to this body of knowledge. She is the author of *Equality in Kenya's 2010 Constitution: Understanding the Competing and Interrelated Conceptions* (Hart Publishing 2021).

Jule Mulder is a Senior Lecturer at the University of Bristol Law School and Co/Editor-in-Chief of the *German Law Journal*. She joined the European equality law network of legal experts in gender equality and non-discrimination (funded by the EU Commission) in 2021 and has published widely on comparative and EU equality law. Her monograph entitled *EU Non-Discrimination law in the Courts: Approaches to Sex and Sexuality Discrimination in EU Law* (Hart Publishing 2017) adopts an innovative critical comparative law methodology to investigate how German and Dutch courts interpret and apply European Equality Law and why their approaches differ widely, despite the common European origin of the laws and the Court of Justice's competence to interpret EU law. Jule has participated in an international comparative research project on the aftermath of the *Laval* and *Viking* judgments. Her most recent project (funded by the Leverhulme Trust) focused on consumer vulnerability within the context of EU consumer and EU non-discrimination law.

Colm O'Cinneide is Professor of Constitutional and Human Rights Law at University College London (UCL). A graduate of University College Cork, he has published extensively in the field of comparative constitutional, human rights, and anti-discrimination law. He has also acted as specialist legal adviser to the Joint Committee on Human Rights and the Women & Equalities Committee of the UK Parliament, and was from 2010 to 2014 Vice-President of the European Committee on Social Rights of the Council of Europe.

Catherine O'Regan is the inaugural Director of the Bonavero Institute of Human Rights and a former judge of the South African Constitutional Court (1994–2009). In the mid-1980s she practised as a lawyer in Johannesburg in a variety of fields, but especially labour law and land law, representing many of the emerging trade unions and their members, as well as communities threatened with eviction under apartheid land laws. In 1990, she joined the Faculty of Law at UCT, where she taught a range of courses including race, gender and the law, labour law, civil procedure, and evidence. Since her fifteen-year term at the South African Constitutional Court ended in 2009, she has amongst other things served as an *ad hoc* judge of the Supreme Court of Namibia (from 2010 to 2016), Chairperson of the Khayelitsha Commission of Inquiry into allegations of police inefficiency and a breakdown in trust between the police and the community of Khayelitsha (2012–2014), and as a member of the boards or advisory bodies of many NGOs working in the fields of democracy, the rule of law, human rights, and equality.

Taís Penteado is a PhD Candidate in Law at FGV Law School of São Paulo (Class of 2024) and holds both an MA degree from the same institution (2020) and an LLM degree from Yale Law School (2022). Along the years, she has received financial support from important Brazilian agencies, such as the São Paulo State Research Foundation, the Coordination for the Improvement of Higher Education Personnel, and the National Council for Scientific and Technological Development, as well as from FGV and Yale Law School funds. Her work has been published in widely read law journals, such as *ICON* and *Yale Journal of Law and Feminism*, and focuses on equality law and critical legal theories.

Amy Raub is Principal Research Analyst at the WORLD Policy Analysis Center, where her work focuses on developing approaches to quantitatively comparing legal provisions that can ameliorate or perpetuate inequalities for all 193 UN member states and translating this data for policy-makers, citizens, civil society, and researchers. Raub is an economist with over two decades of experience working on discrimination and inequality across a range of policy areas, including constitutional rights, work-family, sexual harassment, gender equality, migration, child marriage, disability, child labour, and education, among others. In addition to being a co-author of *Advancing Equality*, Raub has authored more than three dozen journal articles examining the status of constitutional rights globally, legal gaps that undermine equal rights, country progress towards equality over time, statistical analyses of the relationship between policies and outcomes, and assessments of whether countries are meeting their international and regional commitments to advancing health, development, well-being, and equity.

Mary Reader is Research Officer at the Centre for Analysis of Social Exclusion (CASE) at the London School of Economics and Political Science. Her research interests include the causal impact of income, poverty, and social security on families, with a particular focus on health inequalities, early childhood, and larger families.

Aaron Reeves is an Associate Professor in the Department of Social Policy and Intervention at Oxford University, a Fellow of Green Templeton College, and a Visiting Senior Fellow in the International Inequalities Institute at the LSE. He is a sociologist working on the political economy of health and social stratification. He is currently writing a book on the British elite.

Marion Sharples is a feminist activist and gender equality specialist working within the non-profit sector. Most recently, Marion ran the Global Partnerships and Learning programme at the Women's Budget Group and co-chaired the 2022 W7 working group on a Gender-Equal Covid-19 Recovery. Prior to this, Marion was the Project Manager of the Commission for a Gender-Equal Economy set up by the Women's Budget Group (2019–2020). She is also a freelance cycling instructor and teaches refugee women to cycle. Marion holds an MSc in Gender, Development, and Globalisation from the London School of Economics. She is a Clore Social Fellow (2020 cohort, Emerging Leaders) and is trained in the Art of Participatory Leadership (2021).

Aleta Sprague is Senior Legal Analyst at the WORLD Policy Analysis Center at UCLA, where her research focuses on the practical impacts and challenges of legal reforms to advance social and economic equality. An attorney with over a decade of experience working to strengthen equal rights through law and public policy, Sprague is co-author of *Advancing Equality: How Constitutional Rights Can Make a Difference Worldwide* (University of California Press 2020), as well as *Equality Within Our Lifetimes: How Laws and Policies Can Close—or Widen—Gender Gaps in Economies Worldwide* (University of California Press forthcoming 2023). Her writing on topics including equal rights, poverty, paid sick leave, and parental leave has been featured in the *Harvard Human Rights Journal*, the *Columbia Journal of Gender and Law*, the *American Journal of Public Health*, *Health Affairs*, the *Atlantic*, the *Washington Post*, and a range of other media outlets and academic journals. Sprague received her JD from UCLA School of Law.

Lisa Waddington is the European Disability Forum Professor in European Disability Law at Maastricht University in the Netherlands. Her principal areas of research are European and comparative disability law, the UN Convention on the Rights of Persons with Disabilities, and European and comparative equality law in general. She is a senior expert for a number of networks and organizations, including the European Network of Legal Experts in the Non-discrimination Field and the European Disability Expertise network.

Rosalie Warnock is Research Associate in the Department of Social Policy and Social Work, University of York. She works on the Covid-19 Realities and Benefit Changes and Larger Families projects. Her research interests include austerity, welfare bureaucracies, special educational needs, and disability (SEND) support services, family life, care, and emotional geographies.

List of Abbreviations

A1P1	Article 1 of Protocol No 1 (peaceful enjoyment of possessions)
ACIP	Advisory Committee on Immunization Practices
ACT-Accelerator	Access to Covid-19 Tools Accelerator
BAME	Black, Asian, and minority ethnic
BJC	Budget Justice Coalition (South Africa)
BOR	Bill of Rights Ordinance
BSL	British Sign Language
CALD	culturally and linguistically diverse
CEDAW	Convention on the Elimination of All Forms of Discrimination against Women
CEO	chief executive officer
CEPI	Coalition for Epidemic Preparedness Innovations
CERD	Committee on the Elimination of Racial Discrimination
CESCR	Committee on Economic, Social and Cultural Rights
CJEU	Court of Justice of the European Union
CMO	Chief Medical Officer
CRAM	Coronavirus Rapid Mobile Survey (South Africa)
CRC	Convention on the Rights of the Child
CRPD	Convention on the Rights of Persons with Disabilities
CRPD Committee	UN Committee on the Rights of Persons with Disabilities
CSG	Child Support Grant (South Africa)
CSO	Central Statistics Office
CSW	Conference on the Status of Women
DDO	Disability Discrimination Ordinance (Hong Kong)
DPC	Department of Premier and Cabinet (Australia)
DWP	Department for Work and Pensions
ECHR	European Convention on Human Rights
EIGE	European Institute for Gender Equality
EOC	Equal Opportunities Commission
FSDO	Family Status Discrimination Ordinance
FTE	full-time equivalent
GATT	General Agreement on Tariffs and Trade
GAVI	Global Agency for Access to Vaccines
GPI	genuine progress indicator
HAS	Health and Safety Authority
HILDA Survey	Household, Income and Labour Dynamics in Australia Survey
HIV/AIDS	human immunodeficiency virus/acquired immunodeficiency syndrome
ICCPR	International Covenant on Civil and Political Rights
ICERD	International Convention on the Elimination of All Forms of Racial Discrimination

ICESCR	International Covenant on Economic, Social and Cultural Rights
IHREC	Irish Human Rights and Equality Commission
IMF	International Monetary Fund
LAC	Labour Appeal Court (South Africa)
MTBPS	Medium Term Budget Policy Statement (South Africa)
MWRF test	manifestly without reasonable foundation test
NDA	National Disability Authority
NDIS Act	National Disability Insurance Scheme Act 2013
NHIF	National Health Insurance Fund
NHS	National Health Service
NIDS	National Income Dynamics Study (South Africa)
NLS	National Longitudinal Surveys
NPHET	National Public Health Emergency Team
NSNP	National School Nutrition Programme (South Africa)
NS-SEC	National Statistics Socio-Economic Classification
ONS	Office of National Statistics
OPG	Older Persons' Grant (South Africa)
PPE	personal protective equipment
PPP	Paycheck Protection Program
PSED	Public Sector Equality Duty (UK)
PUP	Pandemic Unemployment Payment
RDO	Race Discrimination Ordinance (Hong Kong)
SAR	Special Administrative Region
SDO	Sex Discrimination Ordinance (Hong Kong)
SERs	socio-economic rights
TFEU	Treaty on the Functioning of the European Union
TRIPs	Agreement on Trade-related Aspects of Intellectual Property Rights
UDHR	Universal Declaration of Human Rights
UNCTAD	United Nations Conference on Trade and Development
UNDP	United Nations Development Programme
UNGPs	United Nations Guiding Principles on Business and Human Rights
UNHCR	United Nations High Commissioner for Refugees
UNICEF	United Nations Children's Fund
US(A)	United States (of America)
WGEA	Workplace Gender Equality Agency (Australia)
WHO	World Health Organization
WRC	Workplace Relations Commission
WTO	World Trade Organization

1
Introduction

Exponential Inequalities: What Can Equality Law Do?

Shreya Atrey and Sandra Fredman

1 Introduction

At the start of the pandemic, it seemed that Covid-19 was a great leveller. Everyone was vulnerable, including heads of states and millionaires in the wealthiest parts of the world. The reality has been different. The pandemic has exposed and exacerbated pre-existing inequalities. People with disabilities, older people, people living in poverty, minorities, women, and those at the intersection of these groups have been disproportionately adversely affected, whether in access to medical care, vaccines, schooling, water, sanitation and housing, or safety from violence. Indeed, inequality has not only been the earliest but also one of the most lasting lessons around which consensus has endured, while views on public health measures such as handwashing, masks, quarantine, and vaccines have continued to shift.

The growth in inequality is striking given that high levels of inequality existed before the pandemic too. For example, in 2018, there were about 258 million children and young people out of school.[1] This number, however, has risen to 450 million in 2022.[2] In 2019, 388 million women and girls lived in extreme poverty.[3] This number is estimated to be 450 million in 2021.[4] Meanwhile, the ten richest men in the world have more than doubled their fortunes, from US$700 billion to US$1.5 trillion—while the incomes of 99 per cent of the world's population have worsened since the pandemic.[5] As Michelle Bachelet, the United Nations High Commissioner for Human Rights, summed up, it is both 'the magnitude and scope of inequalities' exacerbated by Covid-19 that has been truly shocking.[6] It is not simply that inequalities have continued to

---

[1] UNESCO Institute for Statistics, Fact Sheet No 65 (2019) http://uis.unesco.org/en/topic/out-sch ool-children-and-youth#:~:text=About%20258%20million%20children%20and,million%20of%20up per%20secondary%20age (accessed 19 April 2022).
[2] 'COVID-19: Education Risks Becoming "Greatest Divider"' *UN News website* (30 March 2022) https://news.un.org/en/story/2022/03/1114932 (accessed 19 April 2022).
[3] 'COVID-19 Is Driving Women and Girls Deeper into Poverty' *UN Women* (17 October 2020) https://data.unwomen.org/features/covid-19-driving-women-and-girls-deeper-poverty (accessed 20 April 2022).
[4] ibid.
[5] 'Inequality Kills' Oxfam Report (17 January 2022) https://policy-practice.oxfam.org/resources/inequality-kills-the-unparalleled-action-needed-to-combat-unprecedented-inequal-621341/ (accessed 20 April 2022).
[6] Statement by the High Commissioner for Human Rights, Half-day Panel Discussion on Deepening Inequalities Exacerbated by the COVID-19 Pandemic and their Implications for the Realisation of Human Rights (September 2021) https://www.ohchr.org/en/2021/09/magnitude-and-scope-inequalities-created-and-exacerbated-covid-19-truly-shocking-high (accessed 20 April 2022).

Shreya Atrey and Sandra Fredman, *Introduction* In: *Exponential Inequalities*. Edited by: Shreya Atrey and Sandra Fredman, Oxford University Press. © Shreya Atrey and Sandra Fredman 2023. DOI: 10.1093/oso/9780192872999.003.0001

exist but the fact that they have *grown in magnitude and scope* and *exponentially so* since the crisis that seems to be significant.

As equality lawyers, we have wondered what, if anything, equality law can do about exponential inequalities. Our interest in the question has been sparked by how little attention has been paid to equality law responding to this dramatic deepening of inequality.[7] We find this perplexing given that the field of equality law—at least in its name—is literally about addressing the very subject of inequality. So where has equality law been in the face of exponential inequalities?

This book is dedicated to answering this question. To do so, it asks two further questions: what are exponential inequalities and how has equality law responded to them across contexts in comparative and international law (especially focusing on the UK, the US, Ireland, the EU, South Africa, Kenya, Brazil, India, Hong Kong, Australia, and Colombia), and across vulnerable groups including elderly persons, disabled persons, women, workers in the informal economy, and people living in extreme poverty.

Drawing on a range of interdisciplinary research, and comparative and international law, the book presents a complex picture of how equality law has been engaged during the pandemic in response to exponential inequalities and why its engagement, even where positive, appears limited not only in undoing exponential inequalities but by its own normative standards. The central argument of the book as a whole is that there is greater potential in equality law to deal with exponential inequalities than the extant doctrine suggests. This introductory chapter maps how the research in the individual contributions to this book lends to this conclusion. In the next two sections, we explain what we mean by exponential inequalities before turning to how they interact with equality law, especially exploring the central argument that there is untapped potential within both the theory and practice of equality law in doing more transformative work in challenging exponential inequalities of the kind that arise in crises such as the current pandemic. The significance of this work, however, lies in exceeding the current context and assessing the relevance of equality law in 'crisis' generally, such as climate emergencies, wars, austerity, recessions, refugee crises, and democratic deficits. Challenging the assumption that equality laws are meant to operate only in ordinary times, the research shows the relevance of engaging equality law in both ordinary times, as well as times of crisis. With more extraordinary global crises looming, the research explores productive avenues for engagement with equality law in the future by drawing on vital lessons which have been driven home by crises we have faced so far.

2 Exponential Inequalities

The book uses the term 'exponential inequalities' to refer to the inequalities that grow rapidly because of crises. Thus, at a minimum, the use of the term draws attention to at least three things. First, it draws attention to *inequality*, which is understood qua

---

[7] cf Meghan Campbell, Sandra Fredman, and Aaron Reeves, 'Palliation or Protection: How Should the Right to Equality inform the Government's Response to Covid-19?' (2020) 20 International Journal of Discrimination and the Law 183.

equality law as disadvantaged people suffer because of their personal characteristics related to race, caste, religion, sex, gender, sexual orientation, disability, age, etc, and as including stereotypes,[8] prejudices,[9] marginalization,[10] the loss of dignity[11] or being demeaned,[12] or the loss of deliberate freedoms,[13] capabilities,[14] autonomy,[15] or substantive equality.[16] Personal characteristics or 'grounds' of discrimination play a key role in identifying disadvantages or inequalities people suffer not simply because of their bad luck, lack of 'merit', or for being singled out arbitrarily, but because they belong to groups which are disadvantaged per se.[17] This distinguishes the use of the term in equality law with the use of the term in other contexts such as economics, where inequalities may not be understood as relating to specific grounds or disadvantaged groups alone. Furthermore, the use of the plural, as in *inequalities*, reaffirms the capacious use of the term to encompass inequalities which result from all forms of direct and indirect discrimination which lead to a whole range of redistributive, recognition-based, or participative harms in an individual, institutional, systemic, or structural sense.[18]

Secondly, the term draws attention to the fact that these inequalities arise *because of* crises; that is, they arise in circumstances which are extraordinary or unusual such as natural disasters, economic downturns, pandemics, wars, and climate emergencies. What determines whether these are extraordinary circumstances or crises is not whether they are foreseen or unforeseen but whether they have the potential to disrupt what may be considered 'normal' or 'ordinary' life in a society. Importantly, however, once generated, exponential inequalities do not disappear when the crisis passes, and life returns to normal (or to a new normal). Thus, exponential inequalities are not restricted during crises. Instead, they may be understood as arising *because of* crises (although not solely), that is, in *interaction* with crises, and unless addressed, they persist beyond crises.

Thirdly, the term draws attention to the fact that these inequalities grow with exceptional *rapidity*. Thus, the term exponential is used in a colloquial (as opposed to mathematical) sense to highlight that inequalities, when they interact with crises, can be exacerbated or made worse both considerably (as opposed to marginally) and at pace (as opposed to slowly).

---

[8] Larry Alexander, 'What Makes Wrongful Discrimination Wrong? Biases, Preferences, Stereotypes, and Proxies' (1992) 141 University of Pennsylvania Law Review 149.

[9] Sophia R Moreau, 'The Wrongs of Unequal Treatment' (2004) 54 University of Toronto Law Journal 291.

[10] Henk Botha, 'Equality, Plurality and Structural Power' (2009) 25 South African Journal on Human Rights 1; Hugh Collins, 'Discrimination, Equality and Social Inclusion' (2003) 66 Modern Law Review 16; Cass R Sunstein, 'The Anticaste Principle' (1994) 92 Michigan Law Review 2410.

[11] Denise G Réaume, 'Discrimination and Dignity' (2003) 63 Louisiana Law Review 1.

[12] Deborah Hellman, *When is Discrimination Wrong?* (Harvard UP 2008).

[13] Sophia Moreau, 'What is Discrimination' (2010) 38 Philosophy and Public Affairs 143; Sophia Moreau, *Faces of Inequality: A Theory of Wrongful Discrimination* (OUP 2020).

[14] Amartya Sen, *Development as Freedom* (OUP 1999); Martha Nussbaum, *Women and Human Development* (CUP 2001).

[15] Joseph Raz, *The Morality of Freedom* (OUP 1998) ch 9.

[16] Sandra Fredman, *Discrimination Law* (3rd edn, OUP 2022).

[17] Tarunabh Khaitan, *A Theory of Discrimination Law* (OUP 2015) ch 2.

[18] Sandra Fredman, 'Substantive Equality Revisited ' (2016) 14 International Journal of Constitutional Law 712.

These theoretical assumptions are borne out by the contributions in the book which paint a vivid picture of the rapid growth in inequality during crises across a range of geographical contexts and vulnerable populations. The contributions, especially in Part I of the book, yield an evidence-based understanding of exponential inequalities, drawn together from sociological, economic, legal, and policy-based perspectives. The accounts of exponential inequalities laid bare in these contributions help extract the common features of exponential inequalities which actually cut across geographical contexts and particularities of inequality across vulnerable groups. Three further features can be identified as defining exponential inequalities as they materialize in the real world. These include the presence of *pre-existing* inequality, the preponderance of *socio-economic disadvantage or poverty*, and the *interrelationship* between patterns of group disadvantage.

The contributions identify *pre-existing* inequality as key to the generation of exponential inequalities. As Aparna Chandra argues, in a perfect world where inequality does not exist, exponential inequalities will not exist either.[19] This is because the perfect world would have redistributive principles which would operate in and beyond crises to prevent, redress, and reverse any emerging inequality. But we are dealing with the real world, which is beset with pre-existing inequality which affects vulnerable groups such as Black people, ethnic minorities, Dalits, indigenous populations, women, disabled persons, elderly people, children, and those at the intersection of these groups. In fact, as Aaron Reeves, Kate Andersen, Mary Reader, and Rosalie Warnock show in their chapter, the pre-existing inequality groups suffer is a result of policies brought before a crisis.[20] They demonstrate the ways in which austerity measures in the UK brought in after the global recession of 2008 have systematically impoverished large families along gendered and ethnic lines. Their work thus reveals the 'path dependence' of inequality on policy choices made by governments before a crisis. Their findings from the Benefit Changes and Larger Families project reveals the devastating impact of policies such as the two-child limit and benefit cap on large families, especially those led by single mothers, during the Covid-19 pandemic.

Likewise, the contribution from Aleta Sprague, Amy Raub, and Jody Heymann shows that is not simply policies, but also laws which leave a gap in protection.[21] In their survey of constitutions of 193 countries, they show that while constitutional protection for workers has considerably expanded to include the right to decent work and equal pay, there is still a gap in protection in relation to issues such as workplace injury compensation and sickness pay, and also in relation to vulnerable populations such as disabled persons and workers in the informal economy.

This analysis sets the tone for discussing how 'well-prepared' equality regimes have been in responding to inequality, especially that which has been exacerbated by crises. Laws which provide less than complete protection in ordinary times naturally

---

[19] See Aparna Chandra's chapter in this book, 'A Life of Contradictions: Group Inequality and Socio-Economic Rights in the Indian Constitution'.
[20] See Aaron Reeves, Kate Andersen, Mary Reader, and Rosalie Warnock's chapter in this book: 'Social Security, Exponential Inequalities, and Covid-19: How Welfare Reform in the UK Left Larger Families Exposed to the Scarring Effects of the Pandemic'.
[21] See Aleta Sprague, Amy Raub, and Jody Heymann's chapter in this book: 'Protecting Workers' Equal Rights During Crisis and Recovery: Constitutional Approaches in 193 Countries'.

fail to provide adequate protection during crisis. Thus, when pre-existing inequalities interact with crisis, especially measures put in place to address the crisis, they only exacerbate those inequalities such as in the case of migrant workers in India who were left to walk thousands of miles to their homes when the first lockdown was announced with less than a few hours' notice, which included a complete shutdown of transport services.[22] The lack of foresight in imagining how migrant and daily-wage workers in the informal economy living across states would have travelled back home, or had their basic needs such as food, water, shelter, and sanitation met, reveals a lack of appreciation of pre-existing inequality, almost as if it did not exist before the pandemic. But indeed, the inequality resulting from the pandemic only seems to build upon the very inequality which existed before.

It is striking that poverty or socio-economic disadvantage seems to be a defining characteristic of exponential inequalities studied in this book. Although we study exponential inequalities through the lens of equality laws which generally do not recognize poverty or socio-economic disadvantage as grounds of discrimination per se, we observe a preponderance of poverty or socio-economic disadvantage both within groups which are protected within recognized grounds and those which fall outside the recognized grounds. In fact, as Beth Gaze's contribution shows, the worst impact of the pandemic has been on the poor, and poverty levels have risen sharply.[23] She argues that pre-existing disadvantage which is socio-economic in nature remains largely unaddressed by Australian equality laws. This is because the laws have been too focused on attributes or identities associated with grounds of discrimination rather than their attendant socio-economic disadvantage. As she states, it is disadvantage, not discrimination, then which seems to be the cause of exponential inequalities.

This is true even in constitutions, such as that in Kenya. In her chapter, Victoria Miyandazi shows that the exponential rise in poverty by 13 per cent from 2019 to 2020 in Kenya impacted those who fell outside of the protection of the traditional grounds of discrimination, such as slum dwellers.[24] Through the case study of evictions at the height of the pandemic with lockdowns in place, her contribution shows the deliberate targeting of slum dwellers who were stigmatized as prone to spreading the virus. Yet even when evictions were stayed by judicial orders out of concern for inequality and socio-economic disadvantage, these orders were frequently disregarded. She shows that even well-meaning constitutional jurisprudence fails to be effective in an environment defined by apathy for inequality and rule of law. Equality laws, whether statutory or constitutional, thus need to be accompanied by effective enforcement to hold exponential inequalities genuinely at bay.

It is not only law but also political economy which has shaped poverty within and beyond status groups. Helena Alviar's contribution demonstrates the intimate relationship between political economy and poverty, especially gendered poverty.[25] Alviar

---

[22] Patralekha Chateerjee, 'The Pandemic Exposes India's Apathy Toward Migrant Workers' *The Atlantic* (12 April 2020).

[23] See Beth Gaze's chapter in this book: 'Responding to Exponential Inequalities in Australia: Beyond the Limits of Equality and Discrimination Law'.

[24] See Victoria Miyandazi's chapter in this book: 'An Equality-sensitive Approach to Delivering Socio-economic Rights During Crises: A Focus on Kenya in the Covid-19 Era'.

[25] See Helena Alviar García's chapter in this book: 'The Interaction of Laws Enabling Gender Equality with Other Legal Regimes: Limiting Progress in Times of Crisis'.

shows that despite a plethora of equality laws enforcing the constitutional guarantee of equality between sexes in the Colombian constitution, the lack of any budgetary allocation for implementing these laws has limited their potential to alleviate gender inequality. Thus, gender inequality has been exacerbated not only by a lack of public resources but also by neoliberal policies. In particular, she shows that decades of neoliberal policies to boost the mining sector in Colombia have essentially made women poorer with very little social and economic investment in either retaining women in the private sector or compensating for their labour at home. Coupled with a diminished role of the state across sectors such as healthcare and housing, these neoliberal policies essentially diminished the Colombian government's ability to respond to the pandemic in an appropriate manner. A fairer redistribution of resources thus remains key to gender equality but in the absence of clear obligations on both public and private sector in linking the two—redistribution of resources and gender equality—crises such as the pandemic only end up worsening the already dire situation of women in Colombia.

Exponential inequalities are also characterized by intersectional disadvantage wherein the worst of inequalities befall those who are disadvantaged because of their membership in two or more disadvantaged groups such as women of colour, single mothers, older women, disabled women, etc. Furthermore, crises too intersect to exacerbate inequality further. Intersectionality in both these senses defines the exponential inequalities studied in this book. In their chapter, Diane Elson and Marion Sharples apply a feminist economics lens to show how the Covid-19 pandemic has had a highly differential impact on workers depending on their gender, race, class, disability, and citizenship status, and in particularly sensitive areas such as essential services and public procurement.[26] They examine the situation in the UK, comparing the differences in public policies across the four nations and the impact they have had in creating exponential inequalities understood in an intersectional sense, that is, compounding the disadvantage suffered by those belonging to several vulnerable groups at a time. They draw on the UK Women's Budget Group research to show that health outcomes which were previously highly differentiated based on income and wealth, and further along racial and gendered lines, only widened in the wake of the pandemic. No singular factor can be isolated as having led to this, not even the pandemic. Their own contention is that economic policies adopted before, during, and after crises play a crucial role in creating and exacerbating exponential inequalities which are intersectional in nature.

Kelley Loper builds on this theme and shows how exponential inequalities result from multiple and intersecting crises.[27] With the example of Hong Kong, she demonstrates the dynamics of interaction of inequalities along multiple axes especially as they transpire when several major crises such as the democratic deficit and the Covid-19 pandemic interact with ongoing socio-political, economic, and cultural conflicts in a country. Loper shows that the lack of democratic participation affects those who

---

[26] See Diane Elson and Marion Sharples' chapter in this book: 'Addressing Intersecting Inequalities through Alternative Economic Strategies'.
[27] See Kelley Loper's chapter in this book: 'Intersecting Crises and Exponential Inequalities: The View from Hong Kong'.

are intersectionally disadvantaged (namely, women of ethnic minorities or immigrant women) worse than others during a crisis like the Covid-19 because they lack a voice to either protect their rights or to preserve the processes through which those rights can be protected during crises. She canvasses the dynamics of this interaction against the template of equality laws in Hong Kong and against the larger backdrop of equality laws in other Commonwealth countries to show how exponential inequalities develop without the intervening force of robust equality laws.

This is further exemplified by Marta Machado and Taís Penteado, who show that the present crisis has only intensified other crises, such as the roll back of reproductive rights in Brazil.[28] In a painstaking review of the current crisis, they map the disturbing impact of the pandemic on women's reproductive rights, especially women who are socio-economically vulnerable, domestic workers, disabled, and belonging to ethnic minorities. They hone in on the intensification of attacks on abortion rights during the Covid-19 pandemic when opportunities to resist those attacks were greatly reduced. The lack of participative democracy during the pandemic (which has been classified as an emergency in many countries) furnished an opportunity for the government to accelerate law and policy reform to make access to abortions and contraception not only scarce but also illegal in Brazil. They thus take this opportunity to resist the proposed criminalization of abortion through a substantive approach to gender equality which they argue is part of Brazilian constitutionalism and its promise of social justice for all groups.

A crisis can thus accelerate inequality and at the same time decelerate democracy and rule of law. The larger point is that, the compounding effects of the intersection of multiple forms of disadvantages and their interaction with multiple crises create a cascade of exponential inequalities which are causally difficult to disentangle as having arisen out of either a specific form of disadvantage or a particular crisis.

3 Equality Law

While the talk of exponential inequalities has been rife in the public discourse, not much seems to be said of equality law and its capacity to address exponential inequalities. The contributions in this book examine this hypothesis and show why equality law in practice has remained marginal despite an exponential rise in inequality.

In most jurisdictions, equality law has *not* been engaged to challenge exponential inequalities. As Colm O'Cinneide states in respect of the UK, 'it is notable that, at the time of writing—two years after the covid epidemic began—no serious equality law challenges have been brought against aspects of UK covid policy'.[29] His chapter thus critiques the structural and temporal limits of the current equality law regime in the UK. He suggests that, while equality law has some innovative features, they are ultimately piecemeal in addressing the exponential inequalities recounted above. He suggests instead that a substantive response to inequality today requires a concerted

---

[28] See Marta Machado and Tais Penteado's chapter in this book: 'Covid-19 and Exponential Reproductive Rights-related Inequalities in Brazil'.
[29] Colm O'Cinneide, 'New Directions Needed: Exponential Inequalities and the Limits of Equality Law'.

move beyond the existing adversarial model of equality law, and towards a much more radical institutional innovation. He explores what this could look like, drawing from the 1960s anti-discrimination institutional architecture, which included community relations boards, public advocates, and other 'tribute'-style mechanisms.

Similarly, in the case of Ireland, Mark Bell confirms that there is 'very little evidence of litigation on discrimination related to the pandemic'.[30] His chapter shows how the current structure of equality law organized around courts and case law remained latent in the present crisis when most of the response was policy-based. Bell critiques the limits of the complaints-based model of equality law in light of the sparse case law it has generated during the crisis, and thus looks to public sector equality and human rights duty in Ireland to provide a different recourse to addressing inequality during the crisis for challenging exponential inequalities.

While there has been a genuine lack of cases being brought forward under equality law in some countries, in others like Hong Kong, as Kelley Loper shows, the limited role of equality litigation is despite the interest in engaging equality law to bring complaints. For example, although the Equal Opportunities Commission—which has the power to investigate discrimination claims in Hong Kong—received 1,448 enquiries related to discrimination and Covid-19 in 2020, it is not clear how many cases were in fact investigated.[31] But it is clear that only one such case was actually adjudicated by a court.[32]

What explains this indifference to equality law? Doctrinal issues such as the reliance on grounds, the number and nature of recognized grounds, the scope of direct and indirect discrimination, the standard of review to be applied to discrimination claims, the range of available remedies, in addition to practical difficulties of time, money, and expertise in engaging equality law, all dictate the extent to which equality law is useful in particular jurisdictions. But prior to these doctrinal issues are issues with the architecture of equality law as a field which affect engagement with equality law at a more fundamental level. Two such broad sets of issues—relating to the material and structural scope of equality law—can be identified as the root causes of the waning influence of equality law in conversations around exponential inequalities during crises.

First, the material scope of equality law appears to be a mismatch for exponential inequalities. A crisis such as the Covid-19 pandemic is exceptional in its scale in that it has indeed impacted *everyone everywhere*, even if not *equally*. Recessions, climate disasters, and wars have a similar impact which is global in nature. This scale of exponential inequalities seems to transcend the personal and territorial scope of equality law.

In terms of the personal scope, both the constitutional right to equality as well as statutory non-discrimination guarantees are framed as individual rights or entitlements. Even though equality law is generally framed in reference to grounds (such as race and sex) and in turn groups defined by grounds (such as Black people and women), the protections themselves accrue to individuals based on their group

---

[30] Mark Bell, 'More than an Afterthought? Equality Law in Ireland during the Pandemic'.
[31] Kelley Loper, 'Intersecting Crises and Exponential Inequalities: The View from Hong Kong'.
[32] ibid.

membership or status related to grounds and not to groups themselves.[33] It is also in this sense that equality law is considered 'symmetrical' in nature, that is, it protects individuals as defined by grounds and not only members of disadvantaged groups alone.[34] Equality law has thus traditionally served individual claimants who have been able to show personal injury or discrimination suffered either individually or as a distinct class. This liberal model of equality law seems to have been a poor fit for challenging exponential inequalities which have arisen out of crises and the particular laws and policies adopted in response to crises which are fundamentally broad-based. Importantly, even where the impact of such laws and policies is not individual but group-based, equality law seems to be of little relevance where rights and entitlements themselves accrue to individuals. The leap from addressing discrimination against individuals belonging to disadvantaged groups, to group inequality per se has thus been difficult despite the conceptual link between the two in equality law.

Similarly, in terms of the territorial scope, both domestic and international equality laws which focus on states as the primary duty-bearers limit the possibility of global action which transcends nation-states or the focus on particular forms of disadvantage within them. Equality or non-discrimination based on grounds is thus conceived very much as a 'domestic' issue even when international law imposes a whole gamut of state obligations in this area. This means that, even though issues of inequality may transcend state boundaries and are truly global in nature, they can hardly be dealt with as such. This comes out in the issue of vaccine equity, which remains an illusion despite widespread agreement that one of the most effective responses—from a healthcare perspective—to the coronavirus is to vaccinate as many people as possible around the world.[35] Catherine O'Regan's chapter examines how international law is navigating the problem of 'vaccine nationalism' or equality in access to vaccines between countries. O'Regan discusses the intersection of three key areas in international law in promoting equality in access to vaccines. These areas include the rights protected in the International Covenant on Economic, Social and Cultural Rights (ICESCR), the international law on intellectual property under Trade-related Aspects of Intellectual Property Rights (TRIPs, especially the Doha Agreement), and the UN Guiding Principles on Business and Human Rights. Her chapter shows that equal access to vaccines remains a far cry, not only because of international human rights law's state-centric approach, but also because of the strong protection for patents in international law under the World Trade Organization's TRIPs agreement. The latter as a regime in fact rejects state-centrism and is actually premised on inter-state equity,[36] being potentially more effective in scalar terms. Trade and patent law thus trumps equality law—whether domestic or international—which is premised on state sovereignty and imposes obligations on states within their territorial boundaries primarily.

---

[33] See for an account of limitations of the grounds-based model of equality law, Kate Malleson, 'Equality Law and the Protected Characteristics' (2018) 81 Modern Law Review 598.
[34] Naomi Schoenbaum, 'The Case for Symmetry in Antidiscrimination Law' (2017) 69 Wisconsin Law Review 70.
[35] See statements made at the 2nd Global Covid-19 Summit https://ec.europa.eu/commission/presscorner/detail/en/STATEMENT_22_3050 (accessed 14 May 2022).
[36] See Catherine O'Regan's chapter in this book: 'Equal Access to Vaccines: Exposing the Limits of International Human Rights Law?'.

Secondly, the structure in which equality law is moulded—of court-centred adjudication—limits the possibilities of engagement with the field in either a proactive or prompt manner. Nearly all contributions to this book identify the predominantly litigious model of equality law as a severe constraint in engaging the field in times of crisis.

At a very basic level is the issue of temporality. Equality law under the litigious model is meant to be reacting to discrimination which has already occurred. Moreover, discrimination that is sought to be addressed under the litigious model is episodic in nature, focusing on a particular action or omission as leading to a particular kind of impact which is deemed discriminatory.[37] The ex post and episodic nature of discrimination that is meant to be remedied by courts, however, sits awkwardly against the nature of crisis which, as discussed above, is broad-based especially in terms of its impact which is multi-causal and predicated on pre-existing inequalities. In fact, the exponential inequalities resulting from a crisis are far from the 'central case' of equality law imagined in the form of discrimination directed towards someone because they are a member of a disadvantaged group.[38]

For example, rejecting a woman for a job because she is a woman, or denial of service to a Black customer because she is Black, are typical cases of discrimination the body of equality law is meant to serve.[39] Even a slight deviance from these—when someone is rejected for a job or denied service because she is a woman *and* Black—complicates matters in equality law, which is imagined to address discrimination based on a single ground alone.[40] This aversion to intersectionality is broadly an aversion to complexity in equality law, where the impact that equality law is meant to address is imagined as discrete and limited to an individual. It serves the adjudicative frame perfectly by streamlining judicial discretion to be applied to a very particular kind of inequality, that is, discrimination based on grounds and in specific cases. In other words, the limited conceptual nature of equality law serves the limited nature of the litigious model in which equality law is moulded. None of this comports with the nature of crisis which requires prompt responses to impact which is extremely broad-based and not limited to an episode concerning an individual alone.

---

[37] Sandra Fredman Discrimination Law (3rd edn, OUP 2022) ch 8.

[38] Shreya Atrey, 'On the Central Case Methodology in Discrimination Law' (2021) 41 Oxford Journal of Legal Studies 776.

[39] Paul Brest, 'In Defense of the Antidiscrimination Principle' (1976) 90 Harvard Law Review 1, 2, 5; Larry Alexander, 'What Makes Wrongful Discrimination Wrong? Biases, Preferences, Stereotypes and Proxies' (1992) 141 University of Pennsylvania Law Review 149, 151; Cass Sunstein, 'The Anticaste Principle' (1994) 92 Michigan Law Review 2410, 2412.

[40] Kimberlé W Crenshaw, 'Demarginalizing the Intersection of Race and Sex: A Black Feminist Critique of Antidiscrimination Doctrine, Feminist Theory and Antiracist Politics' (1989) University of Chicago Legal Forum 139; Sandra Fredman and Erika Szyszczak, 'The Interaction of Race and Gender' in Bob Hepple and Erika Szyszczak (eds), *Discrimination: The Limits of the Law* (Mansell 1992); Sarah Hannett, 'Equality at the Intersections: The Legislative and Judicial Failure to Tackle Multiple Discrimination' (2003) 23 Oxford Journal of Legal Studies 65; Aileen McColgan, 'Reconfiguring Discrimination Law' [2007] Public Law 74; Iyiola Solanke, 'Putting Race and Gender Together: A New Approach to Intersectionality' (2009) 72 Modern Law Review 723; Dagmar Schiek and Anna Lawson, *European Union Non-Discrimination Law and Intersectionality* (Ashgate 2011); Dagmar Schiek and Victoria Chege (eds), *European Union Non-Discrimination Law: Comparative Perspectives on Multidimensional Equality Law* (Routledge Cavendish 2008); Shreya Atrey, *Intersectional Discrimination* (OUP 2019).

Given these 'framework issues' with equality law, some authors in the book suggest exceeding equality law altogether. For example, Jessica Clarke critiques the limited legal model of equality law as focused on 'anti-discrimination' in the US.[41] She contrasts this model with the more capacious understanding of equality in US public policy such as through the principle of 'health equity', which has informed data science and policy responses to inequality. She identifies the public policy approach as showing greater promise than equality law in the US in fighting extreme and entrenched forms of health inequity. In particular, she argues that the public policy approach, including broad guidelines, goals and principles which guide the discretion of public officials, has the potential to address systemic inequalities which have remained beyond the reach of US constitutional law hitherto confined to intentional discrimination based on a narrow set of grounds.[42] The public policy approach also allows designing remedial measures in response to grave statistical disparities or disadvantage—for example in relation to health indicators—which have so far been treated with scepticism by the US Supreme Court and dismissed as evidence of bad luck or misfortune.[43] She identifies this potential as embedded in the conceptual shift from talking about 'equality' as in 'anti-discrimination' in law to 'equality' as in 'equity' in the public policy domain, a shift which she argues breaks free from the clutches of legal rules which have stymied US equality law.

Likewise, Diane Elson and Marion Sharples suggest focusing on the economy and economic principles which give rise to exponential inequalities and to attack those with a paradigm shift to feminist economic principles for the creation of a caring economy which is truly 'equalizing'.[44] They set out an eight-step plan for a caring economy including a central organizing principle which reimagines economy as centred around care work, that is, receiving and giving care. This can be potentially transformative in addressing inequalities in the UK, which have remained largely untouched by the Equality Act 2010—the leading comprehensive state-of-the-art equality legislation in the country.[45]

Others are not so quick in exceeding equality law. They show that despite its framework limitations, equality law remains open to intervention in both new and old ways. In a structural sense, both Mark Bell and Colm O'Cinneide show that there are opportunities beyond the litigious model of equality law which can be tapped into during crises. For example, Mark Bell shows the influence of EU equality law on Irish legislation where a gap in protection excluding workers on maternity or temporary leave from the Temporary Wage Subsidy Scheme was filled by invoking the primacy of EU law and by activating the discretionary provisions of the revenue officers in charge of delivering the scheme.[46] Neither resort to adversarial proceedings; nor was immediate legislative change required. Appeal to equality law by the Irish Human Rights

---

[41] See Jessica Clarke's chapter in this book, 'A Public Policy Approach to Inequality'.
[42] ibid.
[43] ibid.
[44] Diane Elson and Marion Sharples, 'Addressing Intersecting Inequalities through Alternative Economic Strategies'.
[45] Bob Hepple, 'The Aims of Equality Law' (2008) 61(1) Current Legal Problems 1; Bob Hepple, 'The New Single Equality Act in Britain' (2010) 5 Equal Rights Review 11.
[46] Mark Bell, 'More than an Afterthought? Equality Law in Ireland During the Pandemic'.

and Equality Commission was sufficient to convince the government to course correct and to offer social benefits which were not discriminatory towards women or temporary workers.

Similarly, tools which have so far remained dormant too have potential in guiding decision-making during crises. For example, while the public sector equality and human rights duty in Ireland[47] and the public sector equality duty in Great Britain[48] have not been engaged explicitly during the pandemic, there is clear room for activating them either via the Irish Human Rights and Equality Commission (Ireland) or the Equality and Human Rights Commission (UK) or in wider public discourse to insist on equality analysis at the time of adopting, or soon thereafter, measures in response to crises.[49] The pliability of these proactive equality duties makes them much more functional in being put to use by public bodies during crises, especially given that there is great leeway in showing *compliance* with the duty but clear mandates on *engaging* them nevertheless.[50] Similarly, although no model of proactive duties necessarily requires an equality impact assessment before or after a measure is adopted, nothing bars an expansive reading of the existing duties to include an equality impact assessment as such, especially if the bodies or courts in charge of monitoring and/or enforcing these duties consider equality impact assessment as vital. There is a strong case to be made for this in the context of crisis. Given that the measures adopted in response to crisis are extremely broad-based and carry inherent risks in affecting different groups differently based on their vulnerability, an equality impact assessment can be powerful in reckoning with inequalities and responding to them by tailoring the measures appropriately. Furthermore, a group level assessment of measures seems necessary not only from an equality perspective but also from the perspective of the measures themselves to be effective in a crisis. Likewise, the fact that proactive duties are framed in a processual rather than in a reactive mode makes them ply not only at a particular point in time before or after a certain measure is adopted, but throughout its course.

Proactive duties provide a useful antidote to the entrenched dichotomy of courts as the sole guardians, and rights-bearers as victims seeking enforcement of their rights under equality law. They widen the pool of those who use equality law as equal participants, diluting the rigid binary of rights-bearers and duty-bearers.[51] As Alysia Blackham shows, the newly minted gender equality duty in the Gender Equality Act 2020 (Vic) applicable in the Australian state of Victoria, capitalizes on these possibilities by laying down a comprehensive model of proactive duties to

---

[47] Irish Human Rights and Equality Commission Act 2014, s 42(1).
[48] Equality Act 2010, s 149.
[49] Conor Casey and others, 'Ireland's Emergency Powers During the Covid-19 Pandemic' (IHREC 2021) https://www.ihrec.ie/documents/irelands-emergency-powers-during-the-covid-19-pandemic/ (accessed 14 May 2022).
[50] Sandra Fredman, 'Breaking the Mold: Equality as a Proactive Duty' (2012) 60 American Journal of Comparative Law 265; Sandra Fredman, 'The Public Sector Equality Duty' (2011) 40 Industrial Law Journal 405; Alysia Blackham, 'Positive Equality Duties: The Future of Equality and Transparency?' (2021) 37 Law in Context 98.
[51] Simonetta Manfredi, Lucy Vickers, and Kate Clayton-Hathway, 'The Public Sector Equality Duty: Enforcing Equality Rights Through Second-Generation Regulation' (2018) 47 Industrial Law Journal 365; Sandra Fredman, *Discrimination Law* (3rd edn, OUP 2022) ch 8.

consider and promote gender equality through: taking necessary and proportionate action towards achieving gender equality in developing policies and programmes and delivering public services;[52] undertaking workplace gender audits;[53] developing and implementing gender equality action plans;[54] undertaking gender impact assessments when developing or reviewing any policy, or public programme or service;[55] making reasonable and material progress towards workplace gender equality indicators such as gender composition at workplace;[56] publicly reporting on progress every two years;[57] and allowing the government to issue guidelines in relation to the allocation of funding[58] and procurement.[59] Importantly, as Blackham argues, this model of proactive duties mandates *consultation* as a necessary part of discharging the duty, thus strengthening the participative dimension of equality law and imposes a duty to ensure *progress* towards gender equality, thus striking a balance between process and outcomes.[60] Although there are limitations to this model, including the lack of individual enforcement, it shows the potential there may be in setting up equality laws which lack neither ex post individual enforcement nor group-based proactive duties, and are ultimately effective in appreciating what she calls a 'life course approach' to age and gender inequality.

In this regard, Anna Lawson and Lisa Waddington's chapter shows the particular value-added of the anticipatory reasonable adjustment duty under the Equality Act 2010 in Great Britain, to the litigious model of equality law.[61] They examine the 'traditional' nature of reasonable accommodation duty against the more proactive British model which requires an ex ante assessment of needs of disabled persons rather than leaving reasonable accommodation to be triggered when accessibility is already impaired. They show that the anticipatory reasonable adjustment duty, which requires duty-bearers to consider and provide for the needs of disabled people *before* a demand is made, can make a significant difference in preventing exponential inequalities in contrast with the traditional reasonable adjustment duty which is only triggered ex post. In fact, the anticipatory nature of the duty, as Fordham J's reasoning in *R (on the application of Rowley) v Minister for the Cabinet Office*[62] confirms, applies as much in crises as in ordinary times. It thus provides a mechanism for taking into account the needs of the most vulnerable to prevent exposing them to the worst effects of a crisis. Furthermore, since the ex-ante reasonable adjustment duty is group-based, as opposed to the traditional reasonable adjustment duty which is individual specific, it targets a larger cross-section of disabled people than possible under the liberal model

---

[52] Gender Equality Act 2020 (Vic), s 7.
[53] ibid s 11.
[54] ibid s 10.
[55] ibid s 9.
[56] ibid s 16(1).
[57] ibid s 19.
[58] ibid s 48.
[59] ibid s 49.
[60] ibid ss 10(2)(b), 12(3), 16(1), 18(1)–(2), 22.
[61] See Anna Lawson and Lisa Waddington's chapter in this book: 'Disability in Times of Emergency: Exponential Inequality and the Role of Reasonable Accommodation Duties'. See also Anna Lawson and Maria Orchard, 'The Anticipatory Reasonable Adjustment Duty: Removing the Blockages?' (2021) 80 Cambridge Law Journal 308.
[62] [2021] EWHC 2108 (Admin).

of equality law. As Lawson and Waddington argue, this is further confirmed in the unprecedented rise of collective class action claims for disability discrimination under the Equality Act 2010, which could be attributed in large part to the ex-ante duty itself. Indeed, both private actors such as supermarkets, as well as public actors, such as the government have had to change course in light of these claims for making grocery shopping, both online and on site, more accessible for disabled persons; and for making government communication more accessible to persons with hearing difficulties. The extraordinary mobilization of collective disability discrimination claims during the pandemic shows the immense possibility in challenging both the liberal and litigious model of equality law and replacing it with group-based and governance-oriented tools which are pre-emptive, flexible, and user-friendly.

In a substantive sense, Jule Mulder's contribution shows similar possibilities which can be activated, for example, with regards to indirect discrimination.[63] Her contribution seeks to understand whether the EU sex discrimination law can support workers in this more precarious and reorganized setting where a large part of the workforce is working from home, a phenomenon which is probably here to stay. In particular, she focuses on indirect discrimination law to assess whether 'particular disadvantage' can be construed as disadvantage related to reformed workspace, ie home; and whether reasonable accommodation measures can be expected in response to indirect sex discrimination claims. She shows that, while the extant doctrine of indirect discrimination in EU equality law may seem intractable in accommodating flexible work arrangements which have become mainstream since the Covid-19 pandemic, there are yet conceptual possibilities which do not exclude future developments. These include bridging the divide between public and private spheres and regulating private workspaces (including home as workspace), and imposing remedies for structural reform rather than simply reasonable accommodation for the individuals who complain of indirect discrimination. In particular, she argues that an expansive reading of indirect discrimination may well enable these developments and ensure that the future of work is fairer and equitable for women.

In a similar vein, Meghan Campbell's contribution argues that a robust application of the proportionality test at the justification stage of an indirect discrimination claim can enable the courts finding exponential inequalities unlawful.[64] She shows that crises such as the global recession of 2008 triggered economic policies in the UK which were left largely unchecked under the prevailing equality law. It is indeed these policies which have exacerbated the inequalities in the current pandemic, given that the standard of review for challenging these policies under equality law—of proportionality—remains weak. Instead, she argues that the necessity limb of the proportionality test, which requires the government or the decision-maker to show that no less intrusive means was available in responding to a crisis, could be crucial in finding against the government, if considered sincerely.

There is also more to be made of constitutional equality laws, especially where socio-economic rights are part of constitutional bill of rights. Victoria Miyandazi and Aparna Chandra respectively make a strong case for reading the guarantee and enforcement

---

[63] See Jule Mulder's chapter in this book: 'Reorganisation of Work and EU Sex Discrimination Law'.
[64] See Meghan's Campbell's chapter in this book: 'The Proportionality of an Economic Crisis'.

of socio-economic rights—as mandated under Kenyan and Indian constitutions—in conjunction with the right to equality and non-discrimination such that the violations of socio-economic rights are particularly adjudicated from the standpoint of disadvantaged groups. In her chapter, Aparna Chandra examines the disjuncture between socio-economic rights and the right to equality and non-discrimination. As she shows, much of the socio-economic rights litigation in India has in fact involved disadvantaged groups such as women, disabled persons, children, Dalits, Muslims, and those belonging to several of these groups at once.[65] Yet, no group-based analysis of the impact of their unequal position in accessing and enjoying socio-economic rights has ensued. Indeed, claims of socio-economic rights are rarely assessed in reference to vulnerable groups even when vulnerable groups are at the helm of these claims. She argues for centring concerns of group inequality in relation to vulnerable groups such as women, Dalits, disabled persons, etc in socio-economic rights adjudication. Only such an approach to adjudication can be effective in mitigating pre-existing inequalities which give rise to exponential inequalities during crises. Her analysis, together with that of Victoria Miyandazi, reinforces the fact that a co-joint reading of equality rights with human rights can achieve greater equality in the realization of human rights of disadvantaged groups, while its absence aggravates both inequality and human rights violations.

South African jurisprudence remains the exemplar in demonstrating the value of the equality-based approach to socio-economic rights. As Cathi Albertyn shows in respect of *Mahlangu v Minister of Labour*,[66] the South African Constitutional Court has developed a robust approach to tackling not only issues of status-based inequality between disadvantaged groups but also issues of poverty in its post-pandemic jurisprudence.[67] Although *Mahlangu* did not concern the pandemic itself, its intricate analysis weaving in issues of race, gender, poverty, and class in accessing employment injury compensation provides cues to other constitutional courts for tackling complex forms of inequality without losing sight of wealth inequality, poverty, and class.[68] In addition, South African courts have also paved the way for accepting poverty as a prohibited ground and have thus created multiple routes to reckoning with poverty as a form of disadvantage whether as discrimination in and of itself or as contributing to the violation of other rights and freedoms.[69] Nevertheless, Albertyn shows that, although the South African equality jurisprudence has been progressive, it has not been successful on its own in upturning massive patterns of pre-existing disadvantage. In this context, she explains how the current pandemic has only driven home this realization that equality law, while acting as a good mitigator, can hardly be transformative

---

[65] Aparna Chandra, 'A Life of Contradictions: Group Inequality and Socio-Economic Rights in the Indian Constitution'.
[66] [2020] ZACC 24.
[67] See Catherine Albertyn's chapter in this book: 'The Role of Equality Law in Expanding Access to Social Goods and Services in South Africa: Lessons after the Pandemic'.
[68] See also Shreya Atrey, 'Beyond Discrimination: Mahlangu and the Use of Intersectionality as a General Theory of Constitutional Interpretation' (2021) International Journal of Discrimination Law https://doi.org/10.1177/13582291211015637 (accessed 14 May 2022).
[69] *Social Justice Coalition v Minister of Police* [2018] ZAWCHC 181 [57]–[65].

on its own in addressing inequalities of the scale that exist, persist, and continue to generate further exponential inequalities in South Africa.

Thus, both framework issues as well as more jurisdiction-specific doctrinal issues show where the possibilities of engagement with equality law lie in the future. Neither tools beyond equality law nor the traditional model of equality law need be abandoned to activate these other possibilities. But they do need to be explored and actually harnessed because the current practice seems to overlook them entirely. This book hopes to do just this.

PART I
UNDERSTANDING EXPONENTIAL INEQUALITIES

2
Protecting Workers' Equal Rights during Crisis and Recovery
Constitutional Approaches in 193 Countries

Aleta Sprague, Amy Raub, and Jody Heymann

1 Introduction

Across countries, the Covid-19 pandemic has served to bring new light to long-standing inequalities, both within and among countries. In many respects, these inequalities intersect with work. Workers from marginalized groups are over-represented in jobs that subject them to high risks of exposure to the virus.[1] Marginalized workers are also disproportionately concentrated in low-wage, part-time, in-person, and informal work, leaving them more vulnerable to job loss triggered by the pandemic.[2] And beyond those whose positions were terminated, many were forced out of jobs due to other inequalities; in particular, restrictive gender norms have led millions more women to leave the workforce to manage their families' care needs as schools and day-care facilities shut.[3] Compounding all these risks are the gaps in social protection that disproportionately exclude many of the workers with greatest need for financial support, as well as the high risks of employment discrimination against marginalized groups as economies begin to recover.[4]

Constitutional guarantees of equality and fundamental social and economic protections can provide an important practical and normative foundation for protecting the equal rights of marginalized workers amidst and in the wake of crises like Covid-19.

---

[1] See eg Noreen Goldman and others, 'Racial and Ethnic Differentials in COVID-19-Related Job Exposures by Occupational Status in the US' (2021) 16 PloS One 9; Laurent Bossavie and others, 'Do Immigrants Shield the Locals? Exposure to COVID-Related Risks in the European Union' World Bank Policy Research Working Paper No 9500 (2020); Yea-Hung Chen and others, 'Excess Mortality Associated with the COVID-19 Pandemic among Californians 18–65 years of Age, by Occupational Sector and Occupation: March through November 2020' (2021) 16 Plos One 0252454.

[2] International Labour Organization, 'World Employment and Social Outlook: Trends 2021' (2021) https://www.ilo.org/wcmsp5/groups/public/---dgreports/---dcomm/---publ/documents/publication/wcms_795453.pdf (accessed 3 January 2022).

[3] Kate Power, 'The COVID-19 Pandemic Has Increased the Care Burden of Women and Families' (2020) 16 Sustainability: Science, Practice and Policy 67.

[4] Kenneth A Couch and Robert Fairlie, 'Last Hired, First Fired? Black-white Unemployment and the Business Cycle' (2010) 47 Demography 227; Anton Nilsson, 'Who Suffers from Unemployment? The Role of Health and Skills' (2015) 4 IZA Journal of Labor Policy 1; Rebecca Lessem and Kayuna Nakajima, 'Immigrant Wages and Recessions: Evidence from Undocumented Mexicans' (2019) 114 European Economic Review 92; George Gray Molina and Eduardo Ortiz-Juarez, 'Temporary Basic Income: Protecting Poor and Vulnerable People in Developing Countries' (2020) United Nations Development Programme https://www.undp.org/publications/temporary-basic-income-tbi (accessed 24 April 2022).

Aleta Sprague, Amy Raub, and Jody Heymann, *Protecting Workers' Equal Rights during Crisis and Recovery* In: *Exponential Inequalities*. Edited by: Shreya Atrey and Sandra Fredman, Oxford University Press. © Aleta Sprague, Amy Raub, and Jody Heymann 2023. DOI: 10.1093/oso/9780192872999.003.0002

Comprehensive constitutional protections against discrimination have had demonstrated impact as a tool for claiming equal rights to public goods and addressing systemic discrimination in the economy, and hold meaningful expressive value as an affirmation of every person's equal worth and dignity.[5] Constitutional guarantees to social protection and minimum labour standards can help ensure that these fundamental rights and supports are available universally, which is essential to establishing a more equitable baseline for workers rather than only providing remedies for discrimination after the fact.

This chapter examines the scope, potential, and early impacts of these constitutional provisions in mitigating the damage of Covid-19 and addressing the 'exponential inequalities' that have arisen as the pandemic's health and economic shocks layer upon existing disparities. Specifically, this chapter: (1) examines how the pandemic has exacerbated inequality among working adults; (2) reviews early examples of how constitutions provided a tool to address disparities; (3) analyses the extent to which constitutions provide adequate protections for equal rights, decent work, and social insurance in all 193 UN countries; and (4) concludes by identifying gaps likely to leave workers vulnerable if they go unaddressed. We find that explicit constitutional protections for almost all aspects of equal rights, decent work, and social insurance that we examine have become more common over time; moreover, courts from a range of countries have cited these provisions in decisions addressing workers' rights and households' material needs amidst Covid-19. Nevertheless, protections in certain areas that are consequential to equality both during pandemics and more typical years—including safe working conditions, income protection during illness and unemployment, and non-discrimination on the basis of disability—remain underaddressed on a global scale.

2 Covid-19's Economic Impacts on Marginalized Workers

Around the world, the Covid-19 pandemic has had profound consequences for workers from marginalized groups, exacerbating underlying inequalities. Meanwhile, across countries, the most vulnerable workers are often excluded from core labour and social protections like paid sick leave and unemployment benefits. Three months into the pandemic, the United Nations Development Programme (UNDP) reported that nearly four billion people—disproportionately informal and low-wage workers, women, refugees, migrants, and people with disabilities—lacked access to social insurance amidst Covid-19.[6] Moreover, if past crises are any indication, we can expect the disparate economic impacts of the pandemic to continue into recovery.

---

[5] Jody Heymann, Aleta Sprague, and Amy Raub, *Advancing Equality: How Constitutional Rights Can Make a Difference Worldwide* (UC Press 2020).

[6] Molina and Ortiz-Juarez (n 4).

2.1 Risks of Job and Income Loss

Across countries, job losses triggered by the pandemic have been concentrated in fields in which women, migrants, and low-wage workers are over-represented.[7] Statistics from individual countries provide examples: in Turkey, for instance, a May 2020 survey found that 69–87 per cent of refugee households had experienced a job loss due to the pandemic.[8] In South Africa, 24 per cent of manual labourers lost their jobs between February and April 2020, while an additional 11 per cent were furloughed without pay; in contrast, just 5 per cent of the country's professional workers lost their jobs in the same period, and just 7 per cent were furloughed.[9] In the US, over a million more women than men lost their jobs in 2020, and Black and Latina women faced the greatest losses due their over-representation in the leisure, hospitality, education, and health sectors; these gaps were compounded by the increased care-giving demands created by the pandemic, which contributed to 154,000 Black women leaving the US labour force in December 2020 alone.[10]

The crisis has been particularly devastating for the approximately two billion workers in the informal economy, many of whom are self-employed. In Delhi, for example, a survey conducted following the first wave of lockdowns in the spring of 2020 found that 83 per cent of women in informal work had experienced a 'severe' drop in income.[11] These different vulnerabilities also intersect; in Brazil, for example, self-employed workers lost significantly more work hours due to the pandemic than employees, and self-identified Black and mixed race self-employed workers experienced greater losses than the White self-employed.[12] In the UK, Black, Asian, and Minority Ethnic (BAME) migrant workers were three times more likely to lose their jobs than White, UK-born workers during the country's initial lockdown, even after controlling for higher rates of self-employment among BAME workers.[13]

---

[7] International Labour Organization, *ILO Monitor: COVID-19 and the World of Work* (7th edn, ILO 25 January 2021) https://www.ilo.org/wcmsp5/groups/public/---dgreports/---dcomm/documents/briefingnote/wcms_767028.pdf (accessed 3 January 2022).

[8] International Labour Organization, 'Protecting the Rights at Work of Refugees and Other Forcibly Displaced Persons during the COVID-19 Pandemic' (2020) https://www.refworld.org/docid/5ef48e404.html (accessed 3 January 2022).

[9] Ronak Jain and others, 'The Labour Market and Poverty Impacts of COVID-19 in South Africa' Southern Africa Labour and Development Research Unit Working Paper No 264 (2020) 20 http://www.opensaldru.uct.ac.za/bitstream/handle/11090/980/2020_264_Saldruwp.pdf?sequence=1 (accessed 3 January 2022).

[10] Diane Boesch and Shilpa Phadke, 'When Women Lose All the Jobs: Essential Actions for a Gender-Equitable Recovery' Center for American Progress (1 February 2021) https://www.americanprogress.org/issues/women/reports/2021/02/01/495209/women-lose-jobs-essential-actions-gender-equitable-recovery/ (accessed 3 January 2022).

[11] Shiney Chakraborty, 'Impact of COVID-19 National Lockdown on Women Informal Workers in Delhi' Institute of Social Studies Trust (May 2020) https://www.isstindia.org/publications/1591186006_pub_compressed_ISST_-_Final_Impact_of_Covid_19_Lockdown_on_Women_Informal_Workers_Delhi.pdf (accessed 3 January 2022).

[12] Igor Pereira and Pankaj C Patel, 'Impact of the COVID-19 Pandemic on the Hours Lost by Self-employed Racial Minorities: Evidence from Brazil' (2021) 58 Small Business Economics 769.

[13] Yang Hu, 'Intersecting Ethnic and Native–migrant Inequalities in the Economic Impact of the COVID-19 Pandemic in the UK' (2020) 68 Research in Social Stratification and Mobility 100528.

2.2 Risks of Exposure to Covid-19

Marginalized workers also occupy a disproportionate share of front-line jobs, where working conditions heighten their risks of exposure to infection. Globally, women comprise 70 per cent of the health workforce, and an even higher proportion of jobs requiring intensive, hands-on care;[14] migrant women and women from marginalized racial and ethnic groups are also over-represented among women in these roles.[15] Across low- and middle-income countries, sanitation workers and domestic workers, who often work in informal jobs, face higher risks of infection due to exposure risks of their jobs.

2.3 Exclusion from Labour Laws and Social Protection

These occupational risks have been exacerbated by gaps and disparities in social protection. Part-time workers, the self-employed, and many people working in the informal economy—including agricultural, domestic, and gig workers—often lack full access to their countries' social insurance and labour protection laws. For example, our recent analysis of 193 countries found that just 42 per cent guarantee sick leave to the self-employed, while only a third of countries explicitly cover those working part-time.[16] Many countries also exclude some or all non-citizens from eligibility for unemployment benefits and other aspects of the social safety net, and many even extended this approach to Covid-19 emergency measures.[17]

In other words, in many countries, existing labour and social policies have not only offered insufficient support as Covid-19 spreads, but have also made long-standing inequalities worse by disproportionately excluding those workers who already face greater health and economic risks. This failure to provide universal coverage not only widens disparities but also perpetuates the pandemic itself by making it more difficult for workers to access medical care, meet other basic health needs, or stay at home when sick. And globally, the consequences for hunger, homelessness, and economic hardship are vast: since 2019, the number of workers worldwide classified as 'poor' or 'extremely poor'—meaning they subsist on less than US$3.20 per day—has increased by 108 million, erasing five years of progress towards ending global working poverty.[18]

---

[14] World Health Organization, 'Delivered by Women, Led by Men: A Gender and Equity Analysis of the Global Health and Social Workforce' (2019) https://apps.who.int/iris/handle/10665/311322 (accessed 3 January 2022).

[15] Sarah Spencer and others, 'The Role of Migrant Care Workers in Ageing Societies: Report on Research Findings in the United Kingdom, Ireland, Canada and the United States' International Organization for Migration (2010) https://publications.iom.int/system/files/pdf/mrs41.pdf (accessed 3 January 2022).

[16] Jody Heymann and others, 'Protecting Health During COVID-19 and Beyond: A Global Examination of Paid Sick Leave Design in 193 Countries' (2020) 15(7) Global Public Health 925, 930.

[17] Maria Santillana, 'The Impact of Covid-19 on Migrants, Asylum Seekers and Refugees' *International IDEA* (17 June 2021) https://www.idea.int/news-media/news/impact-covid-19-migrants-asylum-seekers-and-refugees (accessed 3 January 2022).

[18] International Labour Organization, 'World Employment and Social Outlook: Trends 2021' (2021) https://www.ilo.org/wcmsp5/groups/public/---dgreports/---dcomm/---publ/documents/publication/wcms_795453.pdf (accessed 3 January 2022).

2.4 Risks of Discrimination in Recovery

Finally, even as some countries' economies begin to recover as vaccines become widely available, the employment inequalities exacerbated by the pandemic are likely to persist or even widen further. A July 2021 report from the ILO forecasted that globally, women would hold 13 million fewer jobs in 2021 compared to 2019, while men's employment would recover to 2019 levels.[19] Further, evidence from past crises also suggests that an increase in discrimination by employers during periods of large-scale unemployment is likely. Studies have found that workers from marginalized backgrounds—including workers with disabilities, migrants, and racial and ethnic minorities—face higher risks of discrimination during economic downturns.[20]

Indeed, some research suggests an increase in discrimination against marginalized workers is already happening: in the US, for instance, research has shown that the portion of the disability pay gap that is 'unexplained'—ie that is not attributable to observed differences in qualifications—increased during the pandemic, suggesting that employer discrimination against workers with disabilities is on the rise.[21] In addition, due to the pandemic's presumed origins in China and the spread of variants across countries, Covid-19 in particular has escalated xenophobic and anti-Asian bias, including in workplaces; in Australia, for instance, the share of Asian–Australian workers who reported experiencing discrimination at work jumped by 15 percentage points between April and October 2020, and Asian–Australians have also sustained more enduring declines in employment than the general population.[22] Globally, however, the scope and comprehensiveness of statutory protections against workplace discrimination vary widely: while a substantial majority of countries prohibit at least some discrimination at work based on sex and race, not all do. Moreover, far fewer countries prohibit discrimination on the basis of migration status or foreign national origin.[23]

In addition, long-standing biases and restrictive underlying norms about work—particularly with respect to gender—further threaten an equitable recovery. The 2020

---

[19] International Labour Organization, 'Fewer Women than Men Will Regain Employment During the COVID-19 Recovery, Says ILO' (19 July 2021) https://www.ilo.org/global/about-the-ilo/newsroom/news/WCMS_813449/lang--en/index.htm (accessed 3 January 2022).

[20] Couch and Fairlie (n 4); Nilsson (n 4); Lessem and Nakajima (n 4); Patrick Taran, 'The Impact of the Financial Crisis on Migrant Workers, Presentation to the 17th OSCE Economic and Environmental Forum. International Labour Office' (2009) https://www.osce.org/files/f/documents/6/d/36454.pdf (accessed 24 April 2022).

[21] Lisa Schur, Yana van der Meulen Rodgers, and Douglas L Kruse, 'COVID-19 and Employment Losses for Workers with Disabilities: An Intersectional Approach' The Center for Women and Work Working Paper 2021-2 (2021) https://smlr.rutgers.edu/sites/default/files/Documents/Centers/CWW/Publications/draft_covid19_and_disability_report.pdf (accessed 3 January 2022).

[22] Nicholas Biddle, Matthew Gray, and Jieh Yung Lo, 'The Experience of Asian-Australians during the COVID-19 Pandemic: Discrimination and Wellbeing' (2020) https://csrm.cass.anu.edu.au/sites/default/files/docs/2020/11/The_experience_of_Asian-Australians_during_the_COVID-19_pandemic.pdf (accessed 3 January 2022); Michelle Toh, Moss Cohen, and Lauren Cook, 'Attacked at Work, Rejected for Jobs and Harassed by Colleagues' *CNN Business* (7 June 2021) https://www.cnn.com/interactive/2021/06/business/asians-workplace-discrimination-covid/ (accessed 3 January 2022).

[23] Jody Heymann and others, 'Legislative Approaches to Nondiscrimination at Work: A Comparative Analysis across 13 Groups in 193 Countries' (2020) 40(3) Equality, Diversity and Inclusion 225.

World Values Survey, which captures views on social issues from more than 100 countries, found that 43 per cent of respondents agreed with the statement that 'when jobs are scarce, men should have a greater right to work than women'. The impacts of restrictive gender norms have also been on full display in how the widespread closures of schools and childcare centres have disproportionately harmed women's employment, making clear that sufficiently addressing care, and comprehensively prohibiting discrimination linked to care-giving responsibilities, will be essential to both households' and countries' economic recovery.

3 The Role of Constitutional Rights to Equality, Decent Work, and Social Protection during the Pandemic: Examples from Case Law

While it's too soon to comprehensively evaluate how constitutions' influence on countries' responses to and recovery from Covid-19, some early case law suggests that rights to equality, social insurance, and decent working conditions have already had impact amidst the pandemic in at least four key ways: by protecting the rights of vulnerable workers, by mandating the provision of material support to households affected by income loss, by invalidating gaps in legislation that exclude marginalized workers from key protections, and by ordering governments to improve working conditions for those in front-line positions.

3.1 Protecting Rights for Vulnerable and Informal Workers

As noted earlier, migrant and informal labourers have faced some of the most severe consequences due to the pandemic. Without an employment contract or access to social protection, informal workers who lose their jobs due to the pandemic or who fall ill and cannot work may have little recourse. For those working abroad, a loss of work can simultaneously trigger loss of legal status in their destination country or increase the risks of being undocumented. A number of court cases have addressed countries' responsibilities to protect the rights of migrant and other vulnerable workers during the pandemic.

For example, in *K Ramakirshna v Union of India*, the High Court of Andhra Pradesh addressed the state's constitutional obligations to help workers from small villages who had been working temporarily in distant cities return home. As the court noted, due to the economic shutdown, thousands of these internal migrants were returning to their homes on foot. Pursuant to a public interest litigation case filed on the basis of the workers' constitutional rights to equality, non-discrimination, and life, the court ordered the government to provide the workers and their families with food, water, medical care, and train transportation to facilitate their journeys home.[24] Similarly, in Nepal, the Supreme Court addressed two similar cases focused on migrant workers

---

[24] *K Ramakrishna v The Union of India*, WP(PIL) 101 OF 2020, 22 May 2020 (High Court of Andhra Pradesh).

stranded in Kathmandu and abroad. Citing the constitution's guarantee of equality, the Court ordered that the workers be provided with transport, food, free Covid-19 testing, and quarantine support if they tested positive.[25]

These cases come on the heels of a transformative ruling in South Africa for another key group of vulnerable workers: those who work in the domestic sphere. In *Mahlangu v Minister of Labor*, which was decided during the pandemic but not specific to its challenges, the Constitutional Court of South Africa found that the exclusion of domestic workers from the country's workers' compensation law—justified by excluding them from the definition of 'employees'—violated the constitution's guarantees of both equality and social security. In discussing these provisions, the court explicitly noted that:

> [The] purpose of social security is to ensure that everyone, including the most vulnerable members of our society, enjoy access to basic necessities and can live a life of dignity. Moreover, social security legislation serves a remedial purpose: namely, to undo the gendered and racialised system of poverty inherited from South Africa's colonial and apartheid past.[26]

Further, in a critical recognition of intersectional discrimination, the court acknowledged how this exclusion perpetuated apartheid-era inequalities and disproportionately harmed Black women.[27]

3.2 Meeting Workers' and Families' Material Needs

In some countries, constitutions have played an important role in how governments address the pandemic's impacts on income loss and poverty risks. For example, in a case decided by the Malawi High Court in September 2020, *Kathumba v The President*, the justices ruled the government could not impose a national lockdown without first putting in place adequate social security measures for marginalized groups. Moreover, the court recommended that any future lockdown measures take into account their likely effects on specific populations, including by considering the impacts on women's

---

[25] *Advocate Bishnu Luitel v Office of Prime Minister & Advocate Pushpa Raj Poudel v Office of Prime Minister*, Supreme Court of Nepal, Writ No 076-WO-0933 (6 April 2020); *Advocate Manish Kumar Shrestha v Prime Ministers' Office*, Supreme Court of Nepal, Writ No 076-WO-0958, 31 May 2020. See also Hardik Subedi, 'How Nepal's Supreme Court Upheld Dignity of Migrant Workers Without Diluting COVID Fight' *The Wire* (28 April 2020) https://thewire.in/law/nepal-supreme-court-migrant-workers (accessed 3 January 2022); Aoife Nolan, 'Constitutional Social Rights Litigation and Adjudication in a Time of COVID-19' *IACL-AIDC Blog* (28 May 2020) https://blog-iacl-aidc.org/social-rights/2020/5/28/constitutional-social-rights-litigation-and-adjudication-in-a-time-of-covid-19 (accessed 3 January 2022); Gopal Sharma, 'Nepal's Top Court Orders Rescue of Migrant Workers Stranded Abroad' *Reuters* (17 April 2020) https://www.reuters.com/article/us-health-coronavirus-nepal-migrants-trf/nepals-top-court-orders-rescue-of-migrant-workers-stranded-abroad-idUSKBN21Z2DO (accessed 3 January 2022); 'Rescue the Migrant Workers Free of Cost: Supreme Court' *New Spotlight Online* (17 June 2020) https://www.spotlightnepal.com/2020/06/17/rescue-migrant-workers-free-cost-supreme-court/ (accessed 3 January 2022).
[26] *Sylvia Bongi Mahlangu v Minister of Labour* [2020] ZACC 24 [63].
[27] ibid [65], [73]–[76], [93], [95], [96], [102], [105].

unpaid care work, children's access to education and school meals, and women's exposure to domestic violence.

In its ruling, the court noted how many Malawians' living conditions and reliance on informal market work made it impossible to follow stay-at-home orders since they needed to 'travel out of their homes as a matter of survival'.[28] The court then determined that the Malawian constitution 'implicitly' protected a right to social security through its right to life, right to livelihood, and directive principle on basic needs, which calls on the government to 'actively develop the health and the welfare of the people by progressively adopting and implementing policies and legislation aimed at achieving' nutrition, health, and substantive gender equality, among other goals. In this way, the decision illustrated how even aspirational rights to social insurance, rather than those that are explicitly justiciable, can and do have impact.

Constitutional rights to basic needs have also had impact for workers' children. In South Africa, the High Court in Gauteng issued a ruling in July 2020 ordering the government to provide a free meal to schoolchildren despite the lockdown, citing their constitutional rights to 'basic nutrition, shelter, basic health care services and social services,' among others.[29]

3.3 Addressing Discrimination and Exclusion in the Law

Beyond addressing material needs broadly, high courts have also issued rulings striking down laws and policies that excluded specific marginalized groups from access to income support and other material assistance during the pandemic. For example, in April 2020, lawyers in the UK brought a case on behalf of the 8-year-old son of a migrant care worker, challenging the 'No Recourse to Public Funds' rule that restricted migrants' access to housing and child benefits and highlighting the risks to public health if migrant families were excluded from these core supports made available to citizens.[30] The applicants sought relief based in part on the Human Rights Act 1998, which is widely considered part of the unwritten UK constitution[31] and which incorporates the European Convention on Human Rights (ECHR) into domestic law. Notably, both instruments include express protections against 'degrading treatment', which prior case law found to be violated when the state 'denies the most basic needs of any human being'.[32] Citing the government's responsibilities 'not to impose, or to

---

[28] *R (on the application of Kathumba) v President of Malawi* [2020] MWHC 29.

[29] *Equal Education v Minister of Basic Education* [2020] ZAGPPHC 306.

[30] Diane Taylor, 'Home Office's Denial of Benefits to Migrant Families Unlawful, Court Rules' *Guardian* (7 May 2020) https://www.theguardian.com/society/2020/may/07/home-offices-denial-of-benefits-to-migrant-families-unlawful-court-rules (accessed 3 January 2022).

[31] Particularly following Brexit, the question of which pieces of UK legislation arise to the level of constitutional status has become increasingly contested. Nevertheless, past jurisprudence and analysis suggest that the Human Rights Act 1998 qualifies as a constitutional instrument. See eg *R (on the application of HS2 Action Alliance Ltd) v The Secretary of State for Transport* [2014] UKSC 3 [207] (Hale J). See also Andrew Blick, David Howarth, and Nat le Roux, 'Distinguishing Constitutional Legislation: A Modest Proposal' The Constitution Society (2014) https://consoc.org.uk/publications/distinguishing-constitutional-legislation-a-modest-proposal/ (accessed 3 January 2022); Farrah Ahmed and Adam Perry, 'Constitutional Statutes' (2017) 37 Oxford Journal of Legal Studies 461.

[32] *R (W, A Child by His Litigation Friend J) v Secretary of State* [2020] EWHC 1299 [40].

lift, the condition of [no recourse to public funds] in cases where the applicant is not yet, but will imminently suffer inhuman or degrading treatment without recourse to public funds' under the Human Rights Act, the Court ruled in the boy's favour.[33]

Similarly, in June 2020, the High Court of South Africa (Gauteng Division) ruled that asylum seekers could not be excluded from the country's emergency unemployment grant enacted to offset the widespread layoffs caused by the pandemic, citing the constitution's 'interrelated' protections for equality, human dignity, and social assistance.[34] As the court noted, 'whilst it cannot be disputed that the Covid-19 pandemic must be fought by all means necessary, it must be constantly borne in mind that the Constitution and the Bill of Rights in particular, ought to be the touchstone against which the formulation and implementation of regulations is measured'.[35]

3.4 Improving Working Conditions for Frontline Workers

Finally, constitutions have served as tools for protecting workers' occupational safety. One key way that workplaces have sought—or failed—to protect workers in essential jobs during the pandemic is by providing adequate personal protective equipment (PPE). In Lesotho, an association of doctors and nurses initiated a lawsuit to compel the government to furnish them with adequate PPE, citing constitutional protections for just and favourable working conditions and the right to life.[36] At issue, however, was whether the constitutional provision on safe working conditions—which was explicitly non-justiciable—could be invoked by the petitioners. Similar to the High Court of Malawi, however, the High Court of Lesotho determined that these directive principles were enforceable when interpreted through the lens of the right to life, a fundamental and justiciable right. Determining that these directives comprised a 'constitutional interpretative guide', the High Court found in the petitioners' favour, ordering the government to provide the doctors and nurses with PPE and rejecting their argument that doing so was too costly.[37]

4 How Widespread Are Constitutional Protections for Decent Work, Social Insurance, and Workers' Equal Rights?

While the preceding examples reflect only a small selection of cases decided during the first few months of the Covid-19 pandemic, their rulings suggest that constitutional provisions for social insurance and decent working conditions can both lay

---

[33] ibid [73].
[34] *Scalabrini Centre of Cape Town and Another v Minister for Social Development* [2020] ZAGPPHC 308.
[35] ibid [41].
[36] *Lesotho Medical Association v Minister for Health* [2020] LSHC 14; Khanyo Farisé, 'COVID-19 and Africa Symposium: The State's Duty to Provide PPE to Health Workers in Lesotho' *Opinio Juris* (12 August 2020) http://opiniojuris.org/2020/12/08/covid-19-and-africa-symposium-states-response-to-covid-19-in-africa/ (accessed 3 January 2022).
[37] *Lesotho* (n 36) [9].

the groundwork for more inclusive and effective protections and reduce backsliding amidst public health emergencies. Moreover, constitutional protections for other fundamental social and economic rights—including health and education—also yielded case law during the first wave of lockdowns that strengthened protections for the social determinants of health.[38] To be sure, constitutional provisions alone are no guarantee that their protections will be realized; the ability of claimants to access the courts, the strength of constitutional wording, and the favourability of judicial interpretation can markedly shape their impacts. Nevertheless, in a range of contexts, constitutional provisions articulating workers' fundamental rights have offered valuable tools for challenging exclusionary policies and practices that exacerbate gender, racial, and socio-economic inequalities both amidst crises and in a typical year.

Recognizing this potential, in this section, we examine how commonly constitutions globally explicitly enshrine four interrelated and mutually reinforcing rights: (1) decent work, including the right to safe working conditions; (2) non-discrimination in all aspects of employment; (3) social insurance, including income support during unemployment and illness; and (4) non-discrimination more broadly. To understand how common these protections are globally, we analysed the constitutions of all 193 UN member states to assess the prevalence and quality of protections for social insurance, decent work, and non-discrimination.[39] For the small number of countries without a written constitution, we analysed those documents widely considered to have constitutional status (eg the Basic Laws of Israel).[40] We examined in detail: (1) prohibitions of discrimination at work; (2) broad approaches to equality or non-discrimination for different groups; (3) guarantees of income security; and (4) guarantees of decent work.

4.1 Variables

4.1.1 Prohibitions of discrimination at work

Our analysis of prohibitions of discrimination at work included general prohibitions of discrimination at work, as well as in the specific areas of hiring, pay, working

---

[38] Firooz Kabir and others, 'The Role of Constitutional Courts in Protecting Health During Pandemics: Early Rulings on Social Determinants of Health' (2022).

[39] For details on methodology see Heymann, Sprague, and Raub (n 5); Aleta Sprague, Amy Raub, and Jody Heymann, 'Providing a Foundation for Decent Work and Adequate Income during Health and Economic Crises: Constitutional Approaches in 193 Countries' (2020) 40 International Journal of Sociology and Social Policy 1087.

[40] In some countries without a single constitutional document, the instruments that have constitutional status have nevertheless been clearly articulated (see eg *Bank Mizrahi v Migdal Cooperative Village* 49(4) PD 221 (Supreme Court of Israel, 1995) which established that the Basic Laws took precedence over ordinary legislation). In others, such as the UK, debates persist about which pieces of legislation comprise the unwritten constitution, particularly following Brexit; for the sake of this analysis, we adopted a more expansive interpretation, based on sources including Blick, Howarth and le Roux (n 30) (describing the Equality Act 2010 as 'arguably constitutional') and Andrew McDonald and Robert Hazell, 'What Happened Next: Constitutional Change under New Labour' in *Reinventing Britain: Constitutional Change under New Labour* (UC Press 2007) 14(describing the Equality Act 2006, a precursor to the 2010 Act, as a 'constitutional statute').

conditions, promotions, and terminations. We did not capture provisions that explicitly only applied to public sector employment. For these variables, we separately distinguished between countries that prohibited discrimination at work broadly for all workers without specifying based on what grounds ('guaranteed generally') and those that limited the prohibition of discrimination to specific characteristics or groups ('guaranteed only to certain groups').

4.1.2 Broad approaches to equality or non-discrimination for different groups
We considered a constitution to take an approach to equality or non-discrimination for a specific group if it (1) prohibited discrimination against the group, (2) guaranteed equal rights to the group, (3) guaranteed equality before the law for the group, or (4) guaranteed overall equality for the group. We separately distinguished between group-specific guarantees ('guaranteed right') and guarantees of equality for citizens generally, but not specifically for the group ('equality guaranteed, not specific to group'). We assessed these broad approaches to equality based on sex and/or gender, race/ethnicity, language, foreign citizenship, foreign national origin, religion, socioeconomic status, disability, sexual orientation, and gender identity.

4.1.3 Income security
Our measures of guarantees of income security examined separately whether constitutions addressed income security during unemployment, old age, illness, disability, work injury, after the birth of a child, or for families in need. In addition to the categories outlined above, we further distinguished among constitutions that explicitly addressed the circumstances ('specifically guaranteed'); constitutions that did not address the circumstances, but guaranteed a broad right to income security ('not explicit, but broad right to social security'); and constitutions that generally guaranteed income support to individuals who needed it ('not explicit, but guaranteed for cases of need or unable to work').

4.1.4 Decent work
Our analysis of constitutional provisions to guarantee decent work included the right to safe working conditions, adequate remuneration, limited working hours, the right to rest, and paid annual leave.

4.1.5 Analysis
For each variable, we analysed overall levels of constitutional protection. For summary measures, we assessed trends in constitutional protections over time. To assess changes in constitutional protections over time, we assessed the prevalence of protections by year of constitutional adoption. Year of adoption is used instead of year of most recent amendment because most constitutional rights are added at the time of first passage and constitutions vary as to the difficulty of amendment. Additionally, older constitutions may be less likely to guarantee rights if they have already been addressed in legislation. All analyses were conducted in Stata 14.

5 Protections for Equal Rights, Decent Work, and Income Security in 193 Constitutions

5.1 Non-discrimination in Employment

A growing number of constitutions address discrimination in various aspects of employment, including pay, working conditions, hiring decisions, promotions, and terminations. Having at least one protection against discrimination has become more prevalent in constitutions adopted in the 1980s and later, although progress on including these protections appears to have stagnated (Table 2.1).

The most common protections are broadly against discrimination and specifically for equal pay. Eleven per cent broadly prohibit employment discrimination (Table 2.2). Likewise, 16 per cent prohibit discrimination in employment against certain groups or aspire to non-discrimination in employment generally. The Constitution of Burkina Faso, for instance, prohibits discrimination 'in matters of employment and of remuneration founded notably on sex, color, social origin, ethnicity or political opinion' (article 19).

In addition, 19 per cent mandate equal pay for equal work, while 10 per cent guarantee this right to certain groups or aspire to equal pay for workers. For example,

Table 2.1 Constitutional Protection from Discrimination in Any Aspect of Work by Year of Constitution Adoption

	All years	Before 1970	1970— 1979	1980— 1989	1990— 1999	2000— 2009	2010— 2017
No specific provision	123 (64%)	36 (88%)	21 (78%)	11 (50%)	33 (55%)	8 (42%)	14 (58%)
At least one aspect guaranteed	70 (36%)	5 (12%)	6 (22%)	11 (50%)	27 (45%)	11 (58%)	10 (42%)

Table 2.2 Prohibition of Discrimination in Different Aspects of Work

	General prohibition of discrimination at work	Equal pay for equal work	Hiring	Promotions	Working conditions	Terminations
No specific provision	141 (73%)	137 (71%)	172 (89%)	181 (94%)	178 (92%)	166 (86%)
Aspirational or guaranteed only to certain groups	30 (16%)	20 (10%)	4 (2%)	7 (4%)	4 (2%)	7 (4%)
Guaranteed universally	22 (11%)	36 (19%)	17 (9%)	5 (3%)	11 (6%)	20 (10%)

Ethiopia's constitution provides that 'women workers have the right to equal pay for equal work' (Art 42(1)(d)). The principle of equal pay for equal work is foundational. However, a significant portion of persisting pay gaps is attributable more to gender or racial/ethnic segregation in the labour market than disparate pay for the same job.[41] Further, industries in which women and racial/ethnic minorities are over-represented are often under-remunerated, relative to the value they contribute to the economy. Accordingly, equal pay for work of equal *value* provides a stronger standard for advancing equity. Some constitutions, such as Guyana's, articulate this stronger protection: 'Every citizen has the right ... to equal pay for equal work or work of equal value' (article 22).

Finally, 9 per cent of constitutions universally prohibit discrimination in hiring, as do 3 per cent in promotions, 6 per cent in working conditions, and 10 per cent in terminations. This specificity is important given that women, marginalized racial or ethnic groups, and people with disabilities are commonly over-represented in lower-level positions and underrepresented in management, which speaks to the need for equal rights in opportunities to advance in the workplace as well equal opportunities to get in the door. At the same time, out of 193 constitutions, just two explicitly provide for reasonable accommodations at work for people with disabilities, which is critical to substantive equality.

Importantly, while some courts have interpreted constitutional protections against employment discrimination to encompass private workplaces, a few constitutions address the private sphere directly, or use broad language that could easily support an interpretation of its application to both public and private employment. Colombia's constitution broadly provides that '[w]omen cannot be subjected to any type of discrimination' (article 43). The Bolivian constitution states that the government will guarantee women 'the same remuneration as men for work of equal value, both in the public and private arena' (article 48).

5.2 Broad Equality and Non-discrimination

There is substantial variation in constitutional guarantees of overall equality and non-discrimination across groups. Constitutions most commonly guarantee equal rights on the basis of sex and/or gender (85 per cent), followed by religion (78 per cent) and race/ethnicity (76 per cent) (Table 2.3). Guarantees were lowest based on gender identity (3 per cent), sexual orientation (5 per cent), and citizenship (22 per cent). A small share explicitly prohibit common types of discrimination that often intersect with gender discrimination but are not always covered by provisions addressing sex or gender, including 6 per cent that ban pregnancy discrimination and 8 per cent that ban discrimination on the basis of marital status. A minority of countries also explicitly address indirect discrimination on various grounds, including 5 per cent that ban indirect sex discrimination and indirect race discrimination, respectively. In 17 per cent of countries, the constitution explicitly permits affirmative measures to address

---

[41] World Economic Forum, 'The Global Gender Gap Report 2017' (2017) https://www.weforum.org/reports/the-global-gender-gap-report-2017 (accessed 3 January 2022).

Table 2.3 Constitutional Guarantees of Equality or Non-Discrimination by Social Group and Year of Constitution Adoption

	All years	Before 1970	1970–1979	1980–1989	1990–1999	2000–2009	2010–2017
Sex and/or gender	165 (85%)	22 (54%)	24 (89%)	20 (91%)	56 (93%)	19 (100%)	24 (100%)
Race / ethnicity	146 (76%)	20 (49%)	21 (78%)	16 (73%)	53 (88%)	17 (89%)	19 (79%)
Religion	150 (78%)	23 (56%)	22 (81%)	15 (68%)	52 (87%)	16 (84%)	22 (92%)
Socioeconomic status	114 (59%)	14 (34%)	11 (41%)	7 (32%)	50 (83%)	12 (63%)	20 (83%)
Disability status	52 (27%)	5 (12%)	3 (11%)	2 (9%)	16 (27%)	9 (47%)	17 (71%)
Language	85 (44%)	8 (20%)	7 (26%)	5 (23%)	38 (63%)	9 (47%)	18 (75%)
Foreign national origin	115 (60%)	18 (44%)	20 (74%)	13 (59%)	38 (63%)	12 (63%)	14 (58%)
Foreign citizens	42 (22%)	3 (7%)	3 (11%)	3 (14%)	24 (40%)	3 (16%)	6 (25%)
Sexual orientation	10 (5%)	4 (10%)	1 (4%)	1 (5%)	1 (2%)	2 (11%)	1 (4%)
Gender identity	5 (3%)	2 (5%)	0 (0%)	0 (0%)	0 (0%)	2 (11%)	1 (4%)

past discrimination and exclusion on the basis of race or ethnicity, which can provide important protection against overly formal interpretations of equal rights that mandate identical treatment in all circumstances.

There is a trend of increasing protections among more recently adopted constitutions. For example, whereas only 54 per cent of constitutions adopted before 1970 guarantee equality based on sex, all constitutions adopted from 2000 to 2017 do so. Similarly, while overall guarantees of equality or non-discrimination for persons with disabilities are low (27 per cent), these have greatly increased. Only 12 per cent of constitutions adopted before 1970 guarantee equality for persons with disabilities, compared to 71 per cent of those adopted from 2010 to 2017.

5.3 Income Security

In the midst of Covid-19, income security during unemployment and illness is critical to ensure individuals and families can meet their basic needs. More than half of countries have made a constitutional commitment to provide income security during periods of unemployment. Twenty-three per cent of countries explicitly guarantee income support during unemployment (Table 2.4). An additional 16 per cent of countries guarantee a broad right to social security without mentioning unemployment and 8 per cent guarantee income support for individuals in need. Fourteen per cent of countries aspire to provide income security during unemployment. Twenty-three per cent of constitutions explicitly guarantee income security during illness.

Targeted income support may also be important to ensure security for individuals disproportionately affected by the pandemic or who are facing critical life transitions.

Table 2.4 Constitutional protection of income security during different circumstances

	Unemployment	Old age	Illness	Disability	Work Injury	Maternity	Paternity	Families in need
No specific provision	76 (39%)	60 (31%)	71 (37%)	68 (35%)	78 (40%)	78 (40%)	81 (42%)	76 (39%)
Aspirational	27 (14%)	32 (17%)	28 (15%)	29 (15%)	27 (14%)	24 (12%)	27 (14%)	27 (14%)
Not explicit, but guaranteed for cases of need or unable to work	15 (8%)	3 (2%)	14 (7%)	7 (4%)	26 (13%)	19 (10%)	29 (15%)	23 (12%)
Not explicit, but broad right to social security	31 (16%)	23 (12%)	36 (19%)	33 (17%)	46 (24%)	42 (22%)	50 (26%)	45 (23%)
Specifically guaranteed	44 (23%)	75 (39%)	44 (23%)	56 (29%)	16 (8%)	30 (16%)	6 (3%)	22 (11%)

Explicit constitutional protections are more frequent for the elderly (39 per cent) and for persons with disabilities (29 per cent), whereas fewer address support specifically for new mothers (16 per cent), new fathers (3 per cent), families in need (11 per cent), or in cases of work injury (8 per cent).

In settings of constrained resources, some constitutions explicitly protect social security rights in aspirational terms or subject to progressive realization. For example, Fiji's constitution obligates the State to 'take reasonable measures within its available resources to achieve the progressive realisation of the right of every person to social security schemes' (article 37).

Altogether, a majority of constitutions (54 per cent) guarantee some aspect of income security, indicating that income support during temporary or permanent unemployment is a widespread commitment. Whereas a third of constitutions (37 per cent) adopted before 1970 guarantee some aspect of income security, nearly two-thirds (62 per cent) of those adopted from 2010 to 2017 do so (Table 2.5).

5.4 Decent Work

Fundamental guarantees of decent work are especially critical during pandemics and other major health crises. Nearly one-third of constitutions (31 per cent) guarantee the right to safe working conditions (Table 2.6). The Dominican Republic's constitution,

Table 2.5 Constitutional Protection of Income Security in any Circumstance by Year of Constitution Adoption

	All years	Before 1970	1970—1979	1980—1989	1990—1999	2000—2009	2010—2017
No specific provision	89 (46%)	26 (63%)	16 (59%)	10 (45%)	20 (33%)	8 (42%)	9 (38%)
At least one aspect guaranteed	104 (54%)	15 (37%)	11 (41%)	12 (55%)	40 (67%)	11 (58%)	15 (62%)

Table 2.6 Constitutional Protection of Decent Work

	Adequate remuneration	Safe working conditions	Limited working hours	Rest	Paid leave
No specific provision	118 (61%)	122 (63%)	144 (74%)	117 (61%)	142 (74%)
Aspirational or guaranteed only to certain groups	13 (7%)	12 (6%)	3 (2%)	6 (3%)	4 (2%)
Guaranteed generally	62 (32%)	59 (31%)	46 (24%)	72 (37%)	47 (24%)

Table 2.7 Constitutional Protection of Decent Work by Year of Constitution Adoption

	All years	Before 1970	1970–1979	1980–1989	1990–1999	2000–2009	2010–2017
No specific provision	97 (50%)	30 (73%)	19 (70%)	8 (36%)	25 (42%)	8 (42%)	7 (29%)
At least one aspect guaranteed	96 (50%)	11 (27%)	8 (30%)	14 (64%)	35 (58%)	11 (58%)	17 (71%)

for instance, mandates that every employer 'guarantee to their workers conditions of safety, sanitation, [and] hygiene [and an] adequate work environment' (article 62(8)).

Slightly more constitutions address the right to rest (36 per cent) and adequate remuneration (32 per cent). Less than a quarter address the right to limited working hours (24 per cent) and paid leave (24 per cent).

These rights have become more prevalent over time. While just 27 per cent of constitutions adopted before 1970 guarantee workers some aspect of decent work, 71 per cent of those adopted between 2010 and 2017 do so (Table 2.7).

6 The Potential of Constitutions to Safeguard Equality amidst the Covid-19 Pandemic and Other Crises

Compared to the constitutions of 50 years ago, contemporary constitutions take much more comprehensive approaches to discrimination, both generally and within workplaces. While just 12 per cent of current constitutions that were adopted before 1970 prohibit discrimination in at least one aspect of employment, 42 per cent of those adopted from 2010 to 2017 do so. A substantial majority of constitutions guarantee overall equal rights on the basis of sex, race/ethnicity, and religion. All constitutions adopted since 2000 protect equal rights regardless of sex or gender, compared to just 54 per cent of those adopted before 1970. Guarantees of equal rights on the basis of disability, race/ethnicity, religion, and socio-economic status are also far more common in more recent constitutions.

Similarly, constitutional protections of the rights to social insurance and decent working conditions are increasingly widespread. In over half the world's countries, the constitution guarantees income security in at least some circumstances. This includes just 37 per cent of constitutions adopted before 1970 compared to 62 per cent of those adopted from 2010 to 2017. Likewise, half of constitutions protect at least some aspect of decent work, and these provisions appear more than twice as often in constitutions adopted from 2010 to 2017 compared to those adopted before 1970.

As some early cases have already suggested, the growing enshrinement of these rights has the potential to support workers during and after the pandemic in four central ways: (1) by translating international human rights commitments into domestic law; (2) by limiting cuts to benefits and services, consistent with the principle of non-retrogression; (3) by providing a foundation for more detailed laws and policies advancing social and economic rights; and (4) by shifting norms and practices within workplaces through their applied and expressive value.

6.1 Constitutions as Mechanisms for Protecting Universal Human Rights

As countries' foundational legal documents, constitutions can be ideal instruments for translating commitments to uphold universal human rights into domestic law. A range of widely ratified treaties guarantee the rights to non-discrimination and decent working conditions, including the International Convention on the Elimination of All Forms of Racial Discrimination, the Convention on the Elimination of All Forms of Discrimination Against Women, and the Convention on the Rights of Persons with Disabilities.

The International Covenant on Economic, Social and Cultural Rights (ICESCR) protects the rights to social security, an adequate standard of living, and safe and healthy working conditions for all. Similarly, the Universal Declaration of Human Rights guarantees 'everyone' the rights to non-discrimination, just and favourable working conditions, a 'standard of living adequate for the health and well-being of himself and of his family', and 'the right to security in the event of unemployment, sickness, disability, widowhood, old age or other lack of livelihood in circumstances beyond his control'. Each of these rights is guaranteed 'without distinction of any kind, such as race, colour, sex, language, religion, political or other opinion, national or social origin, property, birth or other status'.

Low-cost steps and the guarantee of non-discrimination are understood as immediate obligations. For other social and economic rights, the principle of progressive realization requires that countries devote the maximum available resources to realizing these rights universally. As the UN has clarified:

> Governments shall take progressive measures to the extent of their available resources to protect the rights of everyone—regardless of citizenship—to: social security; an adequate standard of living including adequate food, clothing, housing, and the continuous improvement of living conditions.[42]

International organizations have underscored countries' responsibilities to uphold these and other fundamental human rights during the pandemic. For example, in a September 2020 report, the UN Special Rapporteur on Extreme Poverty and Human Rights urged countries 'to ground their responses to the post-COVID-19 economic and social crisis on the right to social security, and to strengthen resilience by adopting a rights-based approach to social protection'.[43] In a paper published the following month, the ILO observed that '[t]he COVID-19 crisis has laid bare the effects of

---

[42] UN Office of the United Nations High Commissioner for Human Rights, *Rights of Non-Citizens* (2006) 25 https://www.ohchr.org/documents/publications/noncitizensen.pdf (accessed 24 April 2022).

[43] Special Rapporteur on Extreme Poverty and Human Rights, 'Looking Back to Look Ahead: A Rights-based Approach to Social Protection in the Post-COVID-19 Economic Recovery' (11 September 2020) https://www.ohchr.org/Documents/Issues/Poverty/covid19.pdf (accessed 3 January 2022).

pervasive discrimination in society. Leaving no one behind and building back better require integrating the principles of nondiscrimination and inclusiveness in all stages of the pandemic response'.[44] As the foundation of nearly every country's legal system, national constitutions that clearly embed fundamental social and economic rights can provide the basis for equitable, comprehensive, and responsive policy-making during crises and recovery.

6.2 Constitutions as a Foundation for Non-retrogression on Social and Economic Rights

One concrete way that constitutional rights to equality and social insurance may benefit workers in the current moment is by offering protection against budget cuts that would dismantle critical health and income support programmes and exacerbate structural inequalities. Alongside progressive realization, the ICESCR's principle of non-retrogression generally prohibits countries from deliberately weakening the realization of fundamental social and economic rights. While the Committee on Economic, Social, and Cultural Rights has recognized that global recessions pose particular challenges to the fulfilment of these obligations, it has also clarified that they remain in effect amidst economic crises; the 'minimum core' of each right—including health, education, decent working conditions, and social security—must be guaranteed, and any cuts enacted pursuant to the crisis must be temporary, necessary, proportionate, and non-discriminatory.[45]

Covid-19 itself has underscored the critical importance of non-retrogression. The austerity measures of the past decade exacerbated the pandemic's health and economic consequences by leaving social and public health systems inadequately funded to respond to the crisis.[46] Systematic underinvestment in the social determinants of health—including decent work, safe and healthy living conditions, and freedom from discrimination—has contributed to worse health and economic outcomes for marginalized groups since long before the pandemic, and will continue to do so in its wake unless countries correct course. By enshrining core social and economic protections like social insurance as fundamental rights, constitutions can provide a foundation for countering proposals to treat these essential supports as optional or discretionary, thereby strengthening countries' responses to the current crisis, better preparing us to

---

[44] International Labour Organization, 'Issue Paper on COVID-19 and Fundamental Principles and Rights at Work' (2020) https://www.ilo.org/wcmsp5/groups/public/---ed_norm/---ipec/documents/publication/wcms_757247.pdf (accessed 3 January 2022).

[45] Ariranga G Pillay, 'Letter to All States Parties to the ICESCR' (16 May 2012) https://www2.ohchr.org/english/bodies/cescr/docs/Lettercescrtosp16.05.12.pdf (accessed 3 January 2022) (addressing and arguably diminishing States Parties' ICESCR responsibilities amidst economic crises); Joe Wills and Ben TC Warwick, 'Contesting Austerity: The Potential and Pitfalls of Socioeconomic Rights Discourse' (2016) 23 Indian Journal of Global Legal Studies 629; CESCR General Comment No 3: The Nature of States Parties' Obligations (article 2(1) of the Covenant); CESCR General Comment No General Comment 19: The Right to Social Security; CESCR General comment No 23 (2016) on the right to just and favourable conditions of work (article 7 of the International Covenant on Economic, Social and Cultural Rights).

[46] Luis Rajmil and others, 'Austerity Policy and Child Health in European Countries: A Systematic Literature Review' (2020) 20 BMC Public Health 1.

address the next, and affirming governments' commitments to uphold minimum core obligations even amidst economic downturns.

Past examples from case law illustrate this potential. While specific courts' application of constitutional rights to healthcare and social insurance will vary depending on a wide range of factors—including the specific wording of constitutional provisions, the degree of deference the judiciary exhibits towards other branches of government, and the particular facts and judicial analysis applied in each case—jurisprudence from a range of countries has relied on constitutional protections for health and social insurance to prevent reductions in basic services that would disproportionately affect access by low-income households. For example, in Portugal, the Constitutional Court rejected efforts to abolish the National Health Service, which was created pursuant to the constitutional right to health, noting that '[t]he constitutional tasks imposed on the State as a guarantee for fundamental rights, consisting in the creation of certain institutions or services, do not only oblige their creation, but also a duty not to abolish them once created'.[47] Likewise, in countries including Bulgaria, the Czech Republic, and Ukraine, top courts have cited constitutional health protections to find that efforts to impose new fees or privatize parts of the public health system violated constitutional health rights.[48] Although these cases may not be representative of all instances in which austerity cuts are challenged as unconstitutional, they support the notion that enshrining explicit protections for social and economic rights in constitutions can provide a basis for mobilization against the erosion of fundamental public supports and services.

6.3 Constitutions as a Foundation for Stronger Legislation on Social and Economic Rights

Constitutional guarantees for social and economic rights can also catalyse the adoption of more detailed policies and legislation advancing their implementation. The relationship between broadly worded rights and more detailed laws may be particularly important in the case of constitutional labour and social insurance rights, which may be most effective when they provide a foundation for more detailed policy-making without permanently establishing precise thresholds or standards. Specifically, constitutional provisions that broadly guarantee decent working conditions and social insurance for those not working for pay due to illness, old age, unemployment, or caregiving responsibilities can create a framework for ensuring everyone is able to meet basic human needs. However, the fine details of how these rights are implemented are indeed probably best reserved for legislatures, which may be better positioned

---

[47] Portuguese Constitutional Tribunal (Tribunal Constitucional), Decision (Acórdão) No 39/84 (11 April 1984) cited in Christian Courtis, 'The Role of Judges in the Protection of Economic, Social and Cultural Rights' Presentation Before the South African Chief Justices Forum Annual Meeting (8 August 2009) https://www.venice.coe.int/SACJF/2009_08_BTW_Kasane/speeches/Courtis_social_rights.pdf (accessed 3 January 2022).

[48] Jan Alexa and others, 'Czech Republic: Health System Review' (2015) 17 Health Systems in Transition 1; Antoniya Dimova and others, 'Bulgaria: Health System Review' (2018) 20 Health Systems in Transition 1; Valery Lekhan and others, 'Ukraine: Health System Review' (2015) 17 Health Systems in Transition 1.

to respond dynamically to shifting economic conditions—including those triggered by crises—and evolving labour standards. By enshrining decent work and a comprehensive social safety net broadly, however, constitutions can provide a mechanism for holding governments accountable for adopting laws to realize these rights fully.

In the context of Covid-19, countries' constitutional guarantees to health and social security have already provided a foundation for advocacy to adopt stronger laws and policies to support workers amidst the pandemic.[49] Some legislators have also proposed stronger protections for social and economic rights in constitutions precisely to support more human-rights based legislation during the pandemic in beyond; in January 2021, for instance, an Irish parliamentarian reintroduced a bill to amend the constitution to enshrine new protections for health, housing, and workers' rights, noting that it would provide 'an anchor for the rights to housing, health and education to be provided for on the basis of need at all times [and] would give Irish citizens a strengthened right to hold the Government to account'. In support of the proposed amendment, a second member of parliament urged that it would establish 'rights that would give a basic threshold below which any Government could not go when it is implementing austerity cuts'.[50]

While the Irish amendment has yet to be adopted, constitutional change has already occurred elsewhere. For example, in Costa Rica, in anticipation of both future pandemics and the impacts of climate change, the legislature adopted a constitutional amendment in June 2020 guaranteeing access to drinking water as a fundamental right, which explicitly calls for more detailed legislation governing water 'use, protection, sustainability, conservation, and exploitation'; as the president noted, '[t]he signing of this law occurs in a context of national emergency (COVID-19), placing the health of people ahead of any interest'.[51] More recently, in a referendum on the government's Covid-19 policies in Switzerland, voters approved a constitutional amendment to improve wages and working conditions for nurses, which requires the government to 'recognize and promote care as an important component of health care and ensure that it is adequate and accessible to all'.[52] To advance its realization, the amendment requires the government to adopt implementing provisions within four years addressing remuneration, working conditions, and training opportunities for care workers in detail.[53]

---

[49] See eg Stephen Devereuz and Alex van den Heever, 'How Social Security Could Make Life Better in South Africa after COVID-19' *The Conversation* (29 September 2020) https://theconversation.com/how-social-security-could-make-life-better-in-south-africa-after-covid-19-146606 (accessed 3 January 2022); Claudeth Mocon-Ciriaco, 'Smoke-free Environment Expansion Pushed to Help Fight vs Covid-19' *Business Mirror* (25 February 2021) https://businessmirror.com.ph/2021/02/25/smoke-free-environment-expansion-pushed-to-help-fight-vs-covid-19/ (accessed 3 January 2022).

[50] Dáil Éireann debate (Wednesday, 27 January 2021) vol 1003 No 5, 'Thirty-seventh Amendment of the Constitution (Economic, Social and Cultural Rights) Bill 2018: Second Stage [Private Members]' https://www.oireachtas.ie/en/debates/debate/dail/2021-01-27/3/ (accessed 3 January 2022).

[51] 'Costa Rica Decrees a Law that Designates Water as a Basic Human Right' *MenaFN* (10 June 2020) https://menafn.com/1100300154/Costa-Rica-Decrees-a-Law-that-Designates-Water-as-a-Basic-Human-Right (accessed 3 January 2022).

[52] Explanations of the Federal Council: Referendum of 28 November 2021 (24 September 2021) https://www.admin.ch/dam/gov/de/Dokumentation/Abstimmungen/November2021/Abstimmungsbroschuere_28-11-2021_de.pdf.download.pdf/Abstimmungsbroschuere_28-11-2021_de.pdf (accessed 3 January 2022); Noele Illien, 'Swiss Voters Approve their Government's Covid Policy in a Referendum' *New York Times* (28 November 2021) https://www.nytimes.com/2021/11/28/world/europe/swiss-voters-approve-covid-green-pass.html (accessed 3 January 2022).

[53] Explanations of the Federal Council (n 52) 19.

6.4 Constitutions' Normative and Applied Role in Creating More Equal Workplaces

Finally, constitutional provisions protecting equal rights, both broadly and specifically in the context of employment, have the potential to provide the normative foundation for ensuring equal rights are prioritized as economies recover. In addition to their practical application, constitutions have an expressive function that communicates values on behalf of the state.[54] In times of crisis or scarcity, the government's responsibility to affirm the equal worth and rights of every person is particularly critical. Survey data also suggests that stronger constitutional protections for equality may support greater public support for equal rights.[55]

Further, constitutional protections against employment discrimination, particularly when designed to reach both public and private workplaces, can help safeguard against the erosion of protections in ordinary laws, which are often easier to amend or repeal. While constitutional rights have traditionally only applied against public actors, some comparative evidence suggests that constitutions' ability to reach the private sphere is expanding, particularly as private actors increasingly provide traditionally public services.[56] These broader interpretations, alongside newer judicial mechanisms available in a minority of countries that enable individual workers to seek court-ordered remedies for private actors' violations of their rights, have had implications for workers; Colombia provides a powerful example, where the constitution's labour and social security protections have provided a foundation for rulings strengthening equal pay for equal work, access to health coverage, and unemployment benefits.[57] Likewise, in South Africa, the constitution's protections against discrimination have been found to extend to private employers, resulting in an important 2008 ruling against a church that fired an employee for being openly gay, in which the court noted that 'right to equality (protected in terms of section 9 of the Constitution) is viewed as foundational to our constitutional order'.[58]

---

[54] Elizabeth S Anderson and Richard H Pildes, 'Expressive Theories of Law: A General Restatement' (2000) 148 University of Pennsylvania Law Review 1503.

[55] Heymann, Sprague, and Raub (n 5) 130–31, 144–45.

[56] Harold J Sullivan, 'Privatization of Public Services: A Growing Threat to Constitutional Rights' (1987) 47 Public Administration Review 461; Andras Sajó and Renata Uitz (eds), *The Constitution in Private Relations: Expanding Constitutionalism* (Eleven International Publishing 2005).

[57] See eg Judgment T-341/94 (Constitutional Court of Colombia) (affirming a pilot's right to social security coverage for her miscarriage); Sentencia No SU-519/97 (Constitutional Court of Colombia) (holding that public and private employers alike must uphold the constitutional right to equal pay for equal work); Sentencia C-051/95 (ruling that a provision in the labour code that established a lower level of unemployment benefits for domestic workers violated the constitution's protections of equality and decent work); Martha I Morgan, 'Taking Machismo to Court: The Gender Jurisprudence of the Colombian Constitutional Court' (1999) 30 The University of Miami Inter-American Law Review 253, 285–87.

[58] Sonu Bedi, 'The Horizontal Effect of a Right to Non-Discrimination in Employment: Religious Autonomy under the US Constitution and the Constitution of South Africa' (2015) 95 Boston University Law Review 1181.

7 Constitutions, Crises, and Exponential Inequalities: Assessing Gaps and Opportunities

As the project giving rise to this volume has emphasized, the current moment demands deep engagement with the inadequacies of existing legal approaches to non-discrimination. However, it also presents an opportunity for stock-taking and identifying emerging trends with the potential to offer more powerful protections if adopted more widely.

This chapter has aimed to seize this opportunity through a combination of global, quantitative analysis of rights protections in 193 pre-pandemic constitutions and a survey of recent case law illustrating how these provisions can make a difference for workers. Our analysis has found that constitutions have increasingly enshrined protections for workers' equal rights, decent working conditions, and access to social protection. Moreover, emerging case law indicates that these protections have had impact.

Nevertheless, critical gaps remain in each area. Even with marked progress on equal rights guarantees in recent decades, some groups of workers receive minimal protections. Just 27 per cent of constitutions guarantee equal rights regardless of disability and just 22 per cent do so regardless of citizenship status, while a mere 5 per cent prohibit discrimination based on sexual orientation and 3 per cent do so for gender identity. Moreover, only 6 per cent address pregnancy and 8 per cent address marital status, which is cause for concern as caregiving norms, expectations, and responsibilities substantially contribute to the pandemic's consequences for women's employment. Meanwhile, just over a third of constitutions take any approach to protecting equal rights specifically in employment, and much more is needed to ensure these protections cover the private sphere.

Further, less than a third of constitutions guarantee the right to safe working conditions, while less than a quarter guarantee income protection during illness or unemployment, respectively. As the economic fall-out of Covid-19 continues and workers in front-line positions face ongoing health risks, gaps in these three protections are especially concerning.

More broadly, addressing the underlying inequalities that have driven the disparate risks and outcomes for marginalized workers during the pandemic is a substantial yet urgent undertaking. Occupational segregation and countries' failure to invest adequately in caregiving, for instance, are long-standing barriers to gender equality in the economy that worsened women's outcomes in the context of a crisis. Inadequate investments in public health, safe living conditions, and access to preventive care have made countless workers—disproportionately from marginalized groups—more vulnerable to severe illness or death.

Constitutional rights on their own cannot solve these immense challenges. Nevertheless, constitutional rights are having meaningful impacts, including by addressing some of the structural discrimination and policy gaps that have worsened outcomes for marginalized workers during the pandemic. Even aspirational rights, such as Lesotho's directive on safe working conditions and Malawi's directive principle on the fulfilment of basic needs, have made a difference in the courts, which offers further proof that even in lower resource settings, social and economic rights in constitutions can provide powerful tools for improving living and working conditions. This evidence suggests that further strengthening constitutional rights to equality, social insurance, and decent working conditions—including by closing the global gaps in protections identified in this chapter—would be a valuable step towards realizing fundamental human rights in both emergency situations and during a typical year, and could provide an important foundation for mitigating the types of exponential inequalities exacerbated by crises like the Covid-19 pandemic.

3
Addressing Intersecting Inequalities through Alternative Economic Strategies

Diane Elson and Marion Sharples

1 Introduction

This chapter examines some inequalities of class, gender, and race in the UK prior to Covid-19—with a focus on income, wealth, and health—and discusses how they have intensified during the pandemic. It notes that UK governments since 2010 have not conducted any systematic and comprehensive equalities impact assessments despite the provisions of the 2010 Equality Act. It suggests that inequalities could be reduced through alternative economic strategies that have been put forward by feminist economists in which public investment in care services plays a central role. In particular it discusses the steps to create a Caring Economy, put forward by the UK Women's Budget Group's Commission on a Gender Equal Economy, and argues this strategy could be strengthened by measures to redress the imbalance between the regimes of commercial property rights (rights to buy and sell resources and to extract profits and rents from their use) and the rights set out in the International Covenant on Economic, Social and Cultural Rights (ICESCR).[1]

2 Inequalities Prior to the Covid-19 Pandemic: Income, Wealth, and Health

When the Covid pandemic hit the UK in early 2020, it arrived in a country which had already been ravaged by austerity measures, introduced by the Conservative and Coalition governments in office since 2010. Cuts to public expenditure were argued to be necessary to reduce the UK budget deficit that had risen steeply as a result of the financial crisis in 2008/9. Far from the government's promise that 'we are all in this together',[2] these measures had different impacts on different groups in society. The UK Women's Budget Group showed that cuts to public services, social security, and changes to the tax system over the period from 2010 to 2020 hit disabled women,

---

[1] International Covenant on Economic, Social and Cultural Rights, adopted by the General Assembly of the United Nations on 16 December 1966, UNTS 999, 171.

[2] David Cameron, 'Prime Minister's Speech on the Economy' (7 June 2010) https://www.gov.uk/government/speeches/prime-ministers-speech-on-the-economy (accessed 13 July 2021).

lone mothers, and women from a Black, Asian, or Minority Ethnic (BAME) group the hardest.[3]

Was this the government's intention? It is hard to know, as the June 2010 budget, which was the budget which began the decade of austerity, was not accompanied by an equality impact assessment. This was despite the requirements of the 2010 Equality Act to carry out impact analysis of significant policy measures on equality. Indeed, since then, while a few piecemeal impact assessments have been published on some individual policies by specific government departments, no comprehensive equality impact analysis has been carried out of any UK Budget or Spending Review since 2010.

Economic inequality between households was high prior to the pandemic: in 2014/16 there was a sixfold difference between the income of the top 20 per cent of households and those of the bottom 20 per cent. Wealth inequality was much worse, with 44 per cent of the UK's wealth owned by just 10 per cent of the population, five times the total wealth held by the poorest half.[4] Child poverty had been rising over the decade to 2020.[5] Children from BAME groups[6] and children living in lone-parent families[7] were significantly more likely to be living in poverty. The number of emergency food parcels issued from Trussell Trust foodbanks increased by 3,900 per cent over the period from 2010 to 2019.[8] The gap between the pay of the richest and the rest widened. In 2017, the average pay of chief executive officers (CEOs) of FTSE 100 companies in the UK was 145 times the pay of the average worker, up from forty-seven times in 1998. Household earnings of the poorest stagnated, with the lowest earning working households earning little more than such households earned in the 1990s.[9] The gap between male and female hourly earnings had been falling but progress stalled and the gap was still 18 per cent in 2018.[10] Although there is undoubtedly some outright discrimination against women in labour markets, a very important factor of the gender pay gap is structural inequalities in the division of unpaid care work. Gender gaps in employment, working hours, and wages intensify after workers become parents. Many more mothers than fathers stop paid work altogether or switch to part-time paid work while taking on the majority of childcare. This has long-lasting, cumulative impacts on women's hourly wages well into the future.[11] In 2015, mothers spent, on average,

---

[3] Women's Budget Group, 'Intersecting Inequalities: The Impact of Austerity on Black and Minority Ethnic Women in the UK' (2017) https://wbg.org.uk/analysis/intersecting-inequalities/ (accessed 13 July 2021).

[4] Richard Partington, 'How Unequal is Britain and Are the Poor Getting Poorer?' *The Guardian* (5 September 2018) https://www.theguardian.com/inequality/2018/sep/05/qa-how-unequal-is-britain-and-are-the-poor-getting-poorer (accessed 13 July 2021).

[5] Joseph Rowntree Foundation, 'Child Poverty Rates by Family Size' (2020) https://www.jrf.org.uk/data/child-poverty (accessed 13 July 2021).

[6] Child Poverty Action Group, 'Child Poverty Facts and Figures' (2020) https://cpag.org.uk/child-poverty-facts-and-figures (accessed 13 July 2021).

[7] ibid.

[8] Charity Works, 'Food Bank Britain' (17 June 2019) https://www.charity-works.co.uk/food-bank-britain/ (accessed 13 July 2021).

[9] Robert Joyce and Xiaowei Xu, 'Inequalities in the 21st Century: Introducing the IFS Deaton Review' (2019) https://www.ifs.org.uk/inequality/wp-content/uploads/2019/05/The-IFS-Deaton-Review-launch.pdf (accessed 13 July 2021).

[10] ibid.

[11] Alison Andrew and others, 'The Careers and Time Use of Mothers and Fathers' Institute for Fiscal Studies (12 March 2021) https://ifs.org.uk/publications/15360 (accessed 13 July 2021).

1 hour and 57 minutes per day providing childcare, comprising 74 per cent of total unpaid childcare. Women also provide the majority of hours spent in unpaid care for adults. On average, both men and women over 50 increased the amount of time devoted to unpaid caring of adults, by 15 per cent and 21 per cent respectively between 2000 and 2015. Women accounted for 59 per cent of this time in 2015.[12]

Regional inequality was higher than in other rich countries: Camden and the City of London, the richest part of the UK, was thirty times richer than the poorest (Ards and the North Down in Northern Ireland).[13] Life expectancy had stopped growing in England, with similar patterns in Scotland,[14] Wales,[15] and Northern Ireland.[16] In England, average women's life expectancy actually declined in the most deprived 10 per cent of areas between 2010 and 2012 and between 2016 and 2018.[17] Health inequalities are related to the climate emergency as well as to austerity: air pollution contributes to 40,000 deaths each year, primarily in deprived areas.[18] More broadly, older people, the very young, people in poor health, tenants, socially isolated people, and people on low incomes tend to be worst affected by the climate emergency.[19]

Before the pandemic hit, health outcomes were already racialized. Black Caribbean, Pakistani, and Bangladeshi people are expected to live between six to nine years fewer without a limiting illness than White British people.[20] Black women are more than five times more likely than White women to die in pregnancy or up to six weeks after giving birth. Women of mixed ethnicity have three times the mortality risk and Asian women have almost twice the risk.[21]

Housing is critical to health and to wealth. The prices of housing to rent,[22] and to

---

[12] Office for National Statistics, 'Changes in the Value and Division of Unpaid Care Work in the UK: 2000 to 2015' (2016) https://www.ons.gov.uk/releases/changesinthevalueanddivisionofunpaidcareworkintheuk2000to2015 (accessed 13 July 2021).

[13] *The Economist*, 'Why Britain is More Geographically Unequal than any Other Rich Country' (30 July 2020) https://www.economist.com/britain/2020/07/30/why-britain-is-more-geographically-unequal-than-any-other-rich-country (accessed 13 July 2021).

[14] *BBC News*, 'Scottish Life Expectancy Improvements Stall' (14 August 2019) https://www.bbc.co.uk/news/uk-scotland-49343732 (accessed 13 July 2021).

[15] NHS Wales and Public Health Wales Observatory, 'Life Expectancy and Mortality in Wales' (2020) https://www2.nphs.wales.nhs.uk/PubHObservatoryProjDocs.nsf/7c21215d6d0c613e80256f490030c05a/75522ac51cc545a18025852000365842/$FILE/LifeExpectancyAndMortalityInWales_2020_v1.pdf (accessed 13 July 2021).

[16] Department of Health, Northern Ireland, 'Life Expectancy in Northern Ireland 2016-18' (2019) https://www.health-ni.gov.uk/sites/default/files/publications/health/hscims-life-expectancy-ni-2016-18.pdf (accessed 13 July 2021).

[17] Institute of Health Equity, 'Health Equity in England: The Marmot Review 10 Years On' (2020) https://www.instituteofhealthequity.org/the-marmot-review-10-years-on (accessed 13 July 2021).

[18] Living Streets, 'Air Pollution' (2019) https://www.livingstreets.org.uk/policy-and-resources/our-policy/air-pollution (accessed 13 July 2021).

[19] Climate Just, 'Socially Vulnerable Groups Sensitive to Climate Impacts' https://www.climatejust.org.uk/socially-vulnerable-groups-sensitive-climate-impacts (accessed 13 July 2021).

[20] Pia Wohland and others, 'Inequalities in Healthy Life Expectancy between Ethnic Groups in England and Wales 2001' (2015) 20 Ethnicity and Health 341.

[21] Royal College of Obstetricians and Gynaecologists, 'RCOG Position Statement: Racial disparities in Women's Healthcare' (6 March 2020) https://www.rcog.org.uk/globalassets/documents/news/position-statements/racial-disparities-womens-healthcare-march-2020.pdf (accessed 13 July 2021).

[22] Office for National Statistics, 'Index of Private Housing Rental Prices, UK: July 2020' https://www.ons.gov.uk/economy/inflationandpriceindices/bulletins/indexofprivatehousingrentalprices/july2020 (accessed 13 July 2021).

buy,[23] have increased substantially since 2010, making an affordable home unachievable for increasing swathes of the UK population. Research by the UK Women's Budget Group has shown that in England, women are less likely to be able to afford housing than men, both to buy and to rent: women need more than twelve times their annual salaries to be able to buy a home in England, while men need just over eight times. There is no English region where the median private rent is affordable on women's median earnings, whereas it is for men in all English regions except London.[24] The number of rough sleepers in England increased since 2010, by around 165 per cent,[25] and more than doubled in Wales since 2008.[26] However, there was a rapid growth in the number of people buying houses in Britain to rent out (and a smaller growth in the number of second homes that people own). Buy-to-let was the fastest-growing part of Britain's multiple property wealth: the total number of outstanding buy-to-let mortgages has risen fifteen times since 2000.[27] Property wealth has accumulated in fewer and fewer hands.

This is one aspect of the rise of a 'rentier' economy, in which businesses make money primarily by buying and selling existing assets—many of which were created using public money and at public risk (such as financial assets, property, care homes, railway companies, and football clubs). Rentiers extract rent, fees, interest payments, dividends, and capital gains from these financial assets, while seemingly making only small profits. This has affected the delivery of public services, which have been outsourced to the private sector. For example, while the UK care home industry is often reported as being on the verge of collapsing, it is estimated that £1.5 billion leaks out of this industry each year in the form of rent, dividend payments, interest payments, fees, and profits before tax.[28] HC-One, the largest care home group, declared a loss every year bar one since its creation in 2011, and yet it paid dividends of £48.5 million in the years 2017 to 2019.[29]

Underpinning inequalities between people and places is the concentration of economic power in the hands of a few big companies. In the UK in the period just prior to the Covid-19 pandemic, six energy companies held 82 per cent of the retail energy

---

[23] Statista, '12 month Percentage Change in House Prices in the United Kingdom (UK) from July 2007 to July 2019' (2020) https://www.statista.com/statistics/751619/house-price-change-uk/ (accessed 13 July 2021).

[24] Housing is considered 'affordable' when it takes less than a third of a household's income: Sara Reis, 'A Home of Her Own: Housing and Women' Women's Budget Group (2019) https://wbg.org.uk/wp-content/uploads/2019/07/WBG19-Housing-Report-full-digital.pdf (accessed 13 July 2021).

[25] MHCLG, 'Rough Sleeping Statistics Autumn 2018, England (Revised)' (2018) https://assets.publishing.service.gov.uk/government/uploads/system/uploads/attachment_data/file/781567/Rough_Sleeping_Statistics_2018_release.pdf (accessed 13 July 2021).

[26] Welsh Government, 'National Rough Sleeper Count' (2020) https://gov.wales/national-rough-sleeper-count (accessed 13 July 2021).

[27] George Bangham, 'Game of Homes: The Rise of Multiple Property Ownership in Great Britain Resolution Foundation (2019) https://www.resolutionfoundation.org/app/uploads/2019/06/Game-of-Homes.pdf (accessed 13 July 2021).

[28] Centre for Health and the Public Interest, 'Plugging the Leaks in the UK Care Home Industry: Strategies for Resolving the Financial Crisis in the Residential and Nursing Home Sector' (2019) https://chpi.org.uk/wp-content/uploads/2019/11/CHPI-PluggingTheLeaks-Nov19-FINAL.pdf (accessed 13 July 2021).

[29] Sheila Smith, 'Termite Capitalism: How Private Equity Is Undermining the Economy' *Open Democracy* (4 June 2020) https://www.opendemocracy.net/en/oureconomy/termite-capitalism-how-private-equity-undermining-economy/ (accessed 13 July 2021).

market; four supermarkets comprised 69 per cent of the grocery sales; five banks had 85 per cent of retail bank accounts; four mobile phone companies retained 89 per cent of customers; and a few firms like Carillion held a very high proportion of outsourced contracts to deliver publicly funded services.[30] The companies operating the major digital platforms dominate the UK market, as they do in almost all the countries in which they operate: in the UK, Facebook controlled 74 per cent of the market for social networks, Amazon was responsible for around 80 per cent of online sales of books, and Google enjoyed 90 per cent of the search-engine market.[31]

3 Unequal Impact of Covid-19

Covid-19 has had unequal impacts on health due to underlying economic inequalities. The impact on health was worse in the most deprived areas of England, Wales, and Scotland.[32] Two-thirds of the people who died from Covid-19 in March to July 2020 were disabled people.[33] Death rates from Covid-19 have been higher for BAME people than White people,[34] most likely a result of the underlying economic inequalities that structure a disproportionately high number of the lives of people from BAME groups, such as poorly paid and insecure employment, overcrowded, poor-quality housing, and living in deprived neighbourhoods with high rates of poverty.[35] There are calls to focus on the underlying, structural causes of unequal health outcomes, including institutional and structural racism, and deeply embedded discrimination.[36]

The psychological burden of the pandemic has been borne differently by different groups. While women overall reported higher levels of psychological distress than men, working class[37] women reported the highest levels of psychological distress of

---

[30] IPPR Commission on Economic Justice, *Prosperity and Justice: A Plan for a New Economy* (Polity Press 2018).

[31] ibid.

[32] Helen Pidd, Caelainn Barr, and Aamna Mohdin, 'Calls for Health Funding to be Prioritised as Poor Bear Brunt of Covid-19' *The Guardian* (1 May 2020) https://www.theguardian.com/world/2020/may/01/covid-19-deaths-twice-as-high-in-poorest-areas-in-england-and-wales (accessed 13 July 2021); Caelainn Barr and Libby Brooks, 'People in Deprived Areas of Scotland More Likely to Die from Covid-19' *The Guardian* (13 May 2020) https://www.theguardian.com/uk-news/2020/may/13/people-in-deprived-areas-of-scotland-more-likely-to-die-from-covid-19 (accessed 13 July 2021).

[33] Disability Rights UK, 'Disabled People Make up Two Thirds of Coronavirus Deaths—ONS' (24 September 2020) https://www.disabilityrightsuk.org/news/2020/september/disabled-people-make-two-thirds-coronavirus-deaths-ons (accessed 13 July 2021).

[34] Public Health England, 'Disparities in the Risk and Outcomes of Covid-19' (2020) https://assets.publishing.service.gov.uk/government/uploads/system/uploads/attachment_data/file/908434/Disparities_in_the_risk_and_outcomes_of_COVID_August_2020_update.pdf (accessed 13 July 2021).

[35] Bridget Byrne and others, *Ethnicity, Race and Inequality in the UK: State of the Nation* (Policy Press 2020).

[36] James Nazroo and Laia Bécares, 'Ethnic Inequalities in COVID-19 Mortality: A Consequence of Persistent Racism. Runnymede and CoDE' (2021) https://www.research.manchester.ac.uk/portal/files/200461103/Runnymede_CoDE_COVID_mortality_briefing_FINAL.pdf (accessed 13 July 2021).

[37] The researchers on this project used the National Statistics Socio-Economic Classification (NS-SEC) to define a 'working class worker' group, combining 'semi-routine' (such as care workers, retail assistants, hospital porters) and 'routine' workers (such as cleaners, waiting staff, bus drivers, bar staff, sewing machinists), and then comparing them with employed people in the other class groupings.

all groups in November 2020, when infection numbers started to creep up again.[38] Higher levels of depression were noted among women, people aged 16 to 39, people unable to afford an unexpected expense, and disabled people.[39] During the first wave of the pandemic in May 2020, work-related anxiety for those working outside the home was highest among BAME people.[40]

Working outside the home during the pandemic, which increases the risk of infection, was not spread equally across groups. The government introduced lockdown measures, requiring most people to stay at home, and where possible work from home using the internet, but this did not apply to 'key workers' who were required to work outside the home to provide essential services, such as health and social care, transport, and food retailing. Women were twice as likely to be 'key workers' than men, with BAME and migrant women overrepresented.[41] In November 2020, 86 per cent of working class women were not working from home (compared with 35 per cent of women in management and professional jobs), and 60 per cent of working class women were in key worker roles—the highest proportion of all class groupings.[42] BAME women are also over-represented in both health and social care,[43] with one in five National Health Service (NHS) workers being from a BAME group.[44] Social care workers have been at the front line of the pandemic, often without adequate protective equipment and with significantly higher mortality rates than the rest of the population.[45]

To support employment and incomes during the lockdowns for those that were neither 'key workers', nor working from home, the government introduced the Coronavirus Job Retention Scheme, through which the government provided finance to companies to pay 80 per cent of workers' wages while they stayed at home on furlough. Some, but not all, companies found the finance to pay the other 20 per cent. Mothers have been more likely to be furloughed than fathers (35 per cent compared

---

[38] Tracey Warren and Clare Lyonette, 'A Year On: Working Class Women and Work During the Covid-19 Pandemic' (2021) https://www.nottingham.ac.uk/vision/working-class-women-work-during-the-covid-19-pandemic (accessed 13 July 2021).

[39] Office for National Statistics, 'Coronavirus and depression in adults, Great Britain: June 2020' (2020) https://www.ons.gov.uk/peoplepopulationandcommunity/wellbeing/articles/coronavirusanddepressioninadultsgreatbritain/june2020 (accessed 13 July 2021).

[40] Women's Budget Group, 'New Data Reveals Crisis of Support for Black, Asian and Minority Ethnic Women' (2021) https://wbg.org.uk/media/new-data-reveals-crisis-of-support-for-bame-women/ (accessed 13 July 2021).

[41] Maja Gustafsson and Charlie McCurdy, 'Risky Business: Economic Impacts of the Coronavirus Crisis on Different Groups of Workers' The Resolution Foundation (28 April 2020) https://www.resolutionfoundation.org/publications/risky-business/ (accessed 13 July 2021).

[42] Warren and Lyonette (n 38).

[43] Lucinda Platt and Ross Warwick, 'Are Some Ethnic Groups More Vulnerable to Covid-19 than Others?' Institute for Fiscal Studies (May 2020) https://ifs.org.uk/inequality/wp-content/uploads/2020/04/Are-some-ethnic-groups-more-vulnerable-to-COVID-19-than-others-V2-IFS-Briefing-Note.pdf (accessed 13 July 2021).

[44] UK Government, 'NHS Workforce: By Ethnicity' (26 January 2021) https://www.ethnicity-facts-figures.service.gov.uk/workforce-and-business/workforce-diversity/nhs-workforce/latest#by-ethnicity (accessed 13 July 2021).

[45] Haroon Siddique, 'Social Care Workers at Increased Risk of Death from Coronavirus, ONS Finds' The Guardian (26 June 2020) https://www.theguardian.com/world/2020/jun/26/social-care-workers-increased-risk-death-coronavirus (accessed 13 July 2021).

to 30 per cent for fathers),⁴⁶ with their overall employment rate dropping from 80 per cent to 70 per cent.⁴⁷

Women were called upon to increase their unpaid work caring for others as schools shut down, and risk of infections led to reluctance to send small children to nurseries and frail elderly relatives to care homes. A study of heterosexual couples with school age children found that both mothers and fathers had substantially increased the time they spent on unpaid care, but more was being done by mothers, even if they had a paid job. Moreover, mothers were more likely to have lost their jobs (either temporarily or permanently) than fathers, with women with the lowest levels of education at most disadvantage.⁴⁸ After the onset of Covid-19, the numbers of unpaid carers for adults increased in 2020 by 4.5 million to over 13.6 million, nearly 58 per cent of them women, nearly 3 million of whom combine paid work with care. A survey of almost 5,900 carers in October 2020 found nearly two-thirds had no respite from their caring responsibilities; three-quarters reported feeling exhausted and worn out; two-thirds said that their mental health had worsened. Eleven per cent of carers reported they had reduced their hours of paid work to manage their caring responsibilities, and 9 per cent had given up paid work because of caring.⁴⁹ These increases in the unpaid care contributed by women and falls in women's employment meant that progress on reducing gender inequality in incomes had been put at risk. A third of nurseries in the most disadvantaged areas of England may be forced to close permanently due to financial difficulties and instability experienced since the pandemic hit.⁵⁰ Gender equality has also been jeopardized by an increase in cases of femicide as a result of domestic abuse in locked-down households; the number of suspected domestic killings more than doubled between 23 March and 12 April 2020.⁵¹ Refuge saw a 950 per cent increase in visits to its website, where women can arrange a safe time to be contacted.⁵²

The financial impacts of the pandemic have been unequal. By November 2020, 42 per cent of high-income households had increased their savings during the pandemic, while unemployed and furloughed households decreased their savings.⁵³ Some ethnic minority groups—such as Bangladeshi and Black African groups—have experienced significant income loss during the coronavirus crisis, and nearly two-thirds of

---

⁴⁶ Alison Andrew and others, 'How are Mothers and Fathers Balancing Work and Family Under Lockdown?' IFS Briefing Note BN290 (May 2020) https://ifs.org.uk/uploads/BN290-Mothers-and-fathers-balancing-work-and-life-under-lockdown.pdf (accessed 13 July 2021).
⁴⁷ ibid.
⁴⁸ Andrew and others (n 11).
⁴⁹ Carers UK, 'Caring Behind Closed Doors: Six Months On' (2020) https://www.carersuk.org/images/News_and_campaigns/Caring_Behind_Closed_Doors_Oct20.pdf (accessed 13 July 2021).
⁵⁰ The Sutton Trust, 'A Third of Nurseries in the Most Disadvantaged Areas may be Forced to Close due to Financial Difficulties' (1 July 2020) https://www.suttontrust.com/news-opinion/all-news-opinion/a-third-of-nurseries-in-the-most-disadvantaged-areas-may-be-forced-to-close-due-to-financial-difficulties/ (accessed 13 July 2021).
⁵¹ Jamie Grierson, 'Domestic Abuse Killings "More Than Double" Amid Covid-19 Lockdown' *The Guardian* (15 April 2020) https://www.theguardian.com/society/2020/apr/15/domestic-abuse-killings-more-than-double-amid-covid-19-lockdown (accessed 13 July 2021).
⁵² Refuge, 'Refuge Reports Further Increase in Demand for its National Domestic Abuse Helpline Services During Lockdown' (27 May 2020) https://www.refuge.org.uk/refuge-reports-further-increase-in-demand-for-its-national-domestic-abuse-helpline-services-during-lockdown/ (accessed 13 July 2021).
⁵³ Bank of England, 'How has Covid Affected Household Savings?' (2020) https://www.bankofengland.co.uk/bank-overground/2020/how-has-covid-affected-household-savings (accessed 13 July 2021).

members of ethnic minority groups (65 per cent, compared with 46 per cent of people in White groups) have struggled with paying bills and paying for essentials during lockdown.[54] Ethnic minority groups have also been less likely to receive any form of sick pay if ill with the coronavirus, even though they have had to self-isolate.[55]

One in five key workers (who are more likely to be women, with BAME and migrant women over-represented) have fallen behind on their bills, compared to fewer than one in ten of non-key workers.[56] Almost twice the proportion of working-class women than women in managerial and professional jobs reported experiencing financial hardship in April 2020, rising even further in November.[57]

The wealth of the world's billionaires has grown by US$4 trillion during the pandemic—and fifty-four of these billionaires are based in the UK. The combined wealth of Britain's super-rich rose by 36 per cent from US$154 billion to US$209 billion.[58]

The power and profits of many large companies, especially those operating online and delivering to homes, increased. A notable example is Amazon, whose UK sales rose 51 per cent to almost £20 billion and whose profits tripled from the start of 2020 to the start of 2021.[59] UK online fashion retailers have also benefited: ASOS saw profits soar from £25 million in 2019 to £113 million in 2020, and Boohoo saw profits increase from £47.5 million to £72.8 million. All three companies have been widely criticized for exploitative employment practices, so the jobs they create are unlikely to combat widening inequality. There were outbreaks of Covid-19 in summer 2020 in Leicester garment factories that supply Boohoo amid claims that pressure to produce fast and cheap led to failure to maintain a Covid-19 secure working environment for a workforce in which British Asian women are the majority.[60]

Other companies benefited from a rapid increase in Covid-19 related public sector outsourcing, mostly awarded without an open competitive public tender as the standard rules were suspended, often to companies with no track record in producing the required goods and services. An investigation by an international anti-corruption non-governmental organization found that twenty-seven contracts worth £2.1 billion for Personal Protective Equipment and Coronavirus testing were awarded to

---

[54] Zubaida Haque, Laia Becares, and Nick Treloar, 'Over-Exposed and Under-Protected: The Devastating Impact of COVID-19 on Black and Minority Ethnic Communities in Great Britain' Runnymede Trust (August 2020) https://assets-global.website-files.com/61488f992b58e687f1108c7c/61c31c9d268b932bd064524c_Runnymede%20Covid19%20Survey%20report%20v3.pdf (accessed 13 July 2021).
[55] ibid.
[56] Citizens Advice, 'Excess Debt: Who Has Fallen Behind on Their Household Bills due to Coronavirus?' (8 September 2020) https://www.citizensadvice.org.uk/about-us/our-work/policy/policy-research-topics/debt-and-money-policy-research/excess-debts-who-has-fallen-behind-on-their-household-bills-due-to-coronavirus/ (accessed 13 July 2021).
[57] Warren and Lyonette (n 38).
[58] Phillip Aldrick, 'The Rich Get Richer Amid the Pandemic' The Times (1 April 2021) https://www.thetimes.co.uk/article/the-rich-get-richer-amid-the-pandemic-0blt3mhwx (accessed 13 July 2021).
[59] BBC News, 'Amazon Hopes Pandemic Habits Stick after Profits Triple' (29 April 2021) https://www.bbc.co.uk/news/business-56937428 (accessed 13 July 2021).
[60] Laurie Macfarlane and Christine Berry, 'Who is Winning from Covid-19?' Scottish Trade Union Centre (19 April 2021) http://www.stuc.org.uk/files/Policy/Research-papers/Who_is_winning_from_covid.pdf (accessed 13 July 2021).

firms with political connections to the governing Conservative Party.[61] For instance, a former Conservative councillor, whose company Platform-14 was awarded £276 million in government contracts for personal protective equipment (PPE), then proceeded to buy a £1.5 million mansion in the Cotswolds.[62]

An enquiry by the cross-party Parliamentary Select Committee on Women and Equalities found that the government did not conduct equalities impact analysis of its policy response to the pandemic. Moreover, it suspended enforcement of gender pay gap reporting requirements on employers with more than 250 employees, which had been introduced in 2017. The Committee called for gender pay gap reporting to be urgently reinstated and for ethnicity and disability pay gap reporting to be introduced. It emphasized that all proposals for post-Covid economic recovery should be subjected to equality impact assessments.[63]

4 Alternative Economic Strategies

A number of strategies for post-Covid recovery have been discussed in the UK, in other countries and in UN agencies. Women's rights advocates emphasize public investment in care services as key to halting the increase in inequalities in paid and unpaid work. Improved and expanded high quality care services, employing well-paid and well-trained workers, reduce the amount of unpaid care that women have to provide. They also provide more and better jobs that, given current employment patterns will likely be mainly taken by women, especially working class, ethnic minority, and migrant women. This will reduce gendered and racialized employment, wage, and income gaps; improve work-life balance; and reduce inequalities in well-being, for both providers and recipients of care.

The UK Women's Budget Group proposed a care-led recovery plan for the UK,[64] arguing that investment in care services will provide more jobs, for both women and men, than investment of a similar size in construction. It is estimated that investing 1 per cent of gross domestic product (GDP) in the care sector would create approximately 2.7 times as many jobs as investing the same amount in the construction sector; 1.1 times as many jobs for men, and 6.3 times as many jobs for women. While investment in construction would increase the gender employment gap, investment in care would reduce it. Moreover, if wages paid in care were raised to the level of those in construction (requiring more than a doubling of wages in care), and care workers had full time jobs at the same rate as construction workers, more jobs overall would still

---

[61] Transparency International, 'Track and Trace: Identifying Corruption risks in UK Public Procurement for the COVID-19 Pandemic' (2021) https://www.transparency.org.uk/sites/default/files/pdf/publications/Track%20and%20Trace%20-%20Transparency%20International%20UK.pdf (accessed 13 July 2021).

[62] Gabriel Pogrund, 'Tory Steve Dechan's £276m in PPE Contracts Lands him a Place in the Country' *The Times* (22 November 2020) https://www.thetimes.co.uk/article/tory-steve-dechans-276m-in-ppe-contracts-lands-him-a-place-in-the-country-zgbmmtn8q (accessed 13 July 2021).

[63] House of Commons Women and Equalities Committee, 'Unequal Impact? Coronavirus and the gendered Economic Impact. Fifth Report of Session 2019-21' (2021) https://committees.parliament.uk/work/319/unequal-impact-coronavirus-and-the-gendered-economic-impact/ (accessed 13 July 2021).

[64] Jerome De Henau and Susan Himmelweit, 'A Care-Led Recovery from Coronavirus' (June 2020) https://wbg.org.uk/wp-content/uploads/2020/06/Care-led-recovery-final.pdf (accessed 13 July 2021).

be created by investment in care than in construction (1.6 times as many jobs), with 0.8 times as many jobs for men and 3.9 times as many jobs for women; and the gender wage gap would also be reduced.

Just as spending on construction is seen as investment in physical infrastructure, spending on care should be seen not as a cost but as investment in social infrastructure, which yields returns to economy and society well into the future in the form of a better educated, healthier and better cared for population, improving both productivity and well-being. Investment in care is also greener: calculations using Eurostat data suggest that investing in the care sector is 30 per cent less polluting in terms of greenhouse gas emissions than investing the same amount in the construction sector.[65] Thus, prioritizing investment in care is also more environmentally sustainable.

The UK government produced a very different kind of recovery plan, titled *Build Back Better*,[66] that emphasizes reducing geographical inequalities in England, primarily through 'levelling up' via special funds for investment in new physical infrastructure in towns and cities where productivity is estimated to be low, plus some additional funding for skills development. This is supposed to increase productivity, and it is assumed that this will improve living standards. It was reported that the criteria for allocating the new funding did not include the index of multiple deprivation, and the funding was distributed disproportionately to towns that had Conservative Party MPs.[67] The plan was supported by substantial tax breaks for corporations but funding for local public services is projected to continue to fall in the 2021 UK budget.[68] This plan did not directly address the inequalities discussed in this chapter but relied on economic growth 'trickling down' to those who are disadvantaged. It was not accompanied by any equalities impact analysis. The recovery plan did not address the issue of investment in care. However, in September 2021 the government announced a 'Health and Social Care Levy', a tax rise of 1.25 per cent on national insurance contributions, to come into force in April 2022, to be paid by employers, employees, and the self-employed. This is a regressive tax increase that would impact more on low-income people. Initially, nearly all the additional revenue was to go to the NHS to address the urgent patient backlog in the healthcare system, with just £5.4 billion over three years allocated to adult social care.[69]

In December 2021, the UK government finally published its long-awaited White Paper, setting out its ten-year vision for adult social care. However, most of the money was allocated to put a cap on co-payments, and not enough funding was allocated to improve pay and conditions of social care workers, to expand the workforce, and to improve access to services and levels of services for the 1.5 million older people

---

[65] ibid.
[66] HM Treasury, 'Build Back Better' (2020) https://www.gov.uk/government/publications/build-back-better-our-plan-for-growth (accessed 13 July 2021).
[67] Kenan Malik, 'Unlevelling Down is the Tories New Vote-winner' *The Guardian* (14 March 2021) https://www.theguardian.com/commentisfree/2021/mar/14/unlevelling-down-is-the-tories-new-vote-winner (accessed 13 July 2021).
[68] Paul Johnson, 'Opening Remarks. Spring Budget 2021' (28 October 2021) https://www.ifs.org.uk/budget-2021 (accessed 13 July 2021).
[69] Susan Himmelweit and Jerome De Henau, 'Autumn Budget 2021: Social Care, Gender and Covid-19' Women's Budget Group (October 2021) https://wbg.org.uk/wp-content/uploads/2021/10/Social-care-Autumn-2021-PBB.pdf? (accessed 13 July 2021).

and many more working-age adults currently with unmet care needs.[70] The Autumn 2021 Budget did include some additional funding for childcare, but nowhere enough to meet the needs of children and their parents.[71] The additional planned spending on care nowhere near matches the scale of investment estimated by the Women's Budget Group and the New Economic Foundation to be necessary for a high-quality universal social care service that satisfies needs and provides good jobs. The additional funding requirement could be met by reforming the tax system, including closing gaps and loopholes in inheritance tax, reducing tax breaks for occupational pension contributions by high income earners, and taxing wealth and income from wealth.[72] However, in October 2022, the planned rise in national insurance contributions was reversed, and funding for care is under threat.

Feminists in Canada argued for a care-led recovery. YWCA Canada and the Institute for Gender and the Economy at the University of Toronto's Rotman School of Management published a Feminist Economic Recovery Plan[73] that called for substantial investment in childcare. A group of academics and activists initiated a Campaign for the Care Economy covering all kinds of care, arguing that public spending on care is investment in social infrastructure.[74] The Government of Canada was more responsive than the UK government, creating a Taskforce on Women in the Economy to advise the government on a feminist, intersectional action plan that addresses issues of gender equality in the wake of the pandemic.[75] In the Spring 2021 Federal Budget, CN$30 billion was allocated over five years for childcare, estimated to create up to 240,000 more childcare jobs, and raise GDP by as much as 1.2 per cent. However, there was very little investment in long term care for frail elderly people, consisting of only CN$3 billion over five years with no proposal to improve standards of care and wages and conditions of work, on a Canada-wide basis.[76]

In the US, feminists helped to create a Carework Network and called for the Biden-Harris administration to take sustained and decisive action to build robust care infrastructure.[77] President Biden put forward bold new policies that are being compared to

---

[70] 'The Government's Social Care White Paper' Women's Budget Group (1 December 2021) https://wbg.org.uk/blog/the-governments-social-care-white-paper-a-good-vision-without-a-meaningful-strategy-for-delivery/ (accessed 19 January 2022).

[71] 'A Lack of Ambition: WBG Response to the Autumn 2021 Budget and Spending Review' Women's Budget Group (October 2021) https://wbg.org.uk/wp-content/uploads/2021/11/Autumn-2021-Budget-and-Spending-Review-full-response.pdf (accessed 19 January 2022).

[72] Sarah Bedford and Daniel Button, 'Universal Quality Social Care: Transforming Adult Social Care in England' New Economics Foundation and the Women's Budget Group (January 2022) https://wbg.org.uk/analysis/reports/universal-quality-social-care/ (accessed 19 January 2022).

[73] Anjum Sultana and Carmina Ravanera, 'A Feminist Economic Recovery Plan for Canada: Making the Economy Work for Everyone' YWCA Canada and University of Toronto (28 July 2020) https://www.feministrecovery.ca/the-plan (accessed 13 July 2021).

[74] The Care Economy, 'Task Force on Women in the Economy' (2020) https://thecareeconomy.ca/ (accessed 13 July 2021).

[75] Government of Canada, 'Task Force on Women in the Economy' (2021) https://www.canada.ca/en/department-finance/task-force-women-economy.html#about (accessed 13 July 2021).

[76] Marjorie Griffin Cohen, 'Budget Promises Childcare but Misses Opportunities in Care Economy' *The Rabble* (20 April 2021) https://rabble.ca/news/2021/04/budget-promises-child-care-misses-opportunities-care-economy (accessed 13 July 2021).

[77] 'Carework Network' University of Massachusetts (2020) https://www.uml.edu/Research/CWW/carework/carework-network/ (accessed 13 July 2021).

Roosevelt's New Deal. They include not only investment in physical infrastructure but also new income transfers, higher taxes on corporations and rich people, support for workers' rights and wages, and investment in health and care services. President Biden included money for home-based care for the elderly and the disabled under the umbrella of infrastructure, as part of a US$2 trillion package he proposed in March 2021. The following month, he proposed more funding for paid family leave, and US$225 billion for childcare.[78] If these policies were to be implemented, they will directly address the kinds of inequalities that have been increasing.

International organizations have also been calling for a care-led recovery. UN Women has developed a post-Covid feminist plan for a sustainable and just economy, with investment in care at its centre.[79] Some of those working on the UN Women plan go beyond this to argue for a more thorough-going paradigm shift,[80] based on four elements. The first element requires a shift in the understanding of the economy from a narrow focus on market production and exchange to one based on social provisioning, with a focus on the processes and practices that lead to human flourishing. The second element is a redirection of resources to sectors that support social and environmental sustainability, including care but also activities such as low-cost clean energy. Thirdly, policy-makers must adopt new ways of measuring economic outcomes to provide alternatives to GDP. Finally, economic policy-making processes must be changed so that they are based on democratic deliberation rather than being reduced to technocratic calculations.

The Commission on a Gender Equal Economy, set up by the UK Women's Budget Group in 2019, called for a paradigm shift to focus on creating a caring economy, and set out an overarching vision and eight practical steps through which this could be realized in the UK.[81] A caring economy is one which prioritizes care of one another and the environment in which we live, so that both human beings and our shared planet can thrive. In a caring economy, care takes priority for all businesses, large or small, owned by shareholders, employees, or members of cooperatives; for all levels of government (local, regional, national) and all kinds of public agencies; for all non-governmental organizations and community groups; for all families, neighbours, and friends. In a caring economy, everyone gives and receives care on the basis of their capacities and needs.

Good-quality care services, such as adult social care, healthcare, and childcare, are critical for a caring economy. But a caring economy extends beyond provision of care services. It means caring about the pay and conditions of workers, especially the low paid, and acting together to ensure that all workers have decent work. It means caring

---

[78] Emily Peck, 'Policymakers Used to Ignore Child Care: Then Came the Pandemic' *New York Times* (9 May 2021) https://www.nytimes.com/2021/05/09/business/child-care-infrastructure-biden.htm (accessed 13 July 2021).

[79] UN Women, 'Beyond Covid-19: A Feminist Plan for Sustainability and Social Justice' (2021) https://www.unwomen.org/-/media/headquarters/attachments/sections/library/publications/2021/brief-plan-for-equal-en.pdf?la=en&vs=4300 (accessed 13 July 2021).

[80] James Heintz, Silke Staab, and Laura Turquet, 'Don't Let Another Crisis go to Waste: The Covid-19 Pandemic and the Imperative for a Paradigm Shift' (2021) 27 Feminist Economics 470.

[81] Women's Budget Group Commission on a Gender-Equal Economy, 'Creating a Caring Economy: A Call to Action' (2020) https://wbg.org.uk/wp-content/uploads/2020/10/WBG-Report-v10.pdf (accessed 13 July 2021).

about deprivation and poverty and acting together to bring them to an end. It means caring about tackling domestic violence and abuse, supporting those who have been subjected to it, and acting together to eliminate it. It means caring about our planet and acting together to ensure we do not pollute and degrade our air, water, and soil. It means acting together to improve well-being rather than to maximize economic growth.

A caring economy cares for all those who live in country regardless of their legal status; not just those who have citizenship, but also migrants, refugees, and asylum seekers. In the case of the UK, a caring economy would take into account that the UK is composed of four nations (England, Northern Ireland, Scotland, and Wales) and learn from their different experiences and divergent approaches. A caring economy also aims to reduce other forms of inequality beyond gender inequality, based on race, disability, class, age, sexual orientation, gender identity, religion, and belief, among others. A caring economy is an equalizing economy.

The vision set out by the Commission is intended to be enabling, setting out principles and recommendations for a caring economy, but the details of its operation would be shaped and adapted according to varying experiences, through deliberative processes at national, local, and community levels. The Commission also recognized that the extent to which a caring economy in any one country can be achieved is dependent on how international rules, relations and regulations facilitate this. The building of caring economies cannot be completed without transformations of international trade and finance.

Step 1 in creating a caring economy is to re-envision what is meant by 'the economy', so that the contribution of unpaid work as well as paid work is fully recognized. It entails seeing time as important as well as money, well-being as well as output, and ecological limits as well as human innovations. The measurement of the economy must go beyond GDP and the overarching objective must extend beyond growth of GDP. Well-being indicators, such as the genuine progress indicator (GPI) should be adopted. The GPI takes account of income inequality, the value of nonmarket household and volunteer labour, and the social and environmental costs associated with market activity, and the specific design of the GPI can be adapted for different contexts.[82] Economic concepts of costs, efficiency, and productivity must be redefined so that social value, environmental value, well-being, and unpaid time are taken into account, rather than only market value. The impact of all economic policies on equalities must be properly assessed before the policy is implemented and action must be taken to address any negative impacts, if necessary by abandoning the policy.

Step 2 is to invest in social as well as physical infrastructure, recognizing that infrastructure encompasses both physical structures, such as roads and bridges, and also public services such as healthcare, social care, and education, and services to address violence against women and girls. Both social and physical infrastructure not only have immediate benefits to users but also a broader positive impact on wider society and the economy with benefits felt over time and beyond the immediate users. Social

---

[82] Günseli Berik, 'Towards More Inclusive Measures of Wellbeing: Debates and Practices' ILO Future of Work Research Paper Series (2018) https://www.ilo.org/wcmsp5/groups/public/---dgreports/---cabinet/documents/publication/wcms_630602.pdf (accessed 13 July 2021).

and physical infrastructure must support well-being on an equitable basis and should be well-funded, accountable to users, designed according to their needs, and managed and provided at an appropriate level for the service. Provision of services should not be outsourced to large private for-profit businesses although, with appropriate quality standards for services and safeguarding of workers' rights, outsourcing to not-for-profit organizations, such as voluntary organizations and social enterprises, is compatible with creating a caring economy.

Step 3 is to transform work, both paid and unpaid, to provide not just more jobs, but better jobs. These jobs would enable women and men to share paid and unpaid work equally. They would provide a secure living income; be environmentally sustainable; and be free from gender stereotypes and discrimination. Governments and businesses must make it easier for workers to combine paid work and caring responsibilities, for instance through introducing equal legal entitlements to paid caring leave for all employees and self-employed people, including equal sharing of parental leave in the first year of a child's life, and leave for caring for elderly/disabled people and older children when required. In addition, they should pursue innovative strategies to reduce the full-time working week to around thirty hours and implement a minimum wage which is based on the real cost of living. Governments should support greater diversity and innovation in forms of business ownership, including cooperatives and social enterprises.

Step 4 is to invest in a caring social security system, based on dignity and autonomy, which helps to ensure people fulfil their capabilities and live a meaningful life, in and out of employment and regardless of migration status, throughout their lives. Governments must ensure that dignity is safeguarded by withdrawing punitive and unreasonable conditions and sanctions; and enhance autonomy by enabling individuals to establish their own claim to benefits, for example so that women are not dependent on husbands for access to benefits. They should improve and extend individual universal non-means-tested benefits to replace means-tested benefits wherever possible.

Step 5 is to transform taxation to make it more progressive, so that richer people pay a higher proportion of their income in tax than do poorer people. In many countries, income tax is much less progressive now than in the past: in the 1970s in the UK the highest rate of income tax on earned income was 83 per cent, in comparison to 45 per cent today. In addition, corporation tax rates have fallen across the world: in the UK in the early 1980s it was 52 per cent, compared to 19 per cent in 2020.[83] To support a caring economy, governments must accordingly: ensure independent taxation of income for each partner in a marriage or civil partnership; abolish poorly designed tax reliefs, allowances, and exemptions which aid tax avoidance and mainly benefit better-off men; overhaul the taxation of wealth and income from wealth, including equalizing the rate of capital gains tax with income tax, taxing unearned income at the same rate as earnings, and converting inheritance tax into a tax on lifetime gifts; and increase the rate of corporation tax and ensure multinational companies are not so easily able to avoid paying tax.

---

[83] Women's Budget Group Commission (n 81) 71.

Step 6 is to focus the overall framework for macro-economic policy (ie for fiscal and monetary policy) on building a caring economy. In the decade before the Covid-19 pandemic, fiscal and monetary policy in UK and most other countries was framed in terms of the objectives of promoting economic growth; keeping inflation low; reducing public expenditure and taxation to promote private sector investment; and reducing the budget deficit and public debt. This was reinforced by financial deregulation that permitted free flows of capital between countries. Fiscal and monetary policy was constrained by rigid rules and targets that reduced fiscal space and left little room for increases in public spending. In middle and low-income countries these objectives were stipulated as conditions for loans from the International Monetary Fund (IMF) and the World Bank. Under the pressure of Covid, in high income countries including the UK, governments abandoned restrictive targets and have borrowed large amounts of money to fund measures to support people and businesses through lockdown. Most middle and low-income countries are not able to expand their borrowing and are still constrained by IMF and World Bank conditions. The latter should change their policies, so that all governments are able to adopt flexible targets for government borrowing and reducing the budget deficit, going beyond narrow financial concerns to take into account human needs. Policy objectives should be directly related to well-being, gender equality, and sustainability. Such policy objectives might include: the creation of good jobs producing social and environmental value, monitored not only with unemployment and employment data, but also data on underemployment and precarious employment, disaggregated by gender, age, ethnicity, disability, and location; the reduction in the proportion of jobs that are in polluting industries, in line with targets for decarbonizing the economy; and the redistribution of unpaid work, measured by whether the share of men in time spent on this work is rising. Gender-responsive budgeting can be used to ensure that the reorientation of fiscal and monetary policy supports gender equality. Policy decisions about budget deficits and government debts should be subject to equality impact assessments and modified if the assessment shows that there would be an overall adverse impact.

Step 7 is to develop an international trade and investment system that is socially and environmentally sustainable. The benefits of trade and investment agreements have been very unequally distributed, channelled mainly to big companies and rich people. Some people have not only failed to benefit, but have been made worse off. Governments must ensure that all trade and investment agreements guarantee no deterioration of environmental, human rights, and labour standards; assess the impact of trade and investment deals on equality; and take action to support any groups who will be negatively impacted (including changing the terms of agreements). Public services should be excluded from trade and investment agreements, and so should investor protection provisions that allow big business to sue governments.

Step 8 is to transform the international financial system, which currently operates in ways that increase inequality and give money mastery over human life. Governments must support the UN General Assembly in organizing an International Economic Reconstruction and Systemic Reform Summit, to promote global transformation in light of the crises triggered by the Covid-19 pandemic. The gathering debt crisis in middle and low income countries must be addressed by supporting sovereign debt restructuring process, ensuring that a country can restructure its entire debt stock in one place in a procedure that involves all creditors (private as well as public), but in ways that are in line with international human rights law and other international commitments.

This eight-step plan for a caring economy does address equality and human rights issues but it could be strengthened with more attention to redressing the imbalance between the regimes of commercial property rights (rights to buy and sell resources and to extract profits and rents from their use) and the rights set out in the ICESCR. Systems of commercial rights are very strong, while the fulfilment of economic and social rights is weak. Commercial rights are disproportionately in the hands of elite men, with the majority of women and minority ethnic groups excluded from ownership of large businesses. The provisions of current systems of commercial rights are often at odds with the fulfilment of economic, social, and cultural rights, on which women and minority ethnic groups are more reliant for their well-being. This imbalance underpins the growth of inequality and must be redressed if we are to create more equal societies.

The UNCTAD has noted that anti-monopoly measures are beginning to be included on agendas at national and regional levels. It calls for existing multilateral agreements, such as the UN's Equitable Principles and Rules for the Control of Restrictive Business Practices, adopted by the General Assembly in 1980, to be strengthened and operationalized with new institutional support such as a global competition authority. It argues that urgent action is required to address 'the price gauging, patent abuse and other anti-competitive practices of pharmaceutical giants and digital platforms.'[84] In the UK, the remit of the Competition and Markets Authority (created in 2013) is narrow, concerning only price, quality, and choice for consumers and not the wider public interest. Meagher has set out a proposal for a fair and comprehensive competition law that limits unfair mergers, enforces accountability, and redistributes power through stakeholder governance.[85]

Weak corporate governance has led to soaring executive pay in many countries, including the UK. In response, pay ratio disclosures have been made mandatory in annual reports of companies listed on the London stock exchange since 2020. The High Pay Centre has called upon the biggest institutional investors to use this information to vote against disproportionate pay awards for executives in future. However, companies have proved reluctant to do this, and it is clear that changes are needed in the governance of companies, including reform of the Companies Act to end the primacy of shareholders' interests, to ensure representation of workers on boards, and to oblige companies to take into account not only the interests of shareholders but also workers, consumers, wider society, and the environment.[86] One suggestion is that 45 per cent of a company board should be elected by the workforce, 45 per cent by the shareholder body, with the remainder representing social and environmental interests, and

---

[84] United Nations Conference on Trade and Development (UNCTAD), 'Trade and Development Report 2020: From Global Pandemic to Prosperity for All' (2020) https://unctad.org/system/files/official-document/tdr2020_en.pdf (accessed 13 July 2021).

[85] Michelle Meagher, *Competition is Killing Us* (Penguin Business 2020).

[86] High Pay Centre, 'Briefing: Using Pay Ratio Disclosures to Inform ESG Strategies and Stewardship Practices' (2021) https://highpaycentre.org/wp-content/uploads/2021/05/AGM-season-investor-briefing-draft-for-circulation.docx.pdf (accessed 13 July 2021).

mandatory profit sharing for workers in companies with more than fifty employees, as exists in France.[87]

In addition, sectoral bodies could be established to monitor fair pay, made up of stakeholders including representatives from business, unions, workers, and government in a similar fashion to the Wages Councils, which were in place in the UK until the 1990s. Their remit could include setting guidelines for minimum wages and pay ratio limits across the sector, using pay ratio disclosures to inform recommendations.[88] Limiting the pay of CEOs and other executives could free up resources to protect at-risk jobs or raise the pay of low-wage workers. A maximum wage of £100,000 per annum could increase the annual median wage by £3,535 and this cap would only affect 2.85 per cent of earners in the UK.[89]

Measures to limit the power and incomes of large corporations, and those who run them, as well as hold shares in them, must be complemented by measures to strengthen labour rights. The UK Trades Union Congress has called for unions to have access to workplaces to tell workers about the benefits of union membership and collective bargaining (following the system in place in New Zealand); new rights to make it easier for working people to negotiate collectively with their employer; a broadening of the scope of collective bargaining rights to include all pay and conditions; reform of the Central Arbitration Committee that adjudicates on union recognition requests, requiring it to take account of the benefits of collective bargaining in its decisions; the establishment of new bodies for unions and employers to negotiate across sectors, starting with hospitality and social care; and the abolition of the Trade Union Act of 2016, as well as allowing unions to use electronic balloting in votes including all internal elections and votes on industrial action.[90]

Enhanced rights are also needed to combat precarious work. Prior to Covid-19, 3.7 million people in the UK were in insecure work, comprising one in nine of the workforce. Black workers, women, and disabled workers were all disproportionately represented in insecure work.[91] Their rights could be strengthened by measures including a ban on zero-hours contracts; robust rules on notice of shifts and compensation for cancelled shifts; a statutory presumption that workers are employed (to combat bogus self-employment); and penalties for misleading workers on their employment status.[92] The question of employment status is vital to the millions who work in the growing 'gig' economy operated by owners of digital platforms that claim to be simply connecting customers to 'self-employed' workers. Some of those workers

---

[87] Mathew Lawrence and others, 'Commoning the Company' *Common-Wealth* (17 April 2020) http://www.common-wealth.co.uk (accessed 13 July 2021).

[88] Rachel Kay and Luke Hildyard, 'Pay Ratios and the FTSE 350: Analysis of the First Disclosures' High Pay Centre (December 2020) https://highpaycentre.org/wp-content/uploads/2020/12/0.1_MUL1564-FOUNDATION-Pay-ratios-report.pdf (accessed 13 July 2021).

[89] Autonomy and the High Pay Centre, 'Paying for Covid: Capping Excessive Salaries to Save Industries' (2020) https://autonomy.work/wpcontent/uploads/2020/10/2020OCT_SalaryCap_Ameneded.pdf (accessed 13 July 2021).

[90] Trades Union Congress, 'A Better Recovery. Learning the Lessons of the Corona Crisis to Create a Stronger, Fairer Economy' (2021) https://www.tuc.org.uk/sites/default/files/TUC%20Report%20A%20Better%20Recovery'%20(2).pdf (accessed 13 July 2021).

[91] ibid.

[92] ibid.

are becoming unionized and, as in the case of Uber drivers in UK, have succeeded in obtaining a court order that they are workers with rights to a minimum hourly wage and holiday pay.[93]

As well as new laws, stronger rights for workers can be supported by ensuring that state support for businesses, including through procurement contracts, is made conditional on upholding these rights. However, stronger rights to and at work—although necessary—are insufficient for creating an equitable economy: workers are always at risk of unemployment due to ill-health and lack of jobs; participation in paid work varies over the life course; and people enter the labour market with different capacities, due to inequalities in education achievement and health status, mainly linked to the income and wealth of their parents.[94] Stronger rights to and at work must be buttressed by stronger rights to social security, health, education, and an adequate standard of living (including housing and food). These rights are best fulfilled through public provision. However, higher public expenditure, although necessary, is alone not sufficient. The ways in which public money is used are critical. Social security and public services must be organized on the basis that people have a right to good quality provision caringly delivered in ways that are consistent with human dignity and are responsive to people's needs.[95]

5 Conclusion

Covid-19 exposed and intensified inequalities of class, gender, and race in the UK, as in many countries. Despite the provisions of the 2010 Equality Act, the UK government failed to conduct equality impact assessments of policies both prior to and during the pandemic. The trend towards higher inequalities can be reversed by adopting alternative economic strategies that give a central role to public investment in high-quality care services, delivered by well-paid and well-trained workers, but also through taking steps to transform the ways in which the economy is understood and the way in which economic policy is formulated. A comprehensive strategy to do this is set out in the report of the Women's Budget Group Commission on a Gender Equal Economy. This strategy could be further strengthened by legal changes that would redress the imbalance between the regimes of commercial property rights (rights to buy and sell resources and to extract profits and rents from their use) and economic and social rights.

---

[93] *Uber BV v Aslam* [2021] UKSC 5.

[94] UN Development Programme, 'Human Development Report 2019: Beyond Income, Beyond Averages, Beyond Today: Inequalities in Human Development in the 21st Century' (2019) https://hdr.undp.org/sites/default/files/hdr2019.pdf (accessed 13 July 2021).

[95] Radhika Balakrishnan, James Heintz, and Diane Elson, *Rethinking Economic Policy for Social Justice: The Radical Potential of Human Rights* (Routledge 2016).

4
Social Security, Exponential Inequalities, and Covid-19
How Welfare Reform in the UK Left Larger Families Exposed to the Scarring Effects of the Pandemic

Aaron Reeves, Kate Andersen, Mary Reader, and Rosalie Warnock

1 Introduction

Covid-19 has put social security systems under immense pressure.[1] In the UK, the number of households on Universal Credit, Britain's main form of social security, had grown by 1.7 million households by mid-May 2020, a 68 per cent increase.[2] Processing all of those new claims presented an enormous administrative challenge. Alongside this, the British government also quickly implemented a furlough scheme that partially covered the salaries of employees in order to keep people attached to firms after the introduction of economic restrictions left many at risk of unemployment. The furlough scheme is estimated to have cost around £70 billion.[3] The government also increased the amount of money that households claiming Universal Credit would receive—the so-called £20 uplift—and provided a generous but rather blunt cash transfer to the self-employed.[4] All of these changes were implemented in a matter of weeks, providing a remarkable level of support for a traditionally 'liberal' welfare regime.[5] However, these relatively generous provisions need to be viewed alongside both the history of welfare reform over the last ten years and how the policy response to the crisis belies a residual concern with providing help to the supposedly 'undeserving'.[6] Indeed, what has been notable about these provisions is the absence of any additional support to households with children.[7] This chapter focuses on the experience of larger

---

[1] Daniel Edmiston and others, 'Navigating Pandemic Social Security: Benefits, Employment and Crisis Support during COVID-19' (2021) http://usir.salford.ac.uk/id/eprint/62042/ (accessed 29 July 2021).
[2] Department for Work and Pensions, 'Universal Credit Statistics, 29 April 2013 to 8 April 2021' (2021) https://www.gov.uk/government/statistics/universal-credit-statistics-29-april-2013-to-8-april-2021/universal-credit-statistics-29-april-2013-to-8-april-2021 (accessed 29 July 2021).
[3] Brigid Francis-Devine, Andrew Powell, and Harriet Clark, 'Coronavirus Job Retention Scheme: Statistics' (House of Commons Library 2021).
[4] Mike Brewer and Karl Handscomb, 'Half-Measures: The Chancellor's Options for Universal Credit in the Budget' (Resolution Foundation 2021) https://www.resolutionfoundation.org/publications/half-measures/ (accessed 29 July 2021).
[5] Gøsta Esping-Andersen, *The Three Worlds of Welfare Capitalism* (Polity 1990).
[6] Ruth Patrick, *For Whose Benefit? The Everyday Realities of Welfare Reform* (Policy Press 2017).
[7] Ruth Patrick, Aaron Reeves, and Kitty Stewart, 'COVID-19 and Low-Income Families: The Government Must Lift the Benefit Cap and Remove the Two-Child Limit' *British Politics and Policy at LSE Blog* (12 May 2020) https://blogs.lse.ac.uk/politicsandpolicy/covid19-children-welfare/ (accessed 29 July 2021).

families (households with three or more children) during the pandemic as a way of illuminating how the policy responses failed to reach those groups who have been treated with some suspicion in policy terms over the last decade.

To illustrate some of the experiences of larger families during the pandemic, this chapter draws on findings from the Benefit Changes and Larger Families project. This project is a collaboration between the Universities of York, Oxford, and the London School of Economics. It is funded by the Nuffield Foundation and the research team is working in partnership with the Child Poverty Action Group. The aim of the research is to understand the impacts of the two-child limit and the benefit cap on larger families using both qualitative and quantitative methods. This chapter uses data from the qualitative longitudinal component of the project, which entails three rounds of interviews with forty-five parents from London and Yorkshire over two years. The first round of interviews reported on in this chapter were conducted in 2021. The interviews were semi-structured and, owing to Covid regulations, the vast majority were conducted over the phone. The data has subsequently been analysed thematically using NVivo. Throughout this chapter, aliases have been used when quoting participants.

This chapter explores the experience of larger families in three ways. First, it unpacks how the government's response to Covid-19 has left larger families in an even more precarious position than many on low incomes already experienced prior to March 2020. Here, we focus on the inadequacy of the £20 per week uplift to Universal Credit, which was applied to everyone irrespective of whether they were single, coupled, or had children. Additionally, the £20 uplift had no impact on those families who were already subject to the benefit cap. Secondly, we situate the experience of larger families in the context of a wider set of reforms to social security—such as the benefit cap, the two-child limit, and the benefits freeze—which have already pushed even more larger families into poverty over the last decade.[8] We draw out how (a lack of) decision-making around welfare policy related to households with three or more children during the pandemic is rooted in many of the assumptions which have informed the last decade of welfare reforms in the UK (and in some cases even earlier).[9] These assumptions (and the reforms built on them) have created the conditions for the scarring effects of the pandemic—including poverty, unemployment, and economic insecurity—to be felt for many years to come. The final section of the chapter draws out how these policy decisions exacerbate inequalities between groups, while alluding to implications for protected characteristics as enshrined in the Equality Act 2010.[10] While we recognize that household size is not a protected characteristic, the policies

---

[8] Helen Barnard, 'End the Benefit Freeze to Stop People Being Swept into Poverty' *JRF* (6 March 2019) https://www.jrf.org.uk/report/end-benefit-freeze-stop-people-being-swept-poverty (accessed 30 March 2019); Carl Emmerson and Robert Joyce, 'If the Cap Doesn't Fit?' (7 April 2020) https://www.ifs.org.uk/publications/14794 (accessed 20 June 2020).

[9] Tracey Jensen and Imogen Tyler, '"Benefits Broods": The Cultural and Political Crafting of Anti-Welfare Commonsense' (2015) 35 Critical Social Policy 470; John Welshman, *Underclass: A History of the Excluded, 1880 - 2000* (Continuum International Publishing 2007).

[10] Meghan Campbell, Sandra Fredman, and Aaron Reeves, 'Palliation or Protection: How Should the Right to Equality Inform the Government's Response to Covid-19?' (2020) 20 International Journal of Discrimination and the Law 183.

that target larger families are far more likely to affect women, some minoritized ethnic groups, and households with a disabled family member.[11]

This analysis not only illuminates how the pandemic has increased gender and ethnic inequalities but also suggests that the degree to which the pandemic was inequality-generating—that is, whether inequalities increased 'exponentially' or not—is rooted in policy decisions made before the pandemic even began. Exponential inequalities have become manifest during this crisis because of the policies, rules, and institutions which were put in place *before* the Covid-19 pandemic hit and which were, in the short-term, hard to change.[12] It is also true, however, that the British government refused to change some policies that were more amenable to rapid reform, and their inflexibility on these issues is reflective of an ideological commitment to certain assumptions about welfare policy-making, such as the distinction between the 'deserving and undeserving' poor,[13] that are not simply washed away by societal shocks. There are, then, two forms of path dependence which informed the responses to the crisis: an institutional path dependence, which created certain policy constraints that limited the choices available to policymakers, and an ideational path dependence, which makes some policy proposals harder to countenance even though they were institutionally feasible.[14] There is little doubt that the pandemic will increase inequality, but the size of the impact is dependent on the policies societies put in place before such crises hit, as well as whether their responses are sensitive to the interactions between societal shocks and existing institutions. Avoiding exponential inequalities in response to future crises requires that policies—and the discourses which surround them—are sensitive to the potential for other kinds of societal shock.

2 Did the Government Protect Larger Families during the Pandemic?

As the seriousness of the pandemic became apparent, governments around the world moved quickly to curb the spread of the virus. Whilst slower to respond than other countries, Prime Minister Boris Johnson eventually announced a series of economic and social restrictions (so-called 'lockdowns') in March 2020. These restrictions had a number of cascading effects, especially for those whose livelihoods and incomes were threatened by the mandate to stay at home. The government moved quickly, and in collaboration with social partners, to implement a number of policies (including the furlough scheme, National Health Service (NHS) volunteer responders, and food vouchers for children ordinarily in receipt of free school meals) to avoid a situation

---

[11] Jonathan Bradshaw and Joseph Rowntree Foundation, *Child Poverty in Large Families* (Policy Press 2006) http://catalog.hathitrust.org/api/volumes/oclc/71667704.html (accessed 15 March 2021).
[12] Paul Pierson, 'Power and Path Dependence' in James Mahoney and Kathleen Thelen (eds), *Advances in Comparative-Historical Analysis* (CUP 2015); James Mahoney, 'Path Dependence in Historical Sociology' (2000) 29 Theory and Society 507.
[13] Welshman (n 9).
[14] Margaret R Somers and Fred Block, 'From Poverty to Perversity: Ideas, Markets, and Institutions over 200 Years of Welfare Debate' (2005) 70 American Sociological Review 260.

in which people were going hungry whilst confined to their homes.[15] Decisive action offered a lifeline to some families.

But there has been a surprising blind spot in these Covid-19 measures in relation to the particular challenges faced by families with children.[16] Before Covid-19 swept across the world, larger families in the UK were already exposed to a higher risk of poverty.[17] In 2018/19, around 42–43 per cent of households with three or more children had household incomes that were less than 60 per cent of the median (after housing costs). In contrast, the poverty rate for households with one or two children was around 24 per cent.[18] While both rates are undeniably high, this differential risk of poverty is partly rooted in the extra costs faced by larger families.[19] Larger families have more people to feed, of course, but they also face different trade-offs between hours worked and the cost of childcare; in part because it can be harder for adults in these households to secure work that fits around childcare arrangements.[20] Recognizing this, all UK governments since the 1990s have used a variety of policy tools, such as financial incentives, subsidized childcare, and—increasingly—benefit conditionality, to encourage people into work.[21] The problem is that the additional challenges larger families face make it difficult for them to respond to these policy changes, and this often leaves them doubly hit by unemployment or poorly paid work with inadequate hours, while also at risk of sanctions and other forms of welfare conditionality. This is particularly the case for larger single-parent families.[22] During the pandemic, the government appears to have been blind to these additional challenges and to have made very few moves to directly address the added burden faced by families with children, regardless of family size. To take one very concrete example, there was no rise in child benefit.[23] This would have been quick and simple to administer, and would have provided exactly the kind of support that acknowledges the additional costs faced by families.

One policy of note, however, is the temporary £20 weekly uplift to Universal Credit (March 2020–September 2021).[24] While seemingly small, it is in fact worth around

---

[15] Rishi Sunak, 'The Chancellor Rishi Sunak Provides an Updated Statement on Coronavirus' (20 March 2020) https://www.rebeccaharris.org/news/chancellor-rishi-sunak-provides-updated-statement-coronavirus (accessed 29 July 2021).

[16] Patrick, Reeves, and Stewart (n 7).

[17] Bradshaw (n 11); Esther Dermott (ed), *Poverty and Social Exclusion in the UK: The Nature and Extent of the Problem* (Policy Press 2017).

[18] Kitty Stewart, Aaron Reeves, and Ruth Patrick, 'A Time of Need: Exploring the Changing Poverty Risk Facing Larger Families in the UK' Centre for Analysis of Social Exclusion (CASE), London School of Economics (28 July 2021) https://sticerd.lse.ac.uk/dps/case/cp/casepaper224.pdf (accessed 30 July 2021).

[19] Eleanor Florence Rathbone, *The Case for Family Allowances* (Penguin 1940); Benjamin Seebohm Rowntree, *Poverty: A Study of Town Life* (Macmillan 1902).

[20] Selma Sevenhuijsen, 'Caring in the Third Way: The Relation between Obligation, Responsibility and Care in Third Way Discourse' (2000) 20 Critical Social Policy 5.

[21] Mike Brewer and others, 'Did Working Families' Tax Credit Work? The Impact of In-Work Support on Labour Supply in Great Britain' (2006) 13 Labour economics 699; Paul Gregg, Susan Harkness, and Sarah Smith, 'Welfare Reform and Lone Parents in the UK' (2009) 119 Economic Journal F38.

[22] Ruth Cain, 'Responsibilising Recovery: Lone and Low Paid Parents, Universal Credit and the Gendered Contradictions of UK Welfare Reform' (2016) 11 British Politics 488.

[23] Child Poverty Action Group, 'Campaign to Increase Child Benefit' (7 April 2020) https://cpag.org.uk/campaign-increase-child-benefit (accessed 30 July 2021).

[24] Brewer and Handscomb (n 4).

£1,000 a year for those families receiving Universal Credit. This was an important lifeline for many families and went against the established general trend toward reducing the adequacy of social security; particularly as a four-year 'benefit freeze' from April 2016 (expected to end in April 2020) meant that the value of social security had fallen in real terms during this time.[25] In fact, this uplift increased the generosity of Universal Credit for unemployed people from around 14 per cent of average weekly earnings to approximately 18 per cent, taking it back to levels last seen in the late 1990s and thereby reversing some of the damage created by the benefits freeze.[26] While relatively generous, this policy was implemented irrespective of household size. For example, this meant that a single person received the same amount as a household with three children. Across these two households, that £20 per week would have had very different implications, providing a strong financial buffer for a single person but doing much less for the family with three children.

Putting the diluted effect of the £20 uplift to one side, there was another major problem with this increased generosity: the benefit cap.[27] The cap places a maximum limit on the amount of social security income that any household can receive from the government in a given period. Since November 2016, the cap has been set at £23,000 a year for families in London and at £20,000 outside the capital.[28] The cap matters because, for those families already affected by it, the £20 uplift had no effect at all, because they could not keep that money.[29] Additionally, for some households, it pushed them *over* the threshold for the cap, perhaps for the first time. For example, a single mother living outside of London and who received £19,500 in social security payments per annum (including to help with housing costs), pre-Covid, will only have received £500 of the uplift over the year because the cap will have removed the other £500.

A significant proportion of capped households are larger families. Notwithstanding the way the cap was clawing back the £20 uplift, the government continued to offer a dogged defence of the benefit cap.[30] Dr Thérèse Coffey, Secretary of State for Work and Pensions, used her statement to the House of Commons to reiterate the government's commitment to the cap, saying that she did not 'think it is necessary right now to change it'.[31] The government has gone further and defended the cap and other benefits-related sanctions on the basis that it is not in children's best interests to grow up in households in which no-one is in paid employment.[32] Yet, according to the government's own logic, there was probably no better time to remove the cap. Originally, it was designed to incentivize people into paid work, but that became difficult to defend during the severe economic restrictions that were in place during

---

[25] Barnard (n 8).
[26] Brewer and others (n 21).
[27] Patrick, Reeves, and Stewart (n 7).
[28] For most families, it is receipt of housing benefit—assistance with the cost of renting a home—that pushes them into the cap. But this is not true for everyone. Couples and lone parents with around six children can also be affected by the cap, even if they are not receiving housing benefit.
[29] Patrick, Reeves and Stewart (n 7).
[30] Ruth Patrick, Aaron Reeves, and Kitty Stewart, 'The Government's Misplaced Confidence in the Benefit Cap' (2021) 168 Poverty 7.
[31] Secretary of State for Work and Pensions, *Covid-19: DWP Update* (HC 2020) 675.
[32] *DA and DS v Secretary State for Work and Pensions* [2019] UKSC 21.

much of 2020, with few new vacancies being advertised during this period.[33] Capped households were, in effect, being punished for their failure to find paid work, despite there being no work for them to take up. Particularly striking was the fact that over the spring of 2020 other forms of welfare conditionality—underpinned by the same logic as the benefit cap—*were* temporarily suspended.[34] That the cap endured while wider forms of welfare conditionality were temporarily halted is a stark inequity that disproportionately harmed larger and single parent families, fuelling existing inequalities yet further.

Findings from the Benefit Changes and Larger Families project illustrate the problems with continuing to apply the benefit cap during the pandemic, particularly during the first lockdown. Several participants reported that they had either lost their jobs or had their paid work hours vastly reduced owing to the pandemic. For these participants, taking on more hours or obtaining a new job was impossible, as one mother explained:

> I lost my job this pandemic and is very hard … I was really hard working; so when there is pandemic everybody starts taking everybody out of the job. But there's no help like when you like lose the job in the pandemic, unless they see another job that they can put you to move, keep you on but there is nothing like that.
>
> Zauna, single mother, four children, subject to the benefit cap

In addition to the lack of jobs, some of the participants were unable to seek paid work during the lockdowns owing to health conditions which meant they had to shield. One participant expressed his frustration at being told he had to work sixteen hours a week to escape the benefit cap while at the same time being instructed to shield on account of his diabetes:

> The part I did see wrong with these benefit cap side of things was, is they put you on benefit cap and tell you you've got to work sixteen hours a week; well for the past, what eight, what was it, about eighteen months in the end, wasn't it, lockdown? … I've got the [local council] sending me letters telling me I shouldn't go out, that because of the diabetes I'm clinically high risk and so on and so forth; so if that's the case how can they keep me on the benefit cap?
>
> Anthony, single father, three children, subject to the benefit cap

The continuance of the benefit cap during the lockdowns also failed to recognize that many people affected by the cap have children and therefore had considerable responsibilities for home-schooling their children. Therefore, several factors made paid work difficult and, in many instances, impossible during the lockdowns, yet the benefit cap was not removed.

---

[33] ONS, 'UK Job Vacancies (Thousands): Total Services' (Office for National Statistics 2021) https://www.ons.gov.uk/employmentandlabourmarket/peopleinwork/employmentandemployeetypes/timeseries/jp9z/unem (accessed 24 April 2022).

[34] Ben Baumberg Geiger and others, 'Claiming but Connected to Work' University of Kent Working Paper (2020) https://kar.kent.ac.uk/id/eprint/83776 (accessed 24 April 2022).

Given the difficulty of undertaking paid work during the pandemic, why has the cap persisted? Neil Couling, the Change Director General for the Department of Works and Pensions, in a 2020 webinar with the Resolution Foundation alluded to the ongoing role that stigmatizing assumptions about benefit claimants have played in these policy decisions.[35] He suggested that the cap continues in part because the government wanted to distinguish between Covid-19-affected claimants and existing claimants. This comes close to replicating the 'deserving and undeserving' distinction, and while Couling did not use these precise words, his argument suggests that some in government thought that pre-Covid claimants were seen as less deserving than newer claimants. The government did not distinguish between newer and older claimants in terms of the help offered, however, because it would have been technically very difficult and slow to introduce.[36] The benefit cap already allowed a grace period of nine months for those who had a stable work history and therefore this allowed the government to informally (and imperfectly) distinguish between those who might be capped because of Covid-19 (those with more complete work histories) and those they believed to be unrelated to Covid-19. Irrespective of the motivation, the perpetuation of the cap's conditionality during lockdown is a new manifestation of the structural inequalities embedded in the system.

3 How Welfare Reform Left Families in a Precarious Position

When the Conservative-led Coalition Government came to power in the UK in 2010, it was elected on a commitment to reduce government spending.[37] A few months later, it announced a raft of reforms aimed at cutting social security expenditures.[38] This included the benefit cap described above, but also other policies which have affected the risk of poverty experienced by larger families.

Perhaps the single most significant change—at least in terms of the impact on larger families to date—was the benefits freeze. Most of the time, the value of social security is up-rated every year to take account of inflation because in the absence of this increase, the real value of the financial support offered by the government diminishes (in that you can buy less with the same amount of money).[39] One of the central methods used by the Conservative-led Coalition to reduce social security spending was to break this link between the value of social security and inflation. From 2013, the annual uprating

---

[35] Resolution Foundation, 'The Safety Net in Action?' https://www.resolutionfoundation.org/events/the-safety-net-in-action/ (accessed 20 June 2020).
[36] ibid.
[37] Peter Taylor-Gooby, 'Root and Branch Restructuring to Achieve Major Cuts: The Social Policy Programme of the 2010 UK Coalition Government' (2012) 46 Social Policy and Administration 61.
[38] Chancellor of the Exchequer, 'Spending Review 2010: Presented to Parliament by Command of Her Majesty' (HM Treasury 2010) https://assets.publishing.service.gov.uk/government/uploads/system/uploads/attachment_data/file/203826/Spending_review_2010.pdf (accessed 24 April 2022).
[39] Adam Corlett, 'The Benefit Freeze Has Ended, but Erosion of the Social Security Safety Net Continues: Resolution Foundation' Resolution Foundation (2019) https://www.resolutionfoundation.org/publications/the-benefit-freeze-has-ended-but-erosion-of-the-social-security-safety-net-continues/ (accessed 30 July 2021).

of most working-age benefits was limited to 1 per cent per year. Then, between 2016 and 2020, the amounts paid were frozen in cash terms, irrespective of inflation.[40]

This kind of policy drift[41] may seem trivial but the impact that this change has had on low-income families is profound. The support that low-income families received in 2019 would have been around 6.5 per cent higher than it was if it had kept pace with inflation. More concretely, people in poverty are on average £340 a year worse off than they would have been in the absence of this policy. This is significant: £340 is approximately eight weeks' worth of food for a low-income family.[42] While this policy is not explicitly targeted at larger families, they have been acutely affected by it, in part because of the increased costs they experience. The benefits freeze policy has, in short, pulled people into poverty, including an estimated 200,000 children.[43]

Alongside the benefit freeze and the benefit cap, a number of other changes have been made to social security provisions for households with children. Both child benefit and child tax credit saw tightened eligibility and, in the case of child tax credit, reduced generosity.[44] Other forms of support for newborns were removed (Baby Tax Credit and Health in Pregnancy Grant) or limited to the first child (Sure Start Maternity Grant).[45] But perhaps one of the most significant changes—one with a very large influence over the long-run—was the two-child limit: under this policy parents and carers do not receive means-tested support for third and subsequent children born from April 2017 onwards,[46] albeit with some important exceptions.[47]

These policy choices have increased poverty rates generally, but their effects have been particularly acute among larger families. Child poverty had, until recently, been falling in the UK.[48] In 1996/97 an estimated 27 per cent of children lived below the standard relative poverty line of 60 per cent of median income before housing costs.[49] By 2013/14, however, this share had fallen to 17 per cent. The six years prior to the start of the global pandemic saw child poverty rising again, reaching 21 per cent in 2019/20. This general trend masks important differences according to family size. Recent work by Stewart and colleagues explicitly addresses this issue, revealing a crucial and neglected fact: a very large part of the aggregate child poverty trend in the UK over the

---

[40] Barnard (n 8).
[41] Jacob S Hacker, Paul Pierson, and Kathleen Thelen, 'Drift and Conversion: Hidden Faces of Institutional Change' American Political Science Association (17 September 2013).
[42] Barnard (n 8).
[43] ibid.
[44] Kitty Stewart and Polina Obolenskaya, 'The Coalition's Record on the under Fives: Policy, Spending and Outcomes 2010-2015' (Centre for Analysis of Social Exclusion (CASE), London School of Economics, Working Paper 12, Social Policy in a Cold Climate 2015) https://citeseerx.ist.psu.edu/viewdoc/download?doi=10.1.1.676.8465&rep=rep1&type=pd (accessed 24 April 2022).
[45] ibid.
[46] Tom Sefton and others, 'All Kids Count: The Impact of the Two-Child Limit after Two Years' (Child Poverty Action Group, 2019) https://cpag.org.uk/sites/default/files/files/All%20Kids%20Count%20report%20FINAL.pdf (accessed 24 April 2022).
[47] One exception has become known as 'the rape clause'. Women who conceive a third or subsequent child without their consent are allowed to claim the child element of Universal Credit of Child Tax Credits. 'Consent' here includes situations such as rape and also conception in the context of abusive relationships.
[48] Pascale Bourquin and others, 'Living Standards, Poverty and Inequality in the UK: 2019' Institute for Fiscal Studies (19 June 2019) https://www.ifs.org.uk/publications/14193 (accessed 23 February 2021).
[49] Institute for Fiscal Studies, *Living Standards, Inequality and Poverty Spreadsheet* (2020) https://ifs.org.uk/tools_and_resources/incomes_in_uk (accessed 24 April 2022).

last twenty-five years has been driven by what is happening in households with three or more children.[50] For example, since 2013/14, the increase in poverty is observed *only* among larger families, with no change in smaller families. These trends matter because they show that, when larger families entered the pandemic, they were already struggling, having seen their risk of poverty increase over the last decade. In other words, larger families were already especially vulnerable to the effects of a major economic shock, such as the pandemic.

If these reforms have made life harder for larger families, why have they been implemented at all? In this respect, the justification for the two-child limit is instructive. It was introduced under the guise of drawing an equivalence between families perceived to be dependent on welfare and those 'hardworking' families whose taxes supported those on welfare. More specifically, the government wanted families receiving benefits to 'face the same financial choices about having children as those supporting themselves solely through work'.[51]

The assumption, therefore, behind many of these policies, is that those receiving benefits are different from those supporting themselves solely through work. But this is simply not true. John Hills'[52] work has explicitly tackled 'the welfare myth of them and us', arguing that it is incredibly difficult to draw a neat distinction between those who are claiming benefits and those who are not. This becomes even more difficult when we look at people across the life course. Hills writes that: 'over our whole lives we are all—or nearly all—considerable beneficiaries from the welfare state', and this includes 'middle-class professionals'.[53] This is because 'most of what the welfare state does and the taxes we pay to fund it is to redistribute across our own life cycles, and so smooth out our available resources from year to year'.[54] Roantree and Shaw have produced a very clear illustration of this phenomena by following a group of people over an eighteen-year period. They observed that nearly half of participants had received a means-tested benefit or tax credit at some point (hence implying that they were on a low-income).[55] If we followed this group over their whole lives, this proportion would be even higher, and this is before we incorporate people who receive a state pension, use the NHS, receive child benefit, or who send their children to a tax-financed school.

In fact, the justification for the benefit cap is a good example of precisely how this kind of distinction actually obscures the reality of social security in the UK. In October 2010, during a speech in which then Chancellor of the Exchequer George Osborne announced the policy, he said that the benefit cap was being implemented to ensure that 'no family should get more from living on benefits than the average family gets from going out to work'.[56] The problem with this comparison is that there is a false

---

[50] Stewart, Reeves, and Patrick (n 18).
[51] Steven Kennedy, 'Two Child Limit in Universal Credit and Child Tax Credits' House of Commons Research Briefing (23 November 2018) https://commonslibrary.parliament.uk/research-briefings/cdp-2018-0263/ (accessed 29 July 2021).
[52] John Hills, *Good Times, Bad Times: The Welfare Myth of Them and Us* (Policy Press 2014).
[53] ibid.
[54] ibid 251–52.
[55] Barra Roantree and Jonathan Shaw, 'The Case for Taking a Life-Cycle Perspective: Inequality, Redistribution, and Tax and Benefit Reforms' IFS Research Report R92 (2014) https://www.econstor.eu/handle/10419/119782 (accessed 29 July 2021).
[56] HM Treasury (n 38).

equivalence between an out-of-work family's *total income* and an in-work family's *earnings*. While this comparison ignores differences between families in their composition and therefore spending needs, it also masks the similarities between these families with a rhetorical sleight of hand. Critically, it overlooks the additional support to which many in-work families are entitled, which increases their *total income*, and helps them meet their needs. That is, an in-work family's earnings are often supplemented by child benefit and housing support.

Moreover, this assumption about the welfare dependence of larger families has a long history which can be traced back to Thomas Malthus' *Essay on the Principle of Population*,[57] first published in 1798. This essay has had a tremendous impact on how British society thinks about poverty.[58] Malthus argued that providing financial support to the poor is counterproductive for societies as a whole because it uncouples the natural check that starvation places on the number of deprived people in a society.[59] The impoverished, in Malthus' view, would refuse to work if they could survive without doing so, and providing them with welfare (in other words, food and shelter) does exactly this. It decommodifies their labour power and therefore erodes their work ethic. On top of this, Malthus also thought that welfare undermined the sexual restraint of the poor, leading to an inexorable increase in unemployment, which, in turn, would produce collective immiseration and eventual societal collapse. Rising unemployment, in this view, is driven by increasing numbers of people who refuse to work and therefore becomes a symptom of the moral decay that will make societies unsustainable. It is this fear of apparent societal collapse that pushes governments to make 'tough choices' to reduce welfare uptake and disincentivize welfare dependency. To this end, Malthus argued that welfare receipt should be stigmatized: 'hard as it may appear in individual instances, dependent poverty ought to be held disgraceful'.[60]

While Malthus himself is rarely mentioned directly in debates about welfare, the imprint of his influence can be seen in almost every major debate about welfare policy over the last 200 years. His ideas directly informed the Poor Law debates of the 1830s[61] and were implicitly central to the welfare reforms of the 1980s and 1990s.[62] Most relevant for the purposes of this chapter, Malthus' ideas were a crucial aspect of the logic used to legitimize austerity policies following the Great Recession.[63] Returning to the language used to justify the two-child limit, the distinction between those receiving benefits as being different from those 'supporting themselves solely through work'

---

[57] Thomas Robert Malthus, *An Essay on the Principle of Population* (Geoffrey Gilbert ed, OUP 2008).
[58] Peter Golding and Sue Middleton, *Images of Welfare: Press and Public Attitudes to Poverty* (Martin Robertson 1982); Steven Harkins and Jairo Lugo-Ocando, 'How Malthusian Ideology Crept into the Newsroom: British Tabloids and the Coverage of the "Underclass"' (2016) 13 Critical Discourse Studies 78; John Macnicol, 'Perspectives on the Idea of an "Underclass"' in John Edwards and Jean-Paul Revauger (eds), *Discourses on Inequality in France and Britain* (Ashgate 1998).
[59] Daniel McArthur and Aaron Reeves, 'The Rhetoric of Recessions: How British Newspapers Talk about the Poor When Unemployment Rises, 1896–2000' *Sociology* (9 April 2019) https://journals.sagepub.com/doi/abs/10.1177/0038038519838752 (accessed 28 May 2019).
[60] Malthus (n 57) III, VI.5.
[61] ibid; Karl Polanyi, *The Great Transformation: The Political and Economic Origins of Our Time* (Beacon Press 2002).
[62] Somers and Block (n 14).
[63] Harkins and Lugo-Ocando (n 58); Jensen and Tyler (n 9).

legitimized welfare retrenchment by 'othering'[64] people in poverty and representing them as part of an outgroup who were lazy, immoral, and living fraudulently at the expense of hard-working taxpayers.[65] In other words, this distinction is explicitly Malthusian. Such anti-welfare narratives have permeated public discourse over this period and in some cases have even had a demonstrable impact on attitudes towards welfare recipients.[66]

The distinction between 'strivers and skivers'[67]—and the ideology which embeds and legitimates it—is also contradicted by how social policy is organized in other areas of our lives. For example, the majority of those affected by the benefit cap are actually not required to look for paid work because they have other commitments (such as raising very young children) or because they face considerable barriers to paid work as a result of serious health conditions.[68] Recognizing this, a 2019 Work and Pensions Committee inquiry argued that the benefit cap should only be applied to those the government expects to be actively seeking paid work. This was not, however, accepted by the government who, in its response to the inquiry, argued that 'the Department firmly believes ... that just because claimants may not be required to look for work under work conditionality rules does not mean that they should not be encouraged to work or to prepare for work'.[69]

On top of this, the evidence examining work intensity and job search effort among the families that are the targets of these policies suggest government's concerns in this regard are largely unfounded.[70] Unemployment among families with three or more children, including families led by lone parents, has been shown to be the result of structural or personal barriers rather than some deficit of desire or effort.[71] Findings from the Benefit Changes and Larger Families project show that, while some parents want to enter paid work at a later date owing to their preferences to care for their children themselves, many want to enter paid work but are prevented from doing so by barriers including the difficulties of finding paid work that is compatible with caring responsibilities, and parental and child health conditions. One single mum with five children (aged ten, nine, four, and two years, and four months) explained how finding paid work was difficult, especially as her 2-year-old went to nursery for only sixteen hours a week and the nursery hours did not match her older children's school hours:

---

[64] Ruth Lister, '"To Count for Nothing": Poverty beyond the Statistics' (2015) 3 Journal of the British Academy 139.
[65] Tracey Jensen, 'Welfare Commonsense, Poverty Porn and Doxosophy' (2014) 19 Sociological Research Online 3.
[66] Aaron Reeves and Rob de Vries, 'Does Media Coverage Influence Public Attitudes towards Welfare Recipients? The Impact of the 2011 English Riots' (2016) 67 British Journal of Sociology 281.
[67] Hills (n 52).
[68] Work and Pensions Committee, 'The Benefit Cap: Government Response to the Committee's Twenty-Fourth Report' (House of Commons 2019).
[69] Work and Pensions Committee, 'Appendix: Government Response' https://publications.parliament.uk/pa/cm201719/cmselect/cmworpen/2209/220902.htm (accessed 29 May 2022).
[70] Stewart, Reeves, and Patrick (n 18).
[71] Sarah Johnsen and Janice Blenkinsopp, 'Final Findings: Lone Parents' Welfare Conditionality: Sanctions, Support and Behaviour Change (22 May 2018) http://www.welfareconditionality.ac.uk/publications/final-findings-welcond-project/ (accessed 24 April 2022).

> All day I'm back and forth ... she does three days full day but it's not so full, I have to get her out at three, I have to stay around for another half an hour for the boys to come out with two little ones; so the whole day is just either come quickly, clean, cook, go quickly, get her, stand around the street, get the other two.
>
> Yasmin, single mother, five children, subject to
the two-child limit and the benefit cap

The children's father did not have regular contact with the children and this participant did not have any friends or family nearby who could help with childcare. Thus, although she wanted paid work and had specific career aspirations, finding a job was practically impossible for her as she was solely responsible for her children's care. Similarly, another participant explained that she wanted to obtain paid work but was frustrated that she could not owing to her youngest child's health condition:

> He is with me because he has a medical condition ... he has a tube feed ... not every childminder will take in. So we're looking for someone willing to get trained, cos I'm trained as well with, from the community, I'm the only person that will take care of him.
>
> Bushra, single mother, seven children, subject to
the two child limit and the benefit cap

Therefore, despite a desire to obtain paid work, many people subject to the cap are unable to obtain a job. However, the benefit cap persists regardless of the significant barriers people face to entering paid work.

Despite evidence to the contrary, these ingrained assumptions about larger families not only informed policy decisions made *before* the pandemic, but also continue to influence the absence of action at the height of the pandemic—and as it continues to roll on. As recently as November 2020, Minister for Employment Mims Davies sought to defend the benefit cap using the very same language as those who had gone before her: 'The benefit cap restores fairness between those receiving out-of-work benefits and taxpayers'.[72] Moreover, the Department for Work and Pensions (DWP) has also defended the continuation in the same terms: 'The benefit cap ... offers fairness for taxpayers while providing a strong safety net for those who need it.'[73] It does not seem that there has been any considerable movement in the discourse surrounding these policies. The failure to act (and the assumptions on which this inaction is predicated) has ensured that the conditions for the scarring effects of the pandemic—on poverty, unemployment, and economic insecurity ---—will be felt for many years to come.

---

[72] Mims Davies, 'Universal Credit: Coronavirus—Question for Department for Work and Pensions' UK Parliament (2020) UIN 115679 https://questions-statements.parliament.uk/written-questions/detail/2020-11-16/115679/ (accessed 29 July 2021).

[73] Patrick Butler, 'Scrap Benefit Cap to Lift 150,000 Children out of Poverty, Says Charity' *The Guardian* (22 December 2020) http://www.theguardian.com/society/2020/dec/22/scrap-benefit-cap-to-lift-150000-children-out-of-poverty-says-charity (accessed 29 July 2021).

4 Covid-19, the Equality Act, and Exponential Inequalities

We have seen how decisions made both before and during the pandemic have potentially put larger families in a precarious situation in the UK, but what is the evidence that these measures have increased inequality and, if so, does this violate the Equality Act 2010? Household size is not a protected characteristic, but policies which target larger families are far more likely to affect women (especially lone parents), some minoritized ethnic groups, and households with a disabled family member. It is important to note that recent legal challenges to the benefit cap and the two-child limit on the grounds that they discriminate against women have been unsuccessful.[74] But here we still take seriously the idea of indirect discrimination that is implied in policies which are (intentionally or not) disproportionately affecting the lives of women and ethnic minorities.

The March 2020 lockdown led to a collapse in working hours and this reduced earnings too. This reduction in income affected a number of different groups, including low-income households and those from ethnic minority backgrounds.[75] It also affected larger families on a low income. Reader and Andersen have shown, using data from Understanding Society, that among families with children, larger families on benefits saw the sharpest falls in working hours.[76] The average number of working hours for those in larger families halved in the first six months of 2020, while they fell by just a third among smaller families on benefits. Larger families experienced this stark decline because they were in occupations that put them at a higher risk of redundancy, reduced hours, or furlough. Many of these households had a household member who was employed part-time and they were more likely to have someone employed in jobs that could not be done from home.[77] Although the proportion of people not working *any* hours rose to a relatively small degree overall during the pandemic, in part because of furlough, there were increases in joblessness among lone parents (a 5.5 percentage point increase and a 4.3 percentage point higher than couples with children) and Pakistani and Bangladeshi households, and it was especially large among lone parent Pakistani and Bangladeshi households.[78] These economic shocks may have increased economic inequalities across these groups.

Beyond the precarious economic position of these households with respect to the lockdowns, another driver of this reduction in working hours among larger families

---

[74] *R (SC and Ors) v SSWP* [2021] UKSC 26.

[75] Thomas F Crossley, Paul Fisher, and Hamish Low, 'The Heterogeneous and Regressive Consequences of COVID-19: Evidence from High Quality Panel Data' (2021) 193 Journal of Public Economics 104334; Michaela Benzeval and others, 'The Idiosyncratic Impact of an Aggregate Shock: The Distributional Consequences of COVID-19' Institute for Fiscal Studies Working Paper W20/15 (2020) https://www.ifs.org.uk/publications/14870 (accessed 19 June 2020).

[76] Mary Reader and Kate Andersen, 'Size Matters: Experiences of Larger Families on a Low Income during Covid-19' in Kayleigh Garthwaite and others (eds), *COVID-19 Collaborations: Researching Poverty and Low-Income Family Life during the Pandemic* (Policy Press 2022).

[77] Robert Joyce and Xiaowei Xu, 'Sector Shutdowns during the Coronavirus Crisis: Which Workers Are Most Exposed?' Institute for Fiscal Studies (2020) http://hdl.voced.edu.au/10707/538124 (accessed 24 April 2022).

[78] Jonathan Cribb and others, 'The Labour Market during the Pandemic' Institute for Fiscal Studies (5 July 2021).

was increased caring and home-schooling responsibilities. Parents in all types of larger families—both low-income and high-income—spent more time helping their children with home-schooling than those in smaller families. However, it was parents in low-income larger families that seemed to be most affected. Parents in these households were spending four hours every day on average helping their kids with schoolwork compared to 2.5 hours among higher-income larger families.[79] It is hard to say whether this additional home-schooling burden is the driver of reduced working time or a response to it, although it is probably a mixture of both. What we do know, however, is that children in low-income larger families did receive less support from their schools and this may have necessitated more parental involvement and supervision. For example, around 39 per cent of smaller families on some form of social security (and so potentially low-income) were able to provide each child a computer for their school work but in larger families on benefits this fell to around 25 per cent.[80] Additionally, there is also clear evidence that closing schools had a particularly acute impact on the mental health of mothers with more than one child.[81] Parents in larger families who were receiving benefits may therefore have had to be more actively involved in home-schooling, and may have struggled more financially and emotionally as a result.

The material consequences of this are clear. The rates of furlough were higher among low-income larger families and they remained higher for longer than for other family types.[82] In September 2020, schools embarked on a full reopening and this allowed (for most families) working hours to return to what they were pre-pandemic. This was not true for low-income larger families who still saw a shortfall in working hours of around four hours per week, meaning incomes remained lower.[83] On top of this, evidence from other data sources noted that around 42 per cent of households with children were finding it harder to make ends meet during the pandemic.[84] This was not only attributable to reduced income but also because larger families saw their costs, including food bills, increase. At the beginning of the first lockdown, when food was scarce in the supermarkets, 10 per cent of low-income larger families reliant on benefits for a non-trivial portion of their income reported having used a foodbank in the last month; more than double what it was for low-income smaller families. The safety nets which should have protected families on a low income proved to have too many holes. Around 30 per cent of households eligible for free school meals did not receive a replacement in the form of a voucher or food parcel, and this was particularly concentrated among the poorest households.[85]

---

[79] A further contributory factor may also be that younger children require more supervision at home, and larger families on benefits are more likely to have slightly younger children due to the link between caring responsibilities, work intensity, and benefits receipt (the average of school-age children among larger families on benefits is 9.9 years compared to 10.4 years for larger families not on benefits).

[80] Campbell, Fredman, and Reeves (n 10).

[81] Jo Blanden and others, 'School Closures and Children's Emotional and Behavioural Difficulties: Institute for Social and Economic Research (ISER)' (ISER Working Paper Series 2021) https://www.iser.essex.ac.uk/research/publications/536633 (accessed 30 July 2021).

[82] Reader and Anderson (n 76).

[83] ibid.

[84] Campbell, Fredman, and Reeves (n 10).

[85] Public First, 'Sutton Trust: UK Parent Poll' (2020) http://www.publicfirst.co.uk/uk-parent-poll-st.html (accessed 12 August 2020).

It is important to emphasize that while most of this data relates to the adults in households with three or more children, these policies have also affected children. While all children have been asked to bear a huge burden during the various lockdowns, this burden varies greatly depending on family circumstances and resources. Lockdowns meant not only social isolation for many children, but some also went hungry because their parents could not afford enough food and the free school meals replacement system did not work properly.[86] The lockdowns led to less interaction with teachers but some children received more help than others (in part from private tutors but also from the schools themselves).[87] The long-term consequences of this are unclear but it is possible that children in larger families may have experienced a greater degree of learning loss than their peers in smaller families, potentially harming their future prospects.[88]

Qualitative research findings from the Benefit Changes and Larger Families project demonstrate some of the difficulties larger families subject to the benefit cap and the two-child limit faced during the pandemic:

> I already had like a food budget and stuff for the kids cos since Covid coming in place it's doubled my food shopping because I've got 'em at home; at least with the school they were getting a free school meal as well. But now I was, you know, budgeting for day meals for them as well. On top of that they were, they were all on laptops from school so my electric meter was, I was constantly topping that up as well so that was a nightmare; and then I had to get an internet, cos obviously with the budgeting and stuff I really couldn't afford Wi-Fi but then with school I had to go get Wi-Fi; so that was another £20/£30 a month for, for Wi-Fi for their school. And I didn't want to be behind school and stuff like that, and you just have that guilt don't yer?
>
> Jyoti, single mother, four children, subject to the benefit cap

As this comment shows, larger families incurred significant costs owing to the pandemic, including increased food, utility, and internet costs. These were difficult to meet in the context of inadequate benefit payments. Another participant explained how having increased costs and constrained financial circumstances made the pandemic more difficult for the family:

> It was depressing, to be honest ... there was not much to do with the kids and I don't have a lot of money; so they will ask me like "Can we have takeaway?" I couldn't really afford it, you know it was horrible ... So the kids eat more when they're at home, people don't notice that but they do ... so it was hard.
>
> Yasmin, single mother, five children, subject to the two child limit and the benefit cap

---

[86] ibid.
[87] 'Closing Schools for Covid-19 Does Lifelong Harm and Widens Inequality' *The Economist* (30 April 2020) https://www.economist.com/international/2020/04/30/closing-schools-for-covid-19-does-lifelong-harm-and-widens-inequality/ (accessed 21 August 2020).
[88] Per Engzell, Arun Frey, and Mark D Verhagen, 'Learning Loss Due to School Closures during the COVID-19 Pandemic' (2021) 118 Proceedings of the National Academy of Sciences e2022376118 https://www.pnas.org/content/118/17/e2022376118 (accessed 30 July 2021).

Yasmin relied on food parcels from a local community centre during the pandemic. The Covid Realties project has also found that low-income families faced extra increased spending overall during the pandemic owing to the extra costs of food, energy, and entertaining, distracting and home-schooling children, which led to financial hardship, stress, and anxiety.[89]

The pandemic and the economic restrictions that were put in place to curb the spread of the virus have increased inequalities, but these increases are not entirely because of pandemic policies themselves. The decisions taken by the government increased inequalities because pandemic policies interacted with existing disparities. Larger families were already at risk of poverty, they were already working fewer hours, and they were already experiencing higher costs. Moreover, larger families were increasingly exposed to policies that left them even more precarious. This was particularly true of larger families led by lone parents or living in minoritized ethnic households. The pandemic has exponentiated these inequalities by creating even more precarity. The government did not intentionally seek to exacerbate inequalities among these communities but their decisions have, it seems, failed to protect these groups and they have not adequately fulfilled their responsibilities to them under the Equality Act. The particularly troubling aspect of how the pandemic has increased inequalities is that these shocks to earnings, working hours, and living standards will have a scarring effect on these families for years to come. It is this long-run impact of the pandemic and the inadequate policy responses to it which have made these inequalities exponential—and they will only continue to grow over time.

5 Conclusion

This chapter has advanced three main arguments. The first is that the government's response to the pandemic failed to be sensitive to the additional pressures faced by larger families. Secondly, that the government's blind spot towards larger families is not merely an oversight during an otherwise incredibly pressurized moment in British policy-making. Rather, the absence of specific protections for larger families is symptomatic of a much longer tradition of policy decisions which appear to be predicated on longstanding but incorrect views of the relationship between social security and family size. Our third claim is that this failure to address the challenges faced by larger families during the pandemic interacted with their already precarious position (created by policies such as the benefit cap and the two-child limit) to exacerbate inequalities between some vulnerable groups and others who received more protection. In particular, some of the evidence we have pointed to indicates that larger families (and by implication women and some minoritized ethnic groups) have been particularly affected by this blind spot.

The pandemic, then, has increased inequality; but the extent and pace of that increase—that is, the exponentiality of it—is rooted in policy decisions made in

---

[89] Mike Brewer and Ruth Patrick, 'Pandemic Pressures: Why Families on a Low Income are Spending More during Covid-19' Resolution Foundation (11 January 2021) https://www.resolutionfoundation.org/app/uploads/2021/01/Pandemic-pressures.pdf (accessed 24 April 2022).

so-called 'normal' times. In other words, exponential inequalities have become manifest during this crisis because of the policies, rules, and institutions which were put in place before the pandemic hit. In some instances, these policies were probably hard to change, or, at least, quite slow to change. Neil Couling, the Change Director General for the Department of Works and Pensions, made exactly this point.[90] To some extent, this is a fair response, especially because kneejerk policy-making often leads to poor decisions.[91]

But merely pointing out that some changes are hard to implement, for example in order to defend the government's failure to stop the impact of the pandemic on child poverty, is inadequate in three respects. First, it ignores the fact that while some changes were hard, the government did pursue other challenging policy approaches. The furlough scheme involved converting an existing policy infrastructure and redirecting it towards new ends.[92] The Eat-Out-to-Help-Out scheme—which proved to be a very expensive disaster in terms of managing Covid-19[93]—was also a similar example of the government trying and succeeding to do something difficult because they thought it was in the best interests of the country. Secondly, while some changes were difficult, this does not mean that all possible avenues for supporting larger families were hard to implement. The government had options available to it which would have been relatively easy (albeit costly). For example, they could have considered increasing the amount of child benefit made available to households.[94] This change may have been as easy to make as the £20 uplift to Universal Credit but it was, as far as we know, never properly considered. Thirdly, the fact that some options would have been hard to implement is itself a choice—the forms of social security were inadequate and hard to change because of how governments had chosen to set them up in the past. The government's response to the pandemic in terms of their support for larger families, then, was not solely the product of decisions made during the first few months of 2020; rather, it was a consequence of the way governments had been thinking about support for larger families over a much longer period.

The government's blind spot of support for households with children more generally and larger families specifically is a product of two kinds of path dependence.[95] The first is institutional path dependence—the way certain choices that have been made in the past constrain the policy space in the present.[96] The absence of any real debate about how to support these families intimates another sort of path dependence, namely, ideational path dependence. Policies such as the benefit cap and the two-child

---

[90] Resolution Foundation, 'The Safety Net in Action? Universal Credit's Role in the Crisis and the Recovery' (27 May 2020) https://www.resolutionfoundation.org/events/the-safety-net-in-action/ (accessed 20 June 2020).
[91] Jen Gaskell and others, 'Covid-19 and the Blunders of Our Governments: Long-Run System Failings Aggravated by Political Choices' (2020) 91 The Political Quarterly 523; Anthony King and Ivor Crewe, *The Blunders of Our Governments* (Oneworld Publications 2014).
[92] Hacker, Pierson, and Thelen (n 41).
[93] Thiemo Fetzer, 'Subsidising the Spread of COVID-19: Evidence from the UK's Eat-Out-to-Help-Out Scheme' 132 Economic Journal 643, 1200.
[94] CPAG (n 23).
[95] Mahoney (n 12).
[96] For example, the UK government did not have the institutional mechanisms in place to provide social security to the self-employed and without this was forced to provide cash assistance to those who could not work using an incredibly blunt instrument.

limit are ideationally embedded in certain ways of thinking about the families targeted by these policies. More concretely, the two-child limit becomes intelligible and even sensible from the viewpoint that families are having children because they know the state will provide financial support for them.[97] This ideational embedding (or this theory of how certain families respond to these incentives) also makes other ways of approaching the challenges faced by these households harder to countenance, even though they may be institutionally feasible. The British government's refusal to change some policies that were amenable to rapid reform is reflective of an ideological commitment to certain assumptions about larger families in particular and welfare policy-making in general.[98] The durability of this ideological commitment to policies which no longer work in the way they were intended, such as the benefit cap, is evidence of a kind of ideational path dependence which means that these policies can continue without being seriously challenged. These ideological assumptions are not simply washed away by societal shocks,[99] but require committed and systemic effort if the fundamental beliefs underpinning the British welfare state are to change.

As we have shown, there is little doubt that the pandemic has increased inequality, but the degree to which inequalities will increase is dependent on the policies in place before such crises hit as well as whether the responses are sensitive to the interactions between societal shocks and existing institutions. Avoiding exponential inequalities in response to future crises requires that policies—and the discourses which surround them—are sensitive to the potential for other kinds of societal shock.

---

[97] Somers and Block (n 14).
[98] Hills (n 52).
[99] McArthur and Reeves (n 59).

5
The Proportionality of an Economic Crisis

Meghan Campbell

1 Introduction

Despite rhetorical invocations to 'Build Back Better', the United Kingdom (UK) has implemented policies that have exacerbated the inequalities revealed by Covid-19. A public sector pay freeze has already been implemented in the UK, the £20 uplift to Universal Credit (the major source of social benefits for those on low income or out of work) has been discontinued, and other punishing restrictions to accessing social benefits (such as the two-child limit and the benefits cap) remain in place. There is a 'bill to pay' for the health care and economic relief measures implemented during the height of the pandemic. In paying that bill it appears the UK will revert back to, or in fact continue to implement, policies of austerity.[1] The regularity of 'unprecedented' fiscal emergencies means there is now a substantial body of social science evidence and jurisprudence that explores the equality impacts and role of the legal right to equality in an economic crisis. One of the key lessons from the recovery measures implemented in light of the 2008 banking crisis is that austerity both cemented and exacerbated pre-existing inequalities. Elson and Sharples, and Reeves and others in their chapters in this collection paint a vivid portrait of the exponentially rising inequalities in the UK under the post-2008 austerity policies. Equality seeking groups in the UK have challenged the discriminatory impact of austerity on individuals with protected characteristics. The results of this litigation are decidedly mixed. More often than not, the courts have accepted that the discrimination against women, children, or disabled persons was justified in pursuit of economic recovery. This chapter explores the jurisprudence from the UK, focusing on the role of justification in reviewing equality impacting measures implemented in response to an economic crisis. This provides a clearer picture on the potential role of courts in reviewing emergency measures implemented in light of Covid-19 or other future crises that undermine the right to equality.

The chapter begins by canvassing the origins of the 2008 economic crisis. To prevent the collapse of the financial sector, governments bailed out the banks using public funds. In response to the increase in debt, the UK implemented austerity, a series of cuts, freezes, and restrictions on public spending and social services. After canvassing the theory and critiques of austerity, Section 2 argues that austerity was used as a tool, by first the Coalition government of Conservatives with the Liberal Democrats and then the Conservative government, to advance its political ideology.

---

[1] Sam Warner and others, 'More Austerity? The Treasury Must Act Against the Grain of its Own History in Responding to the COVID-19 Crisis' LSE BPP (2020) https://blogs.lse.ac.uk/politicsandpolicy/treasury-covid19/ (accessed 9 August 2021).

Austerity operated to disguise the role of the financial sector in the crisis and to blame the rise in fiscal debt on welfare spending as the 'cuts disproportionately [fell] upon the already marginalised and exploited'.[2] Women, children, and disabled persons who bore the brunt of austerity unsuccessfully challenged the welfare reforms as discriminatory under Article 14 of the European Convention on Human Rights (ECHR). Section 3 analyses these cases. The UK Supreme Court (UKSC) generally accepted that the reforms are indirectly discriminatory but held that imposing income poverty on women, children, and disabled persons is a justifiable equality-limiting measure. Through a highly deferential, light-touch review, the role of the economic crisis in prompting the welfare reforms is minimized and, echoing the political rationale for austerity, the recklessness of unchecked welfare spending is emphasized. Section 4 seeks to rebalance the justification analysis by placing the need for discriminatory austerity policies within its full context. A more searching justification analysis, that uses a high intensity proportionality framework, can accurately account for the economic emergency. This in turn shifts the analytical focus at justification stage away from the perceived overdependence of welfare recipients and towards questioning whether it is fair to ask the most vulnerable and marginalized to bear the costs of the crisis. It also unearths the contestable assumptions on the effectiveness of austerity and queries orthodox economic discourse that discriminatory austerity welfare measures are the only method for restoring fiscal health. In undertaking this type of assessment, the courts should not be seen as exceeding their institutional role but as demanding the evidence that is perquisite to justify limiting equality rights. A meaningful interrogation of the government's rationale for austerity must be sensitive to the background of the crisis. And in doing so, courts need not be bystanders in the face of economic emergency but can ensure that due weight is given in policy responses to the equality rights of the most disadvantaged and marginalized.

2 Smoke and Mirrors: the Banking Crisis, Fiscal Deficit, and Austerity

The 2008 economic crisis has been described as the greatest 'bait and switch' in history.[3] The banking industries' recklessness in granting high-risk mortgages and then repackaging that risk through a series of financial products created an economic bubble that ultimately burst. To avoid the collapse of the banks, public funds were used to bail them out. The mistakes, and the costs of those mistakes, were transferred from the banks to the public ledger. After ensuring the solvency of the financial sector, with a staggering level of irony, it was demanded 'that the state get their own house in order or face the prospects of having their credit rating downgraded and their own ability to borrow restricted'.[4] This is a repeated pattern; 'a banking crisis is followed

---

[2] Ben Warwick and Joe Wills, 'Contesting Austerity: The Potential and Pitfalls of Socioeconomic Rights Discourse' (2016) 23 Indiana Journal of Global Legal Studies 629, 631.
[3] Mark Blyth, *Austerity: The History of a Dangerous Idea* (OUP 2013) ch 3.
[4] Ben Warwick, 'Debt, Austerity and the Structure of Social Rights' in Ilias Bantekas and Cephas Lumina (eds), *Sovereign Debt and Human Rights* (OUP 2018) 395.

by a sovereign debt crisis 80 per cent of the time'.[5] Indeed, the pattern of private risks becoming public debts has been true for the UK. Gordon Brown, the Chancellor of the Exchequer during the peak of the crisis, 'spent, lent or otherwise guaranteed about 40 percent of the British [Gross Domestic Product] to save the banks'.[6] The UK debt rose by £850 billion as a result of bailing out and propping up the banks.[7]

Rather than openly acknowledging that the public had taken on banking debts, the fiscal deficit was explained as being the result of proliferate public spending. Cameron's Coalition government, which came to power in 2010, argued that spending cuts were needed to 'get the public finances back under control'.[8] George Osborne, the Chancellor of the Exchequer under the Coalition government, invoked the spectre of Greece and its reputation for careless spending to justify re-engineering the public expenditure: 'you can see in Greece an example of a country that didn't face up to its problems and that is the fate I want to avoid'.[9] The right-wing press was even more explicit. *The Sun* explained that 'the nation is clear who it blames for Britain's debts: LABOUR' and *The Daily Telegraph* blamed irresponsible spending that allowed people to 'wallow in state-sponsored idleness'.[10] Blyth argues that the misdirection on the origins of the economic crisis were used to turn 'the politics of debt into a morality play, one that has shifted the blame from the banks to the state'.[11] This, however, is not the end of the blame game. The fault then shifts to those who depend on the state. These morality twists are evident in 2009, as then Leader of the Conservative Party and soon-to-be Prime Minister, David Cameron, explained that the 'age of irresponsibility is giving way to the age of austerity'.[12]

The smoke and mirrors on the causes of the fiscal deficit is not benign but is used by political actors to legitimatize austerity. This is a political and economic ideology that seeks to reduce public spending so as to restore private-sector confidence and enhance international competitiveness.

Austerity pits the public and private sector against each other. Investment in public services is characterized as money that is directed away from business and as a result private-sector innovation will shift elsewhere in the world. On the flip side, austerity measures are said to generate fiscal savings and reduce the deficit on the assumption that this will create space for the highly prized private market investment. Under this line of thinking, fiscal consolidation will create economic growth as investors 'anticipate long run tax deductions because of cuts in expenditure'.[13] By cutting public

---

[5] Cameron Reinhart and Kenneth Rogoff, 'Banking Crises: An Equal Opportunity Menace' (2008) NBER Working Paper Series 14587.

[6] Blyth (n 3) 59.

[7] Kerry-Anne Mednoza, *Austerity: The Demolition of the Welfare State and the Rise of the Zombie Economy* (New Internationalist 2015)15.

[8] HM Treasury, 'Budget 2010' (June 2010) https://assets.publishing.service.gov.uk/government/uploads/system/uploads/attachment_data/file/248096/0061.pdf (accessed 20 July 2021).

[9] Reuters Staff, 'UK to Dodge Greek Fate with Tough-Budget: Osborne' *Reuters* (20 June 2010) https://www.reuters.com/article/uk-britain-osborne-budget-idUKTRE65J0UX20100620 (accessed 21 July 2020).

[10] As cited in Isabela Fairclough, 'Evaluating Policy as Argument: The Public Debate Over the First UK Austerity Budget' (2016) 13 Critical Discourse Studies 57, 62.

[11] Blyth (n 3) 13.

[12] David Cameron, 'The Age of Austerity: Conservative Party Speeches' (2009) https://conservative-speeches.sayit.mysociety.org/speech/601367 (accessed 9 August 2021).

[13] Stephen Kinsella, 'Is Ireland Really the Role Model for Austerity?' (2012) 36 Cambridge Journal of Economics 232.

spending, there will be a return to economic prosperity. The history of austerity, however, suggests that the equation between consolidation and fiscal growth is false.[14] After canvassing the failures of austerity policies, Blyth succinctly concludes that 'it doesn't work'.[15] It is only effective in a highly specific set of circumstances that arguably no longer exist in the modern world.[16] Despite austerity's dim track record, economists and politicians continuously claim there is no alternative.[17] Any failures of austerity to achieve the promised economic growth, it is claimed, can only be solved with more austerity. This explains why austerity policies, such as in the UK or in Greece, can be in place for over a decade. Little credence is given to other economic theories on how best to respond to the banking crisis and sovereign debt.[18] The fidelity to austerity is, in part, because it reflects a neo-liberal ideology on the role of the state and of markets. Austerity is not only an economic theory but is a set of beliefs on which institutions are better equipped to ensure flourishing and who should benefit from that flourishing.

Austerity measures were proposed in a series of successive budgets by Cameron's Coalition and then the majority Conservative government and solidified in various statutes and regulations. These budgets were presented as the unpleasant, but necessary, medicine needed to correct the supposed overspending on social welfare and to restore the banks' confidence in the UK economy.[19] The theory of expansionary fiscal consolidation was particularly evident in the 2010 emergency budget as the Treasury described it as 'a springboard for a private sector-led recovery'.[20] These successive budgets contain a wide array of austerity measures, but a significant focus was placed on reducing the spending on social welfare benefits.[21] This included, inter alia, the 'bedroom tax', which reduced the housing benefit if the individual living in social housing was deemed to have under-utilized bedrooms.[22] It also included the 'two-child limit', which limited the eligibility for child tax credit, a non-contributory means-tested benefit designed to assist in the costs of raising children, to the first and second children in a family.[23] The central pillar of the austerity motivated benefit reforms was the benefit cap and work conditionalities. Despite being entitled to a range of benefits, the amount any individual could receive is now capped[24] and the income poverty of the cap can only be escaped if a certain amount of work is performed in the

---

[14] Florian Schui, *Austerity: The Great Failure* (Yale UP 2014).

[15] Blyth (n 3) 10.

[16] ibid chs 4–6.

[17] Kolja Möller, 'Struggles for Law: Global Social Rights as an Alternative to Financial Market Capitalism' in Poul Kjaer, Gunther Teubner, and Alberto Febbrajo (eds), *The Financial Crisis in Constitutional Perspective: The Dark Side of Functional Differentiation* (Bloomsbury 2011).

[18] Ruth Pearson and Diane Elson, 'Transcending the Impact of the Financial Crisis in the UK: Towards a Plan F: A Feminist Economic Strategy' (2015) 109 Feminist Review 8.

[19] Andrew Gamble, 'The Economy' (2015) 68(Supplementary 1) Parliamentary Affairs 154.

[20] HM Treasury (n 8).

[21] Women's Budget Group, 'The Impact of Women of Budget 2013: A Budget for Inequality and Recession' (2013) https://wbg.org.uk/wp-content/uploads/2013/10/WBG_Budget-Analysis_2013.pdf (accessed 10 August 2021).

[22] Welfare Reform Act 2012, s 69(3); Housing Benefit (Amendment) Regulations 2013 (SI 2013/665).

[23] Welfare Reform and Work Act 2016, s 13(4); Tax Credits Act 2002, ss 9(3A), (3B); Child Tax Credit (Amendment) Regulations 2017 (SI 2017/387).

[24] Welfare Reform Act 2012, ss 96, 97; Welfare Reform and Work Act 2016, s 96(5A); Benefit Gap (Housing Benefit and Universal Credit) (Amendment) Regulations 2016 (SI 2016/909).

paid labour force.[25] George Osborne claimed that the initial 2010 austerity budget was 'tough but fair'[26] and that the pain of austerity was equally spread as 'those with the broadest shoulders should bear the greatest burden'.[27] Numerous studies have demonstrated the opposite.[28] Elson and Sharples, and Reeves and others in their chapters, forensically investigate the exponential growth of inequalities under austerity. The debt rose by 33.4 per cent of gross domestic product (GDP) between 2009 and 2013[29] and austerity has been argued to have 'set back the economic recovery'.[30] Beyond the balance sheet, there was a rise in exploitative employment, child poverty, foodbank use, and ill-health.[31] Austerity has unnecessarily inflicted 'great misery' and 'wrought the most harm to the fabric of British society'.[32]

3 Unsuccessful Equality Challenges to Austerity

The unequal impact of austerity points towards using the legal right to equality in the courts to challenge these policies. Despite the theoretical promise of equality, the courts have repeatedly held that perpetuating discrimination is justified to ensure the economic well-being of the state. Discrimination becomes the cost of the fiscal crisis. This chapter focuses on a narrow subset of cases where equality seeking groups have challenged the disproportionate impact of austerity. It homes in on the unsuccessful challenges to the benefit cap, bedroom tax, work conditionalities and the two-child limit. These cases were brought by disabled persons, women, and children and, despite some doctrinal twists and turns, epitomize the Court's decontextualized and highly deferential approach to evaluating the government's justifications for austerity. All these claims are brought on the basis of indirect discrimination. Analytically, this requires an investigation into the disproportionately prejudicial effects of a neutral policy.[33] The Court, however, does little to unearth the exponentially unequal impact of austerity policies on protected groups.[34] The aim of this chapter is not to retread these arguments, but to focus on the Court's assessment of the government's arguments to justify limiting equality in response to an economic crisis. This section briefly sketches the nature of the claims and the Court's conclusions on whether

---

[25] Working Tax Credit (Entitlement and Maximum Rate) Regulations 2002 (SI 2002/2005), reg 4(1).
[26] As cited in Fairclough (n 10) 64.
[27] George Osborne, 'Chancellor George Osborne's Summer Budget 2015 Speech' https://www.gov.uk/government/speeches/chancellor-george-osbornes-summer-budget-2015-speech (accessed 21 July 2021).
[28] See eg James Browne and Peter Levell, 'The Distributional Effect of Tax and Benefit Reforms to be Introduced Between June 2010 and April 2014: A Revised Assessment' Institute for Fiscal Studies Briefing Note BN108 (2010).
[29] Oxfam, 'The True Cost of Austerity and Inequality: The UK Case Study' (2013) https://www-cdn.oxfam.org/s3fs-public/file_attachments/cs-true-cost-austerity-inequality-uk-120913-en_0.pdf (accessed 21 July 2021).
[30] Gamble (n 19) 159.
[31] Oxfam (n 29); UN Special Rapporteur on human rights and extreme poverty, 'Visit to the United Kingdom of Great Britain and Norther Ireland' (2019) A/HRC/41/39/Add.1.
[32] ibid [11], [13].
[33] *DH v Czech Republic* (2008) 47 EHHR 3 [184] (ECtHR).
[34] Meghan Campbell, 'The Austerity of Lone Motherhood: Discrimination Law and Benefit Reform' (2021) 41(4) Oxford Journal of Legal Studies 1197.

benefit discrimination was a justified measure needed to restore the fiscal health of the country. In doing so, it argues that the Court employs an overly deferential standard of review to assess the government's rationale for regressive benefits reforms that not only fails accurately to capture the background context of the economic crisis but also contributes to exponential inequalities by stigmatizing poverty.

In *SG and Others v Secretary of State for Work and Pensions*, lone mothers challenged the benefit cap as being indirectly discriminatory against women.[35] The impact of the cap was most felt by those receiving high levels of benefits, namely lone mothers.[36] They challenged the cap as discriminatory under Article 14 of the ECHR read in conjunction with Article 1 of Protocol No 1 (peaceful enjoyment of possessions) (A1P1). The government conceded the cap was indirectly discriminatory.[37] Lord Reed, for the lead majority judgment, held that since the benefit cap involved 'controversial issues of social and economic policy' and the 'determination of those issues is pre-eminently the function of democratically elected institutions', it was only appropriate to subject the benefit cap to a minimal amount of scrutiny.[38] The low level of scrutiny is further explained as the Court failed to engage fully with the multifaceted, exponential inequalities resulting from the imposition of the cap.[39] The Court accepted, on the basis of the manifestly without reasonable foundation (MWRF) test, that:

(i) curtailing welfare dependency by limiting the upper level of benefits any individual could claim from the state was reasonable;
(ii) there was a rational basis to hold that the benefit cap would motivate those on welfare to support themselves exclusively through work in the paid labour force; and
(iii) the cap was a legitimate method for reducing public spending at a time when it was necessary for the economic health of the state.[40]

These justifications entwine to create the impression that the large fiscal debt is a function of welfare dependency and the work-shy behaviour of individuals who live in poverty. They are emblematic of the misdirection of the causes of the sovereign debt crisis, as nowhere in the judgment is there acknowledgement of the role of financial organizations in precipitating the debt. Rather, the judgment tacitly endorses the government's argument that the crisis is the result of welfare spending. By obscuring the true origins of the deficit and accepting the narrative of imprudent public spending, the Court legitimatizes the income poverty imposed upon women through the application of the benefit cap.

The bedroom tax was held in *Carmichael and Rourke and Others v Secretary of State for Work and Pensions* to be lawful discrimination against disabled persons and women who experience gender-based violence.[41] Similar to *SG and Others*, the restrictions on the housing benefits were based on Article 14 taken together with Article

---

[35] [2015] UKSC 16.
[36] ibid [26].
[37] ibid [61], [180].
[38] ibid [93].
[39] ibid.
[40] ibid [4].
[41] [2016] UKSC 58.

1 of A1P1 and Article 8 (right to private life) of the ECHR. Beside a throw-away line in Appendix 2 explaining that the bedroom tax was 'part and parcel of the Government's deficit reduction strategy' in the 2010 emergency budget, there is a glaring absence of any analysis as to whether discriminatorily reducing the housing benefit for supposed under-occupation is a justifiable response to the economic crisis. Should disabled people bear the burdens of mistakes made in the financial sector? Instead of asking this question, using the MWRF test, the Court interrogated the nature of the disability and co-habitation relationships between household members to conclude for all but one of the disabled claimants that the bedroom tax was justified.[42] On a similar basis, the majority of the Court found that it was lawful to discriminate against women in reducing housing benefit for under-occupation of sanctuary homes (homes specially equipped to protect women against domestic violence). There was no 'objective' need for the additional space and thus, according to Lord Toulson, it could not be said that 'the approach taken by the Secretary of State was manifestly without reasonable foundation'.[43] Again, there was no explicit assessment on whether imposing the bedroom tax on women who experienced gender-based violence was a justifiable response to the bank induced fiscal emergency. This decision was partially overruled by the European Court of Human Rights (ECtHR), which held the bedroom tax was discriminatory against women who experienced gender-based violence.[44]

In *DA and Others v Secretary of State for Work and Pensions*, the companion case to *SG and Others*, lone parents (in this case, all lone mothers) challenged the work conditionalities to escape the income poverty imposed by the cap.[45] Owing to their caring commitments, lone parents of young children argued they were less able to obtain sixteen hours of work in the paid labour force. The Court found that there was prima facie indirect discrimination against lone parents of young children based on Article 14 read together with Article 8 of the ECHR and, once again, the majority applied the MWRF test to assess justification. Lord Wilson held, on a narrow basis, that the work conditionality was justified as there was a reasonable foundation to conclude that there were 'better long-term outcomes for children who live in households in which an adult works'.[46] Unlike *SG and Others*, but similar to *Carmichael and Rourke*, the role of fiscal deficit in prompting regressive welfare reforms was absent from the Court's analysis. *DA and Others* emphasized combating welfare dependency. This gives credence to Blyth's arguments that banking debt becomes a morality play, with welfare recipients cast as blameworthy.

And in the final case, *SC and CB v Secretary of State for Works and Pensions*,[47] the UKSC unanimously upheld the two-child limit for receipt of child tax credit, thirteen years after the 2008 banking crisis. The Court held that the reform was prima facie indirectly discriminatory against women and children in households with two or more

---

[42] ibid [51]–[55]. Only with respect to Mrs Carmichael did the Court find there was no reasonable justification for reducing her housing benefit as she could not share a bedroom with her husband due to the nature of her disability; ibid [44]–[46].
[43] ibid [56], [66].
[44] *JD and A v United Kingdom* App nos 32949/17 and 34614/17 (ECtHR, 24 October 2019).
[45] [2019] UKSC 21.
[46] ibid [88].
[47] [2021] UKSC 26.

children. The case once again turned on justification. In light of developments from the ECtHR, the UKSC restricted the application of the highly deferential MWRF test and acknowledged that for suspect grounds, such as gender, weighty reasons were needed to justify discrimination. Lord Reed adopted a proportionality analysis, but the thin application of proportionality raises questions as to whether the Court understood the conceptual difference between the MWRF test and proportionality.[48] In justifying the discrimination, the Court held that the two-child limit was a proportionate measure to manage the fiscal deficit and ensure a fair benefit system that encouraged individuals to reflect on their financial readiness to have additional children.[49] Similar to *SG and Others*, the Court entwined public debt and welfare spending implying a cause-and-effect relationship between the economic ill-health of the country and financially supporting women in poverty in the care of children. The lynchpin of proportionality in *SC and CB* was inquiring whether Parliament decided these aims were sufficiently important to discriminate against women and children. The Court accepted that Parliament had deemed the aims important enough and concluded there was no legal basis for the Court to disagree with the Parliament.[50]

4 Rebalancing the Proportionality of Austerity

In these cases, rather than rigorously protecting the equality rights of women, children, and disabled persons, the Court all too willingly accepts the need for discriminatory cuts to the welfare system. At the justification stage, through light-touch scrutiny, the role of the economic crisis is minimized and even invisiblized. The judgments all implicitly accept that high degrees of welfare dependency are linked to the economic ill-health of the state and thus they contribute to the prejudice against individuals in poverty. Accurately accounting for causes of fiscal debt, however, can reshape this assessment. Given the doctrinal guidance in *SC and CB* that suspect grounds, such as those at stake in these cases, require weighty reasons to justify discrimination, this section applies a high intensity proportionality review. Proportionality can not only ensure that weighty reasons are required for limiting equality rights, but it can also bring to the fore the true causes of the crisis. This is of immense value to using legal equality rights in challenging policy-making after an economic emergency, as it flushes out the demonization of poverty and permits a more transparent weighing and balancing of the burdens of the crisis.

This section uses the proportionality test articulated by the UKSC in *Bank Mellet*, which evaluates whether:

---

[48] Meghan Campbell, 'Might Makes Right: The Two-Child Limit Justifiable Discrimination Against Women and Children' (2021) 43 Journal of Social Welfare and Family Law 467; Charlotte O'Brien, 'Inevitability as the New Discrimination Defence: UK Supreme Court Mangles Indirect Discrimination Analysis' Oxford Human Rights Hub (2021) https://ohrh.law.ox.ac.uk/inevitability-as-the-new-discrimination-defence-uk-supreme-court-mangles-indirect-discrimination-analysis-while-finding-the-two-child-limit-lawful/ (accessed 28 July 2021).
[49] *SC and CB* (n 47) [190].
[50] ibid [199].

(i) the government's objectives are sufficiently important to justify limiting the individual's rights;
(ii) the measures are rationally connected to the government's objectives in bringing in these benefit reforms;
(iii) a less intrusive measure could have been used; and
(iv) having regard to these matters and to the severity of the consequences; a fair balance has been struck between the rights of the individual and the interests of the community.[51]

Acknowledging that the economic situation is not the result of supporting the welfare state but of ideological choices to allow the recklessness of the financial sector and the decision to publicly underwrite the banking debt opens new lines of inquiry at the justification stage. Through a searching proportionality analysis, that places the burden of proof on the government,[52] courts should be demanding evidence that there is a rational connection between the government's aims and austerity, and that austerity is the less intrusive way to respond to an economic crisis; and then conducting a transparent balancing exercise in determining who in the community should bear the costs of the crisis.

4.1 Identifying with Precision the Sufficiency of the Government's Aims

The first step in the proportionality analysis is to assess whether the government's aims in bringing the welfare reforms into effect are sufficient. There is a tendency uncritically to accept the government's aims as legitimate.[53] A closer inspection of the government's objectives is warranted as the Court's approach is highly decontextualized.[54] Under the umbrella of securing the economic well-being of the state,[55] there are a cluster of aims that are repeated throughout the jurisprudence:

(i) to make fiscal savings;[56]
(ii) to incentivize individuals to make certain choices such as moving to smaller accommodation, entering the paid labour force, or reflecting on financial readiness to have children;[57]
(iii) to improve benefit fairness and increase public confidence in the welfare system by not rewarding non-working people with benefits that would exceed the income of average working people.[58]

---

[51] *Bank Mellet v Her Majesty's Treasury* [2013] UKSC 38 [20].
[52] Cora Chan, 'The Burden of Proof Under the Human Rights Act' (2014) Judicial Review 46.
[53] Oddný Mjöll Arnardóttir, 'The "Procedural Turn" Under the ECHR and Presumptions of Convention Compliance' (2017) 15 International Journal of Constitutional Law 9, 29–31.
[54] The UN Committee on Economic and Social Rights has been critiqued for adopting a similar decontextualized approach to its monitoring work in the context of austerity; see Warwick (n 4) 383–85.
[55] *Andrejeva v Lativa* (2009) 51 EHRR 650 (ECtHR).
[56] *SG and Others* (n 35) [63]; *DA and Others* (n 45) [7]; *SC and CB* (n 47) [193].
[57] *Carmichael and Rourke* (n 41) [16]; *DA and Others* (n 45) [7]–[8]; *SC and CB* (n 47) [191].
[58] *SG and Others* (n 35) [66]; *DA and Others* (n 45) [152]; *SC and CB* (n 47) [208].

Through a two-stage process, these three reasons operate not only to camouflage the role of the banking crisis in prompting discriminatory austerity measures but also serve to legitimize demonizing welfare recipients.

The first stage in this decontextualizing process is to obliterate the role of financial sector in precipitating the rise in debt. The Court does this by failing to ask any questions on the origin of the deficit. In *SG and Others* and *Carmichael and Rourke*, the Court accepts that the cap was designed to 'reduce the structural deficit' and 'achieve savings in public expenditure at a time when such savings are necessary in the interests of the economic well-being of the country'.[59] Lord Hughes in *SG and Others* goes so far as to hold that 'at a time of national economic crisis it was also legitimate to seek to reduce overall expense'.[60] At best, this is a vague nod towards the 2008 crash. The economic risk-taking and the political decisions to underwrite the risk that underlie the fiscal deficit and the corresponding cuts in welfare spending play no role in the Court's justification assessment. Although the lower courts do refer to the bedroom tax and work conditionalities as part of the government's austerity package,[61] the term 'austerity' is not used in the UKSC. This linguistic choice obscures the connection between 2008 economic crisis and retrogressive welfare measures. Blyth, however, argues that the crisis does in fact have a specific origin:

> the cost of ... saving the global banking system, has been depending on ... how you count it, between 3 and 13 trillion dollars. Most of that has ended up on the balance sheets of governments ... which is why we mistakenly call a sovereign debt crisis when it is in fact a transmuted and well-camouflaged banking crisis.[62]

In later judgments, this context is stripped out to an even greater degree.[63]

Failing to account for the role of the financial sector in austerity is not merely an inaccurate recounting of recent history, but it creates a vacuum. This leads to the second stage in decontextualizing the aims of the reforms. The government and the Court fill the deficit causation vacuum by characterizing welfare recipients as scroungers who are plunging the state into fiscal ruin. Lord Reed in *SC and CB* explicitly draws these threads together. He explains that 'the excessively high level of public spending on welfare benefits' has led to a 'resulting ... large fiscal deficit'.[64] This implicitly places the blame for debt onto lone mothers needing financial support from the state to care for their children or onto disabled persons who are deemed to under-utilize space in subsidized housing and ignores its macro-economic roots. In a similar vein, by incentivizing work and placing limits on the total amount of benefits, the cap is explicitly framed by the Court in *SG and Others* as a facet of economic well-being.[65] This reinforces the narrative that the economic well-being of the country has been

---

[59] *SG and Others* (n 35) [4], [42], [63]; *Carmichael and Rourke* (n 41) [20].
[60] *SG and Others* (n 35) [135].
[61] *MA and Others v Secretary of State for Work and Pensions* [2014] EWCA 13 [94]; *DA and Others v Secretary of State for Work and Pensions* [2018] EWCA Civ 504 [3].
[62] Blyth (n 3) 5.
[63] *DA and Others* (n 45) [7].
[64] *SC and CB* (n 47) [190].
[65] *SG and Others* (n 35) [64], [65].

jeopardized by welfare spending. The fiscal deficit becomes the result of welfare recipients living unwarranted luxurious lifestyles, with taxpayers shouldering the cost for their irresponsibility and idleness. Regressive welfare reforms are then perceived to be a prudent measure to incentive these wayward members of the community into economically productive lifestyles and to ensure sound management of the state's finances. The decisions of the financial and political elite in precipitating the financial crisis are ignored. By accepting the narrative of over-spending on welfare, it then becomes legitimate to impose discrimination and income poverty on individuals with protected characteristics.

The argument here is neither that the economic well-being of the country is an illegitimate aim nor that ensuring that individuals can support themselves through decent work is unfair. It is that stripping out the context of the economic ill-health of the state and then characterizing the need for austerity in a manner that stigmatizes individuals in poverty is less than legitimate.

4.2 Demanding Evidence of a Rational Connection

Refusing to place the government's aims in pursuing retrogressive and discriminatory welfare reforms in the context of the 2008 financial crisis has knock-on effects on the justification analysis and prevents the Court from grappling with whether austerity is a proportionate economic recovery measure. This is evident at the rational connection step. This limb of the test requires the government to demonstrate that there is a means-end fit between its aims and the measures chosen to achieve those aims. The Court repeatedly fails to demand evidence that there is a rational connection between austerity and economic well-being. This subsection critically assesses the Court's lackadaisical evaluation of rational connection and, drawing on heterodox economics, demonstrates how the justification analysis can be used to expose assumptions surrounding austerity.

Generating fiscal savings through cuts in welfare spending is uncritically presumed to guarantee the economic well-being of the state. At no point in any of the four judgments is the conflation of welfare spending, cuts to public expenditure, and fiscal health questioned. The Court conceptualizes sovereign debt as akin to managing personal or household debt so that the simple solution appears to be to cut spending to reduce costs and create fiscal solvency. Lord Reed repeatedly characterizes welfare funding as 'excessively high'.[66] In *SG and Others*, the Court accepts the government's figures that the cap will result in meaningful savings. The cap is projected to save £110 million in 2013/14 and £185 million in 2014/15 and optimistically, this level of 'savings is expected to continue over the longer term'.[67] In *SC and CB*, Lord Reed held that:

> there is clearly a rational connection between the objectives pursued by the legislation and Parliament's decision to limit entitlement to the individual element of the

---

[66] ibid [66], [96]; *SC and CB* (n 47) [190], [201].
[67] ibid.

child tax credit to the amount [payable] in respect of two children. It is not in dispute that the measure, by imposing that limitation, will achieve savings in public expenditure, and thus contribute to reducing the fiscal deficit.[68]

There are multiple cracks in this equation that should prompt questions as to whether the government has discharged its burden to demonstrate a rational connection. It is not a mathematical certainty that reducing welfare spending will result in increased savings. In recognition of the punishing levels of income poverty imposed by the benefit cap, work conditionality and bedroom tax, the government increased the funding to the discretionary housing payments scheme.[69] These benefits are designed to assist in securing accommodation, for example to 'pay the deposit on a new home and the initial instalment of rent'.[70] Over 2013-15, an additional £100 million was earmarked for discretionary housing payments. The government's projected £295 million in savings does not account for the increased funding for these payments. In *SG and Others*, early in the judgment, Lord Reed does acknowledge this incomplete accounting, also observing that the government has not accounted for the costs of implementing the cap.[71] Despite flagging this issue, later at the justification stage in *SG and Others*, the Court does not demand evidence from the government that the cap actually generates appreciable savings. At a minimum to justify discriminatory welfare measures that are aimed to generate fiscal savings, the government should be required to give a thorough and accurate audit of the economic costs and savings of the measure. When the bedroom tax was challenged in Strasbourg, the ECtHR criticized the government for failing to put forward 'any detailed reasons as to how imposing the measures ... might achieve the stated aims of reducing benefit payments'.[72] Lady Hale in dissent in *DA and Others* undertakes a more robust rational connection analysis that holistically explores the links between fiscal savings and cutting welfare spending. She accounts not only for the increase in the discretionary housing payments, but also the costs of 'rehousing families made homeless as a result of the cap'.[73] This leads her to conclude that the fiscal savings 'are very small and liable to [be] offset'.[74]

The other substantial crack in the rational connection analysis is the unexamined operating background assumption that austerity measures will assist in economic recovery. Pro-austerity economic theory holds that there is a rational connection between imposing discriminatory welfare measures and recovering from the 2008 banking and sovereign debt crisis.[75] A high-intensity proportionality review should place this claim under the judicial microscope. The previous subsection highlighted the Court's reluctance to undertake this contextual analysis. Economic policy-making

---

[68] *SC and CB* (n 47) [193], [204].
[69] *SG and Others* (n 35) [45].
[70] ibid.
[71] ibid [45], [58]; *DA and Others* (n 45) [32]. Lord Carnwath in *SG and Others* (n 35) [127] similarly queries whether the government's estimates are up-to-date.
[72] *JD and A* (n 44) [71].
[73] *DA and Others* (n 45) [153].
[74] ibid.
[75] Alberto Alesina and Silvia Ardanga, 'Large Changes in Fiscal Policy: Taxes Versus Spending' (2009) National Bureau of Economic Research Working Paper 15434; Blyth (n 3) 173–76.

is often presented as a rigorous and neutral science or a strict mathematical exercise.[76] The empirical evidence, however, reveals that austerity is not so much an unimpeachable formula but a reflection of conservative, neo-liberal ideology. The implementation of austerity in Greece, Latin America, and Sub-Saharan Africa resulted in slow and even negative economic growth, destroyed GDP, and increased sovereign debt.[77] In Spain, Portugal, and Italy, 'the interaction between austerity and structural reforms generated a downward spiral of shrinking [GDP] and continued increases in sovereign debt'.[78] For Spain, Greece, and Portugal, austerity resulted in a second recession.[79] The tough medicine of austerity in the UK did not result in the promised balanced budget by 2015.[80] This is not the first time austerity failed in the UK. It was also ineffective in the 1930s.[81] In understanding the intellectual history of austerity, Blyth demonstrates that contemporary and highly influential arguments for the effectiveness of austerity in the last economic crisis boil down to boastful and unsupported claims.[82] The government bears the burden, and the Court should demand evidence that shows a link between discriminatory benefit reforms and economic well-being. Recent history suggests that there is weak rational connection evidence between austerity and economic health. Notwithstanding the repeated failures of austerity, it still has a gravitational pull among policy-makers. It is a quintessential example of zombie economics, a term coined by Quiggin to describe economic theories 'that persist even when the evidence that seemed to support them fails'.[83] Despite the 'ugly facts' of austerity,[84] it survives because it is not purely concerned with economic well-being but reflects political beliefs on the role of private markets being the driver of economic recovery.

Examining the rational connection between welfare reforms, austerity and economic well-being might be argued to be beyond the institutional competence of the Court. For instance, Yowell argues that courts do not have the skill to 'acquire and assess empirical research' and may 'make mistakes in understanding statistical analysis and social science methodology'.[85] Lord Carnwath makes this observation in *DA and Others*. He notes that the Court has been 'faced with detailed submissions based on conflicting factual and statistical evidence' and is sceptical as to whether that evidence can 'be properly tested within the limitation of this court's proper function'.[86] This position misunderstands the role of Courts. Courts are not being asked to rule

---

[76] Allison Corkery and Gilad Issacs, 'Human Rights Impact Assessment and the Politics of Evidence in Economic Policymaking' (2020) 24 International Journal of Human Rights 1268.
[77] Busi Sibeko, 'The Cost of Austerity: Lessons for South Africa' (2019) Institute for Economic Justice 10, 11.
[78] Philip Engler and Mathias Klein, 'Austerity Measures Amplified Crisis in Spain, Portugal and Italy' (2017) 7 DIW Economic Bulletin 89.
[79] Pearson and Elson (n 18) 12.
[80] Fairclough (n 10) 67.
[81] Blyth (n 3) 123–26; Sibeko (n 77).
[82] Blyth (n 3) 174.
[83] John Quiggin, 'Why Zombie Ideas Persist in Economics' (2011) 57 The Chronicle of Higher Education 1; John Quiggin, *Zombie Economics: How Dead Ideas Still Walk Among Us* (Princeton UP 2012).
[84] ibid.
[85] Paul Yowell, *Constitutional Rights and Constitutional Design: Moral and Empirical Reasoning in Judicial Review* (Hart Publishing 2018) 88–89.
[86] *DA and Others* (n 45) [123].

conclusively on competing economic theories. They are tasked with requiring the government to provide evidence for the rational basis for austerity motivated welfare cuts. They fail in their role if they unreflectively and uncritically accept this connection. Courts routinely weigh and balance the veracity of conflicting pieces of evidence. The weak empirical basis for austerity should prompt the Court to demand that the government provide reasons for why austerity was adopted after the crash. The government can respond with arguments such as the epistemic uncertainty of an economic crisis, or circumstances unique to the crisis, to defend the viability of austerity. A robust, context sensitive rational connection evaluation can expose the normative assumptions about markets, the role of government, the causes of the crisis and the work ethic of individuals in poverty that underpin the continued belief in austerity. This is not overstepping the role of the Court but giving due weight to equality rights to ensure discrimination is only justified when it is proportionate.

4.3 Challenging Whether a Less Intrusive Measure than Austerity Could Have Been Used

The less intrusive measures step of proportionality considers whether there are other measures that would achieve the government's goals of economic well-being that do not discriminate against women, children, or disabled persons. The Court is not tasked with 'dreaming up' any potential measure. This would exceed its institutional role and draw courts into inappropriate policy-making, particularly in the context of an emergency where decisions are made in high pressure environments and with incomplete knowledge. This limb of the justification analysis requires the government to present credible evidence that no less intrusive measures other than the benefit cap, the bedroom tax, work conditionalities, and the two-child limit would have been as effective in achieving fiscal health. The decontextualized understanding of the government's aims also skews this stage of the justification analysis as the Court does not consider whether other measures could have effectively and non-discriminatorily responded to the economic crisis, but instead scrutinizes the government's line-drawing exercise in relation to the scope of the specific benefits.

Thus, in the case law, the less intrusive measures stage focuses on tinkering with the boundaries of the various schemes and considering whether exemptions could be crafted. For example, there are two less intrusive measures canvassed in *SG and Others*. The claimants had argued that child-related benefits could have been exempted from being capped and that the cap should have been set at a different level.[87] The Court rejected both of these arguments on the basis that these alternatives would have unacceptably compromised the government's aims. According to the Court, first, 'excluding child-related benefits would reduce the savings and the number of households affected by the cap by 80 to 90%'[88] and 'the fiscal savings would be less' if the level of the cap was raised.[89] According to this argument, the only way to achieve fiscal

---

[87] The cap is set at the average earnings of working households and the argument was the cap should be set at the average income inclusive of benefits; *SG and Others* (n 35) [68].
[88] ibid [77].
[89] ibid [69].

health is to impose income poverty disproportionately on women, disabled persons, and children. There is no engagement with any other line items in the national budget or any exploration of other areas of life in which fiscal savings could be made. In *SC and CB*, Lord Reed notes that spending on child tax credit has trebled over the last ten years and that 'there is no evidence that there has been a comparable increase in expenditure on ... other benefits'.[90] However, this unduly narrows the scope of the assessment to welfare spending and fails to examine the budget in its entirety. Secondly, the government defends against a more generous cap, holding that it 'would have effectively resulted in there being no limit to the amount of benefit a household could receive'.[91] The lead judgment by Lord Reed in *SG and Others* accepts this argument, holding that the harshness of the cap is an inevitable consequence of addressing the perception that welfare spending is excessive.[92] The arguments made at the less intrusive measure stage rely on pernicious stereotypes on individual in poverty as workshy, benefit-suckers and implicitly link welfare spending to the cause of the economic crisis.

In *Carmichael and Rourke*, the analysis is also focused on whether there is a practical or affordable way to exclude disabled persons or women who experience gender-based violence from the bedroom tax.[93] This devolves into an evaluation of whether these are precise, stable and identifiable enough classes so that the exemption would not be too broad or leave out too many.[94] There was also a long assessment of the sufficiency of discretionary housing payments and the Court held that, notwithstanding the indeterminacy and administrative difficulties, the discretionary scheme was a sufficient method to compensate for an overly broad categorization in the welfare system.[95] In *SC and CB*, the argument was that there should be exemptions for consensual unplanned pregnancies or for women who have a third child when they 'believe they will be able to support the child out of their own resources, only for some misfortune to render them dependent on welfare benefits'.[96] The Court held that this would 'be completely impractical'.[97]

The third step of the proportionality analysis in the benefit case law is another form of misdirection. Focusing on the lack of precision in creating categories for welfare benefits obfuscates a more fundamental question on whether there are alternative measures to austerity that would achieve the government's aims without discriminating against marginalized groups. In mainstream economic and political discourse, austerity is presented as the exclusive way for the government to restore 'credibility in financial markets'.[98] The unavoidability of austerity is so ubiquitous that there is now a shorthand language for this position in economic discourse: TINA or 'there

---

[90] *SC and CB* (n 47) [60], [190].
[91] *SG and Others* (n 35) [123].
[92] ibid [96].
[93] *Carmichael and Rourke* (n 41) [21], [22], [26], [36], [40], [63].
[94] ibid.
[95] ibid [9], [16], [20], [41], [60], [77], [78]; *DA and Others* (n 45) [30], [31], [86], [88], [189].
[96] *SC and CB* (n 47) [206].
[97] ibid.
[98] Diane Elson, 'The Reduction of the UK Budget Deficit: A Human Rights Perspective' (2012) 26 International Review of Applied Economics 177, 178.

is no alternative'.⁹⁹ Gamble observes that 'Osborne insisted ... there was no Plan B and the Government would not be deflected from its path'.¹⁰⁰ This tone is echoed in the judgments. Lord Reed repeatedly describes the discrimination against women as 'inevitable' or 'inherent'.¹⁰¹ Even if the boundary-drawing in welfare benefits is broad, this merely amounts to an 'unfortunate consequence'.¹⁰² However, discriminatory austerity is not unavoidable and all too 'frequently [it is] taken without sufficient consideration of less harmful policy options'.¹⁰³ There is a wide range of measures that heterodox economists have proposed that could be employed in light of the banking and then subsequent sovereign debt crisis. This includes raising or imposing taxes on high-income earners, implementing a one-time capital levy, addressing tax evasion, letting the banks fail, tackling corruption, regulating the banking and financial industry, investing in health, education, childcare and other public services, and cutting spending on other areas of life such as defence.¹⁰⁴ The Women's Budget Group demonstrated that a financial transactions tax at only 0.01 per cent would raise approximately £25 billion per year in revenues, alleviating the need for discriminatory welfare cuts.¹⁰⁵

Similar to a robust rational connection argument, the role of the Court under the less intrusive measure limb is not to squarely adjudicate on the effectiveness of different economic policy responses to the crisis. Its task is more nuanced. Taking seriously its commitment to guarantee the equality of marginalized groups, the government needs to demonstrate that other non-discriminatory measures would not have been effective in protecting the economic system of the state. The Court does not need to select or create an economic recovery plan, but it needs positive evidence that discriminatory welfare reforms are in fact necessary to redress the economic crisis of 2008. If the government cannot do this, it has not discharged its burden under the proportionality analysis. In *SC and CB*, Lord Reed held that 'the appellants have not suggested any way in which the legitimate aims of the measure might have been achieved without affecting a greater number of women than men'.¹⁰⁶ The Court confuses the burden of proof. It is not for the appellant but for the government to demonstrate the necessity of austerity by demonstrating that other less intrusive measures fell short of achieving the desired aims.

---

⁹⁹ R Daniel Keleman, 'Commitment for Cowards: Why the Judicialization of Austerity is Bad Policy and Worse Politics' in Tom Ginsburg, Mark Rosen, and Georg Vanberg (eds), *Constitutions in Times of Financial Crisis* (CUP 2019).
¹⁰⁰ Gamble (n 19) 159.
¹⁰¹ *SG and Others* (n 35) [59], [61], [76], [96]; *SC and CB* (n 47) [125], [195], [196], [199].
¹⁰² *SC and CB* (n 47) [206].
¹⁰³ Oliver Hudson and Jefferson Nascimento, 'Human Rights Impact Assessments Must be Part of Economic Reforms: Interview with Juan Pablo Bohoslavsky' (2018) 15 Sur International Journal of Human Rights 165.
¹⁰⁴ Blyth (n 3) 240–45; Sibeko (n 77) 31–34; Pearson and Elson (n 18) 24; Magdalena Sepulveda Carmona, 'Alternative to Austerity: A Human Rights Framework for Economic Recovery' in Aoife Nolan (ed), *Economic and Social Rights After the Global Financial Crisis* (CUP 2014) 40.
¹⁰⁵ UK Women's Budget Group, 'The Gender Impact Assessment of the Coalition Government Budget June 2010' (2010) https://wbg.org.uk/wp-content/uploads/2016/12/RRB_Reports_12_956432831.pdf (accessed 5 August 2021).
¹⁰⁶ *SC and CB* (n 46) [198].

4.4 A Fair Balancing

The last step of the proportionality analysis assesses whether the deleterious effects of discrimination against women, children, and disabled persons via the application of the benefit cap, the bedroom tax, work conditionalities, and the two-child limit are fairly balanced against the benefits of achieving the government's aims. Jackson argues the final balancing process should provide clarification and a degree of transparency of community values.[107] This is not an easy task as it 'entails balancing rights against neoliberal economic "imperatives",[108] but at a minimum it requires a contextualized understanding of the economic crisis as the question of fair balance is sensitive to the underlying factual matrix. The Court's approach ignores the reality of the 2008 economic crisis and defers, or arguably abdicates, balancing to what the Parliament determines is fair. In *SG and Others*, Lord Reed explained that the 'level of benefits ... is inherently a political question on which opinions within a democratic society may reasonably differ widely. It is not the function of the courts to determine how much public expenditure should be devoted to welfare benefits'.[109] This abdication is repeated in *SC and CB*. Parliament has decided that importance of cutting welfare expenditure is fair, economically desirable, and socially acceptable and the resulting discriminatory impacts do not outweigh these aims. Lord Reed holds that there is 'no basis on which this court could properly take a different view'.[110] Drawing on the separation of powers arguments, he further explains that 'democratically elected institutions are in a far better position than courts to reflect ... where the balance of fairness lies'.[111]

Remembering that the government must provide weighty reasons to justify discrimination on suspect grounds, the Court needs to conduct an open assessment of the costs of achieving economic well-being through discriminatory measures.[112] As argued elsewhere, the Court minimizes the exponential inequalities that have arisen as a result of austerity-motivated benefit reforms.[113] On the other side of the scale, the strength of the government's aims is unquestionably assumed by the Court. But the gains from discriminatory welfare reforms do not withstand scrutiny. Piecing together evidence from the judgments raises serious questions on whether the negative impacts are in fact outweighed by the marginal level of fiscal savings. There also should be a more transparent evaluation of whether the burden of economic recovery is fairly distributed. If austerity is the necessary medicine after the fiscal emergency, the reforms can only be proportionate if all groups bear the costs. There were invocations of banding together to recover from the economic crisis.[114] This belies the darker reality that the austerity measures have required individuals in poverty to accept

---

[107] Vicki Jackson, 'Proportionality and Equality' in Vicki Jackson and Mark Tushnet (eds), *Proportionality: New Frontiers, New Challenges* (CUP 2017).
[108] Ben Warwick, 'Socio-Economic Rights During Economic Crisis: A Changed Approach to Non-Retrogression' (2016) 65 International and Comparative Law Quarterly 249.
[109] *SG and Others* (n 35) [72].
[110] *SC and CB* (n 47) [199].
[111] ibid [208].
[112] *SG and Others* (n 35) [188] (Lady Hale, dissenting).
[113] Campbell (n 34).
[114] Fairclough (n 10) 63.

greater disadvantage to save the banking industry and restore the state's financial competitiveness. Blyth argues that 'austerity is not just the price of saving the banks. It's the price that the banks want someone else to pay',[115] and the UK has asked lone mothers, children, disabled persons, and victims of gender-based violence to bear the cost. The Women's Budget Group revealed that 'women shoulder[ed] 70 per cent of the budget cuts, with the cuts fall[ing] especially harshly on [lone] mothers'.[116] Appreciating the origins of fiscal crisis draws attention to whether it is fair to require marginalized groups to bear the costs of the reckless economic decisions by the financial elite in the private sector. Bilchitz argues that a fair approach to austerity would place the burdens on those most culpable for the crisis.[117] By collapsing the last stage of proportionality into an assessment of Parliament's calculation of fairness, the Court fails to engage with these fundamental questions on the proportionality of an economic crisis.

5. Conclusion

In theory, courts are well placed to adjudicate claims for equality in the context of austerity after an economic crisis. A robust proportionality analysis can dissect the government's claims that there is a rational connection between excessive welfare spending and fiscal debt, demand evidence that less intrusive measures were meaningfully considered, and weigh and balance the individual's right to equality against the interests of the state. However, this promise has not been realized.

Through a light-touch review that accepts the political-economic narrative that the fiscal emergency was caused by welfare spending and the idleness of individuals in poverty, the UKSC is unable to evaluate accurately whether discrimination is a proportionate measure to restore economic well-being after propping up the financial sector. The scale and severity of the exponential inequalities against women, children, and disabled persons in poverty demand a searching and context sensitive approach that fully accounts for the role of the crisis. Currently, the Court 'dismisses the legal equality rights of individuals who live in poverty and instead consigns them to political vicissitudes'.[118] These decisions also contribute to a culture of impunity as there is little institutional accountability or responsibility for inequalities that have been exacerbated by the economic crisis. Taking seriously the role of the economic crisis in perpetuating inequalities can challenge the accepted political-economic orthodox narrative and call into question whether the discrimination against protected groups who live in poverty can be justified in the name of austerity.

---

[115] Blyth (n 3) 7.
[116] Carmona (n 104) 34, citing Fawcett Society, 'Single Mothers: Singled Out: The Impact of 2010-15 Tax and Benefit Changes on Women and Men' (2011) https://www.fawcettsociety.org.uk/single-mothers-singled-out (accessed 9 August 2021).
[117] David Bilchitz, 'Socio-Economic Rights, Economic Crisis and Legal Doctrine' (2014) 12 International Journal of Constitutional Law 710, 724.
[118] Campbell (n 48).

6
Intersecting Crises and Exponential Inequalities
The View from Hong Kong

Kelley Loper[*]

1 Introduction

This chapter considers the limits and the potential of equality law[1] to address inequalities arising from intersecting crises, that is, when more than one crisis occurs simultaneously or in close succession. It examines the case of Hong Kong, a Special Administrative Region (SAR) of China, which has recently faced multiple crises with different, but interrelated, root causes and effects. While concurrent crises may have distinct features, their impacts frequently overlap and mutually reinforce each other. As other contributions to this volume illustrate, a single crisis on its own is often enough to exacerbate existing inequalities (or produce new forms of marginalization) in many societies. Indeed, unresolved inequality itself may be characterized as a 'crisis' in its own right, whatever else is happening. Additional traumas are all the more likely to amplify disadvantage.[2]

Unfortunately, equality law in most jurisdictions lacks the capacity to prevent or remedy deep-seated inequalities even in 'normal' times, let alone in situations of single or multiple crises. These shortcomings are well documented.[3] They include, but are not limited to: single-axis approaches that fail to tackle intersectional discrimination; the exclusion of particularly disadvantaged groups, such as non-citizens; overly narrow definitions of discrimination; broad exceptions allowing for unjustifiable differential treatment; individual remedies that do not address group-based, asymmetrical disadvantage; weaknesses and underutilization of enforcement mechanisms; the absence of forums for certain groups to partake in policy-making; and political and

---

[*] Portions of the research for this chapter were supported by a General Research Fund grant awarded by the Hong Kong Research Grants Council, Project code: 17613117.
[1] In this chapter, 'equality law' includes anti-discrimination statutes and constitutional equality guarantees.
[2] On the impact of multiple crises in other contexts see 'Facing Multiple Crises: Covid-19—Impact on Vulnerable Households and Enterprises in Jordan' UNDP Jordan (2020) www.arabstates.undp.org/content/rbas/en/home/library/crisis-response0/facing-multiple-crises--covid-19--impact-on-vulnerable-household.html (accessed 3 May 2022); Michele Binci, 'The Gender Impact of Multiple Crises in Kenya' (2014) 47 Women's Studies International Forum 269.
[3] See eg Sandra Fredman, *Discrimination Law* (2nd edn, OUP 2011); Hugh Collins and Tarunabh Khaitan (eds), *Foundations of Indirect Discrimination Law* (Bloomsbury 2018); Shreya Atrey, *Intersectional Discrimination* (OUP 2019).

ideological resistance to equality law reform. While the inability of equality law to remedy structural inequalities is more evident in multiple crisis situations—and thus the need for law reform becomes more urgent—worsening discrimination can close off (already narrow) avenues for participation and prospects for progressive change.

As the following discussion suggests, such a scenario is especially likely when one of the crises is political in nature, such as a democratic deficit and/or intractable political divisions that impede the effective operation of a democratic system. When coupled with Covid-19 the impact is more pronounced.[4] Although formal democratic processes are insufficient on their own to address substantive inequalities, they are a necessary starting point. Their absence obstructs participation generally and especially for groups excluded from other areas beyond the political sphere, such as education, employment, housing, and healthcare, among others. Deepening crisis entrenches inequalities and opportunities for involvement thus recede, creating a vicious cycle. In other words, as the need for transformation grows, its possibility becomes more remote.

As Sandra Fredman has cogently explained, enhancing participation is a critical element of substantive equality that requires removing obstacles to the inclusion of groups lacking political and social voice.[5] This participative dimension of substantive equality contributes to, and is supported by, other, overlapping aims including redressing disadvantage, tackling stigma, prejudice and violence, dismantling structural discrimination, and accommodating diversity.[6] Courts can contribute to increasing the voices of under-represented minorities through the application of equality laws designed to counter the effects of ongoing disadvantage: in this way the judiciary serves broader democratic values.[7] As Fredman notes, 'courts have begun to see human rights as constitutive of democracy rather than ranged against it. With this has come the emergence of equality as a central democratic principle'.[8] A political crisis implicating judicial independence, such as Hong Kong's, can affect this democratic role. Indeed, when a democratic deficit prevails, the *general* inability to participate, compounded by a worsening, disproportionate lack of representation by marginalized communities, makes it even more difficult to advance equality claims through the courts or the political system.

At the same time, efforts to promote 'universal suffrage' understood solely in a formal procedural sense and divorced from the interconnected dimensions of substantive equality, are insufficient to achieve full participation. During a political crisis,

---

[4] Francesc Amat and others, 'Pandemics Meet Democracy: Experimental Evidence from the COVID-10 Crisis in Spain' SocArXiv (April 2020) https://osf.io/preprints/socarxiv/dkusw/ (accessed 3 May 2022); Sarah Repucci and Amy Slipowitz, 'Democracy under Lockdown: The Impact of COVID-19 on the Global Struggle for Freedom' *Freedom House* (2 October 2020) https://freedomhouse.org/sites/default/files/2020-10/COVID-19_Special_Report_Final_.pdf (accessed 3 May 2022); Todd Landman and Luca Di Gennaro Splendore, 'Pandemic Democracy: Elections and COVID-19' (2020) 23 Journal of Risk Research 1060.

[5] Sandra Fredman, 'Substantive Equality Revisited' (2016) 14 International Journal of Constitutional Law 712, 727.

[6] ibid 727.

[7] ibid 731–32. Fredman cites the famous footnote in *Carolene Products Co* 304 US 144, 152 n 4 (1938) and John Hart Ely's '"Representation-Reinforcing" Theory of Judicial Review' in John Hart Ely, *Democracy and Distrust: A Theory of Judicial Review* (Harvard UP 1980) 46. See also Sandra Fredman, 'From Deference to Democracy: The Role of Equality under the Human Rights Act 1998' (2006) 122 Law Quarterly Review 53.

[8] Fredman, 'From Deference to Democracy' (n 7) 53.

such a singular majoritarian focus may even fuel (rather than ameliorate) discrimination. On the one hand, the Hong Kong experience illustrates this dilemma and the importance of connecting equality law with broader democratic principles. During Hong Kong's political crisis, the complexity of the democracy movement has sometimes given rise to contradictory, even reactionary, impulses.[9] For example, although protesters in Hong Kong have called for greater inclusion through universal suffrage, some have also, simultaneously, forged an exclusionary local identity at the expense of certain groups that fall outside its contours. At its worst, this feature of the movement has contributed to xenophobia and racial discrimination, highlighting the need for more efficacious legal measures. The shortcomings of equality law contribute to the absence of voice and limit its ability to mitigate these aspects of an otherwise progressive cause.

On the other hand, crisis may create opportunities. Exponential inequalities arising from multiple crises starkly reveal the deficiencies of equality law and could thus spark demand for reform and reinvigorated advocacy. This could help overcome previous resistance to law reform and inspire creative non-legal solutions that buttress effective legal strategies. In other words, crises may give rise to counterbalancing forces that could alleviate some of the damaging effects. If crisis leads to an increase in the volume of an array of voices, it could open new avenues for advancing equality. Such an outcome is unlikely without attention to all elements of substantive equality, and would require a degree of transformation difficult to achieve without a representative political system.

Bearing these challenges and possibilities in mind, this chapter considers the limits of equality law but also aspects of the law that could be better leveraged to interrupt self-reinforcing cycles of disadvantage. It investigates these issues in the context of Hong Kong, a territory that has, in recent years, experienced increasing inequalities arising from a democratic deficit, shrinking space for civil society, political and ideological polarization, and strict responses to the Covid-19 pandemic. These crises intersect in complex ways with negative implications for the aims of substantive equality. Although the situation is unique in many respects, insights from Hong Kong may nevertheless inform strategies for dealing with the effects of crisis elsewhere and shed light on broader trends. Indeed, the Hong Kong crises have occurred alongside, and been influenced by, global events including the pandemic, the rise of authoritarian regimes, populist movements, geopolitical tensions, and other threats to democracy and human rights.[10] Also, its four anti-discrimination statutes replicate models from the UK and Australia, while the equality and non-discrimination provisions in the International Covenant on Civil and Political Rights (ICCPR) have been directly

---

[9] André Lecours and Luis Moreno (eds), *Nationalism and Democracy: Dichotomies, Complementarities, Oppositions* (Routledge 2010).

[10] Literature on these trends is vast. See eg Philip Alston, 'The Populist Challenge to Human Rights' (2017) 91 Human Rights Practice 1; Kenneth Roth, 'The Pushback Against the Populist Challenge' *Human Rights Watch* (2017) www.hrw.org/world-report/2018/country-chapters/global-4 (accessed 3 May 2022); Cesar Rodriquez-Garavito and Krizna Gomezet (eds), *Rising to the Populist Challenge: A New Playbook for Human Rights Actors Desjusticia* (2018) www.dejusticia.org/wp-content/uploads/2018/04/Rising-to-the-populist-challenge_1.pdf (accessed 3 May 2022); Lee Morgenbesser, *The Rise of Sophisticated Authoritarianism in Southeast Asia* (CUP 2020).

incorporated into domestic law. Hong Kong courts also rely on comparative case law from around the world. Hong Kong equality law, therefore, contains many of the same constraints and possibilities as equality law in other jurisdictions.

The remainder of the chapter proceeds as follows. Section 2 considers Hong Kong's intersecting crises, their impact on disadvantage, and some of the inequalities that have emerged (or become more evident) since the intensification of political crisis in mid-2019 and the spread of Covid-19. Section 3 then sets out the relevant legal framework and explains why it is ill-equipped to address the disadvantages amplified by crisis. It also identifies opportunities and calls for more consistent application of progressive aspects of existing law. Section 4 concludes that such legal solutions remain remote without democratic reform or a deeper commitment to change. In the meantime, however, greater attention to equality outside the political sphere may still be possible and could support future prospects for a more comprehensive response.

2 Intersecting Crises and Disadvantage in Hong Kong

This section considers the intersecting crises facing Hong Kong in recent years and their impact on growing inequalities. These crises include: (1) what I refer to generally as a 'political crisis', but which encompasses several sub-crises such as a democratic deficit and constraints on political dissent; and (2) local responses to the Covid-19 pandemic. Certain groups have been disproportionately affected, notably those denied full citizenship and associated rights. These include migrant domestic workers from the Philippines and Indonesia, new immigrants from mainland China, refugees, and people of South Asian descent, among others. These communities frequently experience intersectional disadvantage based on a range of identity categories such as national origin, gender, citizenship, and socio-economic status. Members of the political opposition in Hong Kong have also lost opportunities. At the same time, some members of the democracy movement have themselves contributed to discrimination against people from mainland China. As discussed in section 3, Hong Kong equality law has been especially ill-equipped to tackle these forms of discrimination, which are issues at the frontiers of the field of equality law more generally.

2.1 Political Context and the Democratic Deficit

The political crisis in Hong Kong has been particularly pronounced. When China resumed sovereignty over the territory in 1997 after 156 years of British colonial rule, it embarked on a unique constitutional experiment based on the principle of 'one country, two systems',[11] a formula detailed in the 1984 Sino-British Joint Declaration[12]

---

[11] First articulated by Deng Xiaoping, China's pre-eminent leader. See 'Deng Xiaoping on "One Country, Two Systems"' *China Daily* (22–23 June 1984) reproduced in Deng Xiaoping, *Selected Works of Deng Xiaoping 1982-1992)*, vol 3 (Beijing Foreign Languages Press 1994) www.chinadaily.com.cn/english/doc/2004-02/19/content_307590.htm (accessed 3 May 2022).

[12] Joint Declaration of the Government of the United Kingdom of Great Britain and Northern Ireland and the Government of the People's Republic of China on the Question of Hong Kong (19 December 1984).

and the Basic Law, Hong Kong's regional constitutional instrument.[13] The Basic Law guarantees Hong Kong a high degree of autonomy, including a separate common law legal system, an independent judiciary, autonomous immigration controls, the continued application of the ICCPR (although China has not ratified this treaty), and no change to Hong Kong's capitalist system and way of life for fifty years.[14] The Hong Kong Bill of Rights Ordinance (BOR)[15] reproduces most of the rights in the ICCPR and has constitutional status. While the Basic Law entrenches what was already a largely undemocratic governing arrangement during the colonial era, it also promises the gradual introduction of universal suffrage for the election of members of Hong Kong's legislative body, the Legislative Council (LegCo), and Hong Kong's regional leader, the Chief Executive.[16]

The slow pace of political reform, however, has led to growing dissatisfaction, polarization, mass street protests, and a democratic deficit. There have been several moments of tension since 1997, but concerns about the future of the region's autonomy boiled over in June 2019 when millions of people protested an attempt to introduce a law that would have allowed the rendition of fugitive offenders to mainland China.[17] Fears that the law would contribute to the deterioration of Hong Kong's autonomy generated a backlash.[18] Although the government ultimately withdrew the bill, the protests continued with additional demands, including full universal suffrage. Violence ensued on both sides.[19] Partly in response to the unrest, Beijing promulgated a controversial National Security Law (NSL)[20] for Hong Kong in June 2020. These developments have implications for Hong Kong's autonomy, the enjoyment of fundamental rights including freedom of expression, assembly, and association, and judicial independence.[21]

The Chinese government also introduced electoral reforms in 2021 that affected participation in the LegCo elections in December 2021 and the Chief Executive elections in 2022.[22] Only half (thirty-five of seventy) of the seats in the previous LegCo elections in 2016 were returned through broadly representative geographical constituencies.

---

[13] The Basic Law of the Hong Kong Special Administrative Region of the People's Republic of China, adopted by the National People's Congress on 4 April 1990 and took effect on 1 July 1997.

[14] ibid, arts 2, 5, 8, 39, 154.

[15] Cap 383 (BOR).

[16] Basic Law (n 13) arts 45, 68.

[17] Fugitive Offenders and Mutual Legal Assistance in Criminal Matters Legislation (Amendment) Bill 2019 www.legco.gov.hk/yr18-19/english/bills/b201903291.pdf (accessed 3 May 2022).

[18] On the constitutional implications see, Cora Chan, 'Demise of One Country, Two Systems: Reflections on the Hong Kong Rendition Saga' (2019) 49 Hong Kong Law Journal 447; Albert Chen, 'Constitutional Controversies in the Aftermath of the Anti-Extradition Movement of 2019' (2020) 50 Hong Kong Law Journal 609.

[19] Martin Purbrick, 'A Report of the 2019 Hong Kong Protests' (2019) 50 Asian Affairs 465.

[20] The Law of the People's Republic of China on Safeguarding National Security in the Hong Kong Special Administrative Region www.elegislation.gov.hk/doc/hk/a406/eng_translation_(a406)_en.pdf (accessed 3 May 2022).

[21] Carole J Petersen, 'The Disappearing Firewall: International Consequences of Beijing's Decision to Impose a National Security Law and Operate National Security Institutions in Hong Kong' (2020) 50 Hong Kong Law Journal 633.

[22] Basic Law (n 13) Annex I and Annex II as amended by the National People's Congress Standing Committee (30 March 2021); Simon NM Young, 'Introductory Note to the Decision of the National People's Congress on Improving the Election System of The Hong Kong Special Administrative Region' (2021) 60 International Legal Materials 1163.

The new system reduced this to twenty out of a total of ninety seats. Politicians from pro-democracy parties have generally had public support, but the system has precluded any real chance of governing or driving the policy agenda.[23] With some exceptions, these politicians have focused mainly on advocating for universal suffrage and less on substantive equality or social justice issues.[24] Most of the opposition politicians elected as members of LegCo in 2016 have been disqualified, resigned from their seats, and/or been charged with national security and other offences.[25]

Of the remaining seats in 2016, thirty were elected by 'functional constituencies', representing specific professional and industry groups, most with conservative interests.[26] Electors without a vote in traditional functional constituencies elected five other legislators from amongst the district councillors, who themselves had been directly elected. Initially introduced by the colonial government in 1985, functional constituencies allow corporate voting and disproportionately exclude certain groups from the political process based on socio-economic status (wealthier members of society have a greater share of the votes) and gender (the majority of voters in these professional groupings are men).[27] They have generally backed pro-government policies and cemented a powerful alliance between government and business.[28] Their representatives, with notable exceptions, have resisted the introduction of equality laws and socio-economic policies aimed at addressing poverty and housing inequality. In 2021, thirty of the ninety LegCo seats were elected by functional constituencies. An additional 40 seats, for the first time, were returned by a newly constituted Election Committee,[29] the body responsible for electing the Chief Executive. Like functional constituencies, the Election Committee is largely made up of representatives that support the interests of the local and central authorities. The number of eligible voters for members of this body decreased by 97 per cent in September 2021 as compared

---

[23] Basic Law (n 13) art 74; Regina Smyth, William Bianco, and Kwan Nok Chan, 'Legislative Rules in Electoral Authoritarian Regimes: The Case of Hong Kong's Legislative Council' (2019) 81 Journal of Politics 892.

[24] Miguel A Martínez, 'Street Occupations, Neglected Democracy, and Contested Neoliberalism in Hong Kong' (2019) 46 Social Justice 101.

[25] Jeffie Lam and others, 'Hong Kong Opposition Lawmakers to Resign En Masse over Beijing Resolution Empowering Local Government to Bypass Courts and Unseat Politicians' *South China Morning Post* (11 November 2020) www.scmp.com/news/hong-kong/politics/article/3109330/top-beijing-body-makes-patriotism-mandatory-hong-kong (accessed 3 May 2022).

[26] Joseph Chan and Elaine Chan, 'Perceptions of Universal Suffrage and Functional Representation in Hong Kong: A Confused Public?' (2006) 46 Asian Survey 257, 273.

[27] 'Report of the Hong Kong Association of Business and Professional Women on the Initial Report on the Hong Kong Special Administrative Region under the Convention on the Elimination of All Forms of Discrimination Against Women' CB(2)797/98-99(03) (*LegCo*, November 1998) www.legco.gov.hk/yr98-99/english/panels/ha/papers/p797e03.pdf (accessed 3 May 2022); Carole J Petersen, 'Stuck on Formalities: A Critique of Hong Kong's Legal Framework for Gender Equality' in Fanny M Cheung and Eleanor Holroyd (eds), *Mainstreaming Gender in Hong Kong Society* (Chinese University Press 2009) 407, 414.

[28] Christine Loh and Civic Exchange (eds), *Functional Constituencies: A Unique Feature of the Hong Kong Legislative Council* (HKU Press 2006).

[29] Hong Kong Special Administrative Region: Improve Electoral System, 'Method for the Constitution of the Election Committee' www.cmab.gov.hk/improvement/en/ceo-ele-committee/index.html (accessed 3 May 2022); Gary Cheung and Ng Kang-chung, 'Hong Kong Now has a Powerful Election Committee: Will it be a New 'Superstructure' Reshaping City's Political Landscape?' *South China Morning Post* (20 September 2021) www.scmp.com/news/hong-kong/politics/article/3149350/hong-kong-now-has-powerful-election-committee-will-it-be (accessed 3 May 2022).

with elections in 2016.[30] New requirements that only 'patriots'—broadly defined—can take up positions in the three branches of government have excluded many opposition politicians.[31]

2.2 Political Crisis, Marginalization, and Intersections with Covid-19

While political crisis has reduced participation generally, it has particularly affected marginalized communities and their ability to shape or access tools for addressing discrimination. Indeed, the democratic deficit has impeded the introduction of policies aimed at redressing structural inequalities.[32] Policy-makers have refrained from progressive decisions in a polarized climate prioritizing national security and the politicians most likely to advocate reform have resigned or been removed.[33] In addition to exclusion based on political opinion and the disparate impact of the system on women's involvement, other groups have also been left out. For example, migrant domestic workers and refugees cannot acquire permanent residency status and are thus denied the right to vote,[34] further exacerbating the democratic deficit.

These obstacles have played out against a backdrop of severe socio-economic inequality, a vast wealth gap,[35] a shortage of affordable housing, and the Covid-19 pandemic.[36] Immigrants and other marginalized communities disproportionately live in poverty in tiny, substandard flats.[37] Pandemic restrictions have aggravated the

---

[30] In 2021, 8,000 voters were eligible as compared with 246,440 in 2016. The number of registered voters for the geographical constituencies was 4,467,363 in 2021: The Government of the Hong Kong SAR, 'Voter Registration Statistics' www.voterregistration.gov.hk/eng/statistic20211.html#1 (accessed 3 May 2022).

[31] 'The criteria for a patriot are to respect one's own nation, sincerely support the resumption of the exercise of sovereignty over Hong Kong by the Motherland, and not to impair Hong Kong's prosperity and stability': Hong Kong SAR Government, 'CE Statement on NPC's Deliberation on Improving HKSAR Electoral System to Implement "Patriots Administering Hong Kong"' (5 March 2021) www.info.gov.hk/gia/general/202103/05/P2021030500393.htm (accessed 3 May 2022); Chun Han Wong and Natasha Khan, 'China All but Ends Hong Kong Democracy With "Patriots Only" Rule' *The Wall Street Journal* (11 March 2021) www.wsj.com/articles/china-all-but-ends-hong-kong-democracy-with-patriots-only-rule-11615462663 (accessed 3 May 2022).

[32] Michael Tilbury, Simon NM Young, and Ludwig Ng (eds), *Reforming Law Reform: Perspectives from Hong Kong and Beyond* (HKU Press 2014).

[33] Jeffie Lam, Lilian Cheng, and Chan Ho-him, 'Three Hong Kong Opposition Politicians Explain Why They Turned Their Backs on Legislative Council—and Where They Go from Here' *South China Morning Post* (29 November 2020) www.scmp.com/news/hong-kong/politics/article/3111788/three-hong-kong-opposition-politicians-explain-why-they (accessed 3 May 2022).

[34] Po Jen Yap, '*Vallejos Evangeline B v Commissioner of Registration*: Why Foreign Domestic-Helpers Do Not Have the Right of Abode' (2012) 41 Hong Kong Law Journal 611; Nicole Constable, 'Tales of Two Cities: Legislating Pregnancy and Marriage among Foreign Domestic Workers in Singapore and Hong Kong' (2020) 46 Journal of Ethnic and Migration Studies 3491.

[35] Hong Kong's Gini coefficient, a standard measure of income inequality, is one of the highest in the world. Oxfam Hong Kong, 'Hong Kong Inequality Report' (25 September 2018) www.oxfam.org.hk/en/f/news_and_publication/16372/Oxfam_inequality%20report_Eng_FINAL.pdf (accessed 3 May 2022).

[36] Ryan Ip and Iris Poon, 'Hong Kong's Housing Crisis: with Fewer and Smaller Flats, Quality of Life will Only Worsen' *South China Morning Post* (13 May 2021) www.scmp.com/comment/opinion/article/3133072/hong-kongs-housing-crisis-fewer-and-smaller-flats-quality-life-will (accessed 3 May 2022).

[37] Shirley Zhao, 'Living in Subdivided Flats that Nobody Wants—the Grim Struggle to Find a Home for Hong Kong's Poorer Ethnic Minorities' *South China Morning Post* (16 April 2018) www.scmp.com/news/hong-kong/community/article/2141793/living-subdivided-flats-nobody-wants-grim-struggle-find (accessed 3 May 2022).

political and socio-economic crises and lack of attention to inequalities has also exacerbated the impact of Covid-19, creating a vicious cycle.[38] As in other jurisdictions, stringent pandemic measures have affected members of some groups more than others.[39] The government has used such controls to restrict demonstrations and postpone the LegCo elections originally scheduled for September 2020, allowing more time to institute the electoral changes described above. Multiple crises have predominantly impacted groups facing intersectional disadvantage including migrant domestic workers, refugees, mainland immigrants, and people of South Asian origin. While by no means a comprehensive account, the following examples provide context for the subsequent evaluation of the legal framework.

For decades, certain policies have facilitated mistreatment of migrant domestic workers, mostly women from particular national origins.[40] For example, they are required to live with their employers (the 'live-in rule') and must leave Hong Kong within two weeks of the termination of their contracts, making it difficult for some to exit abusive situations.[41] Although migrant domestic workers receive a minimum monthly wage, there are no limits on working hours. During the pandemic, the government singled out this group for mandatory vaccination and weekly testing. The implication that these workers were more likely to spread disease generated a backlash and, although the government backtracked after objections by the Philippine and Indonesian consulates, public discussion of the issues perpetuated negative stereotypes.[42] During a surge of Omicron infections in early 2022, some employers of migrant workers reportedly fired their employees if they became sick or forced them to live on the streets.[43]

---

[38] 'Covid-19 Further Entrenched Income, Health, Racial and Educational Inequalities Across Hong Kong, Experts Say' *South China Morning Post* (28 December 2020) www.scmp.com/news/hong-kong/health-environment/article/3115488/how-covid-19-further-entrenched-income-health (accessed 3 May 2022); Vivian Wang and Tiffany May, 'In "Coffin Homes" and "Cages", Hong Kong Lockdown Exposes Inequality' *New York Times* (26 January 2021) www.nytimes.com/2021/01/26/world/asia/hong-kong-coronavirus-lockdown-inequality.html (accessed 3 May 2022); Roger Yat-Nork Chung and others, 'COVID-19 Related Health Inequality Exists Even in a City Where Disease Incidence is Relatively Low: A Telephone Survey in Hong Kong' (2021) 75 Journal of Epidemiology and Community Health 616.

[39] The Chinese University of Hong Kong Institute of Health Equity, 'Forum on Social Determinants of Health Inequality and COVID-19' (2 June 2020) www.ihe.cuhk.edu.hk/forum-on-social-determinants-of-health-inequality-and-covid-19/ (accessed 3 May 2022).

[40] Thanh-Dam Truong, 'Intersectionality, Structural Vulnerability, and Access to Sexual and Reproductive Health Services: Filipina Domestic Workers in Hong Kong, Singapore, and Qatar' in Thanh-Dam Truong and others (eds), *Migration, Gender and Social Justice: Perspectives on Human Insecurity* (Springer 2014); JTK Cheung and others, 'Abuse and Depression among Filipino Foreign Domestic Helpers. A Cross-sectional Survey in Hong Kong' (2019) 166 Public Health 121.

[41] Raquel Carvalho, 'Study Finds Hong Kong Domestic Helpers Subjected to Employment Terms Abuse by More than 70 per cent of Agencies' *South China Morning Post* (11 May 2017) www.scmp.com/news/hong-kong/law-crime/article/2093836/study-finds-hong-kong-domestic-helpers-subjected-employment (accessed 3 May 2022).

[42] Rina Chandran, 'Hong Kong Pauses Plan to Force COVID-19 Vaccines on Migrant Maids' *Reuters* (4 May 2021) www.reuters.com/article/healthcoronavirus-hongkong-idUSL8N2MQ27N (accessed 3 May 2022).

[43] Kathleen Magramo, 'Domestic Helpers Denied Treatment, Forced to Sleep Rough after Testing Positive During Hong Kong's Fifth Coronavirus Wave' *South China Morning Post* (18 February 2022) www.scmp.com/news/hong-kong/health-environment/article/3167607/domestic-helpers-denied-treatment-forced-sleep (accessed 3 May 2022).

Government policies have also contributed to disadvantage faced by refugees and asylum seekers. Although the 1951 Convention relating to the status of Refugees does not apply to Hong Kong, the authorities introduced a mechanism in 2014 to determine whether applicants would be at risk of serious harm if returned to their countries of origin.[44] Successful claimants are not removed from Hong Kong but are also not granted status and remain illegal immigrants until resettled in a third country.[45] The substantiation rate for *non-refoulement* claims is less than one per cent, much lower than in other jurisdictions with similar systems.[46] In March 2021, new legislation added obstacles for claimants to succeed or even arrive in Hong Kong in the first place.[47] The removal of opposition politicians facilitated the smooth passage of these provisions. Refugees have also been denied socio-economic rights on an unequal basis. Claimants have faced difficulties obtaining sufficient food, housing, and healthcare especially during the pandemic.[48] Even if successful in their claims, many remain stuck in limbo for years before being resettled in another country. They do not have the right to work, although some have been granted temporary permission on a case by case basis.[49]

The protest movement and the pandemic have also amplified discrimination against mainland immigrants.[50] Immigration from the mainland into Hong Kong increased substantially after 1997. Unlike migrant domestic workers and refugees, these arrivals may obtain permanent residency after seven years of ordinary residence, but many live in relative poverty.[51] The majority are women, adding an intersectional dimension that has largely been overlooked.[52] Negative attitudes toward mainland immigrants

---

[44] *Secretary for Security v Sakthevel Prabakar* (2004) 7 HKCFAR 187; *Ubamaka v Director of Immigration* (2012) 15 HKCFAR 743; *C v Director of Immigration* [2013] HKEC 428.

[45] Ada Pui Yim Lai and Kerry J Kennedy, 'Refugees and Civic Stratification: The "Asian rejection" Hypothesis and Its Implications for Protection Claimants in Hong Kong' (2017) 26 Asian and Pacific Migration Journal 206.

[46] Justice Centre Hong Kong, 'Submission to the United Nations Human Rights Committee: List of Issues on the Fourth Report of the Hong Kong Special Administrative Region under the International Covenant on Civil and Political Rights' (May 2020) www.justicecentre.org.hk/framework/uploads/2020/05/Justice-Centre-Hong-Kong-List-of-Issues-Submission-to-Human-Rights-Committee-Final.pdf (accessed 3 May 2022).

[47] Immigration (Amendment) Ordinance 2021 www.legco.gov.hk/yr20-21/english/ord/2021ord007-e.pdf (accessed 8 May 2022); Virginie Goethals, 'Give Refugees and Others a Chance to Speak out on a New Hong Kong Law Set to Curtail Their Rights' *Hong Kong Free Press* (4 February 2021) https://hongkongfp.com/2021/02/04/give-refugees-and-others-a-chance-to-speak-out-on-a-new-hong-kong-law-set-to-curtail-their-rights/ (accessed 3 May 2022).

[48] Refugee Concern Network, 'Parallel Report to the Committee on Economic Social and Cultural Rights' (December 2020) www.justicecentre.org.hk/framework/uploads/2020/12/Refugee-Concern-Network-ICESCR-parallel-report.pdf (accessed 3 May 2022).

[49] *GA v Director of Immigration* (2014) 17 HKCFAR 60.

[50] Fiona Sun, 'Insulted, Humiliated, Shunned: Hong Kong's Mainland Chinese Immigrants Face Unending Discrimination in Struggle to Feel at Home, Survey Shows' *South China Morning Post* (2 October 2021) www.scmp.com/news/hong-kong/society/article/3150851/insulted-humiliated-shunned-hong-kongs-mainland-chinese (accessed 3 May 2022).

[51] Kee-Lee Chou, Kelvin Cheung, and Maggie Lau, 'Trends in Child Poverty in Hong Kong Immigrant Families' (2014) 117 Social Indicators Research 811.

[52] Census and Statistics Department Hong Kong Special Administrative Region, 'Women and Men in Hong Kong, Key Statistics (2020)' 29 table 1.14 (Persons from the Mainland of China Having Resided in Hong Kong for Less than 7 Years by Sex and Duration of Residence in Hong Kong) www.statistics.gov.hk/pub/B11303032020AN20B0100.pdf (accessed 3 May 2022),.

have also intensified over the years.⁵³ The recent social and political movements in Hong Kong have fuelled the emergence of a distinct Hong Kong identity, referred to as 'localism', especially in the aftermath of the 2014 Umbrella Movement and the 2019 protests.⁵⁴ Attempts to shape a Hong Kong identity in opposition to being 'Chinese', however, led to increasing xenophobia toward new immigrants and others from mainland China. People from the mainland have also faced discrimination in access to services. At the beginning of the pandemic in 2020, when news broke of the outbreak in Wuhan, China, at least 100 Hong Kong restaurants supporting the pro-democracy movement refused to serve mainland Chinese customers.⁵⁵

Another group experiencing disproportionate poverty and discrimination are residents of South Asian origin who trace their lineage to countries such as Nepal, India, and Pakistan.⁵⁶ While some are more recent immigrants, many have roots in Hong Kong that go back to the nineteenth century. South Asian minorities have faced difficulties accessing education, employment, housing, and other services for decades.⁵⁷ Covid-19 has exacerbated this situation and has probably increased poverty rates.⁵⁸ In January 2021, the government began what it called 'ambush' lockdowns and their first target was a neighbourhood where many South Asian minority families live. Rather than commenting on the effects of the crowded, substandard living conditions, the head of the Centre for Health Protection claimed that the risk of Covid-19 was high in these communities because they 'like to gather with [their] fellow countrymen to share food and chat together'.⁵⁹ Although the Chief Executive quickly distanced herself from these comments, a local non-governmental organization (NGO) observed

---

⁵³ Siu-yau Lee and Kee-lee Chou, 'Explaining Attitudes Toward Immigrants from Mainland China in Hong Kong' (2018) 27 Asian and Pacific Migration Journal 273; Juan Chen and others, 'Effects of Neighborhood Discrimination Towards Mainland Immigrants on Mental Health in Hong Kong' (2019) 16 International Journal of Environmental Research and Public Health 1025.

⁵⁴ Malte Philipp Kaeding, 'The Rise of "Localism" in Hong Kong' (2017) 28 Journal of Democracy 157; Ying-ho Kwong, 'The Growth of "Localism" in Hong Kong' (2016) China Perspectives 63; Samson Yuen and Sanho Chung, 'Explaining Localism in Post-handover Hong Kong: An Eventful Approach' (2018) China Perspectives 19; Gordan Mathews, 'The Hong Kong Protests in Anthropological Perspective: National Identity and What it Means' (2020) 40 Critique of Anthropology 264.

⁵⁵ Victor Ting, 'Coronavirus: More than 100 Hong Kong Restaurants Refuse to Serve Customers from Mainland China, Investigation Reveals' *South China Morning Post* (5 March 2020) www.scmp.com/news/hong-kong/health-environment/article/3065262/coronavirus-more-100-hong-kong-restaurants-refuse (accessed 3 May 2022).

⁵⁶ Census and Statistics Department Hong Kong Special Administrative Region, 'Hong Kong Poverty Situation: Report on Ethnic Minorities 2016' (February 2018) www.statistics.gov.hk/pub/B9XX0004E2016XXXXE0100.pdf (accessed 3 May 2022).

⁵⁷ Mercado Solutions Associates Ltd, commissioned by the Hong Kong Equal Opportunities Commission, 'Study on Discrimination against Ethnic Minorities in the Provision of Goods, Services and Facilities, and Disposal and Management of Premises' (September 2016) www.eoc.org.hk/EOC/Upload/UserFiles/File/ResearchReport/201609/EM-GSF_Report(Eng)V8_2_final.pdf (accessed 3 May 2022); Loh Ka Yee Elizabeth and Hung On Ying, 'A Study on the Challenges Faced by Mainstream Schools in Educating Ethnic Minorities in Hong Kong' Oxfam Hong Kong (January 2020) www.eoc.org.hk/en/policy-advocacy-and-research/research-reports/2020-4 (accessed 3 May 2022); Centre for Youth Research and Practice Hong Kong Baptist University, commissioned by the Hong Kong Equal Opportunities Commission, 'A Study on Education and Career Pathways of Ethnic Minority Youth in Hong Kong' (June 2020) www.eoc.org.hk/EOC/upload/ResearchReport/20200619_em.pdf (accessed 3 May 2022).

⁵⁸ Interview with Hong Kong UNISON (Hong Kong, 13 September 2021) (UNISON).

⁵⁹ Jessie Lau, 'In Hong Kong, COVID-19 and Racism Make an Ugly Mix' *The Diplomat* (22 January 2021) https://thediplomat.com/2021/01/in-hong-kong-covid-19-and-racism-make-an-ugly-mix/ (accessed 3 May 2022).

a subsequent increase in discrimination against their clients of South Asian origin in employment and the provision of services.[60]

3 Equality Law in Hong Kong: Resistance, Stagnation, and Potential

Can Hong Kong equality law address these problems? In its current state, it is ill-equipped to prevent or remedy such complex disadvantage. Indeed, the law's shortcomings have limited its potential to achieve positive change even in 'normal' times. This section considers the history of equality law in Hong Kong, including resistance to anti-discrimination legislation, problems with the text of the legislative provisions and their enforcement, and the potential (but inconsistent application) of the constitutional right to equality.

3.1 Anti-discrimination Legislation

Although the British colonial government imported a number of laws to Hong Kong, it did not introduce anti-discrimination legislation until the mid-1990s. Indeed, many of the problems discussed above have roots in pre-1997 policies. The colonial government only began to champion more progressive law reform after the Chinese government's response to student protests in Beijing in 1989, which sparked concerns about the future of human rights in Hong Kong under Chinese sovereignty.[61] The BOR directly incorporated the ICCPR in 1991, the British extended the Convention on the Elimination of All Forms of Discrimination against Women (CEDAW) to Hong Kong in 1996, and three anti-discrimination laws—the Sex Discrimination Ordinance (SDO),[62] Disability Discrimination Ordinance (DDO),[63] and Family Status Discrimination Ordinance (FSDO)[64]—were enacted between 1995 and 1997. The legislation also established an Equal Opportunities Commission (EOC) with the power to investigate and conciliate discrimination claims.[65] As discussed below, only one additional anti-discrimination law, the Race Discrimination Ordinance (RDO),[66] was enacted more than a decade later in 2008.

Despite these advances, the piecemeal, single-axis approach has limited the scope and impact of these laws. Anna Wu, a former LegCo member, had tabled a more

---

[60] 'Hong Kong's Lam says Covid-19 Spike has "Nothing to do with Ethnicity" after Health Official's Comments' *Hong Kong Free Press* (19 January 2021) https://hongkongfp.com/2021/01/19/hong-kongs-lam-says-covid-19-spike-has-nothing-to-do-with-ethnicity-after-health-officials-comments/ (accessed 3 May 2022); UNISON (n 58).

[61] Cora Chan, 'Thirty Years from Tiananmen: China, Hong Kong, and the Ongoing Experiment to Preserve Liberal Values in an Authoritarian State' (2019) 17 International Journal of Constitutional Law 439, 441.

[62] Cap 480 (SDO).
[63] Cap 487.
[64] Cap 527.
[65] SDO (n 62) pt 7.
[66] Cap 602.

comprehensive Equal Opportunities Bill in 1994 covering a range of grounds in one cohesive piece of legislation.[67] The authorities, however, opposed the Bill and instead countered with separate draft laws with fewer protected characteristics.[68] The statutes also contain broad exceptions for blatantly discriminatory policies. For example, the SDO incorporates a reservation made to CEDAW preserving the Small House Policy, which grants the right to build small houses to male (but not female) descendants of indigenous inhabitants of the New Territories (those living in villages in an area of Hong Kong near the border with mainland China before 1898).[69] Because of this reservation and constitutional protections for the traditional rights and interests of indigenous villagers,[70] legal challenges to this policy have failed.[71]

Ongoing resistance to anti-discrimination law by powerful interests has impeded further development. The Basic Law entrenches some regressive elements of the colonial executive-led system including the largely unrepresentative legislature and the alliance between business and government. These aspects of the colonial legacy have continued to thwart political reform and limited equality law's ability to address fully the intersectional inequalities described above. A stated commitment to 'free market' ideology—preserved by the Basic Law[72]—underpinned the business community's initial opposition to the introduction of discrimination legislation. Influential business leaders expressed concerns that anti-discrimination law would interfere with employers' freedom and entail burdensome costs.[73] Despite a stated commitment to 'freedom' in this sense, many also opposed democracy.[74] As discussed, the ongoing democratic deficit has contributed to various forms of exclusion within and beyond the political arena; this dynamic has largely foreclosed additional anti-discrimination legislation.[75] After the enactment of the three initial statutes, attempts to introduce legislation prohibiting discrimination on the grounds of race, age, and sexual orientation were unsuccessful. Eventually, LegCo enacted the RDO in 2008 after sustained local advocacy and pressure by UN human rights bodies.[76] At that point, many business groups expressed support, perhaps because the earlier laws had generated a small number of discrimination claims.[77]

---

[67] Petersen (n 27).

[68] ibid.

[69] KW Ma, 'Sustainable Development and Social Policy: A Case of Indigenous Villages in Hong Kong' (2016) 5 Asian Education and Development Studies 305.

[70] Basic Law (n 13) art 40.

[71] *Kwok Cheuk Kin v Director of Lands No 2* (2021) 24 HKCFAR 349.

[72] Basic Law (n 13) art 5.

[73] Carole J Petersen, 'Hong Kong's First Anti-Discrimination Laws and their Potential Impact on the Employment Market' (1997) 27 Hong Kong Law Journal 324; Barry Sautman and Ellen Kneehans, *The Politics of Racial Discrimination in Hong Kong* (Maryland Series in Contemporary Asian Studies 2002).

[74] Alvin Y So, 'Hong Kong's Problematic Democratic Transition: Power Dependency or Business Hegemony?' (2000) 59 Journal of Asian Studies 359.

[75] The government implemented only 8 of the EOC's 78 recommendations. Equal Opportunities Commission, 'Discrimination Law Review, Submissions to the Government' (March 2016) www.eoc.org.hk/eoc/upload/DLR/2016330179502227490.pdf (accessed 3 May 2022).

[76] Carole J Petersen and Kelley Loper, 'Equal Opportunities Law Reform in Hong Kong' in Michael Tilbury, Simon NM Young, and Ludwig Ng (eds), *Reforming Law Reform: Perspectives from Hong Kong and Beyond* (HKU Press 2014) 173.

[77] In 2001, the Home Affairs Bureau commented: 'The results of our consultations indicate that the business sector is more open to legislation than previously, perhaps because it has had time to adapt to the three existing anti-discrimination laws.' Home Affairs Bureau, Government of the Hong Kong SAR, 'Legislating

These four laws together prohibit direct and indirect discrimination on the grounds of sex, marital status, pregnancy, breastfeeding, disability, responsibility for the care of a close family member, race, colour, descent, and ethnic or national origin. Sexual, disability, and racial harassment are unlawful, as is victimization (on all grounds), and vilification and serious vilification based on sex, disability, and race. The statutes cover discrimination in the private and public sectors in employment, education, the provision of goods, facilities and services, and government functions and powers (except the RDO, which excludes many government functions).[78] Although modelled on older anti-discrimination legislation in the UK and Australia, including the UK's 1975 Sex Discrimination Act and 1976 Race Relations Act, the government has not incorporated recent comparative developments that have strengthened discrimination law in other jurisdictions. For example, the definition of indirect discrimination is based on the older UK definition requiring the plaintiff to show the respondent had imposed a 'requirement or condition' with a disproportionate, negative, and unjustifiable impact on a group defined by a protected characteristic. The government rejected proposals to adopt the broader concept of 'provision, criterion or practice' in the UK Race Relations Act, amended in 2003 to implement the European Union Racial Equality Directive.[79] The government has also declined recommendations to add a duty to provide reasonable accommodation in the DDO. While all four laws allow for 'special measures', reasonably intended to ensure equal opportunities, these provisions have not been used.[80]

Although the definition of 'race' in the RDO duplicates the expansive list in article 1 of the International Convention on the Elimination of all forms of Racial Discrimination, it disallows claims of either direct or indirect discrimination related to nationality, citizenship, immigration status, or length of stay in Hong Kong.[81] These exceptions were apparently included to prevent challenges to policies that disproportionately disadvantage migrant groups.[82] In particular, the Hong Kong government took the position that the RDO should not cover discrimination against mainland Chinese since they are of the same 'ethnic stock' as Hong Kong people.[83] They explained: '[t]he discrimination experienced by new arrivals from the Mainland is not based on race. Rather, it is a form of social discrimination and therefore outside the intended scope of the Bill.'[84] As a result, the RDO is unlikely to apply to the exclusion of mainland Chinese from restaurants during the pandemic although this appears to

---

Against Racial Discrimination, a Consultation Paper' (September 2004) [11] www.info.gov.hk/archive/consult/2005/lard-e.pdf (accessed 3 May 2022).

[78] *Sing Arjun v Secretary for Justice* [2016] HKEC 1210; Petersen and Loper (n 76).
[79] Legislative Council, 'Report of the Bills Committee on Race Discrimination Bill' (30 June 2008) [36]–[38] www.legco.gov.hk/yr06-07/english/bc/bc52/reports/bc520709cb2-2478-e.pdf (accessed 3 May 2022).
[80] The UN Committee on the Elimination of Discrimination against Women has expressed concern about this absence of special measures, CEDAW/C/CHN/CO/7-8 (14 Nov 2014) [52]–[53].
[81] RDO, s 8(3).
[82] EOC, 'Submissions' (n 75) 108–109, citing a local NGO report that asylum seekers 'often receive subpar services at healthcare, education and other services for which they are eligible compared to other local residents or foreign visitors'.
[83] Hong Kong SAR Government, 'Legislating Against Racial Discrimination, A Consultation Paper' (September 2004) [24], [25] www.info.gov.hk/archive/consult/2005/lard-e.pdf (accessed 3 May 2022).
[84] ibid.

involve direct or indirect forms of 'origin' discrimination. These exceptions for immigration status and the exclusion of most government functions and powers also undermine the RDO's potential to address discrimination against refugees, asylum seekers, and migrant domestic workers based on their status, or lack of status, in Hong Kong. The government has repeatedly disregarded UN human rights treaty bodies' recommendations to amend the RDO and introduce protections from discrimination on the grounds of nationality, sexual orientation, religion, gender identity, and age.[85]

In addition to these problems with the provisions themselves, implementation has been weak and the available enforcement mechanisms remain underutilized.[86] First, the burden of proof does not explicitly shift to the respondent when the plaintiff makes out a prima facie case of discrimination on the facts.[87] Also, while the legislation grants the EOC significant powers, certain factors have limited its impact. For example, the EOC has a statutory duty to attempt conciliation before providing assistance for meritorious claims not successfully conciliated (and even then, funding is insufficient to support many of them).[88] Early research on the EOC's conciliation mechanism revealed problems with the imbalance of power between claimants and respondents.[89] Shortly after its establishment, the EOC challenged some government policies, including direct discrimination against girls in allocating secondary school places.[90] However, the government did not renew the contract of the EOC chairperson who had initiated those legal actions. Since then, the government-appointed chairpersons have rarely contested potentially discriminatory government policies through litigation.[91] An NGO working with South Asian minorities observed that despite discrimination experienced by members of these groups falling within the RDO, many of their clients are reluctant to approach the EOC due to perceptions that the investigation and conciliation processes are slow, fears of losing their jobs after making a complaint, and a focus on immediate livelihood issues.[92]

Few cases make it to the courts, also limiting the development of anti-discrimination law. Calls to improve access to justice by establishing an equal opportunities tribunal have been rejected.[93] Since the SDO came into force in 1996, the Court of Final Appeal, Hong Kong's apex court, has only decided three related sex discrimination cases.[94] The

---

[85] The Committee on Economic, Social, and Cultural Rights expressed concern 'about the prevalent and widespread discrimination against some disadvantaged and marginalized groups, such as migrants and internal migrants, asylum-seekers and refugees' E/C.12/CHN/CO/2 (13 June 2014).

[86] UNISON (n 58).

[87] EOC (n 75) 75–80.

[88] In 2021, the EOC granted legal aid in 11 of 20 applications www.eoc.org.hk/en/Statistic?year=2021 (accessed 3 May 2022).

[89] Carole J Petersen, 'Investigation and Conciliation of Employment Discrimination Claims in the Context of Hong Kong' (2001) 5 Employee Rights and Employment Policy Journal 627.

[90] *Equal Opportunities Commission v Director of Education* [2001] 2 HKLRD 690.

[91] Puja Kapai, 'The Hong Kong Equal Opportunities Commission: Calling for a New Avatar' (2009) 39 Hong Kong Law Journal 339.

[92] UNISON (n 58).

[93] Equal Opportunities Commission, 'Equal Opportunities Commission's Recommendations to the Government on the Establishment of an Equal Opportunities Tribunal in Hong Kong' (March 2009) www.eoc.org.hk/en/PressRelease/Detail/8144 (accessed 3 May 2022).

[94] *Secretary for Justice & Others v Chan Wah & Others* [2000] 3 HKLRD 641; *Leung Kwok Hung (Long Hair) v Commissioner of Correctional Services* (2020) 23 HKCFAR 456; *Kwok Cheuk Kin v Director of Lands No 2* (2021) 24 HKCFAR 349.

first concerned complex electoral arrangements for village elections in Hong Kong's rural areas that excluded the non-indigenous male spouses of female villagers. The second challenged a requirement that male, but not female, prisoners have their hair cut short. The third contested the Small House Policy, as discussed below. At the time of writing, the courts had considered fewer than thirty claims of disability discrimination and only a handful involving the FSDO and the RDO.

Although these problems with anti-discrimination laws and their enforcement persist, the current political climate has, paradoxically, presented unexpected, if limited, opportunities for reform. For example, ongoing discrimination against people from mainland China has prompted the government's re-evaluation of the initial exclusion of such discrimination from the RDO. The Constitutional and Mainland Affairs Bureau announced in October 2021 that '[w]e are in close liaison with the EOC to study how the anti-discrimination legislation may be enhanced to tackle discrimination or vilification that may be encountered by persons arriving in Hong Kong from the Mainland'.[95] Upcoming reviews by UN treaty bodies of Hong Kong's human rights record under the ICCPR and International Covenant on Economic, Social and Cultural Rights (ICESCR) may have also influenced this decision.[96] Indeed, human rights reviews have sometimes motivated legal changes in Hong Kong, including the introduction of the RDO.[97] The authorities' concerns about Hong Kong's international human rights reputation in the wake of global criticism of the NSL may also encourage reform, at least in less politically sensitive areas. Shortly before the promulgation of the NSL in June 2020, the Chief Executive sent a video to the UN Human Rights Council justifying the new law on human rights grounds.[98] Whether attention to human rights is born out in practice, these attempts to defend Hong Kong's reputation at the international level suggest some room for leverage, at least in fields such as equality law that do not directly challenge primary state interests.

---

[95] Legislative Council Panel on Constitutional Affairs, 'Policy Initiatives of the Constitutional and Mainland Affairs Bureau in Relation to Electoral Arrangements, Promotion of the Constitution and the Basic Law, Promotion of Equal Opportunities and Elimination of Discrimination, Etc.' (October 2021) 23 www.legco.gov.hk/yr20-21/english/panels/ca/papers/ca20211018cb4-1631-1-e.pdf (accessed 8 June 2022).

[96] UN Human Rights Committee, 'List of Issues in Relation to the Fourth Periodic Report of Hong Kong, China' CCPR/C/CHN-HKG/Q/4 (26 August 2020); Committee on Economic, Social and Cultural Rights, 'List of Issues in Relation to the Fourth Periodic Report of Hong Kong, China' E/C.12/CHN-HKG/Q/4 (7 April 2021).

[97] The Hong Kong Government mentioned treaty body recommendations in its brief to LegCo when tabling the draft RDO in December 2006: Home Affairs Bureau, 'Legislative Council Brief: Race Discrimination Bill' [6] www.legco.gov.hk/yr06-07/english/bills/brief/b12_brf.pdf (accessed 3 May 2022); Petersen and Loper (n 76).

[98] 'Carrie Lam Defends National Security Law in Speech to United Nations' (*South China Morning Post*, 30 June 2020) www.scmp.com/video/china/3091249/carrie-lam-defends-national-security-law-speech-united-nations (accessed 3 May 2022); The Government of the Hong Kong SAR Press Release, 'Video Message by CS at the 45th Session of the UN Human Rights Council' (15 September 2020) www.info.gov.hk/gia/general/202009/15/P2020091500878.htm (accessed 3 May 2022).

3.2 Constitutional Right to Equality and Non-discrimination

The constitutional right to equality—which binds the government and public authorities—has been more effective than anti-discrimination legislation and may be better equipped to promote progressive, systemic change. As discussed, judicial review of discriminatory law and policy is an important tool for promoting voice in support of substantive equality and democratic principles.[99] Hong Kong constitutional law is firmly grounded in international human rights, notably the ICCPR, and the Basic Law allows courts to refer to comparative case law for guidance.[100] This openness to external legal influences has encouraged the development of a robust, purposive approach to human rights adjudication generally and in cases involving the right to equality in particular.[101] The courts apply a proportionality test to determine the legitimacy of any restrictions to non-absolute rights and have struck down unconstitutional laws.[102]

Article 25 of the Basic Law guarantees the right to equality before the law and articles 1 and 22 of the BOR (ICCPR, articles 2.1, 3, and 26) require protection from discrimination based on a non-exhaustive list of grounds: 'such as race, colour, sex, language, religion, political or other opinion, national or social origin, property, birth or other status'. When construing these provisions, Hong Kong courts have articulated certain elements of an emerging substantive equality doctrine.[103] The value of human dignity has been an important interpretive tool and supports such a substantive reading.[104] The courts have clarified that discrimination is a denial of dignity and dignity plays a role in determining when government reasons for differential treatment require strict scrutiny. The courts have also recognized that a right to equality prohibits indirect, as well as direct, discrimination and the non-exhaustive list of prohibited grounds has allowed for the inclusion of protected characteristics not explicitly mentioned, especially sexual orientation.[105]

These aspects of substantive equality are evident in the Court of Final Appeal's decision in *QT v Director of Immigration*,[106] a case challenging the refusal to grant a dependent visa to the same-sex partner of an expatriate woman working in Hong Kong. The court held that this policy (based on marital status) amounted to indirect sexual

---

[99] Fredman (n 7).
[100] Basic Law (n 13) art 84.
[101] Sir Anthony Mason, 'The Place of Comparative Law in Developing the Jurisprudence on the Rule of Law and Human Rights in Hong Kong' (2007) 37 Hong Kong Law Journal 299; Albert HY Chen, 'International Human Rights Law and Domestic Constitutional Law: Internationalisation of Constitutional Law in Hong Kong' (2009) 4 NTU Law Review 237.
[102] *Ng Ka Ling v Director of Immigration* (1999) 2 HKCFAR 4; *Leung Kwok Hung v HKSAR* (2005) 8 HKCFAR 229; *Hysan Development Co Ltd v Town Planning Board* (2016) 19 HKCFAR 372 (hereafter *Hysan*); Rehan Abeyratne, 'More Structure, More Deference: Proportionality in Hong Kong' in Po Jen Yap (ed), *Proportionality in Asia* (CUP 2020).
[103] Kelley Loper, 'Human Rights and Substantive Equality: Prospects for Same-Sex Relationship Recognition in Hong Kong' (2019) 44 North Carolina Journal of International Law 273.
[104] Kelley Loper, 'Dignity as a Constitutional Value in Hong Kong: Toward a Contextual Approach?' in Jimmy Chia-Shin Hsu (ed), *Human Dignity in Asia: Dialogue between Law and Culture* (CUP 2022).
[105] *Secretary for Justice v Yau Yuk Lung* (2007) 10 HKCFAR 335.
[106] *QT v Director of Immigration* (2018) 21 HKCFAR 324.

orientation discrimination. In doing so, it cited Lord Walker of Gestingthorpe in *R (Carson) v Secretary of State for Work and Pensions*,[107] who explained: 'In the field of human rights, discrimination is regarded as particularly objectionable because it disregards the fundamental notion of human dignity and equality before the law'.[108] The court affirmed that sexual orientation is among the 'core values' or 'suspect or prohibited grounds ... which, if used as a ground for discrimination, are recognized as particularly demeaning for the victim'.[109] In such cases, 'the government's margin of discretion is much narrowed and the court will subject the impugned measure to "particularly severe scrutiny"'.[110] The government must provide '"particularly convincing and weighty reasons" to justify the challenged difference in treatment'.[111] While the judgment does not expressly mention intersectional discrimination, its fluid consideration of marital status and sexual orientation as prohibited grounds and the reliance on interpretive materials produced by international human rights bodies suggest possibilities for development.[112]

The courts have also applied the right to equality when reviewing potentially discriminatory policies in the socio-economic field. Unlike article 1 of the BOR, article 22 is autonomous and does not limit the equality review only to discriminatory treatment in relation to other civil and political rights.[113] The Court of Final Appeal has explained that '[i]t would be appropriate for the courts to intervene (indeed they would be duty-bound to do so) where, even in the area of socio-economic or other government policies, there has been any disregard for core-values'.[114] Therefore, even in relation to socio-economic policy, if 'the reason for unequal treatment strikes at the heart of core-values ... (such as race, colour, gender, sexual orientation, religion, politics, or social origin), the courts would extremely rarely (if at all) find this acceptable'.[115]

The courts, however, have developed this substantive equality doctrine within a small number of domains and have not applied it consistently to other areas or identified its broader implications. This is especially true in cases involving new immigrants, migrant domestic workers, and refugees who, as discussed, frequently face intersectional disadvantage. For example, the equality jurisprudence has not recognized the possible intersections between immigration status and the 'core values' such as race, sex, etc. Equality was not considered in challenges to the 'live-in rule' and the denial of migrant domestic workers' applications for permanent residency, despite the disproportionate impact on women from certain national origins.[116] The

[107] [2006] 1 AC 173 [49], as cited in ibid [27].
[108] *R (Carson) v Secretary of State for Work and Pensions* [2006] 1 AC 173 [49].
[109] *QT* (n 106) [107], citing *Carson* (ibid) [55].
[110] *QT* (n 106) [108], citing *Fok Chun Wa v Hospital Authority* [2012] 15 HKCFAR 409.
[111] *QT* (n 106), citing: *Carson* (n 108) [58]; *Stec v United Kingdom* (2006) 43 EHRR 47 [52]; *EB v France* (2008) 47 EHRR 21 [91]; *AL (Serbia) v Secretary of State for the Home Department* [2008] 1 WLR 1434 [29]; *Humphreys v Revenue and Customs Commissioners* [2012] 1 WLR 1545 [16]; *Taddeucci v Italy* (Application No 51362/09, 30 June 2016) [89]; *Hysan* (n 102) [111].
[112] UN Committee on Economic, Social and Cultural Rights, General Comment No 20, UN Doc E/C.12/GC/20, (2 July 2009) [17] [27]. Cf Shreya Atrey, 'Fifty Years On: The Curious Case of Intersectional Discrimination in the ICCPR' (2017) 35 Nordic Journal of Human Rights 220.
[113] Human Rights Committee, General Comment No 18: Non-discrimination (10 November 1989) [12].
[114] *Fok Chun Wa* (n 110).
[115] ibid.
[116] *Vallejos and Domingo v Commissioner of Registration* [2013] 2 HKLRD 533; *Comilang Milagros Tecson v Director of Immigration* [2019] HKCFA 10; *Lubiano Nancy Almorin v Director of Immigration* [2020] 5

court also dismissed a constitutional equality claim against higher obstetric charges in public hospitals for non-resident pregnant women, a policy particularly affecting pregnant women from mainland China married to Hong Kong men but who had not yet received permission to settle in Hong Kong permanently.[117] Despite the effects on women immigrants, the judgment did not consider the potential gender-related consequences and determined that these distinctions, based on residency status, were not core values, granting the government a wide 'margin of discretion'. In the only successful case involving discrimination against new immigrants in accessing social welfare, counsel for the applicant abandoned the initial equality argument and relied primarily on the right to social welfare.[118]

Judicial review applicants have invoked equality law on occasion when attempting to contest aspects of the democratic deficit. These efforts have also largely failed, however, and most occurred prior to the political unrest of mid-2019. Although the courts have accepted that 'political opinion' is a 'core value', as an enumerated ground of discrimination in the BOR,[119] they have nevertheless deferred to the executive and legislature in cases involving the exclusion of opposition candidates from the political process. For example, in *Chan Ho Tin v Lo Ying Ki Alan*,[120] the convenor of a political party advocating for Hong Kong's independence challenged the invalidation of his candidacy in the LegCo elections. He argued this decision breached his right to non-discrimination on the grounds of political opinion and his rights to participate in public life and to freedom of expression.[121] The Court of First Instance rejected his claim, explaining:

> [W]hilst the Government bears the burden to justify the legislative restriction as an appropriate or justified one vis-à-vis an alleged constitutional right ... the court would accord a wide margin of discretion to the legislature, as this is pre-eminently a political judgment.[122]

If the court had followed its established approach to 'core values' in relation to equality, as described above, more stringent judicial scrutiny might have been required. An earlier case contesting the functional constituency system on the ground it discriminated based on financial means (although not sex or gender) also failed.[123] In these cases, the courts arguably missed opportunities to apply their robust equality doctrine more consistently and better promote political participation as a dimension of substantive equality.

HKLRD 107; *Fernandez Yvette Dingle v Commissioner of Labour* [2021] HKCFI 307; Kelley Loper, 'Gender, Sexuality and Constitutionalism in Hong Kong' in Wen-Chen Chang and others (eds), *Gender, Sexuality and Constitutionalism in Asia* (Hart Publishing 2023).

[117] *Fok Chun Wa* (n 110).
[118] *Kong Yunming v Director of Social Welfare* (2013) 16 HKCFAR 950.
[119] *Fok Chun Wa* (n 110).
[120] [2018] 2 HKLRD 7.
[121] BOR (n 15) arts 21, 16 (cf ICCPR, arts 25, 19).
[122] *Chan Ho Tin* (n 120) [153].
[123] *Chan Yu Nam v Secretary for Justice* [2010] HKEC 1893.

Kwok Cheuk Kin v Secretary for Constitutional and Mainland Affairs[124] also illustrates the courts' deferential approach to political questions. This case involved election laws barring candidates who had resigned from LegCo from running in by-elections within six months of the resignation. The law aimed to prevent a de facto referendum on universal suffrage and abolishing functional constituencies. The referendum strategy was designed by pro-democracy legislators who intended to resign from their directly elected seats in order to trigger a by-election that would gauge public views on these issues. Although equality law was not invoked, the Chief Justice clarified that 'a wide margin of appreciation' is accorded in cases involving 'matters of national security, defence and foreign policy', and 'political decisions or legislative provisions reflecting political judgments'.[125] He noted this is 'quite different to the position where core values ... are involved'.[126] This reasoning suggests limited possibilities for judicial review, based on equality or other constitutional rights, to challenge the effects of political crisis going forward.

Indeed, political crisis itself can undermine judicial legitimacy and, therefore, the courts' ability to exercise their democratic function. As discussed, judicial review of discriminatory policy, based on equality law, is a critical tool for promoting participation as a key feature of substantive equality and democratic values. The political crisis in Hong Kong, the democratic deficit, and the government's emphasis on national security, however, have put a great deal of pressure on the courts. Some have questioned the future of judicial independence in the new political climate, especially since the promulgation of the NSL.[127] Decisions by a new Committee for Safeguarding National Security are not amenable to judicial review and the Chief Executive has the power to designate judges to handle cases involving national security offences.[128] Some of the foreign non-permanent judges on the Court of Final Appeal have resigned over concerns about the rule of law in the territory.[129]

Even in such an environment, however, there may still be space to promote equality outside the political sphere. Opposing discrimination on grounds such as gender, disability, race, and sexual orientation is likely to be more politically palatable than advocating for other rights, such as the right to vote and the freedoms of expression, assembly, and association. As Yam points out, the courts could enhance their legitimacy through the adjudication of 'medium-stakes cases'.[130] He explains that such cases 'provide valuable opportunities to the courts to earn their reputation with a minimal risk of sanctions' adding, 'The promotion of liberal values is often, in principle,

---

[124] (2017) 20 HKCFAR 353.
[125] *Kwok Cheuk Kin v Secretary for Constitutional and Mainland Affairs* (2017) 20 HKCFAR 353 [41]–[42].
[126] ibid.
[127] Johannes Chan, 'National Security and Judicial Independence: A Clash of Fundamental Values' in Hualing Fu and Michael Hor (eds), *The National Security Law of Hong Kong: Restoration and Transformation* (HKU Press 2023).
[128] NSL (n 20) arts 14, 44.
[129] Gary Cheung, Jeffie Lam, and Jack Lau, 'Veteran Australian Judge James Spigelman Resigns from Hong Kong's top court, Citing National Security Law' *South China Morning Post* (18 September 2020) www.scmp.com/news/hong-kong/law-and-crime/article/3102051/veteran-australian-judge-james-spigelman-resigns-hong (accessed 3 May 2022); Anna Dziedzic, 'Foreign Judges and Hong Kong's New National Security Law' (2020) 25 Commonwealth Judicial Journal 27.
[130] Julius Yam, 'Approaching the Legitimacy Paradox in Hong Kong: Lessons for Hybrid Regime Courts' (2021) 46 Law and Social Inquiry 167.

contrary to the authoritarian ideology, but it does not necessarily contradict China's core interests, including national security.[131] The courts might therefore build on their more progressive constitutional equality jurisprudence even as the NSL closes other avenues for advocacy.

In a context like Hong Kong's with a significant democratic deficit, better implementation of equality law and resolving socio-economic inequality could contribute to inclusion in areas of life beyond the political arena. Indeed, democratic legitimacy is at least partly dependent on the realization of social justice outcomes.[132] There may even be growing political support for measures addressing socio-economic inequalities. The Chinese authorities claimed that poverty and substandard housing were the root causes of the 2019 protests[133] and have encouraged the Hong Kong authorities to address these issues.[134] Although protesters pushed back on this narrative since it ignored calls for political reform, socio-economic inequalities are nevertheless extreme. Advocacy more explicitly highlighting the intersections between poverty and other forms of identity-based discrimination may be feasible.

However, despite these possibilities, and in light of the political challenges, policymakers are unlikely to frame socio-economic inequality as a human rights concern. Also, as discussed above, substantive equality consists of several inter-related dimensions that are co-dependent and cannot be neatly divided.[135] Without opportunities for political participation, the other dimensions of equality, such as redressing economic disadvantage, become more difficult to achieve. The democratic deficit has reinforced—and been reinforced by—poverty, the extreme wealth gap, and the discriminatory denial of socio-economic rights, thus perpetuating a vicious cycle and impacting participation beyond the political sphere. Even when addressed as constitutional issues, the courts have generally been constrained when interpreting and applying socio-economic rights and have not entirely explored the socio-economic components of civil and political rights, such as the right to life.[136] The courts have regularly prioritized civil and political rights as 'fundamental' and have referred to the ICESCR as 'aspirational' or determined that most socio-economic rights are unincorporated and therefore not justiciable. The courts have not heard cases involving socio-economic inequalities arising from the pandemic, although it may still be too early fully to assess the role of the judiciary in this context. At the time of writing, only one case involving discrimination related to Covid-19 had been adjudicated,[137] even though the EOC received 1,448 enquiries related to discrimination and Covid-19

---

[131] ibid.
[132] Robert Post, 'Democracy and Equality' (2006) 603 The Annals of the American Academy of Political and Social Science 24.
[133] 'Behind Hong Kong's Chaos Lie Deep-seated Social Problems' (*Xinhua*, 7 September 2019) www.xinhuanet.com/english/2019-09/07/c_138374167.htm (accessed 3 May 2022); 'Hong Kong: a Glitzy Metropolis with 1 Million in Poverty' *Xinhua* (19 September 2019) www.xinhuanet.com/english/2019-09/19/c_138405650.htm (accessed 3 May 2022).
[134] Alex Lo, 'Beijing to Hong Kong: Resolve Housing Mess for the Poor' *South China Morning Post* (18 July 2021) www.scmp.com/comment/opinion/article/3141572/beijing-hong-kong-resolve-housing-mess-poor (accessed 3 May 2022).
[135] Fredman (n 5).
[136] Loper (n 104).
[137] *Syed Agha Raza Shah v Director of Health* [2020] HKCFI 770 (a race discrimination challenge to quarantine policies impacting Pakistani nationals).

in 2020.[138] It is not clear, however, how many resulted in investigations or triggered conciliation.

4 Conclusion

This chapter recounts the intersectional crises facing Hong Kong in recent years, their impact on existing inequalities, the creation of new forms of inequality, and the general failure of equality law to address these issues, including intersectional disadvantage experienced by the most marginalized groups, such as migrant communities. This is despite available mechanisms, such as a robust constitutional equality doctrine, that could be better utilized to support substantive equality outcomes. As argued in this chapter, the nature of a political crisis affects the aims of equality in complex ways. It reduces participation for all, but has a particular impact on minorities. The lack of political voice expands into other domains of life and reduces prospects for transformation. The democratic deficit extends to the courts and jeopardizes the role of judicial review for enhancing democratic values. Although the Hong Kong case study suggests some opportunities—and remaining space—for equality law to contribute to a broader notion of participation, albeit outside the direct political arena, this is necessarily only a partial democratic project. Indeed, equality rights cannot be fully implemented in isolation. Fostering more comprehensive democratic values requires a holistic approach to substantive equality as well as attention to the complete range of civil, political, economic, social, and cultural rights.

---

[138] Email from the Complaint Services Division of the EOC to the author (15 March 2021).

PART II
ADDRESSING EXPONENTIAL INEQUALITIES

SECTION A
COMPARATIVE AND INTERNATIONAL LAW

7
New Directions Needed
Exponential Inequalities and the Limits of Equality Law

Colm O'Cinneide

1 Introduction

Equality law has had a good run.[1] Over the last half century, it has put down deep roots in the legal systems of most liberal democracies. However, recent events have exposed its limitations. For all its doctrinal and conceptual sophistication, equality law has not succeeded in eliminating overt forms of discrimination, let alone its more subtle manifestations. This was graphically highlighted by the revelations that triggered the #MeToo and Black Lives Matter campaigns of 2015 to 2021, which shone a spotlight on the persisting and often normalized nature of the public and private violence regularly inflicted on women, ethnic minorities, and other disempowered social groups. Equality law has also failed to play a significant role in limiting the discriminatory impact of recent systemic shocks,[2] such as the economic turmoil of 2008 and the Covid-19 crisis of 2020–2022—which, as discussed throughout this book, have amplified existing embedded patterns of social disadvantage and have generated a range of 'exponential inequalities'. Given that such systemic shocks are likely to recur in the coming era of environmental degradation, socio-economic unsettlement and geopolitical turbulence, it is time to take stock of the existing state of equality law. Is it still fit for purpose, half a century after its first emergence in the very different world of the 1960s and 1970s?

This chapter argues that equality law (i) provides comprehensive legal protection against specific types of discrimination; (ii) functions with enough flexibility to accommodate shifts in public understanding of what constitutes discrimination, while maintaining its structural integrity as a legal framework; and (iii) enjoys a healthy degree of insulation from quotidian political dynamics. However, (a) its scope of protection is too narrow and unduly rigid; (b) its enforcement model is inherently limited and excessively technocratic; and (c) its semi-sacrosanct, 'embedded' status is often

---

[1] I use the term 'equality law' here to refer to both the legislative and the public/constitutional law dimension to equality and non-discrimination rights, following in the footsteps of Bob Hepple: see Bob Hepple, 'The Aims of Equality Law' (2008) 61 Current Legal Problems 1.

[2] The term 'systemic shock' is used here to refer to events that disturb the existing socio-economic order enough to drive it out of equilibrium, by analogy to the use of the term in a computing context: see Peter Mitic, 'Systemic Shock Propagation in a Complex System' (2020) 24 Soft Computing 13667. Note that the impact of such shocks is not necessarily confined to a specific timeframe: for example, some of the longer-term consequences of the 2008 economic crisis are still playing themselves out at the time of writing, when it comes to issues such as lack of access to housing for younger people, income stagnation, and persisting political instability. The effects of Covid-19 will in all likelihood play out on a similar time scale.

Colm O'Cinneide, *New Directions Needed* In: *Exponential Inequalities*. Edited by: Shreya Atrey and Sandra Fredman, Oxford University Press. © Colm O'Cinneide 2023. DOI: 10.1093/oso/9780192872999.003.0007

used as a justification to constrain its development. These flaws limit the capacity of equality law to tackle 'ordinary' inequalities. By extension, they also hobble its ability to ameliorate the exponential impact of systemic shocks such as Covid-19. As a consequence, radical new thinking is needed, about how to inject new dynamism into equality law—which may require rethinking old shibboleths, and breaking with some of the established orthodoxies of the last half century.

2 The Emergence of Equality Law

Born in North America in the 1950s and 1960s in response to the emerging civil rights and feminist movements of that era, equality law was designed to fill a gap—namely, the absence in existing common, statute, or constitutional law of any substantive legal prohibition on discriminatory treatment.[3] From the beginning, two modes of legal regulation were used to fill this gap: legislation, and purposive judicial interpretation of constitutional equality clauses. The legislative dimension of equality law took shape with statutes such as the Ontario Fair Employment Practices Act 1951 and the US Civil Rights Act 1964, which effectively made discrimination a tort, enforceable via civil actions brought by individual victims and/or state enforcement agencies. Its constitutional dimension emerged with the development of the equal protection jurisprudence of the US Supreme Court in the wake of *Brown v Board of Education*, and the more limited Canadian case law relating to the equality provisions of the federal Bill of Rights.[4] Both these legislative and constitutional dimensions were mutually influencing, with legislative developments influencing constitutional norms and vice versa. Both also proved to be attractive legal innovations, which were quickly adopted by other jurisdictions. In essence, spreading out from North America, equality law went global.[5]

Its legislative dimension was the first to put down deep roots elsewhere, being picked up and transplanted to other jurisdictions—including, for example, the UK in the form of the Sex Discrimination Act 1975 and the Race Relations Act 1976, and the EEC more generally with the Equal Treatment Directive 76/207/EEC. Gradually, a standard legislative template emerged, influenced by comparative legislative and case law developments as well as 'levelling up' pressure generated by non-governmental organizations and other campaigning groups.[6]

Throughout much of the democratic world, states have now adopted comprehensive anti-discrimination codes based on this template.[7] Such legislation usually prohibits direct, indirect, and associated forms of discrimination over a number of discrete 'protected' grounds, while also specifying applicable defences, the scope of

---

[3] See in general Geoffrey Bindman and Anthony Lester, *Race and Law* (Penguin 1972).
[4] *R v Drybones* [1970] SCR 282. cf *Canada (AG) v Lavell* [1974] SCR 1349.
[5] Anthony Lester, 'The Overseas Trade in the American Bill of Rights' (1988) 88(3) Columbia Law Review 537; Bob Hepple, 'The European Legacy of *Brown v Board of Education*' [2006] University of Illinois Law Review 605.
[6] Hepple (n 5).
[7] Tarunabh Khaitan, *A Theory of Discrimination Law* (OUP 2015) 3–5; Iyiola Solanke, *Discrimination as Stigma: A Theory of Anti-discrimination Law* (Hart Publishing 2017).

lawful positive action, and the procedural mechanisms for bringing individual and group discrimination claims. It also locks in the 'civil liability' model for addressing discrimination, making individual claims as litigated through employment tribunals and civil courts the primary mechanism for securing redress.[8]

A similar transplantation/standardization process has happened at the constitutional level.[9] Most constitutions include written guarantees of equal treatment, or at least can be interpreted as precluding state action which discriminates in an unjustified manner. All the major international human rights instruments contain similar guarantees—including those incorporated instruments that enjoy quasi-constitutional status in multiple different countries, such as the European Convention on Human Rights (ECHR) and the Inter-American Convention on Human Rights (IACHR). As such, most liberal democratic constitutional orders provide potentially fertile soil for the cultivation of constitutional equality jurisprudence. National and international courts have not always been quick to explore these possibilities. However, by slow, incremental steps, constitutional equality jurisprudence has become part of the arsenal of individual rights protection.[10]

Thus, equality law—in both its legislative and constitutional dimensions—has put down deep roots in multiple different legal systems. Furthermore, its development across these different systems has tended to follow a similar pattern, making it possible to speak of 'equality law' as a transnational mode of legal regulation whose specific national manifestations share certain common characteristics.[11]

3 The Achievements of Equality Law

One important characteristic of established equality law is the *comprehensive* protection it provides against the specific forms of discrimination that come within its scope of application.[12] The prohibitions it imposes on direct, indirect and associated forms of discrimination generally apply across the variegated spheres of employment and occupation, service provision, education, housing, transport, and the performance of public functions—with the constitutional dimension of equality law often filling gaps in protection left by its legislative dimension. The exceptions that exist to these prohibitions tend to be narrowly defined, and strictly limited.[13]

Now, as discussed below in further detail, this does not necessarily mean that the protection equality law offers against discrimination is effective, or sufficient. But it

---

[8] In Europe, the provisions of the EU equality directives have played a key role in encouraging its spread: see in general Barbara Havelkova and Mathias Möschel (eds), *Anti-discrimination Law in Civil Law Jurisdictions* (OUP 2019).

[9] Catherine O'Regan and Nick Friedman, 'Equality' in Tom Ginsburg and Rosalind Dixon (eds), *Comparative Constitutional Law* (Edward Elgar Publishing 2011) 473; Susanne Baer, 'Equality' in Michel Rosenfeld and András Sajó (eds), *The Oxford Handbook of Comparative Constitutional Law* (OUP 2012) 982.

[10] See eg Rory O'Connell, 'Cinderella Comes to the Ball: Art 14 and the Right to Non-discrimination in the ECHR' (2009) 29 Legal Studies 211.

[11] Sandra Fredman, *Discrimination Law* (2nd edn, OUP 2012); Khaitan (n 7).

[12] Bob Hepple, *Equality: The Legal Framework* (2nd edn, Hart Publishing 2014) ch 1.

[13] See eg Case C-414/16 *Vera Egenberger v Evangelisches Werk für Diakonie und Entwicklung eV* ECLI:EU:C:2018:257.

does mean that equality law is potentially in play whenever individuals and groups are subject to differences of treatment that can be linked to 'suspect' grounds of discrimination. Thus, for example, national law prohibitions on race discrimination apply to most forms of public and private activity—meaning that, in general, all forms of differential treatment that can be linked to a person's race or ethnicity are vulnerable to legal challenge.[14]

A second characteristic of equality law is its relative *flexibility*. Its basic design features usually are framed in terms of fixed, standard formulae: for example, legal requirements relating to indirect discrimination and reasonable accommodation are generally worded in similar, specific ways, and are applied by courts and tribunals in line with set prescriptions. However, these standard formulae have a certain degree of in-built flexibility, and their application can be adjusted to reflect shifting views of what constitutes unjustified discrimination and the social function of equality law in this regard.

Thus, for example, the comparator requirement that forms part of the standard test for direct discrimination cases is set aside or adjusted when it comes to pregnancy discrimination and sexual harassment claims.[15] Similarly, the objective justification test in indirect discrimination cases is applied with varying degrees of rigour, depending upon the particular discrimination ground at issue, and the nature of the social activity in question.[16]

This flexibility has allowed the set formulae of equality law to keep pace to some degree with an expanding understanding as to what qualifies as discriminatory conduct, and the growing focus on combating structural patterns of group inequality. It has also allowed it to accommodate shifting views as to (i) the nature of individual 'fault' in this regard, with an initial focus on subjective motivation giving way to a central concern with what Zatz has described as 'status causation;[17] and (ii) the animating values that should underpin the functioning of equality law more generally, with 'formal' approaches being adjusted to accommodate greater concern with achieving 'substantive' equality.[18] Furthermore, it has proved to be relatively easy to bolt on new 'suspect' grounds of discrimination to existing equality law frameworks, in response to changing social and political perceptions of what constitutes unjust forms of unequal treatment. In general, this in-built flexibility has allowed the legislative and constitutional dimensions of equality law, originally formulated more than half a century ago, to remain legally relevant—while maintaining its structural integrity as a form of legal regulation.

A third notable characteristic of equality law is its *embeddedness*. Once enacted, it is rare for anti-discrimination legislation to be repealed, or for its scope to be

---

[14] See eg *R(E) v Governing Body of JFS* [2009] UKSC 15.

[15] See eg *Webb v EMO Air Cargo (UK) Ltd* [1994] ECR I-3567; Equality Act 2010, s 26.

[16] To take one example among many, note the contrasting degrees of leeway given to government employment policy relating to older workers in the EU age discrimination judgments of Case C-144/04 *Mangold v Helm* [2005] ECR I-9981 and Case C-45/09 *Rosenbladt* [2010] ECR I-09391.

[17] Noah D Zatz, 'Disparate Impact and the Unity of Equality Law' (2017) 97 Boston University Law Review 1357. See also Sandra Fredman, 'Direct and Indirect Discrimination: Is There Still a Divide?' in Hugh Collins and Tarunabh Khaitan (eds), *Foundations of Indirect Discrimination Law* (Hart Publishing 2018) 31.

[18] Fredman (n 17).

substantively narrowed. Adjustments can be made to the legislative scheme.[19] Courts can give a restrictive interpretation to some of its provisions.[20] New procedural barriers can be placed in the way of claimants.[21] However, it is not common for the substance of anti-discrimination legislation to be rolled back—even in situations where the expansion of equality rights stirs up strong political backlash.[22] The same tends to be true in respect of the constitutional dimension of equality law—although the abstract language of constitutional equality clauses makes them vulnerable to restrictive interpretation.[23] In general, at least when it comes to its core framework of substantive norms, equality law tends to stick around: once it beds down in a particular legal system, it is difficult to uproot. Even the many critics of 'expansionist' understandings of discrimination, or of 'juridification' more generally, are slow to call for the roll-back of equality law as such.

In part, this embeddedness is a by-product of the bi-dimensional nature of equality law: its constitutional dimension tends to reinforce the status of its legislative dimension, and sometimes vice versa. Equality law also benefits from the influence of international human rights law, and in particular the status of the non-discrimination norms set out in UN instruments like the Convention for the Elimination of Racial Discrimination (CERD), as well as provisions such as Article 14 of the ECHR. More generally, non-discrimination tends nowadays to be viewed as a fundamental legal principle: both in the sense of being a core human right, and also an integral element of basic rule of law values.[24] It is also closely bound up with the political equality principle that underpins democratic rule, while chiming nicely with the immanent logic of the dignitarian- and autonomy-based strands of liberalism that have dominated legal thought since 1945.[25] Furthermore, while equality law can operate so as to disrupt certain social hierarchies, it could also be viewed as market perfecting/enabling.[26] As such, it can appeal both to critics and supporters of neoliberal socio-economic ordering, and is generally well insulated against repeal or substantial roll-back.

These general characteristics of equality law, as it has developed in sync across multiple different legal systems—its comprehensiveness, flexibility, and embeddedness—make it a robust form of legal regulation. It provides broad protection against discrimination; it functions with sufficient flexibility to accommodate shifts in public

---

[19] See eg how s 65 of the UK Enterprise and Regulatory Reform Act 2013 repealed the 'third party harassment' provisions of s 40(2)–(4) of the Equality Act 2010.

[20] See eg *Wards Cove Packing Co v Atonio* 490 US 642 (1989). The dilution of the legal prohibition on disparate impact in US law remains perhaps the most prominent example of judicial 'read down' of anti-discrimination legislation—but note that the Civil Rights Act 1991 reversed the impact of the *Wards Cove* judgment, at least in the legislative sphere.

[21] See eg how s 66 of the UK Enterprise and Regulatory Reform Act 2013 abolished the 'questionnaire' procedure set out in s 138 of the Equality Act 2010.

[22] This may seem a controversial claim, given how, for example, gender equality rights have been targeted recently in Central and Eastern European states: Agnieszka Graff and Elżbieta Korolczuk, *Anti-Gender Politics in the Populist Moment* (Routledge 2021). However, it is striking how equality law itself, as distinct from reproduction rights, is rarely targeted directly by such backlash strategies, reflecting its embedded status and in particular how it benefits from inclusion within the *acquis* of superior EU law.

[23] See eg Barbara Havelkova, 'Judicial Scepticism of Discrimination at the ECtHR' in Hugh Collins and Tarunabh Khaitan (eds), *Foundations of Indirect Discrimination Law* (Hart Publishing 2018) 83.

[24] O'Regan and Friedman (n 9).

[25] Jeremy Waldron, *One Another's Equals: The Basis of Human Equality* (Belknap Press 2017).

[26] Alexander Somek, *Engineering Equality: An Essay on European Anti-Discrimination Law* (OUP 2011).

understandings of what constitutes discrimination, while maintaining its structural integrity as a legal framework; and it enjoys a degree of insulation from quotidian political dynamics. As a legal sub-system (to use vocabulary borrowed from autopoietic systems theory), it has been able to operate according to its own internal logic as a distinct area of law, while remaining open to shifts in the external normative landscape. Equality law has therefore been able to evolve in a broadly coherent and consistent manner, at least when viewed from an internal perspective.[27] It has also come to exert a significant influence on wider systems of social governance: its normative framework looms large in the contemporary legal and political framing of 'equality' as aspiration and goal.

More generally, equality law has arguably become the most developed element of the 'rights revolution' that has transformed legal systems since the 1960s. Its influence extends deep into both the public and private sectors, it has acquired plenty of 'hard' legal content, and it impacts directly on individual lives in a way that many legal human rights standards generally do not.[28] Furthermore, equality law has become a significant vector for social change: in areas such as pregnancy discrimination, sex harassment, reasonable accommodation provision for persons with disabilities, and partnership rights for same-sex couples, the requirements of equality law have often played a key role in bringing about radical shifts in societal practices and mores. Indeed, a key factor in the cross-jurisdictional spread of equality law has been the perception that it serves as an effective motor for social transformation. In the eyes of many of the lawyers, academics and activists who work with equality law and analyse its development, it provides compelling evidence that law can sometimes be a redemptive force.[29]

4 The Limits of Equality Law

However, half a century and more after the birth of equality law, the world remains unredeemed. For all its success, it has become clear that legal non-discrimination guarantees, whether legislative or constitutional in form, have finite impact. Recent events have highlighted the limits of their reach, in ways that need to be taken into account in any serious assessment of the functioning of equality law.

To start with, it should be noted that liberal democratic societies are profoundly unequal, and remain riven by multiple different and interlocking forms of social stratification. Indeed, socio-economic inequality has grown significantly since the 1970s, propelled by the dynamics of neo-liberalism.[30] Even the forms of discrimination that are particularly targeted by equality law—such as race or sex discrimination,

---

[27] Khaitan (n 7).
[28] Elaine Rene and others, *Antidiscrimination Law and Shared Prosperity: An Analysis of the Legal Framework of Six Economies and Their Impact on the Equality of Opportunities of Ethnic, Religious, and Sexual Minorities* World Bank Policy Research Working Paper No 7992 (2017) https://openknowledge.worldbank.org/handle/10986/26242 (accessed 15 April 2022).
[29] See eg the descriptive framing of equality law in Owen Fiss, 'The Accumulation of Disadvantages' (2018) 106 California Law Review 1945.
[30] Thomas Piketty, *Capital in the Twenty-First Century* (Harvard UP 2014).

sex harassment, and social exclusion of persons with disabilities—have persisted. Structural forms of such discrimination have proved to have persistent staying power.[31] A person's race, gender, disability, and so on can still have a significant impact on their life opportunities, as reflected in multiple indicators, with such impact often greatly amplified by intersectional factors such as socio-economic disadvantage.

Furthermore, discrimination can still take raw and overt form, despite the comprehensive protection provided by equality law. This was graphically demonstrated by the facts of the Harvey Weinstein case, along with multiple other stories of sexually abusive conduct that hit the news in late 2017 and early 2018 as part of the #MeToo wave of allegations. Much of this alleged behaviour was straightforwardly unlawful, on the basis that it constituted a form of sexual assault under criminal law and/or qualified as a prohibited act of sexual harassment under equality law. But the unlawfulness of the behaviour in question, and in particular its overt breach of the requirements of equality law, did not prevent it persisting for decades.[32]

This problem of persisting inequalities—both structural and overt—means that the marginalized groups that equality law is supposed to benefit often remain lacking in social, political, and economic capital. By extension, this makes them more vulnerable to economic downturns, austerity policies, and other negative twists and turns in social development. A large-scale systemic crisis like Covid-19 can magnify this vulnerability, exposing marginalized groups to greater risk of ill-health, inadequate medical care, economic marginalization, unemployment, and other forms of adverse treatment.[33] As discussed throughout this book, this can convert persisting inequalities into 'exponential inequalities', with the relative social disadvantage suffered by such groups being amplified and even at times turbo-charged by the specific way in which the dynamics of the crisis play out.[34] Existing racial and gender disparities can be greatly exacerbated, embedded modes of social exclusion can be deepened, and persisting patterns of marginalization within democratic, cultural, and socio-economic processes can be reinforced—as highlighted by research generated while the Covid-19 crisis was ongoing.[35] And equality law, along with other modes

---

[31] See eg Nadine White, 'Ethnic Minority Unemployment 70% Higher than White Joblessness for Past 20 Years' *The Independent* (3 November 2021) https://www.independent.co.uk/news/uk/home-news/ethnic-minority-unnemployment-labour-disparity-b1950050.html> accessed 16 May 2022).

[32] The same could be said about the police racism that triggered the Black Lives Matter movement in 2013, and which inspired global protests after the death of George Floyd in 2020.

[33] As Hammonds notes, 'pandemics do not produce inequalities but rather ... they reveal them': Evelynn Hammonds, 'A Moment or a Movement? The Pandemic, Political Upheaval, and Racial Reckoning' (2021) 47 Signs 11.

[34] See further on this point Matthew Sparke and Owain David Williams, 'Neoliberal Disease: COVID-19, Co-pathogenesis and Global Health Insecurities' (2022) 54(1) Environment and Planning A: Economy and Space 15.

[35] See eg Arjun Neil Alim, '1 in 5 Children Short of Food' *Evening Standard* (9 December 2020) https://www.standard.co.uk/news/foodforlondon/food-for-london-now-children-food-shortage-b232967.html (accessed 15 April 2022); Vikram Dodd, 'Met Police Twice as Likely to Fine Black People over Lockdown Breachers' *The Guardian* (3 June 2020) https://www.theguardian.com/uk-news/2020/jun/03/met-police-twice-as-likely-to-fine-black-people-over-lockdown-breaches-research (accessed 15 April 2022); Jamie Grierson, 'Domestic Abusers "Weaponised" Covid in England and Wales, Study Finds' *The Guardian* (25 August 2021) https://www.theguardian.com/society/2021/aug/25/domestic-abusers-weaponised-covid-england-wales-study-finds (accessed 15 April 2022).

of solidarity reinforcement, has not proved to be of much use in combating these trends.[36]

Given current trends relating to global instability, market over-reach and climate change—and the apparent inability of contemporary forms of national and international governance to provide comprehensive solutions to associated global problems such as environmental degradation, migration pressures, and resource scarcity—it is likely that Covid-19-style crises will recur. This means that such exponential effects may become increasingly common in the future. And it is difficult to see how equality law in its current form, which already struggles to address persisting patterns of structural and overt discrimination, is going to be able to engage effectively with such exponential dynamics.

This begs the question of why equality law falls short. Why does it struggle to engage with many forms of structural and even overt discrimination, let alone crisis-amplified exponential inequalities—despite its global expansion, its rapid evolution, and its well-developed qualities of comprehensiveness, flexibility, and embeddedness? From the existing scholarship, it is possible to identify a number of factors which limit the reach of equality law. Some are well documented in the literature; others less well so. But their combined effect adds up to a significant set of constraints whose existence is sometimes downplayed, or glossed over, when shining accounts are presented of the evolution of equality law. Indeed, these limitations are closely bound up with the qualities of equality law that have helped it to thrive: a trade-off sometimes exists between its strength and its effectiveness.

4.1 Limited Scope

To start with, anti-discrimination legislation generally only prohibits discrimination linked to the specified protected grounds that come within its scope.[37] This limits its comprehensive range of protection: it offers depth, but not breadth. Thus, for example, it is rare for socio-economic status, or similar grounds, to receive comprehensive protection as a distinct 'suspect ground'.[38] It is also rare for anti-discrimination

---

[36] For an excellent analysis of the limits imposed on possibilities of solidarity and collective action by the purportedly 'progressive' public nature of the Covid-19 crisis see Myria Georgiou and Gavan Titley, 'Publicness and Commoning: Pandemic Intersections and Collective Visions at Times of Crisis' (2022) 25 International Journal of Cultural Studies 331 doi:10.1177/13678779211060363 (accessed 15 April 2022).

[37] Certain states adopt an 'open ground' model of anti-discrimination legislation. However, the scope of this legislation still tends to be read restrictively, outside of the usual, well-established non-discrimination grounds. See eg the Canadian experience, analysed in Colleen Sheppard, 'Grounds of Discrimination: Towards an Inclusive and Contextual Approach' (2001) 80 Canadian Bar Review 893.

[38] This is beginning to change, in Europe at least: see Tamas Kadar, *An Analysis of the Introduction of Socio-economic Status as a Discrimination Ground* (Equality Rights Alliance 2016). However, coverage of socio-economic status (however defined) remains the exception rather than the norm. Also, even when covered, socio-economic status tends to be interpreted narrowly as a non-discrimination ground, and generate surprisingly little case law: for the Australian experience in this regard with the protected ground of 'social origin' see Angelo Capuano, 'Giving Meaning to "Social Origin" in International Labour Organization ("ILO") Conventions, the Fair Work Act 2009 (Cth) and the Australian Human Rights Commission Act 1986 (Cth): "Class" Discrimination and its Relevance to the Australian Context' (2016) 39 University of New South Wales Law Journal 84.

legislation to cover intersectional forms of discrimination, or other complex forms of inequality that are not reducible to discrimination linked specifically to one of the specific grounds coming within its purview.[39]

These limits of anti-discrimination legislation tend also to be replicated within the constitutional dimension of equality law. Constitutional equality clauses are generally not confined in scope to particular grounds. In theory, they provide a potential basis for reviewing state action based on any 'status' ground. However, in practice, in reviewing state action by reference to the requirements of such equality clauses, courts usually apply highly variable degrees of scrutiny depending upon the type of distinction at issue.[40] Thus, distinctions based on the traditional single grounds of discrimination, such as race and sex, tend to attract strict scrutiny, with other types of distinctions attracting different levels of scrutiny depending upon the degree to which the ground in question is viewed as being inherently 'suspect'. Socio-economic distinctions are usually treated as non-suspect,[41] while intersectional approaches remain radically underdeveloped in most constitutional systems. As a result, the constitutional dimension of equality law tends to track and reflect the limited scope of its legislative dimension.

In general, there is a strong assumption that the 'central case' of equality law—the types of discrimination that are assumed to constitute the principal 'target' and *raison d'être* of both its legislative and constitutional dimensions—remains what it was in the 1960s and 1970s: namely, to combat specific single-ground forms of discrimination, in particular race and sex discrimination.[42] This assumption shapes and limits the horizons of equality law. It is predominantly seen as a vehicle for combating stigmatizing discrimination based on a specific and distinct set of 'ascribed identity' grounds. In contrast, any wider protective or redistributive effects it might generate are viewed as incidental to that core focus.[43] Even where such 'additional' protection is available, it is often applied by courts in a cautious, uncertain, and even grudging manner—as evidenced by how the potentially wide reach of its constitutional dimension has been generally reined in and limited in scope to the contours of the traditional 'central case' of equality law.

This does not mean that equality law can only impact on forms of inequality that are directly linked to protected grounds. The protection it offers against indirect discrimination means that it can be deployed to challenge discriminatory measures based on socio-economic status or other 'external' grounds, as long as claimants can show that the measure also has a differential impact on one of the protected grounds. Thus, for example, the prohibition on sex discrimination can be used to challenge austerity cuts and other measures which contribute to socio-economic inequalities, if it can be

---

[39] See in general Shreya Atrey, *Intersectional Discrimination* (OUP 2019).
[40] See eg *R v SSWP (ex p Carson and Reynolds)* [2005] UKHL 37 [15] (Lord Hoffmann).
[41] See eg *Dandridge v Williams* 397 US 471 (1970).
[42] Shreya Atrey, 'On the Central Case Methodology in Discrimination Law' (2021) 41 Oxford Journal of Legal Studies 776.
[43] This also explains why positive action measures are often viewed as an inherently problematic add-on to the core requirements of anti-discrimination legislation. Their largely redistributive impact is often discounted when it comes to determining their lawfulness, while their use of protected grounds to select beneficiaries of this redistributive impact chafes against the central case's ground-exclusionary logic.

shown that women are disproportionately affected by the cuts in question.[44] However, the requirement that a clear link be established to a protected ground ultimately limits how far equality law can be 'stretched' in practice. It imposes boundary conditions on equality law—conditions which are often vulnerable to being interpreted narrowly, often yet again reflecting the dominance of 'central case' thinking.[45]

In a way, the comprehensiveness of equality law is based upon a trade-off. It provides systematic protection across the protected grounds, but its scope is predominantly restricted to 'central case' scenarios—with its legitimacy often justified precisely on the basis of its circumscribed field of application, which is regularly framed as a narrow and exceptional carve-out from standard freedom of contract norms.

As a result of this limited scope, equality law can only chip away at particular veins within the geological strata of inequalities that make up the bedrock of our current societies. Multiple forms of inequality, in particular those linked to intersectionality and/or socio-economic factors, remain outside its purview. This inhibits the capacity of equality law to deal with structural inequalities.

By extension, it also constrains its ability to address exponential inequalities. The impact of systemic shocks such as Covid-19 plays out across multiple different axes of disadvantage and discrimination, with those caught up in intersecting inequalities often being the most vulnerable to their exponential effects. In response, equality law can only offer a partial response, which provides a two-dimensional, often static, and inherently limited solution to a three-dimensional problem. It can provide a way of challenging certain forms of discriminatory treatment—but the deeper drivers of exponential inequalities, in particular the impact of poverty and socio-economic disadvantage, generally remain beyond its purview.[46]

4.2 Limits on Enforceability

These limits are amplified by a structural feature that is integral to the design and functioning of equality law, and yet can limit its impact—namely its adoption of a civil liability enforcement model. As mentioned already, legal prohibitions on discrimination are primarily enforced through civil law mechanisms, rather than through criminal or administrative/regulatory mechanisms. This liberates equality law from gatekeeper mechanisms, such as police and prosecutorial discretion, which might constrain its development. Instead, individual claimants can bring private enforcement action, which helps to ensure equality law maintains its characteristic flexibility and remains open to new interpretations of its core concepts. However, reliance on

---

[44] See eg *JD and A v United Kingdom* App nos 32949/17 and 34614/17 (ECtHR, 24 October 2019).
[45] See eg the remarkably constricted approach taken to the application of indirect race discrimination analysis in the EU case of Case C-94/20 *Land Oberösterreich v KV* ECLI:EU:C:2021:477. This followed the CJEU's adoption of a similarly narrow analysis in Case C-668/15 *Jyske Finans* ECLI:EU:C:2017:278.
[46] In the UK, the Office of National Statistics (ONS), in estimating the impact of Covid-19 on the national population, has noted that 'the mortality rate in the most deprived areas of England was more than double that in the least deprived areas' for 12 of the initial first 14 months of the epidemic: ONS, *Leaving No One Behind: A Review of Who has been Most Affected by the Coronavirus Pandemic in the UK* (December 2021) https://www.ons.gov.uk/economy/environmentalaccounts/articles/leavingnoonebehindareviewofw hohasbeenmostaffectedbythecoronaviruspandemicintheuk/december2021 (accessed 15 April 2022).

civil liability also has drawbacks—which need to be factored into any analysis of the limits of equality law.

To start with, this approach means that discrimination claims are often litigated through contentious civil proceedings. Individual claimants, usually from disadvantaged or marginalized social groups, are expected to bear the burden of initiating most claims and carrying them through to a conclusion—often in the face of intimidation, or strong social pressure to settle or drop their claim.[47] Employers and others accused of discrimination often 'lawyer up' and fight discrimination claims to the bitter end—in part precisely because accusations of discrimination bring a degree of social opprobrium in their wake, even though intention or 'bad motive' is generally no longer required to ground a breach of equality law.[48] This means that the enforcement of equality law can be a costly, complicated, and emotionally draining affair, for everyone concerned.[49]

Also, as the more obvious and straight-forward forms of discrimination relating to a particular ground tend to be identified early by case law, with social behaviour often (but not always) adjusting accordingly, subsequent litigation often involves less clear-cut cases—either in the sense that the application of law to the specific facts of a claim is complex, or because the legal norms themselves remain unsettled. Either way, this means that as civil litigation in this field progresses, it can become more complex.[50] Also, certain aspects of discrimination law—in particular, indirect discrimination and harassment—have a certain degree of uncertainty built into their normative framework. For example, in indirect discrimination cases, both the selection of comparator pools and the application of objective justification analysis can be a fact-specific and highly value-laden exercise. Similar issues arise in respect of harassment, complicated by the evidence issues that often arise in such claims.[51]

Furthermore, the way equality law has adjusted over the years to accommodate shifts in perception of what constitutes unjustified discrimination—a key element of its success, as mentioned above—can also leave claimants and defendants disorientated. In particular, the shift from a focus on subjective motives to a focus on 'status causation' has arguably opened up a gap between how 'discrimination' is understood by significant segments of the general population and how the term is legally framed within equality law.[52] This can contribute to equality law becoming seen as a technocratic exercise, a type of artificial legal language, which can alienate claimants

---

[47] For a good recent overview of these issues see Women and Equalities Committee, *Enforcing the Equality Act: The Law and the Role of the Equality and Human Rights Commission* (HC 2017–19, 1470) [11]–[23].

[48] See in general Lizzie Barmes, *Bullying and Behavioural Conflict at Work: The Duality of Individual Rights* (OUP 2015).

[49] Nicola Lacey, 'From Individual to Group' in Bob Hepple and Erika M Szyszczak (eds), *Discrimination: The Limits of the Law* (Mansell 1992) 99.

[50] Certain areas are mired in complexity and time delays, such as equal pay: Sandra Fredman, 'Inching Forward: Preliminary Victory for Equal Value at Tesco and Asda' (2022) 51 Industrial Law Journal 166.

[51] Suzanne B Goldberg, 'Harassment, Workplace Culture, and the Power and Limits of Law' (2020) 70 American University Law Review 419.

[52] Samuel R Bagenstos, 'The Structural Turn and the Limits of Antidiscrimination Law' (2006) 94 California Law Review 1). See also Michael Selmi, 'Was the Disparate Impact Theory a Mistake?' (2006) 53 UCLA Law Review 701.

and defendants alike.[53] It can also generate uncertainty about its scope and content, leading to inconsistent decisions and fluctuating case law.

All this ensures that litigation in this context can be a messy business, often resembling a form of trench warfare. Both claimants and defendants often find it to be an alienating, artificial, fraught, and highly legalized process—often exemplifying wider problems with the functioning of the legal system more generally.[54] Claims may take a long time to resolve, adding a temporal drag factor to the impact of even successful actions. Also, success rates for claimants are low.[55]

Unsurprisingly, this discourages engagement with equality law. Potential defendants are often reluctant to engage constructively with allegations of discrimination or to admit wrongdoing before any legal proceedings commence, for fear of exposing themselves to liability. More seriously, many victims of discrimination, reluctant to be framed as 'trouble-makers' or to engage in a protracted legal battle, simply do not complain about their treatment.[56] In general, these structural defects inevitably limit the impact of equality law.[57] They hamper enforcement of its provisions, deter individual claimants, and can turn litigation in this field into an arid, technical, and protracted exercise in legal gymnastics. Equality law may possess an inherent degree of flexibility, but its structural underpinnings constrain its ultimate effectiveness.

All of these factors seem to have contributed to the gaps in enforcement revealed by the #MeToo and Black Lives Matter campaigns. Many of the acts of public and private violence that served as the spark for these social movements were clearly unlawful. For example, the acts of sexual harassment and assault performed by Harvey Weinstein and others within the film and TV industry, as uncovered and exposed by #MeToo campaigners, seem in general to have been straightforwardly illegal behaviour, in both criminal and civil law terms. But their behaviour was not challenged for decades. Their victims' concerns about the consequences of coming forward, and fear about the negative impact of litigation, served to insulate Weinstein and his fellow abusers from legal challenge for many years.[58] The difficulties of challenging seemingly blatant discrimination by police and other public authorities also form part of the background to the Black Lives Matter movement. Taken together, both social movements provide

---

[53] Barmes (n 48).

[54] ibid. See also Marc Hertogh, *Nobody's Law: Legal Consciousness and Legal Alienation in Everyday Life* (Palgrave Macmillan 2018).

[55] Colm O'Cinneide, 'Comparative Perspectives on the Enforcement and Effectiveness of Discrimination Law: United Kingdom' in Marie Mercat-Bruns, David B Oppenheimer, and Cady Sartorius (eds), *Comparative Perspectives on the Enforcement and Effectiveness of Antidiscrimination Law* (Springer 2018) 493.

[56] Even claimants who initiate legal action often settle their claims, signing non-disclosure agreements and other publicity-repressing measures in return for 'hush money'—a problem spotlighted by the Weinstein revelations and the wider #MeToo campaign. See the Women and Equalities Committee of the UK House of Commons, *The Use of Non-disclosure Agreements in Discrimination Cases* (HC 2017–19, 1720).

[57] Lacey (n 49); Bagenstos (n 52). There never was a time when the law in this area was 'simple', or when a clear normative consensus existed about the scope and content of equality law—and yet equality law has continued to evolve, and have a significant impact on wider society. However, the existence of these drag factors does impede its capacity to generate comprehensive social change.

[58] Ronan Farrow, 'From Aggressive Overtures to Sexual Assault: Harvey Weinstein's Accusers Tell Their Stories' *The New Yorker* (23 October 2017) https://www.newyorker.com/news/news-desk/from-aggressive-overtures-to-sexual-assault-harvey-weinsteins-accusers-tell-their-stories (accessed 15 April 2022).

graphic evidence of the limits of the civil liability enforcement model of discrimination law.

These limits also inevitably hamper the extent to which equality law can ameliorate the impact of systemic shocks such as Covid-19. The reactive nature of the civil liability model, and its dependence on individual enforcement, effectively guarantee that its response to systemic shocks will be delayed, partial, and patchy. It is also likely to incentivize public authorities to take a highly defensive approach to claims of discrimination, and to encourage technocratic responses to the exponential inequalities generated by such systemic shocks.

In this respect, it is notable that, at the time of writing—three years after the Covid-19 epidemic began—no serious equality law challenges have been brought against aspects of UK Covid-19 policy. Similarly, in other states, prominent legal challenges to Covid-19 control measures have thus far generally involved assertions of civil and political rights like freedom of association, rather than equality claims.[59] Equality law claims are difficult to bring, and difficult to win. It is therefore perhaps not surprising that discrimination claims are marginal to 'Covid-19 law', broadly defined—despite the well-documented discriminatory impact of the Covid-19 crisis, as outlined above.

4.3 Limits on Ambition

Even the 'embeddedness' of equality law can bring problems in its wake. Claims that stretch the boundaries of existing case law, whether at the legislative or constitutional dimension, are sometimes viewed as threats to its status. In particular, claims that extend well beyond its 'central case', into socio-economic or intersectional terrain, often attract strong pushback from judges and other legal actors. They are regarded as over-extending the elasticity of equality law, by stretching its scope and content beyond its 'natural' limits, and thus as threatening its semi-sacrosanct integrity. Various legal doctrines have thus been developed to limit the reach of equality law into 'inappropriate' terrain.[60]

The embeddedness of equality law can limit its scope in other ways. De Búrca has highlighted the potential value of developing new experimental approaches to address problems of inequality and discrimination.[61] However, such approaches can come into tension with the perceived need to maintain the structural integrity of existing equality law, and by extension its embedded status. In general, there tends to be a widespread reluctance to tinker with the existing framework of equality law, out of fear that this might destabilize its assumed legitimacy, which can discourage innovation.

---

[59] See the global overview of Covid-19-related case law at David Mednicoff, 'The Rule of Law, Covid-19, and the Struggle Against Autocratic Power: Towards a Multi-faceted Approach' *Lex-Atlas: Covid-19* (8 April 2022) https://lexatlas-c19.org/ (accessed 15 April 2022).

[60] See eg the application of the 'manifestly without reasonable foundation test' in the context of UK Article 14 ECHR jurisprudence, as discussed inter alia in the UK Supreme Court judgment of *R(SC) v Secretary of State for Work and Pensions* [2021] UKSC 26.

[61] Gráinne de Búrca, 'The Trajectories of European and American Antidiscrimination Law' (2012) 60 American Journal of Comparative Law 1.

This conservationist approach complicates attempts to extend equality law into new terrain by enlarging its scope: the further its reach deviates from its assumed 'central case', the more problematic such an extension is assumed to be. It also can make equality law unduly rigid—and deter attempts to move beyond the individual model of enforcement. These factors in turn inevitably inhibit its capacity to engage with exponential inequalities. Attempts to invoke equality law to engage with, for instance, the intersectional dimension of systemic shocks like Covid-19 will inevitably run up against fears that its outer boundaries are being stretched too far. Thus, equality law's embeddedness, generally a key strength, can also have a downside. It inhibits its capacity to engage with new frontiers of discrimination, so to speak—in particular those generated by systemic shocks, whose novelty lies precisely in their deviation from the established, embedded norms.

5 Escaping the Limits? The (Partial) Turn towards Substantive Equality

All of these limits of existing equality law are widely recognized. Academics, activists, and policy-makers have invested plenty of time and energy in attempting to overcome them, by extending the scope and 'bite' of equality law, and thus making it a more effective vehicle for combating structural inequalities.

The limited scope of equality law has triggered calls for anti-discrimination legislation to be extended to cover new grounds such as socio-economic status,[62] as well as intersectional discrimination[63]—reforms which have been translated into law in a number of different jurisdictions.[64] Similar arguments have been made in relation to constitutional equality protection.[65]

The enforcement limits of equality law, and its core civil liability operating system, have also generated plenty of proposals for reform. These have generally been focused on reducing dependence on individual legal enforcement, and encouraging employers, service providers and public authorities to adopt more proactive approaches to eliminating discrimination and promoting substantive equality. Examples of such initiatives include the introduction of public sector positive duties, the imposition of gender pay gap auditing requirements, increased use of both voluntary and compulsory positive action measures, and tentative measures to encourage pro-equality initiatives in public procurement.[66]

Attempts have also been made to empower equality bodies to carry out a wide-ranging enforcement and promotion role, including the exercise of investigative

---

[62] Tamas Kadar, *An Analysis of the Introduction of Socio-economic Status as a Discrimination Ground* (Equality Rights Alliance 2016).

[63] Atrey (n 39); Iyiola Solanke, 'Infusing the Silos in the Equality Act 2010 with Synergy' (2011) 40 Industrial Law Journal 336.

[64] Atrey (n 39).

[65] Laurens Lavrysen, 'Strengthening the Protection of Human Rights of Persons Living in Poverty under the ECHR' (2015) 33 Netherlands Quarterly of Human Rights 293; Beth Goldblatt, 'Intersectionality in International Anti-discrimination Law: Addressing poverty in its complexity' (2015) 21 Australian Journal of Human Rights 47.

[66] Sandra Fredman, 'Equality: A New Generation' (2001) 30 Industrial Law Journal 145.

powers, to ease the burden on individual enforcement.[67] In some jurisdictions, the remedial powers of courts and tribunals have also been widened, enabling them to require discriminating employers to adjust their policies and practices in ways that extend beyond the specific context of the individual claim in question.[68]

In the UK, the Hepple Report in 2000 essentially proposed the adoption of a radically new equality law model, with civil liability viewed as supplementary to internal self-regulation, structured by a framework of positive duties.[69] Such a 'responsive regulation' approach would add a new dimension to the flexibility of equality law, potentially opening the door to more participatory, proactive, and context-specific approaches than is possible under the existing model.[70]

More generally, an impressive academic case has been made for the historic 'central case' of equality law to be displaced by a new organizing model, built around a multidimensional, intersectional, 'substantive equality' framework. Fredman has produced the best developed account of how such a framework might be structured: she suggests it could have four analytical dimensions, namely a focus on (i) redressing disadvantage, (ii) tackling misrecognition, (iii) enhancing inclusion and 'voice', and (iv) accommodating difference, which would be applied to combat the marginalization of socially excluded groups.[71]

As Campbell notes, this framework has the potential to address 'the interaction between different facets of inequality' and in particular to capture the socio-economic and intersectional dimensions of social exclusion which currently fall beyond the scope of concern of the dominant 'central case' approach.[72] If widely embraced, it has the potential to reorient established 'central case' assumptions about the role and purpose of embedded equality law, in both its legislative and constitutional dimensions— something which has been already achieved to some degree in Canada and South Africa, in particular.[73]

Taken together, these various reform proposals add up to a cohesive package of measures. If adopted on a comprehensive basis, it could transform both the legislative

---

[67] See eg in the context of the UK, Colm O'Cinneide, 'The Commission for Equality and Human Rights: A New Institution for New and Uncertain Times' (2007) 36 Industrial Law Journal 141.

[68] See eg UK Equality Act 2010, ss 124(2)(c) and 124(3).

[69] Bob Hepple, Mary Coussey, and Tufyal Choudhury, *Equality: A New Framework: Report of the Independent Review of the Enforcement of UK Anti-Discrimination Legislation* (Hart Publishing 2000). For commentary see Joanna Harrington, 'Making Sense of Equality Law: A Review of the Hepple Report' (2001) 64 Modern Law Review 757.

[70] This approach was prefigured by developments in the context of disability discrimination law: Pamela S Karlan and George Rutherglen, 'Disabilities, Discrimination, and Reasonable Accommodation' (1996) 46 Duke Law Journal 1. See also McCrudden's seminal work on public procurement and 'fair employment' duties in Northern Ireland and elsewhere: Christopher McCrudden, *Buying Social Justice* (OUP 2007).

[71] Fredman (n 11).

[72] Meghan Campbell, 'The Austerity of Lone Motherhood: Discrimination Law and Benefit Reform' (2021) 41 Oxford Journal of Legal Studies 1197. See also Sandra Fredman, 'Positive Duties and Socio-Economic Disadvantage: Bringing Disadvantage onto the Equality Agenda' (2010) 15 European Human Rights Law Review 290.

[73] Fredman (n 11). See also the recent judgment of the Inter-American Court of Human Rights in *Case of the Workers of the Fireworks Factory in Santo Antônio de Jesus and their Families v Brazil*, Judgment of 15 July 2020, Ser C/407. See also for discussion of the case Aziz Tuffi Saliba and Mariana Ferolla Vallandro do Valle, 'The Inter-American Court of Human Rights and the Quest for Equality: The Fireworks Factory Case' *EJIL: Talk!* (20 January 2021) https://www.ejiltalk.org/the-inter-american-court-of-human-rights-and-the-quest-for-equality-the-fireworks-factory-case/ (accessed 15 April 2022).

and constitutional dimensions of equality law. In particular, it would extend the scope and flexibility of equality law, and reorient its immanent logic towards a new central focus on combating overlapping and multiplying forms of unjust group disadvantage.

Such a reorientation would arguably enhance the effectiveness of equality law, and do much to redress its existing limitations. Enlarging its scope of application would inevitably enlarge its potential reach, and open up new avenues for disadvantaged groups to challenge social exclusion. Encouraging proactive action by employers, service providers, and public authorities would reduce the emphasis on individual enforcement action. Giving equality law greater flexibility might help to reduce its embedded rigidity, and encourage wider engagement with the drivers of discrimination and social exclusion. Taken together, this comprehensive reform package would thus potentially alleviate some of the inadequacies exposed by #MeToo and Black Lives Matter. It would also clearly enhance its capacity to engage meaningfully with the exponential impact of systemic shocks.

However, there is here a catch here. The essential ingredients of this reform package are well known. They have been staples of academic and policy debate for at least two decades now. They have also acquired enough legal status to be more than just pious ideals. The key contours of the Canadian and South African jurisprudence have been laid down since the early 2000s while, for instance, the UK public sector positive duties have been in place for more or less the same duration. And yet, the existing template of equality law has largely remained untransformed. Outside of a few specific jurisdictions, the 'substantive equality' turn has yielded at best limited results.

This reflects the persisting dominance of orthodox 'central case' thinking. The more reforms deviate from this central case, the more they are viewed as potentially problematic 'bolt-ons' to the embedded legislative and constitutional structure of equality law. As a result, 'substantive equality' reforms, if implemented at all, are often framed and interpreted in a restrictive manner.

Thus, for example, positive duty obligations imposed on employers usually take the form of formalistic procedural requirements—such as an obligation to pay 'due regard', or to report on broad patterns of pay differentials.[74] Positive action measures still tend to be viewed as suspect exceptions to a general rule of non-differentiation.[75] Equality bodies are rarely given the powers and/or resources to play a leading role in securing compliance with equality law, while the remedial powers of courts and tribunals remain generally limited to what is normally available in standard civil liability litigation. Intersectionality receives plenty of lip service, but few if any concrete legal steps are taken to engage with it seriously.[76] The same may be said for the wider substantive equality framework: it is rare to see it explicitly contested, in academic writing or at the political level, but courts and legislators are usually slow to operationalize it in practice.

---

[74] Aileen McColgan, 'Litigating the Public Sector Equality Duty: The Story So Far' (2015) 35 Oxford Journal of Legal Studies 453.

[75] See eg the case law of the CJEU on positive action, as discussed in Lisa Waddington and Mark Bell, 'Exploring the Boundaries of Positive Action under EU Law: A Search for Conceptual Clarity' (2011) 48 Common Market Law Review 1503.

[76] For example, the 'dual discrimination' provisions of s 14 of the UK Equality Act 2010 have not been brought into effect.

Why has conventional 'central case' thinking remained so dominant in this context, despite the well-documented limits of existing equality law? The answer almost certainty is linked to the ambivalent status of equality and non-discrimination norms in contemporary society. They are formally valued, and given constitutional and legislative protection. However, they are also the subject of deep political contestation—not so much perhaps the norms themselves, but rather the extent of remedial action necessary to redress existing and emerging inequalities and how to (re)distribute the costs of such action. As a result, in the unequal societies in which we live, the more substantive and wide-ranging equality law becomes, the more potential controversy and contestation it attracts.

Hence it is predictable that legislators, judges, and other key legal actors, in designing, interpreting, and applying equality law, prefer to stick to the safe terrain of orthodox 'central case' approaches. An established political consensus exists about the need to combat discrimination based on single suspect grounds, in line with the 'central case'; no such consensus exists in respect of more ambitious, wider approaches.[77] Furthermore, judges in particular need to worry about democratic legitimacy: interpreting existing equality law in line with a wide-ranging substantive equality approach may be both normatively attractive and doctrinally justifiable, but the freedom of manoeuvre of courts in this regard will inevitably be limited by the constraints of their place in the separation of powers.[78]

Having said that, wider substantive equality approaches have gained some foothold in many legal systems. They share a close relationship with certain key elements of existing equality law, such as reasonable accommodation requirements and the prohibition on indirect discrimination: this means that they are not completely alien to status quo thinking.[79] Furthermore, the obvious inadequacies of the 'central case' model are widely acknowledged, as is the need for a more proactive and flexible equality law. So, while equality law remains predominantly structured around its historic 'central case' assumptions, more substantive approaches have nevertheless begun to exert influence over its development—as evidenced for example by the greater willingness of governments to consider the introduction of positive action measures, and to take other steps to promote a proactive approach to equality.[80]

This has left equality law in what might be described as a liminal state, mainly structured in terms of its established, constricted template, but increasingly influenced by

---

[77] Also, it is worth noting that the existing framework of equality law is firmly embedded in existing legislation and case law, while the substantive equality turn is still predominantly an academic and conceptual construction, meaning that the principle of inertia inevitably favours the former.

[78] See eg the UK Supreme Court judgment in *SC* (n 60).

[79] For the potential significance of the reasonable accommodation approach as a template for a wider reformulation of the equality law framework see Pamela S Karlan and George Rutherglen, 'Disabilities, Discrimination, and Reasonable Accommodation' (1996) 46 Duke Law Journal 1; Fredman (n 11).

[80] See eg in the UK the inclusion of a general positive duty in s 149 of the Equality Act 2010 and enlarged scope for employers to make use of positive action in s 159 of the same Act, as well as the introduction of the Equality Act 2010 (Equal Pay Audits) Regulations 2014 and the Equality Act 2010 (Gender Pay Gap Information) Regulations 2017. See also at the EU level the European Commission's 'Proposal for a Directive on improving the gender balance among non-executive directors of companies listed on stock exchanges and related measures' COM/2012/0614 final, 2012/0299(COD), although note that this proposed Directive has been repeatedly blocked by certain EU Member States within the European Council.

more substantive approaches. It may be that the pressure of social movements like #MeToo and Black Lives Matter, by spotlighting the limits of the status quo, will provide more impetus for a 'substantive turn'. Systemic shocks like Covid-19 may have a similar effect, especially if their exponential impact on existing patterns of inequality is taken into account. But there is a danger that necessary reform of equality law will come stumbling behind the multiplying, multifaceted inequalities generated by such crises, arriving too late to make much difference.

6 Conclusion: Beyond the Limits?

The achievements of equality law—its spreading global reach, and the way it offers comprehensive, flexible, and quasi-embedded protection against specific forms of discrimination—should be acknowledged. It remains one of the most potent—even perhaps *the* most potent—legal legacies of the post-1960s 'rights revolution'. But it is also necessary to recognize its limitations, which seriously impair its capacity to get to grips with the mushrooming forms of exponential inequality that can be generated by systemic shocks like Covid-19. This lack of capacity risks becoming a serious constraint on the effectiveness of equality law in an era of climate change, socio-economic destabilization, and geopolitical turbulence. In contrast to the dynamism of much of its development over the last half century, equality law may yet have a relatively stagnant future.

There are clearly identifiable reform options, as already discussed, which would enhance the extent to which equality law might ameliorate the impact of such exponential inequalities. But the background factors that constrain the current scope of equality law also limit take-up of these reform proposals, especially those that would advance the 'substantive equality' turn proposed by Fredman and others. Prevailing assumptions as to the 'proper' role and function of equality law remain strong. Legislative and constitutional controls on discrimination are viewed as legitimate insofar as they are restricted in scope, and do not extend too far beyond their established 'central case'. Otherwise, equality law might start eating away at the foundations of the unequal societies in which it takes effect—and, despite plenty of rhetoric to the contrary, its transformative impact has never really been intended to extend that far.

What wider lessons can be drawn from this (pessimistic) exploration of the limits of equality law? How should one respond to its deficiencies, while also taking account of the fragility of the contemporary socio-economic order and its capacity to generate exponentially increasing inequalities? What to do about these seemingly intractable constraints, at a time when the inadequacy of the existing law has been graphically highlighted?

One potential response might be simply to shrug. Laws rarely serve as a perfect solvent for society's problems. So, it could be argued that we should focus on what equality law does well, such as correcting specific types of individual and group injustices, and not worry too much about its limitations—beyond perhaps noting them with a fatalistic sigh, and cautioning equality law enthusiasts not to invest too much faith in legal remedies.[81] There may be no legal solutions to persisting and amplifying inequalities, despite what the professional egotism of lawyers might suggest. Ultimate salvation, insofar as it exists, is likely to lie elsewhere—perhaps in the mobilization of social movements, for example, or other forms of exclusively political activity.

However, such a response risks falling into another trap—namely, downplaying the incremental difference that well-designed laws can make, and the way they can provide disadvantaged groups with a platform to challenge oppressive power structures. Equality law may never be able to 'solve' exponential inequalities, in the way it has failed to provide a comprehensive solution to overt inequalities. But it can open up certain lines of legal challenge, generate expectations as to correct behaviour, and limit the manifestation of particular forms of inequality.[82]

As a result, proponents of reform should not give up. #MeToo and Black Lives Matter may have demonstrated the limits of existing equality law, but they also show that there is considerable political support for its scope and effectiveness to be enhanced. Also, while equality law's embeddedness may have a constraining dimension, it also makes it harder for sceptics to challenge reform proposals that can be framed as amplifying its impact. Furthermore, as consciousness of the historical legacy of colonialism, patriarchal rule, class oppression, and so on grows, and campaigning groups intensify pressure on public and private bodies to respond, the attractiveness of the 'substantive equality' turn is likely to grow.

More generally, it is possible to detect wider signs of a loosening of the grip of orthodox 'central case' thinking: the moral imperative to tackle intersectional factors such as poverty is increasingly acknowledged in public discourse, and chimes with the new politics of the post-2008 era with its avowed commitment (at the rhetorical level at least) to redressing socio-economic inequalities.[83] The much-heralded embrace of substantive equality, and a wider engagement with structural discrimination more generally, may be a long time coming—but that is not a reason for abandoning hope in its eventual arrival.

However, in pushing for legal reform, it might also be good to try and find ways of going beyond equality law more generally, in the sense of escaping the limits of the legal form, or at least reducing its inevitably constricting grip when it comes to determining what qualifies as unjustified discrimination. There may be value in looking to establish new mechanisms that provide opportunities for discrimination allegations to be discussed and resolved in a less juridified manner than that currently provided for by equality law.

Barmes has thus argued for more emphasis on collective dispute resolution processes in this regard, in her groundbreaking work on employment dispute resolution.[84] Similarly, writing with reference to the US context, Goldberg and Sturm have separately made similar arguments—with Goldberg calling for policy measures which will

---

[81] The reservations about the constraining effect of legal form on progressive agendas, as articulated by Carol Smart and other critical theorists, remain perennially relevant: see eg Carol Smart, *Feminism and the Power of Law* (Routledge 1989).
[82] Hepple (n 1).
[83] The work of Piketty and others has been very influential in this regard.
[84] Barmes (n 48).

encourage employers in particular to 'go beyond legal-accountability requirements' and embed flexible, discursive and responsive non-discrimination values within their workplace cultures.[85]

Such initiatives could be seen as an extension of the 'substantive equality' turn proposed by equality law reformers, and in particular of the desire to promote proactive action by employers, service providers, and public authorities that underpins the concept of positive duties. However, crucially, they aim to 'go beyond' equality law, so to speak—to depart from its emphasis on embedding comprehensive controls on discriminatory behaviour in law, and instead to encourage a more 'jurisgenerative' approach (to use Robert Cover's celebrated phrase),[86] whereby the subjects of law start to play a more active role in defining, interpreting, and applying the legal norms that govern their conduct. This approach has obvious risks in the context of equality law, given the disparities of power that form the background to this entire area of law. But, if built with suitable care on the foundations of the embedded architecture of existing equality law, it has the potential to reduce the technocratic drag of the existing legal framework, and possibly to encourage less defensiveness and entrenchment when it comes to the application of its core principles.

Furthermore, it may be possible to scale up such potentially participative, jurisgenerative mechanisms with a view to targeting the type of exponential inequalities generated by systemic shocks like Covid-19. The requirements of equality law, including positive duty obligations, could form a framework for wider, structured debate as to the relevant obligations of public and private sector bodies towards the various intersectionally defined social groups who are particularly exposed to the fallout from such crises—including socio-economically disadvantaged groups, such as 'traditional' working-class communities, who have not always been seen to benefit from the protection of equality law (disability and sometimes sex discrimination aside).

This may well sound like so much hot air: a random application of some of the vague, gesticulatory language invoking pious aspirations towards greater democratization that is currently in vogue. However, it actually involves a return to where this chapter began, namely the origins of equality law in the 1960s—and, in particular, to aspects of the original UK anti-discrimination legislation.

Back then, race discrimination complaints were initially handled by local Race Relations Boards, who would try to achieve some sort of structured resolution to a dispute before it was handed over to courts and the inevitably juridified legal process. Subsequently, the newly established equality and human rights commissions of the 1970s were supposed to play a similar dispute resolution role, combining investigative and mediation functions in seeking to provide both (i) individual redress for victims of discrimination and (ii) more general structural adjustments to pre-empt its future occurrence.[87]

---

[85] Goldberg (n 51); Susan Sturm, 'Second Generation Employment Discrimination: A Structural Approach' (2001) 101 Columbia Law Review 458.
[86] Robert M Cover, 'The Supreme Court, 1982 Term—Foreword: *Nomos* and Narrative' (1983) 97(4) Harvard Law Review 4.
[87] See in general Bindman and Lester (n 3).

Both of these institutional mechanisms were designed to be participative, and to avoid forcing individual claimants to litigate their claims through the court structure. Neither really succeeded: the necessary levels of funding needed to make such a remedial system work were not provided, and juridification took over.[88] However, it might be interesting to look again at the potential of such mechanisms, and how they might build on the nominally participative dimension of the positive duty requirements that have been introduced into law in various states.[89]

It also might be worth thinking of how such mechanisms might work on a scaled-up basis, with an eye on the problems of exponential inequalities. For example, is there a role for appropriately funded representative community bodies, or full-time 'equality advocates', with a wide remit extending into socio-economic and intersectional terrain, to review and report on the equality impact of public policies in specified areas of activity (eg healthcare, or welfare support)? The activities of such bodies might potentially extend well beyond the standard remedial framework of equality law. For example, they could become involved in negotiating structured remedies for past acts of discrimination, or facilitating the design and adoption of positive action measures to head off emerging, crisis-generated patterns of inequality.[90]

Similarly, might there be a case for establishing parliamentary equality committees, or an equality ombudsman, or some other equality-focused state institutional mechanism, and giving them wide-ranging investigative powers, to be exercised on their own initiative, with a view to monitoring and commenting on persisting, emerging, and exponentially amplified forms of inequality? The establishment of special representative structures, to redress the political marginalization of particular social groups, is an old feature of constitutional design, going back to the office of the Tribune within the Roman Republic.[91] It would be difficult, perhaps even politically paralysing, to set up such representative structures for each disadvantaged group within modern democratic societies.[92] But structures charged with a broad equality remit might be a different matter. Fresh imagination is needed when it comes to engaging with the inevitably *political* dimension of equality.

More generally, it is time to ask whether the embeddedness of equality law, which as discussed above is a double-edged sword, needs to be supplemented with more

---

[88] For a comprehensive overview of these developments see John Solomos, *Race and Racism in Britain* (3rd edn, Palgrave Macmillan 2003).
[89] For the argument that highlighting inequalities and enabling marginalized groups to contest structural forms of discrimination should be central to any serious attempt to tackle inequalities see Alice Evans, 'Politicising Inequality: The Power of Ideas' (2018) 13 World Development 360.
[90] At the time of writing this chapter, the Digital, Cultural, Media and Sport Committee of the UK House of Commons was hearing evidence into persisting patterns of structural race and religious discrimination within the context of Yorkshire cricket (https://committees.parliament.uk/event/6230). The revelations this triggered, and the redress mechanisms rapidly put into place as a consequence, highlight what a discursive, participatory approach to such issues may achieve, as distinct from a narrowly focused legal process.
[91] John P McCormick, *Machiavellian Democracy* (CUP 2011).
[92] But note the ongoing debate about the 2014 Uluru Statement from the Heart in Australia, and the call in the Final Report of the Referendum Council of the First Nations National Constitutional Convention for a 'First Nations Voice' to be given constitutional status: see Megan Davis, 'Constitutional recognition for Indigenous Australians must involve structural change, not mere symbolism' *The Conversation* (17 February 2020) https://theconversation.com/constitutional-recognition-for-indigenous-australians-must-involve-structural-change-not-mere-symbolism-131751 (accessed 15 April 2022).

participative, flexible, and wide-ranging mechanisms for engaging with the multifaceted forms of contemporary inequality. There are obvious dangers in experimenting with what has been a generally successful formula. However, given the limits of equality law as it currently stands, such experimentation may be necessary to prevent equality law from stagnating—especially in a new era of systemic shocks, and the exponential growth in inequality that can follow in their train.[93]

---

[93] Such a shift in equality law could be linked to a wider turn towards reimagining our political and legal architecture in the wake of the shared and collective vulnerabilities, as discussed in Martha Albertson Fineman, 'Populations, Pandemics, and Politics' (2021) 21 International Journal of Discrimination and the Law 184.

8
More than an Afterthought? Equality Law in Ireland during the Pandemic

Mark Bell

1 Introduction

It has been widely documented that Covid-19, and the measures taken by governments in response, have had disparate impacts upon certain social groups such as older people, younger people, women, or persons with disabilities. It is, of course, difficult to determine whether a different blend of law and policy responses would have been as effective in protecting public health, but less adverse for specific groups. In exploring that issue, the role of equality law comes under the spotlight. Has it functioned effectively in the midst of this crisis? This chapter explores the answer to that question through a case study looking at the experience of Ireland. In particular, it will focus on the role played by equality law in shaping the actions of public bodies, given the leading role of the state in taking emergency measures. In this respect, the crisis provides insight into whether equality considerations were truly embedded in public decision-making processes, or whether they were swept aside in the midst of the storm.

Section 2 sets the scene by providing an overview of the emerging data on inequalities in Ireland as experienced over the course of the pandemic. Section 3 examines efforts to tackle discrimination arising from the pandemic. There is currently very little evidence of litigation on discrimination related to the pandemic, but this section will illustrate how equality law has proven relevant to debates around the eligibility criteria for various employment and welfare support measures. Section 4 takes as its starting point Ireland's public sector equality and human rights duty. In principle, this should have prompted public bodies to have regard to equality considerations when taking measures in response to the pandemic. Section 4 also considers some initial evidence of whether this happened in practice. Section 5 reflects on what the Irish experience indicates about how equality law functions under emergency circumstances.

2 Inequalities in Ireland during the Pandemic

As in other countries, the pandemic has impacted differently upon different social groups. In terms of health outcomes, older people living in residential care settings form a significant proportion of all deaths related to Covid-19,[1] and—more generally—Covid-19 mortality has impacted older people more severely.[2] Unlike some other jurisdictions, there has been little public discussion of disparities in health outcomes related to ethnicity. Initial evidence indicates that those from minority ethnic communities have higher rates of infection than 'White Irish', but lower rates of mortality.[3] This may reflect the different demographic profiles of migrant communities in Ireland, which have a lower proportion of persons aged over sixty-five. Those from the Traveller community also had an elevated risk of infection, which may reflect overcrowding in accommodation.[4] At the same time, the existing research data has limitations. Analysis of ethnicity of those who died is incomplete and the prevalence of testing may not be comparable across ethnic groups.[5]

As in many countries, the Irish government imposed extensive restrictions on economic and social activities in order to suppress virus transmission. This included three extended periods of 'total lockdown', when most non-essential businesses were required to close and most forms of social activity that involved people gathering were not permitted.[6] It is evident that the effects of these restrictions were particularly severe for certain social groups. For example, children with disabilities and their families were acutely affected by the closure of all schools in spring 2020[7] and again in early 2021. For some adults with disabilities, especially those with intellectual disabilities, day services are a key source of support in terms of employment and personal development activities.[8] These were closed from March to August 2020. Adjacently, the impacts of requirements to stay at home and to limit social interactions were particularly adverse for certain groups, such as those at risk of domestic abuse.[9] In a survey of over 2,000 young LGBTI+ people, 56 per cent reported that they were not fully accepted in their home environment and 58 per cent said that their mental health was bad or very bad.[10]

---

[1] In respect of the first wave of Covid-19 in spring 2020, it has been estimated that 56 per cent of all deaths were residents of nursing homes: Houses of the Oireachtas Special Committee on Covid-19 Response, *Interim Report on Covid-19 in Nursing Homes* (2020, 33 SCCR002) 4.

[2] Central Statistics Office (CSO), 'Analysis of Underlying Cause of Death Data, Including Covid-19' (2021) https://www.cso.ie/en/releasesandpublications/fr/fr-ucd2020/analysisofunderlyingcauseofdeathdataincludingcovid-19januarytooctober2020/ (accessed 7 December 2021).

[3] Shannen Enright and others, 'Covid-19 and Non-Irish Nationals in Ireland' (Economic and Social Research Institute (ESRI) 2020) 12.

[4] ibid 12.

[5] ibid 14–15.

[6] On the pattern of full and eased restrictions during 2020 see Conor Casey and others, 'Ireland's Emergency Powers During the Covid-19 Pandemic' (IHREC 2021) 32. The Covid-19 Law and Human Rights Observatory, Trinity College Dublin, provides an online repository of legal instruments and official guidance adopted during the pandemic. See https://www.tcd.ie/law/tricon/covidobservatory/index.php (accessed 8 December 2021).

[7] National Disability Authority (NDA), 'NDA's Submission to the Oireachtas Special Committee on Covid-19 Response on the Impact of COVID-19 on Persons with Disabilities and the Disability Sector' (2020) 7 http://nda.ie/publications/health/covid-19/impact-of-covid-nda-submission-june-20201.pdf (accessed 8 December 2021).

[8] ibid 8.

[9] Women's Aid reported a 43 per cent increase in contacts in 2020 compared to 2019: Women's Aid, 'Annual Impact Report 2020' (Women's Aid 2021) 13.

[10] BeLonGTo Youth Services, 'LGBTI+ Life in Lockdown: 1 Year Later Key Findings' (2021) 5–6 https://www.belongto.org/wp-content/uploads/2021/06/LGBTI-Life-in-Lockdown-1-Year-Later_BeLonG-To-Youth-Services.pdf (accessed 8 December 2021).

Given the confines of this chapter, it is not possible to provide an exhaustive analysis of the many diverse impacts of pandemic restrictions, but the remainder of this section will focus upon the labour market. Looking initially at loss of employment, this was greater for young people. In May 2020, it was reported that 'younger persons have experienced the highest rates of loss of employment and temporary layoff, with 46 per cent of 15-24 year olds being temporarily laid off and over a fifth (22 per cent) experiencing loss of employment'.[11] This pattern continued during the pandemic. Many workers who were laid off because of the pandemic were eligible for a state benefit called the Pandemic Unemployment Payment (PUP). In November 2020, 48 per cent of those receiving the PUP were aged thirty-four or younger.[12]

Data is also emerging that indicates that certain migrant or minority communities were impacted more heavily in terms of job loss. Research in 2020 found that 13 per cent of PUP recipients were Eastern European nationals, although they constitute only 7 per cent of the labour market.[13] Similarly, non-EU nationals comprised 10 per cent of PUP recipients, but only 5 per cent of the labour market.[14] In part, this reflects the over-representation of these groups in those sectors of the economy that experienced the largest reductions in employment. Enwright and others draw attention to the vulnerability of those who were employed in roles that were neither classified as 'essential' work, nor were amenable to being performed remotely, such as workers in non-essential retail and hospitality.[15] Their research found that Eastern European nationals were over-represented amongst those working in roles that were less conducive to being performed remotely,[16] but despite taking this into account, this alone did not explain the scale of their job losses.[17] The fall in employment was particularly high for Eastern European women.[18] This data underlines the way in which pre-existing socio-economic disadvantage has been accentuated by the pandemic, as existing research already indicated that Eastern European nationals had the highest rates of low hourly or weekly pay in the labour market.[19]

Research for the European Institute for Gender Equality (EIGE) has provided extensive evidence of the disparate impact of the pandemic on women in the labour market.[20] This again highlights the factors of intersectionality and socio-economic disadvantage; it identified young, low-educated, and migrant women as amongst those most adversely affected.[21] EIGE noted that Ireland had the third highest job losses amongst women in the EU in the second quarter of 2020, as well as a greater reduction in paid working hours for women than men.[22] At the same time as paid

---

[11] CSO, 'Employment and Life Effects of Covid-19' (2020) https://www.cso.ie/en/releasesandpublicati ons/er/elec19/employmentandlifeeffectsofcovid-19/ (accessed 8 December 2021).
[12] Kieran McQuinn and others, 'Quarterly Economic Commentary' (ESRI 2020)26.
[13] Enright and others (n 3) 28.
[14] ibid.
[15] ibid 26.
[16] ibid 26.
[17] ibid 31.
[18] ibid 38.
[19] Frances McGinnity and others, 'Monitoring Decent Work in Ireland' (ESRI 2021)69, 73.
[20] EIGE, 'Gender Equality and the Socio-Economic Impact of the COVID-19 Pandemic' (EIGE 2021).
[21] ibid 9.
[22] ibid 10–11.

work was decreasing, there was an increase in the amount of time that women were devoting to unpaid care, such as caring for children, older relatives, and performing housework.[23] While this data captured the initial impact of the first lockdown, information from later points in the pandemic suggests that the impact on overall rates of male and female employment and unemployment has been broadly similar.[24]

Similarly, the standard data does not capture the much larger number of people who are temporarily laid off because of the pandemic. The standard unemployment rate in the first quarter of 2021 was 7.1 per cent, but when adjusted for Covid-19 absences, this rose to 25.7 per cent.[25] As mentioned above, those absent from work are often in receipt of the PUP. On the one hand, in both the first and third lockdown periods, there was a considerably higher number of men than women in receipt of the PUP.[26] On the other hand, the PUP was originally available at four levels of weekly income support, ranging from €203 to €350, which reflected income prior to being out of work. Men comprised the majority of those on the highest rate (€350 per week), while women formed the majority of those on the lower rates.[27]

Data indicates that the experience of compelled working from home, when coupled with school closures and restrictions on the availability of caring services, impacted women more adversely.[28] A survey of 271 organizations identified significant differences in the experience of women workers. Thirty-one per cent of respondents stated that more women than men had requested unpaid leave while 48 per cent said that more women than men had requested changes to working patterns in order to accommodate caring responsibilities.[29]

3 Combating Discrimination during the Pandemic

As described above, it is clear that the measures taken in response to the pandemic have had a disparate impact upon certain groups in society. This part of the chapter explores whether there is evidence of the law being used to tackle instances of alleged

---

[23] ibid 36.

[24] Figure 3.3 Employment rate for those aged 15 to 64 years by sex, Quarter 3 1998 to Quarter 3 2021: CSO, 'Labour Force Survey Quarter 3 2021' (2021) https://www.cso.ie/en/releasesandpublications/ep/p-lfs/labourforcesurveyquarter32021/employment/ (accessed 7 December 2021).

[25] ibid 'Summary Results'.

[26] CSO, 'COVID-19 Income Supports: An Analysis of Recipients March 2020 to May 2021' (2021) https://www.cso.ie/en/releasesandpublications/fp/fp-c19isar/covid-19incomesupports-ananalysisofrecipientsmarch2020tomay2021/pandemicunemploymentpayment/ (accessed 8 December 2021). This may reflect the sectors of the economy affected by restrictions: notably, there were tighter restrictions on the construction sector during the first and third lockdowns.

[27] For example, on 25 May 2021, 63 per cent of recipients of the €350 rate were men, while 56 per cent of recipients of the €203 rate were women: Department of Social Protection, 'Update on Payments Awarded for Covid-19 Pandemic Unemployment Payment and Enhanced Illness Benefit' (25 May 2021).

[28] CSO, 'Social Impact of Covid-19 on Women and Men' (2020) https://www.cso.ie/en/releasesandpublications/er/sic19wm/socialimpactofcovid-19onwomenandmenapril2020/ (accessed 8 December 2021).

[29] In contrast, only 3 per cent of respondents said that more men than women had requested unpaid leave and 3 per cent said that more men than women had requested changes to working patterns in order to facilitate caring responsibilities: IBEC, 'Impact of Covid-19 on Women' (2021) https://www.ibec.ie/connect-and-learn/media/2021/04/18/new-ibec-research-reveals-impact-of-covid-on-women-in-business (accessed 8 December 2021).

discrimination arising during the pandemic. In Ireland, there are two principal statutes that prohibit discrimination. The Employment Equality Acts (EEA) 1998–2021 prohibit discrimination in employment and related areas on nine grounds: gender; civil status; family status; sexual orientation; religion; age; disability; race; and membership of the Traveller community. The Equal Status Acts (ESA) 2000–2018 prohibit discrimination in the provision of services, accommodation, education, and in the activities of certain private associations. The ESA applies to the same list of nine grounds found in the EEA, but discrimination in accommodation is also prohibited on the ground of being in receipt of housing assistance (ie social welfare payments).[30] In most instances, complaints under the EEA and the ESA must be brought initially to the Workplace Relations Commission (WRC), where they are determined by an adjudicator.[31] In certain circumstances, discriminatory measures may also be challenged for their compatibility with the constitutional right to equality.[32] Such proceedings commence in the High Court.

At the time of writing, there are only a few examples of these sources of equality law being relied upon in litigation that relates to measures taken in response to the pandemic. Several complaints have been brought under the EEA and the ESA that involved conflicts arising in retail and hospitality settings because the complainant was not wearing a face mask, and where the complainant argued that they had sufficient medical reasons not to do so.[33] In none of these cases did the WRC adjudicator find that the facts disclosed unlawful discrimination.

It is reasonable to expect that the WRC will face further discrimination litigation connected to the pandemic. An example of the type of situation that may arise can be found in *An Operations Coordinator v A Facilities Management Service Provider*.[34] In this case, the WRC adjudicator held that a worker had been constructively dismissed because of her employer's refusal to permit her to work from home after the outbreak of the pandemic in spring 2020. Although the case was heard under unfair dismissal law, it is noteworthy that the claimant's desire to work from home related to her concern about the risks posed to her husband and father who had underlying health conditions. While the facts of the case do not establish whether her husband or father had conditions that meet the definition of disability, the scenario presented by the case illustrates that an employer's refusal of permission to work remotely might raise issues of discrimination by association on grounds of disability or age.

---

[30] In addition, the ESA construes acts of victimization related to discrimination proceedings as a specific discrimination ground: s 3(2)(j).

[31] Complaints of discrimination in relation to gaining entry to licensed premises (eg pubs) are, however, heard by the District Court: Intoxicating Liquor Act 2003, s 19(2).

[32] Article 40.1 of the Constitution of Ireland states: 'All citizens shall, as human persons, be held equal before the law. This shall not be held to mean that the State shall not in its enactments have due regard to differences of capacity, physical and moral, and of social function.'

[33] *Keegan v Family First Medical Practice* ADJ-00031787 (12 October 2021) (no evidence of disability provided by the complainant who insisted on wearing a face visor rather than a face mask in a medical practice); *Dobson v Mulligan Specsavers Ltd* ADJ-00033635 (28 September 2021) (no discrimination where a store manager sought to establish why a customer was not wearing a face mask); *Winters v Holland and Barrett Ltd* ADJ-00033646 (8 September 2021) (no discrimination or victimization in disciplinary measures taken against an employee following a dispute with a customer. The dispute arose from the employee not wearing a face mask, but she was exempt from that requirement due to disability).

[34] ADJ-00028293 (7 January 2021).

There is also little evidence of discrimination claims being raised in judicial review proceedings before the High Court. The constitutional guarantee of equality was invoked in a case that challenged the emergency arrangements for calculating grades in the Leaving Certificate (the qualification typically taken upon completing secondary education). In 2020, the state examinations were cancelled and replaced by a system for calculating grades, but this excluded some 'out-of-school' students, such as those home-schooled children who received their tutoring exclusively from family members. This was successfully challenged, but the High Court and the Court of Appeal relied upon administrative law principles rather than exploring the alleged breach of equality rights.[35] It is, however, worth noting the reasoning that the Court of Appeal adopted when rejecting the minister's argument that the exclusion of home-schooled students was justified by the dissatisfaction that might arise amongst in-school students if special arrangements were made for the former:

> The Court cannot abdicate its role to protect and vindicate the respondents' constitutional rights nor allow constitutional rights of a minority to be dealt a significant and real blow simply because others in society would be aggrieved by a mechanism which is designed to take account of the minority's (constitutionally protected) special circumstances.[36]

This brief discussion indicates that litigation has not yet played a significant role in tackling instances of discrimination arising during the pandemic. This reflects the typically reactive and remedial role of litigation, which often concerns situations that have already occurred in the past. That said, the binding nature of obligations in equality legislation may play a role in forcing change even outside of the courtroom. This can be seen in the debates that arose over the eligibility criteria for employment and welfare supports.

The first example concerns the Temporary Wage Subsidy Scheme.[37] This provided a wage subsidy for businesses who were able to demonstrate that there would be a reduction in turnover or customer orders by at least 25 per cent in the period from 14 March to 30 June 2020.[38] The wage subsidy was paid directly to the employer, but only in respect of 'an individual who was on the payroll of the employer as at 29 February 2020'.[39] This had the effect of excluding those who were not on the payroll because

---

[35] *Elijah Burke v The Minister for Education* [2020] IEHC 418; *NP (A Minor) Suing by her Mother and Next Friend BP v The Minister for Education and Skills* [2020] IEHC 479; *Elijah Burke v The Minister for Education and Skills; NP (A Minor) Suing by her Mother and Next Friend BP v The Minister for Education and Skills* [2021] IECA 67. A total of 929 candidates for the Leaving Certificate in 2020 were not attached to a school or other authorized educational centre; some were candidates due to sit exams in schools that they previously attended. Of these, 173 candidates were refused calculated grades on the basis that they had no tutor or an unregistered teacher: [2021] IECA 67 [45]–[46]. This included those who were home-schooled by family members. The case did not disclose any further information about the general characteristics of home-schooled children, such as religion or nationality. On equality of opportunity and the method of calculating grades see *Sherry v The Minister for Education and Skills and Others* [2021] IEHC 128 [6], [114] (Meenan J).

[36] [2021] IECA 67 [267].

[37] This was established in the Emergency Measures in the Public Interest (Covid-19) Act 2020, s 28.

[38] ibid s 28(3). This period was later extended to 31 August 2020 by the Financial Provisions (Covid-19) (No 2) Act 2020, s 2(1)(a)(i). A new wage subsidy scheme was created from September 2020.

[39] Emergency Measures in the Public Interest (Covid-19) Act 2020, s 28(1).

they were on maternity leave or other types of unpaid family leave. The scheme was included in an Act covering a wide range of emergency measures that was adopted swiftly by the Oireachtas (Irish Parliament) over the period from 24 to 27 March 2020. Given the speed of the drafting of the legislation, it appears that the effect on those on maternity and other types of leave was an oversight. The risk that arose from this exclusion was that an employer would then face higher costs for such employees' wages. This could incentivize the employer to lay off such employees, given that there was a separate scheme providing a social welfare payment (the PUP) for those temporarily laid off because of the pandemic.

The issue was raised by many deputies in a parliamentary debate on 20 May 2020. The Minister for Finance acknowledged that the problem arose from the terms of the scheme, while stating that 'of course the intention of the legislation was to treat all of our citizens and employees equally'.[40] The minister indicated that his department was exploring how the issue could be rectified but, given that the requirement was found in primary legislation, then legislative amendment might be required. If this was the case, there would be further delay in correcting the problem. On 27 May 2020, Ireland's statutory body for the promotion of equality, Irish Human Rights and Equality Commission (IHREC), wrote to the Minister for Finance arguing that the exclusion of women returning from maternity leave was in breach of EU gender equality law, specifically Article 157 of the Treaty on the Functioning of the European Union (TFEU) on equal pay, Articles 21 and 23 of the Charter of Fundamental Rights, and various provisions of Directives 92/85 and 2006/54.[41] While recognizing that amendment of the legislation might provide the ultimate solution, in the interim IHREC called upon the government to disapply the relevant provision on the basis of the primacy of EU law.

In making this argument, IHREC was able to draw upon a 2018 judgment of the Court of Justice in a case which it had supported.[42] In the latter case, IHREC had provided legal representation to two complainants who challenged the upper age limit of thirty-five for recruitment to the Irish police service as age discrimination. The case posed the question of whether, in the event of a conflict between domestic legislation and a provision of EU law, the WRC had the jurisdiction to disapply domestic legislation. The Court of Justice held that a specialized adjudicatory body entrusted with responsibility for implementing the obligations of EU anti-discrimination law, such as the WRC, should disapply provisions of national law in order to ensure that EU law was fully effective.[43] This was a prominent decision in Ireland, which underscored the obligations that flow from the primacy of EU law.

Two days after IHREC's letter, on 29 May 2020, it was announced that employees returning from maternity or adoptive leave would be admitted to the wage subsidy scheme.[44] This was effective from 8 June 2020 and included employees on other

---

[40] Paschal Donohoe TD, Dáil Deb (20 May 2020) vol 993, no 3.
[41] Letter from Dr Frank Conaty to the Minister for Finance (27 May 2021) https://www.ihrec.ie/app/uploads/2020/05/27-May-2020-IHREC-letter-to-Minister-for-Finance.pdf (accessed 8 December 2021).
[42] Case C-378/17 *Minister for Justice and Equality and Commissioner of the Garda Síochána* ECLI:EU:C:2018:979.
[43] ibid [48]–[50].
[44] Revenue, 'Revenue to Implement TWSS Changes for Employees who have been on Maternity and Adoptive Leave' (29 May 2020) https://www.revenue.ie/en/corporate/press-office/press-releases/2020/

'related unpaid leave'.[45] Employers could retrospectively claim the subsidy in respect of any of the salaries of such employees, if they had returned to the payroll since the scheme started in March 2020. At this point, the legislation had not been changed, but the Minister for Finance subsequently explained that the changes were put into effect by 'the Revenue Commissioners on the basis of their care and management provisions'.[46] Finally, in August 2020, the wage subsidy scheme was amended in order to include those employees who returned to work after 1 March 2020 following maternity and other types of leave.[47]

The episode of the Temporary Wage Subsidy Scheme illustrated the influence that equality legislation can exert, even prior to the initiation of any legal proceedings. It is not clear from information in the public domain why the government decided to rectify the discriminatory operation of the scheme in advance of making the necessary legislative amendment. There was political pressure within Parliament, but it is striking that the legal arguments submitted by IHREC invoked the primacy of EU law in order to demonstrate that there was a legal justification (indeed, a legal obligation) to correct the problem even if this entailed disapplication of a provision of primary legislation. It seems reasonable to doubt whether the government would have acted so swiftly if there had been no obligation in either Irish or EU law to avoid such discrimination. Indeed, a similar pattern of events unfolded in relation to the PUP.[48] After some initial confusion, it was decided that asylum seekers who lost their jobs were not eligible for this benefit if they were resident in direct provision centres.[49] IHREC then wrote to the minister responsible, arguing that the exclusion of this category of workers was in breach of the right to equal treatment in EU law, as well as under the Constitution and the European Convention on Human Rights Act 2013.[50] Several months later, the government altered the PUP rules in order to make this available to residents of direct provision.[51]

---

pr-290520-revenue-to-implement-twss-changes-for-employees-who-have-been-on-maternity-and-adoptive-leave.aspx (accessed 8 December 2021).

[45] Revenue, 'Revenue Confirm TWSS Changes for Employees who have been on Maternity, Adoptive and Certain Other Benefits Paid by DEASP are Now in Place' (8 June 2020) https://www.revenue.ie/en/corporate/press-office/press-releases/2020/pr-080620-revenue-confirm-twss-changes-for-employees-on-maternity-adoptive-other-benefits.aspx (accessed 8 December 2021).
[46] Paschal Donohue TD, Dáil Deb (29 July 2020) vol 996, no 2.
[47] Financial Provisions (Covid-19) (No 2) Act 2020, s 2(1)(b).
[48] The PUP was first introduced on 16 March 2020, but then replaced by the Covid-19 PUP from 5 August 2020: Department of Social Protection, 'Operational Guidelines: COVID-19 Pandemic Unemployment Payment (PUP)' (2021) https://www.gov.ie/en/publication/aa03c-operational-guidelines-covid-19-pandemic-unemployment-payment-pup/ (accessed 8 December 2021).
[49] Direct provision is a scheme of group accommodation and other services provided for those applying for international protection in Ireland. For a detailed account of the administrative deliberations that led to the decision to exclude asylum seekers see Liam Thornton, 'Challenging the Unlawful Exclusion of Asylum Seekers from Pandemic Unemployment Payment' (2020) https://liamthornton.ie/2020/06/04/challenging-the-unlawful-exclusion-of-asylum-seekers-from-pandemic-unemployment-payment/ (accessed 8 December 2021).
[50] Letter from Dr Frank Conaty to the Minister for Employment Affairs and Social Protection (28 May 2020) https://www.ihrec.ie/app/uploads/2020/05/28-May-2020-IHREC-Letter-to-Minister-for-Employment-Affairs-and-Social-Protection.pdf (accessed 8 December 2021).
[51] Department of Social Protection, 'Access to COVID-19 Enhanced Illness Benefit and the Pandemic Unemployment Payment for People in Direct Provision' (7 August 2020) https://www.gov.ie/en/press-rele

The above examples indicate the role that equality legislation plays in influencing political debate around the appropriateness of government measures, even in situations where no litigation or individual complaints have yet arisen. At the same time, arguments based on the requirements of equality legislation were not always successful in bringing about changes. Notably, the statute establishing the PUP specifies that it is not available to those who have attained pensionable age, which is currently sixty-six.[52] This meant that workers who were sixty-six or older and who lost their jobs due to the pandemic were not eligible for this benefit. While such individuals may be eligible for a state pension, this is dependent upon other conditions and the rate of pension payment may be lower than that which they would have received from the PUP.[53] Although this is a difference of treatment on grounds of age, it would not be open to challenge under the ESA. This is because of an exemption in section 14(1): 'Nothing in this Act shall be construed as prohibiting—(a) the taking of any action that is required by or under—(i) any enactment ...'. The term 'enactment' covers both primary legislation and statutory instruments.[54] Consequently, insofar as the conditions for welfare supports are laid down in an 'enactment', then they cannot be challenged as discrimination contrary to the ESA.[55] As EU equality legislation does not prohibit age discrimination in the field of social protection, it is unlikely to assist a potential complainant. It is true that such measures are potentially open to review under the constitutional equality clause. While the Supreme Court has accepted that differences of treatment based on age fall within the ambit of Article 40.1, it has left open the strictness of scrutiny to be applied: 'classification by reference to age or disability may be suspect or may be easily explained. Benefits granted by reference to age or disability may be easy to justify'.[56] All things considered, it is likely that the age limit for receiving the PUP is permissible under the current legal framework, which weakened the arguments for its removal. Indeed, IHREC did not intervene publicly on this issue.

4 Promoting Equality during the Pandemic

The discussion in section 3 of this chapter has begun to illustrate that the main function of equality legislation during the initial period of the pandemic has not been found in the courtroom. This section will develop that theme further by examining the functioning of the public sector equality and human rights duty.

---

ase/90416-access-to-covid-19-enhanced-illness-benefit-and-the-pandemic-unemployment-payment-for-people-in-direct-provision/ (accessed 8 December 2021).

[52] Social Welfare (Covid-19) (Amendment) Act 2020, s 68L(1)(a).
[53] Kitty Holland, 'Older Workers Cry Foul Over Being Refused Covid-19 Benefit' *Irish Times* (14 April 2021).
[54] Interpretation Act 2005, s 2(1) states that '"enactment" means an Act or a statutory instrument or any portion of an Act or statutory instrument'. This reading of s 14(1) was applied by the High Court in *AB v Road Safety Authority* [2021] IEHC 217. See further Judy Walsh, *Equal Status Acts 2000-2011: Discrimination in the Provision of Goods and Services* (Blackhall Publishing 2012) 50–56.
[55] In contrast, in *G v Department of Social Protection* [2015] IEHC 419 [144] O'Malley J expressed the view that a non-statutory social welfare scheme would 'probably' be open to review under the ESA.
[56] *Fleming v Ireland and Others* [2013] IESC 19 [130] (Denham CJ).

4.1 The Public Sector Equality and Human Rights Duty

Section 42(1) of Irish Human Rights and Equality Commission (IHREC) Act 2014 states:

> A public body shall, in the performance of its functions, have regard to the need to—
>
> (a) eliminate discrimination,
> (b) promote equality of opportunity and treatment of its staff and the persons to whom it provides services, and
> (c) protect the human rights of its members, staff and the persons to whom it provides services.

In implementation of this duty, a public body is required to publish its assessment of the equality and human rights issues that 'it believes to be relevant to the functions and purpose of the body', as well as identifying the 'policies, plans and actions in place or proposed to be put in place to address those issues'.[57] It should then report annually on 'developments and achievements' in respect of its implementation of the duty. Although this is a statutory duty, it does not appear to be open to enforcement by a private person before the courts. Section 42(11) states that 'nothing in this section shall of itself operate to confer a cause of action on any person against a public body in respect of the performance by it of its functions'. Instead, IHREC is the main vehicle for enforcement. It is empowered to provide guidance for public bodies on the implementation of the duty; this focuses upon what public bodies must do to fulfil their duties to 'assess', 'address', and 'report'.[58] There is no express obligation on public bodies to conduct equality impact assessments in the policy formulation process. That said, IHREC's guidance flags up the necessity of some process for evaluating the impact of policies and it highlights the relevance of other requirements for impact assessment in public policy-making.[59] If IHREC considers that a body is failing to comply with the duty, then it can invite that body to review its compliance with the duty and/or to prepare a report and an action plan in respect of the duty.[60] So the character of the duty is not one that emphasizes legality in the sense of litigation and court-based enforcement. Instead, it is designed to influence decision-making and organizational practice. This tallies with the statutory objectives of IHREC, which include developing 'a culture of respect for human rights, equality, and intercultural understanding in the State'.[61]

---

[57] IHREC Act 2014, s 42(2).
[58] IHREC, 'Implementing the Public Sector Equality and Human Rights Duty' (2019) https://www.ihrec.ie/app/uploads/2019/03/IHREC_Public_Sector_Duty_Final_Eng_WEB.pdf (accessed 8 December 2021).
[59] ibid 11.
[60] IHREC Act 2014, s 42(5).
[61] ibid s 10(10)(b).

4.2 IHREC and the Equality and Human Rights Duty during the Pandemic

Although the public sector duty was established through IHREC Act 2014, its implementation has been an incremental process.[62] IHREC was given a pivotal role in its oversight, but it was a new organization, formed out of a merger of the pre-existing Equality Authority and the Irish Human Rights Commission. It has gradually expanded the guidance available to public bodies, alongside training events and funding projects on implementing the duty.[63] It has not, however, exercised the power to prepare a statutory code of practice on the duty, which would be admissible in legal proceedings.[64]

The pandemic witnessed the state taking truly exceptional measures such as restricting civil liberties, and curtailing economic and social activities, alongside a significant expansion of publicly funded business and welfare supports for those affected by the restrictions. Given the magnitude of the state's role in this time of crisis, the public sector duty played a potentially important role in ensuring that equality and human rights issues were adequately considered. Indeed, in August 2020 IHREC issued a guidance note for public bodies to clarify that the duty remained applicable during an emergency and that it should be taken into account when such bodies were designing measures in response to Covid-19.[65] IHREC also invoked the duty in its engagement with specific public bodies. In May 2020, it wrote to the Minister for Education and Skills about the arrangements for calculated grades. IHREC noted that the section 42 duty applied to such functions and urged the minister to take further steps in order to ensure the avoidance of any risk of bias in the calculated grades process.[66]

It is, of course, difficult to make any general evaluation of the extent to which public bodies acted upon the equality and human rights duty during the pandemic. Research for IHREC has, however, cast doubt on whether the duty was effectively implemented at the highest levels of decision-making.[67] At the outset of the pandemic, wide-ranging powers to take 'extraordinary measures' in response to Covid-19 were conferred on the Minister for Health.[68] When exercising such powers, the minister was required to have regard to advice from the Chief Medical Officer (CMO). The CMO chaired National Public Health Emergency Team (NPHET) for Covid-19. During the course

---

[62] Niall Crowley, 'A Duty to Value: Implementing the Public Sector Equality and Human Rights Duty' (2017) 65 Administration 141, 156.
[63] These activities are detailed in IHREC's annual reports.
[64] IHREC Act 2014, s 42(4)(b).
[65] IHREC, 'Covid-19 and the Public Sector Equality and Human Rights Duty' (2020) https://www.ihrec.ie/app/uploads/2020/09/Guidance-Note-on-COVID-19-and-the-Public-Sector-Equality-and-Human-Right-Duty.pdf (accessed 8 December 2021).
[66] Letter from Dr Frank Conaty to the Minister for Education and Skills (27 May 2020) https://www.ihrec.ie/app/uploads/2020/05/27-May-2020-IHREC-Letter-to-Minister-for-Education-and-Skills.pdf (accessed 8 December 2021).
[67] Casey and others (n 6).
[68] Health (Preservation and Protection and other Emergency Measures in the Public Interest) Act 2020 amending the Health Act 1947, s 31A.

of the pandemic, the recommendations of NPHET on the restrictions necessary to protect public health were highly influential and often, if not always, followed by the government.[69] Early in the pandemic, a sub-group of NPHET prepared a document on an 'ethical framework for decision-making in a pandemic'.[70] This recognized the 'moral equality' of all human persons and the need to avoid unfair discrimination or stigmatization in the measures taken. It also acknowledged the risk of exacerbating pre-existing health inequalities for socially disadvantaged groups. In response, IHREC wrote to the Minister for Health to express concern that the document did not expressly recognize the *legal* requirements arising from domestic and international equality law.[71] Casey and others observed that:

> NPHET itself gives some consideration to the sort of concerns that are reflected in human rights and equality guarantees, but has neither legal expertise in these matters nor direct insight into the experiences of those who would be affected. While the Government is not bound to follow NPHET's advice, shifting political dynamics may leave the Government with little alternative. Also, there is frequently very little time between NPHET's recommendation and new regulations being adopted. This suggests that by the time NPHET makes its recommendation, it is often too late for any meaningful consideration to be given to human rights and equality concerns.[72]

While recognizing the difficulty of time-sensitive decision-making in an emergency, Casey and others pointed out some practical measures that could have been adopted, such as including the Department of Children, Equality, Disability, Integration and Youth on the government oversight committee that received the recommendations from NPHET, or publishing an equality analysis of public health regulations within forty-eight hours of their adoption.[73]

4.3 The Equality and Human Rights Duty and Working during the Pandemic

In order to explore further the application of the public sector duty during the pandemic, this section examines certain measures taken in respect of the labour market. As indicated in section 4.1, this has been an area which exemplifies disparate impacts. For those who remained in employment, a critical issue has been the safety of the working environment, including both where work took place in an employer's premises and where work was performed elsewhere. A key step was the adoption of

---

[69] See further Casey and others (n 6) 57.
[70] Department of Health, 'Ethical Framework for Decision-Making in a Pandemic' (2020) https://www.gov.ie/en/publication/dbf3fb-ethical-framework-for-decision-making-in-a-pandemic/ (accessed 8 December 2021).
[71] Letter from Tony Geoghegan to the Minister for Health (18 May 2020) https://www.ihrec.ie/app/uploads/2020/07/IHREC-letter-to-Minister-for-Health-18-May-2020-F.pdf (accessed 8 December 2021).
[72] Casey and others (n 6) 61–62.
[73] ibid.

a 'Work Safety Protocol' in May 2020.[74] This was described as a 'collaborative effort' of the Health and Safety Authority (HSA),[75] relevant government departments, and the Health Service Executive,[76] following dialogue with employer representatives and trade unions. The Protocol recognizes that certain workers are more vulnerable than others to becoming seriously ill if they contract Covid-19, which includes older workers and those with conditions that place them in high risk or very high risk categories.[77] If such workers cannot work from home, then measures have to be taken to ensure that they can maintain a 2 metre distance from others in the workplace.[78] Employers are also obliged to take measures to ensure appropriate communication with workers whose first language is not English.[79]

The Protocol acknowledges the impact of the pandemic on mental health and refers to the need for employers to take measures to support workers experiencing anxiety or stress.[80] On the one hand, the Protocol demonstrates a welcome recognition of the diversity of workers. On the other hand, it is notable that it does not expressly mention discrimination or equality, nor does it refer to Irish equality legislation. It is true that much of the Protocol is concerned with the practical measures required to maintain safety at work, such as the use of personal protective equipment, arrangements for cleaning, or responding to cases of infection. Yet it would have been salutary to have reminded employers of the need to ensure that the Protocol was implemented in a manner that did not give rise to any discrimination. For instance, the statutory duty to provide reasonable accommodation for workers with disabilities is undoubtedly relevant for an employer considering her obligations in respect of a worker whose disability gives rise to a higher risk of becoming seriously ill from Covid-19.[81] There is also a risk that certain workers encounter harassment related to Covid-19, such as those of Chinese and other Asian ethnic origins. This would have been an appropriate issue to have recognized in the Protocol.

While the Protocol is concerned with returning to the premises of the employer, the HSA also produced updated guidance on working from home.[82] Indeed, research found that, in spring 2021, Ireland had the highest rate of working remotely in the EU.[83] Given the mandate of the HSA, the guidance is understandably focused on

---

[74] An updated version is available at https://www.hsa.ie/eng/topics/covid-19_coronavirus_information_and_resources/ (accessed 8 December 2021).
[75] The HSA is Ireland's statutory agency with responsibility for promoting and encouraging the safety, health, and welfare of persons at work, and enforcing the relevant legislation: Safety, Health and Welfare at Work Act 2005, s 34.
[76] This is the organization that provides Ireland's public health services.
[77] Work Safety Protocol (n 74) 25.
[78] ibid.
[79] ibid 13.
[80] ibid 41.
[81] While not addressed in the Work Safety Protocol, the HSA has separate guidance on providing reasonable accommodation: HSA, 'Employees with Disabilities: An Employer's Guide to Implementing Inclusive Health and Safety Practices for Employees with Disabilities' (HSA 2021).
[82] HSA, 'Guidance on Working from Home for Employers and Employees' (2021) https://www.hsa.ie/eng/topics/remote_working/homeworking_guidance_9mar21_v8.pdf (accessed 8 December 2021).
[83] As many as 48 per cent were working remotely in spring 2021: Eurofound, 'Living, Working and COVID-19 (Update April 2021)' (2021) 2 https://www.eurofound.europa.eu/publications/report/2021/living-working-and-covid-19-update-april-2021-mental-health-and-trust-decline-across-eu-as-pandemic (accessed 8 December 2021).

ensuring that the home working environment is safe, for example as regards the set-up of the home work-station. Importantly, it recognizes that this is not merely a question of physical health, but that the isolation of working from home poses risks to the mental health of some workers.[84] The guidance also draws attention to the specific needs of certain workers, such as those who are pregnant or those with disabilities.[85] At the same time, it is notable that there is no explicit mention of discrimination or equality; for example, there could have been a reminder to employers that they need to ensure that there is no discrimination in the manner in which home-working is organized or facilitated. While the primary purpose of this document is the protection of workers' health, safety, and welfare, the public sector equality and human rights duty means that equality should be woven into all the functions of the HSA (including the production of guidance). By way of comparison, in 2021, the Workplace Relations Commission prepared a statutory Code of Practice on the Right to Disconnect.[86] Although this is not principally concerned with equality issues, there was clear evidence that these issues were considered and incorporated. The Code of Practice requires employers to develop a workplace policy on the right to disconnect. It advises that this should be 'equality proofed' to take into account the situation of employees with caring responsibilities or disabilities.[87]

4.4 Summary

This short review of how the public sector equality and human rights duty has been applied during the pandemic is not intended to draw firm conclusions about the effectiveness or otherwise of the duty. Clearly, that would demand more extensive and wide-ranging research. Nonetheless, the initial evidence raises questions as to how the duty affected top-level government decision-making, as well as the work of specific public bodies, such as the HSA. This may be symptomatic of general difficulties in gaining sufficient engagement by public bodies, which already existed prior to the pandemic. For example, the Strategy Statement of the HSA for 2019–2021 made no explicit reference to the equality and human rights duty,[88] nor did it otherwise acknowledge that health, safety, and welfare issues may impact workers differentially. Likewise, there is no reporting on its implementation of the duty in its most recent annual report.[89] If equality issues were not on an organization's strategic agenda prior to the pandemic, then it is unlikely that this will have changed in the even more demanding context of an emergency.

---

[84] HSA (n 82) 11.
[85] ibid 13.
[86] Workplace Relations Act 2015 (Workplace Relations Commission Code of Practice on the Right to Disconnect) Order 2021, SI 159/2021.
[87] ibid [6].
[88] HSA, 'Strategy Statement 2019-21' (HSA 2019).
[89] HSA, 'Annual Report 2020' (HSA 2021).

5 Equality Law in Ireland beyond the Pandemic

This chapter set out to examine how equality law functions during an emergency, taking Ireland as a case study. While acknowledging that the body of evidence remains limited, what lessons might be derived from this experience? Three reflections are offered below, but clearly the agenda for reform is potentially much wider.

First, the pandemic has acted as a reminder of the central role of the state during an emergency. This means that equality law needs to apply to all the functions of the state if it is to be fully effective. Section 3 provided examples from Ireland of how the state constructed new welfare supports in ways that excluded certain groups (including those on family leave; those residing in direct provision; and those who were sixty-six or older). On the one hand, equality law was an important means of challenging such exclusions. The risk of litigation was certainly one source of pressure on the state to change the conditions for receipt of these benefits. On the other hand, such examples can also expose deficiencies in existing legislation. As discussed in section 3 above, the exemption in section 14(1) ESA for any action taken under an 'enactment' shields government measures in Ireland from scrutiny if they are required by primary legislation or statutory instruments. Consequently, there was little space to challenge (on legal grounds) the age limit on the PUP.

Secondly, the pivotal position of the state during the pandemic underscored both the value, and the limitations, of duties on public bodies to promote equality of opportunity. These should ensure that equality issues are on the agenda of public bodies when designing emergency responses. The experience in Ireland indicated, however, that there is a risk that such duties may be neglected in the midst of a crisis. In part, this may be attributed to the nature of the Irish duty. It has adopted a 'gentle' approach to encouraging change. The obligation is 'to have regard' to, inter alia, the promotion of equality of opportunity. In contrast, it has been argued that it is preferable for equality duties to adopt more active language, such as a duty to 'take steps'.[90]

In Ireland, the obligations on public bodies are set out in loose and general terms. Arguably, these need greater precision; for example, conducting an equality impact assessment prior to taking significant decisions is one mechanism through which an organization can demonstrate that it has consciously reflected on its compliance with the duty.[91] Similarly, consulting with affected communities and gathering data are necessary elements in the implementation of the duty. While these are recommended by IHREC's guidance, this could be strengthened by putting it on a statutory footing in the form of a code of practice, or incorporating such obligations into primary legislation. As mentioned above, there are few sanctions available in the event of a breach of the duty. Under the pressure of an emergency scenario, does this make it more likely that the duty gets side-lined? Certainly, the options for enforcement in Ireland contrast unfavourably with the equivalent equality duty in Britain,

---

[90] Meghan Campbell, Sandra Fredman, and Aaron Reeves, 'Palliation or Protection: How Should the Right to Equality Inform the Government's Response to Covid-19?' (2020) 20 International Journal of Discrimination and the Law 183, 191.
[91] ibid 194.

where it is possible to seek judicial review of a public body's failure to comply with its obligations.[92]

The third reflection is that the pandemic has illustrated the necessity of a strong and autonomous equality body that can be a voice for equality issues during an emergency. This chapter has noted several examples of how IHREC raised concerns with government about the measures taken during the pandemic. This ranged from questioning how equality matters were taken into account when NPHET formulated public health recommendations, through to interventions on specific matters, such as the conditions for the wage subsidy and PUP schemes. It is not possible to reach firm conclusions on the extent to which IHREC's voice brought about change, but its statutory mandate gives it a platform in the public square to raise equality issues with a certain degree of authority. To consider the counter-factual scenario, it seems likely that the pressure on government would be less if this was purely a matter of lobbying from civil society. The experience in Ireland chimes with evidence gathered by Equinet that many equality bodies issued public statements during the pandemic in an effort to ensure that equality considerations were not overlooked in decision-making.[93]

In conclusion, the experience of the pandemic has provided a reminder of the need for binding and enforceable equality legislation. This offers a safeguard in a time of emergency when rights come under exceptional strain. There are, however, lessons to be learned about ways in which equality frameworks can be strengthened. In that regard, it is timely that the Irish government has now committed to a comprehensive review of equality legislation.[94] Items that the review will consider include whether the existing legislation adequately addresses intersectionality and the possible addition of further grounds to the legislation, with a specific focus on socio-economic disadvantaged status. If such changes are incorporated in legislation, this would provide tangible evidence that the inequalities exposed during the pandemic acted as a spur to future action.

---

[92] Sandra Fredman, 'Breaking the Mold: Equality as a Proactive Duty' (2012) 60 American Journal of Comparative Law 265.
[93] Equinet, 'The Role of Equality Bodies During the COVID-19 Pandemic' (2021) https://equineteurope.org/wp-content/uploads/2021/04/equinet_covid19-factsheet-A4_DEF.pdf (accessed 8 December 2021).
[94] Department of Children, Equality, Disability, Integration and Youth, 'Consultation on the Review of the Equality Acts' (6 July 2021) https://www.gov.ie/en/consultation/066b6-review-of-the-equality-acts/ (accessed 8 December 2021).

9
A Public Policy Approach to Inequality

Jessica Clarke

1 Introduction

In the US, the Covid-19 pandemic has had disastrous impacts for almost everyone, but particularly for members of certain racial and ethnic minority groups, who have been more likely to contract the virus,[1] become seriously ill and die,[2] and report significant financial problems.[3] The pandemic's impacts have also been gendered; although men are more likely to die,[4] women are more likely to suffer economic harm from mitigation strategies,[5] while lesbian, gay, bisexual, transgender, and queer (LGBTQ) individuals are at higher risk of a variety of harms.[6] These results can be described as 'exponential inequalities': systemic patterns of inequality that are exacerbated by crisis.[7]

Although it is concerned with racial and gender injustice, civil rights law in the United States is ill-equipped to address the exponential inequalities that have been exacerbated by Covid-19. The US Constitution guarantees equal protection of the laws,[8] but as critics lament, courts have generally construed it to prohibit only intentional discrimination.[9] Unfortunately, crises like pandemics are often unforeseen, and their unequal effects are rarely traceable to the ill-intent of a particular person or group. A theory of indirect discrimination might recognize disparities as pointing to harmful

---

[1] Erin K Stokes and others, 'Coronavirus Disease 2019 Case Surveillance: United States, January 22–May 30, 2020' (19 June 2020) 69 Morbidity and Mortality Weekly Report 759, 763.

[2] Centers for Disease Control and Prevention (CDC), Disparities in Deaths from COVID-19 (10 December 2020) www.cdc.gov/coronavirus/2019-ncov/community/health-equity/racial-ethnic-disparities/disparities-deaths.html (accessed 28 June 2021).

[3] National Public Radio, Robert Wood Johnson Foundation, and Harvard TH Chan School of Public Health, 'The Impact of Coronavirus on Households, by Race/Ethnicity' (2020) 6 https://cdn1.sph.harvard.edu/wp-content/uploads/sites/94/2020/09/NPR-Harvard-RWJF-Race-Ethnicity-Poll_091620.pdf (accessed 28 June 2021).

[4] Sonia Akter, 'The Gender Gap in COVID-19 Mortality in the United States' (2021) 27 Feminist Economics 30, 34–42.

[5] Titan Alon and others, 'The Impact of Covid-19 on Gender Equality' NBER Working Paper Series (April 2020) www.nber.org/system/files/working_papers/w26947/w26947.pdf>.

[6] Craig J Konnoth, 'Supporting LGBT Communities in the COVID-19 Pandemic' in Scott Burris and others (eds), *Assessing Legal Responses to COVID-19* (Public Health Law Watch 2020) 234.

[7] See in particular the chapters in the first part of this edited collection which draw on interdisciplinary research on the nature of 'exponential inequalities'.

[8] US Constitution, amend XIV s 1.

[9] Critics include Ian Haney-López, 'Intentional Blindness' (2012) 87 New York University Law Review 1779; Charles R Lawrence III, 'The Id, the Ego, and Equal Protection: Reckoning with Unconscious Racism' (1987) 39 Stanford Law Review 317; Reva Siegel, 'Why Equal Protection No Longer Protects: The Evolving Forms of Status-Enforcing State Action' (1997) 49 Stanford Law Review 1111; and David A Strauss, 'Discriminatory Intent and the Taming of Brown' (1989) 56 University of Chicago Law Review 935.

forms of inequality, but the US Supreme Court has held that the Equal Protection Clause does not prohibit indirect discrimination (which it refers to as 'disparate impact'), because that theory would call into question too many of the operations of the government and the market.[10] The Supreme Court has recognized that certain US statutes prohibit disparate impact discrimination in domains including employment and housing,[11] but it has construed those statutes narrowly, and the Court's conservatives have gone so far as to suggest they may be unconstitutional.[12] Conservative jurists often see statistical disparities as the results of 'innocent private decisions' rather than discrimination.[13] In addition to narrowing the scope of disparate impact liability, the Supreme Court has limited the tools available to remedy inequality by holding that remedial policies that classify their beneficiaries by race must meet the highest standard of judicial review, called 'strict scrutiny'.[14]

Although US equality law is generally unresponsive to exponential inequalities, US public policy is not. Outside of the courts, policy-makers exercise their discretion to consider a much wider array of equity concerns than intentional discrimination. For example, federal government agencies, private health care providers, and other governmental and non-governmental actors commonly invoke the idea of 'health equity', a principle that seeks to reduce disparities in health that are linked with systemic forms of social disadvantage.[15] This broader conception of equality—which is attentive to statistical disparities, structural dynamics, and social relations—has more potential to address the exponential increases in inequality unleashed by the Covid-19 pandemic and other crises. It draws on an older tradition in US civil rights law, which recognized indirect discrimination and permitted policy-makers to use a broader array of tools to redress inequality. Yet it is in tension with the dominant legal approach to equality in the US Supreme Court today.

This chapter will discuss why legal and public policy definitions of equality diverge in the United States and explain the implications of this divergence for addressing exponential inequalities. In a series of cases beginning in the 1970s, an increasingly conservative US Supreme Court narrowly construed the project of equality law. But more capacious understandings of equity have continued to influence US policy-makers, acting through legislatures, government agencies, and non-governmental organizations. These more capacious understandings have inspired data collection efforts to identify disparities based on race, sex, class, and other social categories, to explore the causes and consequences of these disparities, and to design interventions to mitigate

---

[10] Reva B Siegel, 'Foreword: Equality Divided' (2013) 127 Harvard Law Review 1, 21.
[11] *Griggs v Duke Power Co* 401 US 424 (1971) (Title VII of the Civil Rights Act of 1964, which forbids employment discrimination on the bases of race, sex, religion, national origin, and colour); *Smith v City of Jackson* 544 US 228 (2005) (Age Discrimination in Employment Act of 1967); *Raytheon Corporation v Hernandez* 540 US 44 (2003) (Americans with Disabilities Act of 1990); *Texas Dept of Housing & Community Affairs v Inclusive Communities Project Inc* 576 US 519 (2015) (Fair Housing Act).
[12] *Ricci v DeStefano* 557 US 557, 595–96 (2009) (Scalia J concurring): '[T]he war between disparate impact and equal protection will be waged sooner or later'; *Texas Dept of Hous & Cmty Affs* (n 11) 589–90 (Alito J dissenting): opinion of four conservative justices that disparate impact law raises 'difficult constitutional questions'.
[13] *Texas Dept of Hous & Cmty Affs* (n 11) 553 (Thomas J dissenting).
[14] *Adarand Constructors Inc v Peña* 515 US 200, 227 (1995).
[15] Dana Bowen Matthew, 'Structural Inequality: The Real COVID-19 Threat to America's Health and How Strengthening the Affordable Care Act Can Help' (2020) 108 Georgetown Law Journal 1679, 1679–80.

them. To avoid legal challenge, interventions to mitigate disparities are crafted so as not to identify beneficiaries based on minority identity and to avoid the perception of zero-sum conflict with majority group interests. Over the longer term, as public policy approaches to equity are proven effective, they may inform legal developments, hastening the demise of legal rules that are out of sync with new understandings of what equity demands.

2 The Legal Definition of Equality

The formal law of discrimination in the United States does little to address exponential inequalities and may even stand as an obstacle to solutions. By 'formal law', I mean those sources that would be considered authorities by lawyers, such as constitutions, statutes, regulations, and judicial opinions.[16] Two related features of the formal law of discrimination render it ineffective in addressing forms of inequality that are exacerbated by crises such as the Covid-19 pandemic. First, it is sceptical of the idea that statistical disparities point to problems of inequality. Secondly, it regards efforts to reduce disparities that classify individuals by race or other such characteristics as forms of wrongful discrimination that are rarely justified.

2.1 Scepticism of Statistics

US equality law is sceptical of evidence in the form of statistical disparities because, for the most part, it conceives of inequality as the result of intentional, interpersonal, individual discrimination. The paradigm case it addresses is one in which a biased perpetrator denies an individual victim some advantage or opportunity in a discrete discriminatory transaction.[17] It imagines inequality to be a result of prejudiced attitudes in an interpersonal setting.[18] It is preoccupied with finding fault in the form of discriminatory intent on the part of the institution to be held liable.[19] It does not generally see negligence as a ground for liability.[20]

The Supreme Court has held that government action violates the Equal Protection Clause only if policy-makers acted with discriminatory intent, meaning they 'selected or reaffirmed a particular course of action at least in part 'because of', not merely 'in spite of', its adverse effects upon an identifiable group'.[21] In 1976, the Court rejected the argument that a law with an unjustified disparate impact on a racial group is unconstitutional, because the disparate impact theory 'would raise serious questions about,

---

[16] Roscoe Pound, 'Law in Books and Law in Action' (1910) 44 American Law Review 12.
[17] Aziz Huq, 'Bostock v BLM' *Boston Review* (15 July 2020) http://bostonreview.net/philosophy-religion-law-justice/aziz-z-huq-bostock-v-blm (accessed 28 June 2021).
[18] Ralph Richard Banks and Richard Thompson Ford, '(How) Does Unconscious Bias Matter? Law, Politics, and Racial Inequality' (2009) 58 Emory Law Journal 1053, 1072–1103.
[19] Haney-López (n 9) 1839–47.
[20] Although US law creates duties of reasonable accommodation, they are generally confined to a narrow set of disability and religious contexts: 42 USC s 12112(b)(5)(A); 42 USC s 2000e(j).
[21] *Personnel Administrator of Massachusetts v Feeney* 442 US 256, 279 (1979).

and perhaps invalidate, a whole range of tax, welfare, public service, regulatory, and licensing statutes that may be more burdensome to the poor and to the average [B]lack [person] than to the more affluent [W]hite'.[22] Statistical disparities, however, are not irrelevant to the Constitution; the Court has acknowledged they may provide circumstantial evidence of discriminatory intent.[23] But US courts have made such claims exceedingly difficult to prove, for fear of hamstringing policy-making.[24] In 1987, the Court rejected the argument that statistics showing a state had applied its death penalty in a racially skewed manner demonstrated a constitutional infirmity, because the theory would call into question 'our entire criminal justice system'.[25] A dissenting justice characterized the majority's concern as 'a fear of too much justice'.[26]

The Constitution is not the only source of US equality law; beginning in the 1960s, the US Congress passed a set of landmark civil rights statutes, some of which were interpreted to create disparate impact liability.[27] For example, under Title VII of the Civil Rights Act of 1964, an employment qualification standard that disproportionately screens out minorities is not permitted unless it is justified by business necessity.[28] Yet in recent decades, courts have limited the reach of statutory disparate impact claims to preserve institutional prerogatives. In the employment context, courts have been overly deferential to employers' arguments that their practices are business necessities.[29] In the housing context, the Supreme Court announced in 2015 that 'serious constitutional questions ... might arise' if a statute were interpreted to impose liability 'based solely on a showing of a statistical disparity', without evidence that the institution lacked a legitimate reason for the policy that created the disparity.[30] In the healthcare context, the 2010 Affordable Care Act prohibits certain forms of discrimination, but government enforcers have filed few actions under the law, and the statute has been interpreted to bar private lawsuits alleging disparate impact.[31]

In addition to the concern that liability for disparities would require radical restructuring of the economy and government, US courts are sceptical that disparities point to problematic forms of inequality. US courts have long accepted arguments that disparities are explained by the choices of disadvantaged group members rather than discrimination: for example, that women earn less because they lack interest in higher

---

[22] *Washington v Davis* 426 US 229, 247 (1976).

[23] *Arlington Heights v Metropolitan Housing Development Corporation* 429 US 252, 266 (1977). Statistical disparities may also be evidence discriminatory intent under Title VII. *International Brotherhood of Teamsters v United States* 431 US 324, 335 n 15 (1977).

[24] *Trump v Hawaii* 138 S Ct 2392, 2417–18 (2018). See also *Department of Homeland Security v Regents of the University of California* 140 S Ct 1891, 1915–16 (2020); Jessica A Clarke, 'Explicit Bias' (2018) 113 Northwestern University Law Review 505, 560–71.

[25] *McCleskey v Kemp* 481 US 279, 315 (1987).

[26] ibid 339 (Brennan J dissenting).

[27] See references cited in n 11.

[28] *Griggs* (n 11) 431.

[29] Michael Selmi, 'Was the Disparate Impact Theory a Mistake?' (2006) 53 UCLA Law Review 701, 769.

[30] *Texas Dept of Hous & Cmty Affs* (n 11) 540.

[31] Matthew (n 15) 1712–13. Similarly, Title VI of the Civil Rights Act of the Civil Rights Act of 1964 has been interpreted to permit disparate impact claims with respect to federally funded programs, but only government enforcers may bring those claims: *Alexander v Sandoval* 532 US 275 (2001).

paying work, or that people of colour are less likely to be employed because they lack job qualifications.[32]

As a result of its hollow definition of equality, US law is unsuited to respond to exponential inequalities. In times of crisis, it is easy to attribute disparate misfortunes to unforeseen events, generalized chaos, and strains on administrative systems, rather than any incident of intentional, interpersonal discrimination. For example, although the federal Stafford Act, which authorizes funding for disaster relief, includes a prohibition of discrimination based on race, economic status, and other characteristics,[33] there are few cases in which plaintiffs have ultimately prevailed under that provision.[34] This is because it has been interpreted to require evidence of discriminatory intent, and 'courts are reluctant to attribute evidence of disparate impact to the federal agency and not the disaster itself'.[35] One court denied a discrimination claim by economically disadvantaged victims of Hurricane Katrina on the ground that 'people who are economically disadvantaged will always be more in need of federal disaster assistance' and 'inevitably those with economic resources will recover more quickly than those without'.[36]

2.2 Limits on Remedial Programmes

US equality law's ability to respond to exponential inequality is also limited by another feature of its definition of discrimination: the US Supreme Court interprets the Constitution to require the same degree of scrutiny for any policy that draws racial distinctions, subjecting affirmative action policies intended to remedy disparities to the same standard as overt policies of segregation and exclusion. This much-criticized feature of US equality law is often described as 'colour-blindness'.[37] The Supreme Court is wary of any sort of racial classification, reasoning that 'it demeans the dignity and worth of a person to be judged by ancestry instead of by his or her own merit and essential qualities'.[38] It has held that the Constitution requires that each person be treated 'with respect based on the unique personality each of us possesses'.[39] On this logic, racial classifications offend the principle of individualism: that each person is

---

[32] Vicki Schultz, 'Telling Stories about Women and Work: Judicial Interpretations of Sex Segregation in the Workplace in Title VII Cases Raising the Lack of Interest Argument' (1990) 103 Harvard Law Review 1749. *Wal-Mart Stores Inc v Dukes* 564 US 338, 355 (2011) provides a recent example of this argument's success in the Supreme Court.

[33] 42 USC s 5151(a).

[34] Hannah Perls, 'US Disaster Displacement in the Era of Climate Change: Discrimination & Consultation Under the Stafford Act' (2020) 44 Harvard Environmental Law Review 511, 540. I have found one example of a discrimination claim under the Stafford Act that resulted in settlements for individual plaintiffs, but it took ten years to resolve and failed to result in systemic changes to government practices: Danielle Zoe Rivera, *Fighting FEMA: Urban Informality and Disaster Response in Rio Grande Valley Colonias* (Lincoln Institute of Land Policy 2019)9 www.lincolninst.edu/sites/default/files/pubfiles/2019_descriptive_fighting_fema_rivera.pdf (accessed 28 June 2021).

[35] Perls (n 34) 541.

[36] *McWaters v Fed Emergency Mgmt Agency* 436 F Supp 2d 802, 824 (ED La 2006).

[37] Neil Gotanda, 'A Critique of "Our Constitution Is Colorblind"' (1991) 44 Stanford Law Review 1, 37.

[38] *Rice v Cayetano* 528 US 495, 517 (2000).

[39] ibid.

'autonomous and free' to choose their own life's path.[40] Thus, policies that differentiate based on race, even those that are arguably benign, must meet the standard of 'strict scrutiny'; that is, they must be narrowly tailored to achieve a compelling governmental interest.[41] Strict scrutiny limits the permissible ends and means of remedial programmes.

With respect to permissible ends, the Supreme Court has held that 'an effort to alleviate the effects of societal discrimination is not a compelling interest' that would justify racial distinctions.[42] Rather, racial classifications which are meant to remedy a racial disparity must link that racial disparity to specific incidents of past intentional discrimination.[43] For example, in a 1998 case, *City of Richmond v JA Croson*, the Court invalidated a city rule requiring that 30 per cent of funds for construction contracts go to minority-owned businesses.[44] The city had evidence that minorities made up 50 per cent of the city's population, but minority-owned businesses had been awarded less than 1 per cent of its construction contracts.[45] The Court was not satisfied with this evidence because the city could not demonstrate that any minority-owned businesses had lost out on specific contracts for which they had applied and were qualified.[46] The Court speculated that disparities may have resulted from 'past societal discrimination in education and economic opportunities as well as both [B]lack and [W]hite career and entrepreneurial choices', rather than discrimination in construction contracting.[47] It derided the city's programme for having the goal of 'racial balancing' which it regarded as based on the 'completely unrealistic' assumption that minorities will choose a particular trade in lockstep proportion to their representation in the local population'.[48]

The Supreme Court has allowed race-based affirmative action for two compelling purposes: to remedy specific instances of intentional discrimination and to achieve a diverse student body in institutions of higher education, which use competitive admissions processes to select students.[49] But even when there is a compelling end, the means used to achieve it must be 'narrowly tailored' in several ways. Notably, narrow tailoring forbids the use of quotas or other inflexible or mechanical criteria.[50] Thus, with respect to diversity in higher education, an applicant's race may only be 'one of many factors' considered by admissions officers in a holistic, individualized review of the candidate.[51] Additionally, the institution must demonstrate there are no workable, race-neutral means that would be sufficient to achieve its compelling interest.[52] The Supreme Court's key affirmative action precedents were decided by a closely

[40] Julie Suk, 'Discrimination and Affirmative Action' in Kasper Lippert-Rasmussen (ed), *The Routledge Handbook of the Ethics of Discrimination* (Routledge 2017) 397.
[41] *Adarand Constructors Inc* (n 14) 227.
[42] *Shaw v Hunt* 517 US 899, 909–10 (1996).
[43] *Parents Involved in Community Schools v Seattle School District No 1* 551 US 701, 720–21 (2007).
[44] *City of Richmond v JA Croson Co* 488 US 469, 498 (1989).
[45] ibid 499.
[46] ibid 498–506.
[47] ibid 503.
[48] ibid 507.
[49] *Grutter v Bollinger* 539 US 306, 335 (2003).
[50] ibid 328–33.
[51] ibid 339–41.
[52] *Fisher v University of Texas at Austin* 570 US 297, 312 (2013).

divided court.⁵³ The Supreme Court will soon revisit the constitutionality of race-based affirmative action in higher education in *Students for Fair Admissions v Harvard College*.⁵⁴ Now that the Court has a six-to-three member conservative majority, it is likely to impose further limits on diversity considerations in higher education, if it does not altogether overrule prior precedents allowing race to be considered for purposes of diversity.

Policy efforts to reduce inequalities exacerbated by disasters like the Covid-19 pandemic are hindered by the Supreme Court's understanding of race-based remedies as morally objectionable. The requirement that government identify very specific incidents of past intentional discrimination would be difficult to meet even without an intervening cause like a pandemic. And during a crisis, when quick action is required, it may not be feasible to give all beneficiaries of relief programmes the sort of holistic, individual consideration that narrow tailoring requires, or to conduct studies to determine if there are race-neutral measures that would be effective.

Some efforts by the US government to remediate the economic harms of the pandemic which have prioritized racial and other minorities have encountered obstacles in the courts.⁵⁵ In March 2021, the US Congress passed the American Rescue Plan, a US$1.9 trillion stimulus bill intended to increase economic growth and strengthen the country's social safety net in response to the pandemic.⁵⁶ One provision of the bill, the Restaurant Revitalization Fund, authorized grants to small, privately owned restaurants to help recoup pandemic losses.⁵⁷ The law provided that for the programme's first three weeks, the applications of establishments at least 51 per cent owned by women, veterans, or 'socially and economically disadvantaged individuals' would be prioritized for processing.⁵⁸ Socially disadvantaged individuals are defined as 'those who have been subjected to racial or ethnic prejudice or cultural bias because of their identity as a member of a group without regard to their individual qualities'.⁵⁹ Certain groups, including Black Americans, Hispanic Americans, Asian Pacific Americans, and Subcontinent Asian Americans, are presumed to be socially disadvantaged, while members of other groups have the burden of proving they meet the definition.⁶⁰

Congress enacted this provision due to evidence that minority-owned businesses were more likely to be impacted by government shut-down orders, located in areas with high rates of Covid-19, and unable to access capital due to discrimination in banking.⁶¹ Additionally, minority-owned businesses had received little funding from

---

⁵³ *Grutter* (n 49); *Parents Involved* (n 43).
⁵⁴ *Students for Fair Admissions Inc v Harvard College* 142 S Ct 895 (2022) (granting petition for writ of certiorari).
⁵⁵ *Vitolo v Guzman* 999 F 3d 353 (6th Cir 2021); *Holman v Vilsack* No 21-1085, 2021 WL 2877915 (WD Tenn 8 July 8 2021); *Miller v Vilsack* No 4:21-cv-0595 (ND Tex 1 July 2021); *Wynn v Vilsack* No 3:21-CV-514, 2021 WL 2580678 (MD Fla 23 June 2021); *Faust v Vilsack* 519 F Supp 3d 470 (ED Wis 10 June 2021); *Greer's Ranch Cafe v Guzman* No 4:21-CV-00651, 2021 WL 2092995 (ND Tex 18 May 2021).
⁵⁶ Pub L No 117-2, 135 Stat 4 (2021).
⁵⁷ ibid s 5003(b)(2)(A), (c).
⁵⁸ ibid s 5003(c)(3)(A); 15 USC ss 632(n), (q)(3), 637(a)(4)(A).
⁵⁹ 15 USC s 637(a)(5).
⁶⁰ 13 CFR s 124.103.
⁶¹ *Supporting Small and Minority-Owned Businesses Through the Pandemic* (US Govt Pub Off, 4 February 2021) 38–39, 60–61, 78, 80 www.congress.gov/117/chrg/CHRG-117hhrg43965/CHRG-117hhrg43965.pdf (accessed 28 June 2021).

a prior pandemic relief programme, the Paycheck Protection Program (PPP), because that programme had distributed funds through commercial banks, and minority-owned businesses are less likely to have relationships with commercial banks and more likely to be denied loans.[62] Congress even considered evidence from a 'matched-pair' study in April 2020 that 'found that Black business owners in Washington, DC were more likely to be denied PPP loans compared to White business owners with similar application profiles due to outright lending discrimination'.[63]

Yet a federal appellate court, which sits just below the Supreme Court in the US court structure, found this evidence of past discrimination insufficiently specific to justify the provisions of the law that gave priority to members of certain racial groups.[64] In *Vitolo v Guzman*, the Sixth Circuit Court of Appeals held that the race-and sex-based aspects of the fund were unlikely to pass constitutional muster, in an opinion by Trump-appointee Judge Amul Thapar.[65] In addition to finding the evidence of past discrimination too tenuous, Judge Thapar asserted that government could have pursued race-neutral alternatives in the form of policies targeting business owners unable to obtain necessary capital, credit, or government funds from prior programmes.[66] The court also regarded the lines drawn by the statute to be arbitrary, noting that, although the plaintiff was a White man, his wife, who owned 50 per cent of their restaurant, was a Hispanic woman.[67] A dissenting judge argued, however, that it was unrealistic to expect Congress to devise a perfectly tailored policy in emergency legislation that aimed to distribute funds expeditiously to address the urgent threat the pandemic posed to the nation's economy.[68] Although the Supreme Court has traditionally held sex-based classifications to the lower standard of 'intermediate scrutiny',[69] the *Vitolo* court applied that standard in much the same way as it did strict scrutiny.[70]

Courts striking down provisions of the American Rescue Plan seemed to be more concerned with the moral impropriety of race-based classifications than with any material disadvantage suffered by White male plaintiffs. In *Faust v Vilsack*, a federal district court concluded that White plaintiffs would suffer irreparable harm as a result of a programme granting debt relief to minority farmers,[71] despite the fact that most of the plaintiffs indicated they were not themselves interested in debt relief; rather, they wished to vindicate the principle of colour-blindness.[72] In *Vitolo*, the court temporarily enjoined the three-week priority programme for women and minorities,

---

[62] ibid 38, 48–49, 61, 78–79, 80, 88.

[63] ibid 61 (discussing Anneliese Lederer and others, *Lending Discrimination within the Paycheck Protection Program* (National Community Reinvestment Coalition 2020)).

[64] *Vitolo* (n 55) 361.

[65] ibid 364–65.

[66] ibid 363.

[67] ibid 363.

[68] ibid 372 (Donald J dissenting).

[69] Intermediate scrutiny requires that the law serve 'important governmental objectives' and that the means employed be 'substantially related' to those objectives: *Miss Univ for Women v Hogan*, 458 US 718, 724 (1982).

[70] *Vitolo* (n 55) 364–65.

[71] *Faust* (n 55) 476–77.

[72] Defendants' Opposition to Plaintiffs' Motion for a Temporary Restraining Order, *Faust v Vilsack*, No 21-C-548, 2021 WL 2409729 (ED Wis 10 June 2021) 13.

even though there was no evidence that Vitolo himself would ultimately have been denied funds.[73] Judge Thapar summed up his objection to the Restaurant Revitalization Fund's minority priorities with an example: 'Imagine two childhood friends—one Indian, one Afghan. Both own restaurants, and both have suffered devastating losses during the pandemic. If both apply to the Restaurant Revitalization Fund, the Indian applicant will presumptively receive priority consideration over his Afghan friend. Why? Because of his ethnic heritage. It is indeed "a sordid business" to divide "us up by race".'[74]

Thus, as a formal matter, US law regards the essence of equality to be the absence of discrimination in the form of intentional disparate treatment based on a suspect classification. It has difficulty understanding the magnification of disparities by a crisis as an issue of inequality, and it stands in the way of solutions that might identify beneficiaries based on race or other such classifications.

3 The Public Policy Definition of Equity

The Supreme Court's constrained legal definition of equality, however, is not operative in every US public policy domain. By 'public policy', I refer to the broad range of governmental and non-governmental initiatives undertaken for purposes of advancing the public interest and solving social problems. Public policy can include formal legal rules, such as those promulgated by legislatures and courts, but those rules do not exhaust its definition.[75] It also encompasses policy in the broader sense of goals and values, as influenced and implemented by administrative agencies, 'street-level bureaucrats', and international and non-governmental actors.[76] In many US public policy domains, disparities based on race, gender, socioeconomic status, and other axes of social stratification are regarded as indicia that the benefits of public programmes are not being distributed equitably. In recent policy debates, progressives have deployed the term 'equity', rather than equality in an effort to signal that their goals are substantive and systemic, rather than formal and superficial. This shift in terminology 'reflects the disappointments of "equality" and "equal protection" as implemented', although the terms 'equity' and 'equality' have historically been used interchangeably and their meanings continue to overlap.[77] An example of the focus on 'equity' in public policy is the influential concept of 'health equity' from public health. The term 'public health' refers to a society's collective efforts 'to assure the conditions in which people can be healthy', as opposed to the provision of individualized medical care.[78] Health

---

[73] *Vitolo* (n 55) 367 (Donald J dissenting).
[74] ibid 364 (quoting *League of United Latin American Citizens v Perry* 548 US 399, 511 (2006) (opinion of Roberts CJ)).
[75] Thomas A Birkland, *An Introduction to the Policy Process Theories, Concepts, and Models of Public Policy Making* (5th edn, Taylor & Francis 2019) 7.
[76] Michael Lipsky, *Street-Level Bureaucracy* (Russell Sage Foundation 1980).
[77] Martha Minow, 'Equality vs Equity' (2021) 1 American Journal of Law and Equality 167, 171, 188.
[78] Institute of Medicine, *The Future of the Public's Health in the 21st Century* (National Academies Press 2003) xi.

equity has featured prominently in public health discussions about how to address the Covid-19 crisis.

3.1 Equity in Civil Rights Enforcement

Administrative agencies in the civil rights era were one site where equity norms developed in US public policy. Rather than relying exclusively on courts, Congress tasked administrative agencies with enforcing the civil rights statutes of the 1960s.[79] These agencies pursued an approach to civil rights that Bruce Ackerman describes as 'government by numbers'.[80] This approach regarded statistical measures of minority underrepresentation as pointing to potential statutory violations.[81] For example, the Equal Employment Opportunity Commission (EEOC), charged with administering statutes that prohibit discrimination in employment, created a national reporting system that requires employers to submit quantitative demographic data on their workforces so that the agency can identify potential offenders and push them to make voluntary changes, with the threat of potential legal action in the background as an inducement.[82] The agency avoided the conservative complaint that it was requiring hiring 'quotas' by not requiring anything; '[i]t was simply telling regulated firms how it intended to deploy its scarce investigative resources to fulfil its statutory mission'.[83]

As Olatunde Johnson has described, many federal administrative agencies in addition to the EEOC pursue a numbers-driven approach in domains including housing, transportation, health, and education, requiring state and local grant recipients to affirmatively ensure that federal funds are used equitably.[84] Rather than focusing on post-hoc remedies for discrimination and bias, this approach requires 'grant recipients to conduct front-end assessment of impacts, evaluate alternatives, and include groups not normally at the table'.[85] For example, recipients of certain federal funds for mass-transit programmes must gather data to provide quantitative measures of whether services are being provided to different racial and ethnic groups, evaluate changes to services and fares for disparate impacts, and take action to correct disparities.[86] On this model, the Biden administration has explicitly adopted 'equity' as a goal in devising the federal budget, prioritizing programmes that would provide health care, transportation, affordable housing, environmental protection, and education to communities that have been 'left behind'.[87]

---

[79] Bruce Ackerman, *We the People: The Civil Rights Revolution*, vol 3 (Belknap Press 2014) 154.
[80] ibid 155.
[81] ibid.
[82] ibid 180–83.
[83] ibid 182.
[84] Olatunde CA Johnson, 'Lawyering That Has No Name: Title VI and the Meaning of Private Enforcement' (2014) 66 Stanford Law Review 1293, 1314, 1339.
[85] Olatunde CA Johnson, 'Beyond the Private Attorney General: Equality Directives in American Law' (2012) 87 NYU Law Review 1339, 1376.
[86] ibid 1380.
[87] Michael D Shear, 'Efforts to Advance Racial Equity Baked in Throughout Biden's Budget' *New York Times* (2 June 2021) www.nytimes.com/2021/05/29/us/politics/efforts-to-advance-racial-equity-baked-in-throughout-bidens-budget.html (accessed 28 June 2021).

3.2 Equity in Public Health

'Health equity', a well-recognized concept in US public policy, is an example of this numbers-driven, expansive understanding of equality. It has several features that distinguish it from the current legal understanding of equality: it originates in human rights discourse; it is focused on ex ante solutions rather than ex post attempts to assign fault; it understands inequality as a structural rather than an interpersonal phenomenon; it is concerned with statistical disparities; it does not suffer from a 'fear of too much justice'; and it eschews colour-blind ideology. While this concept is not the dominant approach to public health, it has been influential, particularly in the public health response to Covid-19 in the US.

By contrast to US legal doctrine, in which the concept of equality developed through judicial interpretation of the US Constitution and civil rights statutes, the idea of health equity draws upon concepts from human rights. For example, Healthy People 2030, an interagency workgroup managed by the US Department of Health and Human Services, is focused on the 'social determinants of health', defined as the economic, environmental, and social forces that, if unaddressed, can lead to 'health disparities'.[88] Rather than citing US legal authorities in support of this concern, it cites reports of the World Health Organization (WHO).[89] The WHO's 1948 Constitution declares health to be a fundamental right of every person, without regard for race and other such factors, and asserts that governments have a responsibility to safeguard health with both medical care and social measures.[90] In 2010 the WHO's Commission on Social Determinants of Health set forth a theoretical framework establishing health equity as a core value, building on human rights principles and the philosophy of Amartya Sen.[91] On this theory, governments are responsible for protecting health equity because health is a prerequisite not just for well-being, but also for individual freedom and agency.[92]

Those concerned with health equity aim to achieve a more equitable distribution of health ex ante, not to pin blame on any specific individual or institution for discrimination ex post. A WHO discussion paper in the 1980s identified practical, economic, and humanitarian reasons for the appeal of health equity, with emphasis on the humanitarian argument that 'national health policies designed for an entire population cannot claim to be concerned about the health of all the people, if the heavier burden of ill-health carried by the most vulnerable sections of society is not addressed'.[93] Rather than focusing on questions of fault or blame, the focus is on whether disparities are unnecessary, avoidable, unfair, and unjust.[94]

---

[88] Healthy People 2030, US Department of Health and Human Services, Office of Disease Prevention and Health Promotion, 'Social Determinants of Health Workgroup' https://health.gov/healthypeople/about/workgroups/social-determinants-health-workgroup (accessed 28 June 2021).
[89] ibid.
[90] Constitution of the World Health Organization (22 July 1946).
[91] Orielle Solar and Alec Irwin, 'A Conceptual Framework for Action on the Social Determinants of Health' (2010) 2 Social Determinants of Health Discussion Paper 12, 13.
[92] ibid 12.
[93] Margaret Whitehead, 'The Concepts and Principles of Equity and Health' (1992) 22(3) International Journal of Health Services 429, 431.
[94] ibid.

In much public health discourse, inequities are thought to inhere in social structures and systems, rather than individual interpersonal transactions. 'Social justice' is often mentioned as an explicit goal of efforts to eliminate health disparities, along with other terms such as 'systemic' and 'structural', which point to causal factors beyond just intentional discrimination.[95] Certainly, health equity discussions recognize that Black and Hispanic individuals receive a lower standard of care in the US due to 'pervasive but subtle forms of racism and discrimination.'[96] But they also recognize that biases on the part of health care providers are just one contributor to health disparities.[97] The Centre for Disease Control and Prevention (CDC) identifies both 'interpersonal and structural' racism as harmful to health, citing scholarship defining 'institutionalized racism' as 'differential access to the goods, services, and opportunities of society by race.'[98] Structural, rather than transactional understandings of inequality may appeal to public health practitioners, because the very field of public health is attuned to social dynamics, by contrast to individualized medical care.[99] This feature connects health equity with other recent progressive social movements; to underscore the connection, some scholars have proposed a shift to the term 'health justice'.[100]

Unlike legal approaches to inequality, health equity is deeply concerned with statistical disparities. One reason may be that the collection of statistics is one of the foundational tenets of the public health movement.[101] An extensive body of public health research documents health disparities that track axes of social disadvantage, such as socioeconomic status, race, and ethnicity.[102] The US government maintains data on health outcomes based on race and ethnicity, as well as sex, LGBT identity, disability, and rural or urban location.[103] Even the right-wing Trump administration, which was generally averse to antidiscrimination projects, required that states provide data on Covid-19 based on race, ethnicity, age, and sex.[104] The majority of US states were concerned about equity in access to Covid-19 vaccines, with forty-one out of fifty collecting and reporting vaccination data on race and ethnicity.[105]

---

[95] Solar and Irwin (n 91) 4, 41, 43.

[96] Institute of Medicine (n 78) 62.

[97] ibid.

[98] CDC, 'Racism and Health' (12 April 2021) www.cdc.gov/healthequity/racism-disparities/index.html (accessed 28 June 2021) (linking to Camara Phyllis Jones, 'Levels of Racism: A Theoretic Framework and a Gardener's Tale' (2020) 90 American Journal of Public Health 1212, 1212).

[99] Institute of Medicine (n 78) xi; Matthew (n 15) 1681–82.

[100] Angela P Harris and Aysha Pamukcu, 'The Civil Rights of Health: A New Approach to Challenging Structural Inequality' (2020) 67 UCLA Law Review 758, 808.

[101] John Duffy, *The Sanitarians: A History of American Public Health* (University of Illinois Press 1992) 8.

[102] Institute of Medicine (n 78) 57–71.

[103] Office of Disease Prevention and Health Promotion, US Department of Health and Human Services, 'Disparities' (23 June 2021) www.healthypeople.gov/2020/about/foundation-health-measures/Disparities (accessed 28 June 2021).

[104] Noah Weiland and Apoorva Mandavilli, 'Trump Administration Sets Demographic Requirements for Coronavirus Reports' *New York Times* (4 June 2020) https://www.nytimes.com/2020/06/04/us/politics/coronavirus-infection-demographics.html (accessed 28 June 2021).

[105] Nambi Ndugga, Samantha Artiga, and Olivia Pham, 'How Are States Addressing Racial Equity in COVID-19 Vaccine Efforts?' Kaiser Family Foundation (10 March 2021) www.kff.org/racial-equity-and-health-policy/issue-brief/how-are-states-addressing-racial-equity-in-covid-19-vaccine-efforts/ (accessed 28 June 2021).

Public health approaches to equity envision a broad scope for policy action, unconstrained by the 'fear of too much justice' that limits the judiciary's imagination. The US Supreme Court generally takes care to articulate the scope of constitutional rights in the most narrow of terms, because it regards 'rights as trumps' that will rarely be subject to balancing against the public interest.[106] By contrast, Healthy People 2030's goals include the ambitious aims of 'eliminat[ing] health disparities' and 'achiev[ing] health equity'.[107] Unlike courts, public policy actors such as agency administrators, international organizations, academics, and participants in civil society often set aspirational goals with the knowledge that their achievement will inevitably be limited by political, budgetary, and other such constraints. Thus, public policy actors can tout the importance of goals like 'eliminating health disparities' without committing to the types of broad-scale redistributive interventions that would be required to achieve them.

In the public health context, unlike the law, the very existence of health disparities along lines such as race is assumed to be morally problematic, rather than the potential result of innocent causes. The concept of 'social determinants' attributes racial disparities to the social sphere rather than to supposed biological or cultural differences that might explain why members of different races make different choices.[108] Even if some disparities could be attributed to individual or group choices, principles of health equity require policy changes to enable people to adopt healthier lifestyles, acknowledging that inequalities with respect to housing, employment, education, and other social dynamics can restrict the ability of members of subordinated groups to make choices conducive to health.[109] As Lawrence Gostin and Madison Powers argue, 'an integral part of bringing good health to all is the task of identifying and ameliorating patterns of systematic disadvantage that undermine the well-being of people whose prospects for good health are so limited that their life choices are not even remotely like those of others'.[110] Such arguments may have more appeal in the health context because Americans are generally less likely blame an individual for poor health than other types of disadvantage.[111]

Unlike the legal concept of equality, health equity is not colour-blind. In the United States, 'health disparities' usually refer to race and ethnicity, rather than some other metric, like a Gini coefficient, that would measure the degree of difference between the sickest and healthiest segments of the population.[112] Race and ethnicity are regarded as important axes of disparity because they result from and compound accumulated patterns of systemic social disadvantage.[113] Moreover, rather than a singular focus on

---

[106] Jamal Greene, 'Rights as Trumps?' (2018) 132 Harvard Law Review 28.

[107] Healthy People 2030, US Department of Health and Human Services, Office of Disease Prevention and Health Promotion, 'Social Determinants of Health' https://health.gov/healthypeople/objectives-and-data/social-determinants-health (accessed 28 June 2021).

[108] Paula Braverman, 'Health Disparities and Health Equity: Concepts and Measurement' (2006) 27 Annual Review of Public Health 167, 181.

[109] Whitehead (n 93) 437.

[110] Lawrence O Gostin and Madison Powers, 'What Does Social Justice Require for the Public's Health? Public Health Ethics and Policy Imperatives' (2006) 25 Health Affairs 1053, 1053.

[111] Craig Konnoth, 'Medicalization and the New Civil Rights' (2020) 72 Stanford Law Review 1165, 1222–37.

[112] Braverman (n 108) 179.

[113] ibid 181.

race, scholars have called for intersectional approaches that 'examine the ways that gender, race, and class are mutually constituted and interconnected' to eliminate health disparities.[114]

The concept of health equity has been a prominent feature of Covid-19 relief efforts, under both conservative and liberal presidential administrations. In July 2020, during the Trump administration, the CDC announced a 'health equity strategy' for reducing Covid-19 disparities.[115] The CDC attributed the disparate racial effects of Covid-19 to '[l]ongstanding systemic health and social inequalities'.[116] Before Covid-19 vaccines were made universally available, the federal government formed an Advisory Committee on Immunization Practices (ACIP), a group of independent medical and public health experts, to offer guidance to the CDC on how to advise the states to allocate scarce vaccine doses.[117] One of ACIP's guiding aims was to 'mitigate health inequities'.[118] In early 2021, the Biden administration created a Covid-19 Health Equity Task Force to provide recommendations on reducing inequities.[119] The focus on health equity in the Covid-19 pandemic has been justified not only by moral arguments, but also by utilitarian ones, for example, that in an 'interconnected world', the failure to address a virus' impact on a particular minority group can affect everyone,[120] and economically worse-off groups are more likely to spread the virus because they are more likely to live in crowded households and less able to mitigate their risks with measures like telework.[121]

Thus, the concept of equity in public policy diverges from US law's vision of equality in ways that make exponential inequalities visible as problems to be addressed. While equality law regards disparities as stemming from innocent private choices or state or market imperatives absent specific proof of intentional discrimination, equity policy, by contrast, sees disparities as the results of complex, intergenerational social structures of disadvantage that must be overcome to extend the benefits of public policy to all. To say that health equity discourse makes exponential inequalities visible is not to say that it resolves them. It is important to note that the concept's practical impact has been limited: while the US government increasingly refers to 'health equity', it continues to prioritize 'disease-specific funding streams' over projects focused on social determinants.[122] Moreover, determining what health equity requires in any particular

---

[114] Keith Mullings and Amy J Schulz, 'Intersectionality and Health: An Introduction' in Leith Mullings and Amy J Schulz (eds), *Gender, Race, Class and Health: Intersectional Approaches* (Jossey-Bass 2005) 3.

[115] CDC, 'COVID-19 Response Health Equity Strategy: Accelerating Progress Towards Reducing COVID-19 Disparities and Achieving Health Equity' (2020) 1, www.cdc.gov/coronavirus/2019-ncov/downloads/community/CDC-Strategy.pdf (accessed 28 June 2021).

[116] ibid.

[117] CDC, 'How CDC Is Making COVID-19 Vaccine Recommendations' (14 May 2021) www.cdc.gov/coronavirus/2019-ncov/vaccines/recommendations-process.html (accessed 28 June 2021).

[118] ibid.

[119] Secretary of Health and Human Services, Charter (COVID-10 Health Equity Task Force, 21 January 2021) www.minorityhealth.hhs.gov/HealthEquityTaskForce/docs/COVID-19%20Health%20Equity%20Task%20Force%20Charter%202.04.2021_508.pdf (accessed 28 June 2021). See also Matthew (n 15) 1680.

[120] National Academies of Sciences, Engineering, and Medicine (NASEM), *Framework for Equitable Allocation of COVID-19 Vaccine* (National Academies Press 2020) 2.

[121] Harald Schmidt, Lawrence O Gostin, and Michelle A Williams, 'Viewpoint: Is It Lawful and Ethical to Prioritize Racial Minorities for COVID-19 Vaccines?' (2020) 324 Journal of the American Medical Association 2023, 2023.

[122] Rachel Rebouché and Scott Burris, 'The Social Determinants of Health,' in I Glenn Cohen and others (eds), *Oxford Handbook of US Health Law* (OUP 2016) 1104–105.

circumstance requires that bureaucrats make difficult and contestable judgments about what disparities reflect social injustice, what interventions will reduce those disparities, and whether the benefits of those interventions justify their costs and potential trade-offs. Nonetheless, the health equity approach is at least a first step toward recognizing exponential inequalities.

4 Reconciling Equity Policy with Equality Law

Equity policy and equality law do not simply diverge in their definitions of the problem; they often come into conflict, as in the litigation over the American Rescue Plan's prioritization of minority-owned businesses. Thus, proponents of equity policy must find ways to reconcile their projects with equality law. Many public policy responses to the Covid-19 pandemic attempt to do so with interventions that are race conscious, meaning they are explicit efforts to reduce racial disparities, but facially neutral, meaning they do not identify beneficiaries based on race or other suspect categories. What it means for a policy to be 'facially neutral' is contested and often depends on whether the intervention is crafted to avoid the perception of zero-sum conflict with majority group interests. Debates over health equity in Covid-19 vaccine distribution plans demonstrate how public policy actors attempt to operate in the race-conscious-but-neutral space.

4.1 Conscious but Neutral?

The extent to which race-conscious but race-neutral interventions should be scrutinized under the Equal Protection Clause is not clear as a matter of US law.[123] Supreme Court decisions assume that these types of interventions are permitted,[124] but the Court has not explained whether they are exempt from strict scrutiny or whether they satisfy strict scrutiny.[125] The opinions of the former Justice Anthony Kennedy, often identified as the 'swing vote' on the closely divided Supreme Court before his retirement in 2018, are illustrative. In a concurrence in a case on whether school districts could assign students to particular schools based on race in an effort to achieve diversity, Justice Kennedy opined that rather than using racial classifications, school districts might achieve diversity with 'race-neutral tools', such as 'drawing attendance zones with general recognition of the demographics of neighbourhoods; allocating resources for special programs; recruiting students and faculty in a targeted fashion; and tracking enrolments, performance, and other statistics by race'.[126] He asserted that such measures are 'unlikely' to demand strict scrutiny because they 'do not

---

[123] Stephen M Rich, 'Inferred Classifications' (2013) 99 Virginia Law Review 1525, 1527.
[124] One example is *Fisher* (n 52) 2208.
[125] R Richard Banks, 'The Benign-Invidious Asymmetry in Equal Protection Analysis' (2003) 31 Hastings Constitutional Law Quarterly 573, 578.
[126] *Parents Involved* (n 43) 789 (Kennedy J concurring).

lead to different treatment based on a classification that tells each student he or she is to be defined by race'.[127]

Yet what counts as 'neutral' is difficult to explain with any sort of bright-line rule. In another opinion by Justice Kennedy, the Court questioned, without resolving, whether a university admissions rule that admitted the top ten per cent of students from every high school in a state was more or less 'race neutral'.[128] Although the policy did not classify students based on race, it was adopted explicitly to 'boost minority enrolment' in light of the fact that the state's high schools are racially segregated.[129] Another example is *Ricci v DeStefano*, a case interpreting a statute prohibiting discrimination in employment.[130] In that case, a city gave an exam to decide which firefighters would be promoted, but when city officials learned the exam would have resulted in almost no minority applicants being promoted, they decided not to honour its results.[131] Rather than announcing any promotions, the city opted to create a new exam.[132] In another opinion by Justice Kennedy, the Court held the city's action constituted intentional discrimination, even though the decision to throw out the exam did not sort applicants by race and it applied to all test takers alike.[133]

Whether the Court deems a policy 'neutral' seems to turn on political considerations. Reva Siegel argues that one theme explaining Supreme Court decisions on avoiding disparities is 'anti-balkanization': the idea that civil rights initiatives should not threaten 'social cohesion' or increase racial conflict and resentment, and that efforts at integration must 'emphasize commonality among citizens and minimize the appearance of racial partiality'.[134] As Siegel explains, 'resentments among the racially privileged matter because, if ignored, they may inhibit the amelioration of racial stratification and because these resentments may reflect displaced expressions of other forms of inequality'.[135] Moreover, racial resentments prevent individuals from relating to one another despite their differences.[136]

Equity-oriented interventions may offend the principle of anti-balkanization when they unsettle the expectations of majority group members who act in reliance on particular schemes of distribution for scarce goods or opportunities, by, for example, acquiring certain qualifications, performing jobs, preparing for particular tests, or even waiting in queues. The anti-balkanization principle explains the problem in *Ricci* as the fact that the city threw out the exam *after* applicants had invested the time to prepare for it and take it, fanning flames of racial resentment.[137] As Siegel observes, the city's action 'invited all White applicants (who did not know their scores) to imagine they would have been promoted but for race'.[138] Resentments can arise when the

---

[127] ibid.
[128] *Fisher* (n 52) 2213.
[129] ibid.
[130] *Ricci v DeStefano* 557 US 557, 579 (2009).
[131] ibid.
[132] ibid.
[133] ibid 579–80.
[134] Reva B Siegel, 'From Colorblindness to Antibalkanization: An Emerging Ground of Decision in Race Equality Cases' (2011) 120 Yale Law Journal 1278, 1282, 1354.
[135] ibid 1300.
[136] ibid 1301–302.
[137] ibid 1333.
[138] ibid.

principle of merit seems to have been subordinated to equity concerns, or even when equity initiatives disrupt the principle of first come, first served.[139] For example, in arguing in opposition to a state policy that prioritized minorities for vaccine distribution, a conservative advocacy group pointed to the distress suffered by '[a] computer-savvy, 85-year-old Virginia man who has tried in vain for weeks to get vaccinated'.[140]

Whether Justice Kennedy's pronouncements on conscious-but-neutral remedies endure is uncertain. The now more conservative Supreme Court could one day conclude that any policy aimed at reducing racial disparities requires strict scrutiny, just as a policy aimed at increasing advantages for White people relative to other groups would.[141] Such a rule would call into question a vast subset of public policy initiatives, including the foundational civil rights era statutes of the 1960s.[142] Public policy actors wary of such a result must therefore craft equity-oriented interventions with care.

4.2 Neutrality Strategies for Addressing Pandemic Health Disparities

In general, health interventions may be less likely to provoke backlash than those involving employment opportunities or limited pots of government funds, because 'health is not a zero-sum game: good health for one group does not require poor health for another'.[143] But in responding to a crisis like the Covid-19 pandemic, governments must make choices about how to allocate scarce resources, such as the life-saving vaccines that were not widely available in the United States until mid-2021.

Some experts argued for vaccine eligibility rules that explicitly considered race; for example, rules allowing Black Americans to receive the vaccine at younger ages, because of data showing that group died from Covid-19 at younger ages than White Americans.[144] A few states used race as an explicit factor in vaccine allocation, but legal[145] and practical[146] concerns stood in the way of broader adoption of such rules.

---

[139] Katharine G Young, 'Rights and Queues: On Distributive Contests in the Modern State' (2016) 55 Columbia Journal of Transnational Law 56, 76–81.

[140] 'Black, Latino Seniors in Virginia Get COVID-19 Vaccine Priority as White 85-Year-Olds Wait' *Judicial Watch* (23 February 2021) www.judicialwatch.org/corruption-chronicles/black-latino-seniors-in-virginia-get-covid-19-vaccine-priority-as-white-85-year-olds-wait/ (accessed 28 June 2021).

[141] Benjamin Eidelson, 'Respect, Individualism, and Colorblindness' (2020) 129 Yale Law Journal 1600, 1601.

[142] Samuel R Bagenstos, 'Disparate Impact and the Role of Classification and Motivation in Equal Protection Law After Inclusive Communities' (2016) 101 Cornell Law Review 1115, 1144.

[143] Harris and Pamukcu (n 100) 792.

[144] Oni Blackstock and Uché Blackstock, 'Opinion: Black Americans Should Face Lower Age Cutoffs to Qualify for a Vaccine' *Washington Post* (19 February 2021) https://www.washingtonpost.com/opinions/black-americans-should-face-lower-age-cutoffs-to-qualify-for-a-vaccine/2021/02/19/3029d5de-72ec-11eb-b8a9-b9467510f0fe_story.html (accessed 28 June 2021).

[145] Based on the US Supreme Court's affirmative action precedents, legal experts argued that policies that gave people of colour priority in the vaccine queue would not survive strict scrutiny: Schmidt, Gostin, and Williams (n 121) 2024; Govind Persad, 'Allocating Medicine Fairly in an Unfair Pandemic' (2021) University of Illinois Law Review 1085, 1098.

[146] Experts argued that race-based vaccine allocation would overlook other social determinants of health; that it would 'increase mistrust in communities of color, because they may suspect a lack of ethical and safety oversight for a new vaccine given a long history of mistreatment by the medical community in the name of research'; and that it would be 'divisive': NASEM (n 120) 133.

Thus, many US public health interventions to address the Covid-19 crisis attempted to reduce health disparities without triggering racial resentments by occupying the race-conscious-but-race-neutral grey area. They did this with four overlapping strategies that I refer to as (1) 'race as one of many factors';[147] (2) community outreach; (3) underlying drivers; and (4) 'place, not race'.[148] These strategies had varying levels of success.

One neutrality strategy is to include membership in a racial minority group as just one of many factors contributing to social disadvantage. For example, the CDC's July 2020 'health equity strategy' for reducing Covid-19 disparities included racial and ethnic minorities as just one among many targeted groups including residents of rural areas, people experiencing homelessness, frontline and essential workers, and people with disabilities.[149] Another example is the 'social vulnerability index', a metric that identifies geographic areas where people are worse-off based on fifteen considerations including race.[150] Although ACIP did not go so far as to recommend vaccine allocation based on the social vulnerability index,[151] approximately half of the states included social vulnerability or other similar indices in their vaccine distribution plans.[152] Under the Biden administration, the CDC allocated US$3 billion to increase 'vaccine confidence', with, for example, door-knocking campaigns in areas 'with a high social vulnerability index, minority communities, and rural areas'.[153]

The one-of-many-factors strategy reflects the progressive insights that '[h]ealth equity is intersectional', and '[i]ndividuals may belong to several groups that historically have experienced discrimination'.[154] That race is but one of many factors suggests it is not necessarily a determinative consideration that would result in any particular White person being denied a scarce resource. It also has the potential to appeal across the political spectrum. The Biden administration explained that its funding was to be spent on, for example, hiring 'workers who do culturally-competent bilingual health outreach', appealing to liberals, but also 'rural, faith-based organizations', who are generally a conservative contingent.[155] The inclusion of faith brings to mind an analogy: just as, in the US constitutional tradition, neutrality as to religion may entail

---

[147] *Grutter* (n 49) 339.
[148] Sheryll Cashin, *Place, Not Race* (Beacon Press 2014).
[149] CDC COVID-19 Response (n 115) 1.
[150] Harald Schmidt and others, 'Covid-19: How to Prioritize Worse-Off Populations in Allocating Safe and Effective Vaccines' (2020) 371 BMJ 3795, 2.
[151] Maya Manian and Seema Mohapatra, 'States Must Factor Race in COVID-19 Vaccine Prioritization' *Law360* (18 April 2021) www.law360.com/articles/1376135/states-must-factor-race-in-covid-19-vaccine-prioritization (accessed 28 June 2021).
[152] Ndugga, Artiga, and Pham (n 105).
[153] White House, 'Fact Sheet: Biden Administration Announces Historic $10 Billion Investment to Expand Access to COVID-19 Vaccines and Build Vaccine Confidence in Hardest-Hit and Highest-Risk Communities' (25 March 2021) www.whitehouse.gov/briefing-room/statements-releases/2021/03/25/fact-sheet-biden-administration-announces-historic-10-billion-investment-to-expand-access-to-covid-19-vaccines-and-build-vaccine-confidence-in-hardest-hit-and-highest-risk-communities/ (accessed 28 June 2021).
[154] CDC, 'COVID-10 Racial and Ethnic Health Disparities: What We Can Do to Move Towards Health Equity' (10 December 2020) www.cdc.gov/coronavirus/2019-ncov/community/health-equity/racial-ethnic-disparities/what-we-do.html (accessed 28 June 2021).
[155] ibid.

official support for both religious and secular communities,[156] neutrality as to race may mean supporting communities defined by race as well as those defined by other factors. This reasoning may work on a political level, but any such analogy seems unlikely to persuade the US Supreme Court, which increasingly regards religious rights as entitled to exceptional protection[157] and, due to opposition to affirmative action in general, is unlikely to extend the 'one of many factors' idea beyond the context of diversity in higher education.

A related and sometimes overlapping strategy is outreach to community partners: collaborations with organizations that serve minority communities. The CDC's Covid-19 response included identifying community groups 'affiliated with racial and ethnic populations placed at increased risk for COVID-19' so as to establish collaborations for providing information and health care.[158] Under the American Rescue Plan, the Biden administration awarded more than six billion dollars to support community health centres providing Covid-19 vaccination, testing, and treatment.[159] This approach has had some success, reaching more minority individuals than other vaccination efforts.[160] Many states launched communications campaigns focused on reaching people of colour by, for example, including information in Spanish.[161] Another example is arguably the federal government's approach to Native American tribes, which have a unique status in the US federal system.[162] Tribes received vaccine allocations directly from a federal agency, the Indian Health Service, and by many reports they were more effective at distributing the vaccine.[163]

Outreach strategies do not seem to provoke political backlash or legal challenges. Perhaps the reason is that they do not appear to allocate zero-sum resources—communications in Spanish can occur alongside communications in English, for example. Moreover, outreach strategies avoid the perception of trade-offs by invoking unfair baselines: because the affluent and tech-savvy were able to use the internet to secure the earliest vaccination appointments, efforts to reach other populations

---

[156] Toni M Massaro, 'Religious Freedom and "Accommodationist Neutrality": A Non-Neutral Critique' (2005) 84 Oregon Law Review 935, 946–49.

[157] Richard Schragger and Micah Schwartzman, 'Religious Antiliberalism and the First Amendment' (2020) 104 Minnesota Law Review 1341, 1342, 1347.

[158] CDC COVID-19 Response (n 115) 3.

[159] Health Resources & Services Administration, 'American Rescue Plan Act Awards' (April 2021) https://bphc.hrsa.gov/program-opportunities/american-rescue-plan/awards (accessed 28 June 2021).

[160] Bradley Corallo, Samantha Artiga, and Jennifer Tolbert, 'Are Health Centers Facilitating Equitable Access to COVID-19 Vaccinations? A June 2021 Update' Kaiser Family Foundation (2 June 2021) www.kff.org/coronavirus-covid-19/issue-brief/are-health-centers-facilitating-equitable-access-to-covid-19-vaccinations-a-june-2021-update/ (accessed 28 June 2021).

[161] Ndugga, Artiga, and Pham (n 105).

[162] Rachel Hatzipanagos, 'How Native Americans Launched Successful Coronavirus Vaccination drives: "A Story of Resilience"' *Washington Post* (26 May 2021) www.washingtonpost.com/nation/2021/05/26/how-native-americans-launched-successful-coronavirus-vaccination-drives-story-resilience/ (accessed 28 June 2021); Kirk Siegler, 'Why Native Americans Are Getting COVID-19 Vaccines Faster' *NPR* (19 February 2021) www.npr.org/2021/02/19/969046248/why-native-americans-are-getting-the-covid-19-vaccines-faster (accessed 28 June 2021).

[163] ibid. For a more thorough legal analysis of the vaccine distribution to Native Americans see Persad (n 145) 1113–17.

through community health centres are not perceived as threatening to the privileged.[164] Additionally, outreach does not appear to entail individual-level racial classifications, because community organizations affiliated with minority communities are not seen as turning away non-minorities. Outreach strategies also invoke the virtues of localism and participation: the idea that programmes designed without attention to the needs of local communities or without on-the-ground input from those communities are likely to fail.[165]

Yet another strategy is to target the underlying drivers of health disparities—such as particular occupations, health conditions, and family structures—to identify beneficiaries of public policy. In December 2020, ACIP recommended that the vaccine be offered early to 'frontline essential workers', such as firefighters, teachers, grocery store workers, and food and agricultural workers, both because these occupations exposed workers to high levels of risk, and because they are disproportionately filled by racial and ethnic minorities.[166] ACIP also recommended that individuals with medical conditions that put them at high risk be prioritized early, a strategy likely to reduce inequities because, due to the social determinants of health, Black and Hispanic individuals are more likely to have high-risk conditions.[167] Many states followed this approach as well.[168] For example, Washington state allowed certain older members of multi-generational households to receive the vaccine early, both because people of colour are more likely to live in multi-generational households, and because these living arrangements increase the risk of at-home transmission to vulnerable elders.[169]

These strategies attempt to avoid the suggestion that race itself is 'an inherent risk factor', recognizing instead that 'COVID-19 disparities reflect the health, environmental, and occupational effects of structural racism'.[170] Unlike the race-as-one-of-many-factors approach, they do not explicitly turn on racial categories; rather, they target the intermediate causes of racial disparities. These intermediate causes increase Covid-19 risks for both non-minorities and minorities, but disproportionately affect minorities. Nonetheless, the underlying-drivers strategy could be susceptible to legal challenge to the extent that an underlying driver was selected because it is a proxy for

---

[164] Lloyd Michener and others, 'Engaging with Communities: Lessons (Re)Learned from COVID-19' (2020) 17 Preventing Chronic Disease https://www.cdc.gov/Pcd/issues/2020/20_0250.htm (accessed 28 June 2021).

[165] ibid.

[166] Kathleen Dooling, 'The Advisory Committee on Immunization Practices' Updated Interim Recommendation for Allocation of COVID-19 Vaccine—United States December 2020' (2021) 59 Morbidity and Mortality Weekly Report 1657, 1658.

[167] Harald Schmidt and others, 'Equitable allocation of Covid-19 Vaccines: An Analysis of the Initial Allocation Plans of CDC's Jurisdictions with Implications for Disparate Impact Monitoring' (1 December 2020) 3 https://papers.ssrn.com/sol3/papers.cfm?abstract_id=3740041 (accessed 28 June 2021).

[168] A few states disregarded equity concerns and adopted rules based exclusively or almost exclusively on age: Govind Persad, Emily A Largent, and Ezekiel J Emanuel, 'Opinion: Age-Based Vaccine Distribution Is not only Unethical. It's Also Bad Health Policy' *Washington Post* (9 March 2021) https://www.washington post.com/opinions/2021/03/09/age-based-covid-vaccine-distribution-unethical/ (accessed 28 June 2021).

[169] April Simpson and others, 'WA Leads on Addressing COVID Risk in Multigenerational Homes' *Crosscut* (1 April 2021) https://crosscut.com/news/2021/04/wa-leads-addressing-covid-risk-multigenerational-homes (accessed 28 June 2021).

[170] Govind Persad, Monica E Peek, and Ezekiel J Emanuel, 'Fairly Prioritizing Groups for Access to COVID-19 Vaccines' (2020) 324 Journal of the American Medical Association 1601, 1602.

race, rather than because it increases Covid-19 risk. A colour-blind court could see such a policy as a pretextual attempt to evade the legal scrutiny reserved for race-based classifications.[171]

Another strategy is 'place, not race', or, as the CDC explains it: a 'populations and place-based focus'.[172] Some states followed the vaccine allocation recommendations of the National Academy of Science, Engineering, and Mathematics to make special efforts to distribute vaccines in areas that score high on indices of social vulnerability, because those indices 'attempt to incorporate the variables ... most linked to the disproportionate impact of COVID-19 on people of colour' without focusing on 'discrete racial and ethnic categories'.[173] In March 2021, the federal government announced a plan to devote nearly US$10 billion in funding from the American Rescue Plan to increase vaccination in 'underserved communities' including 'communities of colour'.[174] Some of this funding was used to establish federally run community vaccination centres in 'hard-hit areas' where 60 per cent of doses went to people of colour.[175] This strategy is akin to the underlying drivers approach in that it attempts to capture disparities caused by 'historical and contemporary redlining and other structural inequalities in housing and services'.[176] But insofar as places are selected based in part on racial demographics, place-not-race strategies resemble the race-as-one-of-many-factors approach.

In some contexts, place-not-race strategies succeeded in avoiding political backlash, while in others, they did not. The conservative state of Tennessee, for example, committed to setting aside a percentage of its vaccines for areas with high social vulnerability, rather than strictly according to population.[177] One Tennessee Republican commented that the social vulnerability approach 'doesn't make distribution a race issue. There's no putting one over another. It's based on health conditions'.[178] However, in Michigan, a state with divided politics, the use of the social vulnerability index resulted in backlash from Republican legislators who argued age-based metrics better reflected the likelihood of death and introduced a proposal to bar the use of 'race, gender, colour, national origin, religion, sex, and socioeconomic status as factors in determining the distribution of COVID-19 vaccines'.[179] The overall effectiveness of place-not-race strategies in undermining disparities may have been impaired by the fact that affluent White people were willing to travel to minority communities to

---

[171] Persad (n 145) 1119.
[172] CDC COVID-19 Response (n 115) 1.
[173] NASEM (n 120) 9.
[174] White House (n 153).
[175] ibid.
[176] Kristin Bibbins-Domingo, Maya Petersen, and Diane Havlir, 'Taking Vaccine to Where the Virus Is: Equity and Effectiveness in Coronavirus Vaccinations' (2021) 2(2) Journal of the American Medical Association Health Forum e210213.
[177] Isaac Stanley-Becker and Lena H Sun, 'Covid-19 Is Devastating Communities of Color: Can Vaccines Counter Racial Inequity?' *Washington Post* (18 December 2020) https://www.washingtonpost.com/health/2020/12/18/covid-vaccine-racial-equity/ (accessed 28 June 2021).
[178] ibid.
[179] Abigail Censky, 'Michigan Officials Wrestle with how to Ethically Distribute COVID-19 Vaccines' *NPR* (9 March 2021) www.npr.org/2021/03/09/975194130/michigan-officials-wrestle-with-how-to-ethically-distribute-covid-19-vaccines (accessed 28 June 2021).

receive vaccines early.[180] In general, despite the many race-neutral efforts to mitigate health disparities, the rate of vaccination for Black and Hispanic individuals lagged behind those of White individuals.[181]

Thus, it is not just public policies that identify beneficiaries based on race, such as the American Rescue Plan's provisions for minority-owned restaurants, that may face legal and political challenges, but also policies that consider the racial demographics of their likely beneficiaries, even if race is but one of many factors considered. This leaves outreach programmes and efforts to target the underlying drivers of disparities as safer options for public policy actors seeking to reduce disparities—although policy-makers would be well advised to take care that their policies are justified for independent reasons other than disparity reduction and to ground policy on the benefits of reducing health disparities for the entire population.[182]

5 Conclusion

Although conscious-but-neutral interventions may not necessarily be ideal, they may be the best short-term hope for addressing exponential inequalities in the US context, considering the conservative makeup of the federal judiciary. The way the current Supreme Court thinks about the constitutional guarantee of equal protection and the nation's foundational civil rights statutes is inconsistent with the basic ideals of equity, fairness, and justice that animate much public policy. Yet the Court's ideology has shifted many times over its history, and it has often reinterpreted its precedents to reflect political and social developments, as well as new data and persuasive arguments. One lesson of the Court's rightward shift toward colour-blind jurisprudence is that the strict scrutiny framework is a malleable one, with room for argument on what constitutes a race-neutral policy, what amounts to a compelling interest, and what narrow tailoring requires. As public policy experts continue to track disparities, study the effects of different policy interventions on alleviating crises, and advocate for programmes that both reduce disparities and improve the well-being of the entire population, their efforts may generate evidence that courts find compelling in dismissing legal challenges to crisis interventions. Over the longer term, the values that animate equity efforts might even exert influence over the legal definition of equality.

---

[180] Abby Goodnough and Jan Hoffman, 'The Wealthy Are Getting More Vaccinations, Even in Poorer Neighborhoods' *New York Times* (4 March 2021) https://www.nytimes.com/2021/02/02/health/white-people-covid-vaccines-minorities.html (accessed 28 June 2021).

[181] Nambi Ndugga and others, 'Latest Data on COVID-19 Vaccinations: Race/Ethnicity' Kaiser Family Foundation (9 June 2021) www.kff.org/coronavirus-covid-19/issue-brief/latest-data-on-covid-19-vaccinations-race-ethnicity/ (accessed 28 June 2021).

[182] A policy motivated by discriminatory intent is not invalid if the government can demonstrate it would have pursued the same policy even if it had not considered an impermissible purpose: *Arlington Heights* (n 23) 270.

10
Responding to Exponential Inequalities in Australia
Beyond the Limits of Equality and Discrimination Law

Beth Gaze

1 Introduction

This chapter considers the impact of the Covid-19 pandemic in Australia, focusing on the inequalities that it generated and exacerbated, the government responses to those inequalities, and the path ahead. All countries have confronted similar issues in dealing with the health emergency of the pandemic: how to protect the population from infection, illness, and death, and how to ensure equitable access to vaccines and treatments for infections while trying to protect individual livelihoods and the economy from damage as far as possible. The issues play out differently in each country as a result of their very different social, economic, political, and legal contexts and specifically their healthcare, legal, and political systems. Many further issues flow from government responses, such as the unequal impact of job losses and the exacerbation of domestic violence during lockdowns. In the same way as the virus threatened exponential spread unless precautions were taken, the social and economic consequences of the pandemic threatened to lead to exponential inequalities unless appropriate responses were adopted.

The pandemic has highlighted just how badly many disadvantaged groups, especially workers, are treated. The pandemic has revealed the truly essential workers on whom we all depend—those in food production and distribution, health care including aged care, and education including childcare. Everyone has an interest in ensuring that the health of these workers is protected, because everyone is at risk if these workers are at risk. However, in its policy responses to the pandemic, Australia exposed its most vulnerable people and disempowered workers to substantial, and in some cases severe, economic and other harm. Equality and discrimination laws were not able to ensure attention to their needs, revealing the weaknesses of the law in this context and the need for a much broader positive approach.

This chapter begins by summarizing briefly the impact in Australia of the pandemic and the government responses to it. The government responses were distinctive, pursuing the goal of controlling and excluding Covid-19 altogether until mid-2021, through public health measures such as lockdowns and border closures. Then it identifies the inequality challenges that have arisen as a result, which groups have been most disadvantaged, and the government responses and non-responses to these challenges. I argue that an adequate response to the disadvantage created both by the pandemic and by government actions requires a much broader approach than can be provided by attribute-based equality and discrimination laws. The harm extends beyond groups protected explicitly, for example to the broader group of people living in poverty. Responses must therefore go beyond the scope of the current equality and discrimination laws, to engage with structural disadvantage and vulnerability.

Disadvantage, not discrimination, is the challenge. The pre-existing disadvantage of the groups most affected was often exacerbated by the steps taken to control the virus, replacing exponential growth of the virus and illness with (potentially exponential) growth of disadvantage. After briefly considering the ways in which governments responded and the impacts of those responses, the chapter proceeds to consider how such engagement with structural inequalities could be understood and implemented in law.

2 The Australian Context

In Australia, consideration of government responses to the crisis is complex because of the nature of the federation and the political interplay between state and federal governments formed by different political parties. As a result, much of the government response has been thoroughly politicized, involving tensions between business-favouring conservative (Liberal Party) governments federally and in some states, and more social justice-oriented governments (Australian Labor Party (ALP)) in other states. In the Australian federation, the Commonwealth has only specific limited legislative powers under the Constitution, including powers to raise taxes and to provide social security payments.[1] In practice, it has taken over the field of income taxation from the states, leaving them only a few less remunerative taxes, even though they have primary responsibility for providing the bulk of services such as education and health. This 'vertical fiscal imbalance' gives the Commonwealth great financial power to influence the way things are done in the states by providing conditional grants for specific purposes.[2] When different political parties are in power at state and federal levels, the political contest provides ample scope for blame shifting and avoidance of responsibility for provision (and funding) of essential services such as childcare, aged care, education, and health services.[3] Responses to the pandemic took place in this highly partisan context.

Politics in Australia has followed a neoliberal approach since the 1980s.[4] Both state and federal governments have been committed to outsourcing and privatization of public sector tasks, to the extent that expertise in the federal public service appears

---

[1] Commonwealth of Australia, Constitution (1901), s 51(xxiiiA), (ii).

[2] Such payments are authorized by the Constitution (n 1) s 96.

[3] The tensions around disability care have been partially resolved by the adoption of the National Disability Insurance Scheme, which provides resources to people with disability to facilitate their living to their full capacity, but is currently under pressure from the Commonwealth government to restrain spending where possible.

[4] John Quiggin, 'Globalisation, Neoliberalism and Inequality in Australia' (1999) 10 Economic and Labour Relations Review 240; David Primrose, Robin Chang, and Rodney Loeppky, 'Pandemic Unplugged: COVID-19, Public Health and the Persistence of Neoliberalism' (2020) 85 Journal of Australian Political Economy 17. Adam Tooze points out that one reason for the conservative dedication to

to have been hollowed out. Instead, governments rely on consultants and contracting out essential work, preferring to pursue low taxes rather than social policies needed to support disadvantaged groups. The expertise to manage the pandemic adequately was not available immediately to either state or federal governments. This led to failures of implementation, like breaches of hotel quarantine from which the virus leaked into the community and sparked further long lockdowns, and the Australian government's failure to order a sufficient early supply of vaccines, which led to Australia being among the last Organisation for Economic Co-operation and Development (OECD) countries to embark on a vaccination programme in 2021.[5] Contracting out public services provides profits to private sector organizations and replaces secure public employment with often precarious employment in the private sector. Many industries providing basic services to vulnerable people are privatized and run for profit, including aged care homes, childcare, and private health organizations, as well as some hospitals and most medical practices.[6] This political environment has affected workplace laws as well. Since the mid-1990s there has been movement under federal laws to weaken labour protections which, together with the rise of gig and fissured employment,[7] has resulted in greater precariousness for many workers. In what follows, two strands of concern emerge: the direct health impact of the pandemic and the impacts on livelihoods and welfare dependence from lockdown and isolation requirements.

The pandemic affected Australia very differently from countries that permitted overseas travel. With the advantage of being an island, once it became clear there was a pandemic, the borders were shut, first to China in February 2020, and then in March 2020 to the rest of the world. Travel to or from Australia remained very restricted until late 2021 as primary protection against the Delta strain of coronavirus, but was eventually relaxed in December 2021 just as the Omicron variant emerged.[8] During this

---

neoliberalism is that it removes decisions from the partisan political arena, thereby placing them ostensibly beyond criticism. See Adam Tooze, *Shutdown: How Covid Shook the World Economy* (Allen Lane 2021).

[5] The Therapeutic Goods Administration approved the Pfizer vaccine in January 2021 and the Astra Zeneca vaccine in February 2021, but stocks of vaccine were very limited until later in the year. From late March 2021, vaccine was available only to health workers and people over 70. As supplies slowly increased, this broadened over the following months to wider and younger groups.

[6] The Australian public health system involves publicly run hospitals and public subsidy of fees for service (note that the term used in Australia for this form of subsidized medicine is 'fee for service' not 'fees') care provision by doctors, as well as a pharmaceutical benefits scheme that subsidizes the costs of medicines to individuals. See Stephen Duckett and Sharon Willcox, *The Australian Health Care System* (5th edn, OUP 2015). Prisons and immigration detention are also privatized industries, but outside the scope of this chapter.

[7] Fissured employment refers to the division of employer's responsibilities among more than one party. One example of increasing importance has been labour hire employment, where workers are hired by a labour provider, often as contractors or casuals, or as subcontractors through further levels of contracting, and supplied to the enterprise that uses their labour. This shifts employment towards smaller entities and allows the apparent 'employer' to avoid the usual responsibilities of employment. Labour rights, including correct pay, may be reduced or difficult to enforce against subcontractors. David Weil, 'How to Make Employment Fair in an Age of Contracting and Temp Work' *Harvard Business Review* (4 March 2017) https://hbr.org/2017/03/making-employment-a-fair-deal-in-the-age-of-contracting-subcontracting-and-temp-work (accessed 7 June 2022); David Weil, *The Fissured Workplace: Why Work Became So Bad for So Many and What Can Be Done to Improve It* (Harvard UP 2017).

[8] This chapter considers events until late 2021. With the rise of the Omicron variant and a change of premier in New South Wales, international and most internal borders were opened despite the risks, and a new phase of government response began. However, the same problems of inequality continued.

time, all passengers, both incoming and outgoing, including citizens seeking to return, had to obtain a permit and complete fourteen days' quarantine in a hotel at their own expense. The main tools used against Covid-19 in this period before the population was widely vaccinated were border closures (by the Commonwealth at the external border and the states and territories at the internal borders) and lockdowns, hotel quarantine, extensive contact tracing (by the states and territories), and public health practices such as mask wearing and density limits. These mechanisms were successful in 2020 to keep deaths overall to around 1,000 for the country as a whole, but in 2021 the outbreak of infection with the Delta variant saw infections and death rates begin to climb again from June onwards.

Lockdowns were the primary domestic tool to suppress or eliminate outbreaks of the virus. An initial national lockdown operated from March to June 2020 to control infections at the outset of the pandemic. The virus was then reintroduced by a leak from hotel quarantine of incoming international passengers through casual subcontracted security guards, who of necessity were working more than one job.[9] This outbreak was eliminated by a further four-month lockdown of Melbourne from August to November 2020. Lockdowns and the border closures were relatively effective to eliminate the virus until the advent of the Delta variant in early 2021, after which further lockdowns from mid-2021 of the two largest cities, Sydney and Melbourne, reduced but did not eliminate the Delta variant, and were abandoned at the same time as the Omicron variant arrived, in December 2021, as vaccination levels increased.[10] Outside these two cities, life continued almost as normal[11] except for a small number of lockdowns for a few days to a few weeks during 2021 to eliminate virus infections when they escaped from quarantine hotels or across state borders. People in these less restricted states could still attend school and work in person, and gather in restaurants and theatres until governments decided to reopen fully in late 2021. The main limits they experienced were inability to travel interstate or overseas, and the impact on industries such as tourism that rely on travel. This approach was very popular with residents of those states, even though a minority of residents were adversely affected by the inability to travel. For those who needed to travel, permits both to leave and enter Australia or other states were difficult to obtain, and many requests were refused, sometimes preventing families from seeing dying loved ones, even when only interstate travel was involved.[12]

Lockdowns also created serious economic problems. The initial lockdown prevented Australia's many international secondary and tertiary students from entering

---

[9] Conditions for this work, which was contracted out by state governments, were subsequently revised to limit spread by ensuring use of effective personal protective equipment (PPE) and preventing staff from working at more than one location.

[10] Sydney was locked down from June to November 2021 and Melbourne from July to November 2021.

[11] The states largely unaffected until late 2021 were Western Australia, Queensland, Tasmania, and South Australia, and the two territories (Northern Territory and the Australian Capital Territory), which adopted border exclusion rules that prevented and limited people from Victoria and NSW entering.

[12] John Quiggin, 'After the Pandemic, Let's Not Keep Families Separated by Borders' *Canberra Times* (31 December 2020) https://www.canberratimes.com.au/story/7070879/after-the-pandemic-lets-not-keep-families-separated-by-borders/ (accessed 30 May 2022).

the country, with a huge impact on the education sector.[13] Businesses that operated face to face like education, hospitality, retail, and tourism were disrupted. During lockdowns, schools and workplaces moved to remote interactions. Any worker who could work from home was required to do so. Many white-collar workers could continue to work almost as normal online, while many blue-collar workers and others doing personal services work either could not work, or were required to continue to attend their workplace in person, potentially exposing themselves and their clients[14] to infection. Workers were required to get a test if they had any symptoms of Covid-19 or were close contacts of an infected person, and to isolate until they received a result. Casual workers are not paid for days they do not work and have no paid sick leave entitlements, so this had a big impact, and there was incentive to avoid testing or isolating. The Commonwealth did not address this problem, and eventually the state governments stepped in, providing lump sum wage replacement payments to workers who had to miss work.[15]

In 2020, most of those deaths were of vulnerable aged care residents, especially during the August to November 2020 wave in Melbourne, when the virus entered aged care homes through their staff, who were low paid, casual workers. Because of industry practices of preferring part-time workers, many had to work in multiple jobs at multiple centres to make a living, which risked spreading the virus. The examples of spread through aged care and the hotel quarantine security guards illustrate how exposure to the virus and its transmission depended on socio-economic and other disadvantages. It occurred through workers who carried out essential tasks and often had casual or precarious work conditions as a result of which they had to continue working and could not easily protect themselves.[16] As well as aged care, childcare, schools, and hotel quarantine workers, this included workers in the food chain such as abattoirs, distribution centres, and supermarkets.

The example of aged care is among the most concerning of the pandemic, as it affected both residents and workers. Serious problems of quality in aged care existed before the pandemic and were recently the subject of a Royal Commission inquiry, which traced issues to industry privatization and the deregulation of care standards.[17] The Royal Commission found that these features have led to an industry run for profit rather than for providing excellent care, but the government agreed to implement only some of the recommendations of the Commission.[18]

---

[13] Peter Hurley, '2021 Is the Year Australia's International Student Crisis Really Bites' *The Conversation* (14 January 2021) https://theconversation.com/2021-is-the-year-australias-international-student-crisis-really-bites-153180 (accessed 30 May 2022).

[14] Senate Select Committee on Covid 19, *First Interim Report* (December 2020) ch 4 https://www.aph.gov.au/Parliamentary_Business/Committees/Senate/COVID-19/COVID19 (accessed 1 June 2022).

[15] See eg Victoria, 'Financial and other support for COVID-19' https://www.coronavirus.vic.gov.au/financial-and-other-support-coronavirus-covid-19 (accessed 18 January 2022).

[16] Senate Select Committee (n 14).

[17] Commonwealth, Royal Commission into Aged Care Quality and Safety, *Final Report: Care, Dignity and Respect* (February 2021).

[18] Aged care in Australia is substantially privatized and run for profit. The Royal Commission identified major problems of neglect in care homes and neglect of adequate responses by governments in its Interim Report of March 2020. In its response of May 2021, the government accepted recommendations concerning governance, but not those regarding better funding and regulation of the area, in particular transparency in relation to the use of public funding: Australian Government Department of Health, 'Australian

Women were also substantially affected by job losses resulting from the direct impact of lockdowns on women-dominated industries like hospitality, retail, education, community services, etc, when men's jobs in industries like construction (which was permitted to continue) were largely unaffected.[19]

A further burden for many women was the need to supervise home schooling or care for pre- and primary school children when childcare and schools were closed. Family stereotypes operated to allocate this work to women, and many experienced substantial career interruption, but this burden appears to have been invisible to the government.[20] There was an escalation of domestic violence as a result of lockdowns, while at the same time leaving an unsafe home environment was made more difficult.[21] Government initiatives to encourage economic activity and job creation were focused mainly on male dominated areas like construction and mining[22] and away from human capital work in which women tend to be employed.[23] In these ways, general government policy responses to the pandemic favoured men's jobs over women's and neglected the needs of disadvantaged individuals and workers. None of these gendered impacts were acknowledged or accounted for by governments. Australia's gender pay gap increased during the period of the pandemic from 13.4 per cent in November 2020 to 14.2 per cent reported in August 2021.[24] In 2021, Australia ranked fiftieth in the World Economic Forum Global Gender Gap Report, having fallen from sixth place in 2006.[25]

In summary, the pandemic had the greatest effect on the least secure and most marginalized members of society. Pre-existing disadvantage came from poverty, insecure employment, and poor employment conditions, as well as the marginalizing of women, indigenous people, people with disability, the elderly, ethnic minorities, and temporary migrants. Their disadvantage was reinforced by migration law, lack of protection in labour law, and inadequate welfare benefits or exclusion from benefits.[26]

Government Response to the Final Report of the Royal Commission into Aged Care Quality and Safety' (11 May 2021).

[19] ibid 84. See also Workplace Gender Equality Agency, 'Gendered Impact of Covid-19' (updated to October 2020) https://www.wgea.gov.au/publications/gendered-impact-of-covid-19 (accessed 7 June 2022).
[20] Danielle Wood, Kate Griffiths, and Tom Crowley, 'Women's Work: The Impact of the COVID Crisis on Australian Women' Grattan Institute (12 April 2021) https://grattan.edu.au/report/womens-work/ (accessed 7 June 2022).
[21] See eg Hayley Boxall and Anthony Morgan, 'Who is Most at Risk of Physical and Sexual Partner Violence and Coercive Control during the COVID-19 Pandemic?' (2021) 618 Trends and Issues in Crime and Criminal Justice 1.
[22] Wood, Griffiths, and Crowley (n 20); see also Per Capita, 'Submission to the Inquiry into the JobMaker Hiring Credit Bill 2020' (October 2020) https://percapita.org.au/our_work/per-capita-submission-to-the-inquiry-into-the-jobmaker-hiring-credit-bill-2020/ (accessed 7 June 2022).
[23] Senate Select Committee (n 14) 97.
[24] Workplace Gender Equality Agency, 'National Gender Pay Gap Statistics Over Time' (August 2021) https://www.wgea.gov.au/publications/australias-gender-pay-gap-statistics#national-gender-pay-gapovertime (accessed 7 June 2022).
[25] World Economic Forum, *Global Gender Gap Report 2021 Insight Report* (March 2021) 18; Madeline Hislop, 'Australia Has Fallen Way Behind on the Global Gender Gap Ranking' *Women's Agenda* (31 March 2021) https://womensagenda.com.au/latest/australia-has-fallen-way-behind-on-the-global-gender-gap-ranking/ (accessed 7 June 2022).
[26] Joo-Cheong Tham, 'The COVID-19 Crisis, Labour Rights and the Role of the State' (2020) 85 Journal of Australian Political Economy 71.

Lockdowns and public health measures created further disadvantage, including loss of livelihoods, health problems (including mental health), and interruptions to social life. Loss of income had pervasive effects, which were ameliorated to some extent by the temporary government payments from 2020 to early 2021. Paradoxically, the pandemic showed that the workers who are really essential are the low paid and casualized staff. But this has not changed the way in which essential jobs in healthcare or food distribution are organized or paid. In 2021, the disadvantage of these groups continued to be reflected in lower rates of vaccination (and consequent greater risk of infection) based on language difficulties, limited government health information, lack of access to information from a trusted source, and greater exposure to misinformation.[27]

3 Government Responses and Their Impact

The pandemic drew attention to the vital importance of public health measures, and the government's role in a health emergency to ensure public health is protected. This goes beyond measures directly targeting health such as lockdowns, closures, and mask mandates, to underlying issues such as ensuring sufficient income to allow precarious workers to isolate when necessary. The threat of Covid-19 to public health was so immediate and serious that action had to be taken urgently to protect the most vulnerable people and then the rest of the community. Responses like border closures and lockdowns affected the economy so deeply but unevenly that measures to protect the most exposed industries became necessary to prevent permanent damage. However, the response of the conservative Australian Commonwealth government to these challenges was limited by its neoliberal orientation,[28] which prioritizes low taxes and tax cuts for the wealthy and then claims that the country cannot afford adequate public service provision or a sufficient level of welfare support for the poor and disadvantaged.

Reluctantly, the Australian government brought in two extra welfare benefits to support the system that required infected workers and their close contacts to isolate and not attend work. The first was a payment called Job Keeper, which was made to employers who estimated that their turnover would fall by 15 or 30 per cent (for profit or non-profit organizations respectively), which was designed to keep employees paid by, and attached to, their employer to ensure the economy could return to 'normal' once the crisis passed.[29] In addition, the unemployment benefit, Job Seeker, and other related welfare benefits were supplemented with an extra fortnightly payment of A$1,100, to replace any supplementary pay the person may have lost when required to isolate and refrain from working to avoid risk to the community.[30] For parents on welfare benefits, this supplement was sufficient to virtually eliminate child poverty while

---

[27] Anne Kavanagh, Helen Dickinson, and Nancy Baxter, 'Opening up when 80% of Eligible Adults are Vaccinated Won't be "Safe" for all Australians' *The Conversation* (31 August 2021).

[28] Pragmatically, this also serves the interests of its major donors, thereby preserving both the party's electoral funding and the possibilities of well-paid jobs for MPs after they leave Parliament.

[29] Senate Select Committee (n 14) 73.

[30] ibid 80–82, [5.83]–[5.84].

it was available.[31] However, it was terminated at the end of March 2021, returning them to below poverty-line payments.[32]

Similarly, subsidies for childcare fees,[33] and for childcare centre staff through Job Keeper were provided for some months at the start of the pandemic to ensure centres did not collapse while most parents were not able to use them during lockdowns, when only children of essential workers were allowed to attend. However, both subsidies were removed in June 2020, well before other industries. This required childcare workers, who are predominantly low paid women, to return to work. It appears that the government did not want Australians to get used to the idea that a service like childcare should be free.[34] Because many parents were still working from home and not using childcare, childcare centres struggled after the withdrawal of fee support, and support was introduced again during the 2021 lockdowns.[35] As noted above, the impact of working from home while also providing childcare and home schooling was largely felt by women, affecting their ability to perform and progress at work.[36]

An important success in 2020 was the safeguarding of the indigenous population, especially in small remote communities where health is poorer and health services much harder to access. Steps taken to protect indigenous communities included closing down access to remote communities. This was driven by government-funded but aboriginal-controlled health services, and was effective until September 2021 when the virus spread to unvaccinated rural Aboriginal communities in western NSW.[37] Although the federal government had identified high priority groups for vaccination early in 2021, including aged care residents and first nations people, apparently little effort was made to carry out those priorities beyond aged care residents, so that remote indigenous communities in far western NSW had not been vaccinated by September 2021 when the virus arrived. This is one example among many of the federal government stating goals but failing to act on them.[38]

---

[31] Sharon Bessell, 'Australia was a Model for Protecting People from COVID-19: And Then We Dumped Half a Million People Back into Poverty' *The Conversation* (12 August 2021) https://theconversation.com/australia-was-a-model-for-protecting-people-from-covid-19-and-then-we-dumped-half-a-million-people-back-into-poverty-165813 (accessed 7 June 2022); Simone Casey and Liss Ralston, 'At Least 2.6 million People Face Poverty when COVID Payments End and Rental Stress Soars' *The Conversation* (24 March 2021) https://theconversation.com/at-least-2-6-million-people-face-poverty-when-covid-payments-end-and-rental-stress-soars-157244 (accessed 7 June 2022).

[32] ibid.

[33] Michelle Grattan, 'Free Childcare Ends July 12, with Sector Losing Job Keeper but Receiving Temporary Payment' *The Conversation* (8 June 2020); Senate Select Committee (n 14) 79–80.

[34] Childcare in Australia is a privatized system run largely by for profit companies with substantial government funding, but the cost of care remains very high. See generally Australian Institute of Health and Welfare, 'Childcare and Early Childhood Education Snapshot' (16 September 2021) https://www.aihw.gov.au/reports/australias-welfare/childcare-and-early-childhood-education (accessed 7 June 2022).

[35] Peter Hurley and Hannah Matthews, 'The Government Has Again Rescued the Childcare Sector from Collapse, but Short-term Fixes Still Leave It at Risk' *The Conversation* (24 August 2021).

[36] Wood, Griffiths, and Crowley (n 20).

[37] Rachel Pannett, 'Australia Made a Plan to Protect Indigenous Elders from Covid19, It Worked' *Washington Post* (9 April 2021); Bhiamie Williamson, 'The COVID-19 Crisis in Western NSW Aboriginal Communities is a Nightmare Realised' *The Conversation* (16 August 2021).

[38] Similar failures have occurred with ordering and supplying vaccines to the population as a whole, but especially to vulnerable groups such as people in aged care and in disability care, both of which are Commonwealth funded and controlled. Mary-Louise McLaws, 'Australia Urgently Needs Mass COVID Vaccination Hubs: But We Need More Vaccines First' *The Conversation* (7 April 2021).

The examples of effective assistance (such as Job Keeper and the Job Seeker supplement) were counterbalanced by targeting or refusal to help other groups. Many affected individuals and groups were ignored, including people in aged care, and people with disability who rely on carers either in residential accommodation or in-home care from visiting carers, as well as the carers for these people. Many temporary visa holders, including all international students, were excluded from any government welfare support, and with the closure of many forms of casual work traditionally open to them, were often unable to support themselves, let alone fund a return to their home countries. They were left dependent on food banks and charity, or assistance provided by the universities.[39] The government varied Job Keeper eligibility several times to ensure that public universities could not access it[40] and, together with the closure of the borders, the universities experienced substantial financial impact with the loss of income from international students.[41] This further led to the loss of an estimated 17,000 staff during 2020 from non-renewal of contracts and redundancies of ongoing staff and more losses in 2021,[42] including the reduction of courses and disciplinary areas in many institutions as a result.

The pandemic demonstrated very clearly the problematic effects of laws permitting insecure work that have disempowered workers and allowed employers in the past few decades to keep labour costs down and workers docile. Such working conditions are inimical to effective public health measures, and are generally imposed on the least powerful workers. Workers who have no paid sick leave or social security entitlements have to go to work whether they are sick or not, unless extra support is provided as the states did in 2020–2021. They not only face the risk of being infected and passing it on to their co-workers and clients, but also of bringing the virus home to their families and communities. An adequate response to the pandemic needs to address these structural workplace issues as a matter of public health. Workplace flexibility can be maintained without completely disempowering workers.

4 The Limits of Anti-discrimination Protection

The role of equality and discrimination laws in protecting the vulnerable will differ depending on their formulation and effect in each country. The limitations of Australia's anti-discrimination laws means that they have been marginal to responding

---

[39] Stephen Clibborn and Chris F Wright, 'COVID-19 and the Policy-induced Vulnerabilities of Temporary Migrant Workers in Australia' (2020) 85 Journal of Australian Political Economy 62; Study Australia 'Covid-19 Student Support' https://www.studyaustralia.gov.au/english/latest-travel-and-visa-advice/study-in-australia-student-support/covid-19-international-student-support (accessed 14 January 2022). See eg Victoria, 'Financial and Other Support for COVID-19' https://www.coronavirus.vic.gov.au/financial-and-other-support-coronavirus-covid-19 (accessed 18 January 2022) (further support for international students in Victoria).

[40] Gavin Moodie, 'Why Is the Australian Government Letting Universities Suffer?' *The Conversation* (19 May 2020); Senate Select Committee (n 14) 75–76.

[41] Eliza Littleton and Jim Stanford, 'An Avoidable Catastrophe: Pandemic Job Losses in Higher Education and their Consequences' The Australia Institute (September 2021). Private universities were eligible for the payment.

[42] ibid.

to the problems of inequality created or exacerbated by the pandemic. Although there has been an increase in inquiries and complaints of discrimination based on race and disability during the pandemic, there has been little increase in reported cases decided, indicating that matters are either settled in conciliation or else abandoned if that cannot be achieved.[43] Despite this, the concepts of equality and discrimination, and the language of anti-discrimination law were influential in analysing both social inequalities and public health measures.

Many of those who suffered the greatest disadvantage from the pandemic and the ensuing government measures are covered by anti-discrimination laws which protect, for example, the elderly, disabled people, first nations people, ethnic minorities, and women. Australia has four federal anti-discrimination laws covering the broad categories of race (including colour, descent, and national and ethnic origin), sex (including sexual orientation, gender identity, intersex status, marital or relationship status, pregnancy or potential pregnancy, breastfeeding, and family responsibilities), disability (defined broadly), and age.[44] In addition, each state or territory has laws that cover these attributes, as well as a much wider range of attributes, such as industrial activity, religion, or political belief, opinion, or activity, spent criminal conviction, and physical features.[45] The existing protections would extend to cover many groups seriously affected by the pandemic, such as temporary migrant workers, international students, and people from culturally and linguistically diverse (CALD) communities tend to work in precarious and personal services work including retail, hospitality, aged care, disability, and childcare work.[46] The difficulty is that the laws are difficult to enforce and not drafted to challenge systemic inequalities.

The anti-discrimination laws do not cover socio-economic disadvantage or discrimination based on poverty, class, or socio-economic status. While many groups protected by equality and discrimination laws are socio-economically vulnerable, not everyone who is socio-economically vulnerable may belong to disadvantaged groups or be protected under this body of law. For example, socio-economically vulnerable

---

[43] Data on complaints is only available for the period to June 2020. The Australian Human Rights Commission received an increase of complaints relating to racial and disability discrimination in that period. Australian Human Rights Commission, *Annual Report 2019-20*, 11, 35. The Victorian Equal Opportunity and Human Rights Commission received many more complaints of racial and religious vilification and an increase in racial discrimination complaints as a result of Covid-19. Victorian Equal Opportunity and Human Rights Commission, *VEOHRC Annual Report 2019-20*, 27.

[44] Racial Discrimination Act 1975; Sex Discrimination Act 1984; Disability Discrimination Act 1992; Age Discrimination Act 1992.

[45] For example, Equal Opportunity Act 2010 (Vic); Anti-Discrimination Act 1977 (NSW); Discrimination Act 1991 (ACT); Anti-Discrimination Act 1991 (Qld); Anti-Discrimination Act 1998 (Tas). All federal and state laws are linked from the Attorney-General's web page. See Attorney General's Department, 'Australia's Anti-discrimination Law' https://www.ag.gov.au/rights-and-protections/human-rights-and-anti-discrimination/australias-anti-discrimination-law (accessed 7 June 2022).

[46] In June 2020, 30 per cent of people living in Australia were born overseas, with those born in England continuing to be the largest group. See Australian Bureau of Statistics, 'Migration, Australia' https://www.abs.gov.au/statistics/people/population/migration-australia/2019-20 (accessed 7 June 2022). The 2016 Census showed that, in 2016, nearly half (49 per cent) of Australians had either been born overseas (28.4 per cent were first generation Australian) or had one or both parents born overseas (20.9 per cent were second generation Australian). More than one-fifth (21 per cent) of Australians spoke a language other than English at home: Australian Bureau of Statistics, *2071.0: Census of Population and Housing: Reflecting Australia: Stories from the Census, 2016* (2016).

people are more likely to work in precarious employment, but neither employment status nor socio-economic disadvantage are recognized as grounds of discrimination under Australian law. Similarly, the laws have little to say to the structurally vulnerable position of precarious workers. For example, the problem of work that requires personal attendance and is more likely to involve risks of infection and spreading the virus is not susceptible to analysis in terms of individual discrimination claims, and needs to be tackled at a systemic level.[47] In addition to this focus on individual claims, the laws also fail to recognize the importance of health and health services.

Two examples demonstrate the gaps in the application of equality and discrimination laws in the pandemic context. In 2020, the Victorian government locked down without advance warning several high-rise public housing towers that were home to many immigrant communities, especially from Africa. The immediate lockdown without time to prepare, for example, by getting food and medicines, was justified by the authorities on the basis of public health needs (rising infections in the tower blocks). But this contrasted with lockdowns in more affluent areas where warnings and preparation time were given. In response to a complaint that this was discriminatory based on race, the Victorian Ombudsman conducted an inquiry and expressed concern about it,[48] but the government maintained that public health justified this response. Equality and discrimination laws were seen as not designed to address this type of differential treatment, and the affected communities had limited ability to access legal advice and take any legal action to challenge this view. The law was shown to be wanting in responding to public health demands. The second example involves the lockdown of Sydney from June to November 2021. This was not uniform across the city, but imposed the harshest measures in parts of south-west Sydney, where CALD migrant communities live, leaving the middle and upper class parts of the city under much weaker restraints. This was justified on the basis that many key or essential workers in the locked down area were infected. Not surprisingly, this left a divided city and some resentment at this differential treatment.[49] Once again, the possibility of justification of such treatment on the grounds of public health made a challenge to the differential treatment difficult.[50] The fact that the justification on the grounds of public health requires no adequate balancing or proportionality test made such a challenge impossible.[51]

Furthermore, Australia's equality and discrimination laws do not go beyond allocating responsibility after the event for harm in specific contexts (whether a claim is

---

[47] Senate Select Committee (n 14) ch 5 [5.32]–[5.33].
[48] Victorian Ombudsman, 'Investigation into the Detention and Treatment of Public Housing Residents Arising from a COVID-19 "Hard Lockdown" in July 2020' (2020) https://www.ombudsman.vic.gov.au/our-impact/investigation-reports/investigation-into-the-detention-and-treatment-of-public-housing-residents-arising-from-a-covid-19-hard-lockdown-in-july-2020/ (accessed 7 June 2022).
[49] By contrast, in Melbourne city--wide restrictions were always used.
[50] Anti-discrimination laws generally contain an exemption for actions to protect health, safety, and property. For example, the Equal Opportunity Act 2010 (Vic), s 86(1)(a) allows a person to 'discriminate against another person on the basis of disability or physical features if the discrimination is reasonably necessary (a) to protect the health or safety of any person (including the person discriminated against) or of the public generally'. The government is likely to argue that the decision was based on disability (avoiding potential infection) not on race, which is not exempted.
[51] ibid. No proportionality test is required by the legislation, which refers only to the action being 'reasonably necessary'.

brought by an individual or a group or class). They have limited preventive capacity beyond the ability to support an interim injunction. The scope of the laws is limited by the attributes protected and the areas covered, and most Australian laws have limited effect against broader government policies or systemic issues.[52] The laws are weak in several ways, such as in failing to provide a shifting onus of proof in direct discrimination, providing only limited challenge to systemic discrimination, and permitting 'reasonableness' as a general defence to indirect discrimination.[53] They provide only ex post facto responses after harm has occurred, and the slow litigious enforcement process sidelines them in a time requiring rapid responses. Enforcing the law is difficult because of the need for expert legal advice to succeed with a claim, and the disincentive of having to pay costs if the case is lost.[54] The laws are limited to discrete impacts on individuals, not understood as designed to respond to the type of systemic inequalities that the pandemic created that apply across disadvantaged groups. Many government actions including actions under other pieces of legislation are exempted from anti-discrimination laws.[55] There is no equality duty like the UK public sector equality duty, and the absence of any constitutional equality protection means there is no constitutional basis to challenge government actions as discriminatory.[56]

It is understandable that tensions between equality claims and public health have not yet been addressed, given the unexpected nature of the pandemic. But now we know that the tensions between these two important areas need to be better reconciled and a proper mechanism for doing this developed. We need a duty to ensure that the rights of the vulnerable are protected as far as possible during crises. But even with reforms to strengthen equality and discrimination laws, which are definitely necessary, a duty limited to the groups protected by those laws will not be sufficient; a more comprehensive formulation is needed encompassing socio-economic disadvantage either as a stand-alone ground or in interaction with protected identity categories. Reform should also require proactive measures such as duties to avoid creating or increasing inequality and disadvantage, and instead reducing it, through assessment of the equality impact of government actions. Mechanisms such as equality impact assessments could provide an important means for doing this, and could be adapted to emergency situations by allowing for emergency action to be taken and to be evaluated as soon as possible afterwards, and adjusted if needed. Finally, and most importantly, any mechanism needs to be readily enforceable by people it is designed to protect, whether through the tribunal or court system or by other mechanisms.

---

[52] Anti-discrimination law in Australia is made complex by the presence of a law in each state and territory as well as five relevant laws at the Commonwealth level. Although they are structured similarly, the content of the laws varies between jurisdictions, with different emphases on different elements. See eg Beth Gaze and Belinda Smith, *Equality and Discrimination Law in Australia: An Introduction* (CUP 2017) ch 3.

[53] ibid ch 7, esp 199–200.

[54] ibid ch 7.

[55] See eg Pt II Div 4 of the Sex Discrimination Act 1984 (Cth), which contains a list of exceptions to liability including s 40, which excludes liability for acts done 'in direct compliance with' a list of many other laws. The Equal Opportunity Act 2010 (Vic) (EOA Vic), pt 5 also has a list of exceptions, including s 75 which excludes liability for discrimination if it 'is necessary to comply with, or is authorized by, a provision of' any other legislation. This ranks the EOA at the bottom of the statutory hierarchy.

[56] EOA Vic, s 15 imposes a duty 'take reasonable and proportionate measures to eliminate that discrimination, sexual harassment or victimisation as far as possible' on any person or organization, public or private, who is potentially liable for these actions. However, there is no specific enforcement provision for this duty.

This will involve provision of adequate resources to enable necessary legal advice and representation. Whether equality laws are the best avenue for these changes is considered below.

5 Public Health, Human Rights, and the Emergency Response

Public health advice was given great authority during the pandemic. Australian governments generally listened to public health experts and acted on their advice to preserve the health of the population. There are good reasons for governments to maintain this focus. The increased likelihood of future zoonotic disease outbreaks, whether more harmful variants of Covid-19 or other zoonotic infections, also suggests that reforming some of the dysfunctional and unfair conditions in employment and service provision may be among the most important measures to minimize and address future general population health risk. In this way, public health requirements support arguments for broader reform, including to equality and discrimination laws.

Social inequality is an important social determinant of (ill-)health in public health theory.[57] Similarly, there is good evidence of the health impacts of inequality, discrimination, and disadvantage.[58] These links between inequality and public health have not been fully developed or articulated in Australia in the context of domestic anti-discrimination law. In the Covid-19 pandemic, those most exposed to the risk of infection have been people in precarious and low-paid work. Public health attention to the social and economic determinants of health demonstrates that the path to improve overall population health is to improve the health of those who are most disadvantaged, often due to social and economic conditions. The link of inequalities with health disadvantage provides a broad foundation for arguments to reduce inequality in the interests of health to serve the whole population. The pandemic has made it harder for governments to deny this connection. However, public health law does not require specific consideration of the equality implications of any directions regarded as necessary to respond to a public health emergency.[59]

Health is almost invisible in equality and discrimination laws in Australia. It is only specifically mentioned as an exception, and would be treated as a service provided by governments or private organizations. The focus of the anti-discrimination laws is almost entirely on individual cases, not systemic impacts. Arguably, there should be greater attention to health inequalities in discrimination laws as an avenue for strengthening protection in the context of pandemics and overall social needs.[60]

---

[57] Michael Marmot, 'Social Determinants of Health Inequalities' (2005) 365(9464) The Lancet 1099; Australian Institute of Health and Welfare, 'Australia's Health 2016', Series no 15, Cat no AUS 199 (AIHW 2016) ch 4.1.
[58] Yin Paradies, 'A Systematic Review of Empirical Research on Self-reported Racism and Health' (2006) 35 International Journal of Epidemiology 888.
[59] Public Health and Wellbeing Act 2008 (Vic).
[60] At present, health and welfare services are mentioned in Australian anti-discrimination laws only in the context of exceptions to the laws (eg for the protection of health and safety), and never as specific areas to which the laws apply.

However, approaching these inequalities through equality and discrimination law still fails to capture the full harm of differential provision of health services and protection. The human right to health could potentially play a role in developing legal protection for the vulnerable in jurisdictions with binding human rights protection. Australia has minimal enforceable legal protection for human rights, despite having ratified all the UN Human Rights Conventions.[61] Human rights protection at federal level is limited to scrutiny of bills[62] and the ability to complain about actions of the Commonwealth, which can be conciliated but not enforced by court action.[63] At state and territory level, human rights legislation has been adopted in several states based on the UK Human Rights Act 1998 model,[64] but these laws cannot be used to invalidate legislation that is incompatible with human rights. Only one of these laws refers to any rights related to health, and that is to provide for a right to access health services without discrimination.[65] Their greatest impact has been in requiring public authorities not to act incompatibly with human rights,[66] but there has not been any litigation during the pandemic that has relied on these laws to protect vulnerable individuals or workers, whether based on equality rights or health rights. The domestic potential of the human right to health in the Australian context remains undeveloped. We must pursue other avenues to support legal change to address persistent inequality and disadvantage.

6 Moving Forward: the Direction of Legal Change

The legislative changes most needed are arguably beyond equality and discrimination laws because of their limited focus on protecting members of groups associated with the enumerated grounds of discrimination. We need social institutions to provide protection for everyone against the risks to health and well-being we all face, without unfairly privileging some and disadvantaging others. This requires that social institutions adequately recognize the vulnerability of people of all ages and conditions,

---

[61] Universal Declaration of Human Rights, UNGA Res 217A (III) (adopted 10 December 1948) UN Doc A/810/71; International Covenant on Civil and Political Rights (adopted 16 December 1966, entered into force 23 March 1976) 999 UNTS 171 (ICCPR); International Covenant on Economic, Social and Cultural Rights (adopted 16 December 1966, entered into force 3 January 1976) 993 UNTS 3 (ICESCR); International Conventions on the Elimination of All Forms of Racial Discrimination (adopted 21 December 1965, entered into force 4 January 1969) 660 UNTS 195; Convention on Elimination of all forms of Discrimination Against Women (adopted 18 December 1979, entered into force 3 September 1981) 1249 UNTS 13 (CEDAW); Convention on the Rights of the Child, (adopted 20 November 1989, entered into force 2 September 1990) 1577 UNTS 3 (CRC); Convention on the Rights of Persons with Disabilities (adopted 30 March 2007, entered into force 3 May 2008) 2515 UNTS 3 (CRPD); United Nations Convention against Torture (adopted 4 February 1985, entered into force 26 June 1987) 1465 UNTS 85; Discrimination (Employment and Occupation) Convention (adopted 15 June 1958, entered into force 15 June 1960) 362 UNTS 31.

[62] Human Rights (Parliamentary Scrutiny) Act 2011 (Cth).

[63] Australian Human Rights Commission Act 2006 (Cth), Pt II Div 3 (Functions Relating to Human Rights, and definitions of 'act' and 'practice' in s 3).

[64] Human Rights Act 2004 (ACT), Charter of Human Rights and Responsibilities Act 2006 (Vic) (Charter), Human Rights Act 2019 (Qld).

[65] Human Rights Act 2019 (Qld), s 37(1).

[66] See eg Charter, s 38.

and provide protection against serious disadvantage, whether on protected characteristics, or on unenumerated grounds such as poverty, social origin, or employment status. Martha Fineman's theory of vulnerability as a universal feature of the human condition that acknowledges the presence of risk for everyone at stages throughout their life could provide a foundation on which to build support for such approaches.[67] This might also entail changes to labour laws to reduce insecurity of employment and to ensure that the health of all workers is safeguarded by their employers. It might involve changes to migration laws to ensure that temporary migrant workers are not left in a position of extreme vulnerability because the conditions of their visas allow them to be exploited. It may also guide changes to anti-discrimination laws to expand the grounds and areas of activity covered, and perhaps to allow for more proactive investigations by equality agencies into systemic inequalities outside the individual complaints model.

Effective models to regulate institutions like employment, education, health services, and social welfare need to reconceptualize these core areas of government responsibility and control as providing public supports for everyone against unpredictable risks of harm. Any regulation needs to be enforceable to ensure that change actually occurs, and an effective enforcement process and responsibility needs to be mapped out in advance to ensure that actual change can occur.

In the Australian context, the absence of constitutional equality protection and the subordination of anti-discrimination laws to other laws means that changes like this can only occur through legislation, not judicial interpretation. There are few legislative examples of positive action requirements or positive duties on institutions and organizations in statutes, but two recent examples illustrate movement in this direction. At the federal level, the National Disability Insurance Scheme is designed to provide disability services to everyone with significant permanent disability. Its primary objective is to give effect to Australia's obligations under the Convention on the Rights of Persons with Disabilities (CRPD), as well as obligations undertaken under the other major human rights conventions.[68] Among its specific objectives are to 'support the independence and social and economic participation of people with disability', to 'provide reasonable and necessary supports, including early intervention supports, for participants', and to 'enable people with disability to exercise choice and control in the pursuit of their goals and the planning and delivery of their support'.[69] It seeks to 'give … all Australians peace of mind if they, their child or loved one is born with or acquires a permanent and significant disability, they will get the support they need'.[70] It provides funding to individuals to access services directly or through a service provider organization. However, the services are not provided by a public sector workforce like previous state and territory schemes, but by an outsourced and privatized workforce. The scheme has encountered teething problems and is already subject to

---

[67] Martha Fineman, 'The Vulnerable Subject: Anchoring Equality in the Human Condition' (2008) 20 Yale Journal of Law and Feminism 1.
[68] National Disability Insurance Scheme Act 2013 (Cth), s 3(1)(i) (NDIS Act).
[69] ibid s 3(1)(c)–(f).
[70] NDIS, 'NDIS: What Does It Mean?' https://www.ndis.gov.au/understanding/what-ndis (accessed 7 June 2022).

government cost-cutting, but it does demonstrate that universal arguments based on vulnerability can be successful at a societal level.[71]

At the state level, the most recent model is the Gender Equality Act 2020 (Vic), which requires all public sector organizations in Victoria to take action to advance gender equality in employment, and to consider gender equality in the development of policy and provision of services.[72] Both these strands can be enforced by the Commissioner for Gender Equality in the Public Sector, who has monitoring and enforcement powers.[73] Gender equality is explicitly defined intersectionally,[74] raising a challenge for organizations of collecting rich and detailed intersectional data as a foundation for assessing progress. The tools for effecting gender equality under the statute include workplace gender audits, gender equality plans, gender impact assessments, and regular reporting to the Commissioner, who can take enforcement action where needed.[75] This model relies primarily on the ground of gender (understood intersectionally) as the basis for action. The Gender Equality Act (Vic) requires specific actions and demonstration of actual change,[76] unlike the public sector equality duty in the Equality Act 2010 (UK), which requires public sector bodies to 'have due regard' to equality considerations, which appears to impose a procedural rather than a substantive duty.[77] If the Gender Equality Act (Vic) mechanisms are effective, they could provide a model for further changes to address issues beyond gender inequality.

Arguments based on universal human vulnerability to risks can strengthen and support claims to improved social security payments, labour laws, and other laws that affect disadvantage. As Fineman argues, such laws could gain support by being framed as providing universal insurance against serious risks for everyone, not merely for a section of the population. Ultimately, law must require public agencies to show they have considered all possibilities of potential harm or disadvantage that could result from their public-facing policies or actions. This would include considering traditional grounds of discrimination, including as they relate to socioeconomic status, as well as other bases of insecurity such as precarious immigration or employment status. Similar to work health and safety requirements, agencies should be required to anticipate risks and address them in policy development and implementation to bring about actual elimination of inequalities. It should be the duty of the agency to consider who are its service users, including those who are currently excluded by how the service is offered, and to ensure the interests of all users are considered, not merely the most vocal or those who are able to take advantage of the services most easily.

---

[71] See Paul Ramcharan, 'Understanding the NDIS: A History of Disability Welfare From 'Deserving Poor' to Consumers in Control' *The Conversation* (6 July 2016).
[72] Gender Equality Act 2020 (Vic), ss 7, 9.
[73] ibid pt 5 'Reporting', pt 6 'Monitoring and Compliance'.
[74] ibid ss 9(2)(c), 11(2)(c).
[75] ibid ss 19–21.
[76] ibid s 16.
[77] Equality Act 2010 (UK), s 149.

7 Conclusion

Reviewing the Australian responses to the pandemic shows some effective responses but also others that were not as effective, in a context of continuing tensions between state and federal governments. Labour laws exposed low paid workers to poor conditions including precarious and part-time work, which made it difficult for them to protect themselves or the people who depend on their work. Anti-discrimination laws do not cover all the workers or individuals who experienced disadvantage, and where they applied, were often not effective to protect individuals. Change is needed in both policies and law. Ideally, a duty is needed on those who choose policies to consider and better protect everyone's human rights, including the right to health, especially for the most vulnerable. The goal would be an effective and enforceable system of advance review of government responses that affect rights, which include enforcement powers with resources and accessible mechanisms to ensure compliance. Clearly, such rights need to be balanced with public health priorities and other human rights, but attention to the protection of the most disadvantaged people in society must be a priority. This will require substantial change to our current equality and public health laws, based on the recognition that we are all vulnerable to unforeseen harms, and that social institutions should be designed to protect all individuals or groups for whom the risks eventuate.

11
The Interaction of Laws Enabling Gender Equality with Other Legal Regimes
Limiting Progress in Times of Crisis

*Helena Alviar García**

1 Introduction

There is no denying that the fight for gender equality has increasingly become mainstream in the last thirty years. This is particularly true in Colombia, the place where this chapter concentrates its analysis. From the establishment of an equality clause in the 1991 constitution (along with the many laws, regulations, and rulings that have interpreted it); the election of their first female vice-president in 2018, to the announcement in March 2022 of an Afro-descendant woman as the vice-presidential candidate for the left-wing party, the importance of women's issues in the political agenda has been gaining central stage.

Despite these encouraging advancements, the terms and conditions on which this equality is fulfilled—or should be exercised—is far from a settled matter. There is an abyss between the conservative vice-president's view (elected in 2018) for whom equality means transforming women into micro-entrepreneurs[1] and consequently designing incentives for them to access credit and banking[2] and the 2022 left-wing candidate's perspective that equality means redistribution of resources across gender, class, and race, where care for the environment is central and intersectionality is key.[3]

The understanding of equality that has been translated into laws, judicial decisions, and policies requires a close analysis to understand why (despite legal reforms, judicial orders, and executive branch regulations) distribution of power and resources across gender continues to be highly unequal in Colombia. This close analysis is particularly relevant after the Covid-19 crisis, which exacerbated gender inequality in Colombia, as it did globally.

---

* The author would like to thank Isabella Brandes for her invaluable help in researching for this chapter.
[1] Redacción Web, '"Bono Soberano" Apoyará Emprendimiento en Mujeres: Ramírez' *El Nuevo Siglo* (17 November 2021) https://www.elnuevosiglo.com.co/articulos/11-17-2021-bono-soberano-consolidara-al-pais-como-nacion-de-emprendedoras-ramirez (accessed 20 April 2022).
[2] Portafolio, 'Mujeres Autónomas en Materia Financiera Escapan de la Violencia' (14 March 2022) https://www.portafolio.co/economia/finanzas/entrevista-marta-lucia-ramirez-mujeres-autonomas-en-materia-financiera-escapan-de-la-violencia-562894 (accessed 20 April 2022).
[3] 'I think that women must center our fight around a more equal distribution of property, a feminist and ecological land reform that centers women's role as life's care takers. I am a peasant woman, and my agenda is centered upon their struggles because they are the ones who are in the most precarious conditions'. Volcánicas, La Lucha es Afuera y la Lucha es Adentro, Entrevista a Francia Márquez (4 November 2021).

In fact, studies published since the early stages of the pandemic have extensively analysed the differentiated impact women faced under lockdowns, halted economies, closed borders, quarantines, and curfews. The situation for Colombian women was dire before the pandemic, and the crisis only exasperated it. Prior to the pandemic, in early 2020, 14 per cent of Colombian women were unemployed. When they were employed, they held precarious jobs that lacked social protection and offered the lowest wages. In total, 56.3 per cent of women were working in the informal sector and 42 per cent were making less than the minimum wage per hour. Of these, 13.5 per cent of those who had jobs were domestic servants or family workers without pay. In addition to paid labour, women dedicated more than seven hours a week to reproductive care.[4]

Given this background, once Covid-19 reached the country, women lost their jobs in greater numbers,[5] had few savings to aid them, saw access to sexual and reproductive health curtailed, were overburdened with child and elderly care,[6] and experienced an increase in gender-based violence as they were locked down at home.[7] Over the course of 2020, the number of unemployed women jumped to 20 per cent.[8] As stated above, Colombian women were over-represented in the informal sector (including retail, beauty parlours, restaurants, bars, and domestic service),[9] which was badly hit by long lockdowns.[10] These jobs have been difficult to replace as many businesses were forced to close permanently.[11] Further, given that public schools were closed during most of the year, women were more likely to lose their jobs and delay returning to work because of increased childcare needs and home care duties.[12] In response to the pandemic's outsized impact on women, Colombia introduced specific gendered policies, including wage subsidies for new hires, with greater subsidies for women, and strengthened support for women entrepreneurs.[13] However, even as the population returned to work, the gendered difference in job losses persisted.[14]

---

[4] DANE and ONU Mujeres, 'Boletín Estadístico: Empoderamiento de las Mujeres en Colombia' (March 2020) https://www2.unwomen.org/media/field%20office%20colombia/documentos/publicaciones/2019/09/boletin%20estadistico%20onu%20mujeres%20-%20marzo%202020.pdf?la=es&vs=3252 (accessed 21 December 2021).

[5] CEPAL, 'Preliminary Overview of the Economies of Latin America and the Caribbean' (January 2022) https://www.cepal.org/en/publications/type/preliminary-overview-economies-latin-america-and-caribbean (accessed 12 May 2022).

[6] Adil Marghub and Elizabeth Martínez De Marcano, 'In Bogotá, Impact Mapping Shows Covid-19's Strain on Women Caregivers' *CommDev* (19 November 2021) https://commdev.org/blogs/in-bogota-impact-mapping-shows-covid-19s-strain-on-women-caregivers/ (accessed 2 May 2022).

[7] Yesid José Ortega Pacheco and Milena Martínez Rudas, 'Domestic Violence and COVID-19 in Colombia' (2021) 300 Psychiatry Research 113925.

[8] CEPAL (n 5).

[9] Jorge Alvarez and Carlo Pizzinelli, 'COVID-19 and the Informality-Driven Recovery: The Case of Colombia's Labor Market' IMF Working Papers 2021, no 235 (September 2021) 1.

[10] Adrienne Arsht, 'A Plan for Colombia's Covid-19 Recovery' Atlantic Council (December 2021) 25.

[11] Jairo Guillermo Isaza Castro, 'El Impacto de la COVID-19 en las Mujeres Trabajadoras de Colombia OIT' *ONU Mujeres* (March 2021) 20–24.

[12] Alvarez and Pizzinelli (n 9) 1.

[13] International Labor Organization, 'Building Forward Fairer: Women's Rights to Work and at Work at the Core of the COVID-19 Recovery' (July 2021) https://www.ilo.org/wcmsp5/groups/public/---dgreports/---gender/documents/publication/wcms_814499.pdf (accessed 20 April 2022).

[14] Emilia Cucagna and Javier Romero, 'The Gendered Impacts of COVID-19 on Labor Markets in Latin America and the Caribbean' World Bank (2021) https://openknowledge.worldbank.org/handle/10986/35191 (accessed 20 April 2022).

As I have argued in my previous work, Latin America in general, and Colombia in particular, was ill-equipped to face a crisis like Covid-19.[15] Decades of neoliberal policies regarding economic growth and the role of the state and market in policy-making constricted the regions' ability to respond to a pandemic, including policies privatizing healthcare, dismantling systems for state intervention, and focusing on conditional cash transfers. As a result, when the Covid-19 pandemic occurred, only a limited set of policy tools were at the disposal of policy-makers. Further, austerity measures, apprehension about spurring inflation, and a regional dependence on the economies of the Global North (due to production and export of primary goods) limited opportunities to increase state spending to foster welfare.

In 2018, 25 per cent of Latin America's population was covered by conditional cash transfers. While these programmes could be directly expanded to support social services during the pandemic, governments struggled to identify the 'hidden poor' located outside of the safety net, whose sources of income dried up during the pandemic or who had always worked in the informal economy.[16] As Latin America's economies recover, among women who are employed, the share of those employed as paid employees has dropped by 8 per cent, indicating a further shift away from formal employment.[17] Further, the privatization of social service provision, particularly of healthcare systems, limited access to health care not only for additionally vulnerable citizens, but the population as a whole during a deadly pandemic. In Colombia, 15 per cent of people reported feeling that Covid-19 had reduced their access to healthcare.[18] These examples illustrate how social policy design is directly correlated with the broader context of historical economic development and legal tools available to governments delivering social services.

This chapter argues that along with the economic challenges that women faced before Covid-19, the legal tools available to attack diverse sources of inequality were superficial, lacked sufficient public resources, and demanded very little from the private sector. Therefore, once faced with a crisis of the magnitude of the pandemic, the instruments available remained weak and insufficient. These legal and institutional problems should invite us to move beyond promises of equality law alone and focus instead on (i) the assignment of resources, (ii) the strength of institutions designed to deploy and distribute those resources across gender lines, and (iii) the use of policies targeted towards women in the informal sector in particular.

The goal of this chapter is to look at factors that limit women's equality and that are going to be determinant in times of crisis, such as a pandemic. An important starting point is to unpack the understanding of equality in Colombian laws, along with the responsibilities they allocate between the state and market. This is important because, as

---

[15] Helena Alviar García, *Legal Experiments for Development in Latin America: Modernization, Revolution and Social Justice* (Routledge 2021).

[16] Katharina Lobo and others, 'Social Assistance for Informal Workers: Analysis of the COVID-19 Response in Brazil and Colombia' Agence Française de Développement (January 2022) https://www.afd.fr/en/ressources/social-assistance-informal-workers (accessed 2 May 2022).

[17] Cucagna and Romero (n 14).

[18] USAID, iMMAP, and Data Friendly Space, 'The Effects of COVID-19 on Sexual and Reproductive Health: A Case Study of Six Countries: World' ReliefWeb (December 2021) https://reliefweb.int/report/world/effects-covid-19-sexual-and-reproductive-health-case-study-six-countries (accessed 20 April 2020).

I have previously argued, the content of equality cannot be separated from discussions regarding economic development and the distribution of resources it designs.[19]

To illustrate this, the chapter will analyse women's access to the mining sector. Mining was selected because of its importance for the Colombian economy: it represents 40 per cent of foreign direct investment, 32 per cent of the country's foreign exchange market, 40 per cent of its total exports, and in some cases up to 80 per cent of the resources distributed to regions for their economic development.[20] Despite its significance, it scarcely employs any women.[21] Further, policies geared towards solving the scarce representation of women in the mining sector are too centred upon a superficial understanding of equality that does not take into consideration how economic development policies promote resource concentration and exclude women in diverse ways. In fact, mining has been central to governmental policies for the last thirty years as Colombia has transitioned from mostly exporting coffee to becoming an oil, gas, and coal producer.[22] During the Covid-19 pandemic, the mining industry was relatively unaffected despite lockdown measures, although some of the largest coal companies did reduce their activities to mitigate the spread of the virus.[23] The chapter will therefore analyse the effects that privileging mining as an economic development goal has had upon women's access to work, public resources, and power, far beyond calls for equality. It will show that equality laws have very little to say about the gendered and environmental effects of granting public resources that privilege mining, and in general about how the protection of labour rights is intertwined with access to property.

The chapter proceeds as follows. In section 2, I will briefly describe the legal landscape of equality. Then, in section 3, I will analyse the importance of the mining industry and women's role within it. This section will illustrate examples of the scale of public resources that the mining sector receives, through economic development policies since the early 2000s. Class will play an important role in this analysis given that the mining companies are exploiting not only workers and natural resources but doing so while receiving significant public subsidies. These companies do not provide a significant number of jobs[24] and in any case employ mostly men.[25] This section will

---

[19] García (n 15); Helena Alviar García and Isabel Cristina Jaramillo Sierra, *Feminismo y Crítica Jurídica* (Siglo del Hombre Editores and Ediciones Uniandes 2012).

[20] Forbes Staff, 'No Podemos Satanizar los Sectores' Duque Sobre la Importancia del Petróleo y el Gas, *Forbes* (25 November 2021) https://forbes.co/2021/11/25/actualidad/no-podemos-satanizar-los-sectores-duque-sobre-la-importancia-del-petroleo-y-el-gas/ (accessed 10 January 2022).

[21] Susana Martínez-Restrepo and others, *Empleo, Informalidad, y Bienestar de las Mujeres en el Sector Minero-Energético En Tiempos de Pandemia* (Inter-American Development Bank 2021).

[22] Pilar Poncela, Eva Senra, and Lya Sierra Suárez, 'Long-Term Links between Raw Materials Prices, Real Exchange Rate and Relative de-Industrialization in a Commodity-Dependent Economy: Empirical Evidence of 'Dutch Disease' in Colombia' (2017) 52 Empirical Economics 777.

[23] EU-Latin America Partnership on Raw Materials, 'The Impact of the COVID-19 Pandemic on the Extractive Industries and Related News' Mineral Development Network Platform https://www.mineralplatform.eu/covid (accessed 17 February 2022).

[24] Preliminary analysis of ILO mining employment data by sex in 2019 reveals that 'Mining and quarrying activities accounted for 0.9 per cent of occupations in Colombia in 2019', with 99.1 per cent of the employed population working in non-mining industries. ILO, 'Women and the Mine of the Future' http://www.ilo.org/wcmsp5/groups/public/---ed_dialogue/---sector/documents/publication/wcms_839703.pdf (accessed 20 March 2022).

[25] According to the national statistics agency, DANE, the mining and electric sector in Colombia employs 160,000 individuals of which 20,000 are women. Portafolio, 'Las mujeres mineras se destacan por su labor en el sector' (8 March 2021) https://www.portafolio.co/negocios/empresas/las-mujeres-mineras-se-desta

then analyse equality laws, executive decrees, governmental programmes, and initiatives led by mining companies aimed at improving women's participation in the sector. The objective will be to unpack the meaning of equality in these laws and other initiatives. The final section will summarize diverse factors that influence women's access to power and resources in the mining sector.

2 The Promises of Equality

Since the constitutional reform in 1991, Colombia has passed more than forty laws aimed at guaranteeing gender equality. In fact, at least seven laws reiterate equality between men and women;[26] four laws protect women heads of households[27] (40 per cent of households were led by women in 2021),[28] and at least eight laws attack violence against women.[29] There is a law that mandates that, at a minimum, 30 per cent of high posts in government are occupied by women and in 2020 the Colombian Congress approved a law that requires all lists for elections of public officials to consist of 50 per cent women. In 2021, there were eighty-eight legal initiatives focused on women. Of the eighty-eight, seven will become laws.[30] These include topics such as: affirmative action programmes for female heads of households in prison; the possibility for women to name their children with their last name (traditionally the father's name comes first); granting a maternity licence for elected officials at the municipal level; a reform of entities in charge of family disputes; and a requirement to teach girls about their rights.[31] In the following paragraphs I describe this legal architecture in greater detail.

Article 13 of the Colombian Constitution establishes the equality clause, which states:

> All individuals are born free and equal before the law, will receive equal protection and treatment from the authorities, and will enjoy the same rights, freedoms, and opportunities without any discrimination on account of gender, race, national or family origin, language, religion, political opinion, or philosophy. The State will promote the conditions so that equality may be real and effective and will adopt measures in favor of groups that are discriminated against or marginalized. The State will especially

---

can-por-su-labor-en-el-sector-549869 (accessed 5 July 2021). Similarly, 'ILO estimates the participation rate for female employees in mining category was 13% in 2019'. See Cucagna and Romero (n 14).

[26] See eg Law 731 of 2002; Law 823 of 2003; Law 984 of 2005; Law 1202 of 2008; Law 1434 of 2011; Law 1482 of 2011; Law 1496 of 2011.
[27] Law 82 of 1993; Law 750 of 2002; Law 861 of 2003; Law 1232 of 2008.
[28] Laura Angélica Ospina Herrera, '¿Qué significó esta legislatura para las mujeres?' *El Espectador* (29 June 2021) https://www.elespectador.com/politica/que-significo-esta-legislatura-para-las-mujeres/ (accessed 5 July 2021).
[29] Law 248 of 1995; Law 294 of 1996; Law 575 of 2000; Law 742 of 2002 (which incorporated the Rome Statute); Law 1542 of 2002; Law 882 of 2004; Law 1236 of 2008; Law 1257 of 2008; Law 1542 of 2012; Law 1639 of 2013; Law 1719 of 2014; Law 1761 of 2015.
[30] Ospina Herrera (n 28).
[31] ibid.

protect those individuals who on account of their economic, physical, or mental condition are in obvious vulnerable circumstances and will sanction the abuses or ill-treatment perpetrated against them.[32]

This constitutional clause has been developed in at least seven key laws.[33] Most of these laws reiterate the Colombian state's commitment to equality between men and women. For example, Law 823 of 2003 has as its main goal to establish the institutional setting guaranteeing women's equality. This law lists a set of obligations for the government in terms of adopting gender sensitive policies, producing data regarding gender, and developing policies within the state that attack gender-based discrimination. It also demands that the executive branch advance the necessary policies to increase women's access to health, education, and employment, expanding upon the previous Law 581 of 2000, which established a 30 per cent quota for women to occupy high-ranking government posts.[34]

The reiteration of equality continued with Law 1202 of 2008 which demanded adequate enhancement of mechanisms to monitor women's capacity 'effectively and concretely [to] exercise their rights'.[35] This law also states that the executive branch has the responsibility for presenting the necessary bills to further advance women's rights as well as the design of education campaigns so that women and girls have adequate knowledge of them.

In 2011, discrimination based on gender became a crime. This followed a 2006 law which was aimed at attacking harassment in the workplace (including sexual harassment).[36] The penalties for this type of behaviour include fines, losing one's job, and having to pay for the costs of psychological services. The denial of equal pay for equal work (which has been part of the labour code since the 1950s) was rephrased as a violation of the non-discrimination principle. The law also included a state obligation periodically to visit industries to enforce this, and to demand the establishment of education programmes to advance the knowledge of these prohibitions. Importantly, the law established that any differential treatment in terms of wages or additional forms of payment is presumed unjustified unless the employer proves otherwise.[37]

Further along in the Constitution, Article 43 states:

> Women and men have equal rights and opportunities. Women cannot be subjected to any type of discrimination. During their periods of pregnancy and following delivery, women will benefit from the special assistance and protection of the State and will receive from the latter food subsidies if they should thereafter find themselves

---

[32] Translation of the Colombian Constitution https://www.constituteproject.org/constitution/Colombia_2005.pdf (accessed 20 April 2022).
[33] Ministerio de Justicia de Colombia, 'Sistema Unico de Información Normativa: Protección y Defensa de los Derechos de las Mujeres' https://www.suin-juriscol.gov.co/legislacion/diadelamujer.html (accessed 31 March 2022).
[34] For a critical appraisal of Law 581 see García and Sierra (n 19) 57–83.
[35] Law 1202 of 2008.
[36] Law 1010 of 2006.
[37] Law 1496 of 2011, s 7.

unemployed or abandoned. The State will support female head of households in a special way.[38]

The special attention provided to female heads of households has been developed in at least four laws. In 1993, Law 82 granted privileged access to education and cultural programmes to female heads of households and their children. It also included an article promising access to resources for those who wanted to develop small businesses and privileged access to housing credits if they were part of a women-only cooperative. These benefits were later expanded and further developed by Law 1232 of 2008, which eliminated the cooperative requirement to access housing credits and promised the creation of a publicly funded line of credit to aid female heads of households. This fund was never established but there are some credit lines which privilege female heads of households. In terms of housing, since 2003, if a house or rural plot belongs to a female head of household, banks are prohibited from taking to take over the property (after a default in payments) if this is the only asset the female head of household owns. This well-aimed law has, however, meant that in some cases women do not have access to credit as financial institutions refuse to lend without a collateral. Along similar lines, in 2020 a law was passed which established that female heads of households could stay at home instead of going to prison.

Despite this detailed legal regulation, in institutional terms, women's equality has historically been underfunded with very few resources. Law 188 of 1995 established the National Bureau for Women's Equity and in 1999 an executive decree transformed this national direction into a Presidential advisory office (*Consejería Presidencial para la Equidad de la Mujer*).[39] In 2019, the office was assigned to the Vice-Presidential office. A telling illustration of its institutional weakness is that the current government allocated no resources for policies specifically designed to reach equality.[40] In addition, the programmes announced are not only vague but are very similar to those that have been stated since the beginning of the twentieth century: promoting gender sensitive budgets, creating an inter-institutional commission to study care, designing policies so that more women enter the labour market, and strengthening mechanisms to help women in their care duties.[41]

Courts have also decided a range of cases regarding equality. The Supreme Court has more than fifteen rulings that deal with the term. The main topics include prohibiting the dismissal of pregnant women from work; protecting women in the workplace from discrimination and sexual harassment; enforcing women's equal access to due process; extending non-discrimination principles to private corporations; mandating equal access to political participation; and protecting the rights of unmarried women

---

[38] Translation of the Colombian Constitution https://www.constituteproject.org/constitution/Colombia_2005.pdf (accessed 20 April 2022).
[39] CIDH, 'Chapter 12: The Rights of Women' in 'Third Report on the Situation of Human Rights in Colombia' *CIDH.org* (5 May 1997) http://www.cidh.org/women/chapter-12.htm (accessed 20 April 2022).
[40] Angélica Bernal Olarte, 'Plan Nacional de Desarrollo: insuficiente para las mujeres' *Razonpublica* (6 May 2019) https://razonpublica.com/plan-nacional-de-desarrollo-insuficiente-para-las-mujeres/ (accessed 25 July 2021).
[41] Diana Milena López, 'Las mujeres en el Plan Nacional de Desarrollo' *Razonpublica* (1 April 2019) https://razonpublica.com/las-mujeres-en-el-plan-nacional-de-desarrollo/ (accessed 25 July 2021).

to health and pension benefits.[42] Colombia also has an administrative law high tribunal, 'Consejo de Estado'. This judicial entity has issued more than twelve rulings regarding women's equality on topics that are mostly related to the state's lack of protection against domestic violence; death during childbirth at public hospitals; and access to public sector jobs.[43] Finally, the Colombian Constitutional Court has issued more than forty rulings defining discrimination and protecting women's access to land, education, and work, as well as sexual and reproductive rights, among others.[44]

In sum, if one were to analyse only the number of laws, executive regulation and judicial protection, there seems to be a narrative of progress. Nonetheless, as was described in the introduction to this chapter, the narrative of progress could be contested. Colombian women continue to be plagued by poverty, exclusion, and the dispossession that comes from the intersection of class, race, and gender. Describing progressive constitutional, legal, and administrative provisions says very little about why these problems persist and even gives the impression that they do not.

3 Economic Development in the Twenty-first Century: Privileging Exports of Minerals

Until the late twentieth century, the growth of Colombia's economy was based on the export of coffee. Two interrelated events in the early 1990s led to the decentralization of coffee in the Colombian economy. First, the shift to neoliberal ideas among the ruling elite which were incompatible with the interventionist, protectionist style of coffee production, export, and foreign exchange management. Secondly, Colombian policy had been slowly shifting from promoting agricultural products (coffee, bananas, and flowers) to creating incentives for the export of oil and minerals. During most of the twentieth century, coffee had been the determinant commodity in the country's balance of payments and had been essential in terms of generating employment and in some cases rural property redistribution (as small land plots were granted to address the shortage of labour).[45]

This shift to an export-led growth model based on minerals and hydrocarbons was translated into a range of governmental policies aimed at creating the necessary conditions to promote the sector. Successive governments since the early 2000s have bet heavily on mining. Colombia represents 10 per cent of global coal production[46] and

---

[42] Corte Suprema de Justicia, 'Jurisprudencia Equidad de Género' (2021) https://cortesuprema.gov.co/corte/index.php/jurisprudencia-genero-sala-civil/ (accessed 2 May 2022).

[43] Summaries and references to these rulings can be found in Consejo de Estado, 'Comisión de Género y No Discriminación: Enfoque Diferencial y Equidad de Género en la Jurisprudencia del Consejo de Estado' (2021) https://consejodeestado.gov.co/documentos/biblioteca/libros/2022/Enfoque%20Diferencial%20y%20Equidad%20de%20Genero.pdf (accessed 2 May 2022).

[44] Ambito Jurídico, '13 sentencias hito de la Corte Constitucional sobre el Género' (3 November 2018) https://www.ambitojuridico.com/noticias/general/constitucional-y-derechos-humanos/13-sentencias-hito-de-la-corte-constitucional (accessed 2 May 2022).

[45] For more on the importance of coffee for Colombia see Helena Alviar García, 'Italian Coffee: Retelling the Story' (2021) 14 FIU Law Review 443.

[46] Silvana Habib Daza, 'Colombia no sería la misma sin su carbón' *Revista Semana* (10 August 2017) https://www.semana.com/contenidos-editoriales/carbon-la-base-de-todo-/articulo/la-importancia-del-carbon-en-colombia/535801/ (accessed 7 July 2021).

from the year 2000 until 2015, coal production almost doubled and represented 12 per cent of Colombian exports.[47] During the two terms of Alvaro Uribe's right-wing government, the area granted for mining multiplied, going from 1.13 to 8.53 million hectares.[48] The trend continued during Juan Manuel Santos' presidency and was strengthened by the creation of institutions where private and public actors cooperated in granting mining and environmental titles (*Agencia Nacional de Licencias Ambientales y Agencia Nacional Minera*). As of 2016, coal was Colombia's second most important export product after oil.[49]

Along with an exponential increase in mining licences, the sector has benefited from enormous tax benefits. In Colombia, as in many parts of the world, tax benefits are granted to promote certain sectors of the economy that are important because of their export capacity, import substitution potential, or as employment generators. The two sectors that have been granted greater incentives have been the financial and mining sectors.[50] Along with these benefits, mining companies can also deduct the resources they invest in social programmes, corporate social responsibility, technological advancement, worker training programmes, family subsidies, and the construction or repair of roads (even if these roads are only used by them).[51] According to some academics, the Colombian government grants almost 30 per cent of tax deductions to mining companies.[52]

How does this framework of policies and tax benefits impact employment and most importantly, for this chapter, female employment? In the following section I will explore public and private initiatives to increase women's participation in this crucial sector and their impact.

4 The Elusive Search for Equality in the Mining Sector

All development goals set out by Colombian governments from the year 2002 until 2018 have mostly concentrated public resources on areas that traditionally employ

---

[47] Claudia Strambo and others, 'Privileged Coal: The Politics of Subsidies for Coal Production in Colombia' (2018) Stockholm Environment Institute http://www.jstor.org/stable/resrep17197.7 (accessed 14 July 2021).

[48] Danilo Urrea and Inés Calvo, 'Conflictos socio-ambientales por el agua en la Guajira' (2014) *Revista Semillas* https://www.semillas.org.co/es/conflictos-socio-ambientales-por-el-agua-en-la-guajira (accessed 14 July 2021).

[49] Feline Gerstenberg and Paula Andrea Villegas González, 'La minería de carbón en Colombia y la situación económica de las mujeres rurales: la comunidad El Hatillo (César, Colombia)' (2019) 23(45) Ambiente y Desarrollo.

[50] Álvaro Pardo, 'El "regalito" tributario a las compañías de minas y petróleos: US 3.300 millones anuales' *Razonpublica* (4 June 2018) https://razonpublica.com/el-regalito-tributario-a-las-companias-de-minas-y-petroleos-us-3-300-millones-anuales/ (accessed 15 July 2021).

[51] Álvaro Pardo, 'Subsidios para la gran minería: dónde están, cuánto nos valen' *Razonpublica* (27 June 2011) https://razonpublica.com/subsidios-para-la-gran-mineria-donde-estan-cuanto-nos-valen/ (accessed 18 July 2021).

[52] Álvaro Pardo, 'Los beneficios tributarios a las empresas están desangrando al país' *Razonpublica* (26 October 2020) https://razonpublica.com/los-beneficios-tributarios-las-empresas-estan-desangrando-al-pais/ (accessed 20 July 2021).

men. These include agri-business,[53] mining,[54] infrastructure,[55] and construction.[56] Public spending includes subsidized credit, tax incentives, and technical assistance. Policies aimed at incorporating women have mostly relied upon increasing the number of women without specifically using financial resources to improve existing conditions.

4.1 Weak Demands for Equality

In 2020, the Ministry of Mining created a report which encapsulates gender policies for the mining sector. It had four objectives:

1. Increasing the number of women directly employed, employed in the communities where mining is developed, and employed in value chains linked to these.
2. Transforming cultural patterns.
3. Coordinating these initiatives among different institutions.
4. Preventing violence against women in the industry and its areas of influence.[57]

These broad objectives are then subdivided into specific goals. Yet, the goals appear rather superficial: 'Increase in female participation in all levels … increase in the hiring of women in high-ranking positions … aiming at parity when promotions are considered.'[58] Similarly, in terms of specific actions to be taken by companies, the demands are weak: 'At least 20 per cent of companies advance one gender-based activity per trimester in the community of influence … at least 50 per cent of companies present data about their employees differentiated by gender.'[59]

The goals are equally disheartening in terms of preventing violence against women: 'At least 50% of the workforce has participated in sensibilization workshops … at least 1 course per company per year which states the available process to prosecute and penalize sexual and workplace harassment.'[60]

---

[53] Men occupy 60 per cent of jobs and women occupy 40 per cent. Ministerio de Agricultura y Desarrollo Rural, 'Situación de las mujeres rurales en Colombia 2010-2018' (Colombia) https://nacionesunidas.org.co/Publicaciones-FAO/Situacio%CC%81n-Mujeres-Rurales-2010-2018.pdf (accessed 25 July 2021).

[54] Employing 8.8 per cent of women in the industrial sector and 70 per cent in artisanal mining (which is also called subsistence mining) which is precarious and mostly takes place in mines without a licence. Ministerio de Minas y Energía, 'Lineamientos de género para el sector minero energético' (March 2020) 5 https://www.minenergia.gov.co/documents/10192/24180065/Lineamientos-de-pol%C3%ADtica-p%C3%BAblica-con-enfoque-de-g%C3%A9nero-del-sector-minero-energ%C3%A9tico.pdf (accessed 22 July 2021).

[55] Employing 40 per cent of women. Portafolio, 'Red busca ganar espacio femenino en la construcción' (7 March 2021) https://www.portafolio.co/economia/finanzas/bolsas-de-valores-colombia-lima-y-santiago-se-unen-en-trabajo-por-la-equidad-de-genero-549871 (accessed 20 July 2021).

[56] Employing 7.2 per cent of women. Revista Semana, 'Mujeres representan solo el 7,2% del total de ocupados en el sector de la construcción de la vivienda en Colombia' (26 April 2021) https://www.semana.com/economia/empresas/articulo/las-mujeres-representan-solo-el-72-del-total-de-ocupados-en-el-sector-de-construccion-de-vivienda-en-colombia/202105/ (accessed 18 July 2021).

[57] Ministerio de Minas y Energía (n 54) 15.
[58] ibid 25.
[59] ibid.
[60] ibid.

The report states the burden of reproductive work as one of the crucial limitations in equal access to jobs provided:

> Women find it increasingly difficult to occupy high ranking jobs where they have to make decisions because they don't have equal access to technical or college education and they can't participate in meetings because of their role as care takers ... women dedicate 247% more hours per week than men (25 versus 7 hours) [towards care work]. This difference applies not only for women who work in pits or in the provision of electricity or gas, it applies for all the jobs that were part of the survey. In addition, women who work in mining, electricity, or gas provision, dedicate more hours per week in average when compared to their male counterparts who have the same job. Thus, the difference per week is 13 hours. In other words, they work almost a day more in similar labor conditions.[61]

Despite these numbers, the specific objective remains vague: 'at least one initiative geared towards an increase in an egalitarian use of time (for example flexible schedules and jobs)'.[62]

The report also describes the low numbers of women in science and technology. The data is striking: the percentage of women who graduated from STEM majors between 2014 and 2015 was 36 per cent.[63] In university degrees such as physics, electrical, and electronic engineering women represent only 25 per cent of graduates.[64] The goal to improve these numbers seems so anodyne it is shocking: 'improve agreements with universities so that they send more women for internships' and including the goal of at least '15 per cent of mining companies being certified as being sensible to gender'.[65]

Not even one of these actions is asking for a commitment of resources to these goals from either the companies or governments, such as allocating public funds in the form of subsidized credit or generating tax incentives. The lack of specific commitment to resources is even more surprising if we consider the fact that companies can deduct costs spent towards meeting these goals from their income tax.

4.2 Beyond Equality: The Gendered Impact of Mining

Large-scale mining transforms the lives of women in many ways. Because it is highly profitable, rural land that was previously dedicated to family-based subsistence is sold to big companies to extract minerals (with coal among them). This legal transfer of property is facilitated by the Colombian state in many circumstances.[66] In addition,

---

[61] ibid 5.
[62] ibid 5.
[63] ibid.
[64] ibid 6.
[65] ibid 21.
[66] OXFAM, 'Divide and Purchase: How land ownership is being concentrated in Colombia' *OxFam Research Reports* https://www-cdn.oxfam.org/s3fs-public/file_attachments/rr-divide-and-purchase-land-concentration-colombia-211013-en_0.pdf (accessed 20 April 2022).

violent dispossession of land occurs to advance mining projects. Women are much more vulnerable to these transfers as their land titles are often informal.[67]

Along with the legal and illegal transfer of land, mining companies privatize the use of rivers or roads, with the extraction often leading to pollution of water sources.[68] Mining has transformed the use of land, propagating environmental damage. In addition, the arrival of mining companies in certain areas has increased respiratory illnesses and compromised women's reproductive health. For instance, in municipalities surrounding the mine in the state of La Guajira—where the mining company El Cerrejón has been exploiting coal for the past three decades—respiratory infections are the second leading cause of death. Furthermore, maternal mortality has increased from seventy-nine of every 100,000 births in 2004 to 181 in 2011. In all, 93 per cent of these deaths were Wayuu indigenous women.[69]

Moreover, while men have been employed in mining jobs, women have been further relegated to care duties where they earn less and depend more on men. Given the lack of formal job opportunities in mining areas, women must work for any job available. Most of these are either as domestic servants, cleaning the offices of mining companies, or sex work.[70]

4.3 Implications

Once again, it is important to note that there are only two laws and one administrative regulation which assign public resources to improve women's participation in secure employment in specific terms: Law 731 of 2002 which includes the funding of preferential credit as well as privileged access to publicly funded collateral instruments and a publicly sourced credit fund for women,[71] Law 1257 of 2008 which is designed to prevent and counteract violence against women, and the national planning department document (CONPES of 2013). Secondly, even though many of the laws demand that the government develop the institutional framework and implement adequate regulation to achieve equality, the only executive decree aimed at regulating this topic was passed in 2013, which illustrates the stagnation that has characterized this effort at the institutional level for the past decade.[72] The lack of regulation along with the scarcity or weakness of the institutions in place to monitor advances in gender equality have

---

[67] Rosa Emilia Bermúdez Rico (coord), Tatiana Rodríguez Maldonado and Tatiana Roa Avendaño, 'Mujer y minería. Ámbitos de análisis e impactos de la minería en la vida de las mujeres. Enfoque de derechos y perspectiva de género' (Cordaid and CENSAT 2011) 13 https://censat.org/es/publicaciones/mujer-y-mineria-ambitos-de-analisis-e-impactos-de-la-mineria-en-la-vida-de-las-mujeres-enfoque-de-derechos-y-perspectiva-de-genero (accessed 20 July 2021).
[68] US Office on Colombia, 'Large-scale mining in Colombia' (May 2013) https://reliefweb.int/sites/reliefweb.int/files/resources/large-scale-mining-full-report.pdf (accessed 20 April 2022).
[69] Rico (n 67).
[70] Jineth Bedoya Lima, 'Campamentos de explotación de niñas en zonas mineras' *El Tiempo* (25 May 2013) https://www.eltiempo.com/archivo/documento/CMS-12824463 (accessed 15 July 2021).
[71] Law 731 of 2002, ss 8, 9, and 10.
[72] CONPES SOCIAL, 'Equidad de género para las mujeres' *Consejo Nacional de Política Económica y Social República de Colombia Departamento Nacional de Planeación* (12 March 2013) https://colaboracion.dnp.gov.co/cdt/conpes/social/161.pdf (accessed 1 May 2022).

been translated into grand promises established in laws, but superficial results on the ground.

In sum, gender equality in Colombia has been characterized by a lack of public and private resources as well as a weak public institutional structure, as the office for women's equality has never been granted ministerial status and at best has been a mid-level post in the Presidential or Vice-Presidential office. In 2019, the government announced that for the first time in Colombian history a gender chapter had been included in the national development plan. When closely analysed, it states very broad goals such as the invitation of local and national institutions to include 'gender sensitive' budgets; the promise to advance in the integration of women in formal labour market and the aim of strengthening of social policies (particularly those related to care work) but, it does not assign a single Colombian peso to women's issues, much less in relation to increasing women's access to employment.[73]

When compared to the number of public resources, relevance, and governmental energy placed in sectors such as mining or agrobusiness, the topic of gender equality has been characterized by broad goals and lofty promises but little institutional or financial support. Colombian feminists should follow public finances in a detailed fashion and demand that tax incentives and subsidies be specifically granted to private enterprises that advance an equality agenda. In addition, activists should demand the strengthening of the institutions set in place to promote gender equality and that more resources be spent to attack the intersection of gender and race inequality. These are the structural causes behind women's disenfranchisement that should be prioritized over the current concentration on legal reform towards individual solutions.

5 Conclusion

This chapter illustrates how an equality clause, and laws that reiterate it or redefine it, are only the beginning of the struggle and indeed require commitment of resources to be effective. This reality has only been amplified by the Covid-19 crisis, wherein resource scarcity became more acute alongside the gender imbalances and women's employment vulnerability.

Therefore, a progressive feminist agenda in Colombia should aim at making sure that there are both public and private resources dedicated to advance the agenda of equality. On the one hand, public resources include not only well-staffed government institutions that monitor advances and set-backs, but also more incentives for economic areas that employ mostly women (in the form of tax breaks or subsidies). On the other hand, more should be asked from the private sector in terms of access to work, improvement of wages, and aid in allowing women adequately to balance productive and reproductive tasks.

---

[73] National Planning Department, 'National Development Plan 2018-2022' https://www.dnp.gov.co/DNPN/Paginas/Plan-Nacional-de-Desarrollo.aspx (accessed 20 April 2022).

12
Equal Access to Vaccines
Exposing the Limits of International Human Rights Law?

Catherine O'Regan

1 Introduction

Half a billion people have been diagnosed with Covid-19 and millions have died of the disease since January 2020.[1] Given the failure, save in a handful of countries, to eliminate the virus, SARS-CoV-2, that causes Covid-19, hopes turned to a safe and effective global vaccination programme to halt its spread. The ability of the virus to produce variants that evade natural immunity arising from infection also reduces the likelihood of the spread of the virus being halted by natural immunity and underscores the need for a global vaccination programme. Nearly 200 vaccines are in development with at least 54 being tested on human subjects and a handful having been widely registered for use. Evidence establishes that the registered vaccines significantly lower the risk of severe illness and death. The successful and rapid development of several vaccines is a remarkable achievement given that the Global Agency for Access to Vaccines (GAVI) estimates that only 7 per cent of vaccines complete preclinical development and only 15–20 per cent of these receive market approval.[2]

Billions of vaccination doses have been administered but unequal access to vaccines is pronounced as by far the highest levels of vaccination have been achieved in the developed world.[3] Notably Africa has seen very low levels of vaccine administration. Many of the vaccines that have been registered are manufactured and distributed by pharmaceutical companies, such as Pfizer, BioNTech, Astra Zeneca, Moderna, and Janssen, although most if not all have been assisted in the development of their vaccines by money from public sources. In the USA, for example, US$13 billion has been paid to Covid-19 vaccine developers through the Operation Warp Speed programme.[4] Of this sum, the NIH and Moderna received just under a billion dollars and Janssen, just under half a billion dollars.[5] Public funding through Operation Warp Speed has supported not only expensive phase III (large scale, efficacy) trials of the vaccines, but

---

[1] See the Johns Hopkins Coronavirus Resource Center https://coronavirus.jhu.edu (accessed 8 April 2022).
[2] Ana Santos Rutschman, 'The COVID-19 Vaccine Race: Intellectual Property, Collaboration(s), Nationalism and Misinformation' (2021) 64 Washington University Journal of Law and Policy 167, 175.
[3] See the Johns Hopkins Coronavirus Resource Center https://coronavirus.jhu.edu (accessed 8 April 2022).
[4] David E Bloom and others, 'How New Models of Vaccine Development for COVID-19 have Helped Address an Epic Public Health Crisis' (2021) 40 Health Affairs 410, 411.
[5] ibid.

also the building of manufacturing facilities.⁶ Once a vaccine has proved efficacious and safe, it needs to be manufactured at scale to enable distribution globally. Despite the substantial public funds invested in supporting manufacturing, assessing the prospects and timelines of manufacturing sufficient vaccines to administer to everyone in the world remains challenging, in part because information about manufacturing is 'scarce and fragmented'.⁷

Covid-19 is the first major global pandemic since the acceleration of globalization in the 1980s. Indeed, it is probably the interconnectedness of the world that has enabled the virus to spread so widely across the world so quickly. With everyone on the planet at risk of severe illness from Covid-19, there are strong moral reasons that everyone should have equal access to vaccines. In addition, there are reasons of enlightened self-interest for that to happen. We know that as the virus spreads, there is a risk that it will produce variants that may be resistant to vaccines. If a high proportion of the world's population were to be vaccinated, the rate of spread of the virus would slow down, minimizing the risk of vaccine-resistant variants. Thus, both moral principle and enlightened self-interest support the achievement of equal access to vaccines.

Unlike many of the chapters in this collection, this chapter considers inequality from a global perspective. Inequality between people across the world has been less of a focus for equality law than equality within countries,⁸ which may partly be a result of the strength of domestic equality laws, as opposed to the principles of equality law in international human rights law. This chapter considers the extent to which international human rights law contributes to ensuring equal access to vaccines. It assesses the International Covenant on Economic, Social and Cultural Rights (ICESCR), in particular Article 12, which protects the right to the enjoyment of the highest attainable standard of physical and mental health, and Article 15, which protects the right of everyone to enjoy the benefits of scientific progress and its applications. As with all rights in the Covenant, state parties guarantee under Article 2(2) that they will meet their obligations under Articles 12 and 15 without discrimination of any kind.

The chapter then turns to consider who the rights holders and correlative duty bearers are in relation to these rights, as well as to outline the key mechanisms for enforcement of obligations under the ICESCR. In so doing it considers the implications of both Article 2 which provides that states parties will 'through international assistance and co-operation' seek to achieve the progressive realization of rights in the charter and the United Nations Guiding Principles on Business and Human Rights (the UNGPs) adopted by the United Nations in 2011. It then assesses the interrelationship between international human rights law and international trade law, in particular the World Trade Organization (WTO)'s Agreement on Trade-related Aspects of Intellectual Property Rights (TRIPs), and the system of compulsory licensing, as

---

⁶ Mocef Slaoui and Matthew Hepburn, 'Developing Safe and Effective COVID Vaccines: Operation Warp Speed's Strategy and Approach' (2020) 383 New England Journal of Medicine 1701.

⁷ See Duke Global Health Innovation Center, 'Launch and Scale Speedometer' https://launchandscalefaster.org/covid-19/vaccinemanufacturing (accessed 8 April 2022).

⁸ For an important early argument that global inequality matters see Marko Milanovic, *Worlds Apart: Measuring International and Global Inequality* (Princeton UP 2005).

amended by the Doha Agreement,[9] as well as the provisions of the General Agreement on Tariffs and Trade (GATT) that permit export restrictions on essential products in certain circumstances.

This chapter argues that, although there are important principles of international human rights that support the global project of equal access to vaccinations, various factors undermine the strength and reach of international human rights. In addition, the strong regulatory framework of TRIPs under the WTO further attenuates the ability of human rights principles to provide a secure basis to promote equal access to vaccines as do international trade law rules that permit export restrictions on pharmaceutical products 'to prevent or relieve critical shortages of foodstuffs or other products essential' to the exporting country.[10]

Nevertheless, principles of international human rights remain of importance in global health governance, as evidenced in the work of international organizations such as the World Health Organization (WHO), and public private partnerships such as GAVI and the Coalition for Epidemic Preparedness Innovations (CEPI), and perhaps most visibly through the COVAX initiative, which will be described in the last section of the chapter.[11]

2 International Human Rights

2.1 Legal and Institutional Framework of the ICESCR

There are two key rights entrenched in the ICESCR that relate to the question of equitable access to vaccines. First, Article 12(1) of the ICESCR provides that the states parties 'recognise the right of everyone to the enjoyment of the highest attainable standard of physical and mental health' and Article 12(2)(c) provides that states parties shall take the necessary steps to prevent, treat, and control epidemic diseases.[12] Determining the content and reach of the right to health is not a straightforward task.[13] The task of refining the content of the right was undertaken by the United Nations Committee on Economic, Social and Cultural Rights (CESCR), the treaty body tasked with monitoring the implementation of the treaty in its General Comment 14 on the

---

[9] See, in particular, Agreement on Trade-related Aspects of Intellectual Property Rights (adopted 15 April 1994, entered into force 1 January 1995) 1869 UNTS 299 (TRIPs) art 32bis (the amendment introduced to give effect to the Doha Declaration).

[10] See General Agreement on Tariffs and Trade (adopted 30 October 1947, entered into force 1 January 1948) 55 UNTS 194 (GATT) art XI:2(a).

[11] GAVI, 'Covax' https://www.gavi.org/covax-facility (accessed 8 April 2022).

[12] Other provisions of international human rights law also provide for the right to health see eg International Convention on the Elimination of All Forms of Racial Discrimination (adopted 21 December 1965, entered into force 4 January 1969) 660 UNTS 195 (ICERD) art 5(e)(iv); Convention on the Elimination of All Forms of Discrimination against Women (adopted 18 December 1979, entered into force 3 September 1981) 1249 UNTS 13 (CEDAW) art 11(1)(f) and art 12; Convention on the Rights of the Child (adopted 20 November 1989, entered into force 2 September 1990) 1577 UNTS 3 (CRC) art 24.

[13] See the discussion in A Katarina Weilert, 'The Right to Health in International Law: Normative Foundations and Doctrinal Flaws' in Leonie Vierck, Pedro A Villareal, and A Katarina Weilert, *The Governance of Disease Outbreaks: International Health Law: Lessons from the Ebola Crisis and Beyond* (Nomos 2017).

right to health, issued in 2000. The General Comment interpreted the Article 12 right broadly to include not only a right to 'timely and appropriate health care' but also a right to the underlying determinants of health such as safe and potable water, sanitation, food and housing, healthy occupation and environmental conditions, and access to health-related education and information.[14] The General Comment developed what has come to be known as the '3AQ model' which are elements of the right to health, that is, that healthcare facilities and other goods and services to enable health should be available, accessible, acceptable (respectful of medical ethics and culture), and of good quality.[15]

The General Comment makes plain that states are under a duty to respect, protect, and fulfil human rights.[16] The duty to respect requires states to refrain from inhibiting or impeding access to health care, and to abstain from discriminatory practices in relation to access to health care. The duty to protect requires states to take measures to ensure that third parties do not impede access to health care or provide it on a discriminatory basis, and the duty to fulfil requires states to have a national health plan for realizing the right. In relation to states' specific duties to prevent, treat, and control epidemics, the General Comment stated that it includes states' efforts to 'make available relevant technologies, using and improving epidemiological surveillance and data collection on a disaggregated basis, the implement or enhancement of immunization programmes and other strategies of infectious disease control'.[17]

Secondly, Article 15(1)(b) of ICESCR provides that everyone 'has the right to enjoy the benefits of scientific progress'. Article 15(4) also provides that states parties should take steps through legislation and policies, 'to promote an enabling global environment for the advancement of science and the enjoyment of the benefits of its applications'. The most recent General Comment issued by the UN Committee on Economic, Social and Cultural Rights, General Comment 25, considered this right. It noted that 'science is one of the areas of the Covenant to which States parties give least attention in their reports and dialogues with the Committee',[18] echoing William Schabas who called the right to science a 'sleeping beauty'.[19] The General Comment defined science broadly to include both the methodology of science and its results[20] and it defined

---

[14] See UN Committee on Economic, Social and Cultural Rights, General Comment No 14: The Right to the Highest Attainable Standard of Health (art 12 of the Covenant) (11 August 2000) E/C 12/2000/4 [11].
[15] ibid [12].
[16] See General Comment No 14 (n 14) [34]–[37]. This three-fold formulation accords with the model developed in Henry Shue, *Basic Rights; Subsistence, Affluence and US Foreign Policy* (2nd edn, Princeton UP 1996). See also Sandra Fredman, *Human Rights Transformed: Positive Rights and Positive Duties* (OUP 2008) ch 3.
[17] See General Comment No 14 (n 14) [16].
[18] See UN Committee on Economic, Social and Cultural Rights, General Comment No 25 (2020) on science and economic, social and cultural rights (arts 15(1)(b), (2), (3), and (4) of the International Covenant on Economic, Social and Cultural Rights) E/C 12/GC/25 (30 April 2020) [2].
[19] William A Schabas, 'Looking Back: How the Founders Considered Science and Progress in their Relation to Human Rights' (2015) 4 European Journal of Human Rights 504, 504. See also Yvonne Donders, 'The Right to Enjoy the Benefits of Scientific Progress: In Search of State Obligations in Relation to Health' (2011) 14 Medicine Health Care and Philosophy 371; Sebastian Porsdam Mann, Helle Porsdam, and Yvonne Donders, '"Sleeping Beauty": The Right to Science as a Global Ethical Discourse' (2020) 4 Human Rights Quarterly 332; Tara Smith, 'Understanding the Nature and Scope of the Right to Science Through the *Travaux Préparatoires* on the Universal Declaration of Human Rights and the International Covenant on Economic, Social and Cultural Rights' (2020) 24 International Journal of Human Rights 1156.
[20] See General Comment No 25 (n 18) [5].

benefits to include the material results of scientific research including vaccinations.[21] As did General Comment 14, the General Comment adopted the 3AQ model to define the elements of the right[22] and recognized that states bear obligations to respect, protect, and fulfil the right. It also provided that a core obligation upon states is the obligation 'to ensure access to those applications of scientific progress that are critical to the enjoyment of the right to health'.[23]

The General Comment also addresses the clear tension that arises from the fact that much scientific research is carried out by non-state actors, and often for profit.[24] This tension has become more acute since the adoption of TRIPs in 1994 and the World Intellectual Property Organization's Copyright Treaty and Performance and Phonograms Treaty in 1996.[25] The General Comment accepts that the protection of intellectual property 'enhances the development of science and technology through economic incentives for innovation' but also recognizes that it may 'negatively affect the advancement of science and access to its benefits'[26] in three ways: by skewing research in favour of what are seen to be profitable research projects, rather than those that might most benefit humankind, by limiting the sharing of scientific information for example through data exclusivity arrangements for patent holders, and by creating obstacles to affordable access to the products of scientific research by providing patentholders with exclusive rights to exploit the products, sometimes for long periods of time. In response to this tension, the General Comment urged that a balance be reached between the protection of intellectual property and the sharing of scientific knowledge.[27] In addition, the General Comment asserted that the right to science could become 'a significant mediator' between the right to health and intellectual property rights. It noted that the WTO Doha Declaration on the TRIPs Agreement and Public Health of 2001 provided that the intellectual property regimes should be 'interpreted and implemented in a manner supportive of the duty of states "to protect public health and, in particular, to promote access to medicines for all"'.[28] Accordingly, the General Comment stated that 'states parties should use, when necessary, all the flexibilities of the TRIPS Agreement, such as compulsory licences, to ensure access to essential medicines, especially for the most disadvantaged groups'. This is a matter to which this chapter will return.

Read together, Articles 12 and 15 of the ICESCR appear to create a strong normative framework which imposes obligations upon states parties to take steps to respect, protect, and fulfil the right to health and to enjoy the benefits of scientific progress. They

---

[21] ibid [8]. It is noteworthy that the General Comment was issued in the first months of the pandemic and so its emphasis on vaccinations, and access to them, is understandably firm.
[22] ibid [15]–[20].
[23] ibid [52].
[24] ibid [58]–[62].
[25] See UNHRC, 'Report of the Special Rapporteur in the Field of Cultural Rights: Copyright and the right to science and culture' (2014) A/HRC/28/57 [17]–[19]. For an account of the discussions during the drafting of the Universal Declaration of Human Rights concerning the tensions between the protection of the moral interests of authors (provided for in art 27(2) of the Universal Declaration of Human Rights and art 15(3) of ICESCR), and copyright law see Johannes Morsink, *The Universal Declaration of Human Rights: Origins, Drafting, and Intent* (University of Pennsylvania Press 2010) 219–20.
[26] See General Comment No 25 (n 18) [60]–[61].
[27] ibid [62].
[28] ibid [69].

make a strong case that states have a duty to ensure equal access to vaccines. However, in assessing the effect of the ICESCR, it is important to understand the broader institutional and structural framework of the Covenant. In this regard, there are two key questions that need to be considered: who are the rights holders and correlative duty bearers under the Covenant? And what are the international mechanisms to monitor and ensure implementation of the obligations under the Covenant?

2.2 Rights Holders and Correlative Duty Bearers

International human rights are probably best understood as having moral, institutional, and legal dimensions.[29] Their legal dimension requires us to identify rights holders and duty bearers, as well as to determine what those rights and duties entail, and how they will be enforced. As Onora O'Neill has argued: 'An understanding of the normative arguments that link rights to obligations underlies daily and professional discussion both of supposedly *universal* human rights, and of the *special* rights created by specific voluntary actions and transactions ... There cannot be a claim that rights are rights against nobody, or nobody in particular.'[30] The legal dimension of human rights should thus be understood as conferring upon a rights holder a claim against a duty bearer to respect the content of the duty that is the correlative of the right.[31]

As a matter of international law, the primary duty bearers under the ICESCR are states parties. That means that the pharmaceutical companies that manufacture and distribute vaccines do not bear direct obligations under human rights law, which inevitably diminishes the reach of international human rights law in this field. Moreover, although the ICESCR has been ratified by 171 states, the United States of America (USA) has signed but not ratified it, which means that it is not a state party to the Covenant and bears no direct obligations under it.[32] Given that the USA is a primary developer and manufacturer of health care products, including vaccines,[33] its failure to ratify the treaty also detrimentally affects the reach and effectiveness of the ICESCR.

Public international law is largely state-centric, and that orientation determines not only who the primary duty bearers in international human rights law are, but by and large the correlative rights holders as well. For the most part, the correlative rights holders for state duty bearers are those who fall within the territory or jurisdiction of the state duty bearer. Leaving aside the thorny question of the extraterritorial effect of human rights provisions, there are at least two exceptions in international human rights law to the principle that it is states who bear obligations in relation to those who fall within their jurisdiction.

---

[29] See Adam Etinson, 'Introduction' in Adam Etinson (ed), *Human Rights: Moral or Political?* (OUP 2018).
[30] See Onora O'Neill, 'The Dark Side of Human Rights' (2005) 81 International Affairs 427, 430.
[31] See Samantha Besson, 'The Bearers of Human Rights' Duties and Responsibilities for Human Rights: A Quiet (R)evolution?' (2015) 32 Social Philosophy and Policy 244, 248.
[32] The website of the Office of the High Commissioner for Human Rights contains a full list of ratifications and signatories to the international human rights treaties. See ohchr.org (accessed 29 April 2022).
[33] Several of the vaccines currently widely registered are manufactured and produced by American companies (Pfizer, Moderna, Johnson & Johnson).

The first is to be found in Article 2 of the ICESCR in terms of which states undertake 'to take steps individually and through international assistance and co-operation, especially economic and technical, to the maximum of its available resources, with a view to achieving progressively the full realisation of the rights' in the ICESCR, including the right to health. The undertaking to provide international assistance in Article 2 of the ICESCR repeats the principle of international cooperation in Articles 55 and 56 of the United Nations Charter.[34] General Comment 14 noted how important this obligation is in relation to the right to health.[35] It provided that states should 'facilitate access to essential health facilities, goods and services in other countries wherever possible and provide the necessary aid when required'.[36] Moreover, the General Comment recognized that providing immunization against infection is comparable to a core obligation,[37] and emphasized the duty on states to provide international assistance and co-operation, especially economic and technical, to enable developing countries to fulfil their core obligations.[38] This duty of international assistance is therefore an important qualification to the principle that states only owe duties to those who fall within their jurisdiction. However, the identity of the rights holders under this obligation is not that clear. Is it other states? Or is it citizens of the globe generally? Some international law initiatives have sought to give greater clarity in this regard.[39]

The second aspect of international human rights law that forms a partial exception to its state-centric character are the United Nations Guiding Principles on Business and Human Rights (the UNGPs), which were adopted by the Human Rights Council in 2011.[40] The UNGPs affirm states' existing obligations to respect, protect, and fulfil human rights, but they also affirm that business enterprises 'as specialised organs of society performing specialised functions, are required to comply with all applicable law and respect human rights'. Finally, the UNGPs assert the need for appropriate and effective remedies when business enterprises violate human rights.[41] The UNGPs are a form of 'soft law', defined by Dinah Shelton as 'normative provisions contained in non-binding texts'.[42] Unlike the provisions of the ICESCR therefore they do not contain

---

[34] See UN Committee on Economic, Social and Cultural Rights, General Comment No 3: The Nature of States Parties' Obligations (art 2(1) of the Covenant) E/1991/23 (14 December 1990) [14]. For a fuller discussion see Magdalena Sepulveda, 'Obligations of International Assistance and Cooperation in an Optional Protocol to the International Covenant on Economic, Social and Cultural Rights' (2006) 24 Netherlands Quarterly of Human Rights 271, 275.

[35] See General Comment No 14 (n 14) [38].

[36] ibid [39].

[37] ibid [44], read with [43].

[38] ibid [45]. See also UN General Assembly, 'Interim report of the Special Rapporteur on the right of everyone to the enjoyment of the highest attainable standard of physical and mental health' (2012) A/67/302 [14].

[39] See, for eg, the Maastricht Principles on Extraterritorial Obligations of States in the area of Economic, Social and Cultural Rights (2011). The Maastricht Principles were adopted by a group of international and human rights law experts at a gathering convened by Maastricht University and the International Commission of Jurists in September 2011. See Olivier De Schutter and others, 'Commentary to the Maastricht Principles on Extraterritorial Obligations of States in the Area of Economic, Social and Cultural Rights' (2012) 34 Human Rights Quarterly 1084.

[40] UN Human Rights Committee, Guiding Principles on Business and Human Rights: Implementing the United Nations "Protect, Respect and Remedy"' Framework (2011) A/HRC/17/31 Annex.

[41] ibid.

[42] Dinah Shelton, 'Normative Hierarchy in International Law' (2006) 100 American Journal of International Law 291, 292.

legally binding provisions. There are intense debates even as to whether the term 'soft law' is helpful, but it is clear that soft law provisions often have some normative effect. As Dinah Shelton has also pointed out:

> [n]ot all arrangements in business, neighbourhoods or families are formalized, but are often governed by informal social norms and voluntary non-contractual understandings. Nonbinding norms and informal social norms can be effective and offer a flexible and efficient way to order responses to common problems. They are not law and do not need to be in order to influence conduct in the desired manner.[43]

The UNGPs thus establish a non-binding duty to respect human rights borne by corporate entities. The scope of this duty is different from the duties to respect, protect, and fulfil rights that states bear under international human rights law.[44] Unlike those duties, the duty to respect human rights under the UNGPs requires 'an ongoing process of human rights due diligence, whereby companies become aware of, prevent and mitigate adverse human rights impacts'.[45] The duty to respect thus appears not to be correlative to the rights conferred upon rights bearers by international human rights law. The UNGPs make plain that companies must know that they bear a duty to respect human rights and show they do so. In addition, the duty to respect human rights is accompanied by a duty to comply with applicable law, which means that corporate entities have a duty to obey the law enacted by states. In this way, the UNGPs are built on an important acknowledgement of states' duty under international human rights law to protect human rights, which entails taking steps, including enacting legislation, to prevent third parties, including corporations, from violating human rights.[46] General Comment 24 sets out in some detail the implications of the positive obligations states parties' bear in the light of their duty to protect human rights under the ICESCR.[47] It also notes in relation to the duty of states parties to fulfil rights, that when designing an intellectual property framework, states parties 'should ensure that intellectual property rights do not lead to denial or restriction of everyone's access to essential medicines necessary for the enjoyment of the right to health'.[48]

Although both the undertaking to provide international co-operation to realize rights and the UNGPs assertion of a corporate duty to respect human rights in some way extend human rights obligations beyond the primary obligations which states parties bear towards those within their jurisdiction, the scope of these obligations remains

---

[43] ibid 322.

[44] See Besson (n 31) 262.

[45] UN Human Rights Committee, 'Business and Human Rights: Towards operationalising the "protect, respect and remedy" framework: report of the Special Representative of the Secretary-General on the Issue of Human Rights and Transnational Corporations and Other Business Enterprises' (2009) A/HRC/11/13 [49].

[46] See for a fuller discussion John H Knox, 'The Ruggie Rules: Applying Human Rights Law to Corporations' in Radu Mares (ed), *The UN Guiding Principles on Business and Human Rights: Foundations and Implementation* (Raoul Wallenberg Institute 2012).

[47] See UN Committee on Economic, Social and Cultural Rights, 'General Comment No 24 on State obligations under the International Covenant on Economic, Social and Cultural Rights in the context of business activities' E/C 12/GC/24 (10 August 2017).

[48] ibid [24].

inchoate. This assessment of the normative framework established by ICESCR in relation to the right of access to healthcare suggests that the state-centric structural framework established by the ICESCR provides a weak framework for asserting the right of equal access to vaccines to everyone in the world for two main reasons. First, vaccine manufacturing and distribution is undertaken by corporate entities that are not primary bearers of international human rights law obligations, and, secondly, states, who are duty bearers, owe their primary duty to those within their jurisdiction not beyond. This weakness is to some extent mitigated by the positive duties, mentioned above, that states parties to the ICESCR bear to enact legal frameworks to prevent third parties such as businesses violating Convention rights. Nevertheless, the state-centric approach of international human rights law has the consequence that, despite the duty to provide international assistance to fulfil rights, states will often act in the first place to fulfil their obligations towards the rights bearers within their jurisdiction.

2.3 Mechanisms for Monitoring and Enforcement of Obligations

The weakness of the international human rights law framework for ensuring equal access to vaccines is further attenuated by the system for the monitoring and enforcement of ICESCR obligations. The primary international forum for monitoring the fulfilment of duties under the ICESCR is the Committee on Economic, Social and Cultural Rights (CESCR), which was established by a resolution of the Economic and Social Council of the United Nations in 1985.[49] The CESCR has eighteen independent members who are recognized human rights experts who serve in their personal capacity. Members are appointed by the Council for four-year terms. One of the primary tasks of the CESCR is to receive and examine the reports that states parties must submit on the measures they have taken to achieve the enjoyment of rights under the ICESCR.[50] A state party must provide its first report within two years of its accession to the treaty and thereafter every five years. The CESCR has issued guidelines regarding the form and content of the reports to be submitted by states parties.[51] Once the CESCR has reviewed the reports, it publishes concluding observations on the reports,[52] which provide an important source of guidance on the interpretation and application of the treaty. In addition, the CESCR issues General Comments on interpretation of specific aspects of the Covenant from time to time. To date, it has issued 25 General Comments, the most recent being the General Comment on the Right to Science, discussed above. The monitoring and implementation framework

---

[49] United Nations Economic and Social Council, Resolution 1985/17 (28 May 1985). Prior to the establishment of the CESCR, monitoring of states parties' implementation of their obligations under the ICESCR was undertaken by the Economic and Social Council of the United Nations.
[50] International Covenant on Economic, Social and Cultural Rights (adopted 16 December 1966, entered into force 3 January 1976) 999 UNTS 3 (ICESCR) art 16(1).
[51] See UN Report of the Secretary General 'Compilation of Guidelines on the Form and Content of Reports to be submitted by States Parties to the International Human Rights Treaties' (2009) HRI/GEN/2/Rev.6.
[52] Concluding observations on individual states' reports have been issued since 1992. See the useful analysis in Ben Saul, David Kinley, and Jacqueline Mowbray, *The International Covenant on Economic, Social and Cultural Rights: Commentary, Cases, and Materials* (OUP 2014).

is an important tool for determining the extent to which rights are being realized. However, although it must provide an incentive to states to seek to enhance the measures they introduce to respect, protect, and fulfil rights under the ICESCR, it does not provide any effective compulsion for states to observe their international human rights law duties.

Since 2013, under the 2008 Optional Protocol to the Covenant, the CESCR has had the jurisdiction to receive individual complaints concerning alleged breaches of the Covenant, in relation to which it issues individual communications. This mechanism enhances enforceability of the rights under the ICESCR but so far only twenty-six states parties have ratified the Optional Protocol. Research on compliance with the individual complaints procedure under the International Covenant on Civil and Political Rights, which has had a much longer experience of individual complaints, suggests that the views of the Human Rights Committee are often not enforced.[53] It is also noteworthy that the Optional Protocol does not appear to contemplate that a complaint may be based on a failure to observe the Article 2 obligation of assistance and cooperation.[54]

Accordingly, the mechanisms for enforcement of the obligations borne by states parties under the ICESCR are weak compared, for example, to those domestic legal systems which provide for judicial enforcement under domestic human rights legislation or fundamental rights entrenched in constitutions. Should a state party fail to provide access to vaccines, or to take steps to ensure that corporations do not violate fundamental rights, the likely consequence (where the Optional Protocol has not been ratified) is that the CESCR will, in its concluding observations after its review of the periodic report of the relevant state, conclude that the Article 12 and 15 rights have been violated, and make appropriate recommendations to the relevant state to take steps to meet its obligations under the Covenant.

2.4 The Fragmentation of International Law

The practical impact of the international human rights law framework needs to be assessed in the light of the overall character of international law. International law contains a series of separate, often specialized frameworks, that are enforced in different ways through different mechanisms, whose jurisdictions may overlap. In an early study, Wilfred Jenks noted that 'law-making treaties are tending to develop in a number of historical, functional and regional groups that are separate from each other and whose mutual relationships are in some respects analogous to those of separate systems of municipal law'.[55]

---

[53] For an assessment see Rosanne van Alebeek and Andre Nollkaemper, 'The Legal Status of Decisions by Human Rights Treaty Bodies in National Law' in Helen Keller and Geir Ulfstein (eds), *UN Human Rights Treaty Bodies* (CUP 2012).

[54] Geneva Academy, 'The Optional Protocol to the International Covenant on Economic, Social and Cultural Rights' (2013) Academy In-Brief No 2, 37.

[55] C Wilfred Jenks, 'The Conflict of Law-Making Treaties' (1953) 30 British Yearbook of International Law 403, cited in Marti Koskenniemi, 'Fragmentation of International Law: Difficulties Arising from the Diversification and Expansion of International Law' Report of the International Law Commission C/CN.4/L/682 (2006) [5].

The range of fields subject to the sphere of international law has expanded particularly rapidly in the last three decades with the emergence of a global world economic order, as has the concomitant need to address global problems, such as trade, intellectual property, migration, terrorism, and now climate change.[56] The expansion of the terrain of international law has thus exacerbated the risks of fragmentation and conflict between these different frameworks. The incoherence and inconsistency that might flow from fragmentation may create risks for the integrity of international law, as Anne Peters has argued, because 'the normative pull of international law is fortified by its stringency and consistency. Understanding this interrelationship means understanding why consistency is particularly important for international law (more so than for domestic law): because its normative power is precarious'.[57] The problems caused by the fragmentation of international law were examined by a study group of experts established by the International Law Commission in 2002,[58] which recommended various techniques to seek to avoid normative conflicts between the different systems of international law.

Scholars and jurists disagree on how severe the problem of fragmentation is.[59] What is clear, however, is that one of the sharpest areas of normative conflict in international law arises between the international law framework that protects intellectual property and international human rights law.[60] That conflict sharpened considerably from the 1990s when intellectual property protection became a key focus of the Uruguay round of multilateral trade negotiations within the framework of the GATT, which led to the adoption of the TRIPs Agreement in 1994. The TRIPs Agreement both consolidated and extended existing international agreements on intellectual property into one treaty, accession to which became a condition of membership of the newly established WTO. Notably, the WTO provided a powerful dispute settlement mechanism. Many countries of the global South that had not ratified the Berne and Paris Conventions (the nineteenth-century international treaties regulating intellectual property) now became bearers of obligations under the TRIPs Agreement, although in most cases there was a transitional period before the obligations became binding. One of the key reasons for the willingness of states of the global South to accede to the TRIPs Agreement related to the trade opportunities it afforded them, particularly in relation to the export of agricultural and industrial goods. In addition to the obligations imposed by the TRIPs Agreement, developed countries have often demanded that developing countries enter into what have come to be known as 'TRIPs Plus agreements' as

---

[56] See Anne Peters, 'Fragmentation and Constitutionalism' in Anne Orford and Florian Hoffmann, *Oxford Handbook of the Theory of International Law* (OUP 2016) 1013–14.
[57] ibid.
[58] UN General Assembly Official Records of the General Assembly Fifty-fifth Session, Supplement No 10 (A/55/10) chap IX A1 [729].
[59] See eg Eyal Benvenisti and George W Downs, *Between Fragmentation and Democracy: The Role of National and International Courts* (CUP 2017) 19–23, who argue that many international law scholars do not appreciate the effects of the fragmentation of international law.
[60] See the recent overview in Laurence R Helfer, 'Intellectual Property and Human Rights: Mapping an Evolving and Contested Relationship' in Rochelle C Drefuss and Justine Pila (eds), *The Oxford Handbook of Intellectual Property Law* (OUP 2018), as well as the careful examination of this problem in Sanya Samtani, 'Diluting the Right of Access to Educational Materials: International Institutional Design' in Sanya Samtani, 'The Right of Access to Educational Materials: International and Domestic Law' (DPhil thesis, University of Oxford 2021).

part of bilateral and regional trade negotiations.[61] TRIPs Plus agreements expand the scope of intellectual property protection in a range of ways.

3 International Law and Patents: TRIPs

The TRIPs agreement is an important agreement regulating intellectual property. The Treaty reinforces existing intellectual property treaties by providing that states parties may not derogate from the obligations they have under them.[62] Its coverage includes pharmaceutical patents. The core provision requires member states to accord the protection for intellectual property provided in the TRIPs Agreement on a non-discriminatory basis to rights holders and users of intellectual property in other member states.[63] The enforcement mechanisms under the TRIPs Agreement are far more coercive than those under the ICESCR. Where a state party fails to comply with its TRIPs Agreement obligations, the matter can be referred to the WTO dispute settlement system, which comprises ad hoc panels and then to the WTO Appellate Body. These forums interpret and enforce the Treaty and have the power to impose retaliatory trade sanctions. As Laurence Helfer has argued, '[t]he strength of the WTO dispute settlement system created a structural imbalance whereby the stronger pressures to adhere to TRIPS undermined states' ability to comply with the rules of other regimes where those rules intersected with TRIPS'.[64]

Many civil society actors were concerned that the effect of the TRIPs Agreement would be to hinder access to essential medicines in the global South.[65] Not long after its introduction, the emergence of the human immunodeficiency virus/acquired immunodeficiency syndrome (HIV/AIDS) pandemic with its devastating impact in the global South, and particularly in southern Africa and Brazil, exacerbated these concerns.[66] A court case launched by forty-one pharmaceutical companies in 1998 against the government of South Africa challenging proposed amendments to legislation, which sought to make medicines more accessible, became a focal point for these concerns. At the time, South Africa was facing a severe public health crisis caused by HIV/AIDS, and local civil society activists perceived the case to be resisting the government's attempts to make pharmaceutical products more accessible. After a vigorous civic campaign both within and beyond South Africa, the case was eventually withdrawn by the companies. Nevertheless, the case sparked the establishment of a global alliance between civil society organizations from many parts of the world as well as the governments of some developing states, that sought to facilitate

---

[61] Kenneth C Shadlen, Bhaven N Sampat, and Amy Kapczynski, 'Patents, Trade and Medicines: Past, Present and Future' (2020) 27 Review of International Political Economy 75.
[62] TRIPs (n 9) art 2(2).
[63] These persons are defined in art 1.3 of the Treaty.
[64] See Laurence R Helfer, 'Regime Shifting in the International Intellectual Property System' (2009) 7 Perspectives on Politics 39, 40.
[65] ibid.
[66] See the accounts in Sarah Joseph, *Blame It on the WTO? A Human Rights Critique* (OUP 2011) 223–25; Holger Hestermeyer, *Human Rights and the WTO: The Case of Patents and Access to Medicines* (OUP 2009) 11–15.

access to patented medicines.[67] The result of this activism was the Doha Declaration on the TRIPs Agreement and Public Health, issued in November 2001, by the WTO Ministerial Conference. The Doha Declaration sought to clarify the scope and application of the provisions in the TRIPs Agreement, 'flexibilities', that permit members to limit intellectual property rights in a range of circumstances.[68] In particular, the Doha Declaration declared that the TRIPs Agreement 'does not and should not prevent Members from taking measures to protect public health'.[69]

Perhaps the most important of the TRIPs Agreement flexibilities is compulsory licensing, which permits a government to licence the use of a registered patent to a third party or to use the patent itself, without the consent of the owner of the patent, in certain circumstances.[70] A compulsory licence does not suspend all the patent owner's rights—the patent owner retains a right to be provided 'with adequate remuneration' for the compulsory licensing. In most circumstances, compulsory licensing is only permitted when the state has first sought to obtain an agreement for voluntary licensing with the owner of the patent. However, in circumstances of national emergency, that condition is removed. The Doha Declaration affirmed that WTO members have the right to grant compulsory licences, as well as the freedom to determine the grounds upon which they are granted. It also confirmed that each member has 'the right to determine what constitutes a national emergency or other circumstances of extreme urgency'.[71]

Under the original terms of the TRIPs Agreement, compulsory licensing was permitted only for the purposes of domestic supply, but under an amendment, first agreed at the Doha Ministerial Conference in 2001, that condition was waived so that compulsory licensing may now be employed to meet the public health needs of least developed countries without domestic manufacturing capacity, although by 2020, that possibility appeared to have been used only once.[72]

It is not clear how effective compulsory licensing has been in fostering access to medications. A recent study identified 100 invocations of compulsory licensing under TRIPs between 2001 and 2016. Developing countries have relied on the compulsory licensing flexibility more than developed countries have and in most cases have done so to enable access to treatment for HIV/AIDS.[73] In eighteen of the 100 cases, the compulsory licence was not actually implemented. A common reason was that the patentholder offered a price reduction or allowed voluntary manufacture. This study thus suggests that the credible prospect of compulsory licensing may have a significant

---

[67] See Ellen 't Hoen and others, 'Driving a Decade of Change: HIV/AIDS, Patents and Access to Medicines for All' (2011) 14 Journal of the International AIDS Society 15.
[68] See Helfer (n 64) 42.
[69] WTO Doha Declaration on the TRIPs Agreement and Public Health (adopted 14 November 2001) WT/MIN(01)/DEC/2 [4].
[70] TRIPs (n 9) art 31(b).
[71] ibid [5(b)–(c)].
[72] By Canada and Rwanda, whereby Rwanda imported an antiretroviral drug produced under compulsory licence from Canada. See Gorik Ooms and Johanna Hanefeld, 'Threat of Compulsory Licences Could Increase Access to Essential Medicines' (2019) 365 British Medical Journal l2098.
[73] See Ellen FM 't Hoen and others, 'Medicine Procurement and the Use of Flexibilities in the Agreement on Trade-Related Aspects of Intellectual Property Rights 2001–2016' (2018) Bulletin of the World Health Organization 185.

impact on the price that manufacturers demand for their products.[74] The study also shows that the reliance on compulsory licensing for HIV treatments reduced after 2007, as voluntary licensing became more common. It is widely agreed that compulsory licensing is administratively burdensome to implement, and of less use to those countries that do not have the domestic capacity to manufacture pharmaceuticals. During the Covid-19 pandemic, a few countries have indicated they intend to rely on the TRIPs flexibilities to promote access to vaccines, and treatments for Covid-19, although it is not clear at this stage how widely this flexibility has been invoked.

More global attention has been paid to the call made by India and South Africa in October 2020 that the WTO agree to a waiver of certain key intellectual property rights under the TRIPs Agreement during the pandemic to ensure that all countries have access to vaccines, medicines, and other technologies required to curb the pandemic.[75] Many countries, including many from the developing world, support the proposal, but so far it has been staunchly opposed by most developed countries including the UK, Canada, and the EU, although early in 2021 President Biden announced US support for a waiver in relation to vaccine access only.[76] Those opposing the suspension argue that existing flexibilities within the TRIPs Agreement, as well as the donor-funded COVAX scheme adequately address the concerns raised by those proposing the suspension. The WTO ordinarily proceeds only by achieving consensus, and given the deep disagreement on the proposed suspension, it seems unlikely that it will be approved.[77]

The intellectual property protections provided in the TRIPs Agreement create obstacles for access to vaccines, although how surmountable those obstacles are remains a matter of debate. The formal mechanisms for the enforcement of the TRIPs Agreement are powerful, but so are the informal mechanisms, where developed states can insist on even more onerous obligations (TRIPs Plus) being accepted in trade negotiations than are imposed by TRIPs itself.

4 International Trade Law and Export Restrictions under GATT

Another way in which international trade law has affected equal access to vaccines is found in the provisions of the GATT. The general approach of the GATT is to prohibit

---

[74] This is further illustrated in an example given by Ooms and Hanefeld, who quote the difference in the price of Sofosbuvir, an antiretroviral used to treat Hepatitis C, in the USA where it costs US$64,680 per treatment and India, where it costs US$539, possibly because of the credible threat of compulsory licensing of the medication in India. See Ooms and Hanefeld (n 72).

[75] See WTO, 'Waiver from Certain Provisions of the Trips Agreement for the Prevention, Containment, and Treatment of Covid-19, Communication from India and South Africa (2020) IP/C/W/669, which seeks 'a waiver from the implementation, application and enforcement of sections 1, 4, 5 and 7 of Part II of the TRIPs Agreement in relation to prevention, containment or treatment of COVID-19', which should remain in place 'until widespread vaccination is in place globally, and the majority of the world's population has developed immunity'.

[76] See the announcement dated 5 May 2021 https://ustr.gov/about-us/policy-offices/press-office/press-releases/2021/may/statement-ambassador-katherine-tai-covid-19-trips-waiver (accessed 8 April 2022).

[77] See Ann Danaiya Usher, 'South Africa and India Push for COVID-19 Patents Ban' (2020) 396 The Lancet 1790.

barriers to trade, such as export restrictions or prohibitions.[78] Yet exemptions are permitted in some circumstances. For example, a state party may impose temporary export prohibitions or restrictions to address 'critical shortages of foodstuffs or other products essential' for the exporting country. Article XX of the GATT also provides for exemptions from the general rule against trade restrictions if 'necessary to protect human, animal or plant life or health'. These provisions of the GATT are expressed in generous terms and may be sufficient to justify severe export restrictions.[79] According to the WTO, by April 2021, twenty-nine countries including the UK, the US, the EU, Thailand, and Colombia had introduced export restrictions during the pandemic to restrict the export of products used to address the pandemic.[80] Notably, in January 2021, India blocked exports of the Astra Zeneca vaccine manufactured at the Serum Institute of India, which disrupted supplies of Astra Zeneca around the world. And in March 2021, the Italian government blocked the export of the Astra Zeneca vaccine to Australia. Restrictions on the export of Covid-19 vaccines led the Paris Peace Forum to declare that one of the five steps that needed to be taken to ensure equal access to vaccines globally was the lifting of export restrictions on Covid-19.[81] The other four steps were the need for vaccine doses to be shared by those countries who had excess supply, the need to scale up manufacturing capacity, improvement in regional and national surveillance and alert systems, and long-term pandemic financing to improve pandemic preparedness.

International trade law has thus generally provided a range of obstacles to ensuring equitable access to vaccines during the Covid-19 pandemic, and so far the principles of international human rights law have not provided any significant basis upon which to counteract or surmount these obstacles. Yet that is not to say that principles of international human rights have been entirely ignored during the pandemic. The institutions of global health governance are clearly concerned about human rights principles, although that concern is perhaps more founded on the moral and political dimensions of international human rights than it is on their legal dimension.

5 Changing Patterns of Global Health Governance

The last two decades have seen significant changes in the pattern of global health governance: a wide array of new collaborative organizations to address global health challenges have emerged. Arguably, one of the drivers of this process was the consortium of civil society actors and developing countries that mobilized to respond to the HIV/AIDS pandemic.[82] These new organizations are often public-private partnerships that

---

[78] See GATT (n 10) art XI(1). See also Armin von Bogdandy and Pedro A Villareal, 'The Role of International Law in Vaccinating Against COVID-19: Appraising the COVAX Initiative' (2020) 46 Max Planck Institute for Comparative Public Law and International Law, Research Paper Series 7, 8; Julian Arato, Kathleen Claussen, and J Benton Heath, 'The Perils of Pandemic Exceptionalism' (2020) 114 American Journal of International Law 627.
[79] Arato, Claussen, and Benton Heath (n 78) 629.
[80] See WTO Committee on Market Access Report by the Secretariat (2021) G/MA/W/168.
[81] See Adrien Abecassis, 'Five Priorities for Universal Covid-19 Vaccination' (2021) 398 The Lancet 285.
[82] See eg the website of the Global Fund to Fight AIDS, TB, and Malaria, which references the United Nations Special Session on HIV and AIDS as a turning point in the establishment of new public private

include international organizations (such as the World Health Organization (WHO) and the United Nations Children's Fund (UNICEF)), private philanthropists, notably the Bill and Melinda Gates Foundation, and governments of a wide range of countries.[83] Burci argues that there are several reasons for the emergence of these partnerships, including the effects of globalization, the growing role of private actors in the field of health, and a lack of confidence in the capacity of international organizations to mobilize the resources to tackle global health problems.[84]

These organizations are generally committed to the protection of human rights and to expanding access to health care and address a range of issues from HIV/AIDs to tuberculosis, malaria, child nutrition, and access to vaccines. These institutions are not traditional state-centric international organizations. They include not only private philanthropists, often with a corporate background, but also civil society actors and institutions, such as Médecins Sans Frontières and corporations, including pharmaceutical manufacturers. For example, the Board of GAVI reserves two seats for vaccine manufacturers.[85]

There are important questions concerning how these multi-stakeholder organizations function, whether they are accountable, whose interests they serve, and whether the term 'partnership' accurately captures the way in which they work.[86] These are empirical questions, which require careful research and investigation, but are beyond the scope of this chapter.[87] Two exemplars of this new form of global health governance institutions that have played a key role in promoting access to vaccines during the pandemic are GAVI and CEPI, both of whom have been central to the COVAX Initiative.

6 COVAX

COVAX is the vaccines pillar of the Access to Covid-19 Tools Accelerator (the ACT-Accelerator), a global collaboration to accelerate development, production, and equitable access to tests, treatments, and vaccines for Covid-19 launched in April 2020. COVAX is led by the WHO, GAVI, and CEPI, with the support of the United Nations Children's Fund (UNICEF). It seeks to expedite the development, manufacturing, and distribution of Covid-19 vaccines to ensure that there is equitable access to vaccines across the world, in a manner that, GAVI asserts, will serve to protect human

---

partnerships to promote health. See The Global Fund https://www.theglobalfund.org/en/specials/2021-06-07-20-years-of-partnership-celebrating-the-heroes-of-the-fight/ (accessed 8 April 2022).

[83] See Gian Luca Burci, 'Public/Private Partnerships in the Public Health Sector' (2009) 6 International Organizations Law Review 359.
[84] ibid 362.
[85] ibid 371.
[86] JS Taylor, 'What the Word "Partnership" Conjoins, and What It Does' (2018) 5 Medical Anthropology Theory 1; Mateja Steinbrück Platise, 'The Changing Structure of Global Health Governance' in Leonie Vierck, Pedro A Villareal, and A Katarina Weilert (eds), *The Governance of Disease Outbreaks: International Health Law: Lessons from the Ebola Crisis and Beyond* (Nomos 2017) 113–44.
[87] Katerini Tamatarchi Storeng and Antoine de Bengy Puyvallee, 'Civil Society Participation in Global Public Private Partnerships for Health' (2018) 33 Health Policy and Planning 928.

rights. COVAX thus has two elements: the first is its commitment to accelerating vaccine development, which it seeks to achieve through providing financial support to promising vaccines in development. The second, the COVAX facility, seeks to ensure equitable access to vaccines globally, which it seeks to achieve through procuring and distributing doses of vaccines.[88] The COVAX facility initially aimed to distribute 2 billion doses of vaccines by the end of 2021 but, by April 2022, they had delivered just over 1 billion doses—still an impressive achievement.[89]

The COVAX facility seeks the participation of states to promote equitable access to vaccines. Participating states are classified into two groups: the first comprises self-financing states and the other funded states. States are allocated to groups based on their per capita gross national income. All those with gross per capita national income above US$4,000 are self-financing states, which means they must contribute to COVAX to receive their share of vaccines, while those who fall below the threshold will receive vaccines from COVAX at no cost. The COVAX Initiative creates a web of contracts with GAVI at its centre. GAVI enters into contracts both with vaccine manufacturers, in which the manufacturer undertakes to supply vaccines,[90] and with the self-financing states. Crucially, COVAX accepts that self-financing states may also receive vaccines through other sources.

COVAX seeks to provide every participating state with access to sufficient vaccines to vaccinate 20 per cent of their population. As at May 2021, there were eighty-five self-financing participating states in the COVAX facility and ninety-two low- and middle-income countries eligible to be funded.[91]

There have been a range of challenges for COVAX in meeting its target. Perhaps one of the most severe has been that wealthier countries have pursued bilateral advance purchase agreements to acquire vaccines, thus competing with COVAX for vaccines as they are produced.[92] In addition, COVAX has been hindered by countries introducing export prohibitions, which have meant that vaccines for which COVAX had contracted have not been delivered on time. Accordingly, although COVAX seemed an important global initiative to ensure equitable access to vaccines globally, so far it has not achieved its goal.

7 Conclusion

International human rights have moral, political, and legal dimensions. The legal dimensions of international human rights law are generally state-centric and based on the jurisdiction of states. The consequence is that any human rights obligations of

---

[88] Mark Eccleston-Turner and Harry Upton, 'International Collaboration to Ensure Equitable Access to Vaccines for COVID-19: the ACT Accelerator and the COVAX Facility' (2021) 99 The Milbank Quarterly 426.
[89] See GAVI (n 11).
[90] See the fuller explanation in Bogdandy and Villareal (n 78) 5–6; Eccleston-Turner and Upton (n 88) 435–436.
[91] See GAVI, 'Covax' (2021) https://www.gavi.org/sites/default/files/covid/pr/COVAX_CA_COIP_List_COVAX_PR_12-05-21.pdf (accessed 8 April 2022).
[92] See Eccleston-Turner and Upton (n 88) 437–41.

the producers of vaccines, which are largely corporate entities and not states, do not derive directly from international human rights law, but largely from domestic law. Moreover, states have attenuated obligations to fulfil the human rights of those who do not fall within their jurisdiction. This chapter has argued that the weakness of international human rights law in relation to equal access to vaccines globally contrasts starkly with the more robust manner in which the obligations of states to protect the intellectual property rights of vaccine manufacturers are enforced under international trade law.

Nevertheless, the political and moral dimensions of international human rights law have force in the global health governance environment, where newly established public private partnerships, such as GAVI and CEPI, and existing international organizations such as the WHO, generally seek to promote equal access to healthcare across the globe in a manner consistent with international human rights. However, so far these partnerships have not succeeded in achieving their goal of ensuring equitable access to vaccines globally. Initial optimism about the COVAX facility has waned. Even at the start, its goal of providing 20 per cent of the vaccine needs of participating countries seemed markedly inadequate, and now it seems even more inadequate in a world in which many developed countries have vaccinated more than 70 per cent of their adult populations, yet low-income countries have vaccinated only a small proportion of the populations. In 2005, Branko Milanovic wondered whether 'in some not-too-distant future we would reach the situation where we would be interested in global inequality—treating all individuals in the world the same, simply as world citizens—the way we are currently interested in national inequality'.[93] A global pandemic in which every citizen of the globe is at risk of disease would seem to be the appropriate moment for us to become interested in global inequality. Yet so far, despite some encouraging signs, a worldwide commitment to act to ensure global equality in relation to access to vaccines remains for the moment elusive.

---

[93] See Milanovic (n 8) 12.

SECTION B
VULNERABLE GROUPS

13
A Life Course Approach to Addressing Exponential Inequalities
Age, Gender, and Covid-19

Alysia Blackham[*]

1 Introduction

Age is critical to our understanding of discrimination and its impacts. Drawing on a 'life course' perspective as a framework to understand how human experiences develop over time, this chapter argues that age (and its corollary, time) is an exponential amplifier of inequality in three ways. First, age discrimination amplifies other forms of inequality[1] by exacerbating other forms of disadvantage[2] and making people vulnerable to particular types of wrong.[3] The very nature of age discrimination changes as it interacts with other protected grounds.[4] Age is therefore both a catalyst and a contributor to other forms of inequality. Secondly, our experience of discrimination over time—that is, over our life course—is often amplified and compounded. Inequalities compound over time, and inequality is exponential over the life course. Thirdly, over time, our experiences of discrimination can have negative impacts on our health, well-being, and life satisfaction.

This chapter draws on a case study of gendered ageism in employment in the Covid-19 pandemic in Australia to consider how age discrimination acts as an exponential amplifier of inequality; and how disadvantage and discrimination is exacerbated over time. To respond to this, legal structures need to prioritize age and age inequality; authentically accommodate lived experiences of discrimination, which are intersectional and overlapping; and adopt a life course approach to addressing inequality. I consider the extent to which 'next generation' positive duties—like the Gender Equality Act 2020 (Vic)—might address these concerns, and propose a life course approach better tailored to address exponential inequalities.

---

[*] This research was funded by the Australian Government through the Australian Research Council's Discovery Projects funding scheme (Project DE170100228). The views expressed herein are those of the author and are not necessarily those of the Australian Government or Australian Research Council.
[1] Women and Equalities Committee, 'Older People and Employment' (HC 2017-19, 359) 13.
[2] Aileen McColgan, *Discrimination, Equality and the Law* (Hart Publishing 2014) 68.
[3] ibid 69.
[4] Australian Human Rights Commission, 'Willing to Work: National Inquiry into Employment Discrimination against Older Australians and Australians with Disability' (2016) 71–74.

2 A Life Course Perspective on Discrimination

A 'life course' perspective sees ageing and human development as involving 'age-graded patterns', embedded in social institutions, history, context, and place.[5] However, life course theories also recognize human agency, seeing 'the individual as an active force in constructing his or her life course through the choices and actions taken.'[6] Thus, while our lives are embedded in social pathways and institutions, our choices and decisions have important repercussions for our future life trajectory.[7]

A 'life course' approach has important implications for our understanding of discrimination and inequality. First, it sees ageing as profoundly social and embedded in social institutions. It sees our lives as linked and interdependent,[8] so that effects on one person also affect others in their network. Experiencing discrimination, then, does not just affect one person; it has ripple effects and consequences for families, communities, and social networks.

Secondly, a life course perspective recognizes that experiencing discrimination at certain critical or sensitive points can have a more significant impact than when discrimination is experienced at other, less critical points.[9] Critical or sensitive points might occur at certain stages of social or intellectual development.

Thirdly, and critically, a life course perspective recognizes that 'the effects of certain types of discrimination may reverberate across the life course and reinforce one another', across different contexts, and across time periods.[10] This can be exacerbated by contextual events and social change; as Elder and others argue: 'Cumulative disadvantages or advantages tend to maximize the contextual influences.'[11] Thus, experiencing discrimination should not be seen as a 'one-off' event, with solely short-term consequences; the effects of discrimination can be long-term, compounding across time and across contexts, and exacerbated by other contextual factors. This draws our attention to the way discrimination may accumulate over time, and the latent and long-term impacts that might emerge from experiencing discrimination.[12] A life course perspective also becomes critical for examining periods of social change or disruption—as, for example, during a global pandemic—and how they might impact on life trajectories.

Fourthly, and critical to our understanding of age inequality, a life course perspective sees ageing itself as a life-long process.[13] This means that age discrimination is

---

[5] Glen H Elder, Monica Kirkpatrick Johnson, and Robert Crosnoe, 'The Emergence and Development of Life Course Theory' in Jeylan T Mortimer and Michael J Shanahan (eds), *Handbook of the Life Course* (Springer 2003) 4 https://doi.org/10.1007/978-0-306-48247-2_1 (accessed 15 November 2021).
[6] ibid 14.
[7] ibid 11.
[8] ibid 13–14.
[9] Gilbert C Gee, Katrina M Walsemann, and Elizabeth Brondolo, 'A Life Course Perspective on How Racism May Be Related to Health Inequities' (2012) 102 American Journal of Public Health 967, 967–68.
[10] ibid 967.
[11] Elder, Johnson, and Crosnoe (n 5) 15.
[12] Gee, Walsemann, and Brondolo (n 9) 969–70.
[13] Gilbert C Gee, Eliza K Pavalko, and J Scott Long, 'Age, Cohort and Perceived Age Discrimination: Using the Life Course to Assess Self-Reported Age Discrimination' (2007) 86 Social Forces 265, 265.

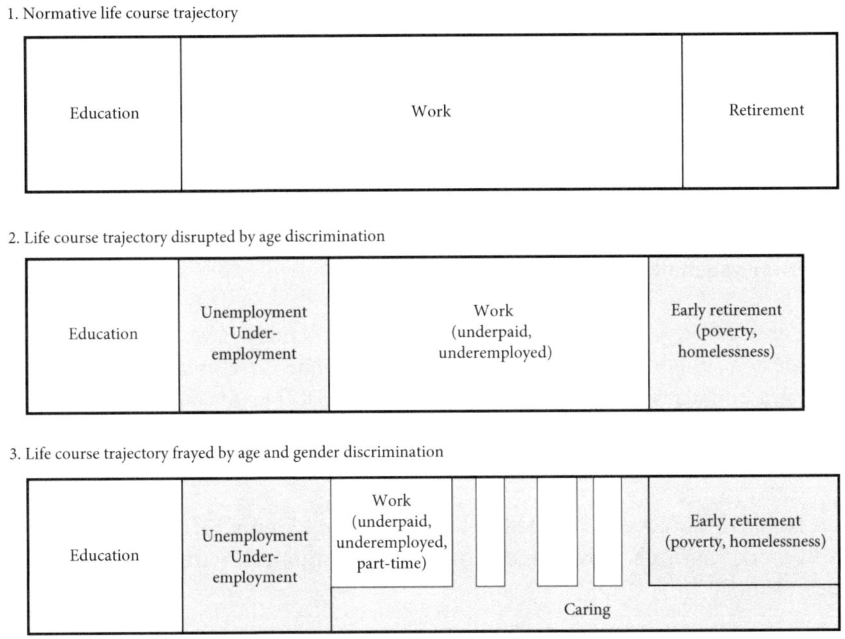

1. Normative life course trajectory

Education	Work	Retirement

2. Life course trajectory disrupted by age discrimination

Education	Unemployment Under-employment	Work (underpaid, underemployed)	Early retirement (poverty, homelessness)

3. Life course trajectory frayed by age and gender discrimination

Education	Unemployment Under-employment	Work (underpaid, underemployed, part-time)		Early retirement (poverty, homelessness)
		Caring		

Figure 13.1 Model of the life course, and with disruption and fraying

not only confined to older age or later life, but 'may ebb and flow across the entire life course'.[14]

Fifthly, a life course perspective posits that exposure to discrimination may be particularly common in life course transitions[15]—from education to work, from work to retirement, and (especially for women) from work to caring. This might explain, then, the prevalence of age discrimination in recruitment and at the end of the working relationship (in redundancy, retirement, and dismissal).[16]

A life course perspective therefore offers us a nuanced lens for enriching our understanding of discrimination and its impacts over time.

3 The 'Disrupted' Life Course

A life course approach has traditionally seen lives as following a linear trajectory, tripartitioning our existence into periods of education, work, and then retirement (see Figure 13.1).[17] However, those who experience discrimination and times of crisis may have a disrupted life course, punctuated by periods of under-employment and

---

[14] ibid.
[15] Gee, Walsemann and Brondolo (n 9) 967.
[16] Alysia Blackham, *Reforming Age Discrimination Law: Beyond Individual Enforcement* (OUP, 2022) ch 6.
[17] Building on Gee, Walsemann, and Brondolo (n 9) 971.

unemployment, poverty, and homelessness. Indeed, in some cases, this trajectory may even be cut short, due to lower life expectancy from experiencing discrimination.

The idea of the 'life course' as something 'linear and cumulative'[18] is grounded in a structured, normative, and gendered view of individual lives and careers, which does not meaningfully encompass women's experiences.[19] Instead, Sabelis and Schilling use the idea of 'frayed careers' to emphasize the rhythm of careers, in contrast to the linearity and upward direction that pervades many views of the life course. In this 'frayed' perspective, stages of working life are interlinked and biographic, but also non-linear and multi-directional:

> Life itself follows a non-linear pattern; social constructions of age and gender constitute and sustain this. Since the traditional masculine career image proceeds in a linear, accumulative way, it is still perceived as a normal or preferable way of work-life design. On this account, female, or patchwork careers are perceived as frayed [and] deviant.[20]

This 'frayed' life course is depicted in the third box of Figure 13.1, with the lines between work, caring and retirement fuzzy and rhythmical, rather than linear and unidirectional.[21]

4 Intersectional Inequalities over the Life Course

Drawing on a life course perspective, we can therefore see experiences of discrimination over time as non-linear and multi-directional, but still interlinked and biographic, punctuating and shaping life stories in unpredictable ways.

This is consistent with empirical data on individual experiences of discrimination. Discrimination is rarely experienced in a siloed way, confined to one context or one protected characteristic. In our study of data from the Australian Bureau of Statistics 2014 General Social Survey (GSS), Jeromey Temple and I found that discrimination was often experienced as multiple discrimination, and across multiple contexts.[22] In total, 38.9 per cent of those who reported experiencing any form of discrimination, reported experiencing multiple types of discrimination; and almost half of respondents (47.7 per cent) reported experiencing discrimination in multiple contexts in the previous twelve months. For those reporting multiple discrimination, the majority reported work (61 per cent) as being a context where they experienced discrimination.

---

[18] Ida Sabelis and Elisabeth Schilling, 'Editorial: Frayed Careers: Exploring Rhythms of Working Lives' (2013) 20 Gender, Work and Organization 127, 127.
[19] ibid.
[20] ibid 129.
[21] Acknowledging, too, that caring can stretch across the life course, including in periods of education; and that caring is not an experience unique to women, just shouldered disproportionately by women: Gerry Redmond and others, 'Projects-of-Self and Projects-of-Family: Young People's Responsibilisation for Their Education and Responsibility for Care' (2021) 43 British Journal of Sociology of Education 84.
[22] Alysia Blackham and Jeromey Temple, 'Intersectional Discrimination in Australia: An Empirical Critique of the Legal Framework' (2020) 43 UNSW Law Journal 773.

While the GSS offers high quality data on experiences of discrimination, it does not fully capture intersectional discrimination; rather, it focuses on individual protected characteristics, allowing us to consider only additive or multiple discrimination. The GSS also only gathered data on individuals' *most recent* experience of discrimination. It therefore does not offer a clear picture of inequality and discrimination over time.[23] That said, respondents of all ages reported experiencing discrimination across a range of protected characteristics, indicating that discrimination is not limited to particular age groups or life periods. Instead, the nature and type of discrimination experienced may shift over the life course. Gee and others' study of longitudinal data from the Mature and Young Women's Cohorts of the US National Longitudinal Surveys (NLS) found that reports of age discrimination are high when women are in their twenties, drop to their lowest at around age thirty-five, then peak around age fifty-five, forming a 'U' shape over the life course.[24] By contrast, experiences of gender discrimination follow an inverted 'U' shape over the life course;[25] the intersection of age and gender discrimination means women are never the 'right' age, and never entirely free from discrimination.[26] Women are also far more likely than men to report experiencing both age and gender discrimination.[27]

Critical to understanding exponential inequalities, then, is acknowledging the way in which experiences accumulate and compound over time, as well as across protected grounds and different contexts. As Moen argues: 'Both advantages and disadvantages cumulate over the life course, widening inequalities within as well as across gender divides.'[28] In relation to race discrimination, for example, Feagin describes how the cumulative impact of what appear to be 'minor' instances of discrimination can build over time: '[W]hen blatant acts of avoidance, verbal harassment, and physical attack combine with subtle and covert slights, and these accumulate over months, years, and lifetimes, the impact on a [B]lack person is far more than the sum of the individual instances.'[29] Individual instances of discrimination do not occur in a vacuum; each experience occurs in an individual, social, and historical context. What might appear minor when viewed in isolation can be 'recurring events reflecting an invasion of the microworld by the macroworld'.[30] When considering exponential inequalities, we therefore need to consider how discrimination is experienced across individual lives, and across generations and communities. Again, the notion of the 'life course'

---

[23] While the Household, Income and Labour Dynamics in Australia (HILDA) Survey offers household-based longitudinal data, its questionnaire on job-related discrimination is only conducted intermittently.

[24] Gee, Pavalko, and Long (n 13) 276.

[25] Gilbert C Gee and others, 'Racism and the Life Course: Taking Time Seriously' (2019) 109 American Journal of Public Health S43, S45.

[26] Catherine E Harnois, 'Age and Gender Discrimination: Intersecting Inequalities across the Lifecourse' in Vasilikie P Demos and Marcia Texler Segal (eds), *At the Center: Feminism, Social Science and Knowledge*, vol 20 (Emerald Group Publishing Limited 2015).

[27] ibid 104.

[28] Phyllis Moen, 'Work Over the Gendered Life Course' in Michael J Shanahan, Jeylan T Mortimer, and Monica Kirkpatrick Johnson (eds), *Handbook of the Life Course*, vol 2 (Springer International Publishing 2016) 253.

[29] Joe R Feagin, 'The Continuing Significance of Race: Antiblack Discrimination in Public Places' (1991) 56 American Sociological Review 101, 114–15.

[30] ibid 115.

can assist here, in illustrating the temporal, communal, and cumulative effects of discrimination.

5 Exponential Inequalities: Gendered Ageism

To better illustrate these issues, this section considers a case study of gendered ageism at work. Gender and age are a particularly harmful combination of protected characteristics. Women experience the 'double jeopardy' of both ageism and sexism.[31] It is not just older women who experience this intersection of age and gender; this affects women of all ages. Women are *never* the right age, as gendered ageism morphs and evolves across the life course. In our study of the GSS, Temple and I found that, of those reporting exposure to any type of discrimination in the last year, women respondents (22.7 per cent) were more likely than men (19.7 per cent) to report experiencing age discrimination, and far more likely than men to report experiencing gender discrimination (22.4 per cent and 8.7 per cent, respectively). Women also reported experiencing discrimination on multiple grounds (40.1 per cent) more often than men (37.5 per cent).[32]

In addition to this intersection of ageism and sexism, gender inequalities compound over time; inequality is exponential over the life course. For example, Grant argues that, having experienced discriminatory treatment throughout their working lives,[33] older women have been culturally conditioned to accept discrimination.[34] This may mean older women are less likely to challenge workplace discrimination, internalizing or accepting discriminatory treatment. Indeed, in my study of the enforcement of age discrimination law in Australia and the UK, I identified gendered gaps in enforcement, especially for older women.[35]

A lack of claiming does not, then, mean that women are unaffected by gendered ageism; quite the opposite. Across the life course, women are over-exposed to insecure work, take on disproportionate caring roles (for children, elders, and partners), and experience a significant gender pay gap. These issues, of course, are inter-related; women may reduce their working time, work in less senior roles, or leave the workforce entirely to accommodate caring responsibilities.[36] This contributes to women's over-representation in insecure work, and the gender pay gap. It also affects women across the life course: women potentially take on caring responsibilities at all life stages. For example, in Moen, Robison, and Fields's study of women and caring roles over the life course, in their sample of 293 women from four birth cohorts in upstate New York, one in four women (24 per cent) became caregivers between ages thirty-five

---

[31] Colin Duncan and Wendy Loretto, 'Never the Right Age? Gender and Age-Based Discrimination in Employment' (2004) 11 Gender, Work and Organization 95, 110.
[32] Blackham and Temple (n 22).
[33] Diane Grant, 'Older Women, Work and the Impact of Discrimination' in Malcolm Sargeant (ed), *Age Discrimination and Diversity: Multiple Discrimination from an Age Perspective* (CUP 2011) 43, 62.
[34] ibid.
[35] Blackham (n 16).
[36] Janneke Berecki-Gisolf and others, 'Transitions into Informal Caregiving and out of Paid Employment of Women in Their 50s' (2008) 67 Social Science and Medicine 122.

to forty-four, and over one in three (36 per cent) became caregivers between ages fifty-five to sixty-four. Those in younger birth cohorts (born 1927–1934) were actually more likely to ever become caregivers (at 64 per cent) than those in the oldest cohort (born 1905–1917, at 45 per cent). The authors concluded, then, that differences in labour force participation had not affected women's caregiving roles.[37] As Moen argues:

> Women are now expected to both hold down jobs and provide care for infirm and disabled family members as well as for dependent children. These differing options and imperatives play out in distinctive trajectories and turning points that shape disparities in men's and women's occupational careers, resource accumulations, and retirement paths.[38]

In Australia, for example, as Table 13.1 illustrates, women are far more likely to work part-time than men, but far less likely to work as independent contractors or other business operators. Part-time work is far more common among the youngest (15–19) and oldest (65+) workers. Women are also over-represented in casual and insecure work (Figure 13.2). This has consequences for pay (during working life) and superannuation (in retirement). The Australian Workplace Gender Equality Agency (WGEA) estimates the gender pay gap for full-time work in Australia to be 14.2 per cent (as at May 2021), up from 13.4 per cent in November 2020. This gender pay gap increases exponentially into retirement; superannuation and pension savings reflect the accumulated gender pay gap across working lives, compounded by investment returns. As Table 13.2 shows, the gender pension gap is two to three times higher than the gender pay gap; and women are more likely than men to have no superannuation savings for retirement (Table 13.3). Age has therefore become an exponential amplifier of the gender pay gap, intensifying the impact of non-linear work careers.[39] As the highlighted age cohorts show in Table 13.2, the gender pension gap increases substantially in mid-life, as women shoulder higher caring loads.

This has significant consequences in practice: older women are now the fastest growing group at risk of homelessness in Australia. Based on longitudinal Household Income and Labour Dynamics in Australia (HILDA) Survey data, in 2018 the number of women aged forty-five years and over likely to be at risk of homelessness was approximately 405,000.[40] For women aged fifty-five to sixty-four in private rental accommodation, the likelihood of being at risk of homelessness was approximately 28 per cent.[41] Notably, the risk of homelessness increased for those who were immigrants from non-English speaking countries; identify as Aboriginal and/or Torres

---

[37] Phyllis Moen, Julie Robison, and Vivian Fields, 'Women's Work and Caregiving Roles: A Life Course Approach' (1994) 49 Journal of Gerontology S176.
[38] Moen (n 28) 254.
[39] Sian Moore, '"No Matter What I Did I Would Still End Up in the Same Position": Age as a Factor Defining Older Women's Experience of Labour Market Participation' (2009) 23 Work, Employment and Society 655, 659.
[40] Laurence Lester and Debbie Faulkner, 'At Risk: Understanding the Population Size and Demographics of Older Women at Risk of Homelessness in Australia' (2020) 4 https://www.oldertenants.org.au/content/risk-understanding-the-population-size-and-demographics-older-women-risk-homelessness (accessed 16 November 2021).
[41] ibid 5.

Table 13.1 Employment by demographic characteristics, Australia, August 2019

	Employees				Independent Contractor					Other Business Operators					Total			
	Full-time in main job	Part-time in main job	Total - Employees	Total employee (% of all employed persons)	Full-time in main job	Part-time in main job	Total - Independent Contractor	Total (% of all employed persons)		Full-time in main job	Part-time in main job	Total - Other Business Operators	Total (% of all employed persons)		Full-time in main job	Part-time in main job	Total - Employed Persons	Total part time (% of all employed persons)
	'000	'000	'000	%	'000	'000	'000	%		'000	'000	'000	%		'000	'000	'000	%
Sex																		
Male	4,324.0	1,020.0	5,344.0	78.7	558.7	201.6	760.8	11.2		537.5	145.8	683.4	10.1		5,420.3	1,367.3	6,788.2	20.14
Female	2,816.9	2,456.2	5,273.1	87.2	106.8	181.7	288.5	4.8		218.0	269.4	487.4	8.1		3,141.8	2,907.3	6,049.0	48.06
Age group (years)																		
15–19	147.4	509.5	656.9	98.8	1.8	4.3	6.1	0.9		0.1	1.4	1.6	0.2		149.3	515.2	664.6	77.53
20–24	639.6	551.3	1,190.9	95.5	24.5	15.4	39.9	3.2		7.4	9.2	16.6	1.3		671.5	575.9	1,247.4	46.16
25–34	2,038.1	660.8	2,698.9	88.3	143.9	60.8	204.7	6.7		93.8	57.8	151.6	5.0		2,275.8	779.5	3,055.3	25.51
35–44	1,695.1	572.1	2,267.2	82.1	158.6	76.6	235.2	8.5		179.9	80.4	260.3	9.4		2,033.5	729.1	2,762.7	26.39
45–54	1,523.5	523.4	2,046.9	78.1	178.5	84.8	263.3	10.0		228.0	81.8	309.9	11.8		1,930.0	690.0	2,620.1	26.33
55–59	595.6	256.1	851.8	75.9	78.4	38.6	117.0	10.4		104.1	48.7	152.8	13.6		778.1	343.5	1,121.6	30.62
60–64	358.6	215.5	574.0	73.6	49.3	41.2	91.0	11.7		69.7	45.3	115.0	14.7		477.6	301.9	780.1	38.70
65 and over	143.1	187.4	330.6	56.5	30.6	61.5	92.1	15.7		72.4	90.4	162.8	27.8		246.1	339.4	585.5	57.96

Source: ABS, 6333.0 Characteristics of Employment, Australia, August 2019, and author's own calculations

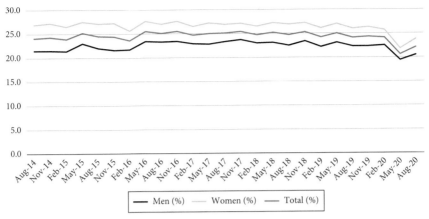

Figure 13.2 Casual employment (%) as share of total employment, Australia, 2014–2020
Source: Australian Bureau of Statistics, Working Arrangements, August 2020.

Strait Islander; and lone parents.[42] The risk was also significantly heightened for those working part-time, out of the labour force or unemployed.[43]

6 Times of Crisis: Covid-19 and Work

If age amplifies other forms of inequality, a time of crisis amplifies the amplifier. Periods of crisis and social change can have significant and profound impacts on life trajectories; this is seen, historically, for example, for individuals and age cohorts who experienced the First and Second World Wars and the Great Depression.[44] That said, events affect people differently, depending on their life stage;[45] and even those of the same birth cohort can be exposed very differently to social change.[46] It is critical, then, that we adopt a nuanced view of how social events affect people over time. At the same time, it is difficult to obtain disaggregated data on how Covid-19 has affected Australian workers and workplaces.

The data that is available, though, indicates that the Covid-19 pandemic—and how governments responded to the Covid-19 pandemic—exacerbated prevailing inequalities in work. Lockdowns, a growth in working-from-home and the closure of schools and early childhood education created additional domestic load, caring and housework, which was disproportionately shouldered by women (though men did take on more childcare responsibility).[47] Widespread lockdowns particularly affected those working in service industries, such as tourism, retail and hospitality, and the arts. As Table 13.4 shows, the brunt of the impact of Covid-19 on work was borne by younger

---

[42] ibid 4.
[43] ibid.
[44] Elder, Johnson, and Crosnoe (n 5) 5.
[45] ibid 12–13.
[46] ibid 9.
[47] Lyn Craig and Brendan Churchill, 'Working and Caring at Home: Gender Differences in the Effects of Covid-19 on Paid and Unpaid Labor in Australia' (2021) 27 Feminist Economics 310.

Table 13.2 Superannuation balance and gender pension gap, by age, 15 years and over, 2009–10 to 2017–18, Australia, estimates (A$)

	2009–10			2011–12			2013–14			2015–16			2017–18		
	Males	Females	Gender gap (%)	Males	Females	Gender gap (%)	Males	Females	Gender gap (%)	Males	Females	Gender gap (%)	Males	Females	Gender gap (%)
Superannuation balance at, or approaching preservation age (55–64 years)															
Mean	291,107	187,417	35.62	283,598	162,229	42.80	344,379	192,528	44.09	321,600	203,663	36.67	332,662	245,126	26.31
Median	138,128	73,445	46.83	120,161	72,930	39.31	160,429	85,562	46.67	172,483	99,558	42.28	183,000	118,556	35.22
Superannuation balance by age group (years)															
15–24															
Mean	6,783	4,588	32.36	6,556	5,153	21.40	7,192	4,512	37.26	6,878	5,854	14.89	6,318	6,100	3.45
Median	3,554	2,369	33.34	3,369	2,360	29.95	3,209	2,139	33.34	2,592	2,281	12.00	3,000	2,237	25.43
25–34															
Mean	31,372	23,933	23.71	32,365	24,638	23.87	32,898	26,754	18.68	39,656	33,206	16.26	41,661	31,618	24.11
Median	21,323	15,400	27.78	21,337	16,845	21.05	21,390	19,251	10.00	26,960	23,855	11.52	30,000	20,000	33.33
35–44															
Mean	74,778	51,704	30.86	75,371	55,327	26.59	83,368	57,391	31.16	95,209	68,192	28.38	100,323	69,252	30.97
Median	48,569	29,607	39.04	50,977	33,690	33.91	53,476	37,433	30.00	67,401	45,946	31.83	70,000	50,000	28.57
45–54															
Mean	149,953	79,559	46.94	153,744	90,689	41.01	162,003	97,163	40.02	186,068	118,488	36.32	196,407	129,086	34.28
Median	82,922	39,092	52.86	84,225	44,920	46.67	96,257	53,476	44.44	114,063	64,533	43.42	131,969	75,000	43.17
55–64															
Mean	291,107	187,417	35.62	283,598	162,229	42.80	344,379	192,528	44.09	321,600	203,663	36.67	332,662	245,126	26.31
Median	138,128	73,445	46.83	120,161	72,930	39.31	160,429	85,562	46.67	172,483	99,557	42.28	183,000	118,556	35.22

65–69															
Mean	358,447	254,699	28.94	326,732	256,602	21.46	379,215	266,507	29.72	426,523	332,748	21.99	404,458	420,259	-3.91
Median	140,504	177,523	-26.35	157,203	145,848	7.22	206,418	159,486	22.74	194,101	182,279	6.09	250,000	217,607	12.96
70 and over															
Mean	300,011	256,962	14.35	300,063	219,351	26.90	323,327	265,904	17.76	383,755	277,969	27.57	409,263	290,054	29.13
Median	142,152	108,983	23.33	114,534	112,300	1.95	139,038	143,473	-3.19	170,170	150,355	11.64	240,000	155,643	35.15
Total superannuation balance															
Mean	123,978	77,966	37.11	125,494	76,918	38.71	144,171	88,888	38.35	158,672	105,406	33.57	168,474	121,322	27.99
Median	41,490	23,692	42.90	44,920	28,075	37.50	49,198	32,086	34.78	62,216	40,440	35.00	65,000	45,000	30.77

Source: ABS, 41250DS0002 Gender Indicators, Australia, December 2020, and author's own calculations.

Table 13.3 Proportion of persons with no superannuation coverage by age and relationship in the household, 15–64 years, 2009–10 to 2017–18, estimates, Australia

	2009–10			2011–12			2013–14			2015–16			2017–18		
	Males	Females	% difference	Males	Females	% difference	Males	Females	% difference	Males	Females	% difference	Males	Females	% difference
No superannuation coverage (15–64 years) (%)	25.0	30.4	5.4	19.6	25.6	6.0	19.9	25.1	5.2	20.1	24.3	4.2	20.5	23.5	3.0
No superannuation coverage (15–64 years) ('000s)	1,827.7	2,237.1		1,472.1	1,930.3		1,497.2	1,912.0		1,538.8	1,894.2		1,603.6	1,882.0	
No superannuation coverage by age group (years) (%)															
15–24	48.2	48.0	−0.2	45.2	45.2	0.0	48.6	47.5	−1.1	50.2	48.4	−1.8	50.3	49.4	−0.9
25–34	16.4	23.6	7.2	11.1	18.0	6.9	12.0	19.5	7.5	12.1	16.9	4.8	14.0	16.0	2.0
35–44	18.7	25.8	7.1	10.6	18.5	7.9	10.1	17.0	6.9	10.2	15.4	5.2	10.1	16.0	5.9
45–54	17.6	22.7	5.1	12.6	18.0	5.4	11.9	16.2	4.3	11.9	18.1	6.2	11.8	16.4	4.6
55–64	23.0	33.2	10.2	18.6	30.3	11.7	16.9	27.3	10.4	16.0	25.6	9.6	16.3	22.4	6.1
No superannuation coverage, by relationship in the household (15–64 years) (%)															
In couple relationship	38.0	50.1	12.1	30.3	47.1	16.8	30.9	45.7	14.8	28.6	44.8	16.2	26.7	41.4	14.7
Not in couple relationship	62.0	49.9	−12.1	69.7	52.9	−16.8	69.1	54.3	−14.8	71.4	55.4	−16.0	73.5	58.5	−15.0

Source: ABS, 41250DS0002 Gender Indicators, Australia, December 2020, and author's own calculations.

Table 13.4 Characteristics of employment, by gender and age, Australia, August 2019, and August 2020

	Employees 2019			Employees 2020			Change 2019 to 2020	
	Full-time in main job	Part-time in main job	Total-Employees	Full-time in main job	Part-time in main job	Total-Employees	Total	%
	'000	'000	'000	'000	'000	'000	'000	%
Sex								
Male	4,324.0	1,020.0	5,344.0	4,245.6	984.7	5,230.3	(113.70)	-2.13
Female	2,816.9	2,456.2	5,273.1	2,794.5	2,361.5	5,156.0	(117.11)	-2.22
Age group (years)								
15–19	147.4	509.5	656.9	115.1	468.6	583.7	(73.18)	-11.14
20–24	639.6	551.3	1,190.9	584.4	519.8	1,104.3	(86.63)	-7.27
25–34	2,038.1	660.8	2,698.9	1,988.5	636.3	2,624.7	(74.17)	-2.75
35–44	1,695.1	572.1	2,267.2	1,676.6	600.2	2,276.9	9.67	0.43
45–54	1,523.5	523.4	2,046.9	1,552.7	495.9	2,048.6	1.65	0.08
55–59	595.6	256.1	851.8	601.2	244.6	845.8	(6.02)	-0.71
60–64	358.6	215.5	574.0	377.1	195.8	572.9	(1.12)	-0.20
65 and over	143.1	187.4	330.6	144.6	185.0	329.5	(1.09)	-0.33

Source: ABS, 6333.0 Characteristics of Employment, Australia, August 2019 and August 2020, and author's own calculations.

workers, especially those aged fifteen to nineteen (with employment down 11.14 per cent from August 2019 to August 2020) and twenty to twenty-four (down 7.27 per cent), reflecting their over-representation in casual employment and in service industries. Employment declined for all ages *except* those aged thirty-five to fifty-four, where employment increased slightly. Women's employment (down 2.2 per cent) declined slightly more than men's (down 2.13 per cent).

Casual (zero-hours) employment overall dropped significantly as a share of total employment with Covid-19-related shutdowns and lockdowns (Figure 13.2). This likely had a disproportionate effect on women and younger workers. This, in part, reflects the nature of casual employment; it is easier to lay-off someone with no entitlement to work. It also, however, reflects the shape of the Australian government's job retention scheme, JobKeeper, which excluded casual workers with less than twelve months 'employed on a regular and systematic basis', those under the age of eighteen, and migrant workers. It is estimated that JobKeeper avoided around 700,000 job losses between April and July 2020.[48] Yet the JobKeeper scheme was ill-designed to support those most affected by Covid-19: women were slightly under-represented among JobKeeper recipients; and young workers were significantly under-represented, reflecting their overrepresentation in short-term casual work, and as migrant workers.[49]

The employment impacts of Covid-19 were largely remedied by December 2020, with a strong recovery in employment in most Australian jurisdictions.[50] This may reflect the largely successful quashing of Covid-19 cases in most Australian jurisdictions; and the JobKeeper job retention scheme.[51] The exception to this overall Australian success story was in metropolitan Melbourne, which experienced the longest lockdown of any city in Australia due to a large second wave of Covid-19 cases.[52] By the end of 2020, lower-skilled older workers in some sectors still experienced significant deleterious effects on employment: long-term job loss for older workers was concentrated in industries such as manufacturing; retail; health care and social administration; transport, postal, warehouse; arts and recreation; and information, media and telecommunications.[53]

The Australian recovery is still jeopardized by two factors: the phase out of JobKeeper in 2021, and continued lockdowns in Victoria and New South Wales over the course of 2021. Thus, the continued impact of Covid-19 on work remains to be seen. It is possible, too, that Covid-19 will have long-term deleterious effects on mental and physical wellbeing, including for those who were working from home while caring for children, and especially for women.[54] In a survey of 988 people

---

[48] James Bishop and Iris Day, 'How Many Jobs Did JobKeeper Keep?' Research Discussion Paper 2020–07 https://www.rba.gov.au/publications/rdp/2020/pdf/rdp2020-07.pdf (accessed 1 April 2022).
[49] Treasury, 'Insights from the First Six Months of JobKeeper' (Commonwealth of Australia 2021) 21 https://treasury.gov.au/sites/default/files/2021-10/p2021-211978_0.pdf (accessed 16 November 2021).
[50] Jane Fry and others, 'COVID-19 and the Australian Labour Market: How Did Older Australians Fare during 2020?' (2021) 5(2) Australian Population Studies 29.
[51] Anthony Forsyth, 'COVID-19 and Labour Law: Australia' (2020) 13 Italian Labour Law e-Journal https://illej.unibo.it/article/view/10812 (accessed 16 February 2021).
[52] Fry and others (n 50).
[53] ibid.
[54] Yijing Xiao and others, 'Impacts of Working from Home During COVID-19 Pandemic on Physical and Mental Well-Being of Office Workstation Users' (2021) 63 Journal of Occupational and Environmental Medicine 181.

working from home, women were more likely to report new physical or mental issues occurring during their time working from home; these problems were strongly associated with experiencing disruptions while attempting to work, perhaps reflecting work-life strain.[55] The equality impacts of Covid-19 are therefore far from over.

7 Reconfiguring Equality Law to Respond to Exponential Inequalities

The foregoing discussion has emphasized the way in which exponential inequalities accelerate over the life course, across grounds and across contexts. These are largely systemic problems, embedded in our approach to work, family, and caring. It is these systemic and structural problems, however, that equality law struggles to address effectively.[56]

To address escalating discrimination and inequality over the life course, interventions must:

- be targeted across the life course, rather than at discrete incidents or periods
- recognize the way in which forms of inequality are overlapping, intersectional and compounding, across grounds and contexts
- be tailored to focus on critical points for inequality or discrimination, as during life course transitions or periods of crisis and
- address the individual, group, and community impacts of discrimination.

Using these criteria, discrimination law appears fundamentally ill-adapted for responding to exponential inequalities. Discrimination law largely depends on individual enforcement, relying on individuals making claims for redress. This model primarily responds to discrete instances or contexts of discrimination, rather than discrimination over the life course. Further, recognition of intersectionality is generally limited;[57] discrimination on the basis of multiple different grounds is treated as raising discrete, disaggregable issues.[58] Both the process of individual enforcement and the remedies that are awarded focus on individual redress, rather than the communal and collective impacts of discrimination.[59] Discrimination law is best used to address instances of overt discrimination, not cases of subtle, systemic inequality.[60] Discrimination law is therefore unlikely to respond to escalating discrimination and inequality over the life course in any meaningful way.

---

[55] ibid.
[56] Susan Sturm, 'Second Generation Employment Discrimination: A Structural Approach' (2001) 101 Columbia Law Review 458.
[57] Shreya Atrey, *Intersectional Discrimination* (OUP 2019).
[58] ibid; Blackham and Temple (n 22).
[59] Blackham (n 16).
[60] Alysia Blackham, 'Why Do Employment Age Discrimination Cases Fail? An Analysis of Australian Case Law' (2020) 42 Sydney Law Review 1.

7.1 'Next Generation' Positive Equality Duties

A potential solution lies in the adoption of 'next generation' positive equality duties. Positive duties themselves represent a 'next generation' of equality law. They offer a radical tool for repositioning equality law to become proactive, focus on cultural change, achieve substantive equality,[61] address deeply embedded structural discrimination,[62] and make equality part of 'core business' in organizations.[63] They are potentially critical tools for addressing exponential inequalities.

However, there remain serious concerns as to how effective positive duties are in practice. The UK Public Sector Equality Duty (PSED), for example, has been criticized for being overly reliant on enforcement via judicial review proceedings,[64] leading to an emphasis on process not outcomes, exacerbating 'box ticking',[65] and proceduralized compliance,[66] at the expense of actual change[67] and inhibiting effective organizational problem-solving.[68] However, examining evidence presented to the 2013 review of the PSED, Manfredi and others identify three positive impacts of the PSED. First, public authorities reported that they had improved their data collection and monitoring systems.[69] Secondly, there were multiple examples of good practice in relation to consultation; thirdly, and relatedly, this participative dimension helped to empower non-governmental organizations to hold government authorities to account.[70] However, the PSED does not require consultation or engagement in England, and it is unclear how widespread these positive impacts have been.

A 'next generation' positive duty may be evolving in the Australian state of Victoria, where the legal framework has been designed specifically to address and respond to the limits of positive duties in other jurisdictions. The Gender Equality Act 2020 (Vic) seeks 'to drive gender equality in the community and the workplace' as 'the first [Act] of its kind in any jurisdiction in Australia'.[71] This Act imposes a positive duty to consider and promote gender equality on defined entities in Victoria,[72] including public sector organizations, universities, and local councils with more than fifty employees.[73]

---

[61] Sandra Fredman, *Human Rights Transformed: Positive Rights and Positive Duties* (OUP 2008)175.
[62] Anne CL Davies, *Perspectives on Labour Law* (2nd edn, CUP 2009)135.
[63] Department for Communities and Local Government, 'Discrimination Law Review. A Framework for Fairness: Proposals for a Single Equality Bill for Great Britain. A Consultation Paper' (2007) 79 [5.3].
[64] Sandra Fredman, 'Breaking the Mold: Equality as a Proactive Duty' (2012) 60 American Journal of Comparative Law 265, 270.
[65] Simonetta Manfredi, Lucy Vickers, and Kate Clayton-Hathway, 'The Public Sector Equality Duty: Enforcing Equality Rights Through Second-Generation Regulation' (2018) 47 Industrial Law Journal 365, 374–75.
[66] Sandra Fredman, 'The Public Sector Equality Duty' (2011) 40 Industrial Law Journal 405, 420; Fredman (n 64) 276.
[67] Fredman (n 64) 276.
[68] Lizzie Barmes, *Bullying and Behavioural Conflict at Work: The Duality of Individual Rights* (OUP 2016)9, 212.
[69] Manfredi, Vickers, and Clayton-Hathway (n 65) 381.
[70] ibid 379–81.
[71] Victoria, *Parliamentary Debates* Legislative Assembly (27 November 2019) 4586 (Gabrielle Williams).
[72] Gender Equality Act 2020 (Vic), s 7.
[73] ibid s 5(1).

Defined entities must take necessary and proportionate action towards achieving gender equality in developing policies and programmes and delivering public services.[74] More specifically, defined entities are required to: undertake workplace gender audits, to assess gender (in)equality in the workplace;[75] develop and implement Gender Equality Action Plans;[76] undertake gender impact assessments when developing or reviewing any policy, or public programme or service;[77] make 'reasonable and material progress' towards workplace gender equality indicators,[78] including gender composition of all levels of the workforce, gender composition of governing bodies, equal remuneration for work of equal or comparable value, sexual harassment, recruitment and promotion practices, availability and utilization of terms, conditions, and practices relating to family violence leave, flexible working arrangements, and working arrangements supporting employees with family or caring responsibilities, gendered segregation within the workplace, and any other prescribed matters;[79] and publicly report on progress every two years.[80] The relevant minister may also issue guidelines in relation to the allocation of funding[81] and procurement.[82]

The duties and responsibilities created by the Act advance existing positive equality duties in three key ways. First, in relation to *intersectionality*, the Act requires defined entities to consider intersectionality when conducting gender impact assessments[83] and workplace gender audits.[84] The Act explicitly requires defined entities to base their gender workplace audit on gender-disaggregated data and, if available, data about aboriginality, age, disability, ethnicity, gender identity, race, religion, and sexual orientation.[85] The Act may therefore encourage defined entities to adopt a more data-driven and intersectional approach to workplace equality, reflecting a more authentic approach to identifying and addressing discrimination.

Secondly, (unlike in England) the Act embeds *consultation* as an essential feature of its procedural requirements. The Act explicitly requires defined entities to consult when preparing Gender Equality Action Plans[86] and to publish Gender Equality Action Plans on their website and notify relevant stakeholders of the publication.[87] It is not yet clear whether this will be sufficient to ensure quality consultation and an action cycle of engagement.[88]

---

[74] ibid s 7.
[75] ibid s 11.
[76] ibid s 10.
[77] ibid s 9.
[78] ibid s 16(1).
[79] ibid s 3.
[80] ibid s 19.
[81] ibid s 48.
[82] ibid s 49.
[83] ibid s 9(2)(c).
[84] ibid s 11(2)(c).
[85] ibid s 11(3).
[86] ibid s 10(2)(b).
[87] ibid s 12(3).
[88] Alysia Blackham, 'Positive Equality Duties: The Future of Equality and Transparency?' (2021) 37(2) Law in Context 98.

Thirdly, the Act does not just impose procedural requirements; it demands *progress* towards gender equality,[89] while also taking into account the specific needs of individual defined entities.[90] The new Victorian Commissioner for Gender Equality in the Public Sector is specifically empowered to issue compliance notices for a failure to make substantive progress towards gender equality.[91] This focus on outcomes, rather than procedure, is unique to the Act; the PSED, for example, contains no specific outcome measures.

7.2 Addressing Exponential Inequalities?

By embedding recognition of intersectionality in its provisions, and demanding progress towards equality, the Act might be seen as a tool for addressing amplifying age inequalities. The Act addresses gender inequality in both the workplace and in the public sphere, engaging defined entities in their multiple roles as employers and public entities. It potentially offers a means of addressing inequality and discrimination across the life course, reflecting the substantial role of the public service in providing education and training, as an employer (in June 2020, employing 322,605 employees of the 3,277,200 employed persons in Victoria), in providing aged care, and in the provision of public services such as housing, health, and transport.

However, key aspects of the Act remain under-utilized. Potentially radical aspects— around gender targets, quotas, and procurement—have been left to the regulations;[92] no targets or quotas have been set to date. Further, the workplace gender equality indicators,[93] which defined entities must make 'reasonable and material progress' towards, exclude superannuation and the gender pension gap, though gender pay gaps are included. This limits the ability to identify and address escalating inequalities over time.

Concerningly, too, there is no provision for individual enforcement of the Act. The duty does not give rise to individual rights to enforcement, create grounds for review or affect the validity of any act.[94] It is unclear what impact this will have in practice, and how it might limit the Act's effectiveness. By contrast, the PSED may be enforced via judicial review proceedings; key progress in relation to the PSED has been made via such claims.[95] Surveying the PSED case law, McColgan concludes that while: 'it would be wrong to suggest that all of the work in the area of equality law is being done by the PSED ... [it is] noteworthy that a duty which began with relatively limited apparent potential has proved so significant in practice'.[96]

---

[89] Gender Equality Act 2020 (Vic), ss 16(1), 18(1)–(2).
[90] ibid ss 16(2), 18(3).
[91] ibid s 22.
[92] ibid s 17.
[93] ibid s 16(1).
[94] ibid s 8.
[95] Helen Carr, 'The Public Sector Equality Duty—a Mainstay of Justice in an Age of Austerity' (2014) 36 Journal of Social Welfare and Family Law 208; Jennifer Sigafoos, 'Using Equality Legislation as a Sword' (2016) 16 International Journal of Discrimination and the Law 66.
[96] Aileen McColgan, 'Litigating the Public Sector Equality Duty: The Story So Far' (2015) 35 Oxford Journal of Legal Studies 453, 481–82.

Much will depend, then, on how the Victorian Act is implemented by public bodies, and the implementation and enforcement action undertaken by the Commission. That said, the processes created by the Act may have their own beneficial equality impacts.[97]

Further, while the Act is grounded in a broad vision of equality as a human right, to which all are entitled,[98] the specific provisions of the Act are primarily focused on the workplace, workforce and 'employees'.[99] The definition of 'employee' explicitly excludes:

(a) a contractor or subcontractor or
(b) an outworker or
(c) a person on a vocational placement or
(d) a student gaining work experience or
(e) a volunteer.[100]

The omission of volunteers from the scope of the Act was driven by practical considerations and the potential 'burden' on defined entities, irrespective of the practical importance of volunteers in advancing gender equality.[101] This raises complex questions about who is included—and excluded—from the push to advance gender equality in the public sector.

This limited scope may have wide-ranging consequences in practice. Non-employees potentially represent a significant proportion of the public sector workforce, though it is difficult to trace how substantial this is in practice. While the Victorian government is attempting to reduce its reliance on contractors and labour hire,[102] in the financial year ending 30 June 2018, Victorian departmental expenditure on contractors, consultants and labour hire was A$1.7 billion.[103] The Victorian Public Accounts and Estimates Committee has found that all Victorian government departments use contractors, consultants and labour hire for information technology and telecommunication skills, and across a range of functions including administration, consulting and strategy, human resources, analyst, accounting, legal, projects, property, economics, research, education and training, marketing and media, governance

---

[97] Manfredi, Vickers, and Clayton-Hathway (n 65).
[98] Gender Equality Act 2020 (Vic), s 6. See also Charter of Human Rights and Responsibilities 2006 (Vic), s 8(3); Victoria, *Parliamentary Debates* (n 71).
[99] Gender Equality Act 2020 (Vic), s 3.
[100] ibid.
[101] Victorian Department of Premier and Cabinet, 'Gender Equality Bill Consultation Feedback Report' 15 https://s3.ap-southeast-2.amazonaws.com/hdp.au.prod.app.vic-engage.files/3915/7481/1417/Gender_Equality_Bill_Consultation_Feedback_Report.pdf (accessed 21 May 2021).
[102] Stephen Easton, 'How the Victorian Government Plans to Wean the Public Service off Labour Hire and Consultants' *The Mandarin* (15 July 2019) https://www.themandarin.com.au/111568-how-the-victorian-government-plans-to-wean-the-public-service-off-labour-hire-and-consultants/ (accessed 26 May 2021); Michael Fowler, 'Unions Rage as Victorian Government Plans to Cut Back Public Sector Wage Growth' *The Age* (15 May 2021) https://www.theage.com.au/politics/victoria/unions-rage-as-victorian-government-plans-to-cut-back-public-sector-wage-growth-20210515-p57s89.html (accessed 26 May 2021). See also the commitments reported in Public Accounts and Estimates Committee, *Report on the 2019–20 Budget Estimates* (Parliament of Victoria 2019) https://www.parliament.vic.gov.au/file_uploads/PAEC_59-03_Report_on_the_2019-20_Budget_Estimates_K8QQBvTH.pdf (accessed April 1 2022).
[103] Public Accounts and Estimates Committee (n 102) 47.

and customer service/call centres.[104] Departments often pay above-market rates for these services.[105] The Department of Premier and Cabinet (DPC) (which includes the Office for Women) in its response to the Public Accounts and Estimates Committee, for example, reported that it engaged the full-time equivalent (FTE) of eleven contractors, one consultant, and twenty-three labour hire arrangements on the last working day of 2017–18; data on FTE was not available for 2018–19 or 2019–20.[106] This FTE data covers only one day in 2017–18; it is likely to be a significant under-estimate of actual contractors engaged. In the financial year ending 30 June 2018, DPC spent A$78.4 million on contractors, A$11.4 million on consultants, and A$15.8 million on labour hire arrangements.[107] That same year, employee expenses for DPC were A$192.7 million; thus, non-employee expenses represented the equivalent of 54.8 per cent of all employee expenses. Figures for OHS training allow us to estimate that there were approximately 934 contractors, 'temps', and visitors at DPC in 2017–18. Despite efforts to reduce consultancies, in 2019–20, DPC reported spending over A$13.8 million on fifty-nine consultancies, compared with A$253.4 million on employee expenses[108] across 1,070 employees; contractors were not reported.

By excluding non-employees, the Act imposes no requirement for public entities to consider or address inequalities in contracting, consultancies, or labour hire arrangements.[109] It also omits consideration of pathways and gateways to work, including through vocational placements, work experience, or volunteering. Unpaid work experience can provide a competitive edge in later obtaining paid employment.[110] Discrimination in work experience may therefore have flow-on effects for the labour market generally.[111] Work experience is often obtained through personal or familial connections,[112] excluding those from non-traditional backgrounds who do not have access to strong personal networks.[113] Gender pay gaps also emerge in work experience placements: men are more likely than women to receive financial compensation in their work experience, including via an allowance or honorarium, and reimbursement of expenses.[114] Given the prevalence of work experience and internship

---

[104] ibid 47–48.

[105] ibid 47.

[106] Public Accounts and Estimates Committee, '2019-20 Budget Estimates General Questionnaire: Department of Premier and Cabinet' (2019) 41 https://www.parliament.vic.gov.au/images/stories/committees/paec/2019-20_Budget_Estimates/BEQ_responses/DPC_2019-20_Budget_Estimates_Questionnaire_response_.pdf (accessed 26 May 2021).

[107] ibid.

[108] Employee expenses comprise all costs related to employment including wages and salaries, superannuation, fringe benefits tax, leave entitlements, redundancy payments, WorkCover premiums, and other on-costs.

[109] It is possible, of course, that non-employees may be captured incidentally by other duties on defined entities, including the duty to consider and promote gender equality in developing policies and programmes and delivering services; and through procurement, although these mechanisms are currently under-developed.

[110] Damian Oliver and others, 'Unpaid Work Experience in Australia: Prevalence, Nature and Impact' (2016) 9, 50 https://docs.employment.gov.au/node/37506 (accessed 19 July 2017).

[111] See eg Andrew Francis and Hilary Sommerlad, 'Access to Legal Work Experience and Its Role in the (Re)Production of Legal Professional Identity' (2009) 16 International Journal of the Legal Profession 63.

[112] Oliver and others (n 110) 36.

[113] ibid 5, 24.

[114] ibid 46.

arrangements,[115] omitting this form of work from the Act's scope may undermine advances towards gender equality in the workplace, particularly from a life course perspective. The Act's limited scope also ignores the fragility and scarcity of the standard employment relationship in the modern workplace.

Despite the Act's radical potential, then, it has serious limitations in addressing exponential inequalities over the life course. The Act does not seek to address age inequality specifically, except as it intersects with gender. The Act's gaps in scope disproportionately affect younger and older people, by omitting internships, work experience, and outsourced labour arrangements from consideration, and excluding consideration of the gender pension gap. These concerns have become even more relevant in times of crisis: for example, the Victorian government outsourced the majority of its Covid-19 testing, tracking, and tracing operations to third parties;[116] in one case, an outsourced call centre was at the centre of a Covid-19 outbreak.[117]

8 Conclusion: Embracing a Life Course Approach to Addressing Exponential Inequalities

While the Gender Equality Act 2020 (Vic) might reflect a missed opportunity for addressing exponential inequalities, there are glimmers of hope in how we might adopt a life course approach to addressing inequality and discrimination. Such a model should leverage the key strengths of government as providers of services, employers, and procurers, across the life course. Public entities must adopt an integrated and solidaristic life course model in their operations. This requires coordinated data monitoring and sharing across different governmental entities, to identify and rectify inequalities as they emerge across the life course.

Further, a life course approach to addressing inequality and discrimination must adopt targeted support for life course transitions, including when moving into and out of education, work, caring, and periods of ill-health. This could be supported, for example, by a guaranteed income, or 'life-course transition payments', which ensure adequate financial support as people move in and out of employment.[118] This approach allows people to transition more smoothly between caring, education, and work; it could particularly support women's workforce participation and financial security

---

[115] ibid.

[116] Legal and Social Issues Committee, 'Inquiry into the Victorian Government's COVID–19 Contact Tracing System and Testing Regime' (2020) Legislative Council PP No 193, Session 2018-2020 99–100 https://www.parliament.vic.gov.au/images/stories/committees/SCLSI/Inquiry_into_the_Victorian_Governments_COVID19_Contact_Tracing_System_and_Testing_Regime_/report/LCLSIC_59-05_Vic_Gov_COVID-19_contact_tracing_testing.pdf (accessed 16 November 2021).

[117] Cassandra Morgan and Paul Sakkal, 'Outbreak Spreads to Contact Tracing Call Centre as State Records 176 Cases' *The Age* (2 September 2021) https://www.theage.com.au/national/victoria/victoria-records-176-local-covid-19-cases-as-families-set-for-small-reprieve-20210902-p58o24.html (accessed 16 November 2021).

[118] Kai Leichsenring and Andrea E Schmidt, 'The Economic Dimension of Population Ageing: From "Silver Economy" to "Ageing 4.0"' (2016) Presentation at the Ninth Meeting of the UNECE Working Group on Ageing https://unece.org/fileadmin/DAM/pau/age/WG9/Presentations/3_EconomicDimension_Ageing_WGA_Leichsenring_20161123.pdf (accessed 1 April 2022).

across the life course, and would serve to normalize and de-stigmatize workforce re-entry at later ages.

In leveraging the role of the public sector, and recognizing the diversity of work arrangements within and outside the public sector, it makes limited sense to constrain equality interventions to support 'employees' alone; a broader view of work must be adopted. This broader view is already adopted in other Australian equality statutes, to include contractors[119] and unpaid work experience within the definition of 'work'. For example, the schedule to the Queensland Anti-Discrimination Act 1991 defines 'work' to include:

(e) work under a work experience arrangement ...;
(ea) work under a vocational placement;
(f) work on a voluntary or unpaid basis; and ...
(h) work under a guidance program, an apprenticeship training program or other occupational training or retraining program.

'Employment' is defined to include unpaid work in South Australia,[120] the Australian Capital Territory,[121] and Tasmania;[122] and 'work' is defined in the Northern Territory to include that 'under a guidance program, vocational training program or other occupational training or retraining program'.[123] Given initiatives like the Gender Equality Act 2020 (Vic) are aimed at achieving radical transformation of the public sector, the scope should also be ambitious.

Finally, as in the Gender Equality Act 2020 (Vic), interventions must embrace the complex compoundedness of intersectionality. It is not easy to operationalize intersectionality; the implementation of the Gender Equality Act 2020 (Vic) has flagged the limited data being collected by the public sector on intersectional inequalities, and the limited understanding of intersectionality among many public bodies.[124] However, even raising these questions has created a degree of movement and change among the Victorian public sector. By identifying and maximizing these glimmers of hope, we can start to tackle even exponential inequalities.

---

[119] Alysia Blackham, '"We Are All Entrepreneurs Now": Options and New Approaches for Adapting Equality Law for the "Gig Economy"' (2018) 34 International Journal of Comparative Labour Law and Industrial Relations 413.
[120] Equal Opportunity Act 1984 (SA), s 5(1).
[121] Discrimination Act 1991 (ACT), dictionary.
[122] Anti-Discrimination Act 1998 (Tas), s 3 ('employment or occupation in any capacity, with or without remuneration').
[123] Anti-Discrimination Act 1992 (NT), s 4(1).
[124] Lauren Ryan and others, 'Laying the Foundation for Gender Equality in the Public Sector in Victoria: Final Project Report' (University of Melbourne 2022) https://doi.org/10.26188/19254539 (accessed 21 April 2022).

14
Disability in Times of Emergency
Exponential Inequality and the Role of Reasonable Accommodation Duties

Anna Lawson and Lisa Waddington

1 Introduction

There is ample evidence that people with disabilities have been disproportionately adversely affected by the Covid-19 pandemic. This relates not only to the risks of contracting the virus and death, but also to their opportunities to access basic necessities such as food, healthcare, and essential public health information. In this chapter, we reflect on the value of legislation which prohibits disability discrimination in such an unprecedented situation. Specifically, we explore whether the reasonable accommodation duty, which is found in disability equality law, is 'fit for purpose' in times of crisis and whether variations of the classic reasonable accommodation duty might be better suited to the task.

Modern disability equality law, at the national and supranational (eg EU and UN) level, goes beyond the prohibition of direct and indirect discrimination, and establishes an obligation to accommodate the needs of disabled individuals. The reasonable accommodation obligation requires duty-bearers, such as employers or service providers, not to ignore disability, as is the case with regard to most protected grounds covered by non-discrimination law, but specifically to take disability into account, and to make an adjustment, alteration or accommodation to their standard practices, policies, and structures in order to meet the needs of a particular disabled individual.

One limitation of the 'traditional' reasonable accommodation duty is that it is ex post, in that it is triggered only when an individual with a disability indicates that they are facing a barrier. This allows duty-bearers to ignore the needs of disabled people up until the point that an accommodation request is made, and not to consider in advance the impact of their policies, even on broad groups of disabled people who have predictable needs, such as blind people or people who use wheelchairs. Other types of reasonable accommodation, adjustment or modification duty adopt a different, more pro-active or ex ante approach. One example is the anticipatory reasonable adjustment duty in the Equality Act 2010 (as applicable in England, Scotland, and Wales). This requires duty-bearers to consider the needs of disabled people, to the extent that they are reasonably foreseeable, in advance of an individual request being made. Duty-bearers are therefore required to provide reasonable adjustments, such as rendering buildings accessible to wheelchair users and providing basic information in Braille and easy to read text, as part of delivering their services or public functions. In this chapter, we reflect on both types of reasonable accommodation duty, reflecting on their respective relevance and contribution in times of crisis.

The chapter begins by presenting evidence of the disproportionately negative impact (or 'exponential inequality') Covid-19 has had on disabled people, drawing on research from across Europe. Secondly, it explores the 'traditional' ex post reasonable accommodation duty, and discusses how it applies to situations of (extreme) disadvantage experienced by disabled people. Thirdly, it reflects on the ex ante anticipatory reasonable adjustment duty in the Equality Act 2010 and its use during the pandemic. We conclude that the latter group-based type of discrimination prohibition seems to have proved much more useful to disabled people during the Covid-19 emergency than the former and reflect on some of the implications of this finding.

2 Exponential Inequality: The Disproportionate Impact of the Covid-19 Emergency on Disabled People

In this section, we draw attention to the disability-related impact of the Covid-19 emergency, drawing on evidence from countries in the EU and the UK. Our aim is not to present an exhaustive account—a project which would be well beyond the scale of what is possible here. Rather, we wish simply to provide readers with an indication of some of the ways in which disabled people were disproportionately—or unequally—affected by this global crisis. We also reflect briefly on the possible causes of this inequality before moving on to our analysis of the effectiveness of reasonable accommodation and related non-discrimination obligations in times of crisis.

While the Covid-19 emergency has touched all population groups, there is growing evidence that it has hit people with disabilities disproportionately hard. The fact that this data has been slow to emerge is itself significant. Writing of the UK, but making observations replicated across many countries,[1] Shakespeare and others note that: 'this population is strangely missing from important analyses which have been published during the Pandemic', including ones which investigate the impact of the crisis on children and its racial and gender disparities, including in the context of care.[2] It is an omission which they rightly describe as 'astounding', especially in light of the important work done by disabled people's organizations throughout the pandemic to draw attention to the particular disability-related impact of the crisis.[3]

---

[1] See eg the Global Covid-19 Disability Rights Monitor https://www.covid-drm.org/ (accessed 5 April 2022).

[2] Tom Shakespeare and others, 'Disabled People in Britain and the Impact of the COVID 19 Pandemic' (2021) 56 Social Policy and Administration 103.

[3] See for relevant UK examples, Greater Manchester Coalition of Disabled People, 'Greater Manchester Disabled People's Panel: GM Big Disability Survey: Covid-19' (2020) 13a Appendix 1 - GM Disabled Peoples Panel 2020-21.pdf (greatermanchester-ca.gov.uk) (accessed 11 March 2022); Inclusion London, 'Abandoned, Forgotten, Ignored: The Impact of the Coronavirus Pandemic on Disabled People: Interim Report' (2020) https://www.inclusionlondon.org.uk/wpcontent/uploads/2020/06/Abandoned-Forgotten-and-Ignored-Final-1.pdf (accessed 11 March 2022); Inclusion Scotland, 'Rights at Risk: Covid-19, Disabled People and Emergency Planning in Scotland' (2020) <Rights At Risk—Covid-19, disabled people and emergency planning in Scotland—a baseline report from Inclusion Scotland. (October 2020)—SCVO (accessed 11 March 2022); Glasgow Disability Alliance, 'Supercharged: A Human Catastrophe' (2020) https://gda.scot/wp-content/uploads/2020/08/GDA-Supercharged-Covid-19Report.pdf (accessed 11 March 2022).

Statistics on the proportion of Covid-19-related deaths of people with disabilities, compared with those of people without disabilities, are not available at the EU level. Nor are they available from most European countries. Where such data is available, however, a clear disability gap is evident. In Croatia, for example, amongst those who had died of Covid-19 prior to January 2021, 38 per cent were disabled people—a figure significantly higher than the proportion of disabled people in the general Croatian population.[4] In the UK, nearly six in ten Covid-19-related deaths between January and November 2020 were of disabled people.[5] Despite making up only 17 per cent of the population, disabled people made up 60 per cent of those who died from Covid-19 in the UK during this period. This data also suggests that the risk of Covid-19-related death is three times higher for more severely disabled people.

These figures are stark. Still more shocking is an earlier report of Public Health England,[6] according to which, of the deaths from Covid-19 between 21 March and 5 June 2020 amongst people aged between eighteen and thirty-four, there were six times as many deaths of people with learning disabilities than of non-disabled people. Also significant is its indication that a third of the people with a learning disability who died of Covid-19 over this period lived in residential care. In the Netherlands too, research indicates a significantly higher Covid-19 death rate for people with intellectual disabilities—in this case, one that is four times higher than the death rate amongst the general population.[7] The Dutch study also revealed that, up to July 2021, 83 per cent of people with an intellectual disability who tested positive for Covid-19 lived in a group home, compared to 16 per cent who lived in their own apartment,[8] suggesting that institutional settings were a particular hotbed of infection.

Data from elsewhere also suggests that a significant number of Covid-19-related deaths were of people living in care homes, many of whom are disabled people. Thus, in Slovenia, 51 per cent of people who died with Covid-19 were residents of long-stay institutional care for older and disabled people.[9] In France, the figure was 43 per cent[10] and in Austria 44 per cent.[11]

---

[4] Ombudsman for persons with disabilities, 'Recommendations for persons with disabilities and the public regarding coronavirus' https://posi.hr/koronavirus/ (accessed 11 March 2022).

[5] Office for National Statistics, 'Updated Estimates of Coronavirus (COVID-19) Related Deaths by Disability Status, England' https://www.ons.gov.uk/peoplepopulationandcommunity/birthsdeathsandmarriages/deaths/articles/coronaviruscovid19relateddeathsbydisabilitystatusenglandandwales/24januaryto20november2020 (accessed 11 March 2022).

[6] Public Health England, 'COVID-19 Deaths of People Identified as Having Learning Disabilities' (2020) https://www.gov.uk/government/publications/covid-19-deaths-of-people-with-learning-disabilities (accessed 11 March 2022).

[7] Sterker Op Eigen Benen and Radboud UMC, 'Factsheet No. 17, Update 2 July 2021', COVID-19 in people with intellectual disabilities (Academic Hospital Radboud, Nijmegen) (2021) 2 https://0da93f8e-6ee7-45d9-be21-eecb55ca3e69.filesusr.com/ugd/d45b6c_424aa975d61c43288eed70c84d4ea798.pdf (accessed 11 March 2022).

[8] ibid 3.

[9] Nacionalni Inštitut za javno zdravje, 'Epidemiološko spremljanje umrlih: covid-19' (2021) https://www.nijz.si/sites/www.nijz.si/files/uploaded/umrli_COVID-19_01022021.pdf (accessed 11 March 2022).

[10] Adelina Comas-Herrera and others, 'Mortality Associated with COVID-19 in Care Homes: International Evidence' (2021) International Long-Term Care Policy Network, CPEC-LSE 1 https://ltccovid.org/wp-content/uploads/2021/02/LTC_COVID_19_international_report_January-1-February-.pdf (accessed 11 March 2022).

[11] ibid.

In relation to access to healthcare for Covid-19, Austria introduced triage checklists which gave many disabled people low priority on the basis of issues such as daily life activity and frailty level.[12] In Slovenia, following public concern about what were termed the 'registers of the written off'[13] the practice of determining in advance that certain care home residents would not be moved to hospital should they contract Covid-19 complications, carried out between March and June 2020, was overturned in July of that year.

The pandemic has also disproportionately impacted disabled people because of withdrawal of, and disruption to, the health-related services on which they depend. Shakespeare and others note that people with disabilities in the UK told them of the cancellation of routine physiotherapy, speech and language therapy, occupational therapy, and annual check-ups.[14] Similarly, a Portuguese survey found that, after the two lockdowns (in April–May 2020 and October 2020), many healthcare services (such as physiotherapy, speech therapy, occupational therapy, medical appointments, and nursing care) remained largely suspended or only partially operational.[15] One study, in May 2020, estimated that the Covid-19 crisis meant that up to 2.2 million people in Europe had had to interrupt rehabilitation treatment.[16]

Another issue, particularly prominent in the UK, was a lack of accessibility of important government communications about Covid-19.[17] Some of the televised Covid-19 briefings from Downing Street were not sign-language interpreted. Further, while these televised broadcasts were helpful in that they could reach people who could not access the internet, Shakespeare and others report that they 'were not sufficient to help people with learning difficulties in particular to understand what they should do differently'.[18] Although issues concerning inaccessible government Covid-19-related communication have had a particularly high profile in the UK, some people with disabilities also encountered similar problems in other countries. In Portugal, for example, a survey found that only 80 per cent of disabled people and care-givers found government information accessible in the first wave of the pandemic, and 69 per cent in the second wave.[19]

A combination of factors intensified the difficulties associated with lockdowns and social distancing experienced by many people with disabilities. Shakespeare and

---

[12] Österreichischer Behindertenrat, 'Triage: Menschen mit Behinderungen mehrfach gefährdet' (2020) https://www.bizeps.or.at/triage-menschen-mit-behinderungen-mehrfach-gefaehrdet/ (accessed 11 March 2022).

[13] Vasja Jager, 'Were the Elders Written Off in Advance?' *Mladina* (15 May 2020) https://www.mladina.si/198410/so-bili-starostniki-ze-vnaprej-odpisani/?fbclid=IwAR3xVmY6lW1JNNqytbcMugcngZcT5ZT_atRwhB_AiLHRRjvy4yq5CWSUIvs (accessed 11 March 2022).

[14] Shakespeare and others (n 2) s 3.1.

[15] Disability and Human Rights Observatory, 'Deficiência e Covid-19 em Portugal' (Pessoas com Deficiência em Portugal: Indicadores de Direitos Humanos, 2020) http://oddh.iscsp.ulisboa.pt/index.php/pt/2013-04-24-18-50-23/publicacoes-dos-investigadores-oddh/item/483-relatorio-oddh-2020 (accessed 11 March 2022).

[16] Stefano Negrini and others, 'Up to 2.2 million People Experiencing Disability Suffer Collateral Damage each day of COVID-19 Lockdown in Europe' (2020) 56 European Journal of Physical and Rehabilitation Medicine 361.

[17] Shakespeare and others (n 2) s 3.4.

[18] ibid.

[19] Deficiência e Covid-19 em Portugal (n 15).

others note that their interviewees drew attention to the major disruption to the provision, repair, and service of assistive equipment and technologies essential to their daily lives. According to one of the participants:

> I've ... been stuck upstairs for fourteen weeks because my [stair]lift has broken down and the local authority has been arguing with me about replacing the lift. They're wanting me to live downstairs. I've stayed in my bathroom, my study and my bedroom after fourteen weeks.[20]

They also found that day centres and large parts of the social care system often became unavailable. The result, for a significant number of the interviewees, was increased social isolation and dependence on family.

Similar developments are noted in a study carried out by the European Disability Expertise network. In many countries, people with disabilities (together with older people) were advised to adopt more extreme social isolation or distancing measures than the rest of the population, but often without mechanisms to ensure their continued access to food, basic necessities, personal assistance, and social care services.[21] In addition, facilities important to the lives of many disabled people closed. For example in Ireland, over 1,000 day centres (offering disabled people opportunities for employment, training, and socializing) ceased offering services from mid-March 2020 to the end of the summer, and even then services were only partially resumed.[22] Poverty is also an important factor, as stressed by the National Council for Disability in Romania, which reported that some of its members were plunged into unprecedented levels of poverty, including not having access to basic necessities such as food.[23]

Compliance with some of the social distancing measures put in place was difficult or impossible for many disabled people. Despite this, exemptions or accommodations to rules (eg to the wearing of face masks, for people with hearing impairments) were sometimes not made. In Germany, for example, some grocery stores required customers to use trolleys, but made no reasonable accommodation for people who could not use them for disability-related reasons.[24] Also in Germany, as in many other countries, people with visual impairments encountered difficulties complying with social

---

[20] Shakespeare and others (n 2) s 3.2.

[21] See the country reports of the European Disability Expertise network on COVID-19 and people with disabilities in Europe, assessing the impact of the crisis and informing disability-inclusive next steps: https://ec.europa.eu/social/main.jsp?catId=1532&langId=en (accessed 29 June 2022).

[22] Health Services Executive and New Directions Subgroup, 'Framework for the Resumption of Adult Disability Day Services: Supporting People with Disabilities in the Context of COVID-19: The Next Year' (2020) 10 https://www.hse.ie/eng/services/news/newsfeatures/covid19-updates/partner-resources/framework-for-resumption-of-adult-disability-day-services.pdf (accessed 11 March 2022). See also Dáil Éireann, 'Select Committee on COVID 19 Response' (2020) 28 Comments from Deputy Pauline Tully https://www.oireachtas.ie/en/debates/debate/special_committee_on_covid_19_response/2020-09-30/ (accessed 11 March 2022).

[23] 'COVID-19 and People with Disabilities: Assessing the Impact of the Crisis and Informing Disability Inclusive Next Steps—Romania' European Commission Report (November 2021) https://ec.europa.eu/social/main.jsp?catId=1532&langId=en (accessed 29 June 2022).

[24] See des Bundes, 'Diskriminierungserfahrungen im Zusammenhang mit der Corona-Krise' (2020) 4 https://www.antidiskriminierungsstelle.de/SharedDocs/Downloads/DE/Dokumente_ohne_anzeige_in_Publikationen/20200504_Infopapier_zu_Coronakrise.pdf?__blob=publicationFile&v=2 (accessed 31 May 2022).

distancing rules, and additional difficulty navigating the public realm, because they were not able to be guided by strangers.[25]

Shakespeare and others note that many of their interviewees who were unable to conform to Covid-19-related guidelines for disability-related reasons encountered increased hostility and stigmatization and/or changed their lifestyle so as to cut out activities they would previously have carried out on their own. In the words of one of them:

> You know, it's the social distancing. [Learning disability], dementia, blind. Oh, yeah. Blind. Yeah. assistance. Dogs are not trained in social distancing. Don't jump the queue and go straight for the door. Can you imagine the social consequences of that? So I've got any number of blind friends with assistance dogs, who are normally really independent, who are now not going out except with family, because they're saying the risk of them bluntly being thumped is too high.[26]

There are also reports of disabled people experiencing harassment and hostility in connection with disability-related exemptions to Covid-19 rules, such as the wearing of face masks.

The pandemic therefore seems likely to have had a particularly intense impact on the social isolation of people with disabilities—a problem even before Covid-19. The percentage of persons with disabilities in the EU declaring feeling lonely all of the time or most of the time prior to the pandemic was 11.9 per cent—significantly higher than the percentage of persons without disabilities, which was 2.9 per cent.[27]

It might be tempting to explain the significantly higher Covid-19 death rate of disabled people in terms of pre-existing co-morbidities, which meant that disabled people were more likely to experience a worse outcome from Covid-19 than non-disabled people. In this respect, Mladenov and Brennan argue that 'government communications and the mainstream media have focus[ed] on the (presumed) enhanced susceptibility of disabled bodies to the virus'.[28] However, this explanation for the adverse outcomes experienced by disabled people is too simplistic. The research identified above has revealed how the pandemic has adversely affected disabled people across Europe in a variety of ways. In addition to any increased health vulnerability, the Covid-19-related risk to disabled people is increased by pre-existing inequalities. Examples of socioeconomic factors that are particularly relevant to people with disabilities, as well as many older people, and which exacerbate risks of transmission and infection and other forms of disadvantage and exclusion, include living in care homes and other congregated institutional settings; more limited access to public health information, including online information, and to hygiene facilities, such as hand-basins

---

[25] See Deutscher Blinden- und Sehbehindertenverband, 'Corona-Ratgeber' (2020) https://www.dbsv.org/corona.html (accessed 11 March 2022).

[26] Shakespeare and others (n 2) s 3.1.

[27] Stefano Grammenos, 'European Comparative Data on Europe 2020 and Persons with Disabilities: Labour Market, Education, Poverty and Health Analysis and Trends' *European Commission* (2021).

[28] Teodor Mladenov and Ciara Siobhan Brennan, 'The Global COVID-19 Disability Rights Monitor: Implementation, Findings, Disability Studies Response' (2021) 36 Disability and Society 1356.

(which again may not be accessible to them); the increased need for physical contact with environmental features, such as handrails, in order to get around; the need for close contact with carers, personal assistants, or assistants in shops, transport settings, and other facilities—particularly where there is no or limited access to personal protective equipment; more limited access to ICT based services such as online shopping, online education and teleworking facilities (because of inaccessibility or being on the wrong side of the digital divide), which thus increases the need to venture into public places; and inability to comply with guidance about wearing face masks (eg because of breathing difficulties) or social distancing (eg because systems depend on markings that are not accessible).[29]

Disadvantages and discrimination experienced in a pre-Covid-19 world have been augmented and increased during the pandemic. Covid-19 has therefore not only created new risks, but importantly 'exposed and magnified existing failings and inequalities'. Disabled people were often 'not protected and the response of the state has compromised their human rights'.[30] This is particularly so for people experiencing intersectional disadvantage—along lines of age, ethnicity, and gender, as well as disability. In the words of the UN Committee on the Rights of Persons with Disabilities (CRPD Committee):

> Pre-existing discrimination and inequality means that persons with disabilities are one of the most excluded groups in terms of health prevention and response actions and economic and social support measures, and among the hardest hit in terms of transmission risk and actual fatalities.[31]

3 Ex Post Reasonable Accommodation Duties

The right of a disabled person to a reasonable accommodation is found in EU law, and across national and international non-discrimination and disability rights legislation. Under EU law, the obligation to provide a reasonable accommodation to disabled individuals was established by Article 5 of the Employment Equality Directive of 2000 (the Directive), which provides:

---

[29] For further information see eg European Parliament Disability Intergroup, 'Summary Report of a Meeting of the European Parliament Disability Inter-Group: Impact of Covid-19 Outbreak to Persons with Disabilities' (30 April 2020); World Health Organization, 'Disability Considerations during the COVID-19 Outbreak' (26 March 2020); International Disability Alliance, 'Toward a Disability-Inclusive COVID19 Response: 10 Recommendations from the International Disability Alliance' (19 March 2020); António Guterres, 'Policy Brief on Persons with Disabilities and COVID-19' (6 May 2020); Office of the United Nations High Commissioner for Human Rights, 'Joint Statement: Persons with Disabilities and COVID-19 by the Chair of the United Nations Committee on the Rights of Persons with Disabilities, on behalf of the Committee on the Rights of Persons with Disabilities and the Special Envoy of the United Nations Secretary-General on Disability and Accessibility' (1 April 2020).

[30] Shakespeare and others (n 2) s 4.

[31] The United Nations Committee on the Rights of Persons with Disabilities, 'Statement on COVID-19 and the human rights of persons with disabilities' (9 June 2020).

> In order to guarantee compliance with the principle of equal treatment in relation to persons with disabilities, reasonable accommodation shall be provided. This means that employers shall take appropriate measures, where needed in a particular case, to enable a person with a disability to have access to, participate in, or advance in employment, or to undergo training, unless such measures would impose a disproportionate burden on the employer.

The obligation to make a reasonable accommodation on the grounds of disability is based on the recognition that, on occasions, the interaction between an individual's impairment and the physical or social environment can result in the inability to perform a particular function, job, or activity in the conventional manner. The characteristic of impairment is relevant in that it can lead to an individual being faced with a barrier that prevents him or her from benefiting from an employment or other opportunity that is open to others who do not share that characteristic. This barrier can be removed through an individualized and tailored reasonable accommodation.[32] Recital 20 of the Directive provides some guidance on what amounts to an accommodation. It states:

> [a]ppropriate measures should be provided, i.e. effective and practical measures to adapt the workplace to the disability, for example, adapting premises and equipment, patterns of working time, the distribution of tasks or the provision of training and integration resource.

The duty to provide an accommodation to a disabled individual is not absolute, being lifted if providing the accommodation would result in a disproportionate burden for the employer. Recital 21 of the Directive refers to some factors which should be taken into account to determine whether a measure amounts to a disproportionate burden. These are 'the financial and other costs entailed, the scale and financial resources of the organisation or undertaking and the possibility of obtaining public funding or any other assistance'. A further limitation is that the duty, under EU law, is confined to the spheres of employment and vocational training.

The duty to provide a reasonable accommodation is also established in the UN Convention on the Rights of Persons with Disabilities (CRPD), to which the EU is a party. Article 2 CRPD defines 'discrimination on the basis of disability' and includes within that definition the denial of reasonable accommodation. Article 5(3) of the CRPD links the equality and non-discrimination norms with the duty to accommodate, and provides that: 'In order to promote equality and eliminate discrimination, states parties shall take all appropriate steps to ensure that reasonable accommodation is provided'. Article 5(3) should be read together with the definition of reasonable accommodation in Article 2, which provides:

---

[32] Text in this paragraph draws on Lisa Waddington, 'Reasonable Accommodation' in Dagmar Schiek and others (eds), *Cases, Materials and Text on National, Supranational and International Non-Discrimination Law* (Hart Publishing 2007).

'Reasonable accommodation' means necessary and appropriate modification and adjustments not imposing a disproportionate or undue burden, where needed in a particular case, to ensure to persons with disabilities the enjoyment or exercise on an equal basis with others of all human rights and fundamental freedoms.

The CRPD therefore explicitly defines an unjustified denial of a reasonable accommodation as a form of discrimination, and extends this duty to all human rights and fundamental freedoms.

The reasonable accommodation duty articulated in the CRPD and EU law is ex post, meaning that it is only triggered once a person with a disability requests an accommodation or otherwise indicates that they are experiencing problems, or the duty bearer becomes aware of this through some other means. It imposes no obligation to consider the predictable needs of groups of people with impairments, such as people who use a wheelchair or who are blind, in advance, and take action to meet those needs before a specific request.

So what does this mean in the context of emergency situations such as Covid-19? Is the reasonable accommodation duty relevant or helpful to disabled people in this context? There are certainly a number of ways in which the duty might be relevant. For example, disabled employees (within the meaning of EU or national law) may request to work from home, or to be excused from carrying out certain tasks, where Covid-19 poses a particular risk to their health. Workers who have a family member with a disability with whom they live and who would be particularly susceptible to Covid-19, including many persons with intellectual disabilities, may also wish to claim this right. The Court of Justice of the European Union (CJEU) held in *Coleman*[33] that certain protections under the Directive applied to people who associated with persons with disabilities, including family members, and, in the *CHEZ* ruling,[34] that 'discrimination by association' extended to indirect discrimination, as well as direct discrimination and harassment. However, the reasonable accommodation duty under the Directive does not seem to extend to non-disabled people, so there may not be a right to claim such an accommodation for 'carers' or other family members. Moreover, an employer is only obliged to provide an accommodation if it does not amount to a disproportionate burden. There are, therefore, important limitations. Nevertheless, this right should serve to give some disabled workers priority in relation to requests to work in a way that reduces their risk of contracting Covid-19. As a matter of good practice, employers may also choose to consider the situation of workers who live or otherwise regularly associate with a disabled person in this context, although there does not seem to be an EU law duty to accommodate such workers. In the future, however, such workers could request flexible working arrangements and carers' leave under national legislation implementing the new Work-life Balance Directive.[35]

Given that European countries went through a period of lockdown in Spring 2020, when all but essential workplaces were closed, workers may have been able to request

---

[33] Case C-303/06 *Coleman v Attridge Law* [2008] IRLR 722.
[34] Case C-83/14 *CHEZ v Komisia za zashtita ot diskriminatsia* [2015] IRLR 746.
[35] Council Directive (EU) 2019/1158 of 12 July 2019 on work-life balance for parents and carers and repealing Council Directive 2010/18/EU [2018] OJ L188/79.

an accommodation in the form of working from home before work resumed in a more face-to-face manner. The first lockdown would thus have given many disabled people a period during which they had the de facto accommodation they required, as well as enabling them to make a timely request for the continuation of such working arrangements. In such an exceptional scenario, the ex post nature of the duty was not problematic.

On the other hand, there are many situations in the current pandemic where an ex post duty involves delays, meaning that barriers are created before the duty to remove them is triggered. Potential examples include online platforms and websites being set up in ways that are inaccessible for people with visual and other impairments, or new systems for organizing public space which unintentionally restrict or exclude access for some disabled people. In such cases, where an ex post duty applies, an individual must first experience a barrier or disadvantage before requesting an accommodation, and the type of accommodation which can be required of a duty-bearer will be assessed in the light of the circumstances applying at that time. The fact that the duty-bearer could have avoided creating the barrier by choosing a different system, or adapting the design, will not be relevant, thus reducing the potential impact and value of the duty—particularly in times of crisis when circumstances for duty-bearers (as well as claimants) are likely to be particularly challenging.

Lastly, it should be noted that in one respect the current crisis may have opened up opportunities for disabled people, for whom working at home is more practical, by increasing the likelihood that relevant types of accommodation will be regarded as appropriate or reasonable in the future. Working from home may be important for people with mobility impairments who find travel difficult or inaccessible; people who require frequent breaks for work for health-related reasons; people who need to remain close to medical equipment at home; and people with unpredictable medical conditions, for whom working consistently on site might be difficult or impossible. The crisis is likely to have made working from home more acceptable, and may lead to employers rethinking how essential work tasks can be carried out, and broadening their view of workplace accommodations. Indeed, working from home may become far more 'normalized' in the future, opening up this possibility to both non-disabled and disabled workers, and reducing possible stigma associated with disability-specific accommodations. The same may be true of having flexible working hours, which have also become more common for non-disabled workers during the current crisis.[36]

Taking a broader perspective, the Covid-19 crisis may have led to more providers of goods and services establishing a permanent online presence, which could reduce barriers to shopping, consumption, and participation for some disabled people, and particularly those with mobility-related impairments. At the same time, inaccessible online platforms and the digital gap (in terms of equipment, skills, and access to Wi-Fi) which disabled people experience may have meant that some disabled individuals experience greater barriers to (online) participation.

---

[36] Lisa A Schur, Mason Ameri, and Douglas Kruse, 'Telework After COVID: A "Silver Lining" for Workers with Disabilities?' (2020) 30 Journal of Occupational Rehabilitation 521; Peter Blanck, 'Disability Inclusive Employment and the Accommodation Principle: Emerging Issues in Research, Policy, and Law' (2020) 30 Journal of Occupational Rehabilitation 505.

4 Ex Ante Reasonable Accommodation Duties

4.1 Equality Act 2010's Anticipatory Reasonable Adjustment Duty

Unlike the ex post reasonable accommodation duty, ex ante or anticipatory reasonable accommodation duties are required neither by EU law nor by the CRPD. This does not mean that they are incompatible with such bodies of law, however. EU law is largely silent on disability discrimination prohibitions outside employment and, in any case, only sets minimum requirements under the Employment Equality Directive. The CRPD includes a general obligation to prohibit disability discrimination and, as explained in the previous section, explicitly specifies that this must include prohibitions of failure to provide ex post reasonable accommodation. It also requires States to ensure progress toward ensuring that facilities and services open to the public, as well as information, communication, and technologies, are made accessible. Ex ante reasonable accommodation duties arguably provide a useful way of supporting such efforts.

An ex ante version of the reasonable accommodation duty was introduced into UK law by the Disability Discrimination Act 1995. This legislation continues to apply in Northern Ireland but is now replaced, in Great Britain, by the Equality Act 2010—a statute which also includes this 'anticipatory reasonable adjustment duty'.[37] What makes disability discrimination prohibitions, such as the Equality Act 2010's anticipatory reasonable adjustment duty, ex ante or anticipatory in nature is the obligation they impose on duty bearers to take steps to remove disability-related disadvantage even before any disabled person has encountered a problem or made a request for an accommodation or adjustment. While other such duties exist,[38] it is the Equality Act 2010's anticipatory reasonable adjustment duty that provides the focus of this section.[39]

The duty can be summed up as imposing, on an ongoing or continuous basis, obligations: first, to identify and anticipate possible ways in which disabled people generally (or broad groups of disabled people such as those with particular types of impairment), might be disadvantaged by provisions, criteria and practices, the absence of appropriate auxiliary aids or services or aspects of the physical environment; and, second, to take reasonable steps to remove, prevent or mitigate these potential problems so that they do not in fact subject disabled people to a substantial disadvantage.[40] Despite being anticipatory or ex ante—in that action is required before a disabled person requests it—the duty gives rise to liability for unlawful discrimination

---

[37] In particular see Equality Act 2010, s 20 as modified by various schedules, such as sch 2.
[38] See eg the analogous duty in the US duty to make reasonable modifications set out in the Americans with Disabilities Act of 1990, 42 USC § 12131(2) (for public bodies) and § 12182(b)(2)(A)(ii) (for private bodies providing services to the public). See also the accessibility duty in the Norwegian legislation, Lov (Nr 61 av 2013) om forbud mot diskriminering på grunn av nedsatt funksjonsevne (diskriminerings- og tilgjengelighetsloven) (the Anti-Discrimination and Accessibility Act) ch 3.
[39] See further Anna Lawson and Maria Orchard, 'The Anticipatory Reasonable Adjustment Duty: Removing the Blockages?' (2021) 80 Cambridge Law Journal 308.
[40] See generally Equality and Human Rights Commission, 'Equality Act 2010 Code of Practice: Services, Public Functions and Associations' (Statutory Code of Practice, 1 January 2011), in particular ch 7.

only if a disabled person does in fact experience a detriment because of the breach.[41] It applies in connection with the provision of services to the public and the discharge of public functions, but not employment under the Equality Act 2010.

The anticipatory reasonable adjustment duty was described by key figures in the Disability Rights Commission (now replaced by the Equality and Human Rights Commission (EHRC)) as 'immensely significant' and 'a major driver in encouraging service providers to think in advance about removing barriers experienced by disabled customers or potential customers'.[42] Despite giving rise to a number of high-profile cases over the years, however, this duty has struggled to gain profile and visibility. Lack of awareness of it was highlighted as a problem by the House of Lords Select Committee on the Equality Act 2010 and Disability.[43] Nevertheless, as discussed below, hundreds of people relied on it to commence actions for disability discrimination during the Covid-19 emergency.

We use the remainder of this section to reflect on the fascinating phenomenon of this turn to the anticipatory reasonable adjustment duty during the pandemic. What happened? Why did it happen? How successful were these initiatives and what do they tell us about the robustness of this aspect of the Equality Act 2010 as a means of enforcing equality standards in times of crisis? Our reflection on these questions is informed by the explanations and perspectives of three key informants who provided their insights in a group interview carried out by Anna Lawson on 2 September 2021.[44] Each of these participants preferred to be identified and named, rather than for their identities to be disguised. They are Catherine Casserley (barrister at Cloisters Chambers), Chris Fry (founder of Fry Law), and Fazilet Hadi (Head of Policy and Research at Disability Rights UK). As professionals actively involved in using litigation or other strategies to secure compliance with the Equality Act 2010 during the Covid-19 emergency, all three provided valuable insights from inside the developments in question. These insider perspectives greatly enriched the current analysis but, unless an opinion expressed in the discussion below is specifically attributed to one of the participants, it should not be assumed that they are in agreement with it.

4.2 Covid-19 Disability-related Litigation and the Anticipatory Reasonable Adjustment Duty

4.2.1 Types of Covid-19-related disability discrimination litigation

As the three participants observed, during the Covid-19 emergency, the Equality Act 2010 was used in three main types of case. First, it was used in cases challenging the

---

[41] Equality Act 2010, s 21(2). cf the question of whether the High Court might be able to issue declaratory and injunctive relief, even where the claimant cannot demonstrate detriment, contemplated by Fordham J in *R (on the application of Rowley) v The Cabinet Office* [2021] EWHC2108 (Admin) [58].

[42] Caroline Gooding and Catherine Casserley, 'Open for All? Disability Discrimination Laws in Europe Relating to Goods and Services' in Anna Lawson and Caroline Gooding (eds), *Disability Rights in Europe: From Theory to Practice* (Hart Publishing 2005) 135, s 4.2.

[43] House of Lords Select Committee on the Equality Act 2010 and Disability, *The Equality Act 2010: The Impact on Disabled People* (2015–16, HL 117) [202]–[208].

[44] Ethical approval for this research was granted by the Business, Environment and Social Science (Area) Faculty Research Ethics Committee at the University of Leeds—ref: LTLLAW-050.

inaccessibility of Covid-19-related government information. Second, it was used in cases challenging Covid-19-related guidance on access to healthcare and hospital visits. Third, it was used in cases concerning access to the services of supermarkets for purposes of buying food and other basic necessities.

Litigation of the first type has resulted in one reported case—*R (on the application of Rowley) v Minister for the Cabinet Office*[45]—relating to the lack of British Sign Language (BSL) interpretation for several of the government's televised briefings on Covid-19. The judgment in this case is interesting and relevant, and will be considered more fully below. The case is also significant because it is the first of many on the same point. According to Chris Fry, there are approximately 270 other similar cases on Fry Law's books which are still pending.[46]

Also noteworthy is the high-profile settlement of a case brought by a visually-impaired woman on the government's 'Extremely Clinically Vulnerable' list. In this case, Sarah Leadbetter successfully challenged the government's practice of providing her with information about 'shielding' in formats that were inaccessible to her.[47] The settlement included government commitments to make improvements in this regard.

The primary example of cases of the second type was the initiation of judicial review proceedings by Fleur Perry and Mark Williams, challenging NHS England's Visitor Guidelines. These provided that there should be no visitors to hospital patients, except in a small number of specific situations, none of which applied to disabled people with high support needs wishing to be visited by a person familiar with those needs and able to fulfil them. This case did not proceed to court because NHS England agreed, after receiving pre-action letters, to change its Guidelines.[48]

In relation to the third type of case, hundreds of disabled people turned to Equality Act 2010 litigation during the first UK Covid-19 lockdown, in the Spring of 2020, to challenge the failure of supermarkets to make adjustments to policies and practices (such as inaccessible websites or rules prohibiting more than one person entering at a time) which severely disadvantaged disabled customers.[49] These cases were supported by Fry Law and, according to Chris Fry:

> We had about 700 supermarket cases at one point, and so we worked very intensively (alongside junior barristers from Cloisters and some other people who provided help pro bono) to write lots of letters to supermarkets threatening legal action.[50]

---

[45] [2021] EWHC 2108 (Admin).
[46] Interview with Chris Fry, Founder, Fry Law (2 September 2021).
[47] See also a similar case brought on behalf of Dan Williams, Chris Fry, 'Second Discrimination Case Launched Against the PM' *Fry Law Briefing* (19 May 2020) https://www.frylaw.co.uk/archives/articles/second-discrimination-case-launched-against-the-pm/ (accessed 10 March 2022).
[48] John Pring, 'Coronavirus: Success for Disabled Duo After NHS England Backs Down on Visitor Policy' *Disability News Service* (2020) https://www.disabilitynewsservice.com/coronavirus-success-for-disabled-duo-after-nhs-england-backs-down-on-visitor-policy (accessed 11 March 2022).
[49] John Pring, 'Coronavirus: Supermarkets face 'biggest class action of its kind' over discrimination claims' *Disability News Service* (23 April 2020) https://www.disabilitynewsservice.com/coronavirus-supermarkets-face-biggest-class-action-of-its-kind-over-discrimination-claims/ (accessed 11 March 2020).
[50] Interview with Chris Fry, Founder, Fry Law (2 September 2021).

He went on to explain that most of these cases were dropped after one major supermarket agreed to change its policies and make adjustments for disabled customers.

The principal focus for Covid-19-related disability discrimination cases against supermarkets then became blanket rules requiring the wearing of facemasks, with no exemptions for disabled people. In April 2021, the Equality and Human Rights Commission issued a statement reminding retailers of the fact that failure to make adjustments to such rules for disabled people is likely to constitute unlawful discrimination.[51] It also reported that it had written directly to a number of companies with such blanket policies (including 'a popular technology store, a luxury department store and a bus company'[52]), reminding them of their legal obligation to make (anticipatory) reasonable adjustments under the Equality Act 2010.

Thus, many Covid-19-related disability discrimination cases have been settled or dropped. It seems likely that the anticipatory reasonable adjustment duty would have played an important role in most of these, had they proceeded, alongside other Equality Act 2010 obligations (such as the Public Sector Equality Duty and the prohibition of indirect discrimination). To date there is only one case in which judgment has been issued—*R (on the application of Rowley) v Minister for the Cabinet Office*[53]—and it was the anticipatory reasonable adjustment argument which proved key to this ruling. This case will therefore now be considered in more depth.

4.2.2 Rowley v The Cabinet Office

In this case, Katie Rowley (a Deaf BSL user) challenged the government's failure to provide any BSL interpretation for two of the televised Westminster Government briefings on Covid-19, broadcast when she was pregnant and living alone. She also challenged its failure to provide on-platform sign-language interpretation for other such briefings. Chris Fry and Catherine Casserley (two of the interviewees in this study) were the legal team acting on behalf of Ms Rowley. The two Equality Act 2010 obligations they argued had been breached were the anticipatory reasonable adjustment duty[54] and the Public Sector Equality Duty.[55]

The most important aspect of the case, for current purposes, is the question of whether the absence of BSL from two of the televised briefings amounted to unlawful discrimination, contrary to the anticipatory reasonable adjustment duty. Fordham J approached this issue methodically, setting out what he described as a 'stepped approach',[56] and drawing extensively on quotes from the EHRC's Code of Practice, as well as on previous authorities.[57]

It was accepted by both sides that Ms Rowley was a disabled person, for purposes of the Equality Act 2010 and that the government was a provider of services (in terms

---

[51] Equality and Human Rights Commission, 'Equality Regulator Warns Against Blanket 'No Masks, No Entry' Policies' (9 April 2021) https://www.equalityhumanrights.com/en/our-work/news/equality-regulator-warns-against-blanket-%E2%80%98no-mask-no-entry%E2%80%99-policies (accessed 11 March 2020).
[52] ibid.
[53] [2021] EWHC 2108 (Admin).
[54] Equality Act 2010, s 29(7)(a).
[55] ibid s 149(1).
[56] [2021] EWHC 2108 (Admin) [19].
[57] ibid [21]–[38].

of providing information about Covid-19) and therefore under a duty to make reasonable adjustments by virtue of section 29(7)(a).[58] Fordham J ruled that the duty had been triggered by the 'comparative substantial disadvantage' test—because Deaf BSL users would have poorer access to the relevant briefings (where the auxiliary service of BSL was not available) than people who were not disabled. On the question of whether providing BSL for these sessions was a reasonable step required of the government by the anticipatory reasonable adjustment duty—the most significant aspect of the decision, to which we will return below—he found that the government had indeed breached the duty. Because Ms Rowley had experienced detriment as a result of this breach, her claim was successful.

The particular context of the Covid-19 emergency featured in the two most contested aspects of this ruling. The first of these concerned the question of whether or not Deaf BSL users had been placed at a 'substantial disadvantage' by the absence of BSL interpretation of the two Covid-19 briefings in question. Fordham J held that such a disadvantage had been established and that it was 'serious' in nature and extent.[59] He pointed out that the briefings were intended to inform the public about 'a subject matter of the greatest public interest and a vital concern—the pandemic'[60] and that:

> In the context of the pandemic, … the circumstances were unprecedented and challenging for Government; but they were also unprecedented and challenging for the public, who needed access to information, to help them to understand and to adhere and to manage their conduct and expectations for the future.[61]

The absence of BSL interpretation resulted in 'a clear barrier' to Deaf BSL users and represented 'a failure of inclusion, suggestive of not being thought about, which served to disempower, to frustrate and to marginalise'.[62] It disadvantaged them because it had the 'substantial, foreseeable and palpable effect' of causing them 'exclusion, and a justified sense of grievance, about which a reasonable person would certainly have good reason to complain, and about which affected people would reasonably say that they would have expected and urged—let alone preferred—to have been treated differently'.[63]

The second aspect of Fordham J's ruling in favour of Ms Rowley to which the context of the national emergency was relevant, was the question of whether the government had taken reasonable steps to avoid disadvantaging Deaf BSL users even though there had been no BSL interpretation of these two briefings. The government argued that it had discharged its anticipatory reasonable adjustment duty because it had entered into an arrangement with the BBC (the broadcaster) for the provision of BSL interpretation for the televised briefings and was entitled to rely on the BBC to ensure this was provided. Prior to the first of these two briefings—a new type of briefing led by government scientists and without a government minister present—the government

---

[58] Albeit that it was also discharging a public function. See Equality Act 2010, s 29(7)(b).
[59] [2021] EWHC 2108 (Admin) [28].
[60] ibid.
[61] ibid.
[62] ibid.
[63] ibid.

had been unaware that there would be no BSL interpretation.[64] It also relied on the fact that subtitles had been provided, even though BSL was absent.

Fordham J rejected these government arguments, despite the emergency context—a context which the government argued (and he accepted) was an important contextual factor. In his words:

> Events were unfolding at speed—sometimes day by day, sometimes hour by hour—in circumstances which were quite exceptional. The Government response to the pandemic was evolving, often at pace, with decisions made and reviewed on an ongoing basis. Government was making difficult judgment calls, including about medical and scientific issues. It was doing so after taking advice from relevant experts, in the context of powerfully expressed conflicting views about many of the measures being taken and about how various balances should be struck. It was identifying appropriate measures and policies to address the pandemic. That included broad political questions as to how to respond to the needs of particular groups. Government was acting under huge pressure, responding to this public health and economic emergency.[65]

In light of this, he stressed that it was 'wrong to "zoom-in" on one aspect of accessibility of one species of communication, without appreciating the "overall picture" or 'to use "hindsight"' or be 'wise after the event'.[66]

The government's defence, based on its arrangement with the BBC was rejected because, while it was 'entirely appropriate' for such arrangements to be made, it remained the responsibility of the government, as service provider, 'to ensure delivery of the discharge of the reasonable adjustments duty'.[67] The nature of this agreement, however, was informal and undocumented and this 'Undocumented informality produced an unknown, unknowable, uncontrollable and unalerted Gap' in the provision of BSL interpretation of government briefings.[68] In considering the reasonableness of the steps taken by the government, Fordham J placed particular stress on the proactive and anticipatory nature of the duty, and the fact that the government should have been aware that failure to provide BSL interpretation would cause disadvantage. Subtitles were not an adequate substitute—dismissing the idea that they were, Fordham J described it as 'a stereotypical opinion' amounting to 'prejudice'.[69]

In response to the government's reliance on the particular difficulties caused by the Covid-19 emergency, he observed that:

> It is right, of course, that Government was dealing with an unprecedented public health and economic emergency ... But that was also the context for the public and for Deaf BSL users. Yes, this increased the burden of the challenges on Government. Yes, this informs the appreciation which any Court must have when considering

---

[64] ibid [34].
[65] ibid [11]–[12].
[66] ibid [12].
[67] ibid [35].
[68] ibid.
[69] ibid [35] (referring to Equality and Human Rights Commission, 'Technical Guidance on the Public Sector Equality Duty' (2014) [3.38]).

actions in extremely challenging circumstances. However, it also increased the importance of information and its accessibility, particularly for groups and subgroups of people with different disabilities.[70]

There was, he stated, no evidence that BSL interpretation would have been impractical or that 'anything would have been sacrificed, or detracted from' had it been provided.[71] In short, he found that: 'Secure and clear arrangements had not been made. The problem was not anticipated. Those are features not of excusability, but rather of non-compliance.'[72]
Additional arguments that the government had not given 'due regard' to the importance of ensuring its briefings included on-platform BSL interpretation (whereby the BSL interpreter is physically present with the speakers and thus filmed with them) did not succeed—for reasons unconnected with the emergency context in which the briefings took place. The Public Sector Equality Duty argument on this point failed because the government submitted an equality impact assessment to the Court demonstrating that it had given 'due regard' to this issue—albeit that this was 'produced in the context of the judicial review proceedings, and "at the door of the Court"'.[73] The claim based on the anticipatory reasonable adjustment duty on this point also failed. This was because, although Fordham J accepted that on-platform provision approximated most closely to the type of access to the information granted to other members of the public,[74] the government demonstrated that it presented difficulties for the presentation of the type of detailed data slides commonly shown in briefings. Accordingly, the provision of in-screen BSL interpretation was a reasonable alternative means of making the service available to Deaf BSL users and there was therefore no breach of the duty.[75]

4.3 Implications of the Anticipatory Reasonable Adjustment Duty Litigation in Times of Crisis

4.3.1 The *Rowley* reasoning relating to the emergency context

As explained above, the Covid-19 emergency and all the demands it placed on the government, were recognized by Fordham J in *Rowley* to be an important contextual factor. This said, it seems clear that it was not a factor that in any way weakened or undermined the claimant's case. Fordham J repeatedly acknowledged the significance of the emergency for individuals, particularly Deaf BSL users—and the government's reliance on communication with the public as a key means of containing and responding to the crisis. His approach is refreshingly free of the deference to government during a crisis that might perhaps have been expected. Instead, it demonstrates a solid grasp of the policy behind the Equality Act 2010's anticipatory reasonable

---

[70] ibid [35].
[71] ibid.
[72] ibid.
[73] ibid [43] (Fordham J).
[74] ibid [55].
[75] ibid [56], [57].

adjustment duty and a meticulous application of the Equality Act 2010, guided by the relevant code of practice as well as by previous cases.

The extent to which this strong approach to the application of equality law was enabled by the anticipatory or proactive nature of the applicable duty is a question worth pondering. In other words, if the relevant duty had been ex post or reactive in nature, would more weight have been attached to the demands the emergency was placing on government and would it have been more difficult for the claimant to succeed? The answer seems likely to be yes. When asked how significant she considered the anticipatory nature of the duty to have been to the upholding of equality standards in this case, Catherine Casserley responded that it had been 'extremely significant indeed' and that 'a lot of weight was placed on the fact the government should have been planning in advance for BSL and putting in place systems to make sure it happened'[76]—a view shared by Chris Fry.

4.3.2 The rise of collective legal action

The Equality Act 2010's anticipatory reasonable adjustment duty is, as explained at the beginning of this section of the chapter, group oriented. It is triggered by the likelihood of group disadvantage. It might therefore be expected that it will, from time to time at least, be relied on in class actions where many individuals experience similar sorts of disadvantage. Until the Covid-19 crisis, however, this did not happen. What then was it about the emergency which led so many disabled people to bring essentially the same case for breach of the anticipatory duty?

The numbers of disabled litigants involved is staggering. As mentioned above, Fry Law was at one point dealing with 700 cases against supermarkets in connection with access to food and other groceries, as well as nearly 300 cases against the government in connection with BSL interpretation for the televised Covid-19 briefings. This sort of mass mobilization behind litigation is unprecedented in UK disability equality legal history. The pandemic, and policy responses to it, are themselves key to understanding why this happened at this time. In the words of Catherine Casserley: 'The emergency meant that lots of disabled people were all experiencing the same problems at the same time.'[77] Chris Fry, known amongst the disability community for his work on disability discrimination cases, added that:

> We just kept getting call after call from disabled people all with the same problems and the same questions. This gave Cathy [Casserley] and me the idea of using online and social media platforms to get advice out to people on mass. So we set up 'Disability Rights TV' which was on twice a week at the beginning but which is now about once a month.[78]

The shared nature of the hardship experienced by many disabled people at the same time, together with access to online legal advice and information, thus seem to be two important explanations of the impressive numbers of disabled people who turned to

---

[76] Interview with Catherine Casserley, Barrister, Cloisters Chambers (2 September 2021).
[77] ibid.
[78] Interview with Chris Fry, Founder, Fry Law (2 September 2021).

disability discrimination litigation during Covid-19. Another factor, suggested by Fazilet Hadi, was the fact that during the lockdowns, online collaboration, support, and communication between different disabled people's organizations across the country increased dramatically—a development which she attributed to the general increase in online activity, the reduction in the face-to-face activities of these organizations, and a focus on particular issues of shared concern.[79] This increase in civil society collaboration was significant at many levels. For present purposes, however, particularly relevant was the platform the collaboration provided to identify key concerns for disabled people, to share information (eg about the opportunities to seek legal information and advice through Disability Rights TV) and to strengthen a sense of solidarity.

Another factor, perhaps the most important one, which helps to explain the phenomenon of mass disability discrimination litigation during the Covid-19 crisis, articulated by Catherine Casserley, was the fact that: 'Disabled people were desperate. As with any crisis, disabled people are always hit very hard.' Litigation provided a means of trying to make their voices heard and push for change. The fact that Fry Law (the firm which supported the hundreds of BSL and supermarket claims) operated on a 'no win no fee' basis, helped reduce the financial barriers facing potential claimants. However, as Chris Fry noted:

> We were delighted that the cases against supermarkets resulted in a change early on— so that it became easier for disabled people to access groceries. And that's why we did that work. But it did create a bit of a financial headache for us. As we are paid on a 'no win no fee' basis, and had put a lot of time into writing letters in these 700 cases which then of course didn't make it to court or to a 'win', we didn't end up getting any money for all the work we'd put in.[80]

The multiplicity of very similar claims demonstrates the need for an effective class action mechanism in UK equality law. The absence of such a mechanism presented practical and financial problems which undermine the impact and effectiveness of equality law and the pursuit of justice. In relation to the BSL cases, for example, Chris Fry explained that:

> It costs money to initiate each case in court. Because of this, we decided to start off with one case—*Rowley*—and see how it went before launching all the others. Now that *Rowley* has been successful, we want to lodge the rest but the government is raising procedural objections which is making this difficult. For example, it's insisting that we lodge (and therefore pay for) each case separately rather than lodging some of them together.[81]

---

[79] Interview with Fazilet Hadi, Head of Policy and Research, Disability Rights UK (2 September 2021).
[80] ibid.
[81] ibid.

4.3.3 Achieving success or reflecting failure

On the face of it, the anticipatory reasonable adjustment duty appears to have achieved success in upholding equality standards in the Covid-19 emergency, both in the private and public sectors. In the private sector, it was referred to in solicitors' letters threatening litigation, which quickly brought about a change in policy and practice in some supermarkets, thereby removing some of the barriers to accessing groceries faced by disabled people. In the public sector, it helped achieve changes in government practice (eg to the formats used to communicate with blind people about 'shielding') through cases settled at a relatively early stage. It was also used in *Rowley* to hold the government to account for its failure to make adequate provision for BSL interpretation of key televised briefings on the emergency.

These successes are important. Disabled people would clearly be in a weaker position to challenge the inequalities they experience without the Equality Act 2010 and the anticipatory reasonable adjustment duty. However, their success should be judged in light of the following questions asked by Fazilet Hadi:

> Should we flip this around? Given that there were many other terrible things for disabled people that happened during the crisis … isn't it surprising that there hasn't been more litigation challenging more issues? And if the anticipatory reasonable adjustment duty was really successful, wouldn't we expect it to be shaping practice and policy on a continuing basis so that government, supermarkets etc would have got things right in the first place?[82]

These questions bring to the fore a key point—equality law standards will have little chance of ensuring equality considerations are prioritized in times of emergency unless they are effectively embedded and enforced in more ordinary times.

5 Conclusion

In conclusion, it is clear that the Covid-19 emergency had the effect of exponentially increasing the inequality experienced by disabled people across Europe. This has in large part been due to pre-existing forms of inequality and marginalization, such as reliance on models of institutional living and the predominance of inaccessible information—issues which equality law arguably could and should have been doing more to challenge and contest prior to the Covid-19 crisis.

There has been surprisingly little evidence of Covid-19-related litigation based on the traditional ex post reasonable accommodation duty. This may of course be because individual adjustments are being made for disabled people in contexts such as employment. It may also be because disabled people who are not being accommodated in the ways they need are being advised against bringing cases based on the ex post duty because of uncertain prospects of success. The fact that this duty focuses on the circumstances existing at the time the disabled person encounters the problem and

---

[82] Interview with Fazilet Hadi, Head of Policy and Research, Disability Rights UK (2 September 2021).

makes a request for accommodation, is likely to work against disabled people in times of emergency. At such times, duty-bearers are likely to be dealing with complex and demanding situations which judges are likely to view as making the implementation of requested accommodations less practicable.

The ex ante anticipatory reasonable adjustment duty in the Equality Act 2010, by contrast, has been heavily used during the Covid-19 crisis. The fact that it focuses attention on what duty-bearers should have been doing to avoid creating disadvantage, rather than on simply what they can do to remove it once in place, is perhaps more useful in times of crisis than the narrower temporal focus of the ex post duty. Nevertheless, it too is limited by the need to show that the claimant has actually experienced a detriment or disadvantage before liability can be established. Furthermore, the exponential increase in litigation based on the anticipatory reasonable adjustment duty would not have been necessary had there been greater awareness and embedding of that duty in the day-to-day operations of duty-bearers.

In short, reasonable accommodation duties and equality law more generally have clearly not been enough to prevent a widening and deepening of disability-related inequality as a result of the Covid-19 emergency. This said, it has provided some protection and a mechanism through which disabled people have been able to challenge the exclusion and injustice they experienced. Without it, their position would have been worse. There is, however, much more that needs to be done to build a legal framework that robustly embeds disability equality into emergency and non-emergency times.

15
Remote Working, Working from Home, and EU Sex Discrimination Law

Jule Mulder

1 Introduction

The worldwide pandemic and the national responses to control the spread of Covid-19 have exposed and potentially increased many of the existing social inequalities. Not only did the virus pose a severe risk for some vulnerable groups within society, but the public health attempts to contain and prevent its spread also imposed significant burdens on some segments of society. The structurally vulnerable were likely to be negatively affected by the lockdowns, business closures, and stay at home orders. This, in itself, is not a surprising finding. Indeed, it has long been recognized under the scope of indirect sex discrimination that apparently neutral measures can have different effects on men and women because of structural inequalities that situate them differently within the employment market and wider society.[1] In terms of gender inequality, one may for example consider gender roles, predominantly female part-time work, or different care responsibilities that often place women differently from men within the employment market and wider society and thus make it more difficult for them to comply with expectations and standards that are perceived as the norm, but in fact benefit men.[2] Moreover, disadvantages that are only linked to certain sectors or especially burden the poorer part of the population are likely to have a different effect on men and women within a gendered labour market.[3] These aspects became visible in the context of Covid-19-related public health policies that had serious impacts on the organization of work and private life. Since women are more likely to work in the particularly hard-hit retail and hospitality sectors, they were more likely to lose their work during the lockdown, due to (temporary) business closures. Simultaneously, the heightened demands on the care industry increased work burdens within another sector that predominantly employs women on low wages.[4] There is also clear

---

[1] First developed by the CJEU in Case C-96/80 *Jenkins v Kingsgate* [1981] ECR 00911 and Case C-170/84 *Bilka v Weber von Hartz* [1986] ECR 01607. For a legal definition see Council Directive 2006/54/EC of 5 July 2006 on the implementation of the principle of equal opportunities and equal treatment of men and women in matters of employment and occupation [2006] OJ L204, art 2(1)(a).

[2] *Bilka* (n 1); Case C-486/18 *Re v Praxair MRC* [2019] ECLI 379; Case C-116/08 *Meerts v Proost NV* [2009] ECR I-10063; Case C-109/88 *Handels- og Kontorfunktionærernes Forbund i Danmark v Dansk Arbejdsgiverforening, agissant pour Danfoss* [1989] ECR 03199.

[3] Case C-236/98 *Jämställdhetsombudsmannen v Örebro läns* [2000] ECR I-02189; Dagmar Schiek, 'Revisiting Intersectionality for EU Anti-Discrimination Law in an Economic Crisis: A Critical Legal Studies Perspective' (2016) 2 Sociologia del Diritto 23.

[4] Kristalina Georgieva and others, 'The COVID-19 Gender Gap' *IMF Blog* (21 July 2020) https://blogs.imf.org/2020/07/21/the-covid-19-gender-gap/ (accessed 1 April 2022); Liana Christin Landivar and

evidence that women provided the bulk of the additional in-home childcare and home-schooling that was required due to school and nursery closures, irrespectively and alongside any work responsibilities.[5] This suggests that gender roles remain relevant within families and limit women's bargaining power when negotiating child and other care responsibilities. Stay at home orders also specially burdened the poorer segment of society who are likely to live in more confined living spaces, including single parents. Accordingly, public health policies to contain the virus have posed a particular burden for women and other structurally vulnerable groups. Efforts to ease that burden throughout the year of the crisis continued to view the household as secure, adequate, and separate from society, thus ignoring the needs of those that did not enjoy such living conditions.[6]

However, the lockdowns and stay at home orders have also disrupted some of the standard work practices that potentially disadvantaged women. While women did provide most of the additional in-house care, fathers working from home increased their provision of childcare too, which potentially disrupted traditional gendered division of labour. Men were thus more involved with childcare than prior to the pandemic.[7] Whether this increased involvement can be sustained may then depend on the larger legal framework regulating care.[8] While working from home certainly posed many challenges for those who simultaneously had to take care of children, it also forced employers to adapt to the new reality of remote flexible working that had to be combined with childcare and thus invited a degree of messiness into the workday.[9] During the lockdown, it was simply impossible for employers to insist on constant uninterrupted availability during prescribed working hours, unless strictly necessary for work performance, and businesses were encouraged to reorganize their workflows to accommodate their employees' remote work activity. Many of these new work arrangements or a blended version of the old and new are likely to stay because they potentially reduce cost of office space, rationalize work processes, and expand the pool

---

others, 'Early Signs Indicate that Covid-19 is Exacerbating Gender Inequality in the Labor Force' (2020) 6 Socius: Sociological Research for a Dynamic World 1.

[5] T Murat Yildirim and Hande Eslen-Ziya, 'The Differential Impact of COVID-19 on the Work Conditions of Women and Men Academics During the Lockdown' (2021) 28 Gender Work Organ 243; Gundula Zoch, Ann-Christin Bächmann, and Bascha Vicari, 'Who Cares When Care Closes? Care-arrangements and Parental Working Conditions During the COVID-19 Pandemic in Germany' (2021) 23 European Societies 576; Jonas Jessen and others, 'Sharing the Caring? The Gender Division of Care Work during the COVID-19 Pandemic in Germany' IZA Discussion Paper No 14457 http://ftp.iza.org/dp14457.pdf (accessed 1 April 2022); Alison Andrew and others, 'The Gendered Division of Paid and Domestic Work under Lockdown' IZA Discussion Paper No 13500 http://ftp.iza.org/dp13500.pdf (accessed 1 April 2022).

[6] Jackie Gulland, 'Households Bubbles and Hugging Grandparents: Caring and Lockdown Rules during COVID-19' (2020) 28 Feminist Legal Studies 329.

[7] Alice Margaria, 'Fathers, Childcare and COVID-19' (2021) 29 Feminist Legal Studies 133; Karyn E Miller, 'The Ethics of Care and Academic Motherhood Amid COVID-19' (2001) 28 Gender Work Organ 260.

[8] See generally Jule Mulder, 'Promoting Substantive Gender Equality Through the Law on Pregnancy Discrimination, Maternity and Parental Leave' (2018) 1 European Equality Law Review 39.

[9] Danielle L Couch, Belinda O'Sullivan, and Christina Malatzky, 'What COVID-19 Could Mean for the Future of 'Work from Home': The Provocation of Three Women in the Academy' (2021) 28 Gender Work Organ 266.

of potential recruits beyond those that are in proximity to the workplace. There is also evidence that jobs advertising working from home are on the rise.[10]

Against this background, the chapter considers the advantages and disadvantages associated with these new work arrangements, namely remote working, in the light of EU non-discrimination law, with a specific focus on indirect sex discrimination. Considering gender roles, gendered division of labour, and gendered wealth inequality (specifically in the context of single parenting), it discusses how the possible changes in standard work organization can potentially enable women's workplace participation and promote gender equality within employment. As this will heavily depend on the precise design of the flexible work arrangements, it will evaluate how EU non-discrimination law can facilitate access to and enjoyment of this new workplace organization and protect employees from disadvantages associated with them. Within the context of indirect sex discrimination law, two aspects seem particularly relevant. First, it is uncertain to what degree disadvantages within the private sphere can be recognized as disadvantages under the scope of indirect sex discrimination.[11] Accordingly, while the way work is organized constitutes working conditions and thus clearly falls within the scope of the Recast Directive 2006/54/EC, it is not clear to what degree disadvantages experienced in private life due to the work organization can be considered as a 'particular disadvantage' under the scope of indirect sex discrimination. While the Court of Justice of the European Union (CJEU) has often upheld a separation between the public and private sphere, such distinction is difficult to draw when work is indeed conducted within a private setting. Secondly, it is unclear to what degree employers indeed need to accommodate the access to remote work rearrangements.

To explore these issues, the chapter will first consider the variable ways flexible remote work arrangements can be understood and how they can enhance women's opportunities in the labour market. It will then discuss how EU indirect sex discrimination law can apply to remote flexible work arrangements and explore uncertainties. While the chapter focuses on EU law only, its findings may very well become relevant within national legal systems which are influenced by EU non-discrimination law even if not formally bound by EU supremacy.

2 Are Flexible Work Arrangements Beneficial for Gender Equality?

Measures ensuring or promoting flexibility at work including remote working are the new flag ships that are supposed to enable workers with care responsibilities to reconcile professional and domestic responsibilities. While rules and measures on flexible working are usually gender neutral, often referring to parents and/or carers,[12] they do

---

[10] Leanna Byrne, 'Working from Home Job Adverts Rise' *BBC News* (11 August 2021) https://www.bbc.co.uk/news/business-58160245 (accessed 1 April 2022).
[11] *Bilka* (n 1).
[12] See eg Council Directive 2019/1158/EU of 20 June 2019 on work-life balance for parents and carers and repealing Council Directive 2010/18/EU [2019] OJ L188/79.

not tackle gender roles or directly encourage fathers' increased or equal involvement with (unpaid) domestic responsibilities, such as childcare. By themselves, they are unlikely to ensure fathers' continued involvement in childcare that was picked up during the exceptional time of lockdowns and stay at home orders.[13] Specifically, they do not challenge the stigma of flexible work arrangements as long as they are associated with care and atypicality that seem to reduce fathers' willingness to take up such flexible work arrangements.[14] However, flexible work arrangements can potentially make it easier for those with care responsibilities to coordinate (full-time) employment and care responsibilities. If the working time and place is flexible, workers can organize their working hours around their domestic care responsibilities, without necessarily reducing their overall working time, productivity, or pay. If successful, these rules will primarily assist women as a group, as women still carry out most unpaid domestic care responsibilities and are more likely to reduce their paid work activities in the interest of unpaid domestic care work. Flexible work arrangements thus mostly contribute to gender equality within employment by accommodating primary care givers. They do not directly challenge the status quo of gender roles and gendered division of labour. Notwithstanding, fathers may be more likely to take advantage of these arrangements too, once they are normalized and lose the stigma of being atypical or contrary to the standard working arrangement. If flexible remote working does indeed become a new normal, fathers are more likely to take advantage of these possibilities to contribute to domestic unpaid care work. This could potentially contribute to a more equal division of labour in the long term and carries significant benefits for fathers, their children, and their partners.

However, flexible remote work arrangements can also work to the detriment of workers with care responsibilities, namely if flexibility is demanded from the worker. The CJEU has long assessed that if a criterion of mobility 'is understood as the employee's adaptability to variable hours and varying places of work, [it may] work to the disadvantage of female employees, who, because of household and family duties for which they are frequently responsible, are not as able as men to organize their working time flexibly'.[15] In *London Underground Ltd v Edwards*, the UK Court of Appeal assessed that a flexibility requirement, namely to work shift work, disadvantaged single parents, most of which are women, and excluded them from accessing employment.[16] Flexibility in this context is understood as something that is demanded from the employee. Workers with pressing domestic responsibilities that cannot be delayed or handed over on short notice will find it difficult to comply with flexibility that is demanded by patterns of irregular working time and place. This is especially problematic within sectors where flexibility is inherent to the contractual design, ie contractual

---

[13] For that, policies actively encouraging fathers to care seem to be necessary. See Mulder (n 8).
[14] Alina Ewald, Emilee Gilbert, and Kate Huppatz, 'Fathering and Flexible Working Arrangements: A Systematic Interdisciplinary Review' (2020) 7 Journal of Family Theory and Review 27; Lane C Powell, 'Flexible Scheduling and Gender Equality: The Working Families Flexibility Act under the Fourteenth Amendment' (2013) 20 Michigan Journal of Gender and the Law 359.
[15] *Handels- og Kontorfunktionærernes Forbund i Danmark* (n 2) [21].
[16] United Kingdom, Employment Appeal Tribunal, *London Underground Ltd v Edwards (No 2)* [1995] IRLR 355 and United Kingdom, England and Wales Court of Appeal, *London Underground Ltd v Edwards (No 2)* [1998] IRLR 364, [1999] ICR 494.

arrangements that reward and require work once it is needed. For instance, zero-hour or on-call contracts can potentially require workers to adapt to changed working patterns at short notice and much of the gig or platform economies in practice require their workers to be available during peak times. It has been noted that these peak times often coincide with fixed childcare responsibilities, such as nursery and school pick up, which makes it more difficult for carers to work during these hours.[17]

Flexible work arrangements do not necessarily advance carers' employment opportunities as they do not always enable the reorganization of work around care responsibilities. They can thus be perceived as negative as well as positive. This is also true in the context of remote working or working from home. On the one hand, remote working can enable a carer to work while also being present at home to be available for those in need of care. If combined with flexible working time determined by the worker, it may also enable them to complete larger chunks of their paid work in the evening once their care role is less demanding. Overall, it may enable a more time efficient organization of the day, as it reduces commuting time or time spent in meetings and resists strict separation of private and professional sphere. Indeed, the lockdown and stay at home orders during the Covid-19 crisis may have allowed for a degree of blending of professional and care responsibilities that makes it more likely for those arrangements to be deemed acceptable in the future. After all, it created a type of messiness that allowed private life to interfere with professional tasks as children's background noises, interruptions, and short-term absences due to care were deemed normal and acceptable and not limited to women's working conditions only.[18]

On the other hand, remote working does create several issues that can potentially be gendered. Working from home is not easy to arrange while providing care and being at home may consolidate one's role as primary carer. Studies about care involvement during the pandemic suggest that the care work done by women working remotely from home was especially high.[19] The opportunity to work from home can then easily turn out to be a poisoned apple. It can also significantly interfere with the way the home is enjoyed as it will require that space is made available to work around the needs of other members of the family, and behaviour potentially has to be controlled in order to ensure acceptable working conditions and/or acceptable service provision. It may require additional investment in working space, equipment, and infrastructure. If women are indeed poorer than men as they are more likely to be engaged in lower paid work, are more likely to be single parents, and are more likely to bear the majority of domestic responsibilities including care, it is more likely for them to face challenges in that regard and end up working in an environment that is unsuitable for remote working, for example because of lack of space or lack of out of house childcare, and less ability to offset the employers' withdrawal from ongoing workplace investment in infrastructure, including costs related to issues as mundane as heating or internet access. Moreover, if employers closely monitor the worktime and conduct at home, employees will not reap the benefits from working remotely and will potentially

---

[17] Susanne D Burri and Sussane Heeger-Hertter, 'Discriminatie in de platformeconomie juridisch bestrijden: geen eenvoudige zaak' (2018) Ars aequi 1000.
[18] Couch, O'Sullivan, and Malatzky (n 9).
[19] Jessen and others (n 5).

experience some intrusion into their privacy. It is reasonable to assume that working time and conduct is more closely monitored in lower skilled jobs that are more focused on covering certain shifts than on the outcome of work processes.

The hidden costs of flexible remote working arrangements that can produce disadvantages are often ignored. During the lockdown, employers' willingness to accommodate remote working was generally applauded, without considering the amount of investment that was required by the employee, including costs that would usually be covered by the employer. Working from home arrangements simply take for granted that the home can support economic life.[20] Similarly, while childcare facilities were closed and received financial support, the actual childcare work did not vanish but simply moved to the private home, where it was not considered as part of the country's productivity.[21] Ignoring these factors of production within the context of flexible remote working can increase gendered disadvantages.[22] Finally, it is not clear whether remote working indeed lost its stigma of an unproductive and disrupted work environment and has become the new normal. While children's interruptions were tolerated as most people worked from home, such occurrences may easily be deemed unprofessional again. The atypical nature of remote flexible working may resurface and may crystallize in negative performance reviews, lack of inclusion, or difficulties within promotion procedures. Moreover, employees working from home may be perceived to receive an unfair benefit, which needs to be remedied. The brieve discussion in the UK around the reduction of civil servants' pays for those who work from home and do not have to commute is only one example of potential pitfalls.[23]

3 The Application of EU Sex Discrimination Law

We will now turn to EU non-discrimination law and specifically consider whether and to what degree indirect sex discrimination law can be used to challenge some of these disadvantages arising from flexible remote working arrangements. The application of EU sex discrimination law to flexible remote working conditions seems uncontroversial. Article 14(c) Recast Directive 2006/54/EC[24] prohibits sex discrimination within employment and explicitly refers to working conditions. Flexible work arrangements that allow for remote working fall within that scope, as they determine how the work is conducted and the wider context work can be confined. One may also consider Article 14(a) that refers to access to employment, if working conditions indeed impede that access.

---

[20] Fiona Jenkins and Julie Smith, 'Working-from-home during COVID-19: Accounting for the Care Economy to Build Back Better' (2021) 32 The Economic and Labour Relations Review 22.
[21] ibid.
[22] Joanne Conaghan, 'Covid-19 and Inequalities at Work: A Gender Lens' (2020) 13 Futures of Work https://futuresofwork.co.uk/2020/05/07/covid-19-and-inequalities-at-work-a-gender-lens/ (accessed 1 April 2022).
[23] 'Covid-19: Home-working Officials Won't Get Paid Less, Says Minister' BBC News (9 August 2021) https://www.bbc.co.uk/news/uk-politics-58144187 (accessed 1 April 2022).
[24] Recast Directive (n 1).

The CJEU conceives working conditions widely. They are not limited to the content of the employment contract or employers' actions or regulations but can also be national law including social security law, if the subject matter is concerned with the material scope of the Recast Directive.[25] More importantly for us, Article 14(c) now explicitly includes dismissal and pay under its scope, and has been referenced in a wide range of working conditions, including part-time schemes for older employees,[26] access to types of short term parental leave to coordinate childcare and employment activities,[27] and disadvantages that may arise from these working conditions.[28] This includes the way work is organized, when and where work is conducted, and what benefits or disadvantages are linked to taking advantage of flexible work arrangements available to the employees. Within that context the negative as well as positive connotation of flexible working arrangements can matter. EU non-discrimination law thus requires that access to existing flexible work arrangements must be provided without sex discrimination and the work arrangements themselves may not discriminate, or more specifically disadvantage, workers of one sex.

Moreover, EU sex discrimination law bans direct as well as indirect discrimination. While the clear distinction between both concepts is somewhat blurred,[29] direct discrimination bans distinctions that are directly based on the protected characteristic, while indirect discrimination bans measures, practices and criteria that are apparently neutral but create disadvantages for members of the protected group, unless justified. The latter thus focuses on the effect and broader implications of the measure. While both potentially can be relevant within the context of flexible remote work arrangements, we will focus on indirect sex discrimination as it considers the de facto possibility to access them and the effect of their use.

Indirect sex discrimination can address various disadvantages related to accessing and working under flexible work arrangements without requiring a specific link to the protected characteristic. Most obviously, it can challenge disadvantages that directly flow from using flexible remote work arrangements as long as there is indeed a gender imbalance regarding the use. Such gender imbalance is likely, as long as remote flexible work arrangements are explicitly or implicitly linked to care and are thus primarily used to coordinate unpaid care and paid work responsibilities. Within this context a parallel can be drawn to the CJEU case law on disadvantages related to parental leave. The CJEU has held repeatedly that disadvantages that flow from taking parental leave can constitute indirect sex discrimination since the overwhelming majority of workers taking advantage of such leave are women.[30]

However, there are limits to that approach within the context of leave. Parental leave traditionally provides long-term or short-term leave to parents to enable them to take

---

[25] Case C-63/91 *Jackson and Cresswell v Chief Adjudication Officer* [1992] ECR I-04737; Case C-116/94 *Meyers v Adjudication Officer* [1995] ECR I-02131.
[26] Case C-187/00 *Kutz-Bauer v Freie und Hansestadt Hamburg* [2003] ECR I-02741.
[27] Case C-222/14 *Konstantinos Maïstrellis v Ypourgos Dikaiosynis, Diafaneias kai Anthropinon Dikaiomaton*; C-104/09 *Pedro Manuel Roca Álvarez v Sesa Start España* [2010] ECR I-08661.
[28] C-7/12 *Riežniece v Zemkopības ministrija* [2013] EqLR 826.
[29] Sandra Fredman, 'Direct and Indirect Discrimination: Is There Still a Divide?' in Hugh Collins and Tarunabh Khaitan (eds), *Foundations of Indirect Discrimination Law* (Hart Publishing 2018) 31–55.
[30] Case C-486/18 *RE v Praxair MRC* EU:C:2019:379.

care of their children without losing their work. During that leave, workers are not at work, their employment is suspended, and are not necessarily entitled to benefits that are linked to performance, eg pay or bonuses.[31] In fact, the substantive rights provided in the Parental Leave Directive[32] (now Work-Life Balance Directive[33]) de facto have limited the type of claims that can be made under the scope of indirect sex discrimination law. Regarding pay, this means that workers on parental leave are only entitled to payments as recognized within the Work-Life Balance Directive.[34] Moreover, the CJEU has rejected claims of indirect sex discrimination regarding the scope of entitlements under the parental leave provisions simply because the Parental Leave Directive did not provide for such a right. Accordingly, in *Ortiz Mesonero* the CJEU has accepted national provisions that require a reduction of working for the purpose of parental leave.[35] The claimant aimed at reorganizing his working time and argued that a reduction of working time should not be required because it carried a particular disadvantage for women, given that they were most likely to take parental leave.

However, the new Work-Life Balance Directive does not only focus on leave but also considers a right to request flexible work arrangements, including remote working, under its scope.[36] National law also at times recognizes an, albeit weak, right to access flexible work arrangements.[37] These arrangements do not necessarily reduce the overall workload but allow workers to reorganize the place and time the work is completed. Accordingly, much of the CJEU case law that limits claims of indirect sex discrimination linked to parental leave is not relevant here. Reduction of pay, tendency to more negative performance reviews or exclusion from promotion processes because of criteria that are easier to fulfil at the workplace than at home are all disadvantages that can potentially be considered under its scope. Such disadvantages flowing from using flexible work arrangements can thus be challenged under its scope as long as women are more likely to take up the leave more often than men.

Indirect sex discrimination can also remain relevant if remote working arrangements indeed become mainstream and are in practice decoupled from care responsibilities. Specifically, access can be impeded if linked to criteria that are more difficult to fulfil by a protected group and the experience of remote working can be less than ideal (eg reduced competitiveness and productivity) if it cannot happen in a work conducive environment. While the demonstration of a particular disadvantage for a protected group depends on the circumstances of the case, it is certainly plausible that women could suffer detrimental effects. If women do indeed provide the majority of childcare,

---

[31] Case C-333/97 *Susanne Lewen v Lothar Denda* [1999] ECR I-07243.
[32] Council Directive 2010/18/EU of 8 March 2010 implementing the revised Framework Agreement on parental leave concluded by BUSINESSEUROPE, UEAPME, CEEP and ETUC and repealing Directive 96/34/EC [2010] OJ L68/13.
[33] Work-Life Balance Directive (n 12).
[34] ibid art 8.
[35] Case C-366/18 *José Manuel Ortiz Mesonero v UTE Luz Madrid Centro* [2019] IRLR 1112.
[36] Work-Life Balance Directive (n 12) arts 3(1)(f) and 9.
[37] Susanne D Burri, 'Care and the Workplace: The Dutch Approach to Part-time Work, Flexible Working Arrangements and Leave' in Loraine Gelsthorpe, Perveez Mody, and Brian Sloan (eds), *Spaces of Care* (Hart Publishing 2020) 143–64; Richard Croucher and Clare Kelliher, 'The Right to Request Flexible Working in Britain: The Law and Organisational Realities' (2005) 21 International Journal of Comparative Labour Law and Industrial Relations 503.

are more likely to be single parents, are generally poorer than men, and are more likely to be engaged in low-skilled and/or low-paid work, they are likely to have less access to remote working arrangements and fewer opportunities to ensure a work-conducive environment at home. Remote working may be reserved for higher skilled positions that are considered to require less input and management. For example, prior to the pandemic it was already commonplace for academic university staff to work remotely depending on the discipline, while it seemed much less likely for administrative or professional services staff, supporting the academic activities, to do so. Lower skilled remote working may also invite more control over the working time and interference with the private home that potentially compounds the negative consequences of remote working. Single parents and generally poorer parts of the population are more likely to live in small living spaces that make effective remote working more difficult, potentially encroaches onto other peoples' living spaces, and undermines the worker's competitiveness. However, it is not at all clear how EU indirect sex discrimination law can indeed react to these kinds of disadvantages and whether they are deemed to fall within the responsibility of the employer and sphere of employment.

4 Remote Flexible Work Arrangements under the Scope of EU Indirect Sex Discrimination Law

We will now consider some areas of uncertainty within the context of EU indirect sex discrimination law that may hinder proper oversight of flexible remote working arrangements within the context of EU sex discrimination law. Specifically, the chapter is concerned with three aspects: the comparability of work done at home and at the employers' premises, the potential blurring of the public/private within the context of remote flexible working, and the potential of reasonable accommodation within the context of indirect sex discrimination to assist carers working from home.

4.1 Comparability of Work

As remote flexible working is organized rather differently from working within the employers' premises, one may challenge the comparability, specifically regarding their working conditions. The potential lack of comparability can then cause issues within equal pay cases as well as equal treatment cases. The question of comparability is a contentious issue within the context of indirect sex discrimination. While direct discrimination usually requires a sufficiently similar situation for there to be comparability, indirect discrimination in principle only considers the outcome. After all, it is the situational difference that means that apparently neutral measures, practices, or criteria have a different effect on different groups. Comparability thus has limited relevance within the context of indirect sex discrimination law. However, it seems difficult to demonstrate a 'particular disadvantage compared with persons of the other sex' (Article 2(1)(b) Recast Directive 2006/54/C) without some sort of comparative exercise. After all, EU non-discrimination law is not prescriptive as such, as it does not generally determine the nature of the treatment or minimum benefits but only that the treatment is equal. While real and hypothetical comparators can be considered, it has to be shown that the claimant as a member of a disadvantaged group faces a particular disadvantage in comparison with other groups. Identifying that correct pool of comparators is not always easy and creates several problems within the context of remote working arrangements. In principle, two potential pools of comparators could be considered depending on the disadvantage. One may want to compare oneself with other remote workers that do not experience the same disadvantage; or with workers that work on the employer's premises and do not experience the same disadvantage. It is the latter group of comparators that may be deemed an inappropriate pool of comparators.

In the most uncontroversial sense, comparability is relevant within the context of equal pay. The right to equal pay extends to like work or work of equal value.[38] It thus has to be possible to compare the work to determine its equalness or equal value.[39] Instead of considering the entire pay structure that may mean lower pay for women than men on average, as suggested in early case law,[40] the CJEU usually requires a detailed consideration of the pay structure and each factor influencing the pay. As a starting point, the CJEU requires that each element of remuneration is considered separately and only allows for an overall assessment if the pay structures lack transparency.[41] Accordingly, a lower basic pay cannot be justified by reference to other (financial or other) benefits that compensate for it. This means that a lack of commute alone cannot justify lower pay that remunerates performance. For that, the employer would have to offer commuting supplements. Therefore, remote working contracts should follow the *pro-rata temporis* approach and remunerate each hour worked accordingly if the work is indeed deemed of equal value.

However, one may question whether remote workers can be compared with other workers. In *Royal Copenhagen*, the CJEU held that the arbitrary formation of groups of men and women for the purpose of comparison must be avoided. Instead, the pool of comparators should include 'two groups each encompass[ing] all the workers who, taking account of a set of factors such as the nature of the work, the training requirements and the working conditions, can be considered to be in a comparable situation'.[42] Considering these criteria, can we compare those working from home and those working at the employers' premises? One may view their working conditions to be rather different as they create different challenges of communication, productivity, and managerial control. There may also be different training requirements. While one may consider these differences irrelevant for the purpose of equal pay as long as the output or service provided can be considered of equal value, it adds an additional layer of complication.

---

[38] Consolidated Version of the Treaty on European Union [2012] OJ C326/01, art 157.
[39] Case C-381/99 *Brunnhofer v Bank der Osterreichischen Postsparkasse AG* [2001] ECR I-04961 [39].
[40] Case C-237/85 *Rummler v Dato-Druck* [1986] ECR 02101.
[41] *Jämställdhetsombudsmannen* (n 3) [43]; Case C-262/88 *Barber v Guardian Royal Exchange Assurance Group* [1990] ECR I-01889 [34].
[42] Case C-400/93 *Specialarbejderforbundet i Danmark v Dansk Industri* [1995] ECR I-01275 [36]–[38]; *Brunnhofer* (n 39) [43]; Case C-427/11 *Margaret Kenny v Minister for Justice, Equality and Law Reform* EU:C:2013:122 (28 February 2013) [27]; Case C-309/97 *Angestelltenbetriebsrat der Wiener Gebietskrankenkasse* [1999] ECR I-2865 [17].

Comparability outside of equal value of work for equal pay is much more controversial. As stated above, situational differences should in principle not matter, because these differences are precisely the reason for the different effect on groups. Moreover, different value work may explain different hourly pay, but it does not necessarily justify different promotion opportunities, different access to vacation, different pay of expenses, or different sick leave policies. However, the CJEU has at times considered comparability as a prerequisite issue. In *Wipple* a worker on a zero-hour contract could not compare herself to other full- and part-time employees, because her contract was not comparable.[43] As such, she could not challenge the slow erosion of her working time. Without reference to comparability, the CJEU in *Kachelmann* considered a redundancy selection based on social factors justified, although it only considered part-time workers for selection.[44] The claimant worked part-time and was selected for dismissal. Had the selection for redundancy based on social factors included part and full-time workers, another (full-time) worker would have been selected for redundancy. Kachelmann argued that she was willing to work full-time, as required by the employer, there was thus no need for the separate consideration of full and part-time workers. Nevertheless, the CJEU considered it justified as a joint consideration would de facto enable the claimant unilaterally to transform her part-time contract to a full-time contact.

In both cases, the CJEU seems to suggest that differences that go to the very heart of the contractual agreement are not challengeable directly or indirectly as they would fundamentally change the nature of the employment status.[45] Thus, workers can challenge conditions that may have been agreed within the contractual arrangements, including pay, but they may not challenge the nature of the contract itself. If that is indeed correct, differential treatment that is required to keep key contractual arrangements in place cannot be challenged under indirect sex discrimination law, either because the contractual arrangements make the work incomparable or because the differential treatment can be justified.

The way comparability can become an issue within the context of remote working is thus twofold. First, comparability can become an issue within the context of pay if the flexible remote working conditions indeed mean that the value of work is different than the value provided by those working on the employers' premises. Secondly, comparability can also become an issue if the 'particular disadvantage' can only be addressed by substantially changing arrangements that go to the heart of the contractual agreement. To what degree flexible remote work arrangements can indeed be considered substantially different may very well depend on the specific arrangements. In terms of construction, it will at times be difficult to find and apply the right pool of comparators in making out a case of indirect sex discrimination in off-site online home-based flexible work arrangements.

---

[43] Case C-313/02 *Nicole Wippel v Peek & Cloppenburg GmbH & Co KG* [2004] ECR I-09483.
[44] Case C-322/98 *Bärbel Kachelmann v Bankhaus Hermann Lampe KG* [2000] ECR I-07505.
[45] Jule Mulder, *Indirect Sex Discrimination in Employment: Theoretical Analysis and Reflections on the CJEU case Law and National Application of the Concept of Indirect Sex Discrimination* (Publications Office of the European Union 2021) 112–14.

4.2 Blurring the Lines of the Professional and Private Divide

Once work is done remotely at home, the lines between private and professional life are blurred, as professional activities are conducted within a private setting that may require attention and responses in its own rights. This was particularly obvious during the school and nursery closures when both were mingled and children were present during working hours and potentially disrupted work processes usually sheltered from private family life. It has been suggested that the lockdown experience is a chance for a cultural shift within the work environment,[46] as their common nature normalizes such interruptions and thus protects those affected from being deemed unprofessional or distracted. If a normal work environment includes children that will almost inevitably disrupt the working day, those with care responsibilities, and thus mostly women, are better able to coordinate working time and care without experiencing disadvantages within their employment. In the same vein, once such remote work environments are normalized, fathers are more likely to take advantage of them and, once they are at home, accept more childcare responsibilities.

However, blurring the lines between private and professional life can cause difficulties for the application of EU non-discrimination law. Specifically, it is unclear whether disadvantages that are related to remote working but originate from the private sphere can indeed be recognized under the scope of EU non-discrimination law. First, while EU indirect sex discrimination does not require that *all* women are disadvantaged because of a particular measure, it does require that it is *predominantly* women who are disadvantaged by it. Whether that is indeed the case is not immediately obvious. While there is a sense that during the Covid-19-related lockdown remote working mothers were more likely to organize their working time around childcare needs than remote working fathers and thus carried most of the burden related to remote working, it is of course easier to organize alternative childcare arrangements in less extreme circumstances. If the remaining disadvantages connected to remote working affect men and women alike, we certainly reach the limits of EU indirect sex discrimination. However, while further gendered disadvantages related to remote working are not too obvious, they are certainly conceivable, if women are indeed on average poorer than men and take up fewer leadership roles that can result in lack of recognition of needs and circumstances. For example, poorer or single parent households may be less able to ensure a productive work environment at home due to lack of space or resources. Accordingly, if female workers are indeed more likely to experience disadvantages than men while working at home, for example because their work environment reduces their productivity, then working from home, especially if required, could be a practice that creates a particular disadvantage.

This bring us to the second challenge, how to assess and identify these disadvantages that are linked to the private sphere. The CJEU has considered that measurements of productivity that consistently measure women's performance as inferior are likely to be discriminatory metrics, because it is inconceivable that women persistently

---

[46] Couch, O'Sullivan, and Malatzky (n 9).

perform on a lower level than men.[47] However, in its equal pay case law, it has often required that every single component of the pay is compared rather than the overall pay, shifting the burden of proof only in case of lack of transparency that makes such comparison impossible.[48] For example, the Court considered that a piece work pay scheme would not be discriminatory even if it consistently disadvantaged women, as long as the same unit of measurement was adopted and the difference could be down to individual outputs.[49] Similarly, promotions or seniority can be based on de-facto performance without too much focus on the reason the differences in performance appear. Accordingly, if remote working arrangements indeed lead to lower productivity because of less-than-ideal working conditions at home, it will be difficult to challenge the consequences of that, such as lower pay or promotion rate, because of the prima facie uncontroversial principle that pay, and promotion can depend on quality or value of performance.

All that is left then, is to challenge the work environment itself. The requirement to work remotely could then be deemed as creating a particular disadvantage for women. However, to what degree the Court would recognize these disadvantages that originate in the private sphere is not at all clear. Traditionally, the CJEU has not had the best track record in recognizing burdens and disadvantages that originate and express themselves in the private sphere as they fall outside the scope of the employer's responsibility. Indeed, in *ÖGB* the Court upheld the public/private divide by refusing to consider absences from work due to military service and parental leave to be comparable.[50] Specifically, it considered the former to amount to civic duty or service and the latter to be a private choice. Accordingly, the absences could be treated differently within the context of seniority irrespectively of the overwhelming gender divide that very much questioned the de facto voluntary nature of taking parental leave.

Helmig may provide further hints on the type of disadvantages the CJEU is willing to recognize. The case was concerned with a pay scheme that offered an overtime supplement for the time worked over and above regular full-time hours. It was argued that it disadvantaged part-time workers, because they did not receive the overtime supplement for every hour they worked overtime, but only once they worked more than regular full-time hours. The CJEU disagreed. Instead, it simply compared each additional hour worked and found that each hour was remunerated the same.[51] Therefore, there was no discrimination. Specifically, the CJEU considered that the proposed pay scheme would in fact benefit part-time workers because it would provide them with higher remuneration while working the same hours, thus being contrary to *pro-rata temporis*. The case turned on the issue of comparability of different hours worked. While the claimants considered contractually agreed working hours and overtime separately, the CJEU considered them together.

---

[47] *Handels- og Kontorfunktionærernes Forbund i Danmark* (n 2) [20].
[48] Case C-400/93 *Specialarbejderforbundet i Danmark v Dansk Industri* [1995] ECR I-01275 [10]–[16].
[49] ibid [21].
[50] Case C-220/02 C-220/02 *Österreichischer Gewerkschaftsbund, Gewerkschaft der Privatangestellten v Wirtschaftskammer Österreich* [2004] ECR I-05907.
[51] Case C-399/92 *Stadt Lengerich and Others v Helmig and Others* [1994] ECR I-05727, later confirmed in Case C-300/06 *Ursula Voß v Land Berlin* [2007] ECR I-10573.

This can be criticized from multiple angles.[52] First, it seems to contradict the Court's own approach that requires the separate consideration of each element of pay.[53] Secondly, within the context of direct discrimination the CJEU assesses whether a situation is sufficiently similar and thus comparable with reference to the specific focus on the purpose and aim of the benefit or measure in question. For example, the similarity of (same-sex) civil unions and (opposite-sex) marriages within the context of sexuality discrimination needed to be assessed with the specific benefit in mind. Thus, no overall abstract assessment of both unions was necessary. Rather the comparability assessment must be carried out 'in a specific and concrete manner in the light of the benefit concerned'.[54] Advocate General Bobek suggests the comparability assessment thus requires an examination of whether 'in relation to a given quality (that is, *tertium comparationis*, which may be a value, aim, action, situation, and so on), the elements of comparison (such as persons, undertakings, products) demonstrate more similarities or more differences'.[55] It is not obvious why the approach to equal pay and the comparability of different hours worked should not take a similar approach.

The purpose of the overtime supplement should thus be relevant. Such purposes could be an additional reward for working more than the contractually agreed hours or compensating for the additional (physical or mental) burden that working overtime poses. Both purposes could suggest that part-time workers need to receive the overtime supplement for each hour they work beyond their contracted hours. However, this depends on the way the additional burden is understood. If we consider the additional burden in absolute terms, ie the burden arises only once more than forty hours of work are provided and thus more than full-time, one would exclude part-time workers working fewer hours from the supplement. For that to be the only burden to consider, one can only and exclusively consider the work environment and exclude external or private additional demands. Once we consider additional private burdens such as unpaid care responsibilities, we will quickly see that overtime worked by part-time workers will often not be comparable with regular hours worked by a full-time employee. Indeed, the critique of the case within literature often highlights that the CJEU excludes the private sphere from its consideration and thus ignores that each additional hour worked is not necessarily the same for part and full-time workers.[56] Certainly, it will be much more difficult for a part-time worker to arrange availability during these extra hours, as they were unexpected, and part-time workers

---

[52] Mulder (n 45) 53–54.
[53] *Jämställdhetsombudsmannen* (n 3) [43].
[54] Case C-267/06 *Tadao Maruko v Versorgungsanstalt der deutschen Bühnen* [2008] ECR I-1757 [67]–[69]; Case C-147/08 *Jürgen Römer v Freie und Hansestadt Hamburg* [2011] ECR I-3591 [42]; Case C-267/12 *Frédéric Hay v Crédit agricole mutuel de Charente-Maritime et des Deux-Sèvres* EU:C:2013:823 (12 December 2013) [33].
[55] AG Bobek in Case C-143/16 *Abercrombie & Fitch Italia Srl v Antonino Bordonaro* EU:C:2017:235 (19 July 2017) [40].
[56] Cathryn Costello and Gareth Davies, 'The Case Law of the Court of Justice in the Field of Sex Equality since 2000' (2006) 43 Common Market Law Review 1567; Tamara Hervey and Jo Shaw, 'Women, Work and Care' (1998) 8 Journal of European Social Policy 43; Nicole Busby, 'The Evolution of Gender Equality and Related Employment Policies: The Case of Work–family Reconciliation' (2018) 18 International Journal of Discrimination and the Law 104; Susanne D Burri, 'Tijd delen: Deeltijd, gelijkheid en gender in Europees en nationaalrechtelijk perspectief' (2000) vol 66 (dissertation, Utrecht University Europese Monografieën, Kluwer).

are less likely to have significant alternative care support available to them. However, the CJEU did not consider these additional burdens relevant as they were a private matter.

This does not bode well for the consideration of disadvantages arising from the work environment at home, if it indeed impacts work performance or disadvantages the worker in other ways. The way the working environment is set up at home certainly, prima facie, seems to be a private matter. However, once the private and professional spheres are meshed because of actions that fall within the employers' responsibility, this distinction between both becomes more difficult to draw. Certainly, if the home is the foreseen workspace as required by the employer, its environment should be relevant within the context of employment. Thus, if the requirement to work at home creates a particular disadvantage because of the factors within that private context, the disadvantages should fall within the sphere of employment. Moreover, employers may be responsible for the work environment to the extent they would be at their own premises. Thus, the investments employees may have to make to have a reasonable workspace at home certainly falls within the sphere of employment especially if remote working is indeed required.

The blurring of private and public sphere within the context of remote working may nevertheless have its most potential in the context of challenging stigmas around remote working. De facto disadvantages suffered by remote workers that cannot be explained by reference to performance certainly fall within the scope of indirect sex discrimination. As such, it can help to challenge assumptions of the distracted inattentive remote worker that may be reflected in performance reviews. It also requires employers to provide inclusionary measures to ensure that the physical absence of remote workers does not pose a detriment to them within the work processes. All of this can potentially necessitate a significant recalibration of work processes, expectations, and communication.

4.3 Reasonable Accommodation

The question is then to what degree employers indeed have to accommodate effective remote working arrangements and reduce the negative effects of and disadvantages connected to remote working. Of course, EU equality law does not impose a specific duty of reasonable accommodation outside the scope of disability.[57] However, there is significant overlap between the reasonable accommodation duty and the concept of indirect discrimination. The former acknowledges that removing disability as an irrelevant factor from the employer's consideration will do little to advance the equality of disabled people, but instead reinforces particular norms and perpetuates disadvantages as long as disabled people are impaired from conforming with these norms.[58] Similarly, indirect sex discrimination acknowledges that practices can have

---

[57] Council Directive (EC) 2000/78 of 27 November 2000 establishing a general framework for equal treatment in employment and occupation [2002] OJ L303/16, art 5.

[58] Sandra Fredman, 'Disability Equality, A Challenge to the Existing Anti-Discrimination Paradigm?' in Anna Lawson and Caroline Gooding (eds), *Disability Rights in Europe: From Theory to Practice* (Hart Publishing 2005) 199–203.

disadvantaging effects on groups, without directly referring to sex, because women (or men) may find it more difficult to benefit within the parameters set out in the practices. Accordingly, many have suggested that reasonable accommodation duties are not necessary for the other protected characteristics under the scope of EU non-discrimination law because the concept of indirect discrimination already entails a duty akin to it.[59] A particular disadvantage that stems from the refusal to provide certain reasonable accommodation may than potentially fall within the scope of indirect discrimination.[60] Within our context this could for example be the case because the policy lacking accommodation measures fails to recognize the living environments and structural context within which remote working takes place. Once the prima facie case of indirect discrimination is established the employer would have to justify the lack of accommodation. Within the justification, it will then have to be considered whether the lack of accommodation is indeed suitable to achieve the legitimate aim and whether less burdensome alternatives are available.[61]

However, the difference lies in the detail. While de facto outcomes may be similar in practice, indirect sex discrimination tackles collective structural barriers since there is nothing inherent to the female sex itself outside the scope of pregnancy that hinders women's equal access and opportunities. Reasonable accommodation duties relate to the individual. While they can relate to social factors that disable people as highlighted by the social model of disability, they neither require structural change as such nor are they limited to reducing or abolishing social barriers.[62] The duty under the scope of indirect sex discrimination is thus wider, as it requires structural change, and narrower as it only considers structural collective barriers not individual needs.[63] This is not to suggest that indirect sex discrimination is a form of positive action to ensure substantive equality. Rather, its symmetric nature will always only focus on the removal of barriers that disadvantage individual members of some groups without considering their experience of disadvantages in more general social, cultural, or economic terms. This has led some to argue that non-discrimination law is not concerned with structural change at all but rather focuses on individual wrongs.[64] One may also concede that EU non-discrimination law should not be conflated with market-based welfare norms that provide substantive minimum rights, but aims at preventing cultural exclusion that expresses itself within the market.[65] My point is that the barriers that are potentially challenged under indirect sex discrimination are those that are of a structurally exploitative nature. Employers do not have to ensure equal outcomes or

---

[59] Andrea Broderick and Philippa Watson, 'Disability in EU Non-discrimination Law' in Delia Ferri and Andrea Broderick (eds), *Research Handbook on EU Disability Law* (Edward Elgar Publishing 2020) 121, 130; Lisa Waddington, 'Reasonable Accommodation' (2011) 36 NJCM-Bulletin 186; Erica Howard, 'Indirect Discrimination, Reasonable Accommodation and Religion' in Daniel Cuypers and Jogchum Vrielink (eds), *Equal is Not Enough* (Intersentia 2016) 73–91.
[60] Lucy Vickers, *Religion and Belief Discrimination in Employment* (European Community 2007) 21–22.
[61] *Bilka* (n 1) [36].
[62] Dagmar Schiek, 'Intersectionality and the Notion of Disability in EU Discrimination Law' (2016) 53 Common Market Law Review 35.
[63] Waddington (n 59).
[64] See eg Michael P Foran, 'Discrimination as an Individual Wrong' (2019) 39 Oxford Journal of Legal Studies 901.
[65] Dagmar Schiek, 'On Uses, Mis-uses and Non-uses of Intersectionality before the Court of Justice (EU)' (2018) 18 International Journal of Discrimination and the Law 82; Schiek (n 3).

equal opportunities, but they are prevented from exploiting structural inequality, and because of that, work structures that produce a particular disadvantage will have to change, unless they can be justified.[66]

Accordingly, accommodation duties arising from indirect sex discrimination refer to needs arising from structural inequality experienced by the protected group, not the individual struggles of some workers. However, de facto wider structural barriers can express themselves in an individual worker. While it may be difficult to demonstrate the disadvantage by statistical means only, depending on the number of workers negatively affected by the measure and their statistical significance, a qualitative assessment of the measures in question may nevertheless identify a 'particular disadvantage', even if it is not apparent within the pool of employees. Indeed, the CJEU at times simply assesses the potentially disadvantaging effect without reference to statistical data.[67]

Such qualitative assessments have been criticized for reintroducing gender stereotypes rather than letting the facts, ie the statistical burden, speak for themselves.[68] If we simply assume that women are more likely to take care of children, struggle with flexibility requirements or take parental leave and assess measures based on that assumption, we will not be sensitive to social changes that in fact make these correlations less common or certain. Qualitative assessments may also struggle to recognize the counterintuitive effects of measures. However, the combination of a qualitative and quantitative assessment can reduce the weaknesses of the qualitative reasoning significantly. Such an approach should combine sector or nationwide statistical data with the group or individual circumstances of the workers specifically affected by the measure, policy, or criterion in question. Thus, it would invite the use of more flexible statistical data that can engage with and demonstrate systemic inequalities.[69] This would also allow the inclusion of individuals that belong to the generally privileged group but nevertheless suffer alongside the disadvantaged groups within the context of sex discrimination;[70] fathers working part-time and/or being the primary carer being the most prominent example.

What does that mean in the context of remote working arrangements? Most obviously, employers promoting and enabling remote working will have to ensure equal access to it. This concerns the initial right to access it but, more importantly, can also concern the way it is organized. Regarding the latter, it maybe be more difficult for

---

[66] In one understanding, the objective justification is then primarily concerned with the question of causation. Once the 'particular disadvantage' is identified, the employer can demonstrate that the measure in fact is not linked to the protected characteristics via the objective justification defence. Evelyn Ellis and Philippa Watson, *EU Anti-Discrimination Law* (2nd edn, OUP 2012) 169, 173; Dagmar Schiek, 'Indirect Discrimination' in Dagmar Schiek, Lisa Waddington, and Mark Bell (eds), *Cases, Materials and Text on National, Supranational and International Non-Discrimination Law* (Hart Publishing 2007) 441–43.

[67] *Handels- og Kontorfunktionærernes Forbund i Danmark* (n 2); Case C-173/13 *Blandine Leone v Garde des Sceaux* ECLI:EU:C:2014:209 (17 July 2014).

[68] See for general discussion Schiek (n 66) 397–99.

[69] Marie Mercat-Bruns, 'Systemic Discrimination: Rethinking the Tools of Gender Equality' (2018) 2 European Equality Law Review 1.

[70] Within the context of race discrimination, the CJEU has recognized that the person suffering the disadvantage does not have to belong to the disadvantaged group as long as the particular disadvantage has been established. See Case C-83/14 CHEZ *Razpredelenie Bulgaria AD v Komisia za zashtita ot diskriminatsia* ECLI:EU:C:2015:48 (16 July 2015). For further discussion see Mulder (n 45) 78–96.

those with care responsibilities to access the remote working schemes if the private home environment is not taken into account. Depending on the specific recognized gendered disadvantages this could include investments within the physical work environment, such as investment into workplace (including ongoing cost) and equipment, as well flexibility in terms of time of work, modes of communication, and expectations on the workplace environment, for example level of noise. For example, if women are more likely to be put in a position where they need to negotiate work and private demands while working remotely, practices that prevent them doing so effectively would need to be justified. Quasi duties of accommodation thus push towards flexibility within the way remote work is organized for the benefit of the worker.

The duties of structural change can then only be limited within the scope of the objective justification. Given that a cost argument alone cannot justify indirect discrimination,[71] the necessity and appropriate test may then narrow the scope of objective justifications significantly, especially if we consider how the employer can benefit from remote working arrangements. While remote working arrangements may require some flexibility from the employer and can benefit the employee, it seems often forgotten in the public discourse that remote working arrangements encumber employees with significant running and investment costs that are usually the responsibility of the employer.[72] Given that, it does not seem unreasonable to suggest that remote workers should be provided with support regarding the financial and organizational cost of remote working to ensure that all workers have equal access to and similar experience of remote working.

5 Conclusion

The pandemic related measures to curb the spread of the virus sent shockwaves through the employment market, many of which will be felt for many years to come. While inequalities have been exposed and worsened during the process, the rushed reinvention of work procedures and policies forced upon employers by stay-at-home orders and lockdowns, can also be a chance to develop a somewhat more inclusive work environment that provides wider access and thus more opportunities for vulnerable groups within society. Specifically, there is clear evidence that future work in many sectors foresee remote or blended work arrangement where employees are expected or permitted to work from home for some or most of their working days.

For this development indeed to ensure wider inclusion and opportunity, I argue for a strong adherence to the concept of indirect discrimination law. By focusing on the EU concept related to sex discrimination, the discussion highlights how it can indeed advance inclusive policies regarding remote working as well as their potential limits. Once work activities are moved from the employers' premises into the private home,

---

[71] Case C-77/02 *Erika Steinicke v Bundesanstalt für Arbeit* [2003] ECR I-09027; Case C-243/95 *Hill and Stapleton v Revenue Commissioners* [1998] ECR I-03739; Case C-343/92 *M A De Weerd, née Roks, and Others v Bestuur van de Bedrijfsvereniging voor de Gezondheid, Geestelijke en Maatschappelijke Belangen and Others* [1994] ECR I-00571.

[72] Jenkins and Smith (n 20).

the private and professional dimensions of life become more visibly intertwined. While this may be a chance for a cultural shift that makes the interaction of private and work-related tasks throughout the day more normal and thus helps those with care responsibilities, the messiness also creates difficulties for the common application of EU sex discrimination law. Specially, the CJEU has not been particularly good at recognizing disadvantages and choices that originate from the private sphere but have negative impacts on working conditions or pay. Instead, the CJEU has at times questioned the comparability of the working conditions and choices made, as well as rejected the inclusion of disadvantages that only indirectly relate to the working sphere. While the shortcomings of the CJEU's approach can be criticized in general terms, the chapter also argues that a separation of private and public sphere is difficult to uphold given that it is the employers' work arrangements that places the work within a private setting. Further, the chapter considers how indirect sex discrimination law includes duties akin on duties of reasonable accommodation and what that could specifically mean within the context of remote working arrangements. It concludes that besides technical and physical support provided within the home environment, working remotely will often require additional flexibility requirements to ensure women are not disadvantaged by the arrangements. Employers will thus only be able to limit flexibility within the home context if they can justify this objectively. As such, indirect sex discrimination law may be able to foster a fair organization of remote working arrangements that does not disadvantage women.

16
Covid-19 and Exponential Reproductive Rights-related Inequalities in Brazil

Marta Machado and Taís Penteado[*]

'The pandemic showed to the distracted (because I believe there are distracted people in Brazil) who had not seen before the tragedy that systemic racism produces on us, Black women and men. But if someone hadn't seen it before, the pandemic lenses helped to see it.

Jurema Werneck[1]

1 Introduction

Aggravation of gender inequalities[2] is a consequence of the Covid-19 crisis in different countries around the globe. The diagnosis is indisputably applicable to Brazil, a country with prevailing structural inequalities. Notwithstanding, instead of acting to minimize the negative gendered effects of the pandemic, the federal government occupied by the right-wing populist president, Jair Bolsonaro, promoted an escalation of attacks on sexual and reproductive rights.

During the Covid-19 crisis, the government accelerated the process of hollowing out access to contraception and legal abortion services in the public health system. But going even further, an executive measure was issued to impose new formal barriers

---

[*] This chapter was produced with the support of the Mario Henrique Simonsen Teaching and Research Scholarship and CAPES-PROSUP Scholarship.
[1] Executive Director of Amnesty International in Brazil and founder of the NGO Criola, in defence of the rights of Black women. Victoria Damasceno, 'Lentes da pandemia ajudaram a ver racismo, diz diretora da Anistia Internacional no Brasil' *Folha de S Paulo* (24 July 2021) https://www1.folha.uol.com.br/cotidiano/2021/07/lentes-da-pandemia-ajudaram-a-ver-racismo-diz-diretora-da-anistia-internacional-no-brasil.shtml (accessed 1 May 2022).
[2] The literature on gender and the law has been contesting the universality of the category 'gender' for a long time now. While gender is a useful category, all gendered experiences are also constituted by the interaction with other categories such as race and class, for instance. In this chapter the authors adhere to an intersectional approach and, as such, whenever the terms 'women' and 'gender' are used, they should be understood as non-universal, non-abstract, non-isolated categories, but rather as complex and dynamic, constituted by other intersecting categories. See Kimberlé W Crenshaw, *On Intersectionality: Essential Writings* (The New Press 2017).

to access the right to legal abortion. Ordinance (Portaria) No 2282 of 27 August 2020 made it mandatory for health professionals who attend to patients in cases of rape to notify the police and bureaucratized access to the procedure. The combination of the Covid-19 crisis with the anti-abortion offensive created a critical juncture that favours the analysis of structural consequences of the denial of reproductive rights, vastly affecting Black and economically deprived women.

This chapter aims to bring to the forefront the equality dimensions of the intensification of attacks on abortion rights in Brazil during the pandemic. If considered an individual rights issue, the reinforcement of criminalization of abortion would have little to do with the moment in which we live—or could be arguably related to the increase of sexual violence. Instead, if considered as a gender equality issue, deeply related to reproductive work, women's roles as caretakers and devalued domestic work, recent attacks on abortion rights could be understood as a cause of exponential growth of intersectional gender inequalities already aggravated by the pandemics.

We will use the case of Ordinance (Portaria) No 2,282 as an entry-point to our analysis. In response to the Ordinance, two lawsuits challenging the constitutionality of the measure have been proposed before the Brazilian Supreme Court. The first one argues that the measure is inadequate, first, because health officials do not have the expertise to deal with criminal records; and, secondly, because the procedure established by the Ordinance would reiterate the trauma of the sexual violence. The second lawsuit argues that the measure harms women's rights to health, dignity, privacy, and intimacy and that to put women through this process is analogous to torture. None of the constitutional claims is based on the equality principle. Equality had no role, neither in the legal strategy for the measure, nor in the public debate. Consequentially, the Covid-19 crisis context also does not appear in the court cases, not even to flag the increase of sexual violence in the period.

Based on these insights, the chapter aims to unearth the equality dimensions of the denial of sexual and reproductive rights during the pandemic. The uncovering of this reality, that is often obscured in debates, is important in itself. But, seeing how the restrictions arise from and perpetuate inequalities also enables the formulation of legal challenges through the mobilization of the equality principle.

In the next section, we set the stage for the discussion, by presenting the Government's exponential attacks on abortion during the crisis, that culminated in the Ordinance referred above. In section 3, we present the two lawsuits that challenged the Ordinance and call attention to the lack of assessment of the gendered consequences of the Covid-19 crises in the legal debate in the court. Section 4 is then devoted to presenting an equality-based argument against the Ordinance. Adopting the reproductive justice framework for scanning reality, we argue that abortion in Brazil is part of a broader realm of reproduction. This realm has been historically permeated by inequalities, but has become particularly unequal during the crisis, with the increase in sexual violence and the allocation of care work to Black women. As such, we argue that abortion restrictions in general, and the Ordinance in particular, are a tool for exacerbating women's subordination and, therefore, clash with the Brazilian Constitution's multiple equality provisions.

2 Bolsonaro Government's Exponential Attacks on Abortion During the Crisis

It is unsurprising that the Bolsonaro Government would oppose sexual and reproductive rights. He was elected with an openly misogynistic speech. He has publicly defended wage inequality between men and women and, in its most radical version, has openly incited violence against women and the LGBTQIA + population. The fight against 'gender ideology' was a key promise in his inauguration speech and a total ban on abortion was included among the strategic targets of his government. Damares Alves, nominated as Minister for Women, Family, and Human Rights,[3] is a former evangelical priest, anti-abortion activist, and former parliamentary adviser of several parliamentarians linked to the Evangelical Caucus in the Congress. At the Sixty-third UN Conference on the Status of Women (CSW), Damares spoke up against abortion, affirming that 'in the understanding of the current Brazilian government, right to life means protection of life from the moment of conception' and Brazil became allied with ultra-conservatives on gender and sex at the United Nations.[4]

Under the Bolsonaro Government, the erosion of women's and LGBTIQIA + rights is happening through different strategies, combining formal measures and informal practices. The word 'gender' has been ruled out of all official documents. The Ministry of Health removed educational material aimed at the health of trans women from the official website. Within its space of discretion, the government is interrupting public policies and placing obstacles to services. Budgetary cuts are happening in all public policies regarding women and LGBTQIA + rights. In her first year in office, Damares Alves has not used a cent of the R$13.6 million reserved to the construction of the 'Brazilian Women Houses', an important public policy aimed at creating referral centres offering health, legal and support services to women in situations of domestic violence. Amidst the rise of domestic and sexual violence during the pandemic,[5] the National Secretariat of Policies for Women used only half of the R$121.9 million overall budget available for the year.[6]

In the case of sexual and reproductive rights, erosion[7] is happening through the dismantling of the network of women's health and legal abortion services and through the creation of obstacles to accessing health services, such as budgetary cuts, disincentives, and technical regulations. This informal strategy had already been launched

---

[3] The name of the ministry has changed to include 'Family'.

[4] Lara Bartilotti Picanço and Anya Prusa, 'At the United Nations, Brazil Allies with Ultra-Conservatives on Gender and Sex-Ed' *Think Brazil, Wilson Center* (22 July 2019) https://www.wilsoncenter.org/blog-post/the-united-nations-brazil-allies-ultra-conservatives-gender-and-sex-ed (accessed 30 July 2021).

[5] Eliane Gonçalves, 'Violência doméstica: Pandemia tornou o lar um ambiente ainda mais hostil' *Agência Brasil* (10 June 2021) https://agenciabrasil.ebc.com.br/radioagencia-nacional/direitos-humanos/audio/2021-06/violencia-domestica-pandemia-tornou-o-lar-ambiente-ainda-mais-hostil (accessed 30 July 2021).

[6] Constança Rezente and Thiago Resende, 'Pasta de Damares esvazia verbas para combater a violência contra mulher' *Folha de S Paulo* (20 September 2020) https://www1.folha.uol.com.br/cotidiano/2020/09/pasta-de-damares-esvazia-verbas-para-combate-a-violencia-contra-mulher.shtml (accessed 30 July 2021).

[7] We are expanding Pozen and Scheppele's analysis of autocratic strategies during the pandemic. See David Pozen and Kim Lane Scheppele, 'Executive Underreach, in Pandemic or Otherwise' (2020) 114 American Journal of International Law 608.

by the previous government, the one that took over after the impeachment of Dilma Roussef (Brazil's first woman president) but was immediately undertaken and deepened since the beginning of the Bolsonaro Government.

Scarcity of services deepened further in the pandemic, when even distribution of contraceptives was reduced or interrupted. The offer of legal abortion services has shrunk, which is specially tragic as it happens amidst the increase in sexual violence against women and girls during the Covid-19 crisis.[8]

In the context of quarantine and lock-down measures, disproportionate negative consequences to women—such as unwanted pregnancies—were expected, as was the disruption in health services. These concerns led WHO and local mobilizations to urge authorities to take measures to minimize Covid-19's negative effects on health issues. WHO's guidance to address the Covid-19 crises recommended expanding access to information, to modern contraception and to legal abortion services.[9] However, moving in the opposite direction, the government actually took active measures to curtail sexual and reproductive rights and further harm women and girls.

In the first weeks of the pandemic, the distribution of contraceptives was impaired. Trying to mitigate the situation, two officials of the Ministry of Health issued a technical note reinforcing policies on reproductive rights that were previously provided and reiterating general recommendations from the WHO for the expansion of access to family planning, information, contraception and legal abortion services.[10] After being thoroughly criticized by the President and the Minister for Women, Family, and Human Rights, the officials were dismissed, which is a serious and exceptional measure for public servants. In view of the Technical Note, besides the government's reaction, conservative Congressmen proposed six different projects aiming to revoke it.[11]

A turning point to more aggressive governmental anti-abortion moves during the pandemic was the case of a ten-year-old girl who, after facing all kinds of hurdles, including pressure from the government, finally had access to legal abortion services in a public hospital. After being systematically raped by her uncle, the girl fell pregnant and, together with her family, sought a legal abortion procedure. She was denied the proceeding in the reference hospital of her home state and had to travel to another state in order to have her right granted. During the whole process, however, the case was reported by the media, with contrasting responses by the public and, as an important conservative voice, Minister Damares was strongly against the procedure.

---

[8] Joana Oliveira, 'Abortos legais em hospitais referência no Brasil disparam na pandemia e expõem drama da violência sexual' El País (30 August 2020) https://brasil.elpais.com/brasil/2020-08-30/abortos-legais-em-hospitais-referencia-no-brasil-disparam-na-pandemia-e-expoem-drama-da-violencia-sexual.html (accessed 30 July 2021).

[9] World Health Organization, 'Continuing Essential Sexual Reproductive, Maternal, Neonatal, Child and Adolescent Health Services during COVID-19 Pandemic', Operational guidance for South and South-East Asia and Pacific Regions (17 April 2020) hps://apps.who.int/iris/bitstream/handle/10665/331816/SRMNCAH-covid-eng.pdf?sequence=1&isAllowed=y (accessed 1 May 2022).

[10] Nota técnica no 16/2020-COSMU/CGCIVI/DAPES/SAPS/MS (2020) https://kidopilabs.com.br/planificasus/upload/covid19_anexo_46.pdf (accessed 1 May 2022).

[11] Indicação n. 626/2020, Requerimento de Informação no 573/2020, Projeto de Decreto Legislativo no 250/2020, Projeto de Decreto Legislativo no 251/2020, Projeto de Decreto Legislativo no 259/2020, Projeto de Decreto Legislativo no 271/2020 (2020).

Besides public statements, the minister sent government officials to try to persuade the girl not to abort and then was said to have leaked information about the place and time of the scheduled medical procedure, so that anti-abortion protesters could promote a blockade in front of the hospital. The girl entered the hospital hiding in the boot of a car, amidst screams calling her a murderer, in a tragic spectacle of revictimization.[12]

This event led the Executive to move more poignantly towards the creation of barriers to access the right to legal abortion. The Ministry of Health promulgated Ordinance (Portaria) No 2282, of 27 August 2020, which expressly revoked a 2005 Ordinance regarding abortion protocols in cases of rape.[13] The 2005 Ordinance was considered a victory of the pro-sexual and reproductive right mobilization within the state, for having de-bureaucratized access to legal abortion, making the presentation of a police report in order to access the procedure unnecessary.[14] By contrast, this Ordinance aims at re-establishing all obstacles. The new rule makes it mandatory for health professionals who attend patients in cases of rape to notify the police, and offer information about the possibility of visualizing the embryo or foetus via ultrasound (even if not requested). It also created the Justification and Authorization Procedure for Terminating Pregnancy, with four stages, bureaucratizing access to the procedure.[15]

In the face of the Ordinance, two lawsuits were proposed and, on the eve of the judgement of the injunction, the Ordinance was replaced by another one, Ordinance No 2561/2020, which attenuates the language of the previous one, without changing the content. This was considered a move, from the part of the Health Ministry, to drain out the lawsuits.[16]

In October 2020, another move was made aiming to restrict reproductive rights. A decree, instituting the 'Federal Strategy for Brazilian Development from 2020 to 2021', was promulgated and, among other goals, adopted as a guideline the promotion of 'the right to life from conception to natural death, observing the rights of the unborn child, through responsible parenthood policies, family planning and protection for pregnant women'.[17] A total ban on abortion became a government goal and has significant support in a conservative leaning Congress composition. For the first time in eight decades, Brazilian abortion regulation is about to retrogress.

---

[12] Thaiza Pauluze and João Valadares, 'Menina de dez anos entrou em hospital em porta-mala enquanto médico distraía religiosos' *Folha de S Paulo* (18 August 2020) https://www1.folha.uol.com.br/cotidiano/2020/08/menina-de-dez-anos-entrou-em-hospital-na-mala-do-carro-enquanto-medico-distraia-religiosos.shtml (accessed 12 December 2021).

[13] Portaria PRT MS/GM 1508/2005 (2005) https://portaldeboaspraticas.iff.fiocruz.br/biblioteca/portaria-n-o-1-508-interrupcao-da-gravidez-nos-casos-previstos-em-lei-no-sus/ (accessed 1 May 2022).

[14] Marta Rodriguez de Assis Machado and Debora Alves Maciel, 'The Battle Over Abortion Rights in Brazil's State Arenas, 1995-2006' (2017) 125 Health and Human Rights Journal 19 https://www.hhrjournal.org/2017/06/the-battle-over-abortion-rights-in-brazils-state-arenas-1995-2006/ (accessed 17 December 2021).

[15] Portaria no 2282/2020 (2020).

[16] Tiago Angelo, 'Lewandowski retira de pauta ações que contestam portaria sobre aborto' *Conjur* (24 September 2020) https://www.conjur.com.br/2020-set-24/lewandowski-retira-pauta-acoes-contestam-portaria-aborto (accessed 30 July 2021).

[17] Decreto No 10531/2020.

3 Judicial Challenges against Legal Abortion Barriers during the Pandemics

In face of the Ordinance (Portaria) No 2282, two lawsuits were proposed in the Brazilian Supreme Court, challenging the constitutionality of the measure. The first one (ADPF 737) was proposed by five left-wing parties in September 2020.[18] The petition argues, in sum, that the Ordinance violates the principles of human dignity, separation of powers, legality, due legislative process, and the rights to health, privacy, and intimacy, as well as the constitutional protection against torture and degrading treatment.[19]

The constitutionally protected right to health—which, according to the claimants, arises from the principle of human dignity—is conceptualized as having not only the negative character of protection from undue interference in the body, but also a positive character: it imposes a duty of promotion on the state. Part of this right, according to the claimants, is the protection of sexual and reproductive rights, which involves the right to abortion in cases of sexual violence and the duty of the state to promote it. The Ordinance, in this context, creates hindrances to the access of legal abortion and, therefore, is in violation of the right to health enshrined in the Constitution.[20]

ADPF 737 also argues that the Ordinance violates the right to health to the extent it harms the intimacy and privacy of the victims, as it prevents the medical observance of the duty to professional secrecy.[21] Along the same lines, it is argued that to demand policing activities from doctors perverts the logic of care, necessary in abortion procedures.[22]

The right to health is seen as also being violated by the fact that the Ordinance imposes the duty of providing information about the negative aspects of abortion in a disproportionate fashion—information that is intended to dissuade women from interrupting pregnancies and cause the feeling of guilt. This, according to the claimants, violates a series of international treaties that delineate the best practices in promoting health.[23]

Regarding the constitutional prohibition of torture and inhumane treatment, ADPF 737 argues that women and girls who are survivors of sexual abuse are revictimized by the consequences of the violence suffered, and therefore, have their dignity violated by the practices provided for in the Ordinance.[24] In this context, the fact that women are impotent in the face of doctors, because of their gender, vulnerability caused by prior violence, and power asymmetries that arise from their dependency on doctors and other health providers, is seen as key in the configuration of degrading treatment.[25]

---

[18] Brazilian Supreme Court, Claim of Non Compliance with Fundamental Precept no 737, Judge-Rapporteur: Min Ricardo Lewandowski, Filed in 3/9/2021 (ADPF 737).
[19] ADPF 737 (n 18) Initial Petition, 7.
[20] ibid 23–33.
[21] ibid 33–36.
[22] ibid 31.
[23] ibid 37.
[24] ibid 46.
[25] ibid 50.

Finally, ADPF 737 advances the argument that the Ordinance violates the principle of legality, to the extent that it goes beyond the powers of the Ministry of Health. The Ordinance imposes restrictions on rights, which cannot be done without the due legislative process and certainly cannot be done by an organ which is part of the administration, violating the separation of powers.[26]

The other lawsuit, ADI 6552, was proposed by the Brazilian Institute of Social Health Organizations, an association that consists of non-profit entities responsible for the management of hospitals.[27] The claimant argues that, from a technical perspective, the Ordinance imposes duties on health professionals that go beyond their attributes and qualifications and that, therefore, could have negative impacts in the offering of legal abortion services.[28] Health providers should provide safe spaces for victims, not prosecutions. From a human perspective, it is argued that the Ordinance extends the suffering of sexual abuse victims, by constraining and threatening them.[29] As a consequence, it violates women's and girls' rights protected by the Constitution and many international treaties.

As can be seen, both the lawsuits primarily frame the abortion issue as being health-related and related to the woman's fundamental rights, albeit in different ways. In the first one, abortion in cases of sexual violence is seen as a materialization of the constitutionally protected right to health—understood as physical and mental integrity. All other principles and rights that are violated by the Ordinance—such as human dignity, privacy, intimacy—are conceptualized by the claimants as flowing *from* the right to health. The second lawsuit, in its turn, was proposed not by political actors, but by a health-related organization, which explains the great importance that is given to how the Ordinance could unduly interfere with doctors and other health professionals' activities, to the detriment of victims.

As the Ordinance has impacts in medical settings, it is intuitive to rely on health rights and technical arguments about health professionals' activities. They are also in tune with how the issue has been legally framed by the pro-reproductive health movements in the broader abortion dispute.[30] The right to health frame has also been recognized before by the Judiciary. In the first constitutional case on abortion ruled by the court, the anencephalic pregnancy case (ADPF 54), the possibility of therapeutic interruption of pregnancy in cases of foetal anencephaly was understood by several justices as a health matter—both in individual and public policy terms.[31] Since then, the health framework reappeared in a decision in which one of the court's chambers declared, in *obiter dictum*, the unconstitutionality of the criminalization of abortion

---

[26] ibid 51.
[27] Brazilian Supreme Court, Claim of Non Compliance with Fundamental Precept no 6552, Judge-Rapporteur: Min Ricardo Lewandowski Filed in 2/9/2020 (ADI 6552).
[28] ibid 13.
[29] ibid 13.
[30] Marta Rodriguez de Assis Machado and Debora Alves Maciel, 'The Battle over Abortion Rights in Brazil's State Arenas, 1995-2006' (2017) Health and Human Rights Journal 19 https://www.hhrjournal.org/2017/06/the-battle-over-abortion-rights-in-brazils-state-arenas-1995-2006/ (accessed 17 December 2021).
[31] Marta Rodriguez de Assis Machado and Rebecca J Cook, 'Constitutionalizing Abortion in Brazil' (2018) Journal of Constitutional Research 185 https://revistas.ufpr.br/rinc/article/view/60973 (accessed 30 July 2021).

up to twelve weeks and in the Initial Petition of the lawsuit that aims the full declaration of unconstitutionality of the criminalization of abortion up to twelve weeks.[32]

4 Reproductive Justice and Substantive Equality-based Considerations on Abortion

As demonstrated above, the pandemic, governed throughout by a misogynist populist government, created a critical juncture resulting from the coincidence of a policy of hollowing out reproductive rights, with the exacerbation of the burdens on and vulnerability of women, particularly Black, poor women.

Despite this hyperbolic situation, the equality principle had no role in the constitutional challenges against the government's obstacles to sexual and reproductive rights. In this section, we propose to reflect on the current situation in Brazil regarding sexual and reproductive rights under the lens of intersectionality and reproductive justice.

The reproductive justice framework was built in opposition to the liberal take on abortion that somewhat predominated among north-American feminist circles in the United States in the 1990s. The critique was based on the fact that, when looking at how women of colour experience reproduction in real life, the liberal approach was not able to deal with problems they faced. While the subject had been formulated in terms of a 'reproductive freedom framework', women of colour were in need of 'justice'.[33]

Such an approach—which is grounded in reality and constructed from the perspective of those at 'the bottom'[34]—allows us to consider how social, economic, and political conditions impact on reproduction. There is, therefore, a direct link to intersectional approaches, calling attention to the different experiences that different groups of women experience towards reproduction.

The examination of reproduction in context has shown that abortion is not an isolated phenomenon, with individual implications, experienced by all women equally. On the contrary, the reality of women of colour brought attention to the fact that all steps of reproduction (ie sexuality, fertility, pregnancy, mothering, excessive care work) are deeply permeated by structural inequalities (like lack of education, information and access to contraceptives) that mutually influence each other, creating the need for abortions.[35]

Theorizing from the ground-up, the reproductive justice approach brings to the forefront the myriad of factors that are involved in reproduction: material factors, like

---

[32] Brazilian Supreme Court, Sentence, Claim of Non Compliance with Fundamental Precept no 54, Judge-Rapporteur: Justice Marco Aurélio, Brasília, DF (30 April 2013); Brazilian Supreme Court, Claim of Non-compliance with Fundamental Precept no 442, Justice-Rapporteur: Justice Rosa Weber, filed on 8/03/2017.

[33] Loretta J Ross, 'Conceptualizing Reproductive Justice Theory: A Manifesto for Activism' in Loretta J Ross and others (eds), *Radical Reproductive Justice: Foundation, Theory, Practice, Critique* (The Feminist Press at CUNY 2017) 173.

[34] Mari J Matsuda, 'Looking to the Bottom: Critical Legal Studies and Reparations' (1987) 22 Harvard Civil Rights-Civil Liberties Law Review 323.

[35] Loretta J Ross and others, *Radical Reproductive Justice: Foundation, Theory, Practice, Critique* (The Feminist Press at CUNY 2017).

how an unwanted pregnancy comes to be and why women need abortions (Did she have access to contraceptives? Does she want it? Does she want it, but has to abort because she cannot support a child?), but also factors related to how systems of oppression shape reproductive experiences. Do unwanted pregnancies happen out of the blue or because of inequality-related issues, like sexual violence or lack of safe conditions to exercise motherhood, for instance? Abortion is inserted into the broader realm of reproduction, which, in turn, is inserted in the broader context of structural inequalities.[36]

Because reproduction is a process that involves multiple mutually constitutive steps, the underlying imperative of the framework is that the reproductive experience should be considered holistically. And a consequence of this new way of reflecting about reproduction is the demand that women be given not only negative rights to non-interference in the body (on which liberty-driven pro-choice authors rely on but also positive rights: the State *must* provide all the resources for the exercise of reproductive rights.[37] This is why the reliance on individual framing to advance the right to abortion, especially on liberty-based arguments focusing on the right to choose, does not at all match how women of colour experience reproduction, and, therefore, does not encompass their needs. For Black women, the freedom to choose is not *the* element at stake.[38]

Reproductive justice activists, in this context, preferred to characterize reproductive-related matters in terms of justice, rather than freedom or equality. Freedom was seen as an illusion—as it had little space in a world of inequality. The liberal Aristotelian conception of equality, however, with its focus on 'difference of treatment', was also seen as insufficient to enclose all the demands. Many inequalities that permeate reproduction are not the fruit of differentiated treatment between men and women or Blacks and Whites, but of asymmetries of power that arise from interlocking systems of oppression. And, as such, they 'cannot be addressed or even imagined by antidiscrimination law'.[39]

Scepticism regarding formal equality is not restricted to the reproductive rights movement. Its limitations have been exposed and challenged for many years now.[40] However, the criticism directed at the principle did not lead to an abandonment of law's potential in addressing, at least, some inequalities derived from subordination. Instead, the adoption of critical methodologies has led to the formulation of the anti-subordination perspective of equality. This perspective provides both an analytical framework that directs inquiries to inequalities that happen on the

---

[36] ibid 8.
[37] ibid 10.
[38] Andrea Smith, 'Beyond Pro-Choice versus Pro-Life: Women of Color and Reproductive Justice' in Loretta J Ross and others (eds), *Radical Reproductive Justice: Foundation, Theory, Practice, Critique* (The Feminist Press at CUNY 2017) 242.
[39] Dean Spade, 'Intersectional Resistance and Law Reform' (2013) 38 Signs 1031, 1034.
[40] Owen Fiss, 'Groups and the Equal Protection Clause' (1976) 5 Philosophy and Public Affairs 107; Catharine A MacKinnon, *Feminism Unmodified* (Harvard UP 1984) 40; Kimberlé W Crenshaw, 'Demarginalizing the Intersection of Race and Sex: A Black Feminist Critique of Antidiscrimination Doctrine, Feminist Theory and Antiracist Politics' (1989) University of Chicago Legal Forum 139; Neil Gotanda, 'A Critique of "Our Constitution is Color-Blind"' (1991) 44 Stanford Law Review 1; Catharine A MacKinnon, 'Substantive Equality: A Perspective' (2011) 96 Minnesota Law Review 1.

ground—substantive inequalities—and provides a tool for the translation of these inequalities into the language of law: the anti-subordination principle.[41]

Despite the scepticism of the reproductive justice framework in relation to rights' discourse, we aim to show that the concrete problems that permeate reproduction can be translated into the language of rights, by the use of the mediating principle of anti-subordination. The social texture of the Brazilian Constitutional order represents a legal and political opportunity to frame reproductive justice claims into law.

Subordination is complex and dynamic: it manifests in many ways. As a consequence, challenges can take many forms. However, all anti-subordination-based arguments share a common animus: the dismantling of hierarchies. From a substantive standpoint, to equalize treatment is not enough; real equality demands improvements in many stances. One comprehensive approach, for instance, sees substantive equality as multidimensional. This means that anti-subordination initiatives should take into account: (i) redressing disadvantage; (ii) redressing of stigma, stereotyping, humiliation, and violence; (iii) the increase in social inclusion and political voice; and (iv) the accommodation of difference and structural change.[42] Restrictions on abortion, in general, involve conceivably all of the dimensions of substantive inequality. The Brazilian context under Covid-19 and Bolsonaro exponentiate inequality in all these dimensions as well. Although interconnected, we will try to disentangle them below.

4.1 Structural Inequalities, the Power Point of View, and Abortion Restrictions

Structurally speaking, abortion restrictions are formulated from the point of view of power.[43] That is, abortion regimes—and the Ordinance discussed, in particular—are detached from how the phenomenon of abortion actually happen in the lives of women.[44] While the Ordinance adopts a view of women's and foetuses' relationship in opposition (like murder, for instance), the decision to abort is much more complex.[45] The decision is shaped by what happens before, during and after an unwanted pregnancy. Unwanted pregnancies are inserted in the realm of sexuality, which, in unequal societies like Brazil, is often permeated by imbalances of power. Inequalities are behind the lack of sexual education and information, poor distribution of contraceptives and sexual violence in general. Such experiences of inequality were deeply exacerbated during the crisis: access to contraceptives were actively boycotted by the government and lockdown measures, and unemployment and other factors enormously

---

[41] Ruth Colker, 'Anti-Subordination Above All: Sex, Race, and Equal Protection' (1986) 61 New York University Law Review 1003, 1007.

[42] Sandra Fredman, 'Substantive Equality Revisited' (2016) 14 International Journal of Constitutional Law 727.

[43] Some feminist authors call this the 'male point of view'. In here we adopt the term 'power point of view', because power better reflects the idea of interlocking systems of oppression.

[44] This argument is developed in the context of the US by Catharine A MacKinnon. See Catharine A MacKinnon, 'Reflections on Sex Equality Under Law' (1991) 100 Yale Law Journal 1281.

[45] A similar argument was developed by Taís Penteado, focusing on pre-Covid-19 inequality-related matters in Brazil. Taís Penteado, 'A questão do aborto no Brasil: uma discussão na chave da igualdade' (MA dissertation, FGV Law School of São Paulo 2020).

contributed to the increase of sexual violence—especially of girls.[46] Part of the decision of whether or not to abort are also considerations concerning the hurdles of the gestational process. During Covid-19, pregnant women faced higher health risks and a shortage of pre-natal and maternal public services.[47] A large group of women, particularly Black women, were pushed into situations of greater vulnerability. Deciding to terminate pregnancy is also shaped by considerations as to what comes after childbirth. In Brazil, women are already disproportionately burdened with care work, which is becoming more dramatic with progressive implementation of austerity measures.[48] The Covid-19 crisis has aggravated such a situation, especially with the deepening of structural inequalities with intersectional dimensions. Almost 8.5 million women left the labour market in the third quarter of 2020 alone.[49] Single mothers, of whom there are more than 11.5 million in Brazil, were pushed into a situation of deeper risks and lack of livelihoods, besides mental and material overload. More than 1.5 million positions were lost in the domestic work sector, one that is mostly made up of Black women.[50]

Part of structural change is to recognize the mismatch between the law and women's reality. In the case of abortion, prohibitive regimes, and the Ordinance particularly, are alienated from women's experiences and the extreme situation they were exposed to by the Covid-19 crisis. Such alienation has structural roots and arises also from women's subordination and exclusion from the formulation of laws and policies. It is not a coincidence that Bolsonaro's Government has one of the worst female participation rates in the executive among all countries in the world, with only two women ministers among twenty-two (9 per cent) while, on average, the international rate is 20.7 per cent of ministries occupied by women.[51] Such misogyny materializes with an array of policies that harm women, particularly Black and indigenous women.

---

[46] Fundo das Nações Unidas para a Infância (UNICEF); o Instituto Sou da Paz & Ministério Público do Estado de São Paulo (MPSP), 'Análise das ocorrências de estupro de vulnerável no Estado de São Paulo (2020) https://soudapaz.org/o-que-fazemos/conhecer/analises-e-estudos/analises-e-estatisticas/boletim-sou-da-paz-analisa/?show=documentos#4484 (accessed 15 April 2022).

[47] Rossana Francisco, Lucas Lacerda and Agatha S Rodrigues, 'Obstetric Observatory BRAZIL: COVID-19: 1031 Maternal Deaths Because of COVID-19 and the Unequal Access to Health Care Services' (2021) https://doi.org/10.6061/clinics/2021/e3120 (accessed 15 April 2022).

[48] OXFAM Brasil, 'Tempo de Cuidar: O trabalho de cuidado não remunerado e mal pago e a crise global da desigualdade' (2020) https://www.oxfam.org.br/justica-social-e-economica/forum-economico-de-davos/tempo-de-cuidar/; Instituto Brasileiro de Geografia e Estatística (IBGE), 'PNAD Contínua' (2020) https://www.ibge.gov.br/estatisticas/sociais/trabalho/17270-pnad-continua.html?edicao=27762&t=resultados (accessed 15 April 2022).

[49] Instituto Brasileiro de Geografia e Estatística (IBGE), 'PNAD Contínua' (2020) https://www.istoedinheiro.com.br/pandemia-deixa-85-milhoes-de-mulheres-fora-do-mercado-de-trabalho/ (accessed 15 April 2022).

[50] Ian Prates and others, 'Desigualdades raciais e de gênero no mercado de trabalho em meio à pandemia' (AFRO-CEBRAP 2021) https://cebrap.org.br/wp-content/uploads/2021/02/Informativo-7-Desigualdades-raciais-e-de-ge%CC%82nero-no-mercado-de-trabalho-em-meio-a%CC%80-pandemia.pdf (accessed 17 December 2021).

[51] Jamil Chade, 'Participação de mulheres no governo Bolsonaro é uma das menores do mundo' *UOL* (12 March 2021) https://jamilchade.blogosfera.uol.com.br/2019/03/12/participacao-de-mulheres-no-governo-bolsonaro-e-uma-das-menores-do-mundo/ (accessed 17 December 2021).

4.2 Stigma and Stereotyping

Abortion restrictions typically involve stigma and stereotyping. The regulations and the public debate are loaded with stereotypes and views about expected behaviours of women as mothers and caregivers. Women are the ones blamed for unwanted pregnancy and expected to risk their health[52] and life plans for a pregnancy. The high number of single mothers and children that do not even have their father's name in their documents shows that men are not confronted with that same responsibility. Women are punished for their sexuality and even rape exceptions can be read as exceptions for those women who did not choose to engage in sexual activities, thus violating expectations of chastity.[53]

During Covid-19, stereotypes about women became even more evident. Women were the ones overwhelmed by reproductive work and expected to abdicate from everything to care for others. Many women had to quit their jobs to care for children and the elderly. A national survey showed that 50 per cent of women had to take care of someone during the pandemic, among which 52 per cent were Black women and 46 per cent were White women. Among those who undertake care work, 72 per cent affirmed that the monitoring work within the household increased a great deal and 40 per cent of the women said that the pandemic and the situation of social isolation put the livelihood of their homes at risk.[54] Domestic workers had to risk their lives, as the work was considered 'essential', reproducing colonial stereotypes about the devaluation of their lives. It is not a coincidence that one of the first fatal victims of Covid-19 in Brazil was a domestic worker, a Black woman in Rio de Janeiro, who contracted Covid-19 from HER employers, who had recently arrived from Europe.[55]

The Ordinance is particularly permeated by stereotypes about women. Two opposing ideas underlie it, that women lie about rape and that women should be protected from abortion proceedings. The first portrays women as malicious, who would use the rape exception to resort to abortion as mere contraceptive methods. Hence the rising demand for corroborating documents and evidence. The second assumes motherhood as natural and the interruption of motherhood as a trauma, from which women should be warned and protected. The Ordinance is also paternalistic, mainly based on the idea that women are incapable of making up their minds about abortion without the interference of physicians. Instead, there is no consideration about the difficult concrete situations women are experiencing, on top of lack of access to public services and welfare policies, and much less about the psychological harm and pain produced on women by the proceeding itself.

---

[52] Brazilian regulation exempts the abortion ban only in cases of life risk.
[53] This argument is developed, in the context of the US, by Reva Siegel. See Reva Siegel, 'Reasoning from the Body: An Historical Perspective on Abortion Regulation and Questions of Equal Protection' (1992) 44 Stanford Law Review 261.
[54] Jonas Valente, 'Metade das mulheres passou a cuidar de alguém na pandemia' *Agência Brasil* (30 August 2020) https://agenciabrasil.ebc.com.br/geral/noticia/2020-08/metade-das-mulheres-passou-cuidar-de-alguem-na-pandemia (accessed 30 July 2021).
[55] Maria Luisa de Melo, 'Primeira vítima do RJ era doméstica e pegou coronavírus da patroa no leblon'*UOL* (13 March 2022) https://noticias.uol.com.br/saude/ultimas-noticias/redacao/2020/03/19/primeira-vitima-do-rj-era-domestica-e-pegou-coronavirus-da-patroa.htm (accessed 1 May 2022).

4.3 Violence and Humiliation

Many unwanted pregnancies result from sexual abuse. The pandemic was responsible for increasing the instances in which sexuality of women and girls were exploited. Since sexual violence is primarily practised in the private environment, by members of the family or people that are known to the victims, lockdown measures exacerbated such abuses and the closure of schools meant the loss of an important resource for the safety of girls, for education professionals are key actors in uncovering abuses.[56] Sexual violence is the most obvious issue. However, many other kinds of gender violence permeate restrictions of abortion in general: lack of support, subjection to unsafe proceedings, and revictimization.

The problem of revictimization is especially acute in the case of the Ordinance, as explored by one of the court cases. The Ordinance obliges women who seek abortion after rape to go through emotionally costly proceedings aimed at dissuading them from access the proceeding. Such treatment was characterized as torture by one of the initial petitions.[57]

Questions about violence also surround the prospects of rearing children, particularly Black children, with shortage of resources and public services, in an extremely violent society, with high rates of violence within the domestic environment, permeated with racism and institutional violence against young Black people. For instance, of the 34,918 violent deaths committed against young people from 2016 to 2020, 80 per cent were Black adolescents and men.[58] The increase in violence took place significantly in the northern and northeastern regions of the country and is linked to disputes between criminal factions, but also to structural issues, such as the population's educational level, inequality, income and racism.[59]

4.4 Disadvantage

Finally, reproductive rights are intimately related to disadvantage. In the input, many times, abortion happens because women are already disadvantaged. Abandonment, loneliness, domestic violence, lack of resources, precarious prenatal care, obstetric violence, discrimination, lack of public policies, among other structural intersected issues are disadvantages that deeply influence the decision to abort.

On the output, restrictions perpetuate those disadvantages. Reproductive rights have an important role in the broader perspective of feminization of poverty. In a

---

[56] Bruna Ribeiro, 'Pandemia aumenta risco de abuso e exploração sexual de crianças' *Estadão* (25 June 2021) https://emais.estadao.com.br/blogs/bruna-ribeiro/pandemia-aumenta-risco-de-abuso-e-exploracao-sexual-de-criancas-e-adolescentes/ (accessed 1 May 2022).

[57] ADPF 737 (n 18) Initial Petition, 7.

[58] Lola Ferreira and Igor Mello, Forum: negros são vítimas de 80% das mortes violentas de jovens no Brasil *UOL* (22 October 2021) https://noticias.uol.com.br/cotidiano/ultimas-noticias/2021/10/22/mortes-violentas-criancas-e-jovens-brasil.htm (accessed in 15 April 2022).

[59] Leandro Machado, 'Atlas da Violência: os fatores que levaram Norte e Nordeste a serem as regiões com mais homicídios no Brasil' *BBC News* (5 June 2019) https://www.bbc.com/portuguese/brasil-48517967 (accessed 15 April 2022).

country like Brazil with a general great imbalance in the distribution of reproductive work, which is reinforced by the government's rhetoric, pregnancy disproportionately affects the lives of women. They often take care of their children alone or are forced to move away or reduce their availability for work. Early pregnancy diverts adolescents from the educational path and directly affects their possibilities of formal employment in the future. The pandemic created numerous disadvantages for women (overload, unemployment, economic deprivation, lack of assistance) and imposed many pressures, which impacted reproduction in many ways: from the burdened and vulnerable positions women were put into as mothers to the impacts of an unwanted pregnancy. The closure of day care centres and schools for extremely long periods (re-opened later than restaurants and bars) caused many children to require full-time care at home. Some women had to give up their paid work, while others lost their jobs since the sectors that employed mostly women were the most affected.[60] In sum, women were even more relegated to reproductive activities and left the labour market *en masse*, which is reflected in the high female unemployment rates—affecting mostly Black women. Many of them were put in even more vulnerable situations, as solo mothers, with no assistance to resort to.

4.5 Legal Opportunities for Substantive Equality in the Brazilian Normative Order

As the above demonstrates, translating the social problem of criminalization of abortion into an equality-based argument in the form of anti-subordination became even more pressing and convincing in face of the Covid-19 crisis. The coincidence of a public health crisis with gendered and racialized effects and government attacks against women's rights represented a critical juncture that exponentiated inequalities in the reproductive reality of women.

The Covid-19 crisis puts a magnifying glass on such structural issues and creates an opportunity for advancing the debate in structural terms. Inequalities were exponentiated in *intensity*, in a way that occurred along lines of pre-existing social divisions, rather than due to different treatment.

Advancing an anti-subordination-based equality argument either for the decriminalization of abortion in general, or defending the unconstitutionality of the Ordinance, is not utopian or external to the Brazilian legal order. The Brazilian Constitution has provisions securing individuals from unjustified differentiations. The equal rights clause, equality in the marital relation and the condemnation of discrimination based on sex were certainly a victory of women's mobilization. But the text of the Constitution also imposes positive duties on the State for the promotion of welfare, social justice, and 'full citizenship'.[61]

---

[60] Jornal Nacional, 'Mulheres formam maioria dos que perderam o emprego em 2020' *G1* (8 December 2021) https://g1.globo.com/jornal-nacional/noticia/2021/12/08/mulheres-foram-maioria-entre-os-que-perderam-emprego-em-2020.ghtml (accessed 15 April 2022).

[61] Brazilian Federal Constitution (5 October 1988).

In its first, third, and fifth articles, the Constitution states that the Brazilian Democratic State has as its foundations, among other principles, the citizenship, the dignity of the person, the building of a free, just and solidarity society, the eradication of poverty, marginalization and social inequalities, as well as the promotion of the well-being of all the people, without prejudice on grounds of origin, race, sex, colour, age, and any other forms of discrimination. Article 6 lists the Constitutional social rights to be sought, among them the right to health, which has fuelled pro-abortion mobilization in the last decades.

This more substantive conception of equality has been embraced by the court in a number of cases involving discrimination. Among others, in the past few years the court has understood that affirmative action is a means of promoting racial citizenship; specific protection of women in cases of domestic violence was not reverse discrimination, having in mind their subordinate status; and the prohibition of blood donations by bi and homosexual men and LGBTQ phobia perpetuate subordination.[62]

The social character of the Brazilian Constitution gives strong grounds for the formulation of powerful equality-based arguments such as the one we envision—one that is able to deal with the empirical consequences of barriers to contraception and to reproductive rights within complex forms of intersecting inequalities. These dimensions are obscured if we frame abortion within more restrictive equality provisions based on the prohibition of different treatment by the state; they are also not equated through the liberal individual rights mobilized to resist the matter (privacy, dignity, intimacy).[63]

5 Conclusion

The exponentiation of gender inequalities during the pandemic and the centrality of care work in this equation make the Covid-19 crisis a critical juncture that exposes the inextricable relationship between sexual and reproductive rights and equality.

The Covid-19 crisis created exponential sexual and reproductive inequalities in Brazil. In this context, access to reproductive health policies become even more fundamental. WHO and specialists widely recommended that state measures should be taken to facilitate access to information, contraception, and legal abortion services. However, under a populist anti-gender crusader administration, the opposite happened. Reproductive rights suffered many attacks, the most prominent being Ordinance 2282, which created obstacles to the access of legal abortion in Brazil.

---

[62] Adilson Moreira, 'Discourses of Citizenship in American and Brazilian Affirmative Actions Court Decisions' (2016) 64 American Journal of Comparative Law 455; Brazilian Supreme Court, Declaration of unconstitutionality no 5.543/DF, Justice-Rapporteur: Justice Edson Fachin (8 May 2020) https://redir.stf.jus.br/paginadorpub/paginador.jsp?docTP=TP&docID=753608126 (accessed 27 August 2021); Brazilian Supreme Court, Declaration of unconstitutionality by omission no 26, Justice-Rapporteur: Celso de Mello (13 June 2019) https://redir.stf.jus.br/paginadorpub/paginador.jsp?docTP=TP&docID=754019240 (accessed 27 August 2021); Brazilian Supreme Court, Sentence, Declaration of Constitutionality no 19, Justice-Rapporteur: Justice Marco Aurélio, Brasília, DF (17 February 2012) https://portal.stf.jus.br/processos/detalhe.asp?incidente=2584650 (accessed 4 December 2021).

[63] Taís Penteado, 'The Abortion Jurisprudence in Brazil: An Analysis of ADPF 54 from Feminist Equality-based Perspectives' (2021) 19 International Journal of Constitutional Law 1664.

This chapter has tried to advance an equality-based argument against Ordinance 2282. Adopting the reproductive justice approach as a tool for scanning the Brazilian reality, we have unearthed the relations between the retrogression of reproductive rights and exponential gender inequalities in its intersectional dynamics, during the Covid-19 crisis in Brazil. In this framework, abortion restrictions emerge as a part of the broader realm of reproduction that, in Brazil, is permeated by inequalities. As the Ordinance raises equality issues on the ground, it can be challenged in law through equality-based arguments. For that, we adopted a substantive approach to equality that problematizes hierarchies rather than different treatment. This approach allowed us to read the recent attacks from the government as an instance of the exacerbation of reproductive injustices, uncovering how the effects of criminalization of abortion are disproportionately distributed among certain groups, affecting particularly Black, poor women. The Covid-19 crisis happening simultaneously to increased inaccessibility to reproductive health services put this group of women in a situation of exacerbated vulnerability and risk.

To frame abortion as an equality issue is an important legal move for the protection of women, but also a political choice. To present a formulation giving clear substantive content to the equality provision is a way of securing the resilience of strong protections over time, avoiding manipulations of this open-ended principle in times of conservative turns. While the social character of the Brazilian Constitution is a legal-political opportunity for a substantive equality argument, it has been under strong attack in the past few years. Therefore, bringing forward its promises of social justice is also a way to resist its erosion.

17
A Life of Contradictions
Group Inequality and Socio-economic Rights in the Indian Constitution

Aparna Chandra

On the 26th of January 1950, we are going to enter into a life of contradictions. In politics we will have equality and in social and economic life we will have inequality. In politics we will be recognizing the principle of one man one vote and one vote one value. In our social and economic life, we shall, by reason of our social and economic structure, continue to deny the principle of one man one value. How long shall we continue to live this life of contradictions? How long shall we continue to deny equality in our social and economic life?

Dr BR Ambedkar, Chairperson, Drafting Committee,
Indian Constituent Assembly[1]

1 Introduction: A Crisis in Utopia

Imagine a perfectly equal world. A time in the future where the structures of oppression and domination have been dismantled, systemic patterns of discrimination and disadvantage no longer exist, material deprivations have been redressed, and people assert identities that they value without fear of reprisal. In such a world, would a calamity result in exponential inequalities?

I would argue not. Certainly, the calamity may cause significant losses and disruptions. The impact of such a crisis may also be spread unevenly around the world. However, in the utopia imagined above, a crisis will be addressed in a manner that accounts for and redresses such inequalities. This is because, to move from our current world to this imagined utopia, we will require deeply entrenched and widely accepted normative principles of equal (re)distribution of resources, burdens, and opportunities, as well as institutional structures that consider the removal of systems of oppression, discrimination, and exclusion a matter of the highest priority. Once such norms and structures are in place, they are likely to continue to operate during times of crises and ensure redress for emergent inequalities.

---

[1] Constituent Assembly Debates 25 November 1949, vol 11 (Lok Sabha Secretariat 1986) (Ambedkar).

This thought experiment provides an important insight into thinking about exponential inequalities: calamities do not result in exponential inequality on their own. The state's—and society's—response determines whether a crisis perpetuates or further exacerbates inequality. Thus, if we could address 'everyday' structural/systemic inequality, if we had the institutional set up, the norms, and the commitment to address inequalities in 'ordinary' times, a calamity may not result in a crisis of exponential inequality.

The current pandemic has taught us that material disadvantages and economic vulnerabilities that result from a crisis operate differently, and with greater intensity, on persons who face oppression, discrimination, and other forms of disadvantage because of their group identity. As the UN Special Rapporteur on Extreme Poverty has noted: '[f]ar from being the "-great leveller", COVID-19 is a pandemic of poverty ... race, gender, religious, and class discrimination have skewed access to housing, food, education, and technology in ways that have yielded radically different outcomes'.[2] These comments highlight how antecedent group inequalities exacerbate the unequal impact of crises. A policy response that does not account for such antecedent disadvantage cannot effectively redress the conditions of crises and might even exacerbate its unequal impact by failing to account for the specific needs of disadvantaged groups.[3] For these reasons, this chapter focuses on group inequality and the obligations of the state to redress such inequalities, so that in the event of calamity, it does not lead to exponential inequalities.[4]

Addressing exponential inequalities will require adopting a normative principle that obliges the state to ameliorate conditions of inequality through a positive duty to redress antecedent disadvantages based on group identity. It is not enough for the state to abstain from actively discriminating against disadvantaged groups. On its own, a negative duty of non-discrimination does not address the underlying structures and systems that perpetuate material and social deprivations and act as barriers in accessing rights and entitlements.[5] If, as a result of antecedent inequality and systemic disadvantage, certain groups are more vulnerable to material deprivations, then the state would have to affirmatively acknowledge and remedy these 'structures of oppression and domination which exclude these identities from participation in an equal life'.[6] Hence, redressing group inequality requires imposing positive obligations

---

[2] Report of the Special Rapporteur on extreme poverty and human rights, 'The Parlous State of Poverty Eradication' UN Doc A/HRC/44/40 (2 July 2020) 9.

[3] See eg *Solidarity obo Members v Minister for Small Business Development* [2020] ZAGPPHC 133 (30 April 2020) [37].

[4] I use the term group inequality to refer to an individual's experience of facing inequality and discrimination because of their group identity. While the claim is based on group membership, the claim is made by an individual, and not by the group collectively.

[5] Sandra Fredman, 'Providing Equality: Substantive Equality and the Positive Duty to Provide' (2005) 21 South African Journal on Human Rights 163, 167; Siobhan Mullally, 'Substantive Equality and Positive Duties in Ireland' (2007) 23 South African Journal on Human Rights 291, 315.

[6] *Indian Young Lawyers Assn (Sabarimala Temple-5 J) v State of Kerala* (2019) 11 SCC 1 [420] (Chandrachud J concurring). See also Fredman (n 5) 166; Catherine Albertyn, 'Contested Substantive Equality in the South African Constitution: Beyond Social Inclusion towards Systemic Justice' (2018) 34 South African Journal on Human Rights 441, 461.

on the state to take affirmative steps to achieve substantive equality.[7] In the words of Catherine Mackinnon, substantive equality would require that 'what law has done, it must undo, and what it has not rectified, it should'.[8]

Are we there yet? I ask this question in relation to the Supreme Court of India's equality jurisprudence. This chapter focuses on how the Court engages with questions of material disadvantage in conjunction with group inequality in ordinary times, to lay the groundwork for addressing inequalities during a crisis.

Section 3 shows that, while the Supreme Court has understood the Constitution's equality code as encompassing a substantive vision of equality, by and large, the Court has not read into these provisions any judicially enforceable *positive obligation* on the state to redress group disadvantages. As such, state *failure* to secure substantive group equality remains non-justiciable. On the other hand, as section 3 demonstrates, the Court *has* read in positive obligations of redistribution into its socio-economic rights jurisprudence; however, it has not engaged with questions of group equality in understanding the scope and content of these rights, the concomitant positive obligations on the state, or in the remedial action ordered by the Court. This gap between the constitutional guarantees of equality and of socio-economic justice leaves unaddressed the 'life of contradictions' of the constitutional project about which Dr Ambedkar was concerned.[9] I argue for bringing these two bodies of jurisprudence into conversation with each other in dealing with group inequalities and redressing material disadvantage. This raises the question: even if they have the willingness, should judges adjudicate and enforce positive state obligations? Section IV examines this issue and argues that a focus on group equality can actually address some of the concerns with the Court's extant practices and processes regarding the adjudication of socio-economic rights. Section 5 concludes by bringing together the various strands of my argument.

2 Equality, Non-discrimination, and Positive Duties

2.1 Equality in the Constitutional Project

Securing equality and socio-economic justice are core values of the Indian constitutional project.[10] The Constitution mandates ending state and societal discrimination on the basis of group identity,[11] protecting those elements of group identity that bring value to peoples' lives (eg religious, linguistic, and cultural identities),[12] and redressing

---

[7] Sandra Fredman, 'Positive Rights and Positive Duties: Addressing Intersectionality' in Dagmar Schiek and Victoria Chege (eds), *European Union Non-Discrimination Law: Comparative Perspectives on Multidimensional Equality Law* (Routledge-Cavendish 2009) 74.

[8] Catherine Mackinnon, *Sex Equality* (Foundation Press 2001) 21. See also Nicola Lacey, 'From Individual to Group? A Feminist Analysis of the Limits of Anti-Discrimination Legislation' in Nicola Lacey, *Unspeakable Subjects: Feminist Essays in Legal and Social Theory* (Hart Publishing 1998) 36.

[9] Ambedkar (n 1).

[10] Constitution of India 1950, preamble. See also Sigrid Boysen and Aparna Chandra, 'Equality and Diversity in Constitutional Discourses' in Philipp Dann and Arun K Thiruvengadam, *Democratic Constitutionalism in India and the European Union* (Edward Elgar Publishing 2021) 104.

[11] Constitution of India 1950, arts 14, 15(1), 15(2), 16(1), 16(2), 17, 29(2), 325.

[12] ibid arts 15(1), 25, 26, 29(1), 30.

material deprivations with a particular focus on the needs of socially and economically disadvantaged groups.[13]

To redress group inequalities, the Constitution permits the state to make 'special provisions' for certain groups. Thus, in the context of group inequality, the equality provisions embody a substantive vision of equality, and recognize the need for differential treatment to address antecedent disadvantage through affirmative action.[14]

Substantive equality requires that the state should not only redress inequality imposed by the law but should also act affirmatively to redress societal and structural inequalities.[15] The Indian Constitution speaks directly to this obligation in Part IV of the Constitution, titled Directive Principles of State Policy, which imposes binding (although not justiciable) obligations upon the state to redress social and economic inequalities, particularly inequalities in income, status, facilities, and opportunities.[16] The state has a particular obligation to 'promote with special care the educational and economic interests of weaker sections of the people … and protect them from social injustice'.[17]

Further, the Supreme Court has interpreted fundamental rights in general as imposing negative as well as positive obligations upon the state,[18] to 'ensure that conditions in which these freedoms flourish are maintained … The state is duty bound to ensure the prevalence of conditions in which of those freedoms can be exercised'.[19] In keeping with this reading, the Court has constructed an elaborate normative, institutional, adjudicative, and remedial architecture of socio-economic rights which target state inaction in securing such rights.[20] However, as I discuss below, despite these provisions and interpretations, the Court has been reticent in reading positive state obligations into the equality provisions of the Constitution for redressal of group inequalities.

2.2 The Absence of Positive Duties to Secure Group Equality

2.2.1 The prohibition of discrimination

The focus of the Indian Supreme Court's anti-discrimination jurisprudence has been on state *action* that leads to discrimination, and not on state *inaction* that results in discriminatory outcomes. For example, while recognizing that the Indian Constitution contains a substantive vision of equality, the Supreme Court has said that the 'primary enquiry to be undertaken by the Court towards the realization of substantive equality

---

[13] ibid arts 15(4), 16(4), 46.
[14] *Joseph Shine v Union of India* (2019) 3 SCC 39.
[15] Patricia Hughes, 'Recognizing Substantive Equality as a Foundational Constitutional Principle' (1999) 22 Dalhousie Law Journal 5.
[16] Constitution of India 1950, arts 37, 38(2).
[17] ibid art 46.
[18] See eg *S Rangarajan v P Jagjivan Ram* (1989) 2 SCC 574 (positive obligations with respect to freedom of speech); *Puttaswamy I v Union of India* (2017) 10 SCC 1 (positive obligation with respect to right to privacy); *Puttaswamy II v Union of India* (2019) 1 SCC 1 (positive obligations with respect to the right to life).
[19] *Indibly Creative Pvt Ltd v Govt of West Bengal* (2020) 12 SCC 436.
[20] See discussion in section 4 below.

is to determine whether the *provision* contributes to the subordination of a disadvantaged group of individuals'.[21] Even when the Court has dealt with cases of state inaction that directly result in group identity-based discrimination and disadvantage, the Court has generally focused on the violation of other rights, such as those of life and liberty, without alluding to the state's positive obligations with respect to equality and non-discrimination.[22]

The Court has understood the non-discrimination provision contained in Articles 15(1) and 16(2) as prohibiting both direct and indirect discrimination. The doctrine of indirect discrimination prohibits state action that has a disparate impact on protected groups in a way that exacerbates antecedent disadvantage and 'contributes to the subordination of a disadvantaged group of individuals'.[23] While indirect discrimination can be understood as restraining the state from discriminating even by use of facially neutral criteria, this restraint also implies a positive duty to take disadvantage seriously, and to account for and ameliorate the disparate impact of its laws and policies.[24] As such, indirect discrimination does impose a positive obligation upon the state to secure group equality.[25] However, this obligation is limited to those situations where the state chooses to act. It does not oblige the state to redress group inequality absent prior state action. Thus, the focus of indirect discrimination law is still on prohibiting state *action* which, while facially neutral, has a disparate impact on protected groups because of antecedent disadvantage.

2.2.2 Affirmative action

The Constitution itself provides for affirmative action to redress certain types of group inequality. Here too, the Court has not interpreted these provisions as imposing any positive obligation on the state to redress inequality. Instead, it views these provisions as enabling powers that the state can *choose* to deploy at its discretion, rather than as positive *duties* to redress disadvantage.

On the one hand, the Court has categorically rejected an earlier view that affirmative action is an exception to equality,[26] and has instead interpreted affirmative action provisions to be a facet of the right to equality and non-discrimination contained in Articles 14, 15(1), 16(1) and 16(2).[27] On the other hand, the Court has refused to interpret the equality provisions as imposing a positive duty on the state to remove structural and systemic barriers that perpetuate group inequality. It has instead repeatedly taken the view that these provisions 'do not confer any fundamental rights

---

[21] *Joseph Shine* (n 14) [172] (Chandrachud J).
[22] See eg *Shakti Vahini v Union of India* (2018) 7 SCC 192; *Tehseen S Poonawalla v Union of India* (2018) 9 SCC 501.
[23] *Nitisha v Union of India* (2021) SCC OnLine SC 261 [59].
[24] Christopher McCrudden, 'Changing Notions of Discrimination' in Stephen Guest and Alan Milne (eds), *Equality and Discrimination: Essays in Freedom and Justice* (F Steiner Verlag Wiesbaden 1985) 90; Jeremy Waldron, 'Indirect Discrimination' in Stephen Guest and Alan Milne (eds), *Equality and Discrimination: Essays in Freedom and Justice* (F Steiner Verlag Wiesbaden 1985) 96.
[25] Benjamin Eidelson, *Discrimination and Disrespect* (OUP 2015) 39, 68.
[26] *M R Balaji v State of Kerala* [1963] AIR 649.
[27] *State of Kerala v NM Thomas* (1976) 2 SCC 310 (Mathew J) [75]; *Indra Sawhney v Union of India* (1992) Supp (3) SCC 217 (Reddy J, plurality) [741]. See also *BK Pavitra v Union of India* (2019) 16 SCC 129 [112].

nor do they impose any constitutional duties but are only in the nature of enabling provisions vesting a discretion in the State to consider providing reservation.[28]

Overall, then, the Court has focused its equality jurisprudence on state action, and not on state inaction. A more thoroughgoing positive obligation to engage in systemic, structural reform for addressing group disadvantage, has largely been absent from the conversation around the equality doctrine under the Indian Constitution.

2.3 An Emerging Canon?

Having said this, the Court has shown some incipient, although by no means established, signs of recognizing positive duties upon the state to redress group disadvantage. Perhaps the best known example is *Vishaka v State of Rajasthan*,[29] where the Supreme Court held that the state's failure to enact a law to provide redress for sexual harassment in the workplace was a violation of women's right to equality, their freedom of occupation, and their right to life with dignity.[30] The state had failed to fulfil its 'primary responsibility for ensuring such safety and dignity through suitable legislation, and the creation of a mechanism for its enforcement'.[31] Thus, the Court read in an affirmative and *mandatory* constitutional obligation on the state to protect women from sexual harassment, an obligation that can be enforced through the judicial process.[32]

In the same vein, in *National Legal Services Authority v Union of India* (NALSA),[33] the Supreme Court held that state inaction that perpetuates and exacerbates group inequality violates the state's obligations under the Constitution's equality guarantee. In this case, petitioners argued that the state's failure to give legal recognition to the gender identity of transgender persons, and the assumption of binary genders that pervades the entire legal system, violates various fundamental rights of transgender persons, including their right to equality and non-discrimination.[34] Agreeing with this, the Supreme Court catalogued the various forms of discrimination, exclusion, and disadvantage that transgender persons face as a result of the state's failure to accord legal recognition to their gender identity.[35] The Court interpreted Article 14 as placing a 'positive obligation on the State to ensure equal protection of laws by bringing in necessary social and economic changes, so that everyone including [transgender

---

[28] *Ajit Singh (II) v State of Punjab* (1999) 7 SCC 209 [31]; *CA Rajendran v Union of India* (1968) 1 SCR 721 [6]; *M Nagaraj v Union of India* (2006) 8 SCC 212 [123]; *Indra Sawhney v Union of India* (1992) Supp (3) SCC 217 (Pandian J, Thommen J, RM Sahai J, Kuldip Singh J, and Sawant J expressly stating that art 16(4) is an enabling provision and not a compulsion); *Mukesh Kumar v State of Uttarakhand* (2020) 3 SCC 1 [12]; *P&T Scheduled Caste/Tribe Employees' Welfare Assn (Regd) v Union of India* (1988) 4 SCC 147; *State Bank of India Scheduled Caste/Tribe Employees' Welfare Assn v State Bank of India* (1996) 4 SCC 119. See generally MP Singh, 'Are Articles 16(4) or 15(4) Fundamental Rights?' (1994) 3 SCC (Jour) 31; Parmanand Singh, 'Fundamental Right to Reservation: A Rejoinder' (1995) 3 SCC (Jour) 6.
[29] (1997) 6 SCC 241.
[30] *Vishaka v State of Rajasthan* (1997) 6 SCC 241 [3].
[31] ibid.
[32] ibid.
[33] (2014) 5 SCC 438.
[34] *National Legal Services Authority v Union of India* (2014) 5 SCC 438 [2].
[35] ibid [48], [53], [62].

persons] may enjoy equal protection of laws and nobody is denied such protection'.[36] Additionally, the Court held that given the extent of social exclusion faced by transgender persons, they constitute 'socially and educationally backward classes of citizens' who are entitled to affirmative action under the Constitution.[37] Holding that the state is *required* to take affirmative action to redress the disadvantages faced by the community, the Court directed the state to extend affirmative action policies to transgender persons.[38]

Likewise, in *Jeeja Ghosh v Union of India*,[39] the Court noted that persons with disabilities face extensive discrimination and exclusion, and that the state has an obligation to take 'positive measures to ensure that in reality persons with disabilities get enabled' to exercise their guaranteed rights.[40] Building on this, in *Vikash Kumar v UPSC*,[41] the Court held that the principle of reasonable accommodation, which places affirmative obligations upon the state, is part of the guarantee of equality and non-discrimination under the Constitution.[42] In this case, the petitioner was denied a scribe for writing a state examination, despite needing such services due to a medical condition called dysgraphia.[43] In examining whether this refusal was in consonance with the Rights of Persons with Disabilities Act 2016, the Court held that prohibiting discrimination is not enough for giving effect to the equality and non-discrimination rights of disabled persons; instead, 'additional support and facilities' have to be provided to overcome barriers faced by disabled persons.[44]

These cases recognize far-reaching positive obligations upon the state to redress group inequality. However, the notion that Indian equality law imposes positive duties upon the state to redress group inequality is by no means well established in the Court's jurisprudence and these cases are not the norm.[45] By and large, Indian equality jurisprudence is located within a negative duties model.

In other jurisdictions, failure to incorporate positive fundamental rights obligations is often grounded in concerns about the institutional capacity and authority of judges to engage with questions of policy and material re-distribution. This argument does not hold force in India, where courts have created an extensive positive obligations jurisprudence in relation to socio-economic rights which expressly seek to redress material disadvantage. However, as I argue in the subsequent Part, group inequality concerns are missing from this body of jurisprudence.

---

[36] ibid [61].
[37] ibid [67].
[38] ibid [67], [135.3].
[39] (2016) 7 SCC 761.
[40] *Jeeja Ghosh v Union of India* (2016) 7 SCC 761 [43].
[41] (2021) 5 SCC 370.
[42] *Vikash Kumar v UPSC* (2021) 5 SCC 370 [66], [67].
[43] ibid [1].
[44] ibid [43].
[45] See eg *Shakti* (n 22); *Tehseen S Poonawalla v Union of India* (2018) 9 SCC 501.

3 Socio-economic Rights, Positive Duties, and the Absence of Group Inequality Concerns

The Supreme Court has constructed an elaborate jurisprudence on socio-economic rights which includes positive state obligations to realize such rights. These positive duties are often derived from constitutional obligations to secure socio-economic justice contained in the Directive Principles of State Policy. The constitutional framers incorporated these principles into the Constitution to guide the state on how to exercise its power.[46] As Dr Ambedkar stated in the Constituent Assembly, these directive principles sought to augment the principles of legal equality ('one person, one vote', or what he termed 'political democracy') with socio-economic equality ('one person, one value': 'economic democracy').[47] Therefore, the Directive Principles require the state to endeavour to eliminate inequalities of status,[48] as well as to 'promote with special care the educational and economic interests of weaker sections of the people'.[49]

Thus, the Constitution provides for substantive equality, which as Sandra Fredman has argued, takes seriously questions of power, domination, and subordination in structuring the lives, opportunities and material realities of those who are 'disadvantaged, demeaned, excluded, or ignored'.[50] Substantive equality requires the state affirmatively to 'redress disadvantage; address stigma, stereotyping, prejudice, and violence; enhance voice and participation; and accommodate difference and achieve structural change'.[51] The Supreme Court of India has also underscored that substantive equality requires 'recognition of and remedies for historical discrimination which has pervaded certain identities. Such a notion focuses on not only distributive questions but on the structures of oppression and domination which exclude these identities from participation in an equal life'.[52]

However, as I argue in this section, in its socio-economic rights jurisprudence, the Supreme Court does not engage with questions of group discrimination, disadvantage, exclusion, stereotyping, or intersectional forms of subordination, even though these questions are central to the realization of the rights under consideration. As a result, the Court's socio-economic rights jurisprudence fails to craft remedies that redress socio-economic deprivations faced by disadvantaged groups.[53]

I use counterexamples to show that where the Court does recognize group disadvantage, it makes rights more robust and inclusive. However, these cases are few and

---

[46] Constituent Assembly Debates 19 November 1948, vol 7 (Lok Sabha Secretariat 2014) 494 (BR Ambedkar).
[47] ibid.
[48] Constitution of India 1950, art 38.
[49] ibid art 46.
[50] Sandra Fredman, 'Substantive Equality Revisited' (2016) 14 International Journal of Constitutional Law 712, 713.
[51] ibid.
[52] *Indian Young Lawyers Assn (Sabarimala Temple-5 J) v State of Kerala* (2019) 11 SCC 1 [420] (Chandrachud J).
[53] Sandra Liebenberg and Beth Goldblatt, 'The Interrelationship Between Equality and Socio-Economic Rights under South Africa's Transformative Constitution' (2007) 23 South African Journal on Human Rights 335, 351.

far between, and a substantive equality focus is not part of the general approach of the Court when engaging with socio-economic rights.[54]

3.1 Reading Socio-economic Rights into Article 21

In *Francis Coralie Mullin v Administrator, Union Territory of Delhi*,[55] in a petition regarding the rights of detainees to meet with their lawyers and family members during incarceration, the Court discussed the meaning of the 'right to life' under Article 21 of the Constitution. It held that the right to life includes the right to live with human dignity, and 'all that goes along with it, namely, the bare necessaries of life such as adequate nutrition, clothing and shelter and facilities for reading, writing and expressing one-self in diverse forms, freely moving about and mixing and commingling with fellow human beings'.[56]

This dictum of the Court has been repeatedly cited in socio-economic rights cases under Article 21 of the Constitution.[57] And while the Court initially understood socio-economic rights as imposing a negative duty on the state to not deprive persons of such rights without due process,[58] it soon read in positive content into these rights.[59] However, as I show below using examples from adjudication of various types of socio-economic rights, the Court has failed to address the group-differentiated needs and antecedent disadvantage of marginalized groups in accessing such entitlements.

3.2 Right to Education

In *Mohini Jain v State of Karnataka*,[60] petitioners challenged the constitutionality of a law that allowed medical colleges to charge exorbitant tuition fees. In its decision, the Court interpreted the right to life alongside directive principles on social justice and education, and held that the right to life with dignity includes a positive state obligation to secure the right to education for all citizens.[61] The Court held that the state could discharge its positive obligation either by directly establishing or by giving recognition to educational establishments at all levels, and by ensuring that access to these institutions is not denied in an arbitrary manner.[62] It held that permitting educational institutions to charge exorbitant fees was an arbitrary denial of the right to education.

---

[54] See Nicholas Robinson, 'Structure Matters: The Impact of Court Structure on the Indian and US Supreme Courts' (2013) 61 American Journal of Comparative Law 173.
[55] (1981) 1 SCC 608.
[56] *Francis Coralie Mullin v Administrator, Union Territory of Delhi* (1981) 1 SCC 608 [8].
[57] See generally Anup Surendranath, 'Life and Personal Liberty' in Sujit Choudhry, Madhav Khosla and Pratap Bhanu (eds), *The Oxford Handbook of the Indian Constitution* (OUP 2016) 756.
[58] *Francis Coralie Mullin v Administrator, Union Territory of Delhi* (1981) 1 SCC 608 [8]; *Olga Tellis v Bombay Municipal Corporation* (1985) 3 SCC 545 [33].
[59] See eg *KS Puttaswamy (Aadhaar-5J) v Union of India* (2019) 1 SCC 1 (Sikri J).
[60] (1992) 3 SCC 666.
[61] *Mohini Jain v State of Karnataka* (1992) 3 SCC 666 [9], [12]–[14].
[62] ibid [14], [17].

In understanding the content of the positive duty imposed on the state to secure the right to education, the Court did not engage with group differentiated barriers. This is particularly surprising because barring access to education for women and marginalized castes has been a defining way in which social hierarchy has been maintained and reproduced in India. Recognizing this, Article 46 of the Constitution specifically mandates the state to secure the educational interests of weaker sections. Accordingly, Article 15(4) empowers the state to make special provisions for the advancement of 'socially and *educationally* backward classes of citizens'. Article 29(2) likewise prohibits discrimination in admission to state maintained or funded educational institutions on the basis of certain markers of group identity.[63] However, the element of discrimination, segregation, and exclusion, both in accessing educational institutions and in the treatment meted out to students from disadvantaged groups within such institutions formed no part in the Court's articulation of the scope of the right to education. Thus, the Court's understanding of the duties of the state to give effect to the right to education focused on establishing educational institutions at all levels, and not also in removing barriers to accessing the institutions that were already in existence.

It could be argued that group differentiated barriers to access was not an issue before the Court. While that is true, the Court could also have decided the case on the basis of the doctrine of arbitrariness *simpliciter*, without going into the question of the right to education at all. By going into this question, and giving content to the right, the Court shaped the discourse on the right to education for years to come.[64] A more robust content may have given a different impetus to the politics of securing the right to education in a more equitable manner.

The correctness of the decision in *Mohini Jain* was called into question in *Unni Krishnan v State of Andhra Pradesh*.[65] The Court upheld *Mohini Jain* on the point that Article 21 encompasses a right to education which places a positive mandate on the state to realize this right. It differed with *Mohini Jain* in finding that this right is limited to mandatorily providing education only up to the age of fourteen, beyond which the state had to secure this right in tune with its economic capacity. This reading followed from a directive principle which had, at that time, mandated the state to provide free and compulsory education up to the age of fourteen.[66] While the Court noted, as *Mohini Jain* had not, that Article 46 directs the state to pay special attention to the educational needs of weaker sections, Scheduled Castes and Scheduled Tribes, the Court's focus remained on establishing schools either directly, or through recognizing private educational institutions, without any discussion on barriers to access to education in these schools.

This one-size-fits-all approach to socio-economic rights, which does not account for group-based disadvantages, does not address the social and material contexts in which these rights are accessed and therefore the specific types of barriers that may be experienced by disadvantaged groups, or the distinct set of obligations required to

---

[63] The prohibited grounds are religion, race, caste, and language.
[64] See n 147, n 148, n 149, and accompanying text on a discussion on this point.
[65] (1993) 1 SCC 645.
[66] Article 45 as it stood prior to the Eighty-sixth Constitutional Amendment 2002.

be imposed upon the state in order to ameliorate these deprivations.[67] For example, centring the experiences of women in accessing education would highlight how access to education for women is mediated not only by lack of facilities but also because of the treatment meted out to women students within educational institutions. Further, segregation in schools, stigma, stereotyping, and discrimination against marginalized groups are often reinforced by the curriculum. A focus on these aspects of deprivation faced by disadvantaged groups could expand the dimensions of the right to education, moving it beyond access to facilities towards a more robust right to an inclusive education. Thus, a substantive equality approach to socio-economic rights can play a constitutive role in shaping the scope and content of these rights, the obligations imposed on the state, and how these obligations ought to be realized.[68]

3.3 Right to Health

The Supreme Court has also read the right to health into Article 21 of the Constitution.[69] As a result, a range of concerns regarding access to healthcare are within constitutional purview. In *Parmanand Katara v Union of India*,[70] and *Paschim Banga Khet Mazdoor Samity v State of West Bengal*,[71] for example, the Court interpreted the right as imposing a positive duty on the state to secure access to emergency medical aid.[72] These decisions were based on the reasoning that the state has a proactive obligation to preserve life under Article 21 of the Constitution. In *Parmandand Katara*, the cause of lack of access comprised hospitals turning away emergency 'medico-legal cases' for fear of getting involved in the legal process. And in *Paschim Banga Khet Mazdoor Samity*, the cause of lack of access was identified by the Court as the lack of adequate healthcare facilities for providing emergency medical aid. The lack of access to medical aid in these cases was framed as a lack of resources, which the state was obligated to provide and to not hinder access to. Without a focus on group inequality, neither of these cases understood lack of access also as a matter of discrimination against marginalized groups which results in exclusion even in existing medical facilities.[73]

Recognizing group inequality in accessing healthcare is not only a matter of extending healthcare to hitherto excluded groups, but can also shape what healthcare itself encompasses.[74] A focus on the differentiated needs of marginalized groups may show how the very understanding of what counts as a matter of health is contested, and access to healthcare can be made meaningful for such groups by focusing on their distinctive health needs and the barriers they face in realizing the right, such as mental

---

[67] Sandra Fredman, 'Engendering Socio-Economic Rights' (2009) 25 South African Journal on Human Rights 410, 411.
[68] ibid 417.
[69] *CESC Ltd v Subhash Chandra Bose* (1992) 1 SCC 441; *Consumer Education & Research Centre v Union of India* (1995) 3 SCC 42 [24].
[70] AIR 1989 SC 2039.
[71] (1996) 4 SCC 37.
[72] *Paschim Banga Khet Mazdoor Samity v State of WB* (1996) 4 SCC 37 [9].
[73] cf *Navtej Johar v Union of India* (2018) 10 SCC 1 (Chandrachud J).
[74] See eg *Ramlila Maidan Incident, In re* (2012) 5 SCC 1 [316] (Chauhan J), where the Court expressly omitted rights of homeless persons when addressing the right to sleep/rest as part of health and well-being.

health services as part of emergency healthcare, or access to contraception or safe abortion services for women.[75]

Devika Biswas v Union of India[76] provides a counter-example. Various state governments were conducting mass sterilization camps in a manner that led to adverse health outcomes for the persons undergoing sterilization. The Court determined that not following proper procedure to conduct sterilization procedures violated patients' right to health which, according to the Court, includes a right to reproductive health.[77] The Court also examined the differential impact of such procedures on disadvantaged groups. It noted that the government efforts disproportionately targeted women for sterilization, offending gender equality.[78] At the same time, it noted that often in 'mass sterilization' camps, it was mostly women from vulnerable communities, and especially indigenous communities, who faced the brunt of sterilization procedures. The Court held that the policy of the state to set informal targets and create incentives for government officials for sterilizing people exposed already vulnerable groups to coercive sterilization.[79] Stating that 'the policies of the Government must not mirror the systemic discrimination prevalent in society but must be aimed at remedying this discrimination and ensuring substantive equality',[80] the Court directed ending the policy of target setting for sterilizations, and the policy of conducting mass sterilization camps.[81] At the same time, it required the state to include, as part of its standard operating procedures, counselling patients in the local language, and a cooling-off period for them to consider whether they want to undergo the sterilization procedure, in order that they might provide genuinely informed consent to such procedures.[82]

In *Devika Biswas* the Court went beyond a one-size-fits-all approach to the right to health to look at the differential impact of sterilization policies on men and women, and on persons from vulnerable groups, to craft a remedy that addressed this group differentiated denial of rights. Infusing a group inequality analysis into the right to health helped the Court formulate the scope and content of the right and obligation relating to health in a manner that is responsive to the lived realities and the specific needs of disadvantaged groups.[83]

---

[75] On the lack of focus on abortion as a healthcare right in India, and barriers to accessing abortion, see Aparna Chandra and others, *Legal Barriers to Accessing Safe Abortion Services in India: A Fact Finding Study* (Center for Reproductive Rights, 2021) http://opac.nls.ac.in:8081/xmlui/bitstream/handle/123456789/812/Legal-Barriers-to-Accessing-Safe-Abortion-Services-in-India_Final-for-upload.pdf?sequence=1 (accessed 3 May 2022).
[76] (2016) 10 SCC 726.
[77] ibid [107]–[108].
[78] ibid [105], [112].
[79] ibid [112].
[80] ibid.
[81] ibid [113.9]–[113.10].
[82] ibid [113.2].
[83] Fredman (n 67) 440.

3.4 Right to Shelter

The right to shelter is another example of the Supreme Court extending positive duties as part of the right to life.[84] In *Shantistar Builders v Narayan Khimalal Totame*,[85] the Court had to decide the constitutionality of a housing policy for 'weaker sections' of citizens. The Court stated that the right to life includes the right to 'a suitable accommodation to live in'.[86] Based on this understanding, the Court set out guidelines on how the state should make allocations under the housing policy. Importantly, while the Court linked the relevant statutory provision to the constitutional obligation under Article 46 to pay special attention to the needs of weaker sections, Scheduled Castes and Scheduled Tribes,[87] it determined the criteria for deciding who belongs to a weaker section on economic means alone.[88] A group inequality analysis was entirely absent from this decision, and therefore the Court was not alive to the intersections between group inequality and economic deprivations which reinforce each other and produce distinct patterns of disadvantage and exclusion in accessing shelter.[89]

The Court also directed the state to make one allotment per family—with the family presumed to consist of a husband, wife, and children.[90] The adoption of a heteromarital nuclear family as the basis for allocation disadvantages persons who live in non-normative familial settings, or who, for reasons such as domestic abuse, have moved out of their marital or natal homes. A substantive equality lens would be alive to (and seek to redress) inequalities in property holding between men and women in the same household, as well as the socio-economic disadvantages these cause and exacerbate for women. The court lost the opportunity to redress such disadvantages by redistributing property rights within families in a more equitable manner.

In *Chameli Singh v State of Uttar Pradesh*,[91] the Supreme Court had to decide whether the state had been justified in using an urgency clause for acquiring land under the Land Acquisition Act 1894. This clause allowed the state to adopt a truncated procedure for acquiring land. The state claimed land was needed urgently to provide housing to persons from Scheduled Castes and Scheduled Tribes. Validating the exercise of this power, the Supreme Court stated that the right to shelter is part of the right to life under the Constitution, and is indispensable to the exercise of other fundamental and human rights.[92] The Court understood the right to shelter as comprising more than 'a mere right to a roof over one's head but right to all the infrastructure necessary to enable them to live and develop as a human being'.[93] Thus, a person's right to shelter encompasses 'adequate living space, safe and decent structure, clean

---

[84] See eg *PG Gupta v State of Gujarat* (1995) Supp (2) SCC 182; *State of Karnataka v Narasimhamurthy* (1995) 5 SCC 524; *Gauri Shanker v Union of India* AIR 1995 SC 55.
[85] (1990) 1 SCC 520.
[86] ibid [9].
[87] ibid [11], [12].
[88] ibid [20].
[89] Liebenberg and Goldblatt (n 53) 339–40.
[90] *Shantistar Builders* (n 85) [17].
[91] (1996) 2 SCC 549.
[92] *Chameli Singh v State of Uttar Pradesh* (1996) 2 SCC 549 [8].
[93] ibid.

and decent surroundings, sufficient light, pure air and water, electricity, sanitation, and other civic amenities like roads etc. so as to have easy access to his daily avocation'.[94] The state, according to the Court, has a positive duty to secure this right to citizens.[95] In particular, the Court recognized that want of shelter limits the ability of persons belonging to Scheduled Castes and Scheduled Tribes to participate meaningfully and on an equal basis in national life, and that the state therefore has an obligation to secure such a right for these disadvantaged groups.[96]

In this case the Court specifically considered the right to shelter for disadvantaged castes and tribes. The Court could have understood the content of the right to shelter in a manner that addressed the specific barriers to accessing shelter faced by such groups, like housing discrimination and segregation.[97] However, these concerns did not factor into the Court's conception of the right. So also, even though the Court stated that the right to shelter encompasses more than a roof over one's head, since it did not focus on barriers to accessing housing, the access concerns of disabled persons found no place in the Court's articulation of the content of the right to shelter.[98]

This may be contrasted with the approach of the Court in *Ahmedabad Municipal Corporation v Nawab Khan Gulab Khan*,[99] where the Court underscored the importance of looking at the right to shelter in the context of the directive principles to minimize inequality and to redress disadvantages of 'weaker sections', especially Scheduled Castes and Tribes. Centring this perspective, the court noted the particular vulnerability of such groups to being forced out of their tenements by 'slum-lords', as well as the housing discrimination and segregation they faced. The court accounted for these concerns in the specific directions it issued to the state.[100]

3.5 Right to Work and Livelihood

The Supreme Court has recognized the rights to work and to livelihood as the largely negative right to not be arbitrarily deprived of work and livelihood.[101] It has placed limited positive obligations on the state with respect to the right to work: that of providing safe and healthy work conditions. In these cases, the Court has read the right to work alongside other positive rights under Article 21 such as the right to health and the right to a dignified work environment.[102]

---

[94] ibid.
[95] ibid.
[96] ibid.
[97] Report of the Special Rapporteur on Adequate Housing as a Component of the Right to an Adequate Standard of Living, and on the Right to Non-Discrimination in this Context, on her mission to India (10 January 2017) UN Doc A/HRC/34/51/Add.1.
[98] Liebenberg and Goldblatt (n 53) 339.
[99] (1997) 11 SCC 121.
[100] *Ahmedabad Municipal Corporation v Nawab Khan Gulab Khan* (1997) 11 SCC 121 [29].
[101] *Olga Tellis v Bombay Municipal Corporation* AIR 1986 SC 180; *Sodan Singh v New Delhi Municipal Committee* (1989) 4 SCC 155; *K Rajendran v State of Tamil Nadu* (1982) 2 SCC 273.
[102] See eg *Bandhua Mukti Morcha v Union of India* (1984) 3 SCC 161 [10]; *Consumer Education & Research Centre v Union of India* (1995) 3 SCC 42 [18], [24].

Vishaka v State of Rajasthan[103]—discussed in the previous section—is a case in point. In *Vishaka*, the Court determined that sexual harassment of women in the workplace violated, inter alia, their right to equality and to a safe and dignified work environment. The case itself was filed as a public interest litigation by an NGO, in response to the gang rape of Bhanwari Devi, a Dalit woman working as a *sathin* (a voluntary worker assisting in the implementation of social schemes) employed by the State of Rajasthan. Dominant caste men raped Bhanwari Devi in retaliation against her attempt to stop a child marriage as part of her work. In the trial court, the judge acquitted the accused inter alia on the ground that it was inconceivable that men belonging to a 'higher' caste would rape a 'lower' caste woman. Thus, the violence inflicted on Bhanwari Devi was mediated as much by her gender as by her caste.[104] However, while the Court used the equality lens to examine the disadvantages women face in the workplace, the specific vulnerabilities of women from marginalized castes were absent from the Court's understanding of sexual violence and in its guidelines for redress.[105] The informal and unorganized nature of Bhanwari Devi's work, which is the case with the overwhelming segment of workers in India and women workers in particular, was also absent from the Court's consideration.[106] As a consequence, the guidelines framed in *Vishaka* were designed to be implemented in the organized workforce,[107] and through internal processes against co-employees. Workers who are not part of such workplaces, such as domestic workers, were not provided any remedy. The lack of an intersectional analysis mediated by caste and class meant that Bhanwari Devi's own experience of sexual violence would not be covered by these guidelines. The Court was also completely silent on accessing redress in courts for rape particularly for women from marginalized communities, and the barriers to access that they face in getting their complaints taken seriously, investigated and adjudicated, as Bhanwari Devi's own experience exemplified.[108] A substantive equality lens requires being alive to such intersectional forms of discrimination.[109] The absence of this intersectional perspective meant that even when the court was alive to questions of group discrimination, it understood discrimination along a single axis (of gender), which limited its ability to provide redress for intersectional forms of group discrimination and disadvantage.

---

[103] *Vishaka* (n 30).

[104] Shreya Atrey, *Intersectional Discrimination* (OUP 2019) 68.

[105] After noting that the petition is *Vishaka* was filed in the context of the gang rape inflicted on Bhanwari Devi, the Court set aside this context stating that 'no further mention of it, by us, is necessary'. *Vishaka* (n 30) [2].

[106] Shiney Chakraborty, *Women in the Indian Informal Economy* IWWAGE Report (February 2021) https://www.indiaspend.com/uploads/2021/03/26/file_upload-446784.pdf (accessed 3 May 2022).

[107] Requiring for example, that the guidelines against sexual harassment should be made part of orders issued under the Industrial Employment (Standing Orders) Act 1946: *Vishaka* (n 30) [17].

[108] For an account of Bhanwari Devi's experiences in securing redress from the police and courts, see Geeta Pandey, 'Bhanwari Devi: The Rape that Led to India's Sexual Harassment Law' *BBC News* (17 March 2017) https://www.bbc.com/news/world-asia-india-39265653 (accessed 3 May 2022).

[109] Atrey (n 104) 68.

3.6 Right to a Clean Environment

As a final example, let us take the Supreme Court's elaborate jurisprudence on the right to a clean environment as part of the right to life under Article 21 of the Constitution.[110] The Court has held that this right imposes a positive duty on the state 'not only to ensure and safeguard proper environment but also an imperative duty to take adequate measures to promote, protect and improve both the man-made and the natural environment'.[111] It has sought to balance the right to a clean environment with the right to development, particularly in the context of infrastructure projects that have a harmful ecological impact.[112] In doing so, it has not focused on the impact of such projects on disadvantaged groups.[113] The Court has weighed the benefits of the projects to the population at large and harms of such projects to a smaller subset of people without accounting for the nature and intensity of the harm caused to the latter. Such a calculus can then easily be weighted in favour of the larger community by dint of sheer numerical strength.[114]

For example, in *Narmada Bachao Andolan v Union of India*,[115] petitioners contested the state's decision to set up a hydro-electric power plant on the Narmada river, inter alia, because of its impact upon indigenous populations who would be displaced as a result. The Court discounted the impact of such displacement on the cultural and associational rights of indigenous communities, and held instead that while such displacement would 'undoubtedly disconnect them from their past, culture, custom and traditions ... it becomes necessary to harvest a river for the larger good'.[116]

The lack of a group inequality lens has shaped not only the Court's articulation and instantiation of right, but the very manner in which it understands the issue before it, as well as the remedies and reliefs it provides. For example, in *Almitra Patel v Union of India*,[117] while conferring on concerns relating to solid waste management in the city of Delhi, the Court framed the issue as one of aesthetics—of the impact of solid waste on how clean and beautiful the city looked.[118] The alternative framing of the issue as one of livelihood of thousands who are involved in urban waste management and sanitation, such as rag pickers, who not only face economic precarity, but are overwhelmingly from marginalized castes, was not a consideration for the Court. If anything, the Court's approach actively harmed such communities, because, in framing

---

[110] *Virender Gaur v State of Haryana* (1995) 2 SCC 577 [7]; *Vellore Citizens' Welfare Forum v Union of India* (1996) 5 SCC 647 [16].
[111] *Virender Gaur* (n 110) [7].
[112] *ND Jayal v Union of India* (2004) 9 SCC 362 [11].
[113] See generally Prashant Bhushan, 'Sacrificing Human Rights and Environmental Rights at the Altar of "Development"' (2009) 41 George Washington International Law Review 389, 397; Nivedita Menon, 'Environment and the Will to Rule: Supreme Court and Public Interest Litigation in the 1990s' in Mayur Suresh and Sidhdharth Narain (eds), *The Shifting Scales of Justice: The Supreme Court in Neo-Liberal India* (Orient BlackSwan 2014) 59.
[114] See eg *T N Godavarman Thirumulpad v Union of India* (2002) 10 SCC 606 [35]; *G Sundarrajan v Union of India* (2013) 6 SCC 620.
[115] (2000) 10 SCC 664.
[116] *Narmada Bachao Andolan v Union of India* (2000) 10 SCC 664 [241].
[117] (2000) 2 SCC 679.
[118] *Almitra Patel v Union of India* (2000) 2 SCC 679 [7], [9], [11].

the issue as one of aesthetics, the Court moved from management of urban waste, to 'slum clearance' as a requirement for a clean city. In doing so, the Court frowned upon resettlement of communities living in such informal settlements on the ground that '[r]ewarding an encroacher on public land with a free alternative site is like giving a reward to a pickpocket'.[119] This case exemplifies how the absence of a substantive equality lens not only excludes the concerns of disadvantaged groups but can also further exacerbate the disadvantages and exclusions they face.[120]

The examples could be multiplied, but the larger point is that while the Court has developed an extensive socio-economic rights jurisprudence including positive state obligations to secure such rights, this jurisprudence does not generally address concerns of group inequality in the realization of socio-economic rights. The cases that do are few and far in between. Factoring in group inequality is not part of the general *modus operandi* of the Court while dealing with socio-economic rights. By not centring a group inequality lens within its socio-economic rights jurisprudence, the Court fails to understand why and how socio-economic rights are violated, and how such violations should be remedied. The exclusion of group-based experiences of deprivation, disadvantage, and exclusion, attenuates the scope and content of socio-economic rights, the positive obligations cast on the state in securing these rights, and the remedies for their violation.

4 Equality of What, Whom, How?

The discussion above indicates that there are two parallel conversations taking place in Indian jurisprudence on redressing material disadvantage. One, on group inequality, imposes negative duties of restraint upon the state, but no positive obligations to redress group inequality. The other, on socio-economic rights, imposes positive obligations on the state to redress material disadvantage but does not consider issues of group inequality. This, I argue, is a missed opportunity to take group disadvantage seriously by infusing socio-economic rights with substantive equality.[121]

However, even if the Court were to bring together these two bodies of jurisprudence, it would have to answer subsequent questions: equality of what? Of whom? And how is this to be achieved—or rather, how should these rights be enforced?[122] I argue below that a conjoint reading of substantive group equality and socio-economic rights will not only answer these questions but will also address some of the institutional concerns around the Court's adjudication of socio-economic rights.

---

[119] ibid [14]. For a critique, see Usha Ramanathan, 'Illegality and Exclusion: Law in the Lives of Slum Dwellers' (International Environmental Law Research Centre, Working Paper 6, 2004) http://www.ielrc.org/content/w0402.pdf (accessed 3 May 2022); Lavanya Rajamani, 'Public Interest Environmental Litigation in India: Exploring Issues of Access, Participation, Equity, Effectiveness and Sustainability' (2007) 19 Journal of Environmental Law 293.

[120] See also *MC Mehta v Union of India* (31 August 2020) Writ Petition (Civil) No 13029/1985.

[121] cf Shreya Atrey, 'The Intersectional Case of Poverty in Discrimination Law' (2018) 18 Human Rights Law Review 411.

[122] Marc Galanter, *Competing Equalities: Law and the Backward Classes in India* (OUP 1984) 394–95.

4.1 Conjoint Reading of Substantive Group Equality and Socio-economic Rights

A conjoint reading of articles 15 and 16 with article 21 can furnish a response to the first two questions. Even to the extent that the Court has recognized positive group equality obligations, such as in *Vishaka*,[123] *NALSA*,[124] and *Vikash Kumar*,[125] it has tied these obligations to securing other rights. In each of these cases, the Court catalogued the various rights of women, transgender persons, and disabled persons, respectively, that were infringed because of state inaction, resulting in such groups facing discrimination and disadvantage.

In this context, socio-economic rights can play an important role in giving robust substantive content to positive equality obligations, since the deprivation of such rights is often exacerbated by group membership, and their redress can reduce group disparity. I have discussed in the previous section how centring group inequality in socio-economic rights jurisprudence can help to articulate more inclusive rights and remedies for socio-economic deprivations.[126]

A positive obligation to achieve substantive equality raises further questions: equality between whom? Again, Article 15 (generally), Article 16 (in the context of public employment) and Article 29 (in the context of education) furnish an answer. These provisions contain guidance on group inequalities towards which the Constitution requires the state to pay special attention. As discussed in section 2 above, at least since *State of Kerala v N M Thomas*[127] the Supreme Court has held that the non-discrimination provisions in Articles 15 and 16 embody a substantive notion of equality.[128] A conjoint reading of Article 21 and the equality code would impose a positive obligation on the state to ensure that in fulfilling its mandate to secure socio-economic rights, the specific disadvantages, deprivations, and exclusions faced by constitutionally recognized disadvantaged groups is accounted for.[129]

At the same time, we should recognize that the protected categories mentioned in Articles 15 and 16 are limited by the imaginations and the political mobilizations of the founding moment. Other grounds of group disadvantage, most particularly that of disability, do not find express mention in the Constitution. Courts in other jurisdictions, most notably the Canadian Supreme Court, have developed doctrines which extend constitutional protections for expressly recognized disadvantaged groups to analogous groups.[130] Such an approach would require the Court to develop a theory of the common characteristics underlying the protected grounds under

---

[123] *Vishaka* (n 30).
[124] *NALSA* (n 34).
[125] *Vikash Kumar* (n 42).
[126] See also Victoria Miyandazi's contribution to this collection, which makes a similar point about Kenya.
[127] (1976) 2 SCC 310.
[128] *Indra Sawhney v Union of India* (1992) Supp (3) SCC 217 [741] (Reddy J); *KC Vasanth Kumar v State of Karnataka* (1985) Supp SCC 714; *Ashoka Kumar Thakur v Union of India* (2008) 6 SCC 1.
[129] See eg *Maneka Gandhi v Union of India* AIR 1978 SC 597, where the Court read arts 14 and 21 together, albeit in a different context.
[130] *Corbiere v Canada* [1999] 2 SCR 203 [60].

Article 15 and 16 and extend these protections to other analogous forms of group inequality.[131]

4.2 Addressing Institutional Concerns with Adjudicating Positive State Obligations

This brings us to the third question: that of implementation. More specifically, does the judiciary have the capacity (including expertise and the ability to deal with polycentric issues), authority (due to the separation of powers), and legitimacy (due to lack of democratic accountability in setting budgetary priorities) to adjudicate positive state obligations to redress group inequality in securing socio-economic rights?[132] I argue that, to the contrary, infusing the Court's socio-economic rights jurisprudence with substantive equality will ameliorate many of the concerns of capacity, authority, and legitimacy that otherwise arise in judicial enforcement of socio-economic rights.

Judicially enforceable positive obligations are already part of Indian jurisprudence, and the Court has crafted its own strategies to address such concerns. For example, while the Court has interpreted Article 21 broadly to read in extensive socio-economic rights, it provides rather limited remedies for their violation. Although the Court uses the broad interpretation of rights to bring the matter within the scope of justiciability, its subsequent interventions focus on determining whether the applicable state policies are compliant with basic norms of reasonableness and non-arbitrariness, and on monitoring their implementation.[133] As a general matter, the Court does not fundamentally reset the budgetary policies of the state.[134] Further, the Court has crafted sophisticated institutional mechanisms such as setting up expert committees and commissions to augment its capacity to engage with questions beyond its own expertise, as well as to gather evidence required for evaluating state policies and failures.[135]

The Court's general approach to socio-economic rights adjudication is broadly aligned to that of other jurisdictions which have adopted 'weak-form' review mechanisms to walk the tightrope between accountability for violations of socio-economic rights on the one hand, and concerns about judicial capacity, legitimacy, and authority on the other.[136] As the Court has itself begun to recognize, in socio-economic rights adjudication, it acts as a forum for dialogue between the court, the political branches, and other stakeholders regarding the realization of the socio-economic entitlement at stake.[137] This 'bounded-deliberative

---

[131] *Navtej Johar v Union of India* (2018) 10 SCC 1 [638.3]–[639] (Malhotra J); Tarunabh Khaitan, 'Reading Swaraj into Article 15: A New Deal For All Minorities' (2009) 2 NUJS Law Review 419.

[132] Fredman (n 5) 168.

[133] Madhav Khosla, 'Making Social Rights Conditional: Lessons from India' (2010) 8 International Journal of Constitutional Law 739.

[134] cf *Paschim Banga Khet Mazdoor Samity v State of West Bengal* (1996) 4 SCC 37.

[135] Ashok H Desai and S Muralidhar, 'Public Interest Litigation: Potential and Problems' in BN Kirpal and others (eds), *Supreme But Not Infallible: Essays in Honour of the Supreme Court of India* (OUP 2000) 159.

[136] Mark Tushnet, 'Reflections on Judicial Enforcement of Social and Economic Rights in the Twenty-First Century' (2011) 4 NUJS Law Review 177.

[137] *In Re Distribution of Essential Supplies and Services During Pandemic* (2021) SCC OnLine SC 355 [7]. See also Upendra Baxi, 'The Avatars of Indian Judicial Activism' in Shailendra Verma and Kusum Kumar (eds), *Fifty Years of the Supreme Court of India: Its Grasp and Reach* (OUP 2000).

approach'[138] creates accountability for state actions and failures by requiring the state to publicly justify its actions and the 'rationale behind [its] policy approach'.[139]

These possibilities for accountability and justification are enabled by procedural techniques that the court adopts in socio-economic rights adjudication. For example, socio-economic adjudication is not a 'one-off' affair where the Court declares the existence of a right and issues a one-time negative or positive injunction as remedy. Rather, through a series of hearings, the claimants, the state, other intervenors, court appointed *amicus curiae* and other experts—and the judges themselves—deliberate upon the issue; seek further information either from the state, or through court directed independent evidence gathering; require the state to provide its rationale for its (in)actions; discuss this information and what it reveals about the state's response to socio-economic imperatives; determine and direct remedial measures, or ask the state to engage in such determination; require the state to report back after taking action; monitor the implementation of such actions; receive feedback from the state and other stakeholders on such implementation; and revise directions in response to this feedback.[140] Through the device of 'continuing mandamus',[141] the Court uses a finding of socio-economic deprivation as the basis to generate public deliberation and accountability for state actions, and to 'improve ... public administration making it more responsive than before to the constitutional ethic and law'.[142]

This form of adjudication has the potential to provide high visibility to issues of socio-economic deprivations, reveal information about such deprivations in the public domain, and thus facilitate accountability for state failures in the court of public opinion by 'preserv[ing] its memory in ... public records'.[143] The Court's interventions can shape political discourse by facilitating a 'culture of justification' by requiring the state to publicly disclose the rationale behind its policy choices.[144]

This is not to say that there are no valid concerns regarding the Indian Supreme Court's intrusion into the arena of socio-economic rights.[145] Questions such as whose concerns, whose voice, what priorities, and—underlying these—what ideologies and interests are centred in the Court's adjudicatory process; which experts are invited to the table; and concomitantly who is silenced, who is ignored, what worldviews, interests and concerns are absent in framing rights and imagining remedies, are all relevant

---

[138] *In Re: Distribution of Essential Supplies and Services During Pandemic* (n 137), citing Sandra Fredman, 'Adjudication as Accountability: A Deliberative Approach' in Nicholas Bamforth and Peter Leyland (eds), *Accountability in the Contemporary Constitution* (OUP 2013); Sandra Fredman, *Comparative Human Rights Law* (OUP 2018) 91–95.

[139] *In Re: Distribution of Essential Supplies and Services During Pandemic* (n 137).

[140] Sandra Fredman, *Human Rights Transformed* (OUP 2008) 233–47.

[141] *Vineet Narain v Union of India* (1998) 1 SCC 226. On the use of the device of continuing mandamus in socio-economic rights adjudication, see Desai and Muralidhar (n 135).

[142] Upendra Baxi, 'Taking Suffering Seriously: Social Action Litigation in the Supreme Court of India' (1985) 4 Third World Legal Stud 107, 122.

[143] *In Re: Distribution of Essential Supplies and Services During Pandemic* (2021) SCC OnLine SC 355 [70].

[144] On the accountability function of socio-economic adjudication see Fredman (n 5) 175; Etienne Mureinik, 'Beyond a Charter of Luxuries: Economic Rights in the Constitution' (1992) 8 South African Journal on Human Rights 464.

[145] Desai and Muralidhar (n 135); Rajamani (n 119); Fredman (n 137) 247–72; Anuj Bhuwania, *Courting the People: Public Interest Litigation in Post-Emergency India* (CUP 2013).

to the present inquiry.¹⁴⁶ A group inequality lens, I would argue, would help the Court address these challenges. Institutionalizing a focus on group inequality at least requires courts to be more reflexive about the constitutional choices they make. Such a lens emphasizes the role of privilege and disadvantage in constituting legal subjectivity and displaces assumptions about the neutrality of these choices. Such a reflexive process is more likely to lead to inclusivity than the *status quo*.

However, in the facts of many of the cases discussed above, questions of group inequality were not directly before the Court. Is it not unfair to criticize the Court for not paying attention to group inequality in such cases?

I would argue that, in fact, many of these cases did not require the Court to go into questions of socio-economic rights in the first place. Both *Chameli Singh*¹⁴⁷ and *Mohini Jain*¹⁴⁸ could have been decided on general principles of judicial review of administrative decisions. Even *Francis Corallie*,¹⁴⁹ the progenitor of the Court's socio-economic rights jurisprudence grounded in an entitlement to a right to life with dignity, did not require the Court to go into the scope of the right to life. The Court was dealing with conditions of detention under a preventive detention law. It could have decided the case on an interpretation of the right to personal liberty. However, by expounding on the scope of the right to life, the Court paved the way for a transformation in the kinds of claims that can legitimately be made upon the state. Recognizing certain claims as rights makes them legible on the legal register and enables claimants to compel courts to implement laws and policies which may be enacted on paper but are not implemented in reality. Such recognition also enables political mobilization and social action outside the courts, by granting visibility and legitimacy to such claims in political discourse, as well as by shaping societal conceptions of justice and political expectations from the state.

So, for example, the Court's recognition of a positive obligation on the state to provide education in *Mohini Jain*¹⁵⁰ and *Unni Krishnan*,¹⁵¹ gave an impetus to social activism around this issue. This ultimately culminated in a constitutional amendment that shifted this obligation from the directive principles of state policy to a fundamental right, and in the enactment of the Right of Children to Free and Compulsory Education Act 2009. The Court's dicta on the right to information and the right to know gave impetus and legitimacy to mobilization around a right to information legislation in India, leading to the enactment of the Right to Information Act 2005.¹⁵² Recognition of the right to food as a constitutional right and a state imperative paved the way for the enactment of the National Food Security Act 2013.¹⁵³ The Court's decision in *Vishaka*¹⁵⁴ recognized sexual harassment as a form of gender discrimination,

---

¹⁴⁶ See Mayur Suresh and Siddharth Narrain (eds), *The Shifting Scales of Justice: The Supreme Court in Neo-Liberal India* (Orient BlackSwan 2014).
¹⁴⁷ *Chameli Singh* (n 92).
¹⁴⁸ *Mohini Jain* (n 61).
¹⁴⁹ *Francis Corallie* (n 56).
¹⁵⁰ *Mohini Jain* (n 61).
¹⁵¹ *Unni Krishnan* (n 65).
¹⁵² *State of UP v Raj Narain* [1975] AIR 865; *SP Gupta v Union of India* [1981] Supp SCC 87; *Union of India v Association for Democratic Reforms* (2002) 5 SCC 294; *PUCL v Union of India* (2003) 4 SCC 399.
¹⁵³ *PUCL v Union of India* (2001) Writ Petition (Civil) No 196/2001.
¹⁵⁴ *Vishaka* (n 30).

and spurred activism around legislation to address sexual harassment in the workplace, culminating in the Sexual Harassment of Women at Workplace (Prevention, Prohibition and Redressal) Act 2013.

This is not to say that legislative action on these issues would not have taken place without court intervention. However, the recognition by the Court of these rights as entitlements under the Constitution invests them with legitimacy and urgency, and provides impetus for claims by civil society organizations for their provisioning by the legislature. As such, norm articulation by the Court structures the possibilities of politics inside and outside of courts.

In this light, there is value in infusing group inequality into the scope and content of socio-economic rights even when the immediate facts of the case do not raise group inequality issues. In many of these cases discussed above, the Court was articulating particular socio-economic rights and establishing their contours for the first time. The Court's articulation of the scope and content of such rights shape their trajectories inside courts as well as in the political arena. By not linking the right to education, for example, to the express constitutional mandate to redress group differentiated access barriers to education, this was a missed opportunity to frame the discourse on the right to education in the country. Beyond influencing the political possibilities of socio-economic rights, how the Court understands the scope and content of the right will also determine how the Court adjudicates the right, its standards for reviewing state (in)action, the justifications and accountability it requires, the positive obligations it places upon the state, and the remedial measures that the Court orders as redress.

Centring group inequality in socio-economic rights adjudication does not mean that the Court should know every barrier faced by every protected group, or the specific disadvantages imposed on them. Rather, it will require the Court to create doctrinal and institutional structures where these concerns can be articulated, engaged with, and addressed. If, as a matter of doctrine, the Court requires the state to take group inequality seriously in implementing its positive obligations to realize socio-economic rights, and be conscious of disadvantage, discrimination, and antecedent structures of oppression, then the State will have to justify how it accounted for group-inequality in its policies. Failure to do so, would render the policy un-constitutional, and may require the state to go back to the drawing board.[155]

Reviewing state actions to determine whether they are consistent with the demands of (group equality-infused) positive obligations of the state would facilitate a culture of justification for socio-economic entitlements that puts concerns of group inequality at the heart of the constitutional project of securing socio-economic justice. In judging the reasonableness of state (in)action, the Court will ask questions and seek evidence about how the state (in)action intersects with the lives of disadvantaged groups and whether it places additional burdens, or alternatively, accounts for and addresses the differential needs and specific barriers faced by such groups in accessing the relevant entitlements.[156] Essentially, by infusing socio-economic rights with group

---

[155] See eg *Government of Republic of South Africa v. Grootboom* [2000] ZACC 19; *Minister of Health v Treatment Action Campaign* (2002) 5 SA 721 (CC). See also Liebenberg and Goldblatt (n 53) 353.
[156] Fredman (n 5) 182.

equality, the Court will hold the state accountable for its policies by reference to this standard.[157]

As Sandra Fredman has argued, group equality concerns can be meaningfully incorporated into decision-making by requiring 'decision-makers to hear and respond to the voices of groups sharing a protected characteristic rather than imposing top-down decisions'.[158] In this sense, substantive equality-infused socio-economic rights adjudication would require the State to explain not only what policy is made, but how it made its decisions. The Court can question the state on how its policies were made, who was consulted, who was left out, and how the policy takes into account the concerns of disadvantaged groups.[159] Institutionalizing requirements of consultation and responsiveness to community views can have the effect of making the state's policy making processes more inclusive beyond the confines of specific litigations.

Adopting a substantive equality approach to socio-economic rights adjudication also calls for judicial restraint in imposing policy prescriptions without hearing from impacted groups. The Court's own adjudicatory processes can exclude disadvantaged groups—their voices are not heard, and the decision is imposed on them top-down through judicial fiat. The Court's capacity to deliver on substantive equality in socio-economic rights adjudication will require re-thinking adjudicatory practices which limit the voices of disadvantaged groups from being represented in Court. In particular, ensuring greater participation will require the Court to review its institutional and procedural mechanisms that support socio-economic rights adjudication (such as committees, commissions, amici curiae, intervenors, etc), to determine how best to ensure that disadvantaged groups are centred in the conversation.

Overall, then, infusing group equality into socio-economic rights adjudication requires courts to take group disadvantage seriously and centre the consideration of group differentiated barriers and needs into its doctrine, standards of review, adjudicatory processes, and remedies in its socio-economic rights jurisprudence.

5 Conclusion: Taking Group Disadvantage Seriously

Centring concerns of group inequality in socio-economic rights adjudication can make rights more robust and relief more meaningful, by acknowledging and affirmatively redressing disadvantage caused by stigma, discrimination, and other forms of exclusion on grounds of one's group identity. Institutionalizing the infusion of positive socio-economic rights with substantive equality can also address many of the concerns about court-mediated socio-economic rights jurisprudence and lead to more inclusive adjudicatory practices.

If the Court can institutionalize taking group disadvantage seriously, then in times of crisis the state will have the institutional capacity, commitment, as well as

---

[157] David Dyzenhaus, 'The Politics of Deference: Judicial Review and Democracy' in Michael Taggart (ed), *The Province of Administrative Law* (Hart Publishing 1997).

[158] Sandra Fredman, 'Emerging from the Shadows: Substantive Equality and Article 14 of the European Convention on Human Rights' (2016) 16 Human Rights Law Review 273, 283.

[159] See generally Anne Philipps, *The Politics of Presence* (OUP 1998).

compulsion, to affirmatively redress the unequal impacts of the crisis. As the Covid-19 pandemic and its response have shown, times of crisis involve fast-changing situations, uncertainty, and many moving parts. Courts may not have the institutional or informational wherewithal to intervene in policy decisions in such situations. Yet if they can institutionalize the norm that the claims of disadvantaged groups have to be centred in how the state responds to crises, courts can take a light touch approach to judicial review in such situations. In such situations, the Court does not have to decline to intervene in the state's policy response to a crisis (as the Indian Supreme Court initially did in response to the migrant labour crisis that resulted from the first pandemic-induced lockdown in India).[160] On the other hand, judicial intervention also does not imply taking over the role of the state in policy-making. As the Indian Supreme Court recognized in the context of adjudicating the state's policy on Covid-19 vaccine distribution, the role of the Court in such situations is to require the state to 'justify the rationale behind their policy approach which must be bound by the human rights framework ... [including] the right to life under Article 21 and right to equality under Article 14 of the Constitution'.[161] Ultimately, courts cannot create utopias. But they can push the state to work towards creating a more just world. Therein, perhaps, lies their greatest role.

---

[160] Sanya Talwar, ' "We Don't Plan to Supplant Wisdom of Govt with Our Wisdom", CJI Says On Relief Measures For Migrant Workers' *Live Law* (7 April 2020) https://www.livelaw.in/top-stories/sc-on-pil-seeking-wages-for-unorganised-workers-154889 (accessed 3 May 2022).

[161] *In Re: Distribution of Essential Supplies and Services During Pandemic* (2021) SCC OnLine SC 355 [7].

18
An Equality-sensitive Approach to Delivering Socio-economic Rights during Crises
A Focus on Kenya

Victoria Miyandazi

1 Introduction

Kenya's poverty rate had greatly declined before the pandemic struck. In 2006, 46.3 per cent of Kenyans were considered as living in poverty—ie living on less than US$1 a day.[1] This number declined to 36.1 per cent in 2015 to 2016,[2] and further to 28.9 per cent in 2019.[3] However, once the pandemic hit, the country's poverty rate shot up to 41.9 per cent in 2020, a 13 per cent increase in absolute poverty in just one year.[4] The rise in the number of Kenyans facing poverty is mainly attributed to loss of employment, food shortages, the high cost of living experienced during the pandemic, and the lack of equality-sensitive interventions by the government.[5] These challenges have had a disproportionate impact on vulnerable groups already suffering from pre-existing entrenched inequality, intensifying their experience of disadvantage. This is evidenced by the increase in inequality from a Gini coefficient of 0.391 pre-pandemic to 0.402 in 2020.[6]

This chapter examines the duty of the state to apply an equality-sensitive approach in its delivery of socio-economic rights (SERs) generally, and, particularly when coming up with laws, programmes, and policies to address the adverse effects of a nationwide socio-economic crisis. Section 2 sets out the textual basis in Kenya's 2010 Constitution for the application of an equality-sensitive approach in the development of laws, policies, and programmes touching on SERs. It argues that the wording of Article 43, when read together with Article 20(5) of the Constitution on how SERs

---

[1] Kenya National Bureau of Statistics (KNBS), *Kenya Budgetary Household Survey 2005-2006* (2006).
[2] KNBS, *Basic Report on Well-Being in Kenya: Based on the 2015/2016 Kenya Integrated Household Budget Survey (KIHBS)* (2018) 44–45.
[3] Nancy Nafula and others, 'Poverty and Distributional Effects of Covid-19 on Households in Kenya' (2020) African Economic Research Consortium Working Paper 8.
[4] ibid.
[5] See Kenya National Commission on Human Rights (KNCHR), 'Nationwide Survey on Human Rights for Vulnerable Groups During the COVID-19 Pandemic: A One Year Perspective on the "Unrelenting Virus"' (KNCHR, March 2021) 7; Monica K Kansiime and others, 'COVID-19 Implications on Household Income and Food Security in Kenya and Uganda: Findings from a Rapid Assessment' (2021) 137 World Development 105199, 2; Nafula and others (n 3).
[6] Nafula and others (n 3). The Gini coefficient measures inequality of income distribution within a country, with 0 representing complete equality and 1 absolute inequality.

should be implemented, creates a textual link between redistributive and status-based equality. This particularly relates to the requirement in Article 20(5)(b) that the state should give priority to vulnerable groups and individuals when realizing SERs, which adds a status-based equality component to the implementation of these rights. Section 3 interrogates how the various direct and indirect effects of the pandemic, as well as interventions adopted by the government to mitigate the spread of Covid-19 have exacerbated poverty and inequality, further compounding the vulnerability of disadvantaged groups in Kenya. Lastly, section 4 explores how the application of an equality-sensitive approach to addressing socio-economic disadvantage during a crisis, can avoid reinforcing inequality. It shows that in the final analysis, the needs of the most vulnerable in society should be prioritized when states implement initiatives to respond to crises. This is what is constitutionally mandated in Kenya.

2 The Kenyan Constitution's Equality-sensitive Approach to Implementing Socio-economic Rights

An equality-sensitive approach is one which recognizes the interconnection between status-based inequality and socio-economic deprivation, and thus obliges the state to prioritize the needs of vulnerable groups in addressing socio-economic disadvantage. Such an approach requires the consideration of four key interrelated factors as set out in Fredman's four-dimensional view of substantive equality[7]—first, the consideration of recognition harms such as stereotypes, prejudices and stigma (the recognition dimension); secondly, the consideration of pre-existing redistributive inequalities (the redistributive dimension); thirdly, the participation of vulnerable groups and inclusion of their voice (the participative dimension); and fourthly, the prioritization of the needs of disadvantaged groups with the aim of achieving structural change (the transformative dimension).[8] This approach is grounded on a substantive understanding of equality because, 'instead of aiming to treat everyone alike, regardless of status ... [it] focuses on the group which has suffered disadvantage'.[9]

There is a constitutional mandate in Kenya to apply an equality-sensitive approach in the provision and implementation of socio-economic rights, so as not to reinforce socio-economic disadvantage.[10] Article 43 of Kenya's 2010 Constitution mandates the state to provide, protect, and fulfil every person's socio-economic rights. These include the rights to the highest attainable standard of health, adequate housing, reasonable standards of sanitation, adequate food of acceptable quality, clean and safe water, social security, education, and emergency medical treatment. Article 20(5)(b) then goes on to provide that the state should give priority to vulnerable groups and individuals when realizing the socio-economic rights listed in Article 43 of the

---

[7] See Sandra Fredman, *Discrimination Law* (2nd edn, OUP 2011) 25–33; Victoria Miyandazi, *Equality in Kenya's 2010 Constitution: Understanding the Competing and Interrelated Conceptions* (Hart Publishing 2021) 189, 191.

[8] Fredman (n 7).

[9] ibid 26.

[10] See Sandra Fredman, 'Redistribution and Recognition: Reconciling Inequalities' (2007) 23 South African Journal of Human Rights 214, 215.

Constitution. The provision specifically states that in allocating resources for realizing the socio-economic rights in Article 43: 'the state shall give priority to ensuring the widest possible enjoyment of the right or fundamental freedom having regard to prevailing circumstances, including the vulnerability of particular groups or individuals'.

The requirement in Article 20(5)(b) thus adds an equality component to the way in which SERs should be implemented in the country as it requires the government, in provision of socio-economic infrastructure, to take positive steps to remedy the socio-economic inequality experienced by vulnerable groups. Article 21(3) of the Constitution reinforces this point by requiring all state organs and public officers to address the needs of vulnerable groups, 'including women, older members of society, persons with disabilities, children, youth, members of minority or marginalized communities, and members of particular ethnic, religious or cultural communities'. These provisions are over and above the general equality and non-discrimination guarantee in Article 27 of the Constitution. They are also in addition to the specific socio-economic rights and equality guarantees for children, persons with disabilities, the youth, minorities and marginalized groups, and the elderly, set out in Articles 53–57 of the Constitution.

In fact, these constitutional provisions highlight the growing recognition of the relationship between the right to equality and SERs with a goal of furthering redistributive equality. This relationship is underscored by the fact that poverty, or socio-economic deprivation, mostly affects individuals belonging to groups that have suffered from pre-existing discrimination. As Brodsky and Day rightly note: 'Poverty affects disadvantaged groups disproportionately' and members of vulnerable groups mostly populate the group termed as 'poor people'.[11] For instance, as will be further discussed below, when the Covid-19 pandemic hit, the government's abrupt closure of learning institutions countrywide for over a year disproportionately affected learners from poor backgrounds.[12] Most private educational institutions moved to online learning almost immediately, while, sometime afterwards, numerous public learning institutions also shifted to online education. Learners who had access to smartphones, laptops, and televisions were able to remain engaged with their learning, while those who did not were adversely impacted.[13] Aside from putting learning to a complete halt for under-privileged children, the closure of learning institutions also led to them being more susceptible to violence, child labour, child marriage, teenage pregnancies, sexual exploitation, mental health challenges, and lack of access to proper nutrition through the School Meals Programme.[14] Likewise, social distancing rules intensified the disadvantage that persons with visual disabilities and wheelchair users faced as they needed close assistance from their aides or other people, for instance, to access public transport which, in Kenya, is not disability friendly.[15]

---

[11] Gwen Brodsky and Shelagh Day, 'Denial of the Means of Subsistence as an Equality Violation' (2005) Acta Juridica 149, 162.
[12] KNCHR (n 5) 66.
[13] ibid 62, 63, 66.
[14] ibid. On School Meals Programme, see Republic of Kenya, 'National School Meals and Nutrition Strategy 2017–2022' https://docs.wfp.org/api/documents/WFP-0000116843/download/ (accessed 12 May 2022).
[15] Open Institute, 'Impact of COVID-19 on Kenyans with Disabilities' (27 April 2020) https://openinstitute.africa/impact-of-covid-19-on-kenyans-with-disabilities/ (accessed 12 May 2022).

The above-mentioned examples show how, in the wake of the Covid-19 pandemic, the measures put in place by the state to curb the spread of the virus actually compounded the inequality and disadvantage vulnerable groups already faced. This has long been recognized in international human rights law, such as by the UN Committee on Economic, Social and Cultural Rights (CESCR) in its observation that: 'individuals and groups of individuals continue to face socio-economic inequality, often because of entrenched historical and contemporary forms of discrimination'.[16] But despite the constitutional and international legal landscape, this understanding did not filter through in the responses to the Covid-19 pandemic in Kenya. The next section explores why this was the case and how an equality-sensitive approach could actually be realized.

3 A Critical Look at Government Interventions to Mitigate the Spread of Covid-19

Once the global pandemic was declared in March 2020, the Kenyan government embarked on putting in place measures to mitigate the spread of the virus. Unfortunately, many of these measures were not equality-sensitive and their implementation ended up adversely affecting vulnerable groups. This section looks at how governmental measures to control the spread of Covid-19, by not taking an equality-sensitive approach, intensified the disadvantage already experienced by vulnerable groups.

3.1 The Case of Slum Dwellers

It is now widely acknowledged that poverty is multidimensional and not just identified by, or associated with, a person's low income and, consequently, low living standards, as it was traditionally understood.[17] Markers of poverty also include the lack of access to food, shelter, sanitation, healthcare, low life expectancy, literacy, freedom and security.[18] If we apply Amartya Sen's capabilities approach, we are concerned with a person's lack of capability 'to be well nourished, literate ... have shelter or be safe', which is usually dependent on 'a range of personal and social factors, such as gender, health, metabolic rates, pregnancy, age or education'.[19] As we can see from these dimensions and markers of poverty, the pattern of who is poor is largely intertwined with one's identity characteristics that make them susceptible to discrimination. It is

---

[16] UNCESCR 'General comment No 20: Non-discrimination in economic, social and cultural rights' (2 July 2009) UN Doc E/C.12/GC/20 [2].

[17] Oxford Poverty and Human Development Initiative (OPHI), 'Multidimensional Poverty' www.ophi.org.uk/research/multidimensional-poverty/ (accessed 12 May 2022).

[18] ibid; The World Bank and OUP, 'World Development Report 2004: Making Services Work for Poor People' (2004) 2; Nanak Kakwani and Jacques Silber (eds), *The Many Dimensions of Poverty* (Palgrave Macmillan 2007) xv.

[19] See Amartya Sen, 'Development as Capabilities Expansion' (1989) 19 Journal of Development Planning 41, 44–47; Amartya Sen, 'Human Rights and Capabilities' (2005) 6(2) Journal of Human Development 151, 154; Sabine Alkire, 'Capability Approach and Well-Being Measurement for Public Policy' (2015) 94 OPHI Working Paper 1, 3; Miyandazi (n 7) 185.

the maldistribution of socio-economic goods and services along with these systemic patterns of disadvantage that mainly lead to poverty, which is effectively the lack of access to basic minimum of social goods essential for a person's survival.[20]

In Kenya, poverty mostly affects slum dwellers who make up a significant percentage of the population. For instance, in Nairobi and Mombasa, Kenya's largest and second largest cities respectively, as of 2020, slum dwellers consisted of between 60 and 70 per cent of the population, which approximates to more than 4.6 million people (ie over 9 per cent of the total population of Kenya).[21] Slums in Kenya are usually characterized by: 'high population density, small informal dwellings, lack of access to clean water, multi-generational households, shared sanitation facilities among multiple households, a high level of inter- and intra-social mixing within slums and other areas'.[22]

Accordingly, slum dwellers were both at a high risk of contracting Covid-19 and adversely affected by measures put in place to mitigate the spread of the virus. This was because, first, overcrowding and shared sanitation facilities in slums made social distancing rules to control the spread of the virus challenging to implement;[23] secondly, the added economic implications of the rise in public transportation costs by 51.7 per cent due to the mandatory public social distancing rules in public transport made movement for work challenging;[24] thirdly, while poor access to water in slums is a perennial problem, handwashing was deemed essential to the prevention of the spread of the virus;[25] fourthly, there was lack of access to essential information on Covid-19 for households with low literacy levels making them more prone to misinformation on treatments and vaccines, negatively affecting their access to the same;[26] and, fifthly, most slum dwellers who are daily wage earners working in the informal sector and live from hand-to-mouth (accounting for an estimated 83.6 per cent of total employment for urban informal settlement dwellers in the country),[27] were adversely affected by public health measures such as national lockdown, movement restrictions, and closure of open-air markets, as 'a large share of informal workers had no opportunity to work from home' and had 'less diversified income streams'.[28] Accordingly, over 37.7 per cent of the country's population was reported to have lost their incomes by the first week of May 2020. Nairobi and Mombasa, where slum dwellers make up

---

[20] Miyandazi (n 7) 179, 183.
[21] Karen Austrian and others, 'COVID-19 Related Knowledge, Attitudes, Practices and Needs of Households in Informal Settlements in Nairobi, Kenya' (Preprint) Bull World Health Organ (6 April 2020) 3; Amnesty International, 'The Unseen Majority: Nairobi's Two Million Slum-dwellers' (2 July 2009) 3 https://www.amnesty.org/en/documents/afr32/005/2009/en/ (accessed 8 June 2022); Amnesty International, 'Driven Out for Development: Forced Evictions in Mombasa, Kenya' (5 October 2015) 4 https://www.amnesty.org/en/documents/afr32/2467/2015/en/ (accessed 8 June 2022).
[22] Austrian and others (n 21) 3.
[23] ibid 2–4, 11.
[24] KNBS, 'Survey on Socio Economic Impact of COVID-19 on Households Report: Wave 1' (15 May 2020); Oxfam International, 'COVID-19 and Vulnerable Hardworking Kenyans: Why it's Time for a Strong Social Protection Plan' (November 2020).
[25] ibid.
[26] Austrian and others (n 21) 7–9.
[27] Kansiime and others (n 5) 3; Nita Bhalla, 'Forced Evictions Leave 5,000 Kenyan Slum Dwellers at Risk of Coronavirus' *Reuters* (6 May 2020).
[28] Kansiime and others (n 5) 2.

more than 60 per cent of the population were the worst hit, with 52 per cent (3.1 million) of residents losing their incomes.[29]

Furthermore, the poor healthcare system in slum areas worsened the impact of the pandemic on slum dwellers.[30] It is reported that the lack of public healthcare facilities in Kenya's slum areas led to 'the mushrooming of several small substandard clinics that are unable to offer integrated primary healthcare, yet they serve a huge slum population'.[31] In one of the main slum areas in Nairobi, out of the twelve primary healthcare facilities present, only one is a public government-owned facility.[32] The other eleven are either private-for-profit, faith-based, or health facilities run by non-governmental organizations.[33] While healthcare in public hospitals is free for services like maternity care or more affordable for those with a national health insurance cover, the aforesaid private healthcare options usually charge a fee, albeit small for some.[34] This means that, with most slum dwellers not having health insurance coverage, they would pay out-of-pocket for healthcare services.[35] In addition, as the Kenya National Human Rights Commission notes, during the pandemic, in terms of affordability, while there were increased charges for treatment and services at health facilities, '[t]here was minimal or no waivers on fees and charges to the vulnerable groups'.[36] This is despite Article 43(1)(a) of the Constitution mandating that every person in Kenya has a right to the highest attainable standard of health and Kenya committing to the universal health coverage as one of its four key developmental pillars for the years 2017 to 2022.[37]

More broadly, these issues show that there was a lack of application of the equality-sensitive approach required by the Constitution. Constitutional safeguards under Articles 20(5)(b), 27, and 43 require the government to put in place adequate social protection measures for vulnerable groups.[38] Slum dwellers seem to have been largely overlooked, however, in the design and implementation of measures to respond to the pandemic.

In fact, the measures put in place by the state to ameliorate the adverse direct or indirect socio-economic impact of the pandemic only targeted a small fraction of the country's population. For instance, the President, on 25 March 2020, at the onset of the pandemic, announced the allocation of Ksh10 billion (US$87.2 million) for monthly cash transfers of Ksh2,000 (US$17.5) to households living with elderly persons aged

---

[29] Nafula and others (n 3) 9.
[30] See Syed A K Shifat Ahmed and others, 'Impact of the Societal Response to COVID-19 on Access to Healthcare for Non-COVID-19 Health Issues in Slum Communities of Bangladesh, Kenya, Nigeria and Pakistan: Results of pre-COVID and COVID-19 Lockdown Stakeholder Engagements' (2020) 5 BJM Global Health e003042; Abdu Mohiddin and Marleen Temmerman, 'COVID-19 Exposes Weaknesses in Kenya's Healthcare System. And What Can be Done' *The Conversation* (27 July 2020).
[31] Peter O Otieno and others, 'Access to Primary Healthcare Services and Associated Factors in Urban Slums in Nairobi-Kenya' (2020) 20(1) BMC Public Health 1, 2, 7.
[32] Ahmed and others (n 30) 3.
[33] ibid.
[34] ibid.
[35] Otieno and others (n 31) 7; Israel Nyaburi Nyadera and Francis Onditi, 'COVID-19 Experience Among Slum Dwellers in Nairobi: A Double Tragedy or Useful Lesson for Public Health Reforms?' (2020) 63(6) International Social Work 838, 839.
[36] KNCHR (n 5) 19, 29.
[37] See 'The Big 4' https://big4.delivery.go.ke (accessed 12 May 2022).
[38] Article 43(1)(e) as read together with Article 20(5)(b) of the Constitution of Kenya, 2010.

between sixty and seventy years, orphans, and vulnerable children.[39] Persons over seventy years, persons with severe disabilities and those facing food insecurity were not included as they were to benefit from ongoing cash transfers. The target population was poor households whose monthly adult equivalent consumption (welfare) was less than Ksh3,040.[40] The initiative, though seemingly equality-sensitive, only covered a small proportion of households, about 1,094,323, ie less than 17.8 per cent of the total households living in poverty as of the year 2020.[41]

One survey also highlighted the fact that cash transfers to the vulnerable poor (between sixty and seventy years, orphans, and vulnerable children) were more effective in rural areas where older members of society mostly reside.[42] However, tax reliefs were more effective in tackling poverty in urban areas 'because urban centres constitute a large proportion of people working in the most affected sectors such as in retail and wholesale trade, accommodation and food services, teachers in private schools and transport'.[43] The tax reliefs put in place from 25 March 2020 to 31 December 2020 included the reduction of Income Tax (Pay-As-You-Earn and Corporation Tax) from 30 per cent to 25 per cent, 100 per cent tax relief for persons earning a monthly income of Ksh24,000 (US$200) and below, and reduction of Value Added Tax from 16 per cent to 14 per cent.[44] These tax reliefs are not as effective in rural areas because most residents rely on agricultural activities in the informal sector. The same applies for slum dwellers who mostly work in the informal sector. Notably, as much as the agricultural sector makes up 34.3 per cent of Kenya's economy and employs an estimated 77 per cent of the population, its economic activities are largely unregulated and untaxed.[45] But even large-scale farmers in rural areas, were affected by losses as a result of 'market disruptions at the local and international level', rather than loss or reduction of income from taxed monthly earnings.[46] Tax reliefs were thus bound to be ineffective in addressing the disadvantages faced by the rural poor and slum dwellers during the pandemic.

A final example which bears mention is of forced evictions. Housing in Kenya's slum areas mostly consists of small informal dwellings. For slum dwellers, 'however decrepit' their accommodation may be, living precariously has become their lived reality and such settlements remain 'home to their existence, their aspirations, and their very humanity'.[47] Such precarious living is further compounded by the ever-increasing unlawful forced evictions of informal settlers.[48] Such unlawful and inhumane evictions

---

[39] Government of Kenya (GoK), 'Presidential Address on the State Interventions to Cushion Kenyans Against Economic Effects of COVID-19 Pandemic' (25 March 2020) https://www.president.go.ke/2020/03/25/presidential-address-on-the-state-interventions-to-cushion-kenyans-against-economic-effects-of-covid-19-pandemic-on-25th-march-2020/) (accessed 12 May 2022).
[40] Nafula and others (n 3) 6, 20.
[41] Oxfam (n 24) 9. See also Nafula and others (n 3) 14–15 (highlighting that 6,162,640 Kenyans, nationally, fell into poverty in 2020) and text accompanying nn 1–4 on poverty levels in the country as of 2020.
[42] Nafula and others (n 3) 8–9, 22.
[43] ibid 8–9.
[44] GoK (n 39).
[45] Institute of Economic Affairs, *Informal Sector and Taxation in Kenya* (2012) 29 The Budget Focus 1.
[46] Nafula and others (n 3) 8–9.
[47] *Mitu-Bell Welfare Society v Kenya Airports Authority & 2 Others* [2021] eKLR [144].
[48] See *Fatuma Khamis Bilal & 3505 Others v Kenya Railways Corporation & 6 Others* [2021] eKLR; CADASTA, Rapid Mapping of Areas Marked for Demolitions and Evictions in Nairobi during COVID-19 (2020) https://cadasta.maps.arcgis.com/apps/MapJournal/index.html?appid=17855a9c855c4f3dadbb3

exacerbate the dire conditions of this group and further pushes them to the margins of society. The Supreme Court in *Mitu-Bell Welfare Society v Kenya Airports Authority & 2 Others* rightly observed that this state of affairs is perpetuated by 'the fact that [the Kenyan] society is incredulously unequal, with the majority of the population condemned to grinding poverty, [such that] the right to accessible and adequate housing remains a pipe-dream for many'.[49]

Such hardships are heightened in times of crises like the Covid-19 pandemic. For instance, in the first two weeks of May 2020, over 9,000 vulnerable persons living in Ruai and Kariobangi informal settlements, located in Nairobi, were forcefully evicted without relocation or compensation, and their houses demolished.[50] The evictions were conducted in heavy rainfall, in the evening during curfew hours and, in one of the two evictions, with only a verbal notice being given two days before the eviction.[51] Consequently, evicted residents were left exposed to the elements as they slept out in the cold without alternative shelter, food, access to water and sanitation. This was compounded by the fact that the nationwide lockdown restricting movement from county to county was also in place, meaning that those evicted could not—even if they had the finances to cover travel costs—move back to their rural homes.

Some of the evictions, for instance the Kariobangi one, were conducted despite court orders prohibiting the same, pending the hearing and determination of the cases on ownership of the disputed public lands.[52] Notably, the government had announced that it would put in place a moratorium restricting all evictions during the Covid-19 pandemic, but the same kept taking place nonetheless.[53]

Despite evictions for unlawful occupation of public land being allowed under section 152B of the Land Laws (Amendment) Act, 2016, there are rules regulating such evictions that are covered in sections 152C–152I of the said Act. These provisions require that for evictions from public land, like in the aforesaid scenarios, to take place, the National Land Commission is to cause a decision for such an eviction to take place to be notified to all affected persons in writing through a notice in the Kenya Gazette, one newspaper with nationwide circulation, and by radio announcement in a local language. Such notification should be made at least three months before the intended eviction. Article 43(1)(b) of the Constitution further provides for the right to housing, which consists of the negative duty not to deprive people of their right to housing

---

b90719de04a (accessed 23 May 2022); *Mitu-Bell Welfare Society v Attorney General & 2 Others* [2013] eKLR; *Satrose Ayuma and Others (on behalf of Muthurwa residents) v Kenya Railways Staff Benefit Scheme and Others* [2013] eKLR; *Ibrahim Songor Osman v Attorney General & 3 Others*, High Court Constitutional Petition No 2 of 2011.

[49] *Mitu-Bell* (n 47) [149].

[50] See UNOHCHR, 'COVID-19 Crisis: Kenya Urged to Stop All Evictions and Protect Housing Rights Defenders' (22 May 2020) https://www.ohchr.org/EN/NewsEvents/Pages/DisplayNews.aspx?NewsID=25901&LangID=E (accessed 15 May 2022).

[51] ibid; Siago Cece, 'Kariobangi Demolition Victims Sue State, Want CSs Fired' *The Nation* (8 June 2020).

[52] Cece (n 51); Alphonce Mung'ahu, 'Court Stops State from Evicting 8000 Families' *People Daily* (4 May 2020) https://www.pd.co.ke/news/national/court-stops-state-from-evicting-8000-families-35452/ (accessed 15 May 2022).

[53] Maureen Kinyanjui, 'State Breaks Promise, Leaves Thousands Homeless in Ruai' *The Star* (17 May 2020) https://www.the-star.co.ke/counties/nairobi/2020-05-17-state-breaks-promise-leaves-thousands-homeless-in-ruai/ (accessed 15 May 2022).

rendering them homeless. This gives rise to the duty to provide alternative housing or compensation to protect evictees' right to housing.[54]

Likewise, Kenyan courts have held that evictions are unlawful and illegal if they do not follow the proper legal procedures. These include adequate consultations with the persons to be evicted, adequate and reasonable notice of at least ninety days prior to the eviction, bar on evictions in bad weather or at night unless the evicted persons consent, and the provision of alternative accommodation or compensation.[55] However, evictions in the early days of the pandemic were conducted in total disregard of the law, threatening the lives and health of thousands of Kenyans.[56]

Indeed, neither did the government consider the vulnerability of slum dwellers as such, nor did it consider the vulnerability of disadvantaged groups within slum dwellers (women, children, persons with disabilities, and the elderly). The inhumane and unlawful forced evictions of these disadvantaged groups exacerbated their dire conditions and pushed them further to the margins of the society.

3.2 The Right to Education of Disadvantaged Learners

The right to education is a multiplier and empowerment right as, besides being a human right in itself, it is indispensable to the realization of other human rights.[57] Article 43(1)(f) of the Kenyan Constitution guarantees every person a right to education. Article 53(1)(b) then goes on to provide for the rights of every child to free and compulsory basic education. The Covid-19 pandemic has exposed the vulnerability of groups like children living in poverty and those with disabilities, and how their vulnerabilities are heightened in times of a crisis; hence highlighting the importance of linking equality concerns with the right to education, by considering the pre-existing socio-economic disadvantage of vulnerable children when developing measures to address the unique challenges a crisis poses.[58] This link is often overlooked in educational initiatives whose purpose is to ensure learners from vulnerable and disadvantaged groups enjoy equal access to education.

For instance, as schools shifted to online education amid the pandemic, the digital divide greatly affected regions that lack electricity, internet connectivity and network

---

[54] *Mitu-Bell* (n 47) [151]–[153].

[55] *Fatuma Khamis Bilal & 3505 Others v Kenya Railways Corporation & 6 Others* [2021] eKLR; CADASTA, Rapid Mapping of Areas Marked for Demolitions and Evictions in Nairobi during COVID-19 (2020) https://cadasta.maps.arcgis.com/apps/MapJournal/index.html?appid=17855a9c855c4f3dadbb3b90719de04a (accessed 23 May 2022); *Mitu-Bell Welfare Society v Attorney General & 2 Others* [2013] eKLR; *Satrose Ayuma and Others (on behalf of Muthurwa residents) v Kenya Railways Staff Benefit Scheme and Others* [2013] eKLR; *Ibrahim Songor Osman v Attorney General & 3 Others*, High Court Constitutional Petition No 2 of 2011; UN Committee on Economic, Social and Cultural Rights (CESCR), General Comment No 7: The right to adequate housing (art 11.1): forced evictions (20 May 1997) UN Doc E/1998/22; Republic of Kenya, Ministry of Lands, 'Eviction and Resettlement Guidelines' (October 2009).

[56] See Cece (n 51); Kinyanjui (n 53); Bhalla (n 27).

[57] CESCR, General Comment No 13: The Right to Education (art 13) (8 December 1999) UN Doc E/C.12/1999/10 [1].

[58] UN Committee on the Rights of the Child 'The Committee on the Rights of the Child warns of the grave physical, emotional and psychological effects of the COVID-19 pandemic on children and calls on States to protect the rights of children' (8 April 2020) INT/CRC/STA/9095/E [7].

resilience, as well as families without access to smart phones, laptops, and televisions. Notably, the Kenya National Bureau of Statistics' 2019 census report reveals that a mere 22.6 per cent of Kenyans from the age of three years have access to the internet and only 10.4 per cent are computer literate.[59] This means that the move to e-learning had the effect of leaving out most learners from under-privileged backgrounds.

The move to e-learning was made too hastily without consulting key stakeholders on how to mitigate its potential adverse impact on learners who are 'children with disabilities; children living in poverty; children in street situations; migrant, asylum-seeking; refugee, and internally displaced children; minority and indigenous children; [and] children with underlying health conditions'.[60] On this matter, the United Nations Committee on the Rights of the Child (CRC), in its statement on Covid-19 called on states to '[p]rovide opportunities for children's views to be heard and taken into account in decision-making processes on the pandemic'.[61] Thus, the state's failure to apply the participative dimension of an equality-sensitive approach by consulting key stakeholders—including those likely to be adversely affected by the measure, such as the poor and persons with disabilities—ended up exacerbating access to education challenges under-privileged learners already face.

On the issue of public participation, various courts have held that, especially on matters involving children's right to education, the state has an obligation to respect, protect and fulfil the paramountcy of the best interests of the child in all matters concerning them, as set out in Article 53(2) of the Constitution. This requires the state, inter alia, to ensure that there is public participation in such decision-making and consult with key stakeholders like parents, before policy decisions are taken or implemented.[62] This issue has been raised in cases challenging the shift to e-learning in schools.[63] For instance, in *OAPA (Suing as Parents and/or Guardians of student minors currently schooling at Oshwal Academy) v Oshwal Education Relief Board & 2 Others*, the petitioners correctly pointed out important issues that should have been considered and addressed through a consultative process before the move to e-learning. These include internet connectivity, power blackouts, and the approach to be taken in the teaching of students with special needs.[64]

In *Joseph Enock Aura v Cabinet Secretary, Ministry of Education, Science & Technology & 3 Others; Teachers Service Commission & 6 Others (Interested Parties)*, the Court held that the state acted ultra vires in prolonging the open-ended closure of schools from 16 March 2020 to the time of the judgment, 19 November 2020.[65] This was said to be particularly the case as there were no prior consultations with parents and guardians of school-enrolled children, affected learners in diverse learning

---

[59] Kenya National Bureau of Statistics, '2019 Kenya Population and Housing Census Volume IV: Distribution of Population by Socio-Economic Characteristics' (December 2019).
[60] UN Committee on the Rights of the Child (n 58) [7].
[61] ibid [11].
[62] *Joseph Enock Aura v Cabinet Secretary, Ministry of Education, Science & Technology & 3 Others; Teachers Service Commission & 6 Others (Interested Parties)* [2020] eKLR [141(c)]; *OAPA (Suing as Parents and/or Guardians of Student Minors Currently Schooling at Oshwal Academy) v Oshwal Education Relief Board & 2 Others* [2020] eKLR [86].
[63] *OAPA* (n 62).
[64] ibid [3].
[65] *Joseph Enock Aura* (n 62).

institutions, and the respective County Education boards, among other entities.[66] The lack of consultation contravened sections 4 and 70 of the Basic Education Act. These provisions provide for the values, principles, and rules guiding the delivery of basic education, such as the requirement for consultations with key stakeholders.[67]

Other key contentions raised by parents and guardians in various right to education cases filed following the outbreak of the Covid-19 pandemic touch on the lack of resources to facilitate the e-learning programme at home as this required access to laptops, desktops, tablets, or smartphones, alongside internet accessibility.[68] This was particularly burdensome, financially, for those with more than one child, and those who were already experiencing financial strains as a result of job losses and salary cuts.[69] In addition, it has been averred that since the e-learning programme was to take place at home, this required constant adult supervision that substantially added to parents and guardians' responsibilities, and, many a time, this left parents/guardians with no option but to resign from their jobs.[70] The closure of schools also had an adverse impact on girls, with increase in sexual exploitation, teenage pregnancies, child labour, and child marriages.[71] This shows how discrimination on the basis of sex intersects with other identities like social status to deepen girls' experience of disadvantage. These issues touch on the recognition and redistributive dimensions to be considered in taking an equality-sensitive approach.

Worse still was the impact of the pandemic on learners who are persons with disabilities, particularly the deaf and blind. As Bhandari aptly observed, 'those who are already disadvantaged, due to economic or structural inequalities … suffer[ed] greater digital exclusion during the pandemic'.[72] Notably, as many schools shifted to e-learning, thousands of children with visual disabilities lacked access to assistive devices such as Braille paper and reading materials at home.[73] Further, children with hearing impairments would need online classes and lessons broadcasted on television to have sign language interpreters.[74] Lack of reasonable accommodation for persons with disabilities, at the advent of the pandemic thus exacerbated the socio-economic disadvantage they already face (transformative dimension).

The *Joseph Enock Aura* case also raised pertinent issues on learners' access to education, amidst the President's addresses on 15 and 16 March 2020 on suspension of schooling and the open-ended closure of schools as a measure to curb the spread of Covid-19.[75] The petitioner averred that the National Council for Children's Services, which is composed of, inter alia, the Principal Secretary for Health, Principal Secretary for Education and the Attorney General, failed to safeguard the best interests of the child in light of the open-ended closure of schools because of the Covid-19 pandemic.

---

[66] ibid [141(c)].
[67] Basic Education Act No 14 of 2013, ss 4(t), 70(c).
[68] *OAPA* (n 62) [2].
[69] ibid [3]–[4].
[70] ibid.
[71] KNCHR (n 5) 66.
[72] Vrinda Bhandari, 'Improving Internet Connectivity during COVID-19', Digital Pathways at Oxford Paper Series No 4 (2020) 2.
[73] Open Institute (n 15).
[74] ibid.
[75] *Joseph Enock Aura* (n 62).

This was said to be a violation of Article 53(2) of the Constitution, as read together with section 32(2) of the Children's Act, on the paramountcy of the best interests of the child.[76]

It was explained that the best interests of the child, as set out in the Child Rights Committee's General Comment No. 5, 'requires active measures throughout Government, parliament and the judiciary ... by systematically considering how children's rights and interests are or will be affected by their decisions and actions'.[77] Further, that considering the Committee on Economic, Social and Cultural Rights' General Comment No. 13, the state should 'avoid measures that hinder or prevent the enjoyment of the right to education ... [and that] [t]he obligation to protect requires states parties to take measures that prevent third parties from interfering with the enjoyment of the right to education'.[78] Citing various research reports from recognized and authoritative sources, the petitioner argued that in times of crisis, the state can restrict the enjoyment of certain human rights to protect public health, but that the restrictions should be necessary, proportionate and kept at a minimum. That, in response to a pandemic, 'restrictions and decisions on allocation of resources' should 'reflect the principle of the best interests of the child'.[79] In light of this, it was argued that various research surveys and reports highlighted the fact that Covid-19 posed low risks to school-aged children.[80] This was especially the case in the emerging evidence from Eastern and Southern Africa, where schools were found not to be associated with significant increases in community transmission of Covid-19.[81] Given this, the conclusion was that 'in-person learning is in the best interest of students, when compared to virtual learning'.[82]

In deciding whether in-person schooling or elearning was appropriate for children in the face of the Covid-19 pandemic, the Court referred to comparative jurisprudence in the 2020 judgment of the Ontario Superior Court of Justice in *Zinati v Spence*.[83] In this case, the Court set out some of the relevant factors to be considered in determining the appropriate educational plan for a child, taking into account their best interests, as including:

i. The risk of exposure to Covid-19 that the child will face if she or he is in school, or is not in school.
ii. Whether the child, or a member of the child's family, is at increased risk from Covid-19 as a result of health conditions or other risk factors.

---

[76] ibid [70]–[85]; Children Act 2001, CAP 141, Laws of Kenya.
[77] ibid [83]; UN Committee on the Rights of the Child, General Comment No 5 (2003): General Measures of Implementation of the Convention on the Rights of the Child, UN Doc CRC/GC/2003/5 [12].
[78] *Joseph Enock Aura* (n 62) [84]; CESCR, General Comment No 13 (n 57) [47].
[79] UN Committee on the Rights of the Child (n 58) [1].
[80] *Joseph Enock Aura* (n 62) [89]; Centres for Disease Control and Prevention, 'Operating Schools During COVID-19' https://www.cdc.gov/coronavirus/2019-ncov/community/schools-childcare/schools.html (accessed 15 May 2022); UNICEF, 'Supplement to Framework for Reopening Schools: Emerging Lessons from Country Experiences in Managing the Process of Reopening Schools' https://www.unicef.org/media/83026/file/Emerging-lessons-from-countries-experiences-of-reopening-schools-2020.pdf (accessed 15 May 2022).
[81] ibid.
[82] *Joseph Enock Aura* (n 62) [89].
[83] *Zinati v Spence*, 2020 ONSC 5231.

iii. The risk the child faces to their mental health, social development, academic development, or psychological well-being from learning online.
iv. Any proposed or planned measures to alleviate any of the risks noted above.
v. The child's wishes, if they can be reasonably ascertained.
vi. The ability of the parent or parents with whom the child will be residing during school days to support online learning, including competing demands of the parent or parents' work, or caregiving responsibilities, or other demands.[84]

Applying these factors, Justice Akbarali in the *Zinati* case concluded that it was in the minor's best interest to resume in-person learning. This was because, among other considerations, she was both at risk of contracting coronavirus in school and at home. Moreover, the risk at home would be increased because her stepmother was a frontline healthcare worker who was at increased risk of exposure to the virus due to the nature of her work.[85]

Similarly, in the *Joseph Enock Aura* case, upon considering the decision in the *Zinati* case, Justice Makau rightly held that the Court's role is not to make a determination on educational plans for individual families, children, or the government. This is especially because 'the government has access to public health and educational expertise which is not available to the Court'.[86] Nevertheless, he observed that, as much as it is not up to courts to 'second guess the government's decision-making', the Court can determine whether a decision is reasonable and an educational plan in the best interests of the child.[87] From this, and applying the criteria set in *Zinati*, the learned judge held that:

> Upon considering all the relevant factors, as well as authorities relied upon, I find that the benefit of the petitioner's school going children and other school children attending school in-person out-weighs the risks of COVID–19 ... provided the respondents ensures that COVID—19 measures and safety protocols are put in place and fully complied with in each and every school by both the learners and the teachers. This being complied with, I find that the school going children will reasonably be safe in school given that health conditions that may place children at health risk are given priority. Further this Court notes that it is important for school-going children to have the social interaction and academic development that can be ripped only from in-person learning. The best interest of any child is to be in school in-person as there is more control, guidance and provision of health [and] safe[ty] measures in the school than leaving the children roaming in the villages or shanties or towns as the case may be without observing any Covid-19 Health Protocols.[88]

Based on this holding, the Court ordered the Cabinet Secretary for the Ministry of Education to 'direct the re-opening of in-person learning institutions and schools in

---
[84] ibid [27].
[85] ibid [28]–[39].
[86] *Joseph Enock Aura* (n 62) [94].
[87] ibid.
[88] ibid [95], [100].

Kenya, observing the health and safety Guidelines', within sixty days from the date of the judgment, 19 November 2020.[89]

The emerging jurisprudence on the right to education in the wake of the pandemic, especially the *Joseph Enock Aura* and *OAPA* cases, show the acknowledgement by courts of the importance of an equality-sensitive approach requiring the state to consider the recognition, redistributive, participative, and transformative dimensions of substantive equality. Cases such as *Joseph Enock Aura*, discuss pertinent issues, touching on all four dimensions, that the state, when adopting measures to mitigate the effects of a pandemic should consider so as not to exacerbate the vulnerabilities of learners in accessing their right to education.

3.3 The Right to Healthcare of Vulnerable Groups

Article 43(1)(f) of the Kenyan Constitution guarantees every person in the country the right to the highest attainable standard of health, which includes the state's obligations to fulfil the right to healthcare and prevent threats to the right, especially for vulnerable persons as per Article 20(5)(b). Treating Covid-19 is a costly affair, particularly for the poor and low-income earners. Over 1.7 million Kenyans are said to have lost their jobs during the national lockdown restricting county to county movements from the end of March 2020 to the end of June 2020.[90] The numbers are much higher if we consider informal workers—particularly daily wage earners, casual labourers, and small-scale traders—who are often unaccounted for in such statistics.

The rise in unemployment rates during the pandemic also led to a spike in mental health-related ailments such as depression, particularly for the poor and vulnerable, as households failed to meet basic necessities due to lack of income.[91] Another health implication of the economic hardships was poor nutrition. The poor and vulnerable living in crowded informal settlements with limited access to water and sanitation were also at a higher risk of contracting the Covid-19 virus.[92]

Two quarantine-related challenges can be discerned. First, in some instances, the period of compulsory quarantine was arbitrarily extended from fourteen to up to thirty days.[93] Further, individuals were detained for failure to pay the required costs, despite section 27 of Kenya's Public Health Act requiring the government to foot the costs of compulsory quarantine.[94] Second, several government designated quarantine

---

[89] ibid [141(f)].

[90] Constant Munda, '1.7m jobs lost during COVID-19 lockdown' *Business Daily* (2 September 2020).

[91] See Ministry of Health, 'Interim Guidance on Continuity of Mental Health Services During the COVID-19 Pandemic' (2020) https://www.health.go.ke/wp-content/uploads/2020/05/INTERIM-GUIDANCE-ON-CONTINUITY-OF-MENTAL-HEALTH-SERVICES-DURING-THE-COVID-19-PANDEMIC_compressed-2.pdf (accessed 15 May 2022).

[92] Maureen Were, 'COVID-19 and Socioeconomic Impact in Africa: The Case of Kenya', WIDER Background Note 2020/3, Helsinki: UNU-WIDER (2020).

[93] See Allan Maleche and Nerima Were, 'Kenya's Growing Anti-Rights Public Health Agenda During COVID-19' Harvard Law Petrie-Flom Center, Bill of Health: Examining the Intersection of Health Law, Biotechnology and Bioethics (21 May 2020) https://blog.petrieflom.law.harvard.edu/2020/05/21/kenya-global-responses-covid19/ (accessed 15 May 2022).

[94] ibid.

facilities were said to be in a deplorable state, being inadequately maintained and having shared sanitary facilities, putting compulsorily detained persons who were Covid-19 free at risk of contracting the virus from those quarantined because of the virus.[95]

Furthermore, much of the Covid-19 policy responses focused on urban areas as compared to rural areas. This only exposed the necessity of addressing the reality that most of the public health care facilities in rural areas were inadequate and subpar in a health crisis. This was particularly the case with the number of beds in public health care facilities, especially for intensive care units; stocking of essential medicines; infrastructure and supplies for conducting essential tests; and staffing (particularly in ensuring healthcare facilities have the necessary professional staff).[96]

Hence, the provision of SERs needs to take an equality-sensitive approach in extending benefits enjoyed by well off counties to rural and marginalized areas to ensure full and equal enjoyment of such rights as guaranteed in Article 27(2) of the Constitution. Indeed, Article 43 of the Constitution specifically mandates that SERs like the right to healthcare services should be guaranteed to 'every person'. This introduces an equality requirement that quality healthcare services, essential medicines and the necessary professional staff, among other healthcare-related benefits provided to one region or county, should be equally and equitably extended to those that lack the necessary health infrastructure.[97] When these provisions are read together with Article 20(5)(b) of the Constitution on prioritizing the needs of vulnerable groups, it becomes apparent that, as Bilchitz rightly asserts, it is truly '[t]he urgent interests of beings [that] provide the reasons for many of our duties to others. Talk of duties alone fails to indicate that it is our connection to others who have interests that is of crucial importance, and which imposes obligations upon us'.[98] Programmes to benefit the people during a nationwide crisis like Covid-19 also need to be cognizant of this fact and ensure that the delivery of socio-economic benefits like those related to healthcare are equitably distributed.

Further compounding the negative health effects of the Covid-19 pandemic was the fact that most insurance policies do not cover epidemics and pandemics. On 24 July 2020, the National Health Insurance Fund (NHIF) announced that it would support all Covid-19 policy holders and their declared beneficiaries who get admitted to the Ministry of Health's designated health facilities.[99] This was a positive move that mostly benefitted poor and vulnerable groups since the NHIF is the cheapest public health insurance cover in Kenya, which all Kenyans above eighteen years working in the formal (compulsory) and informal (optional) sector are required to have.[100] It was also a sigh

---

[95] ibid.
[96] See B Njeru, 'COVID-19: list of Counties with ICU beds' *The Standard* (28 March 2020); A Mohiddin and M Temmerman, 'COVID-19 Exposes Weaknesses in Kenya's Healthcare System: And What Can Be Done' *The Conversation* (27 July 2020); Netherlands Enterprise Agency, Kenya Health Care Sector: Opportunities for the Dutch Life Sciences & Health Sector (2016).
[97] Miyandazi (n 7) 182.
[98] David Bilchitz, *Poverty and Fundamental Rights: The Justification and Enforcement of Socio-Economic Rights* (OUP 2007)73.
[99] See David Indeje, 'NHIF to Cover Partial Covid-19 Expenses in Designated Government Hospitals' *Khusoko* (29 July 2020) https://khusoko.com/2020/07/29/nhif-to-cover-partial-COVID-19-expenses-in-designated-government-hospitals/ (accessed 15 May 2022).
[100] See National Health Insurance Fund http://www.nhif.or.ke/healthinsurance/ (accessed 8 June 2022).

of relief for many due to the exorbitant costs attached to Covid-19 related treatment pre-vaccination, especially for those worst hit by the virus and needing to be put on ventilators.

Similarly, the lack of sign language inclusivity for persons with hearing impairments, denied many the access to essential information related to the pandemic and access to healthcare services, increasing their vulnerability to the virus.[101] For instance, before intervention by the Kenya National Gender and Equality Commission, government communication on Covid-19, similar to other messaging on the pandemic by media outlets, was not accessible to persons with hearing impairments due to the absence of sign language interpreters during press briefings to the nation.[102] There were also accessibility challenges in receiving information on Covid-19 for those without televisions and access to the internet.[103]

As of end of June 2020, approximately 491,921 registered refugees and asylum seekers resided in Kakuma/Kalobeyei and Dadaab refugee camps. They came from Somalia (53.7 per cent), South Sudan (24.7 per cent), Congo ((9 per cent), Ethiopia (5.8 per cent) and other nations including Rwanda, Eritrea, Burundi, and Uganda (6.7 per cent).[104] The number excludes urban refugees and asylum seekers. Aside from the common challenges applying to both Kenyans and non-Kenyans in accessing healthcare, refugees, particularly registered and unregistered urban refugees, faced unique barriers. These included 'discrepancies in healthcare costs between refugees and local Kenyan clients, requirements for documentation before service, threat of harassment and language barrier'.[105] Further, refugees did not have access to the National Health Insurance Fund which greatly reduced the cost of accessing healthcare services. Also, as much as the United Nations High Commissioner for Refugees (UNHCR) facilitated the provision of free or subsidized healthcare services for refugees in some government healthcare facilities, this only applied to registered and not unregistered urban refugees.[106] Aside from this, while refugee camps were equipped with healthcare facilities mostly provided free of charge, the number of such facilities paled in comparison with the population they were to serve.[107]

The discussion in this section confirms that to ensure equitable access to SERs like social protection, education, and healthcare—particularly for vulnerable groups—equality-sensitive approach is required. First, the participation of key stakeholders, including representatives of vulnerable groups, in decision-making affecting access

---

[101] John Ndavula and Jackline Lidubwi, 'Access to Health Information for Persons with Disabilities During the COVID-19 Pandemic in Kenya' (2021) 11(4) African Journal of Social Work 172; Open Institute (n 15).

[102] NGEC, 'Advisory on consideration of the Welfare of Persons in Vulnerable Situations, by the Government, in its Efforts to Combat the Covid-19 Pandemic' (31 March 2020) https://www.ngeckenya.org/news/8238/covid-19--advisory-on-consideration-of-the-welfare-of-persons-in-vulnerable-situations (accessed 15 May 2022).

[103] Ndavula and Lidubwi (n 101) 179.

[104] Julie Jemutai and others, 'A Situation Analysis of Access to Refugee Health Services in Kenya: Gaps and Recommendations—A Literature Review' (2021) 178 CHE Research Paper 1.

[105] ibid 4.

[106] ibid 5.

[107] ibid 5.

to and provision of SERs is imperative in ensuring inclusivity (participative dimension), and to ensure that the needs of vulnerable groups are accommodated to avoid reinforcing structural patterns of disadvantage (transformative dimension). Secondly, when developing laws, policies and programmes to address a crisis, states should actively consider their likely impact on pre-existing material disadvantage (redistributive dimension) in terms of access to the socio-economic rights at issue, especially as it relates to vulnerable groups (recognition dimension), once again, to avoid reinforcing inequality (transformative dimension). In other words, government ministries and policy-makers need to have the equality agenda in mind when seeking to make SERs a reality for the people, especially those from vulnerable and marginalized groups already facing ongoing inequality challenges. As this chapter has shown, this is mandated in Article 43, read together with Articles 20(5)(b) and 27 of the Kenyan Constitution.

4 Conclusion

This chapter has shown that Kenyan laws provide the necessary legal framework and impetus for applying an equality-sensitive approach in delivering socio-economic rights in times of crisis. However, as much as such an approach is constitutionally ordained and the government is mandated to apply it, it is not actually implemented by those who are in charge. The challenge is, therefore, the lack of application of laws in practice, especially when producing laws, programmes, and policies to facilitate the implementation of SERs in times of crisis.

A case in point is forced evictions. As section 3.1 discussed, forced evictions were conducted unlawfully, even where there was a court order prohibiting the same and a government moratorium stopping evictions from taking place during the pandemic. Such disregard for court orders and the law, specifically by state officers, shows that even where the law requires an equality-sensitive approach to be taken, it fails to translate to actual practice. This may be attributed to the inattentiveness, intransigence, or lack of knowledge of those who wield power.

In particular, contempt of court orders has become a great impediment to the safeguarding of human rights in Kenya. Decisive steps need to be taken by the legislature, civil society organizations, and 'fourth branch' institutions protecting democracy like quasi-governmental human rights and equality commissions to ensure that human rights do not remain mere pipe dreams but are actually implemented and enjoyed by the people. Applying an equality-sensitive approach as an interpretive tool in addressing actual or potential violations of SERs, especially where vulnerable groups are affected, may mean the enactment of laws to best tackle contempt of court orders. Such laws should prescribe adequate punishment to state organs and officers who fail to implement and follow court orders and the law.

On the whole, the discussion in the chapter demonstrates that, particularly in times of crisis, the needs of the most vulnerable in society should be prioritized and should be the guiding light when states are brainstorming on initiatives to combat rising crises. This is what the Constitution requires in Kenya. From dismantling the systemic structures of inequality faced by vulnerable groups, to avoiding exacerbating the same, requires the state to remember the constitutional duty in Article 20(5)(b) to prioritize the needs of vulnerable groups when implementing the SERs in Article 43 to ensure their widest possible enjoyment.

19
The Role of Equality Law in Expanding Access to Social Goods and Services in South Africa
Lessons after the Pandemic

*Catherine Albertyn**

1 Introduction

South Africa, with its origins in slavery and colonialism, has always been a place of extreme inequality, especially of race and its intersections with gender and class. Only under democracy did it acquire the constitutional and legal tools to address this in the Constitution of the Republic of South Africa, 1996 and accompanying legislation.[1] In drafting this Constitution and legislation in the 1990s, South Africa was able to draw on the experience of established democracies, where equality law was based on older (and often more limited) understandings, to establish a robust framework of equality law and entrenched socio-economic rights. Indeed, the powerful commitments to a just and egalitarian society expressed in that Constitution grounded an early optimism about the African National Congress government's political will to address a legacy of structural socio-economic inequalities, coupled with the potential for constitutional litigation by civil society to accelerate and monitor this process.[2]

In legal terms, the record suggests an ambitious jurisprudence, with mixed outcomes. It demonstrates the power of equality law in extending recognition to status groups (especially based on sexual orientation, gender, and nationality) and in defending race-based preferential and distributive measures.[3] Socio-economic rights litigation concerning the provision of social goods and services, characterized by a jurisprudence of reasonableness, allowed claimants to hold government to account for the progressive realization of rights, although at more minimum levels of programmatic compliance and meeting the needs of the 'most desperate', and without the substantive bite initially hoped for.[4]

---

* This work is based on research supported wholly by the National Research Foundation (NRF) of South Africa (Grant Number 115567). Opinions expressed and conclusions arrived at are those of the author and are not necessarily to be attributed to the NRF.

[1] Especially the Employment Equity Act 55 of 1998 (workplace inequality); the Promotion of Equality and Prevention of Unfair Discrimination Act 4 of 2000 (inequality across the public and private sectors).

[2] Karl Klare, 'Legal Culture and Transformative Constitution' (1998) 14 South African Journal on Human Rights 168.

[3] Catherine Albertyn, '(In)equality and the South African Constitution' (2019) 36 Development Southern Africa 751.

[4] See eg Sandra Liebenberg, *Socio-economic Rights: Adjudication Under a Transformative Constitution* (Juta 2010); Danie Brand, 'The Proceduralism of South African Socio-economic Rights Jurisprudence or "What are socio-economic rights for"' in Henk Botha, Andre van der Walt, and Johan van der Walt,

In political and economic terms, initial improvements after 1994 gave way to deepening inequality and poverty over the past decade. By 2020, when the Covid-19 pandemic erupted, South Africa was defined by structurally high unemployment and low economic growth. The effects of pandemic-induced lockdowns were devastating on livelihoods and the economy, as inequalities grew exponentially. A R500 billion aid package provided some relief, and an economic bounce-back after the relaxation of lockdowns marginally improved prospects for economic growth. Nevertheless, the pandemic cast a harsh light on South Africa's persistent and deep problems of joblessness, hunger, poverty, and inequality.

For social justice lawyers in South Africa, these events have raised deeper questions about the role of equality and socio-economic rights law in economic and redistributive questions and in addressing longer-term, structural socio-economic inequalities exposed by the pandemic. This chapter focuses on the narrow question of the role of equality rights (unfair discrimination and positive measures) in section 9 of the Constitution and the Promotion of Equality and Prevention of Unfair Discrimination Act, 4 of 2000, (the Equality Act 2000) in achieving more egalitarian and substantive outcomes in the provision of social goods and services.[5] This has been a neglected area of research and litigation, given the prominence of socio-economic rights in South Africa.

The next section briefly recounts growing poverty, inequality, and uneven access to sufficient social goods and services to secure substantive freedom and equality. This reveals multiple and intersecting categories of exclusion, beyond poverty or class, that provide some traction for discrimination and equality arguments. Section 3 briefly evaluates socio-economic rights and equality jurisprudence, to suggest that equality has played a powerful role in securing substantive outcomes in socio-economic rights cases and has multifaceted potential for securing a more egalitarian distribution of social goods and services. Section 4 develops this by mapping the jurisprudential contours of the constitutional value and right and/or the Equality Act 2000 in distributing social goods and services, in four illustrative categories: (i) expanding the scope of existing social goods by adding new groups (who qualifies); (ii) challenging the distribution of resources underpinning goods and services (shifting resources from more privileged towards disadvantaged groups); (iii) preventing the regression of goods and services; and (iv) the judicial development of a positive equality duty (under section 9(2)) to implement policies and laws concerning socio-economic rights with due regard to substantive equality. To conclude, I discuss what this reveals about the role of equality law and courts, and the conceptual and institutional spaces, limits, and opportunities in equality law to address structural and exponential economic inequalities and poverty in South Africa.

Rights and Democracy in a Transformative Constitution (Sun Press 2003); Stuart Wilson and Jackie Dugard, 'Taking Poverty Seriously: The South African Constitutional Court and Socio-economic Rights' (2011) 22 Stellenbosch Law Review 664.

[5] Section 9 generally applies in challenging or interpreting legislation and the Equality Act 2000 in all other instances. The jurisprudence is similar, as the Act was developed on the basis of extant section 9 jurisprudence.

2 Fault Lines of Inequality and Poverty: Before and after Covid-19

Poverty and inequality are deeply entrenched in South Africa's history, as 'land and water, then minerals, capital for investment and finally human capital were accumulated over centuries primarily (although not exclusively) into white hands'.[6] Throughout this time, intentional and discriminatory policies and laws embedded racial inequality, exclusion, and oppression.[7] Addressing this legacy of structural inequality was always going to demand more than a mere reversal of racial laws and policies. After 1994, the Reconstruction and Development Programme[8] that prioritized social spending and a highly distributive fiscal policy, especially on social grants, education, health, and free basic services, meant that poverty and inequality improved slightly in the first fifteen years. For example, the rate of extreme poverty was cut by half, from 34.4 per cent to 16.5 per cent between the end of apartheid and 2011,[9] and overall inequality decreased, albeit slightly, between 1993 and 2014.[10] Official statistics suggested continual improvements to non-monetary well-being in access to formal housing, piped water, electricity, free basic education (through fee exemptions), and healthcare; however, the effects of social spending and the non-income parts of social wage on the levels of poverty and inequality are disputed.[11] Even with an overall positive increase in access to basic services,[12] the impact has varied greatly across provinces and the rural/urban divide, and is also affected by levels of corruption, social struggles, and affordability (as growing poverty cuts into household ability to pay in the context of inadequate basic provision).

In the end, without fundamental changes to South Africa's extractive economy based on mining and resources, little can been done to secure meaningful economic development (with growth averaging only 2.1 per cent between 2010 and 2016),[13] and arrest growing levels of unemployment, especially amongst young people.[14] Indeed, unemployment and education (low years of schooling) remain the top two contributors to poverty[15] as poverty levels and inequality (in income, wealth and power)

---

[6] Francis Wilson, 'Historical Roots of Inequality in South Africa' (2011) 26 Economic History of Developing Regions 1, 12.

[7] ibid.

[8] African National Congress, *Reconstruction and Development Programme* (1994).

[9] World Bank, 'South African Economic Update: Fiscal Policy and Redistribution in an Unequal Society' (2014). See also Arden Finn and Murray Leibbrandt, 'The Dynamics of Poverty in South Africa' SALDRU Working Paper No 174 (2017).

[10] See Janina Hundenborn, Murray Leibbrandt, and Ingrid Woolard, 'Drivers of Inequality in South Africa' SALDRU Working Paper No 194 (2016).

[11] Charles Meth, 'Social Income in South Africa, An Economy Marred by High Unemployment, Poverty and Extreme Inequality' Research Report Centre for Poverty, Employment and Growth, Human Sciences Research Council (2008) 12, 13.

[12] Statistics South Africa, 'The State of Basic Service Delivery in South Africa: In-depth Analysis of the Community Survey' Stats SA Report No 03-01-22 (2016).

[13] David Francis and Edward Webster, 'Poverty and Inequality in South Africa: Critical Reflections' (2019) 36 Development Southern Africa 788, 794.

[14] ibid.

[15] Victor Sulla and Precious Zikhali, 'Overcoming Poverty and Inequality in South Africa: An Assessment of Drivers, Constraints and Opportunities' World Bank Report (2018).

increased again from 2015.[16] Adequate social provisioning thus remains critical to achieving South Africa's constitutional vision.

In this context, the hard lockdowns under the state of disaster[17] occasioned by the Covid-19 pandemic shattered livelihoods. Within a month of lockdown, the labour market shed three million jobs (an 18 per cent decline in employment).[18] One in three income earners had no income in April 2020, skewed towards the informal economy[19] and the most disadvantaged groups: women (two-thirds of job losses), manual workers, youth, black persons, and those with less education and lower incomes.[20] Nearly one-third of those retrenched lived in households with no grant protection.[21] Nearly half of households (47 per cent) ran out of money to buy food in April 2020.[22] Despite some improvements as lockdown eased, with some people able to go back to work,[23] overall those who were poor, rural, female, unskilled, and less educated continued to experience the largest declines in employment.[24] Levels of food insecurity dropped somewhat, but remained high.[25] Any bounce-back with the relaxation of lockdowns was limited as Statistics South Africa reported that, in October 2020, the national unemployment rate increased to a seventeen-year high of 30.8 per cent.[26] By the end of that year, 42.7 per cent of small businesses closed[27] and it was predicted that one-third of middle class families (mostly Black) would fall into vulnerability.[28]

As highlighted by the pandemic, inequality, poverty, and disadvantage are clustered at the intersections of race,[29] gender, class,[30] age, and other vectors of inequality,

---

[16] See Statistics South Africa, 'Poverty Trends in South Africa' Report No 03-10-06 (2017); Statistics South Africa, 'Inequality Trends in South Africa' (2017); Francis and Webster (n 13) 792.

[17] Declared in terms of the Disaster Management Act, 57 of 2002.

[18] National Income Dynamics Study (NIDS) Coronavirus Rapid Mobile Survey (CRAM), 'NIDS-CRAM Synthesis Report Wave 1' (15 July 2020) 3 https://cramsurvey.org/reports/#wave-1 (accessed 5 August 2021).

[19] ibid 4.

[20] ibid 4–5.

[21] ibid 5.

[22] This was more than double the already unacceptable levels of hunger measured in 2020, at 21 per cent: ibid 6–7.

[23] NIDS-CRAM, 'Synthesis Report NIDS-CRAM Wave 2' (30 September 2020) https://cramsurvey.org/wp-content/uploads/2020/10/1.-Spaull-et-al.-NIDS-CRAM-Wave-2-Synthesis-Report.pdf (accessed 5 August 2021) 1–2.

[24] ibid 1–3.

[25] ibid 8–9.

[26] Statistics South Africa, 'Quarterly Labour Force Survey. Quarter 1:2020' (2020) <https://www.statssa.gov.za/publications/P0211/P02111stQuarter2020.pdf (accessed 31 May 2022).

[27] 'Lockdown forced nearly half of small businesses in South Africa to close' *BusinessTech* (7 December 2020) https://businesstech.co.za/news/business/455100/lockdown-forced-nearly-half-of-small-businesses-in-south-africa-to-close-study/ (accessed 18 April 2022).

[28] 'South Africa's middle-class is being wiped out' *BusinessTech* (26 March 2021) https://businesstech.co.za/news/finance/478819/south-africas-middle-class-is-being-wiped-out/ (accessed 18 April 2022). This was based on the number of people in debt, who were relying on credit. See also United Nations Development Programme, 'Socio-Economic Impact of COVID-19 in South Africa' (19 August 2020) https://www.za.undp.org/content/south_africa/en/home/library/socio-economic-impact-of-covid-19-on-south-africa/ (accessed 18 April 2022).

[29] For example, almost half (46.6 per cent) of households headed by Black African people live below the upper-bound poverty line (R1,268 per person per month), compared to less than 1 per cent of White people. Statistics South Africa, *Men, Women and Children: Findings of the Living Conditions 2014/15* (29 March 2018) 17.

[30] Class has become an important driver in South Africa as inequality has grown within racial groups. For example, in 1993, inequality within race groups accounted for 48 per cent of overall inequality, but by

confirming that membership of classically disadvantaged groups—defined both intersectionally and on a single axis—is inextricably linked to low economic status and poor socio-economic outcomes. Within this, Black women remain the poorest overall group in South Africa. Indeed, if one of the gains of the democratic era was that people were 'lifted from extreme poverty through a mixture of social support, better primary healthcare and employment equity policies', then Covid-19 illustrated their reversal. The pandemic thus raised the spectre of more growth in poverty and '[i]nequalities along traditional lines of race, gender, occupation, earnings, location and education' in South Africa,[31] and even less access to social goods and services.

Solutions to the growing need for social provisioning, amidst South Africa's structural problems of persistent low growth and growing unemployment, are subject to highly contested economic policy debates in the political branches and civil society around redistribution and social spending, taxation and revenue, fiscal caution, and acceptable budgetary deficits, as well as state capacity and corruption.[32] However, there are also clear issues around the delivery and distribution of social goods and services that implicate questions of race, gender, age, social origin, and so on, that could potentially ground equality claims around discrimination and positive measures in courts. Given this intensely contested policy space, how far can we rely on courts and equality law to secure a more egalitarian and just distribution of social goods and services?

3 Equality Law and Socio-economic Rights

There is little disagreement that a commitment to building an egalitarian society based on substantive equality, dignity, and freedom is at the heart of the South African constitutional project. Fundamental to addressing the inequalities of the past was the task of remaking the policies, laws, and institutions that governed and regulated society and the economy, to (re)distribute rights, resources, goods, and benefits. To do so successfully also required ongoing political will, state capacity, and resources, as well as society's ability to transform deeply entrenched racialized, gendered, heteronormative, and other prejudicial social roles, norms, attitudes, and conduct cultivated over centuries. Alongside government action, two distinct bodies of activism, research, litigation, and jurisprudence emerged to address inequality and poverty: equality law and socio-economic rights. While the former focused on redressing inequality in the form of discrimination (substantively understood), the latter targeted poverty.

2008 this had increased to 62 per cent: Murray Leibbrandt, Arden Finn, and Ingrid Woolard, 'Describing and Decomposing Post-Apartheid Income Inequality in South Africa' (2012) 29 Development Southern Africa 19.

[31] NIDS-CRAM (n 18) 2.

[32] This is largely a clash around levels of austerity in a declining economy, pitting more cautious versus more distributive approaches. See eg the criticism by the Budget Justice Coalition (BJC) of the Medium Term Budget Policy Statement (MTBPS): BJC Submission on MTBPS to the Select and Standing Committees on Finance (3 November 2020) https://iej.org.za/submission-by-the-budget-justice-coalition-in-response-to-2020-medium-term-budget/ (accessed 18 April 2022).

Equality jurisprudence developed in two directions. The section 9(3) jurisprudence on unfair discrimination—at its best—enabled a contextual and intersectional investigation of the impact of the impugned law or conduct on disadvantaged groups, mediated by concerns of dignity (equal concern and respect) and remedying disadvantage.[33] Although its interpretation and application has found formalist, inclusive and transformative outcomes, the dominant application of discrimination law has been a liberal egalitarian concern to treat everyone with equal concern and respect.[34] This has resulted in powerful inclusive outcomes as status groups, defined by different kinds of misrecognition and disadvantage (but especially sexual orientation, gender, and nationality), have been brought into the framework of rights and legal protection. The second category of jurisprudence under section 9(2) has developed constitutional and legal protection for positive measures in the form of race and gender-based preferential treatment.[35] Here, across different standards of rationality, reasonableness, and proportionality, and different balancing acts between collective equality and individual dignity; the courts have generally defended such measures in the workplace, the economy, and decision-making structures.[36] Until recently, section 9(2) of the Constitution and relevant legal provisions have constituted a shield—rather than a sword—for positive measures.

Overall, with notable and injurious exceptions,[37] equality law in South Africa has been a powerful tool in eradicating legal inequalities for disadvantaged groups, often in terms of social inclusion and recognition, but with some distributive consequences (especially in extending rights to property and inheritance in family, trust, and succession law; public and private forms of social protection; and enabling the redistribution of employment and economic opportunities).

Socio-economic rights jurisprudence has generally focused on securing goods and services for the poor, particularly access to adequate housing, healthcare services, social security, sufficient food and water, and basic education.[38] Wary of separation of powers concerns, the courts have emphasized the reasonableness of government action, in practice an evaluation of process and governance according to—what I categorize as—principles of recognition/dignity, equality, and accountability/democracy. If no action has been taken to deliver a particular good or service, government is required to recognize and treat a community with dignity and respect by introducing programmatic measures to secure socio-economic rights over time (the dignity

---

[33] This test was first set out in full in *Harksen v Lane* [1997] ZACC 12. For fuller exposition of equality law in the first two decades see Catherine Albertyn and Beth Goldblatt, 'Equality' in Stu Woolman and Michael Bishop (eds), *Constitutional Law of South Africa* (2nd edn, Juta 2007).

[34] Catherine Albertyn, 'Contested Substantive Equality in the South African Constitution: Beyond Social Inclusion Towards Systemic Justice' (2018) 34 South African Journal on Human Rights 441.

[35] South African Constitution, s 9(2). See also Employment Equity Act, 55 of 1998; Equality Act 2000.

[36] Catherine Albertyn, 'Adjudicating Affirmative Action within a Normative Framework of Substantive Equality and the Employment Equity Act: An Opportunity Missed? South African Police Services v Solidarity Obo Barnard' (2015) 132 South African Law Journal 711; Chris McConnachie, 'Affirmative Action and Intensity of Review: South African Police Service v Solidarity obo Barnard' (2015) 7 Constitutional Court Review 163.

[37] *S v Jordan* [2002] ZACC 22 (equality claim for decriminalizing sex work denied); *Volks v Robinson* [2005] ZACC 2 (equality claims for recognition of rights if heterosexual cohabitating partners denied).

[38] South African Constitution, ss 26, 27, 29.

principle);³⁹ if the needs of 'the most desperate' are not accounted for in policy, they must be included and met in the short-term (dignity and equality principles);⁴⁰ if a disadvantaged group is unreasonably excluded from an existing good or service, it must be extended to them⁴¹ (the equality principle); and if government has not engaged a community or been sufficiently flexible in its response, it must so engage and act⁴² (the accountability/democracy principle).⁴³ With stronger constitutional provisions *and* supportive legislation, the courts have enabled more substantive outcomes under section 26(3), on limiting homelessness after eviction,⁴⁴ and under section 29(1) (right to basic education), to order that goods and services provided for in the supporting regulatory framework are delivered (including textbooks, desks and chairs, educators).⁴⁵ The Constitutional Court has consistently refrained from engaging in policy debate, and has confirmed and extended existing policies and laws, rather than overturning them.⁴⁶ Although subject to criticism for avoiding substance and not giving content to normative standards to define minimum thresholds in the quality and quantity of goods,⁴⁷ the role of the courts in catalysing solutions and enhancing accountability and participation has also been welcomed as a strategic response to difficult questions.⁴⁸

In one of the few analyses of equality rights and socio-economic rights in 2007, Goldblatt and Liebenberg argue that the rights' common focus on substantive equality requires them to be interpreted in a complementary fashion, noting their parallel jurisdiction.⁴⁹ It is often argued that socio-economic rights should be infused with the value of substantive equality.⁵⁰ However, equality law has rarely been seen as an

---

³⁹ As first set out in *Government of the RSA v Grootboom* 2001 (1) SA 46 (CC) [44] (provision must be made for the needs of the most desperate), and illustrated recently in *Mshengu v Msunduzi Municipality* [2019] ZAKZPHC 52 (government ordered to plan and implement the provision of basic sanitation, sufficient water and refuse collection of refuse for farm occupiers and labour tenants, in accordance with extant policies).

⁴⁰ *Grootboom* (n 39).

⁴¹ *TAC v Minister of Health* [2002] ZACC 15 (extension for anti-retroviral treatment to poor women attending public hospitals where state capacity existed); *Khosa v Minister of Social Development* [2004] ZACC 11 (extension of Older Persons Grant to destitute permanent residents).

⁴² The principle of meaningful engagement was developed, via cases on evictions, in *Occupiers of 51 Olivia Road v City of Johannesburg* [2008] ZACC 1. The principle of a flexible and responsive government, amending policy as required, was confirmed in *Mazibuko v City of Johannesburg* [2009] ZACC 28.

⁴³ Sandra Liebenberg, 'Participatory Approaches to Socio-Economic Rights Adjudication: Tentative Lessons from South African Evictions Law' (2014) 32 Nordic Journal of Human Rights 312, 330; Marius Pieterse, 'Socio-economic Rights Adjudication and Democratic Urban Governance: Reassessing the "Second Wave" Jurisprudence of the South African Constitutional Court' (2018) 51 VRÜ Verfassung und Recht in Übersee 12, 34.

⁴⁴ Section 26(3) provides for negative enforcement and is given further content by the Prevention of Illegal Eviction from and Unlawful Occupation of Land Act 19 of 1998. See eg *City of Johannesburg Metropolitan Municipality v Blue Moonlight Properties 39 (Pty) Ltd* [2011] ZACC 33.

⁴⁵ Section 29 is not qualified by progressive realization and supported by an extensive regulatory system that underpins successful court orders.

⁴⁶ *Residents of Joe Slovo Community, Western Cape v Thubelisha Homes* [2009] ZACC 16; *Mazibuko* (n 42).

⁴⁷ See also references in n 4.

⁴⁸ Katherine Young, 'A Typology of Economic and Social Rights Adjudication: Exploring the Catalytic Function of Judicial Review' (2010) 8 International Journal of Constitutional Law 385; Pieterse (n 43).

⁴⁹ Beth Goldblatt and Sandra Liebenberg, 'The Interrelationship Between Equality and Socio-Economic Rights Under South Africa's Transformative Constitution' (2007) 23 South African Journal on Human Rights 335. See also Sandra Fredman, 'The Potential and Limits of an Equal Rights Paradigm in Addressing Poverty' (2011) 22 Stellenbosch Law Review 566.

⁵⁰ Sandra Liebenberg, 'Towards an Equality-producing Interpretation of Socio-economic Rights in South Africa: Insights from the Egalitarian Liberal Tradition' (2015) 132 South African Law Journal 411.

independent source of social provisioning, even though it is arguable that the few immediate, material outcomes in socio-economic rights jurisprudence are primarily due to equality as a principle of, and right to, inclusion. The success in *TAC* was driven by the unreasonable, even irrational, exclusion of a disadvantaged group of poor, Black women seeking to prevent mother-to-child transmission of HIV.[51] The positive result in *Khosa* was underpinned by the discriminatory exclusion of a classic outsider group defined by citizenship status.[52] Both speak to under-inclusivity in existing policy or law and are—in fact—discrimination arguments, although only *Khosa* acknowledges that.

More recent jurisprudential developments indicate that equality, as a value and a right, can directly and independently enhance the provision of goods and services. This chapter builds on earlier work to evaluate the current potential of equality law to play a greater role in the provision of social goods and services. In particular, can equality law—with its promise of more immediate outcomes—overcome the questions of institutional comity, economic concerns and policy caution that have stalked socio-economic rights cases? In seeking to understand the independent role of equality law, alongside socio-economic rights, the next sections map four areas of jurisprudence to evaluate their scope and opportunities.

4 Expanding the Scope of Social Goods: Adding New Categories of Disadvantaged Groups (Limited Redistribution by Inclusion)

The ability of law to address status-based discrimination in the provision of social goods and services is widely recognized, and discrimination law has enabled the inclusion of disadvantaged groups in different categories of social provisioning in many jurisdictions.[53] However, it is clear that courts are wary of claims by groups defined directly or indirectly by poverty-related grounds, rather than the more traditional status grounds,[54] and/or claims that take courts into contested economic terrains.[55] Where claims traverse these boundaries, courts take more deferent approaches via tests of rationality (does government have reasons for the policy choice?) and/or adopting more procedural rather than substantive outcomes (has a group been *treated* with equal concern and respect?).[56] This has generated debate around the forms of equality law that best enable substantive evaluation and economic accountability. I suggest that much of this is encapsulated in the 'best interpretation' of South African equality law which requires a contextual, impact-focused, and value-based evaluation

---

[51] *TAC* (n 41).

[52] ibid.

[53] Fredman (n 49). See also Magdalena Sepúlveda Carmona, 'Ensuring Inclusion and Combatting Discrimination in Social Protection Programmes: The Role of Human Rights Standards' (2017) 70 International Social Security Review 13, 43.

[54] Fredman (n 49).

[55] See eg Judy Fudge, 'Substantive Equality, the Supreme Court of Canada, and the Limits to Redistribution' (2007) 23 South African Journal on Human Rights 235.

[56] ibid. See also Fredman (n 49).

of claims of discrimination, and a proportional enquiry into their justification that balances economic arguments against the effects of the discrimination. Of course, this will not always result in successful claims, given legitimate separation of powers issues in some cases, but it should always enable more substantive adjudication for vulnerable groups, and thus respect constitutional commitments to participation and accountability.[57]

Litigation and advocacy under South African discrimination law have generally widened the scope of access to social goods and services by expanding the groups that qualify for a particular good or service. The most well-known case is *Khosa v Minister of Social Development*[58] where the Constitutional Court concluded that section 9(3) and section 27 (right of access to appropriate social assistance) required the inclusion of destitute permanent residents in the social grant system, especially the Older Persons' Grant (OPG). In making this finding, the Court noted that the discrimination was on the basis of their non-citizenship status, which resulted in impermissible stigma and stereotypes in the content and effects of the law. In relation to the latter, the exclusion of the *Khosa* applicants from public benefits forced them into 'relationships of dependency upon families, friends and community ... relegated [them] to the margins of society [and] ... cast [them] in the role of supplicants'.[59] In *Khosa*, the exacerbation of material disadvantage and destitution reflected an absence of equal concern and respect.[60] These effects on dignity outweighed the state's financial and immigration policy justifications.[61]

Often classified as a socio-economic rights case, it is an outlier in that jurisprudence (using different standards of reasonableness).[62] However, it is an easy discrimination case, bringing a classic outsider group into the scope of eligibility for *an existing benefit*, motivated by dignity concerns.

In the slipstream of *Khosa*, the direct and indirect use of equality (unfair discrimination) in advocacy and litigation helped secure a range of social grants and statutory social insurance for status groups. Amongst these were age discrimination claims to justify the expansion of the Child Support Grant (CSG) from children of fourteen to eighteen years;[63] sex/gender discrimination claims to seek the equalization of the OPG at sixty for women and men;[64] and intersectional race/gender/social origin claims to

---

[57] See preamble and s 1 of the South African Constitution.
[58] *TAC* (n 41).
[59] ibid [74], [76], [77].
[60] ibid [80]–[82].
[61] ibid [54]–[67], where they overlap with the reasonableness enquiry of s 27.
[62] ibid.
[63] *Mahlangu v Minister of Social Development* (Transvaal Provincial Division 2005, Case Number 25754/05). See also Margaret Sagan, 'Monitoring the Right of Access to Social Security and Appropriate Social Assistance in South Africa: An Analysis of the Policy Effort, Resource Allocation and Expenditure and Enjoyment of the Right to Social Security' (14 September 2017) Studies in Poverty and Inequality Institute Working Paper, 15.
[64] *Roberts v Minister of Social Development* (Transvaal Provincial Division 2005, Case Number 32838/05). Although government successfully defended the age difference as a s 9(2) positive measure benefitting a disadvantaged class of older, Black women in court, in wider policy debates it agreed to phase out the distinction. By 2010, both men and women qualified for the old age grant at sixty: Beth Goldblatt, 'The Right to Social Security: Addressing Women's Poverty and Disadvantage' (2009) 25 South African Journal on Human Rights 442.

include domestic workers, in private households, in social insurance for disability or death arising from injury or disease sustained in the course of employment, under the Compensation for Occupational Injuries and Diseases Act, 130 of 1993.[65] Most recently, in a claim under the Covid-19 pandemic that was able to rely directly on *Khosa*, the case of *Scalabrini Centre for Cape Town v Minister of Social Development*[66] saw a successful challenge to the exclusion of asylum seekers and special permit holders[67] from receiving emergency social assistance by way of the Social Relief of Distress grant (a limited monthly cash grant of R350 that was then set to expire in April 2021).

As poverty and inequality deepen in South Africa, new questions emerge about the scope and potential for discrimination claims to form a basis for widening access to social goods and services for vulnerable and marginalized groups. A new generation of lawyers is bringing creative, intersectional claims to court and asking whether one is limited to expanding the scope of provision, be it grants, water, or housing, or whether discrimination can found 'new' goods, such as a new grant or a new category of housing provision, such as shelters for women? There is limited space to address this in detail. However, the debate inevitably circles around both *conceptual* and *institutional* concerns: conceptual concerns relate to how we interpret and apply discrimination law, while institutional concerns relate to the role of courts in economic policy choices.

4.1 Conceptual Issues: Context, Grounds, Intersectionality

Arguably South African jurisprudence is well placed for innovative uses of equality law that nudge law's traditional boundaries, given its commitment to contextual enquiries into the impact of exclusion on disadvantaged groups,[68] which can be defined intersectionally and can include the grounds of poverty. Most recently, in *Mahlangu v Minister of Labour*,[69] domestic workers were able to demonstrate their position as a group of Black, working class women (at the intersection of race and gender), subject to poverty and historical disadvantage and in need of legal protection to secure inclusion in the Compensation for Occupational Injuries and Diseases Act. The ability to target particularly marginalized and vulnerable groups in discrimination claims has been given further traction in a recent Discussion Paper of the South African Law Reform Commission to secure maternity benefits for self-employed women working in the informal sector. Targeting both labour and social assistance law, these policy proposals centre intersectional sex, gender, pregnancy, race, and social origin (denoting class and poverty) discrimination in making their case.[70] This bodes well for the greater legal protection (inclusion) of vulnerable groups of workers (defined at

---

[65] *Sylvia Bongi Mahlangu v Minister of Labour* [2020] ZACC 24. In line with the dual development of equality and socio-economic rights, the court also found this to be unreasonable under s 27 as it excluded a vulnerable group: *Mahlangu* [27]–[67].

[66] [2020] ZAGPPHC 308.

[67] Special permits are granted, on application, to persons from Angola, Lesotho, and Zimbabwe, meaning they are lawfully resident in South Africa: *Scalabrini Centre for Cape Town* (n 66) [30]–[33].

[68] *Harksen v Lane* (n 33) [46]–[53].

[69] *Mahlangu* (n 65).

[70] South African Law Reform Commission, 'Maternity and Parental Benefits for Self-Employed Workers in the Informal Economy', Project 143: Discussion Paper 153 (23 June 2021) 55–62. Another intersectional

the intersection of race, gender, and social origin, or poverty). And, as *Mahlangu* again demonstrates, even if not a ground, poverty can be addressed via the court's interpretation of history, context, and impact.[71] For both policy advocacy and litigation, these developments signal a moment of potential for South African equality law.

Over and above inclusion in laws, targeted claims can reveal how groups are indirectly discriminated against in the content of policies and laws and/or in how they are implemented. For example, feminist scholars point to the gendered effects of benefits rules such as family size, or how women's care roles might affect access to social goods.[72] This has not been widely used in South Africa, with the exception of *Social Justice Coalition v Minister of Police*,[73] discussed further below, which revealed how an apparently neutral formula for distributing services resulted in a discriminatory race and poverty impact.

Liebenberg and Goldblatt suggest that equality law might even ground new claims for goods and benefits, for example, gender and race discrimination might support claims for state-provided child-care to address the disadvantage faced by poor women in managing their care roles.[74] A revitalized debate in South Africa, in the wake of the exponential inequalities under the pandemic, concerns the amount of some grants (currently below the poverty line), as well as the introduction of a basic income grant to bring a large group of unemployed people into social protection.[75] Here, the group is primarily defined by poverty—even if it has clear race and gender implications. The ground itself is not necessarily a hurdle. Although the Constitutional Court did not formally accept the constitutional ground of 'social origin' (seen to be a marker of poverty and class) as an intersectional ground in *Mahlangu*, it did recognize that domestic workers experience 'racism, sexism ... and class stratification'.[76] In addition, in an earlier Equality Court case, *Social Justice Coalition*, the court accepted that poverty met the test for a 'prohibited ground' under the Equality Act 2000, in that differentiation on the basis of poverty caused or perpetuated disadvantage, undermined dignity, and/or adversely affected the equal enjoyment of socio-economic rights.[77]

There has been some debate around the role of poverty, social origin, social condition, or socio-economic status as grounds in discrimination law.[78] Many agree that

---

argument, although adjudicated under socio-economic rights is *Mshengu* (n 39), where the group of labour tenants and farm workers denied basic services was defined by race and social origin (class, rural, poor).

[71] *Mahlangu* (n 65) [87]–[104]. Shreya Atrey makes this argument in 'The Intersectional Case of Poverty in Discrimination Law' (2018) 18 Human Rights Law Review 411.
[72] Fredman (n 49).
[73] [2018] ZAWCHC 181.
[74] See also Fredman (n 49).
[75] See eg Black Sash, 'Social Protection in a Time of Covid' (2021); Institute for Economic Justice 'Financing Options for a Basic Income Grant in South Africa' (2021).
[76] *Mahlangu* (n 65) [90], [96].
[77] *Social Justice Coalition* (n 73) [57]–[65].
[78] Goldblatt and Liebenberg (n 49); Fredman (n 49); Sarah Ganty, 'Poverty as Misrecognition: What Role for Anti-discrimination Law in Europe?' (2021) 21(4) Human Rights Law Review 962; Juan Carlos Benito Sánchez, 'Towering Grenfell: Reflections around Socioeconomic Disadvantage in Antidiscrimination Law' (2019) 5 Queen Mary Human Rights Law Review 1. On the different but related ground of class see Alex Benn, 'The Big Gap in Discrimination Law: Class and the Equality Act 2010' (2020) 3 University of Oxford Human Rights Hub Journal 1.

a discrimination claim on poverty is workable where it addresses exclusion based on stigma, stereotype, and misrecognition (whether in credit, housing loans, housing, education, or employment). Beyond this, such challenges can have powerful symbolic effects,[79] an effect perhaps prefigured in the *Khosa* judgment, whose invocation of poverty, framed as a failure of recognition or to treat destitute people with equal concern and respect, has resonated across the years.

Arguably, therefore, discrimination—as a concept in South African law—is capable of poverty-based challenges (intersectional or single-axis) to inadequate social provisioning. However, the core problem is a well-known one and generally keeps policy advocacy on augmented or new social grants out of courts and confined to the political domain: these cases raise complex, polycentric budgetary issues, and choices that courts will generally treat with caution and distance.

4.2 Economic Policy Choices in the Courts

Properly applied, section 9 allocates questions of affordability and/or economic policy to the limitation enquiry under section 36, while the Equality Act 2000 envisages a single comprehensive evaluation of fairness that balances the effects of discrimination against the respondent's justifications.[80] Although South African courts have not shied away from questions of budgetary allocation, like all courts they are cautious when human rights cases implicate budgetary issues. So it is perhaps not surprising that in all the successful cases discussed above, economic issues were not determinative. Increases in budget occasioned by expanding access to grants were either not an issue at all (because government has accepted the responsibility, as in the CSG and OPG) or seen to be minimal in the balance with the dignity concerns implicated by exclusion and destitution on the basis of prohibited grounds, as in *Khosa*.[81] No case implicated underlying economic policy arrangements and choices in a fundamental way. Thus, none serve as precedent for more than the important principles that government must make its economic justifications in court or risk-averse findings,[82] and dignity concerns can outweigh budgetary concerns. Equally important is the strategic lesson of doing the advocacy work necessary to get government onside concerning budgetary issues. As discussed below, in section 6, challenges that entail significant budgetary allocation are less likely to succeed. Before that, I discuss the potentially radical finding in *Social Justice Coalition*, suggesting that courts might be used to redistribute resources from privileged to disadvantaged groups and thus to engage underlying principles of distribution.

---

[79] Sánchez (n 78).
[80] Equality Act 2000, s 14(2)–(3).
[81] *Khosa* (n 41) [44], [82].
[82] *TAC* (n 41) [60]–[62], [871].

5 Changing the Distribution of Socio-economic Rights: Challenging the Underlying Distribution of Goods and Services

Equality typically addresses exclusion from social goods and services by virtue of membership of an outsider group, which is remedied by (greater) inclusion. It rarely goes to the underlying distribution of resources. The *Social Justice Coalition* case[83] is particularly compelling in that it addresses this underlying redistribution by looking at not whether, but how, groups are included.

In 2016, the Social Justice Coalition approached the Equality Court alleging indirect discrimination on the basis of race and poverty in the allocation of policing services. It argued that the statistical formula by which police were allocated to different areas of the Western Cape resulted in disproportionately fewer personnel being sent to poor, Black areas than wealthier, middle-class, and predominantly White areas. The Equality Court found the formula to discriminate on the basis of race and poverty (finding poverty to be an additional ground as discussed above). It issued a declaratory order to this effect and postponed the determination of the remedy to a later date. It is unhappily still to be resolved, a point I return to in the conclusion.

The case arguably goes beyond the more accepted use of poverty as a source of stigma and misrecognition to address distributive issues, in this case the distribution of police personnel. However, insofar as the case sought the reallocation or redistribution of *existing and available* policing resources, rather than the addition of new ones, it did not trigger the economic concerns identified above. Thus, it does not act as precedent for claims that seek to *expand* economic resources (beyond existing ones) on poverty grounds, or indeed any other ground.

Also important is that the case flows from an earlier Commission of Enquiry into policing in Khayelitsha (a Cape Town Black township) which had also found the statistical formula for allocating resources to be problematic.[84] It was dependent on this history, as well as substantial litigation resources (expertise, funding etc.) for its successful outcome. This does not render it unique, but rather suggests claims around fairer and more just distributions are possible, although complex, and require extensive research and long term strategizing to be successful.

6 Halting Regression in the Provision of Goods and Services

In recent times in South Africa and the Global South, systems of social protection expanded, while those in the Global North were retracting.[85] However, in South Africa a declining per capita income, a markedly slower growth in tax revenue, and increases

---

[83] *Social Justice Coalition* (n 73).
[84] ibid [41].
[85] Kevan Harris and Ben Scully, 'A Hidden Counter-Movement? Precarity, Politics and Social Protection Before and Beyond the Neoliberal Era' (2015) 44 Theory and Society 415, 416.

in national debt occasioned by economic decline (including the effects of state capture and corruption)[86] mean that the pool for redistribution has been shrinking. This situation worsened under the perfect storm of Covid-19, triggering exponential increases in inequality and economic decline, thus raising difficult questions about social provisioning in a shrinking economy. A recent projected decline in provision for basic socio-economic rights, including below inflation social grant increases and reductions in spending on education and healthcare, has generated intense economic policy debate.[87]

Sandra Liebenberg recently emphasized the importance of harnessing international socio-economic rights norms, under the doctrine of retrogression, to evaluate regressive measures that reduce previous levels of progress in the enjoyment of socio-economic rights.[88] She identifies the procedural and substantive criteria that make up the burden of justifying a regressive measure, including the requirement that it does not result in discrimination, particularly against vulnerable and disadvantaged groups. Non-discrimination is, of course, an independent constitutional and legislative requirement in South Africa, leading to the possibility that a demonstration of unfair discrimination alone might be sufficient to challenge a regressive measure. This is briefly examined in this section.

Here, the nub of the problem in discrimination law has been that discrimination challenges to austerity cuts elsewhere have often been met with minimal justifications of (economic) rationality. Meghan Campbell recently analysed cases challenging austerity motivated reforms in the UK's benefit system, which disproportionately affected single mothers. She argues that the UK Supreme Court consistently defined these to be issues of economic inequality and income poverty, subject to tests of rationality ('manifestly without reasonable foundation'), rather than the more rigorous and contextual proportionality test required when a measure discriminates against identified status groups.[89] As noted above, South Africa's substantive guarantees of equality and against unfair discrimination theoretically provide more powerful defences against a regression in benefits. However, this jurisprudential history is no guarantee that courts will not similarly resort to rationality arguments (including formalist legal reasoning and formal equality arguments) when confronted with claims concerning the reduction of benefits. Here the minority judgment of Jafta J in *Mahlangu*[90] is of concern, as he interprets the differentiation formalistically to relate to a group of (domestic) workers, unconnected to the grounds of race and gender, and applies the threshold rationality standard of section 9(1) to find that this differentiation has no rational purpose.[91] While this did not affect a positive outcome, it reflects a worrying trend in the Constitutional Court to rely on rationality, rather than unfair discrimination in cases

---

[86] Francis and Webster (n 13) 795.
[87] Sash (n 75).
[88] Sandra Liebenberg, 'Austerity in the Midst of a Pandemic: Pursuing Accountability Through the Socio-Economic Rights Doctrine of Non-retrogression' (2021) 37 South African Journal on Human Rights 181.
[89] Meghan Campbell, 'The Austerity of Lone Motherhood: Discrimination Law and Benefit Reform' (2021) 41 Oxford Journal of Legal Studies 1197.
[90] *Mahlangu* (n 65).
[91] ibid [159], [161]. This reflects the majority judgment in *S v Jordan* (n 37) where sex work was found not to constitute indirect sex discrimination, nor was it found to be irrational.

where a classification clearly tranches on prohibited grounds.[92] Although a discrimination enquiry must follow a failed rationality test, it cannot do so if judges fail to see the connection to the grounds, especially where this is indirect and intersectional.

Thus far, the limited case law on regressive measures has provided little space for discrimination arguments. The recent case of *Equal Education v Minister of Basic Education*[93] concerned the cancellation of the National School Nutrition Programme (NSNP) while schools were closed under the Covid-19 lockdown, affecting nine million children who relied on a school-based meal for adequate nutrition. In ordering the reinstatement of the NSNP, the court relied on the section 29(1) right to basic education and the section 28(1)(c) right to basic nutrition (and the linkages between the two).[94] However, it is worth considering how section 9 and unfair discrimination might fit in, by developing the relationship between section 9(2), which was relied on in the judgment, and section 9(3). This would assist in developing the relationship between socio-economic and equality rights as equal, separate, and complementary partners in protecting social goods.

It was undisputed that the NSNP was a section 9(2) positive measure, enacted to create substantive equality via an equal educational dispensation for all children, which included sufficient food. As the respondents stated: 'the NSNP has a historical context and was implemented to achieve substantive equality and to protect and advance children disadvantaged by unfair discrimination in terms of section 9(2) of the Constitution'.[95] The applicants argued further that regression was not possible and that section 9(2) does not allow the state to confer benefits that it can retract at will.[96] This is not developed further as an equality argument. However, the regression does constitute unfair discrimination. The policy was explicit in targeting African children, who were particularly disadvantaged, and removing the benefit of NSNP was thus indirect discrimination on the basis of race and poverty (following *Social Justice Coalition*). This demonstrates that regression of a section 9(2) measure can trigger section 9(3) unfair discrimination, and can be challenged on that basis, alongside socio-economic rights jurisprudence.

Significantly, economic arguments did not form part of the case (the reason for halting the NSNP was school closure under the pandemic, not cost-related). However, economic arguments would apply in many cases on regressive measures, especially in contemporary South Africa where, as noted, the medium term budget anticipates a variety of cuts. If claims did come to court because they constituted discrimination, what would happen to the economic arguments? Properly addressed under equality law, claims should not be limited to the threshold analysis of rationality,[97] but proceed as claims that constitute unfair discrimination on the basis of gender, race, and/or poverty and courts should consider the impact of the budgetary choice, such as

---

[92] See eg *Ruhabe v Rahube* [2018] ZACC 42; *Herbert NO v Senqu Municipality* [2018] ZACC 42.
[93] [2020] ZAGPPHC 306.
[94] A fuller discussion is beyond scope of this chapter, but see Faranaaz Veriave and Nurina Ally, 'Legal Mobilisation for Education in a Time of Covid' (2021) 37 South African Journal on Human Rights 230; Liebenberg (n 88).
[95] *Equal Education* (n 93) [35].
[96] *Equal Education* (n 93) Applicants Heads of Argument [138].
[97] As set out in *Harksen v Lane* (n 33).

below-inflation grant increase, on the claimant group. If this impact is found to be discriminatory, substantive economic considerations enter the justifications enquiry.[98]

Here, one would expect that the more the issue affects core budgetary allocations, the less likely courts are to intervene, beyond insisting on accountability. A recent Labour Appeal Court (LAC) case on government's reduction of public sector wages in the third year of a collective agreement raises interesting questions in this respect.[99] The applicant trade unions sought to enforce the agreement. Government and Treasury argued that the increase had become unaffordable, and that its implementation would affect social grants and other social services. The matter turned on an interpretation of the governing regulations.[100] The LAC found these to allow Treasury to halt the increase due to budgetary constraints, and declined to exercise any residual discretion to enforce the agreement or suggest a compromise remedy.[101] Here, it is worth noting that the Court was deeply concerned about the polycentricity involved in budgetary decisions; the significant role of Treasury in constitutional (and fiscal) governance; the parlous state of the fiscus; the relative privilege of employees in secure salaried jobs versus the provision of social grants to 'millions of vulnerable people' and healthcare costs of the pandemic; and the impact of enforcing the agreement on 'the normative vision of the Constitution which aims that everyone living in the country should live a dignified life and hence those most in peril should be assisted first'.[102]

This judgment has been subject to critical debate about economic policy, the role of Treasury, and the public sector.[103] Nevertheless, it supports rule-governed and accountable economic decision-making and the role of courts in ensuring this (courts can and should insist on economic justifications even if they refrain from greater intervention). It suggests that courts should seek a broad constitutional understanding of these decisions, based on these justifications, even if they avoid detailed interrogation.

This leaves open the question of how far courts might go when called upon to intervene in situations where it is the poor and marginalized who come to court to enforce spending in their favour, such as a challenge to below-inflation grant increases. At minimum, courts can and should require constitutionally informed justifications, even as they avoid polycentric decisions. In certain instances, it might be possible to build on the potential of *Social Justice Coalition* to ask courts to assist in cases where a clear prioritization of resources for the privileged, over the disadvantaged, results in unfair discrimination in existing resources. Here, courts might require a more

---

[98] This aligns with the socio-economic rights requirement of a compelling justification, but tailored within the equality analysis. See Liebenberg (n 88) for suggestions on how this might work in socio-economic rights jurisprudence.

[99] *Public Servants Association v Minister of Public Service and Administration* [2020] ZALAC 54.

[100] ibid [11]. In effect, this turned on budgetary issues, ie whether a Cabinet agreement in 2018 bound Treasury or whether Treasury could raise budgetary constraints in subsequent years. The LAC found that Treasury could do so: ibid [15]–[33].

[101] ibid [34]–[48].

[102] ibid [46]. See also [1], [21], [30]–[33], [44]–[46]. This approach was generally confirmed by the Constitutional Court: *National Education Health and Allied Workers Union v Minister of Public Service and Administration* [2022] ZACC 6 [99]–[104].

[103] Dick Forslund, 'Law and Austerity: Constitutional Court Hears Unions' Appeal on Public Sector Wage Agreement' *Daily Maverick* (23 August 2021).

egalitarian distribution of these resources, although they are unlikely to specify how this should be achieved.

7 Mandating Egalitarian Delivery: A Section 9(2) Duty to Engage Equality Outcomes and Enable Social Provision?

Section 9(2) endorses a positive, restitutionary, and redistributive idea of equality,[104] by permitting the state to take 'legislative and other measures designed to protect or advance persons, or categories of persons, disadvantaged by unfair discrimination'. This protects positive measures that meet the criteria of section 9(2). The Constitutional Court has generally supported race-based measures to achieve substantive equality, but thus far section 9(2) has been viewed as a permissive and defensive provision, without imposing obligatory positive duties on the state. In litigation, it has acted as a shield for positive measures, not a sword to mandate positive action by the state.

Recently, the High Courts have drawn more consistently on constitutional commitments to equality to strengthen the implementation of socio-economic rights and equality measures via regulatory frameworks. They do so by interpreting the relevant law to promote the values of dignity, equality, and freedom, as required by section 39(1) of the Constitution, and often with explicit reference to the positive duties of substantive equality under section 9(2).

This was implicit in *Adonisi v Minister for Transport and Public Works*,[105] where the court drew on the constitutional goal of substantive equality to conclude that the state bore positive duties to implement legislative and policy commitments to housing in a manner that addressed historically-based, spatial inequality.[106] Insofar as government had failed to meet these constitutional and statutory obligations, it had acted unlawfully and was directed to comply with such obligations and report back on steps taken.[107]

The interpretation of legislation, with due regard to positive equality duties, is even more explicit in three cases related to the Covid-19 pandemic. In the *Equal Education* case discussed above, the court relied on section 9(2) and the positive duty to achieve substantive equality as core constitutional imperatives in confirming the state's positive 'constitutional and statutory duty to ensure that the NSNP provides a daily meal to all qualifying learners, to ensure the proper exercise of the rights of learners to education and to enhance their learning capacity, whether they are attending school or studying away from school as a result of the Covid-19 pandemic'.[108]

Two further cases concerned the use of race-based preferences in the allocation of economic relief to small businesses.[109] The applicants generally argued that such

---

[104] *Minister of Finance v Van Heerden* [2004] ZACC 3 [28].
[105] [2020] ZAWCHC 87.
[106] ibid [71].
[107] ibid.
[108] ibid [103.3], [35], [53], [55], [56].
[109] *Solidarity Obo Members v The Minister of Small Business Development* [2020] ZAGPPHC 133; *Democratic Alliance v President of the RSA* [2020] ZAGPPHC 237; *Democratic Alliance v the President of the RSA* [2020] ZAGPPHC 326. For a wider discussion see Catherine Albertyn, 'Section 9 in a Time of

preferences were not permitted by the Disaster Management Act, which required a more neutral approach to assisting those who were (economically) affected.[110] In both instances, the courts disagreed to find that, in the context of historical disadvantage, there was indeed a positive duty on government to consider the application of historic criteria of discrimination, such as race and gender, in determining conditions for obtaining economic relief under Covid-19.[111] Here, they explicitly draw on section 39(2) to find that the duty to interpret legislation 'to promote the spirit, purport and objects of the Bill of Rights' brings 'key constitutional rights such as equality ... and the remedial measures which are permitted in terms of s 9(2) of the Constitution' into play.[112] Indeed, 'the very presence of s 9 (2) of the Constitution together with the range of socio-economic rights contained in sections 26, 27, 28 and 29' confirmed its 'commitment to historical redress and the priority that must be given to those most in need'.[113]

These cases suggest that the high courts are willing to draw on section 9(2) to defend and mandate positive duties on the part of government to act in ways that address race and gender disadvantage and eliminate unfair discrimination. Over and above reliance on progressive realization under sections 26 and 27, this provides an additional and positive constitutional obligation on government to implement its many progressive laws, policies, and programmes in relation to socio-economic rights in a manner that addresses historic and structural inequalities.

8 Conclusion: Equality Law in the Context of Exponential and Structural Inequalities

What does this tell us about the role of equality law in South Africa, a country of deep existing structural inequalities which suffered an exponential rise under the Covid-19 pandemic?

In general, this chapter suggests that, by drawing on the best interpretation of the law and hoping for like-minded judges, it is possible to widen the scope of social provision to outsider groups, including those disadvantaged by poverty, or at the intersection of race, class, and gender. The law enables advocacy and litigation of behalf of targeted vulnerable groups and it enables detailed accountability by government, even where cases appear to breach separation of powers concerns. Further, and particularly compelling, is the possibility of using equality law to challenge discrimination in the distribution of social goods and services, thus touching on the manner in which underlying resources are allocated. Whilst not easy, and certainly requiring careful

---

COVID: Substantive Equality, Economic Inclusion and Positive Duties' (2021) 37 South African Journal on Human Rights 205.

[110] *Solidarity* (n 109) [11]; *Democratic Alliance* (n 109) [31], [36].
[111] *Solidarity* (n 109) [36]–[37]; *Democratic Alliance* (n 109) [41].
[112] *Democratic Alliance* (n 109) [41].
[113] ibid [47].

strategy and detailed research and resources, this suggests potentially transformative equality claims can be made—and won. However, as the *Social Justice Coalition* case suggests, the real challenge lies in the remedy. In that case, the hearing on the remedy was postponed to a date to be arranged by the parties.[114] After two and half years of attempting to secure a remedy through the Equality Court, the applicants appealed to the Constitutional Court to assist.[115] Finding that it did not have jurisdiction as the matter was still before the Equality Court, that Court declined to hear the appeal.[116] The matter remains unresolved four years later.

The brief discussion of the case law also suggests that equality law can facilitate a detailed accounting by government. First, courts are mandating government to act positively to secure substantive equality and overcome disadvantage in implementing policies and laws. Secondly, courts can and should require justifications for economic decisions. Properly applied, equality jurisprudence enables courts to act against government where it fails to provide detailed accounting and to make decisions that require additional budgetary allocations where dignity and disadvantage are at stake. Where these involve more significant expenditure or universal budgetary choices, courts can, at best, ascertain whether the decision broadly aligns with the spirit and values of the Constitution. One should expect, therefore, a degree of normative engagement with budgetary choices. This allows for a range of policy choices and courts thus become part of wider policy debates and engagements on social and economic change in a way that leaves the actual decision-making to the political branches.

Under the pandemic, equality law was deployed to widen access to social relief of distress grants and to defend government's policy choices to include race-based criteria in its conditions for economic relief. Here, the cases are successful because they are limited claims, able to be brought on a relatively urgent basis, that can draw on extant jurisprudence. What is possible in a pandemic seems to be dependent on the law in place. But the pandemic—in its devastating effects on inequalities—also provides a context for developing and strengthening that law to redress historic and structural disadvantage (rather than shore up privilege), and provide new opportunities for transformative litigation and adjudication.

In this sense, one can see possibilities for equality law in engaging the socio-economic consequences of economic decline. The emerging jurisprudence on regressive measures can, and should, be developed to draw on the benefits of equality law. Further, the courts—through equality law—can, at a minimum, provide fora in which to engage normatively with wider policy debates. Courts are not the solution to structural inequalities, and there are many instances where judges should not be anywhere near them. However, even if only by facilitating greater inclusion through widening 'who qualifies', courts redistribute resources to poor and disadvantaged groups. Over and above that, the possibly radical potential in triggering a more just distribution of

---

[114] *Social Justice Coalition* (n 73) par 94.
[115] *Social Justice Coalition v Minster of Police* [2022] ZACC 27 paras 23–39.
[116] ibid paras 139–151.

existing resources through equality law allows courts to make significant interventions. Overall, equality law's role, alongside socio-economic rights jurisprudence, strengthens the ability of claimants and civil society not to resolve structural and exponential inequalities, but—at the very least—to nudge social and economic policy towards more egalitarian distributions of social goods and services, and to advance substantive equality.

Index

For the benefit of digital users, indexed terms that span two pages (e.g., 52–53) may, on occasion, appear on only one of those pages.

adversarial/litigious model 7–8, 11–12, 73, 79, 107–8, 110, 113, 124–25, 133, 134–35, 138, 143, 145, 149, 150, 154, 159, 175, 193–94, 195–96, 266–67, 272–73, 274–75, 325, 330, 343, 351, 353, 354, 357, 361–63, 365, 369, 370–71
age 12–13, 36, 49, 55, 56, 126, 151, 153, 159, 192, 233–54, 320, 338–39, 343–44, 361–62
Australia 2, 5, 12–13, 23, 130–31, 136, 143, 183–99, 226–27, 233–54

Brazil 2, 7, 21, 137, 224–25, 295–310
budget
    budgetary allocation/cuts 5–6, 37, 43–44, 52–53, 57, 82–83, 84–85, 90–91, 92–93, 131–32, 170, 173, 206, 212, 297, 329, 357, 364, 367–68, 371
    UK Women's Budget Group 6, 43–44, 45–46, 51–53, 54, 60, 93–94, 95–96

class 43, 47–48, 50, 51, 55, 60, 69, 142, 173–74, 192–93, 200, 203–4, 207, 312, 325, 353, 354, 356–57, 362–63, 365, 370–71
climate change 2, 3, 8, 39, 45, 130, 140, 223
Colombia 2, 5–6, 40, 200–12, 226–27
Comparative Law 1–16, 40, 115–16, 124, 346
constitutions 19–20, 37–38, 40, 100–1, 112–17, 124, 125, 126–27, 128, 131, 135, 136, 137–38, 139, 140, 143, 148–49, 150, 152, 153, 161–62, 163–64, 165–67, 171, 178–79, 182, 184, 193–94, 197–98, 200, 204, 205, 206–7, 222, 296, 300, 301–2, 303, 304, 308, 309, 313–15, 316–17, 318, 319, 320, 321, 326, 328–29, 330–34, 335–37, 338, 340, 343, 344, 345–46, 348, 349, 351–52, 353, 354, 355–56, 357, 358, 360–61, 363, 366–67, 368–70, 371

Covid-19/pandemic 1–2, 4, 6–7, 8, 14, 19–24, 43–51, 60, 61–63, 64, 67, 73–76, 77, 79, 98, 99–100, 103–7, 123–24, 129–30, 132, 135, 136, 139–40, 142, 145–46, 148, 155–57, 161–62, 163, 167, 169–70, 171, 172, 174, 175, 177–78, 179, 180–81, 183, 185–87, 189, 195, 200, 201, 202, 203, 212, 213–14, 225–27, 228–29, 233, 241–47, 253, 255, 256, 257, 258, 260–61, 263, 264, 266–67, 268–69, 270, 271–73, 274–75, 276–77, 280, 295–96, 298, 304–5, 306, 308, 309, 310, 312, 329, 333–34, 335, 337, 338, 340–41, 342, 343–44, 345–46, 348, 349–50, 351, 354, 356–57, 365–66, 367, 369–70
crisis 1–2, 3, 4–5, 6–7, 8, 10, 12, 13–14, 21, 36–38, 40, 43–44, 61–62, 63, 76–77, 79–96, 97–99, 100–1, 103–7, 115, 117, 123, 129–30, 135, 143, 145, 155, 159, 161, 165, 167, 169–70, 177–78, 181–82, 184, 189–90, 201, 202–3, 224–25, 235–36, 241–47, 253, 255, 256, 258, 264, 271–72, 274, 275, 280, 295–96, 304–5, 308, 309, 310, 311, 312, 313, 333–34, 335–36, 343, 346, 349, 350–52

democracy 7, 84, 95, 98, 99–100, 101, 103, 105–6, 108, 112, 114, 115, 116–17, 124–25, 127, 128–30, 139, 142, 143, 351, 353, 356–57, 358–59
disability 2, 4, 6, 7, 13–14, 20, 23, 29, 31, 32, 33, 35, 36, 41, 43–44, 47, 51, 53–54, 55, 56, 57, 59–60, 62–63, 73, 84–85, 109, 110–11, 115–16, 128–29, 142, 145, 146, 148–49, 153, 156, 157–58, 172, 178, 188–89, 191–92, 197–98, 249, 255–75, 290–92, 337, 340–41, 343, 344, 345, 361–62

economy
  care economy 11, 43, 53, 54–58
  feminist economy 11, 53, 54
  gig economy 279–80
  informal economy 2, 4–5, 20–24, 202, 356
  political economy 5–6, 46, 54, 59–60, 202–3, 207–8, 223, 355–56, 365–66
  recession 2, 4, 8, 14, 20–24, 70–71, 73, 79, 90–91, 123, 129–30, 131–32, 241
Equality Act 2010 (UK), 11, 13–14, 43, 44, 62–63, 73–76, 126–27, 136–37, 138, 139, 198, 255–56, 265–67, 268–69, 271–72, 274, 275
equity 9, 11, 30–31, 162–63, 169–82
EU 2, 11–12, 14, 19, 124–25, 126–27, 131–32, 138, 139–40, 147–48, 151, 152, 153, 255, 256, 257, 260, 261, 262, 263, 265, 276–94
exponential inequalities
  interdisciplinary research 2, 47–51, 61–78
  meaning 2–7, 20, 41–42, 63, 73–77, 78, 83–84, 95–96, 99, 129–30, 132, 135, 136, 140, 141, 142, 143, 161, 162–63, 165–66, 174–75, 182, 183, 184, 233, 237–41, 247–53, 254, 256, 275, 296, 304, 308, 309, 310, 311, 312–13, 363, 365–66, 371–72

family 4, 19, 24–27, 29, 32–34, 36, 44–45, 54, 61–78, 82–83, 107, 109, 150–51, 159, 180, 188, 192, 210–11, 239, 247, 249, 259, 260, 263, 307, 323, 346, 363
flexible work 14, 64, 210, 249, 263, 264, 276–94

gender 2–3, 4, 5–6, 7, 12–13, 19, 23–24, 25, 26, 27–28, 29, 30–32, 35, 43, 44–45, 49, 51–52, 53, 54, 56, 57, 63, 84–86, 93, 95–96, 100, 102–3, 113, 114, 115–16, 128–30, 136, 148–49, 151, 161, 169–70, 173–74, 181–82, 198, 200, 201, 202, 203, 204–5, 206, 207, 209, 210–11, 256, 261, 276–79, 280–81, 282, 287, 292–93, 295, 296, 297, 300, 307, 308, 309, 310, 312, 322, 325, 331–32, 350, 353, 356–57, 358, 361–63, 366–68, 369–71
Gender Equality Act 2020 (Vic) 12–13, 198, 233, 248, 249, 253, 254
gender identity 29, 31–32, 41, 55, 109–10, 192, 249, 328, 333
grounds 2–3, 5, 8, 28–29, 31–32, 73, 85–86, 95–96, 107–8, 109, 111, 112–13, 114, 115–16, 124–26, 128–29, 130–32, 136, 139, 148–49, 153, 160, 161, 172, 192–93, 196–97, 198, 233, 237–38, 247, 250, 252–53, 255, 262, 309, 328–29, 333, 360–61, 362–64, 365, 366–67

health 5–6, 9, 11, 20, 22, 26–28, 34–35, 36, 37–38, 39, 40, 41, 43–47, 48, 49, 52, 53–55, 59–60, 66, 71, 72, 73–74, 82–83, 129–30, 145–46, 155–56, 157–58, 160, 162, 169–70, 171, 174–75, 183, 184–85, 188–89, 190, 193, 195–97, 205, 206–7, 215–16, 217–18, 219, 224–25, 227–28, 230, 233, 246, 250, 253–54, 255, 257, 260–61, 270–71, 297–98, 321–22, 336–37, 339–40, 343, 344, 347–48, 349–50, 355
Hong Kong 2, 6–7, 8, 61–78

impact assessment 12–13, 43, 44, 51, 57, 60, 154, 159–60, 194–95, 198, 271
India 2, 4–5, 14–15, 24–25, 226–27, 311–34
indirect discrimination 2–3, 8, 14, 31–32, 73, 83–84, 85, 109–10, 126, 131–32, 133, 139, 161–62, 193–94, 255, 263, 268, 276–77, 282, 284–85, 290–91, 293–94, 315, 365, 367
international law 2, 9
  ICESCR 9, 36, 111, 214, 215–17, 221–22
  TRIPS 9, 214–15, 217, 223–26
intersectionality 1, 4, 6, 19, 21, 25, 31–32, 43–60, 97–98, 100, 103–7, 108, 112–14, 116, 117, 128–29, 130–31, 132, 135, 136, 137, 138, 141, 142, 143, 147–48, 160, 173–74, 178–79, 198, 200, 207, 212, 233, 236–38, 247, 249, 250, 254, 261, 296, 302, 304–5, 310, 318, 323, 325, 345, 356–57, 358, 361–63, 364, 366–67
Ireland 2, 8, 12, 145–60

Kenya 2, 5, 14–15, 335–52

migrant workers 4–5, 6–7, 21, 24–25, 48, 50, 55, 100, 103–4, 105–6, 109–10, 113–14, 145–46, 147–48, 192, 196–97, 239–41, 246, 333–34

poverty 1, 4, 5, 22, 25–26, 29, 79–80, 82–84, 86, 89, 91–93, 95–96, 102–3, 106–7, 116–17, 132, 141, 183–84, 188–90, 192–93, 196–97, 207, 235–36, 259, 309,

335, 337, 338–39, 340–42, 343, 344, 354, 355–57, 360–61, 362–64, 365, 366–67, 370–71
  extreme poverty 1–2, 36–37, 312, 355, 356–57
  gendered poverty 5–6, 25, 51, 85, 92–93, 96, 307–8
pre-existing inequality or historical disadvantage 1, 4–5, 10, 14–16, 43–47, 63, 79, 147, 159–60, 178–79, 184, 188–89, 206, 241, 260–61, 274, 308, 311, 312–13, 335, 336, 337, 343, 350–51, 363, 369–70
proactive duties 10, 12–13, 194–95, 196–97, 248, 321
  anticipatory reasonable adjustment duty (UK), 12–14, 255–56, 265–66, 268, 269–70, 271–72, 274, 275
  equality and human rights duty (Ireland), 12, 145, 153, 154, 155–58
  positive duty under Gender Equality Act 2020 (Vic), 248, 250, 251–52, 254
  public sector equality duty (UK), 12, 138, 142, 143, 193–94, 248, 268, 271
proportionality 14, 79–80, 85–96, 112, 193, 358, 366–67
public policy 61–65, 67, 68–69, 84, 86, 90–91, 92, 94, 97–98, 101–2, 103, 143, 154, 272, 274, 297, 301–2, 307, 349–50, 355, 357, 358–61, 362–63, 364, 365–66, 367, 368, 369, 371–72
public policy approach 11, 61–78, 162–63

race 8–9, 21, 23, 29, 31–32, 35, 36, 43–44, 55, 59–60, 76, 107, 109, 125–26, 128–29, 131, 142, 161–62, 163, 166–67, 169, 171, 172, 173–74, 175–76, 178–79, 180–82, 191–92, 212, 237–38, 249, 256, 353, 358, 362–63, 365, 366–67, 370
reproductive justice 7, 113–14, 201, 206–7, 210, 211, 212, 295–96, 297–99, 300, 301–4, 306, 307–8, 309, 310, 322

sex/sex discrimination 14, 29, 31–32, 44–45, 49, 51, 55, 56, 73, 107, 124, 128–29, 131–32, 142, 162–63, 168, 172, 181–82, 192, 238, 276–77, 278, 281, 282–85, 286, 287, 291–92, 293–94, 361–63
sexual harassment 205, 206–7, 249, 316, 325, 331–32, 337, 345

social benefits/social security 4, 11–12, 22, 26–27, 35–36, 40, 56, 62–63, 64–66, 67–68, 69–71, 72, 73–74, 79, 81–86, 87, 88–89, 90–91, 92–94, 95–96, 159, 188–90, 206, 259, 261, 358–59
socio-economic rights 14–16, 19–20, 27–28, 35–38, 203, 214, 215–17, 221–22, 313, 317, 318–19, 320–21, 327, 328, 329–31, 332–33, 335–37, 350–51, 353, 354, 357, 358–60, 361, 363, 365–66, 367, 369–70, 371–72
South Africa 2, 15–16, 21, 25, 26, 27, 40, 137, 138, 224–25, 226, 353–72
substantive equality 2–3, 31, 98–100, 101–2, 112–14, 115, 116–17, 136–40, 141, 142, 169–70, 248, 291–92, 303–4, 309, 310, 312–13, 314–15, 318–19, 322, 325, 326–27, 328, 329, 333, 336, 348, 354, 357, 359–60, 367, 369, 371–72
sustainability 57

UK 4, 7–8, 14, 26–27, 43–60, 61–78, 79–96, 123–44, 195–96, 226–27, 255–75, 279–80
USA 11, 21, 124, 141–42, 161–82, 213–14, 218, 226–27, 237

vaccine 1, 9, 23, 171, 172, 174, 175, 177–78, 179, 180, 181–82, 183, 184–85, 213–30, 339–40
violence 1, 25–26, 49, 54–55, 84–85, 93, 95–96, 101, 123, 134–35, 183, 188, 201, 204, 206–7, 209, 249, 296, 297, 298, 300, 301, 303, 304–5, 307, 309, 318, 325, 337

women and girls 1–2, 4, 5–7, 19, 20, 21, 22, 23, 41, 59–60, 79–80, 83–86, 92–94, 95, 96, 103, 104, 131–32, 145, 147–48, 161, 188–89, 190, 192, 200–12, 235, 236, 237–47, 252–54, 276–77, 278–81, 282–84, 285, 287–88, 290–92, 293–94, 297, 298, 300, 307, 320–22, 323, 325, 328, 331–32, 337, 343, 356–57, 359–60, 361–63
  domestic workers 7, 25, 104, 201, 202, 306, 361–63, 366–67
  migrant women 6–7, 48, 50, 104, 113–14, 147–48
  single mothers 6, 43–44, 62–63, 73, 76
  women of colour 6–7, 21, 25, 30–31, 43–44, 48, 123, 147, 295, 296, 303, 304–5, 306, 307–8